ROCK CHRONICLES

GALLAGHER
MARRIOTT
DERRINGER
& TROWER

Their Lives
and
Music

Dan Muise

HAL•LEONARD®
CORPORATION

Published by Hal Leonard Corporation
7777 West Bluemound Road
P.O. Box 13819
Milwaukee, WI 53213, USA

Trade Book Division Editorial Offices:
151 West 46th Street, 8th Floor
New York, NY 10036

Visit us online at:
www.halleonard.com

Visit the artists online at:
www.rorygallagher.com
www.humble-pie.org.uk
www.rickderringer.com
www.members.shaw.ca/stevesplace

Library of Congress Cataloging-in-Publication Data has been applied for.

Printed in the United States of America
First edition

10 9 8 7 6 5 4 3 2 1

DEDICATED TO THE MEMORIES OF THOSE WHO PLAYED FOR ALL THE RIGHT REASONS

Duane Allman • Joe Baptista • John Belushi • Mike Bloomfield • Marc Bolan

Tommy Bolin • John Bonham • Roy Buchanan • Jeff Buckley • Tim Buckley

Paul Butterfield • Glen Buxton • David Byron • Toy Caldwell

Wilgar Campbell • Eddie Cochran • Allen Collins • Chad Conrad

Sam Cooke • Jim Croce • Rick Danko • Miles Davis • Steve Gaines

Rory Gallagher • Marvin Gaye • Lowell George • Bill Graham

Woody Guthrie • Pete Ham • George Harrison • Dan Hartman • Michael Hedges

Jimi Hendrix • Randy Jo Hobbs • Buddy Holly • Nicky Hopkins

Richard Hughes • Waylon Jennings • Brian Jones • Janis Joplin • Terry Kath • Alexis Korner

Paul Kossoff • Ronnie Lane • John Lennon • Phil Lynott • Bob Marley

Steve Marriott • Harold Melvin • Freddie Mercury • Jimmy Miller

Alain Montpetit • Keith Moon • Jim Morrison • Harry Nilsson • Roy Orbison

Jaco Pastorius • Dave Peverett • John Phillips • Jeff Porcaro • Cozy Powell

Elvis Presley • Carl Radle • Otis Redding • Keith Relf • Mick Ronson

Guy Stevens • Ian Stewart • Stu Sutcliffe • Darrell Sweet • Gary Thain

Peter Tosh • Dave Von Ronk • Ronnie Van Zandt • Townes Van Zandt • Stevie Ray Vaughan • Frank Zappa

CONTENTS

PREFACE

Growing up in the late 60s to mid-70s, music was instilled in our minds as far more than just entertainment. It was an education. Most of the messages sent out on vinyl and through performances were of a consistent nature. Stop the war. Love your brother and sister. Rebel against oppression. But what made the message even stronger were the messengers. The ones whose lyrics and music helped shape and define the characters of those willing to see the world through their eyes.

The integrity of these artists was, and is, crucial to me. Had the musicians I followed all these years never received a recording contract, their vocation would not have changed. We would have been the sorrier for never having heard of them but they would still have played their music. Of the people I write, a "regular" job was never an option. They had to do what they did. Whether a divine force led them to discover their talents or whether they were victims of circumstance, we are the ones who have benefited.

The list of those who defined the ideals of millions runs into the hundreds. After much consideration, I narrowed the list down to four. There are so many more to discuss but I will use that as incentive to continue with my writing. This group of artists caused me to run to record stores and watch my weekly allowance disappear. When these bands came to town, it was an event. The thrill of the announced date. The procurement of guaranteed entry. The day before the show. The day of the show. Going there. Entering the hall. The "click of the switch" when the lights went out.

The first time I saw Springsteen. The chill when, after the drum intro in total darkness, the lights kicked in for "Rock'n'Roll" by Zeppelin. Having a limited knowledge of Rory Gallagher, I watched as he and his band walked on stage, plugged in and blew my face off. He was the first "rock star" I ever met. And I have been fortunate to have met many others since then. Bruce and Zep don't need me to tell the public about them but the artists compiled in this book deserve my respect. Enough so that I've made it a passion to remind those of us who followed them. And to introduce them to a new generation that will never be lucky enough to have experienced what I did and at a time that shall never be repeated for more than the obvious reasons.

These are four studies of some of the most blessed of human characters.

– Dan Muise

ACKNOWLEDGEMENTS

I would like to indulge myself and pay recognition to the people whose faith, confidence and patience played an important part in my life before and during the three years it took to write this book.

Thank you to David Alexander, Brian Atkinson, Andre Bourgeois, Scott Cheverie, Tom Deveaux, Beatrice Doucet, Tammy Drougel, Asher and Laura Fischer, Darryl Gaines, Tim Hopton, Julie Jepsom, Barry Kent, Les Krifaton, Stephen Lawrence, Mike Logan, Rickey Mason, A.J. McDonald, Jeff Nearing, Reese Nearing, Phil Nolin, Rick O'Grady, Rick Pottie, Bob Powers, Paul Ranson, Chris Reiser, Norman Roach, Rhonda Ronayne-LeBlanc, Kathleen Roseveare, Sabrena Smith, Mike Smuck, Blaine Touesnard and Bruce Van Feggelen.

A professional thank you to Donal Gallagher, Rudi Gerlach, Fred Goodman, Dino McGartland, Steve Shail and Derek Sutton. To my agent Jim Fitzgerald of the Carol Mann Agency and Brad Smith from Hal Leonard. And to the best in the business, my editor Ben Schafer, who taught me more than I knew there was to learn.

A thank you to Bruce Springsteen for making me understand the importance of family.

Much appreciation to M. Lee Cohen of Halifax for all the legal advice.

A tip of the hat to my right-hand man on this project, Jerry Shirley.

A very special thanks to John Keogh who was there upon conception of this idea as well as many times before and since.

To the memories of Alain Montpetit and Chad Conrad.

A most special thank you to my parents, Ambrose & Leona, who have always had faith in me, my sister Lisa, ny nephew Zachary and sister-in-law Kathleen.

A debt of gratitude that can never properly be repaid to someone who was *always* there and helped in many ways, my brother Rick.

And to the person who understands me most and is my inspiration, the love of my life, my wife Gabriella.

GALLAGHER
MARRIOTT
DERRINGER
& TROWER

RORY GALLAGHER

"He was a gentleman who had time for his audience and his friends. He had great respect from his peers. He was one of the earliest Irish guitar ambassadors who brought his driven style of the blues, without the compromise of given commercial success, to the world. He paved the way for Horslips, U2, Thin Lizzy, Gary Moore, Them, and as a serious musician added credibility to the then Irish music business which only had the showbands. Who, whilst they were superb, were only copycats of the U.K. and U.S. charts and did not have an export possibility. Today the story is very different. And in his own way Rory was certainly a musical and spiritual inspiration to the musicians and bands that followed him and conquered the world."

–Alan O'Duffy, May 2000

Daniel Gallagher was raised in the North, specifically Derry. His wife Monica was from Cork, in the South. A good blend of what Ireland is all about. After serving with the neutral Irish Army during the Second World War, Daniel played piano and accordion in a dance band but only as an evening sideline. During the day Daniel provided for his family by performing construction work on the Ballyshannon Dam.

Daniel and Monica had two sons: Rory, born March 2, 1948, in Ballyshannon, and Donal, born August 9, 1949, in Derry. When the Ballyshannon Dam project ended in 1956 Daniel became a victim of religious prejudice. As scarce as work was, it was even more difficult to find if you were Catholic. Monica could read the writing on the wall. Since she had made the initial move to leave her hometown for his, it was only fair that the reverse be applied to better their chances. She suggested trying her side of the border. The further away from the divide the better. They moved to MacCurtain Street, City Cork, Southern Ireland. By this time, Rory was two to three years into making guitars out of a school ruler, elastic bands and a round cheese box. You had fiddles and accordions. Banjoes were also around. But a guitar was an instrument you only heard about. And Rory had heard about guitars. He had seen Roy Rogers and Gene Autry on the film screen.

Rory Gallagher: "When I was a kid, I said, 'I cannot play this thing.' But you step over that psychological bridge. OK, you may never be Segovia. But you have to get cheeky with your fright, you know?"

Rory was exposed to American Forces Radio and at the age of seven was listening to European broadcasts that appealed to a much older group of folks. "Voice of America" played a lot of blues music as well as the current hits. There was the "Jazz Hour." And gospel music. The sounds touched a nerve in Rory. He shared a sense of drama with blues legend Big Bill Broonzy. Homegrown talent Lonnie Donegan, the biggest name in the U.K. at the time, was interpreting and exposing people to the music of Woody Guthrie. By listening to Donegan's music Rory was led to Leadbelly. By the age of eight he was telling younger brother Donal about Chuck Berry and Muddy Waters, whom he had seen pictures of in *Melody Maker*.

Rory Gallagher: "One night I heard Muddy Waters on FM radio and it changed my life."

Rory badgered his parents until they bought him a plastic ukulele. He quickly graduated to an authentic acoustic guitar and an obsession began. Young Gallagher studied tutorials and honored his self-professed God-given gift with hours of daily practice. He convinced brother Donal and two friends to form a band with him as opposed to joining a street gang. Instead of playing games after school Donal would find himself banging the bottom end of a bucket, the perfect snare drum. When a tea chest bass (similar to a washtub bass) and a washboard were added Rory had a rhythm section. Rory started developing physical movements to accompany his playing in order to motivate the rest of the quartet, especially during the Chuck Berry numbers.

By the age of ten it was well known in the Gallagher family that Rory was a musician for life. His father, who regularly reminded his son of the importance of something to fall back on, expressed the only skepticism. Music was nighttime work. You had to have a day job. Developing a nest egg was the responsible thing to do.

Rory began entering talent competitions, community events, school concerts, anything that would give him more experience performing in front of an audience. In 1960 a photograph of Rory in short trousers on the front page of Cork's "Evening Echo" heralded him as the winner of a talent contest held at City Hall. Though amateur shows dictated that the performers choose to perform "tame" selections, Rory rarely complied. And it was being noticed. Even Donal, at the age of nine, saw the extraordinary potential.

Donal Gallagher: "I was very much hanging on to Rory's coattails all the way through. First of all, he had good taste. And being younger than him, your big brother is always right. Or so he told me!"

In 1961 Rory's biggest supporter, mother Monica, accompanied him on a visit to see Michael Crowley, who owned "the" music store in Cork. There she registered as guarantor for the purchase of an electric guitar, a Rosetti Solid 7. Rory was to pay the equivalent of $1 a week. He ran errands, saved his pocket money, and even gave up his favorite pastime: the cinema.

There was a week-long talent show at his school, North Monastery C.B.S. For the first three nights Rory played a quiet cowboy tune, "The Four Legged Friend." On the fourth night the tape machine broke down. The Brother putting on the show told Rory to go out and fill some time. Rory tried to explain that he didn't know any other "appropriate material" and was told to "Play anything you like." He launched into rock 'n' roll.

Donal Gallagher: "The Brothers went absolutely insane! Rory was taken out of the show from that moment. The Brothers felt that he had played the devil's music! But he knew what to expect. He took it in stride. And basically rock 'n' roll is in its best form when it's rebelling, isn't it? Probably Rory had a huge kick out of it."

He knew what he wanted but there were few places where Rory could play. So he gave in. The ad in the *Cork Examiner* read, "Guitarist wanted for showband." He wasn't a fan of showbands but when you're fifteen your options are limited. The group worked regularly around Cork, Limerick and Kerry. The idea of traveling by van to other counties and playing through an amplifier appealed to him.

Rory auditioned for and joined The Fontana Showband. Fronted by bandleader Bernie Tobin on trombone and saxophone, Tobin's brother Oliver played bass, John Lehane was on saxophone, Eamon O'Sullivan was on drums and Declan O'Keeffe played rhythm guitar. The band was typical of those in that time period in that it was expected that you would have both a rhythm section and a brass section, and that most of the musicians would be able to play another instrument besides their primary one. Any bands with fewer members were considered a "beat group" and didn't play the bigger venues.

The IFM (Irish Federation of Musicians) controlled both sides of the live music business, regulating the bands not only in format but also in the size of the lineups. The set lists consisted of the top songs of the day as well as country and western and Irish standards. The IFM believed it took between seven to nine musicians to properly interpret the music. They insisted on total compliance to their rules from all the venues and enforced this with the threat of being blacklisted. In return the musicians were guaranteed more money by receiving union scale. Since there were no exceptions every group of musicians obeyed.

The Fontana either rehearsed or played every night. There was steady work at The Arcadia in Cork where they opened for top showbands such as The Monarchs, from Belfast, featuring Van Morrison on saxophone. Fontana would also open for touring British acts such as The Animals and The Searchers.

From the moment Rory joined The Fontana Showband, at age fifteen, he basically took it over. Musically, Rory was light years ahead of the other members. No one minded when he began running rehearsals. Rory showed Oliver bass lines and instructed Eamon on patterns. He would play scores on the piano for the brass section to learn. He was very much a "shape up or ship out" young man but he also had the ability to motivate people. Rory would have preferred to form his own group but couldn't, so he worked from the inside out. Rory steered the band away from stock renditions of pop and country and western songs and towards proper rhythm and blues. After a while he was allowed to introduce a limited mix of musical styles from Chuck Berry and Eddie Cochran. There was also the energy of The Beatles and The Rolling Stones. Said Rory, "I knew from day one I was just passing through."

At city gigs two bands usually alternated sets. But anything away from those areas and you were on your own. Gigs usually ran from nine to two or three a.m. After a couple of hours musicians would switch instruments and play songs that needed fewer bodies so everyone could have a break for a beer and a sandwich. They would leave Cork in the late afternoon for out of town gigs and try and get home before daybreak. Rory was still going to school. The band would park around the corner and Rory would race to the van after class to begin the drive to the gig. He would do his homework on the back of an amp and change clothes en route. He was left to get whatever sleep he could on the ride back.

Rory Gallagher: "I was able to cope because, at that age, you can live without sleep. I'd come home early in the morning after a journey in a slow van. I managed."

The Fontana was regularly playing four or five nights a week. Most showbands emulated the syncopated moves of The Shadows but Fontana took it a few steps further. They were more than a showband. Shaking. Jumping. Bernie Tobin used to literally hang from his heels over a railing above the stage at The Arcadia while playing his sax. They would ride on each other's backs. Rory was performing five-minute guitar solos that were accentuated by his physical performance. He paid tribute to Chuck Berry by performing his well-rehearsed version of "the duck-walk." He mimicked Buddy Holly to perfection. But there was something else that Holly had that Gallagher wanted: a Fender Stratocaster guitar.

Jim Connolly, guitarist for The Irish Showband, went to Crowley's Music Store in Cork to buy a Fender Stratocaster. They had to be individually ordered directly from the factory in California, a world away from Cork. Connolly ordered the cherry red model, just like the one owned by Hank Marvyn of The Shadows. But when it arrived it was sunburst in color. Michael Crowley

reordered the cherry red model and let Connolly use the sunburst in the interim. When the correct model arrived, the switch was made and the sunburst was put on sale as a second-hand item. It cost £100, an absolute fortune at the time. Rory talked Donal into taking the day off school and accompanying him to see the Strat. They went down and stood in front of the shop window and eyed it. Says Donal, "It was the proverbial Holy Grail! The contours … it was an icon of instruments. 'The Guitar!' He had a look of determination on his face." Rory bolted in and cornered Michael Crowley. Within moments he had traded in his Rosetti for a fifth of the price of the Fender guitar and had Donal nod in agreement that their mother approved of transferring the guaranteed debt. Then Rory walked out with the Strat.

The exchange had to be kept secret, at least for the time being. Rory hid it under his bed. He or Donal would have to sit guard anytime an adult went near their bedroom. But Monica soon got wise. One night she asked Rory to play for her and he explained that he didn't have the Rosetti. He confessed that he had deceived Crowley into giving him an extra line of credit, which she was the guarantor for. But he explained to her that this would be his instrument for life. He would master playing lead "and" rhythm on the Strat, eliminating the need for a rhythm guitarist.

Rory had been successful at keeping the Christian Brothers, the clergy that ran the school, ignorant of his musical life. "I'd liken them as being taught by the fundamental clerics of Iran," said Donal Gallagher. "You weren't allowed to enjoy yourself." But it blew up in Rory's face. The Fontana Showband landed a two-week run backing Bridie Gallagher, no relation, who was topping the charts in Ireland at the time. Though she was known as a good performer, she was also known for not turning up on occasion. While the band was waiting for her arrival in a fairly rural town the locals sensed the impending no-show and took it out on the bands' instruments. Rory grabbed his Strat and hid under the grand piano, managing to avoid any damage. The police were soon called in to get things under control. It's easy to understand how such an event would warrant front-page coverage the next day. Not only were the fight participants named, so were the band members. This was brought to the attention of the Brothers and Rory was summoned.

Rory (second from left) with The Fontana Showband, Cork, Ireland, 1964. Tom O'Driscoll, extreme left in Beatles jacket, handing out band photos. Courtesy Strange Music Inc.

Donal Gallagher: "We shared a bedroom. One night I'd spotted that his leg had festered and had gone septic. I was quite alarmed. And then he explained to me what they'd done. They'd caned him, basically. They used sticks that they'd got from the hedge groves. That was their sort of temperament at the time. He'd take a suffering and not say anything, which was Rory. I went against his wishes and informed my mother that he needed medical attention. He was upset at me and don't think he ever trusted me after that!"

Monica made sure the wound was properly dealt with and went to see the Brothers. She expressed what she thought of them and took Rory out of school. She told family and friends that he had the flu while she tried to come up with a solution for how to continue Rory's education.

Monica went and saw Pierce Leahy who ran St. Kieran's College in Camden Place, Cork, a semi-private school. She explained that her son was a musician but only fifteen and still needed an education. She would see to it that Rory did the work needed to pass his exams if Leahy could be lenient and allow him to leave early for a particular concert or excuse him should he be late. It was agreed. Leahy, a blind man who later became Lord Mayor

of the city, was frowned upon by most of Cork for being progressive, but he ran a good school and one that suited Rory's needs perfectly. He graduated at sixteen in 1964.

Rory Gallagher: "In Ireland the young students are just hitting it. I mean, it's worse than Amsterdam now. Let me tell ya, when I was a kid it was so strict nobody drank, more or less. There was no such thing as drugs. Kids should play the game and keep everything cool. If the students start going crazy the real heavy right starts getting crazy. It's not good. Some of these people are very privileged to have this education. They didn't have to go out and work through the nights to educate themselves or have their mothers and fathers working and tough times. But you can't say this to these guys. They don't listen. I don't know what's going on. Look, let's not get pessimistic. But I tell ya, the thing my folks had to do to get me through school … I won't even talk about it."

By the time he started at St. Kieran's, Rory had trimmed The Fontana Showband down to a six-piece and really started to make a name for himself. They regularly outplayed the headliners they were opening for. The members of The

Fontana Showband all wanted to achieve "success" but the word had a different meaning for everyone. For Rory, success meant playing the right music to fill houses while being new and inventive. To the others it was cars and being with girlfriends every night. But they were more than happy to go along in accordance with Rory's definition. After all, he was the main attraction. He was a talented, good-looking young man. And he was among the first in Ireland to have long hair. When Gallagher appeared on "Pickin' The Pops" it was the first time anyone had seen a showband musician with long hair. He took a lot of "stick" about that and it infuriated Donal. A lot of people would try and provoke a reaction but Rory, being a pacifist, never allowed anyone to faze him. Donal's temper was enough for both of them.

Gallagher was having fun playing the local circuit but it didn't satisfy the purist side of him. He wanted to play music that touched his soul. He wanted to venture out and begin the journey of developing his true musical passion. In the early part of 1964 he saw how The Beatles had established the idea of rock bands as independent, self-defined units that wrote and performed original songs. Rory began to lobby for an image change for The Fontana.

At certain times of the year, Lent in this case, the clergy didn't like entertainment or dancing going on. It was a time for church so most of the dance halls were closed, making work for musicians very scarce. There was an exodus of showbands that would go to England for the six weeks leading to Easter. Those who had immigrated to the London area had set up a network of Irish ballrooms and were quite welcoming to the showbands. Rory convinced the band to go to London. He was looking forward to a break from the limitations of a ballroom and to exposing himself to new influences. On his nights off Rory would visit "The Marquee Club" to drink in the ambience and see original bands. He was inspired to make another change.

Donal Gallagher: "Rory was very taken with The Beatles and The Stones. He felt that Fontana and that whole showband thing wasn't going anywhere so he got the band to be given a complete makeover. He got the name to be 'The Impact,' which was a far more group-based name."

The name change also brought a minor shuffle in the lineup. John Lehane's brother, Michael, joined on organ and Johnny Campbell replaced Eamon O'Sullivan on drums.

In late spring of 1965 Rory decided to obtain management to secure work abroad. Peter Prendergast, who owned The Arcadia, recommended his brother Phillip, who quickly obtained a six-week residency for The Impact at an American Air Force base outside Madrid, Spain. The Americans wanted to hear R&B and rock 'n' roll. Gallagher had more in common with them, sharing love for the blues, as opposed to entertaining ballroom dancers.

Back in Ireland and armed with a more aggressive manner, Rory refused to be governed by showband conventions. Soon after recording a demo of the Larry Williams song "Slow Down," the band was booked to appear on "Pickin' The Pops," broadcast from Dublin. The show's panel booked acts by listening to the latest releases. The Impact had rehearsed the number they were they had been designated to play, the Buddy Holly-penned ballad "Valley Of Tears." But at the very last minute Rory informed the band that they were going to perform "Slow Down." There wasn't anything anyone could do about it. The show was live. Instead of giving them the usual dross, Rory got them off their seats. He took a terrible tongue lashing from the panel but didn't particularly care.

As opening act to the top bands, Rory regularly provoked the wrath of dance hall managers and promoters by working the crowd into such a frenzy that they would stop dancing to watch him. If people were watching the band it stopped the flow of the dance, creating tension amongst the management. The Impact also risked losing work by upstaging headline acts such as The Royal and The Dixies. They were told, "Either you quit doing those numbers or no more gigs." As an opener you were supposed to keep it simple. Don't be "too" good. But The Impact didn't hold back. Their attitude was if the headliner were better, so be it. If they weren't, then tough luck.

Gallagher became increasingly disillusioned with the showband circuit and considered starting his own group. His talent was miles ahead of everyone else. Declan O'Keeffe remembers Rory as having something special from the beginning. Manager Prendergast had prepared a press release for The Impact and asked each member to list his favorite composer. O'Keeffe listed Gallagher, who had recently written a few compositions. "You Fooled Me All The Time" and "I Want You To Be Happy" were but two of a half dozen. They were fairly derivative of the beat groups of the time.

Donal Gallagher: "Oddly enough I've got a recording of 'You Fool Me All The Time' on acetate. Back then it was a novelty that they would do one or two numbers of their own. And as The Impact progressed it was welcomed when Rory would try and introduce an R&B song into the set. He would have probably been starting to develop some of the early Taste stuff like 'Blister On The Moon.' He was very driven. It was quite exciting to see where this would take him. The whole new culture of The Beatles, The Stones, the whole Liverpool sound. It was easier for a teenager to identify with that as it was to identify with the older forms of music, which was a little bit more sentimental. 'Schlagger music' [laughs] is the only word I can think of."

Donal had started working with his brother, doing things from helping lift equipment to booking ferry tickets. But his involvement was of a more personal nature. Rory needed an ally to back his convictions. He was quite happy to keep The Impact together even though there were certain limitations within that lineup. He got the band used to a recording environment and started to rehearse more. Rory enjoyed playing in London, earning money and spending time frequenting The Marquee. He would watch bands such as The Graham Bond Organization and some of the early John Mayall lineups. Spencer Davis. Georgie Fame. The Lovin' Spoonful. The Impact opened for The Byrds. London was the epicenter of the music business and the place to be.

In late 1965, when offered a three-week stint in Hamburg, Germany, they jumped on it. The Liverpool bands were all cutting their teeth in Hamburg. It was a very vibrant, active scene. Some of The Impact became disenchanted because they didn't like being away from home and the hard work. By the time they got to Hamburg they were down to a three-piece. It was Rory, Johnny Campbell on drums and bass player Oliver Tobin.

Most clubs demanded a four-piece beat group so Rory got a friend to pose with an organ for a publicity photograph. Rory managed to talk the club owner into allowing them to do it as a three-piece by saying the organ player had come down with a case of appendicitis on the ferry over. But rather than let the promoter down they would entertain in the meantime. The trio proved so popular that the owner booked them into his other clubs. The metamorphosis was complete. At this point Rory was only eighteen.

The sleaze pits of Hamburg opened Rory's eyes to a world far removed from that of the showbands. The Beatles had set the standard for the atmosphere in Germany. The gigs lasted seven, eight hours a night. A quarter hour break on the hour. The forty-five minute sets were grueling but it allowed the bands to play as much of the music they liked as they wanted to. He remembered times when there would be nobody left in the club at 3:30 a.m. It was hard-gained experience but paved the way for dates there with Taste later on.

Rory never felt his future would evolve around playing six nights a week with a showband. He wanted to get into a serious group, to play his own brand of music. He'd compromised his art enough and wanted out of the showband environment. Upon returning to Ireland, The Impact broke up. It marked Rory's rock 'n' roll liberation.

•   •   •

In 1964 Eric Kittringham hooked up with two friends in Cork, guitarist Peter Sangquist and drummer Norman Damery. They took on the name The Axills. "We were diabolical!" said Kittringham. The trio went into the musician's union hall on a Sunday morning, the time dues were paid and auditions were held. They performed a couple of numbers as a few Federation members sat and listened. The Axills were accepted but it was suggested that they add a few members for dance hall gigs and they refused, so their dance hall appearances were restricted to being the opener. Yet the band was working a steady three nights a week and getting their fair share of weddings and the like. Their set list consisted strictly of cover songs from Spencer Davis to The Rolling Stones to The Beatles.

In 1966, at a time when Rory was looking for musicians to play with, guitarist Sangquist left The Axills, forcing Kittringham and Damery to look for a replacement. They approached Rory about filling the void on guitar. Rory jammed with them at The Cavalier Club and things went well. At a later meeting in a local eatery, Rory was asked if he would be interested in replacing Sangquist and the answer was an emphatic "no." But when he asked them if they would be interested in starting something new they agreed. Contrary to tales of deep relevance to musical pedigree, they had seen a floor mat advertising Guinness beer and the word "taste" was on it. They called themselves Taste. They started playing in small venues as Rory began to write.

Eric Kittringham: "We did a few practices in my mother's house. Rory used to have numbers that he used to sing and I had a few numbers I used to sing. We basically started off doing mostly covers with a couple of early numbers that he had penned himself. And then he took over doing 99.9 percent of the singing and nearly all his own work. It felt right from the beginning."

While the new band started coming into its own, Donal got a job at a club called The Cavereign doing everything from DJing to tearing tickets at the door. He made the owner aware of Taste and they soon started playing there and quickly developed a following. It seemed that every time the band ventured out of the city, The Cavereign would sell out their return as quickly as the tickets were put on sale. People were soon hanging from the rafters. Taste also played the ballrooms in Cork to strong opposition from showbands. Promoters met three musicians and thought they were being shortchanged when told there was nobody else in the band. The IFM had rules about the minimum number of musicians required and even sent representatives to the halls to count heads. The bouncers would tip off Taste if the union rep was coming to check on the band. There was usually a keyboard off to the side. Donal just walked on stage, somebody else would pick up a tambourine and it was a five-piece.

The Federation came down hard on Taste when they got their first booking at the Arcadia and tried to prevent the dance from going ahead. The controversy split the union locally. Showband elements that felt threatened were against allowing a three-piece to perform. Younger musicians in the beat groups opposed them. The showbands were under pressure in 1967. Many bands found it difficult to survive with so many musicians in their lineups. An extraordinary union meeting was called at the Metropole Hotel one Sunday morning. If Taste agreed to do an audition for the Federation, they would consider giving the gig their blessing. Rory was insulted. "I've been in a showband long enough and I've proven myself. I'm not going to do an audition for anybody." The union backed down and the performance went ahead. It was a significant victory.

Taste then ventured to Hamburg, Germany, where Rory's reputation preceded them. They played seven hours a night. It was hard going but they loved it.

Eric Kittringham: "I enjoyed it immensely. Three raw Irish mommies' boys out there liking all of it. Anything goes, ya know? We had some great times and some scary ones as well."

Taste fulfilled Rory's vision. A rhythm section and lyrics that were based around his guitar. The band barely earned enough to keep itself on the road but that was all they needed.

At home, Southern promoters started bringing bands down from the North of Ireland, which was a drastic step at the time. There was a little bit of a trading of ideas between the various musicians from the North and the South. Rory had played a few clubs in Dublin but Dublin was more of a "soul" town. Promoters may have been blind to Gallagher's talents, but accomplished touring musicians, who shared dates with Taste in Cork, recognized his flair. Belfast's Dave Glover Showband bassist George Jones spoke to Rory and complimented him on his playing, remarking on how advanced he was. Being a huge blues fan, Jones found it very difficult to believe that a young Corksman had enveloped himself so thoroughly in the art form. He declared Rory's guitar playing to be as advanced as Jimi Hendrix. Jones recommended that Rory get to Belfast and try to break into the budding blues scene there.

Taste hooked up with ex-Axills guitarist Peter Sangquists' brother, Kevin, to manage them. He headed a national magazine based out of Dublin called *Spotlight*. He had contacts in Belfast and arranged a weekend for Taste to play there. Van Morrison had a club called The Maritime, which had changed its name to The Club Rado. It was a church hall and seaman's mission. There was also Sammy Houston's Jazz Club, where Van had played as well. "Them" were the band of the day in Belfast but by then they'd moved to London. Taste played Sammy Houston's the first night and went down like an absolute storm. The audience loved them. The next night they played The Club Rado. Belfast was more in tune with Rory's love of the blues. Taste secured a residency at The Club Rado in the summer of 1967.

Donal Gallagher: "The reaction was phenomenal. First of all, to take the music out of it, for a band from the South to make the effort to go up and play in the North … the Northern people will say to you, 'There's no border between us and the South. But it's the people in the South that make the border because they don't venture up to the North.' For obvious reasons [laughs]! So for someone to take that giant foot forward…"

The manager of The Club Rado was Eddie Kennedy. His partner was Marvyn Solomons, whose brother Phil was managing Van Morrison. The Solomons controlled the whole marketing and distribution of records in the North of Ireland. Solomons Sr. was a key figure in Decca Records and had given Phil a subsidiary label, Major-Minor Records, to manage. As soon as Kennedy saw Taste play he approached them and said straight out, "I want to manage you." He explained his contacts in London. He was involved with the NEMS crowd, Brian Epstein's people, and working with an up-and-coming Robert Stigwood.

Eddie continued to drop the names of his legitimate contacts and Taste gave him the chance to concern himself with their business affairs. Eddie Kennedy also managed a band called Cheese, whom Rory was familiar with. Bassist Richard "Charlie" McCracken and drummer John Wilson had come up through the showbands and that common thread led to a meeting in Hamburg in 1966 where the three first met each other.

The first order of business for Taste was to get to London to perform and record. Eddie Kennedy had secured them work in London as part of an exchange. Peter Green had just left John Mayall's Bluesbreakers and had formed Fleetwood Mac. Cream and Mick Taylor were also playing in Belfast and Taste would open for these bands. In return they were given similar positions in London at The Marquee, the venue Rory had always wanted to play. Once Taste got into The Marquee they were a success and were offered a residency.

Roy Eldridge was a young journalist with *Melody Maker*.

Roy Eldridge: "I got to *Melody Maker* in '68. In those days Rory was playing the odd gig at places like The Speakeasy and little sort of clubby-type gigs. *Melody Maker* was going through a bit of a transition. You had a jazz page; you had a blues page. And I guess people like Rory, at the time, really weren't quite sure where they fitted in. So in those early days with *Melody Maker* Rory was sort of an interest to the blues purist. And then there was sort of a younger generation of which I guess I was one, where there was this different 'rock' thing happening. Rory fitted in on both sides of that coin. Then they exploded very quickly."

Taste was getting a lot of work in England and continental Europe. And whenever they went back home it bordered on a hero's welcome. There was overwhelming support for Rory and the band. They would play at City Hall and the shows would sell out instantly.

Joe O'Herlihy: "But Cork is a great leveler kind of place. If you get a little too big for your boots they'll put you back on the ground very quickly! It's an Irish trait, which is a little unfortunate, but there's a whole lot of begrudgers out there. And in Rory's case there was quite a few. It was one of those things that you would have to make it on the international stage, on that scale, then everyone then would welcome you back to Cork. They knew you all your life and you were a hero. But certainly getting to that stage … you probably got there with a bit of a nudge and a wink and a hunched shoulder every now and again. You'd have to prove yourself ten times over to make it in Cork. Whereas if you made it from London and came back they'd be dancing at your feet in seconds."

Though Rory was adamant about not releasing a single, Kennedy and Solomons were anxious to see how the band would fare. There was a demo-studio above the Solomons-Pierce store where Major-Minor Records did their distribution. Taste laid down thirty minutes of original material. Rory brought a unique professionalism into the studio by having Donal bring in slabs of street pavement and placed them under the drums to get a brightness in a very dead room, to get a crisp recording sound. He was also experimenting with overdubbing and guitar tones. The engineer was immediately frustrated. He was used to country-and-western acts going in and doing what they were told. Suddenly there was someone telling him what "he" wanted. The tension was evident but it delivered good results. Major-Minor released a single, "Blister On The Moon." Rory repeated his opposition to it. A hit single could pigeonhole an artist for life. Not only did he not want to get branded, he also didn't want to compete with himself. He didn't want his focus to be how to follow up his last single. He had seen too many acts go that way. This led to a management conflict between Kennedy and Solomons. But when Eddie realized where his bread and butter came from, he sided with Rory and the release wasn't promoted.

The band was becoming very well known but there was no money to speak of. Eddie Kennedy was handling everything and, for the most part, everyone felt secure with the arrangement. The band was given an allowance with Rory earning in the vicinity of £15 a week.

Eric Kittringham: "We actually ended up sharing a basement flat with an old school chum of mine that he was renting in Belgravia, London. We had absolutely nothing. My chum's buddy had a cousin named Tony Faulkner. He worked for this fruit and veg wholesaler and used to deliver veggies around to all the restaurants and bistros in London. He'd siphon off about twenty mushrooms out of each basket. Not enough to be missed but we used to have fried mushrooms for dinner. That was it."

Norman Damery came from an insurance background and had a good head for figures. Eric was more into the fun and the image of it. But they were both constantly after Kennedy about where the funds were going. Rory couldn't have been bothered. To him, the music was all that mattered. But Donal was also starting to worry, especially after one particular night in Cork.

Donal Gallagher: "They were too big to play the club that they were associated with. So I took the task on of promoting the band in the City Hall, which was a very large venue for that size of band. To go from having to play two or three nights to 200 people to go up to a place that actually housed over 2,000 people was a massive leap. I promoted that gig and did it very successfully, only to discover that the manager arrived on the night and did the box office. He basically said that he'd banked all the money for us and everything had been taken care of."

By mid 1968 Polydor Records started sending different reps to The Marquee to check out Taste. The club had its own recording studio at the back of the venue, Marquee Recording Studios. The band played there one afternoon under the watchful eye of a few Polydor executives and everyone returned to their respective corners to await comment following a meeting between Polydor and Eddie Kennedy. When Eddie sat down with Rory and Donal he informed them of Polydor's decision. They would offer Taste a recording contract if Eric and Norman were replaced with a new, stronger rhythm section. And not to worry because Eddie had Charlie McCracken and John Wilson, the rhythm section of Kennedy's other client, Cheese, sitting in the wings. It all seemed a little too perfect. Rory really didn't have the heart to let Eric and Norman go. Donal was convinced Polydor would have signed the band irrespective of the rhythm section. They had never heard this request directly from Polydor, only from Eddie.

Eric Kittringham: "Rory was totally, and I mean this in the nicest way now, totally focused on his career. He knew exactly what he wanted. And, without sounding cruel, I don't think it mattered to him once he got there. From that point of view I don't think there was that much loyalty there. All Rory had to do was say, 'No Eddie. Hold on. We started off together. The lads have been through the hardest times

with me.' Which we had. I didn't mind, to be honest with ya. I was actually totally fed up with it. I loved the music and I loved the time. But I felt we could have been that way forever and made nothing. I was tired of starving. And there were always questions about Kennedy. Eddie had Rory bamboozled as well, to be honest. Kennedy was a devious bastard to put it quite bluntly. He wasn't up front, do you know what I mean? And we were forever on to Kennedy about where the money was. 'What the fuck's happening with this? Why we weren't getting this and when are we gonna get it right?' We never, ever let up. This really pissed him off! In my heart and soul I really do believe that Eddie got us tossed because of our constant demanding of where the money was going. In fact, McCracken and John Wilson, that band were the best Gallagher band of all. To my mind. They were two superb musicians. I have to give them that."

John Wilson: "Eddie Kennedy approached me and Charlie. He said that he was ready to sign a record deal for Rory but that the record company insisted that he have a new bass player and drummer. They didn't think Eric and Norman were up to it. Subsequently, years later, we realized it was a lie. That it was Eddie's idea to change the band. The little tight unit, socially and from a friendship point of view that the old group had, was completely gone. It was a 'divide and conquer' situation. And Eddie realized he would have that. All through the time in the band he would be telling me and Charlie one thing and telling Rory something totally different. And that suited his purposes. His intention all along was to get as much out of us as he possibly could."

It was certainly well known that John Wilson was a gifted drummer. He had a great reputation. Donal knew him from the time he was a DJ at The Cavereign and John was playing with The Misfits as well as having played with an early version of Them. He was the best drummer Donal had seen at that time. Eddie took pride in proclaiming himself an empire builder, a budding Robert Stigwood. He tried to break Cheese in at the same time as Taste but Cheese disintegrated amongst themselves. This was seen as a way to keep those close to him together and avoid having to account for funds that Eric and Norman were constantly on him about. Rory had never made any reference to Donal about the lack of musical abilities that Eric and Norman supposedly had. Yet Donal agrees that, whatever Eddie's reasons, changing the rhythm section was good for the band. An opinion that John Wilson himself disagrees with.

John Wilson: "I'm sure that it caused Rory a great amount of personal pain. They were very close and they had done a lot of trailblazing together. It was totally unfair that Norm and Eric got the criticism that they would have got by Eddie casting aspersions that maybe they weren't good enough players. They certainly were good enough players and Taste was very exciting and very successful. Maybe not successful in terms of making someone lots of money. But if they played to two people or they played to 2,000 people, everybody went away happy."

Rory hooked up with Taste part II. In August of 1968 Rory, Charlie, John and Donal drove to Scotland and played three nights. They then premiered the new lineup at The Marquee and it went over extremely well. Taste was born again, this time with an impending record contract looming. As the band hit the road on their limited budget, Donal took on more responsibilities. He drove the band, set up the gear, shuttled the musicians from the hotel to the gig and back, was responsible for sound and lights and dealing with promoters and the like. And they were performing six or seven nights a week.

Donal Gallagher: "The cutting edge was the live work. It was really where you were creating your record buyers. Rory didn't worry too much about the day-to-day record company thing. It was like being a football team. Every day was the next match. It took on those proportions. You had to go away with a win at every gig. And their reputation as a live band was second to none. Rory had come up through the school of the showbands, entertaining people. That was how he had learned his craft. It wasn't about how you could exploit via records. He was too honest to cheat on his records by orchestrating or adding, or 'guilding the lily,' as it were."

At this same time a bootleg live Taste was released, catching Rory totally off guard. There were no entertainment lawyers around and copyright laws hadn't yet evolved. He tried to find out how this illegal pressing had been released but couldn't. It was entitled "In Concert." The performance was held at The Marquee, which made it easy to run lines to the studio, and the concert was filmed for eventual use as a base for a documentary, though this never happened. The audiotapes surfaced because of the film recording. The culprits are still being tracked down as of the time this book is going to print.

John Wilson: "The fact that some of those live things came out was awful. I know from friends that there is one where a side ends in the middle of a drum solo. And you turn it over to the other side and the drum solo starts again [laughs]!"

When Taste went in to record their debut they were given two days. There were no formal rehearsals. It was go in, play and get out. The pressure was enormous. Gallagher was very good at stretching the limits and talking his way into a little more studio time but he still didn't feel there was enough. Rory was trying to develop a sound and the next thing he knew there was a cover on it, and he wasn't happy with that either. Polydor and Kennedy had taken the tapes and released them as quickly as possible. Gallagher had reservations but getting airplay widened booking possibilities throughout England. And as soon as the record came out Taste hit the road. Hard. An impressionable Gerry McAvoy was a witness.

Gerry McAvoy: "I saw Taste in Belfast when I was quite young. Totally knocked out by the band. It was like a breath of fresh air when they came to Belfast. The main band at the time was a band called The Few, playing John Mayall and the Bluesbreakers stuff. And Taste came on and just wiped the floor with them! Absolutely amazing! After Van Morrison and the high energy people had left and moved to the States or England, there was sort of a lull there for quite a few years. Taste picked everybody back up again. To see energy at that level was quite amazing. It took everybody by surprise. What came across was Rory in the forefront. And his amazing guitar playing. It's hard to describe. You had to be there in The Maritime Club and to see a packed audience when Taste played. Rory playing with his battered Strat, an old Army shirt, a pair of jeans, a pair of white sneakers. They were all just dripping with sweat. The atmosphere was just unbelievable. And Belfast became Rory's second home."

John Wilson: "Nobody really knew how to react to us. And because of the difference in Rory on and off stage, can you imagine how record company executives would react? Rory wasn't into wearing clothes like Jimi Hendrix or trying to carry a superstardom image like Cream. Rory always used to say that he never wanted to be famous. Because if he became big, there was only one way to go. And that was back down again. So Rory's attitude was he wanted to be there. He envisioned himself being like a jazz musician. Jazz musicians play until they drop dead. Whereas pop stars have to go when their hair falls out. Rory just wanted to be a musician. Just a guy playing his music. But that's not what record companies wanted to hear. They wanted to hear of guys who wanted to have Rolls Royces and villas in the South of France. And that meant they were going to have to sell records. Rory wasn't interested."

London was where Taste anchored themselves. Rory basked in the capitol because he could see the bands he wanted to see. His residency at The Marquee promoted Taste to the National Jazz and Blues Festival, which has now evolved into the Reading Festival, going from an audience of 800 to 10,000. But through it all financial worries were reawakened.

Rory Gallagher: "Money? In the Taste days I had to borrow money from my mother. And she had to work to keep me on the road."

Donal Gallagher: "I think she helped him when they were away, particularly in England. Sometimes they'd run out of money or get into difficulties. She certainly would have supported him and was very keen to do so. She knew he was following his profession, if you like. She was a woman who should have been on the stage. She loved singing and drama and probably at another time she would have done very successfully as an actress."

Rory wanted to get to America. He had a very close young friend who emigrated with his family in the early 60s and was hanging out at The Café A Go-Go. He had seen The Doors and there was a lot of swapping of notes and records. Rory developed a mental image of where he would be playing in New York and where to go and what he should be doing. And to go beyond that, to Chicago, New Orleans, the blues homes. Rory saw headlining The Marquee as a springboard to that.

Rory was much happier with the results of the sessions Taste achieved when they returned to the studio to record "On The Boards" in late 1968. But again Kennedy released a single, "What's Going On," without Rory's knowledge. It had not been released in the U.K. but it went to number 1 in Germany before Rory found out. Eddie explained it away, "Oh, the Germans must have done it without permission but it's too late to stop it now. It's already in the Top 10." It seemed that Kennedy couldn't get a firm understanding of what it was that Rory wanted to establish.

Donal Gallagher: "There was always a bit of conflict going on because Kennedy wanted the release of singles which Rory was completely anti. A manager would have a far more commercial take on things. Coming from the old school of showbands it was very hard for a guy like Kennedy to understand an artist having his own integrity. Musicians were people that were told what to do and what to play. So this new breed of independent musician that was coming through at the time was completely alien."

Wilson and McCracken agreed with the direction that Rory wanted to take. Polydor wanted them to be like Cream and become a "supergroup" and have "personalities." But Taste just wanted to play the music. They were a record company's nightmare. And the results of the band's financial concerns weren't helping.

Donal Gallagher: "Early on I'd seen the possibilities of what could happen to the finances. Eddie would say that I was too young to understand about money so he put it away for me 'cuz I would only spend it. Everyone was on a salary at that time. It was meager. It was more like a per diem. There was no money to buy an improved P.A. system or equipment. Everything had to be repaired. And this was at a time when the band was making a good turnover. A concern set in. But it was always going to be rectified. The next thing you're into the second album and you get a bit of a wages uplift. But things really weren't improving."

In the spring of 1969 the band hit a new peak. On a return visit to The Marquee, Taste broke an attendance record that had been set by Jimi Hendrix. It meant great publicity for the record company and management. To Taste it was just another gig. But it reminded Robert Stigwood of them, who was first impressed with Taste when they were booked on Cream's farewell concert at Royal Albert Hall. Stigwood held a party at his offices to announce a U.S. summer tour of newly formed Blind Faith featuring Steve Winwood, Rick Gretsch, Ginger Baker and Eric Clapton. Delaney, Bonnie & Friends were second on the bill. And Taste was supporting both.

Donal Gallagher: "We flew to New York. It was extremely exciting. The buzz of going to America for the first time."

Charlie McCracken: "Showbands had gone to America before but they played Irish clubs. We had no idea what to expect. It was our biggest tour on the road at that time. We were basically playing 20,000-capacity arenas. We'd done some open-air gigs and there would have been quite a few people there but not enough to be playing to that kind of number every night. We were in the deep end straight away, that's for sure. And I don't think Rory was ready to do that. I don't think he liked doing that too much."

Donal Gallagher: "The Stigwood agency had decided that Chris Blackwell's band, Free, would get some dates. We didn't play New York. We went down to see Blind Faith, Delaney, Bonnie & Friends and Free at Madison Square Garden. That was the first venue I ever saw in the States. It was packed. But that tour was an absolute disaster from an organizational point of view. Blind Faith were playing through the house P.A. system at Madison Square Garden. On a rotating stage. So you can imagine what the sound was like. It was atrocious."

John Wilson: "We weren't given any time to do anything. There were no sound checks or anything like that. We just went on and then did whatever we had to do. It was sort of a 'them and us' situation. Delaney and Bonnie; they were all over Eric Clapton. And eventually Eric was going on stage with them before Blind Faith came on. Which obviously didn't go over well with Robert Stigwood Management! Because he was preempting the whole thing. It was a pretty weird tour. And from our point of view, as Taste, it didn't help us at all."

Donal Gallagher: "A lot of the audience that Blind Faith were getting weren't happy with them because they weren't satisfying the Cream fans nor were they satisfying the Traffic fans. And the only thing that they could recognize was when Ginger Baker did 'Do What You Like.' Because to the Cream fans, it was 'Toad.' It was Ginger doing his solo [laughs].

"It was a Sunday afternoon gig in the Hartford Stadium. And the promoter provided what looked for all the world like a preacher's caravan. You know, they opened the two sides, with little column speakers on the stage to play to the stadium. And they had a very bad turnout. Delaney and Bonnie weren't going to play. Winwood didn't want to play. Clapton was trying to keep everybody happy. Taste went on and played and did their bit. Blind Faith eventually did go on and play without Winwood. Clapton, Baker and Gretsch did something and a few people helped out. I recall Janis Joplin being at the gig. There was only four crew on that tour and forty-nine musicians. So you were expected — 'all hands on deck.' Because Ginger was the difficult one I was allowed to go near him. And I remember walking back with him from the stage. Joplin came running over and said 'Hi, Ginger. You know what? You guys sucked [laughs]!'

"We started to make noise about the fact that there was no P.A. system. We went down to the Spectrum in Philadelphia and again had to play through the house system on a rotating stage. All the band equipment was at the boot of the bus. And then you had Ginger or whoever shooting up, holding the whole bus up for hours. As the opening act we were always getting it in the back of the neck. The bus would arrive late. We would have to panic.

"So we got a hold of this guy Hannolly to do the P.A. system. We said, 'The tour is killing everyone.' We'd come all this way and there won't be a tour to do because the reviews were bad for Blind Faith. And it was going to affect the box office. Their album cover had been banned. This was all having a negative effect on the tour. But we got the right guys in for production. We got a tractor-trailer unit on the road and suddenly the whole tour picked up. We had some dates that we couldn't do because Hannolly's P.A. had to go up to Woodstock. I remember sitting on the street in New York, the musicians discussing whether they would go up and play Woodstock or not. We kept saying, 'Yeah, let's do it.' Clapton said, 'Yeah, it sounds like fun.' But Winwood wouldn't do it. And the Delaney and Bonnie band said, 'Aw, we'll never get paid.' So we didn't. And it was a shame. One of those bits of history. So we sat in this bloody bus instead and drove to Milwaukee."

By this stage everybody knew something was wrong. Rory didn't socialize inside or outside of Taste. Everyone associated with the tour felt that having Rory and Eric Clapton sharing transportation would bring the talented guitarists together. But it never happened. Rory just sat at the back of the bus on his own.

John Wilson: "I just think that's the way the guy was. The way I used to describe it, Rory only existed for two hours of the twenty-four. Those were the two hours he was standing on stage. The other twenty-two hours he was some other guy hanging around waiting to be Rory again. Kids would come and see us at gigs and think Rory was this really wild guy, leaping about and going crazy and doing all this stuff. And yet anyone who met him offstage, he was always very timid, polite, shy. At that time, he didn't really drink or anything. He didn't party at all. He didn't hang around with girls. He just played the gig and disappeared. He spent a lot of time on his own. Playing and writing and reading books and buying records and stuff like that. He surprised people. Until they got to know the guy. But that was one of the great things about Rory. The fact that this person could appear. And for someone like me to have the privilege to work with the guy, you looked forward to every gig. Because you couldn't wait for the guy to come back out again. I liked the guy offstage but I loved the guy onstage."

A probable cause of Rory's solitude may have been the fact that Eddie Kennedy came over with his son, Billy, and that he took the attitude that this was a sort of vacation. Eddie was content in just hanging around and letting everyone know that he managed a band.

Eric Kittringham: "Billy was a nice fellow but a bit of a shit. Daddy had plenty of money and he wasn't shy to let you know."

Donal Gallagher: "Eddie was a fun guy but he was a bit of a dictator. Rory felt that here was a manager and he was

allowed to be on a musician's bus and that he was creating a business vibe about the tour rather than a music vibe. Rory just didn't like the way it was being operated and that Eddie was doing it just for the fun of it. Rory felt that we should be staying on instead of doing four or five weeks for that summer. Rory would have sooner been playing clubs to his own audience than playing to 20,000 to 30,000 people in an arena. He hated those big shows."

The best way to see Rory was in a small, sweaty club where, as he used to say, "You can see the whites of their eyes." To suddenly become confronted with daytime gigs in a baseball stadium or a hockey arena was very foreign to him. Often they would have to go on and play while most of the audience was still trying to find their seats.

All the traveling was done by bus resulting in a lot of down time being spent trying to catch up on sleep. Taste invariably had to stay at cheaper hotels than the rest of them.

Donal Gallagher: "Occasionally you stayed at the same hotel but there were usually three different hotels being used. We used to get picked up first thing in the morning. Go over then to pick up the Delaney and Bonnie people, who were the lion's share of the number of people; twenty or twenty-five bodies. You can imagine getting them onto the bus. And then over to Blind Faith's hotel and wait until Ginger had surfaced. It was a nightmare! Bum cramps from sitting on the bus waiting around for everybody else. And I don't actually remember money passing hands. Your bills were covered and you got an allowance."

But Rory did take full advantage of being in America.

Donal Gallagher: "Seeing Muddy Waters play. I remember Winwood, Clapton, Rory and Baker coming along. Guys from the Delaney group. But being American, I don't think they appreciated Muddy as much as the Europeans had the respect for Muddy. That was Rory's first acquaintance with Muddy. Clapton didn't want to get up and jam. In fairness to Clapton he didn't refuse. I remember we all went down to Ungano's to see Muddy Waters and there was a very small turnout of public. The audience was made up of mostly musicians. Everybody from Steve Marriott to Hendrix, Buddy Miles, it was just an incredible turnout of people. And I think Clapton's view was that, 'If I get up and start jamming I won't be able to hear Muddy Waters.' He was being more modest about it by saying, 'Well, let's hear Muddy.' Marriott got up. And I remember Buddy Miles playing drums. And still, to this day, it was one of the finest, most understated drum solos I've ever heard in my life.

"There were situations like that when we got to Chicago. I remember the Polydor rep; it would have been Atco in those days. We had a day off and they provided a limo for the day [laughs]. Well, after a bus! Rory kept the limo after getting chummy with the driver. And there were really 'no go' areas at the time. Chicago areas where the blues were played. I mean, you had race riots, the Vietnam thing; you had the problems of the day. I don't know how he got this limo driver to go down there but we survived it! I think it was Hound Dog Taylor. And the people couldn't believe that someone would take the time to come out. The car was a bit of a defense because they probably thought, 'Well, he must be a star! We'd better be nice [laughs]!' They let us in there and they gave us a table. They were so hospitable. They started bringing down a lot of the local kids. We had a record company guy. The next thing we're doing a talent showcase for all the musicians in the area, all thinking they were going to get signed up. And there were some phenomenal players.

"By the time we got west the L.A. date had been cancelled. One of the tasks I'd been given was to look after Bonnie Bramlett. I was sort of chaperoning her. We rolled into Los Angeles. It was my birthday, the ninth of August. The plan was that we would have a big party. And that was the day of the Tate murders. That had just hit the streets. And the fear! It had been associated with the music thing immediately. And drugs and all sorts of things. And Bonnie's friend was murdered at the Tate house. Jay Sebring, her hairdresser. She was completely devastated. I was sort of consoling her. It was quite a freaky thing! We were so disappointed. We were so looking forward to getting to the West Coast. Rory had supported The Byrds when they came to London and he was looking forward to seeing them again. We spent a few hours in L.A. and we were back on the road, this time to Seattle.

"The summer of '69 was a peculiar time. From an American point of view. With Vietnam. We had guys who were draft dodgers on the bus, smuggling them into Canada to get them out of there. There was man landing on the moon. I remember playing Washington or Baltimore that night. The audience was waiting for Blind Faith to go on stage. And Ginger absolutely refusing until he saw Neil Armstrong step on the moon. The audience had to wait for over an hour [laughs]! The Mansons and the Woodstocks. It was really a brilliant experience. We made a lot of fans. But Rory was determined then to go back to the States and, where possible, play in his own right. He'd sooner have played to fifty people that were there for him rather than play for thousands who were there for somebody else."

John Wilson: "We would have been better off not doing the Blind Faith tour. We would have been better off going to America and playing clubs."

While Taste was touring as an opening act in America their popularity in Europe was rapidly increasing. Sales of "On The Boards" were brisk through the aid of press. No one back home seemed to know how the band was doing on the other side of the ocean. They would get the odd blurb in *Music Express* but getting a copy of that particular magazine in Ireland wasn't easy.

Donal Gallagher: "It was starting to come to a head. They had broken on a European scale. 'On The Boards' was Top Ten in the U.K. The single had taken off in Germany and had gone straight to Number One. They were the biggest thing in Europe. There was no two ways about it. France, where it was the early days of rock 'n' roll. Holland had come on board. In 1968 Taste was the top group in Denmark … had broken Scandinavia. So they were going back to Europe as opposed to London if you like. And had gone from The Marquee to playing The Lyceum in London, which had a bigger capacity. We were doing major festivals in the U.K. as headliners. We got back in late August/September, 1969. I was looking back the other day at the *Billboard*s. First week on the charts with a bullet. The Blind Faith album had come out simultaneously with 'On The Boards.' There was only something like five place points between them. And the first Taste album had surprisingly gone into the *Billboard* charts. Even though I was there at the time, I hadn't realized. And this was part of the friction. This information was vital to Rory and he wasn't getting it. He felt Kennedy had used the whole trip as a holiday as opposed to cultivating agencies or venues or promoters.

"I don't mean to be unkind to Kennedy but he saw the whole exercise of America as a huge investment to fly everybody there, the cost of doing it. He felt out of his depth. And it would require somebody else to be manager/agent in America and he'd lose control. Where they had sewn up Europe, making very good money for the time. Having lots of success. And he had friendships with the guys that were the heads of Polydor, which was a German company. So there were two distinct different views. Rory wanted to come over and work America for all it was worth. Kennedy wanted to remain in Europe. If success came from America, so be it. If not, sod it."

Had the money been reinvested in the band the situation may have been tolerable. But they were still traveling in a small version of an Econoline van that didn't have proper seats. A second vehicle would have been appreciated. The way things were, the band had to arrive hours early for gigs to allow Donal to set the gear up and would have to wait for the stage to be struck and the van loaded before they could leave.

Donal Gallagher: "The venues had gotten larger and the audiences were massive. But the group was playing through the P.A. system that Rory had inherited from the showband. It had 140 RMS watts, which would be the equivalent of 300 American watts."

Rory finally started making inquiries. Kennedy's response was always the same. "When you come back in three weeks from the German tour I'll have all the accounts ready for you." And there was always another tour. As Rory was starting to express his uneasiness, Eddie started solidifying his relationships with John and Charlie. When Wilson got married that year, Kennedy approved a mortgage for a house to allow John to bring his bride to London. The band was told that it was an advance against what they were rightfully owed.

John Wilson: "From there on in it was a struggle. We came back and we did other gigs as good as ever. The music never suffered, ever! No matter what was going down personally. When we went on stage, we played the music and we did our thing. And that's the one thing that used to bring us back together again. But really what was happening was the fact that Rory started to think, 'Well, here we're playing bigger gigs. We're selling records. Where's the money?' All we got was our salary, just to pay the bills."

Donal Gallagher: "Eddie knew that the money was gone. As soon as it came in it was gone. He had his ways and means but the money was not there. Kennedy was living in comfort, in the best of style on a par with the Stigwoods in London. His luxuries were being financed at our expense. And Rory could smell that. There were rumors that Stigwood was going to take over management of the band. So we waited to see what happened. And more importantly Rory didn't want to show any chinks in the armor to the likes of Polydor. You wanted them to believe in the band and do more for the record. It was a very tough path for him to take, to walk both sides.

"Rory felt all the success on paper can wait. 'Let's invest in the band itself. Let's get some comfort in here.' Rory had always seen the band basically as his because he was bandleader. He had Taste Mach I. He had brought it to Belfast and broken all the barriers. And suddenly his authority was being challenged. It was no longer his band. It was Eddie Kennedy's band. And he was being coerced into publishing deals that no one knew about at the time. There were a lot of deals being done behind his back. He was being made to sign things that he didn't understand. Ultimately, we got all that resolved. He was under twenty-one at the time so he couldn't have been made to sign."

Charlie McCracken: "It was a very frustrating time for everybody. And it just manifested itself in different ways."

John Wilson: "There were situations when people weren't speaking prior to playing. It was very difficult to shut that off when you went on stage. If you haven't spoken to someone for two or three days and you have to go onstage in front of a lot of people and play and communicate that way, it causes problems. There were a couple of occasions where Rory would do things that Charlie and myself may have thought, 'Why would he want to do this?' We'd start to play something and then he would just stop and start to play something completely different [laughs]. A cruel thing to do. No problem with it. But at that particular stage it seemed like a problem. All I can say is it never was as big as anybody might think it was. There was one occasion I personally can remember, near the end, where I'd said to Charlie, 'This is stupid. I'm not going to put up with this anymore.' We'd finished the set and people were screaming for more. And I said, 'No, we're not gonna go on.' And I didn't go on. Rory went on his own and did three, four encores. Charlie said to me, 'What have you proved? You're not proving anything.' And he was right. I was just being stupid."

Donal Gallagher: "John's attitude was he was going through his 'jazz phase.' I saw him quoted from an interview that his view on what they'd done in the previous two years was crap. My question to him was, 'Well, why didn't you leave the band then if you were such a strong musician or if you held such strong views?' I think that was just sour grapes. Rory knew how to entertain an audience without compromising his musical skills. Rory was an entertainer. And I think that was being viewed by John as 'That's not cool.'

"He liked Richard (Charlie). He admired John's drumming. He liked the band. It just became very difficult with the personalities. He went to them and said, 'Look, we really have a serious problem here. This is my band. This is where I want to take it. I don't trust the manager. None of us are getting anything. We're still on salaries. This is ridiculous. We haven't had an accountant so we've got to confront the manager.' But Kennedy had gotten to the other two first and said, 'Hang on a second. Rory wants to take all the money. Because it's his band, he's looking to me for the accounts. But he wants to take everything. And he's just using you guys as paid employees.' "

Rory felt he couldn't trust anyone anymore. He began a self-imposed isolation from all but Donal. Though he had been quite interactive with everyone to that point his dissatisfaction with what was going on around him caused him to develop a "loner" personality. He didn't want to share anything that concerned business or activities that occurred offstage.

Charlie McCracken: "I don't blame him. I think after the problems we had business-wise, he wanted control of everything. From my point of view, I thought that was fair enough. He calls the shots."

After successfully touring Europe for close to a year, Taste had been booked as a featured act at the Isle of Wight Festival in the summer of 1970. Onstage the band played as well as ever. As far as the public was concerned, everything was fine and it was just a matter of time before a European tour would begin and another album would follow. But the interior of the organization was quickly crumbling.

Donal Gallagher: "It did come to a head. Very much at the Isle of Wight Festival. That was a situation where John got very cocky about his role in the band. He saw himself as a jazz drummer. John wanted to go all out into Billy Cobham or whatever vein. The John McLaughlin/Mahavishnu vibe for the band, which Rory didn't want. John felt that they shouldn't be playing encores. That was passé. He felt that Rory was playing to the gallery, that he was playing popular R&B three-chord songs.

"I could feel the cracks as we left the Isle of Wight and went on and did other gigs. For the autumn of '70, Polydor had invested a huge amount of money in putting Taste out on tour. Kennedy had sold them the tour. They were actually the promoters of it. And it was great because they were going to really publicize the albums. They put a package together. A guy called Jake Holmes from America. He was kind of wrong for the tour in a way. He was a singer/songwriter who had written an album for Sinatra (Watertown). And another band, Stone The Crows, featuring Maggie Bell and James Dewar, who were co-managed by the late Peter Grant, Led Zeppelin's manager. There was a huge amount of money invested. So when Rory turned around and said he was leaving the band, all hell broke loose. It was on the eve of the tour being announced. Rory had become extremely sullen and depressed about it and wouldn't even talk to anybody about the tour. I felt that maybe it was the right way to end it all. But I could see it impacting badly on Rory that Polydor would view that he was a difficult artist.

"Against Rory's wishes at the time, I went down and put money in a pay phone and rang up Clive Wood, the press officer at Polydor, who I felt would have a sympathetic ear. Which he did. And I explained it to him. Polydor then made sure that Rory got his rightful share for that tour paid in advance. And certain conditions were laid down as to how the band traveled, how it was all organized. It marginalized Kennedy's role. Rory and I traveled together in a transit van and there was a bus to transport everyone else. There were strange tensions because you had a situation where they had to meet up at the gig and get tuned up. Sound checks were tense. And there was always only one restaurant open after the gig [laughs]!"

John Wilson: "The thing I remember from the period was we knew that we were going to be splitting at some stage during that European tour so there was obviously a bit of apprehension. Everybody knew it was gonna happen. And

that was it. Again, and I mean this sincerely, I can't recall any real bad vibe about it all. At the time I certainly wouldn't have had the band break up. Who would?"

Charlie McCracken: "It was a farewell tour as far as we were concerned. I'm not sure if it was public knowledge at that time. It wasn't billed as that. We knew that after the tour, that was that."

John Wilson: "What caused the real crunch of the thing was Eddie Kennedy had been telling Charlie and myself that anything the band was earning would be a three-way split. And that's not what he was telling Rory. Rory was led to believe that it was his band and that Charlie and myself would only be getting a proportion. But it turned out we didn't get anything! That's what I say about this 'divide and conquer' thing. Eddie Kennedy would tell us one thing and tell Rory something else."

Donal Gallagher: "Taste was Rory's band. But what he couldn't do was extract the funds from the manager to even

Taste (l-r, John Wilson, Charlie McCracken, Rory Gallagher) Isle of Wight Festival, 1970. Courtesy Dino McGartland.

get to that stage of saying, 'Well, this is a three-way split. Or it won't be. Or what are the views on it?' Whatever the way the split occurred had to be discussed, obviously. Rory had soon realized that Kennedy had done various contracts, which were dogged up until recently. Contracts with individuals that tried to stitch them up for life. No one was quite sure what the plot was to begin with. In effect, John and Richie (Charlie) were being told this is a three-piece. Rory held the view that it was his band plus two musicians. But he had accepted the fact that it had grown into a trio. It was something that had to be adjusted. But more importantly, whose band was it anyway?"

Author: "Had Eddie Kennedy ever told you, face to face, that it was to be a three-way split?"

Charlie McCracken: "(pause) Yeah, he did. Sure. We were three Irish guys who were twenty years old. The things that are the norm in the business now, that acts, management and record companies take for granted, have evolved over the years. At that time, there was no norm. It was cowboy land! You did what you could, got what you could get. And if you got anything, you were bloody lucky."

In compiling research for this book many cases have come up where people had been subjected to a carrot being dangled in front of their nose with the promise of fulfilling the dreams that each had since he was eleven years old. Damned be the consequences for the moment, though you end up paying for it down the road.

Charlie McCracken: "Exactly 100 percent right. Through the music in Ireland, we were making very little money. All of a sudden, you get the chance to come to London. You get your foot in the door at least. 'I'm gonna give it a shot!' And you're gonna get paid for it. Who could refuse that? The next thing you know you're playing hockey rinks in Chicago but the money doesn't change an awful lot. So you know something's not quite right.

"John really took it to heart after the breakup because he couldn't understand it to the depth at that time that Rory had been told a pack of lies. Eddie Kennedy ripped everybody off. I think Rory probably thought we were in cahoots with him or something at that stage."

John Wilson: "I still couldn't believe it, when the band broke up, that Eddie would do that. It wasn't even until a year after Taste broke up that I found the truth out. And by that stage it was really far-gone. It's well known that none of us got anything, financially. And that has always been the way with musicians and the entertainment industry. It's a fact of life. But it hurts when it's as close as Taste was. It's different for guys suddenly arriving in the big city of London and being signed up to managers whom they've only just met. Eddie Kennedy was from our hometown and we all knew him. So you don't expect someone like that to do what he did.

"I think it well could have been a case of not wanting to rock the boat. From both our sides. Eddie would probably have had more social connection with myself and Charlie than he would have had with Rory. 'Cuz Rory liked being on his own. And we'd known Eddie prior to Taste and he always came across as a decent sort of guy. We had no reason not to trust him. Just because we didn't actually see any money, it doesn't mean to say that he wasn't doing what he said. Investing the money or putting it someplace where it could earn some money. I was never concerned because I just believed what I was being told."

Charlie McCracken: "We just did it and went through with it. It was a sad way to bow out. But in retrospect I know why Rory was feeling like that at the time. He thought that everybody was ripping him off. Which wasn't the case of course. It was only coming from a certain quarter. Everybody was being played off against everybody else. That was just a mess, really. In fact, considering what was going on, we did very well to get through that tour and do some very good gigs too."

Donal Gallagher: "We played a venue called Guildford. It was one of the last dates. I got there with all the equipment and the truck. Because it was so close to London, Rory decided to travel down a little later. I set up and got everything ready. And I ran into this large man, Peter Grant, and I didn't know who he was [laughs]. He was inquiring where the bands were, where was everybody. I explained that I was there on my own setting up the P.A. system. And he said,

'Have you got a beer?' As it happened I had a bottle of wine in the van, opened it up and shared it with Peter. And we had a good chat. He was aware of my phone call to Polydor. He suggested that Rory go have a chat with him. And I said, 'Rory is being put in a very peculiar situation because he's signed to the management contract which he's been told that he won't be allowed to get out of. But he's been coerced into signing a new deal with Polydor. And they'll pay off the manager. So it doesn't look like a good way to go forward.' Anyway, Rory went and saw Peter who was very helpful with advice. He went in and negotiated with Polydor on Rory's behalf. Got him a reversion of rights. A higher royalty rate. And that the copyright of the recordings remain with the artist. But it never got into the publishing situation.

"Though Rory respected Peter he was still very wary. Particularly that Peter could be a very heavy person. Those stories are legendary anyway. But he was certainly never that way to musicians or artists. He was a pussycat when it came to musicians. Robert Stigwood's organization headed publishing. And the various people who ran that were very keen on continuing the relationship. For Stigwood it was guilt by association. With all due respect to those people, they weren't beyond giving Eddie a kickback. There were one or two instances where he was getting a kickback where favorable introductions were affected.

"So Rory saw the tour out to the bitter end. I think the last gig was New Years Eve at Queen's University in Belfast."

Soon after Taste broke up, another financially motivated "situation" occurred.

Eric Kittringham: "One morning, at home, I received a check for £139 for royalties for this LP that had been released. I wasn't married too long at that stage so that went straight away to pay for things. The following day I had a phone call from Donal Gallagher. 'Eric, did you get a check there from Solomons?' So I said, 'I did.' He says, 'I hope you haven't spent this.' I said, 'Donal, it's cashed and gone [laughs].' He said, 'Look, I tell you what. I'm coming to you with a check for the money and a covering letter. I want you to send it back.' So the covering letter more or less said, 'Dear Mr. Solomons, thank you for blah,

blah, blah. But I understand there is a legal wrangle going on at the moment between Mr. Gallagher and yourself. Therefore, under the circumstances, I find that I cannot accept the money and I am returning same.' "

Donal Gallagher: "That was against Marvyn Solomons. This went back to when Taste was taken into a demo studio in Belfast over the Solomons-Pierce store where they had the distribution. After Taste had split up this suddenly appeared from nowhere. This album, called 'In The Beginning.' Contractually, because of the early agreements he entered into or was coerced into, there wasn't much he could do about it. I took legal action against the album because it had come out in the U.S. on a label called Springboard as 'Take It Easy Baby.' We injuncted the album in the U.S. and successfully repressed it. We call it the European version in the high court in the U.K. And the reason I gave Eric the money to return to those people was that I didn't want them to think that cashing the check was approval.

"The problems were that they were just demos and the infringement on Rory's copyrights in terms of the songs. They had put it under their own publishing banner; I think Bruno or something like that. Which was Eddie Kennedy's dog's name. So that's as much imagination as they had."

Eric Kittringham: "And then Norman and myself were called out to Rory's house. We were given legal letters and told, 'Look, we want you to sell us the right to bring Marvyn Solomons to court. What we're doing is claiming all the money that he made from the LP. Every last bob. In the event of us winning, the money will be split three ways.' So we both signed our names and we were off down the drive of the house. And I said to Norman, 'Jeez, Norm, wouldn't it be grand for a nice little sum to get on with it if they win the case?' And Norman turned around and looked at me and says, 'Eric, we're never gonna hear about that again.' And he was right. That is the one not too good memory I have of Rory."

It was time to develop a new direction. Rory was licking his wounds but knew the importance of hitting the ground running. It was easy to get locked into a situation of holding auditions in London and feeling potential players out. But too long a wait and he risked losing the momentum he had worked so hard to build. Deep Joy was a Belfast band whose biggest paydays were the numerous times they had supported Taste. Rory made it a point to always hang out with his opening acts and had developed a friendship with the band. Since Taste broke up there wasn't much work for Deep Joy anymore. Rory offered bassist Gerry McAvoy and drummer Wilgar Campbell a chance to spend a few hours playing to see if a positive feel would develop.

Gerry McAvoy was born in Belfast on December 19, 1951. His sister got him into Buddy Holly, The Beatles and The Rolling Stones. At thirteen he purchased a Muddy Waters album from an old second-hand record store in Belfast. Said McAvoy, "I couldn't believe it. It changed my life."

Gerry McAvoy: "It was a tossup at Christmas between getting a pool table or a snare drum. And my father said, 'You're not having any. You can have a guitar.' So I got this old cheap guitar. The neck was more like a bow than a guitar. It was a semi-acoustic thing. I was about twelve, thirteen. Eventually a bunch of guys that lived in my area came around. We used to get together in someone's front room and just flash out the rock 'n' roll songs of the day."

The first semi-serious venture was with a schoolmate, Brendan O'Neill, who played drums. Both were fourteen years old and full of inquisitive energy. They drafted a bass player and a lead singer named Tom Kidd, who's currently serving a life sentence for murder in the U.S., and called themselves Pride.

Gerry McAvoy: "The bass player was also a butcher in training so he'd turn up at rehearsal with lots of cuts on his fingers. Eventually he couldn't play the bass guitar so he left and there was no one to replace him. So I started to play the bass.

"Deep Joy followed on from Pride. We decided to change our name one night in a fit of madness. I thought Pride was a good name. There was sort of poetry on a Small Faces album, and the words 'deep joy' were there. The same sort of music. Tons of Motown and 60s pop music. Brendan left and we got another drummer in. Wilgar Campbell."

Wilgar had been in a trio called The Method, Belfast's answer to Cream. Or at least that was how their publicity promoted them.

Gerry McAvoy. Courtesy Strange Music Inc.

Gerry McAvoy: "Deep Joy and Taste broke up more or less at the same time, December 1970. But towards the end of our career in London, we used to play a lot of clubs. Rory and his brother Donal would show up every now and then. Just grab a table, have something to eat and watch the band. It happened three or four times. I found it a bit unusual. At that stage we didn't know that Taste were breaking up. We went back to Belfast. I tried to get another band together. Wilgar had stayed in London and he and Rory had kept in touch. After two months I got a phone call. Rory asked me to jump on a plane the next day and have a bit of a blow, a jam. And that was it.

"He never actually asked me to join the band. We did a rehearsal and I flew back to Belfast. I didn't hear anything for about four weeks. Then he rang up again and asked me to play on the album. Which I did. The 'Rory Gallagher' album. That's what Rory was like. I suppose from the early days with Taste, there was so much contractual shit that went down he wanted to stay away from that. He just wanted to have a bunch of guys with him. And to enjoy doing what we were doing as much as he enjoyed doing it. And to have some respect and realize that Rory was the main man. Which you couldn't help but do. That was part and parcel of being in the band. He was the main man and everyone else was a sideline.

"I think me being nineteen years of age, he could see something in me that he could nurture. It was a learning process for me and he was very patient in allowing me to develop. The first couple of months were amazing. The early years were the fun times for me because I was traveling with a band. We were setting up our own equipment. We were touring the States in two station wagons with the equipment in one and the band in the other. And we played massive festivals."

In order to avoid the financial mishaps from Taste, Rory quickly set out to lay down parameters that his new band could understand.

Donal Gallagher: "I don't think it was viewed by Rory that it had to be a three-way split. Most blues musicians were getting ripped off. He knew that his musicians, at the end of the day, at least got their hundred-dollar bill and a bottle of whiskey. They got something out of it. There were so many cases where the percentages of this and the difference between the net and the gross means you get nothing. And suddenly the promoter and your management have the money after having worked your ass off. It was a fairly organic thing to do. 'I will pay, out of my pocket, the musicians. To make sure they're paid. And do it as a band-leader and see where that takes us.' "

It was important that Rory keep his cards to his chest. He was reluctant to allow any business dealings that included anyone but he or Donal. He didn't want to have management of any kind. He was shy and hesitant to tell a promoter, a studio employee or someone from the record company where to get off. But he learned that you "could" say those things. He didn't see the need for a manager to tell him how to play guitar or what he should be wearing. Back at that point in time managers were hired to give the artist an image, to get the right look, to offer introductions,

things Rory didn't need. What Rory wore onstage was what he wore offstage. And he certainly didn't want anyone controlling his financial affairs. Many assumed Donal was now wearing managerial robes.

Donal Gallagher: "I was never officially appointed Rory's manager or he never gave me the official appointment. It just happened organically. I'd say to Rory, 'Well, look, let's do a split management situation.' Covering all the bases proved to be more difficult all the time. I was very much on my own. Taking a truck full of equipment and building the equipment. We were building our own P.A. in Germany at the time, designing it for the band's needs. So it was 24 hours a day. Looking after Rory personally and logistically was a full-time job."

Rory, Gerry and Wilgar got together for rehearsals to prepare to record their first album.

Gerry McAvoy: "We would rehearse but a rehearsal was like a live show. You'd go in and have a sweatbox for two and a half, three hours and then come out again. You wouldn't rehearse all day. You'd go in at six o'clock at night and finish at nine."

Rory invited a friend to lay down a few piano tracks. The late Vincent Crane was then playing with Atomic Rooster who were quite popular in their own right. Most of the material was carried over from the Taste days, which made the transition for Rory's fans an easy one. But he allowed his current band members the room to add their flavor to the mix. If Rory had an idea for a bass line, he'd mention it. But for the most part he allowed everyone the chance to play and contribute. Rory booked Advision Studios, which had recently obtained a state-of-the-art, 24-track board.

Gerry McAvoy: "And also the engineer, Eddie Offord, who had worked with Taste on 'On The Boards.' He had quite a reputation. There was excitement. There was trepidation. There were all these feelings rolled into one. And I think that actually helped the album. In those days you'd go in at ten o'clock in the morning and you'd finish at eleven o'clock at night. Where in later years, you thought you had to play music at the proper time. Which I think is rubbish. Where you go in at six o'clock at night and stop at six o'clock in the morning. I think that defeats the objective sometimes."

Donal Gallagher: "The first album didn't quite come out at the same time in America. It came out eventually on Atco. Atlantic and Atco and the relationship with Polygram was a strange one. On the first release and 'Deuce,' I don't think Atco put a whole lot of effort into those albums. Atlantic and Atco had found that success with Zeppelin and weren't particularly bothered in promoting another heavy rock band. I wouldn't classify 'Zeppelin' as a blues band but they traded on the fact that they were doing blues songs. Especially when they took 'You Need Love.' Rory knew that he had a recording of it by Muddy Waters in 1965 from the Monterey Jazz Festival. It was, in fact, a number he did with Taste. I recall that being a Gallagher riff. And they certainly weren't performing that song before they went to see Taste.

"Where possible Rory would credit the original author, which wasn't always easy to locate. When Rory couldn't locate the writer and he'd heard it on a Sonny Boy Williamson record, he'd credit him. He was very diligent about that. He felt that it was to the conscience of each person to do the right thing. I know, in the case where the action was going to take place over the particular song 'Whole Lotta Love,' Rory was asked for his views by the lawyers involved. He was considered to give the view that this was the done thing at that time. Which he wasn't prepared to say. And declined to support the theory that it was OK to do."

After a stint in Europe, The Rory Gallagher Band headed off to America to finally tour the country and promote the debut album by playing in the intimate confines of the bar circuit.

Gerry McAvoy: " '77 Sunset Strip.' We flew in to Los Angeles the day of the gig. We had three sets at the Whiskey A Go Go. We drove from LAX to the Hyatt House on Sunset Blvd. I was totally aghast! It was L.A.! You grew up watching these things on television. The American way had a big influence on Ireland 'cuz a lot of people emigrated from Ireland. There was that connection. When I was a kid I used to buy American comics. DC Comics. Dell Comics. I was so influenced by America. And to actually get there! As a kid I used to watch '77 Sunset Strip' on television. I drove past 'Dano's Lounge!' and I said, 'I'm here!' And as we drove by the Whiskey A Go Go … it was amazing. Up on the billboard it said, 'Rory Gallagher and Little Feat,' who were meant to be the support. I was a fan of Little Feat. And I thought, 'How the hell can we follow Little Feat?' But they pulled out at the last moment. The first night, a Tuesday night, the first of five nights, there were about thirty people there. By the Saturday night it was jam-packed. And that was just word of mouth.

"The first time we hit Chicago we did the club thing. As a matter of fact, every time we hit Chicago we did the club thing. You had to go to the clubs and see these people before they became extinct. And we'd always try and hit as many as we could [laughs]."

Rory would often take the opportunity to go up and jam with these authentic bluesmen. The patrons of the clubs and the musicians who performed were quite taken with this talented European white boy.

Gerry McAvoy: "I think there was a lot of respect. And a lot of jealousy. I remember Rory telling me a story. He got up and jammed with Albert King once. In Montreaux. And there wasn't a lot of respect for Rory from Albert King. For whatever reason, I don't know. But the main man, Muddy Waters, had total respect for Rory. Hence Rory playing on his albums. It was just different people. I don't think color or race had anything to do with it. It's a personal thing."

Donal Gallagher: "At that point in time, due to certain types of advice which we took from several sources, the first album came out through copyright control. And then Rory established his own publishing company, Strange Music, which was the way to go forward."

Upon returning to Britain, Rory wanted to enter the studio as soon as possible to lay down tracks that got him away from Taste entirely. To lay a foundation for his new band and his music. He called it "Deuce."

Donal Gallagher: "He wanted to use Tangerine Studios, which was up in North London. It was a studio that had been built by a guy called Joe Meek who has since been brought out as a godfather of production. He had a lot of hits but he's never been recognized for his production value. There was a 'Joe Meek sound' kind of renaissance.

It's become a famous one over here. And he liked the environment. It was at the side of a bingo hall. And a point of fact, the reason he'd go back after gigs was because during the day you could hear bingo calling next door and he'd have to do a retake of a number!"

Gerry McAvoy: "After a while it would get on your nerves. But when you think back on it, it was quite fun. And there was a great pub around the corner. We used to go in there for an hour and have a couple of pints of Guinness and come back and keep on going."

Donal Gallagher: "I remember Rory'd get up at midday. We'd work through the afternoon and we'd pack up the equipment at around four o'clock and belt down the freeway to do a gig. And come back from the gig and set up the equipment again in the studio and record or mix until two or three in the morning. It was a frantic rate of work."

Gerry McAvoy: "There was a time limit on that album. But you were young enough to cope with it."

Donal Gallagher: "Robin Sylvester was the house engineer. We'd gotten to know Robin from another source, one of the support bands that were doing a lot of work with us, a band called Byzantium. He was friends with them. So he'd turned up at a few gigs. Robin was a session bass player in the area. He kind of suited Rory because he was quite a calming kind of character."

Gerry McAvoy: "Robin had a good ear. 'Deuce' took on a different level. The first album was reasonably laid back, recording-wise. It didn't jump out of the speakers. Where 'Deuce' was distorted. You could hear the distortion on the record. Which is great. And the bass is distorted. And that was down to Robin. He was like a kindred spirit as far as bass players were concerned."

When "Deuce" was released the Gallagher band toured the same venues throughout Europe and, as usual, the gigs were always well attended. The performances were what was selling the band and keeping the name

alive. There were very few live albums at the time and Polydor was shocked when Rory said, "Now I want to do a live album." Tape machines were kept rolling during shows in Germany, France and the U.K. Once the tracks were selected and mixed, the album "Live In Europe" was released in 1972 and its success was immediate.

Gerry McAvoy: "Things got easier. We started to drive in a car instead of a van. And the venues grew. The hotels got better."

Donal Gallagher: "We had a few allies within the new Polydor. There was a chap named Tommy Noonan who went on to become CEO of *Billboard*. Polydor had consolidated its own company and I think it certainly jumped out at them. The first two albums had come out on Atco. Even though Polydor had the worldwide contract they didn't have a position in America. So they used to license Polydor stuff. Atco picked up the first two albums as a result of that. So the first official Polydor album in the U.S. would have been 'Live In Europe' and that was really breaking through. But it very much became a thing where they wanted to release 'Going To My Hometown' as a single. I recall being in Washington, D.C. They sent down an executive, who came with an edit of 'Going To My Hometown.' And he told Rory, 'This is being released as a single.' Rory hit the roof! I recall the guy saying to Rory, 'This will be Number 1 in the States!' Rory completely refused. He was quite angry that they had actually gone in and edited it. It was stopped. I wouldn't say it soured the relationship but it certainly didn't create the best impression."

Gerry McAvoy: "They pushed and pushed and pushed. And it could have been a hit. It was a very popular track and the record company could see that. And see the benefits of doing it. But Rory stuck to his guns. He swore he would never release a single. And that was the end of story."

While touring America to promote "Live In Europe" in 1972, *Melody Maker* magazine named Rory "Guitarist Of The Year."

Donal Gallagher: "It was extraordinary at the time because so much could have been made of it. But he was slightly embarrassed by it. And by then it was well deserved because the other guitarists of the day weren't touring. They were all hibernating in their cottages in Sussex. They weren't out entertaining and being there for the fans. And the 'Live In Europe' album was so thrilling. He had such a large hardcore audience. It was inevitable. Plus the versatility. Rory was switching instruments. He introduced the acoustic set in at a time when people didn't dare bring out an acoustic instrument to a rock audience.

"Going back to the award itself, he was very pleased. We received the news while we were playing in Memphis. We were there for five nights in a venue supported by a band called Pure Prairie League. And the thrill of being in Memphis, to Rory, was so great! There was a poll concert, where Melody Maker would present the awards, but it clashed with us being in Memphis. I remember saying to Rory, 'Let's postpone these dates. We can jump on a plane and get back.' And not that he wanted to snub it or anything but he took a clear decision that, 'This is an award. Next year someone else will get it. I don't want to rest my laurels on it.' He didn't play the game regarding the press. He was totally against the grain. Which is a good thing. He knew his course and he was focused on that.

"Unfortunately, the magazine may have taken it as a snub."

Donal Gallagher: "For a magazine that was really supporting the artist, a 'cooling off' occurred. Saw it in lack of print."

Author: "Who did Rory consider to be a good guitarist?"

Donal Gallagher: "Well, from the folk world, Martin Carsey. Bert Yance. Certainly he had great admiration for Hendrix. I'm probably gonna do so many people an injustice on this one. He was very keen on Doc Watson. Keith Richards. He liked that kind of rhythm, loose feel. He was very fond of Clapton's playing. I think he felt that Eric went into a different direction than what he'd liked. He was a fan of most guitar players. He was a huge record buyer. His albums would surprise people, what he had in there. All forms of music. Particularly if they had a guitarist in the band. Classically, Manitas de Plata. He adored Django Rheinhardt. He had all Django's records. Segovia. He liked country players as well. He loved James Burton. The pickers, especially the Telecaster pickers."

Rory Gallagher: "We played Poland and we had to be officially invited by the Jazz Society of Warsaw. Now, we're not a jazz group, right? And we sent some albums over and the lyrics, in case there was any anti … you know what [laughs]. And, I mean, they cleared the lyrics. But, I mean, when we got there it didn't matter. It's crazy, these restrictions. The communist wing is coming back heavily in lots of places. But get me three people that can understand what B.B. King is singing about. It's funny. But B.B. doesn't care. You know what he spends his money on? Gambling. Las Vegas. What is he? 64 or 65. No heart troubles, no problems. He fines the band. He's worse than James Brown. Then he goes back to Las Vegas, he goes back to the craps tables and he spends it all. That's his drug, you know. Gambling. Why the hell does he keep doing it? He's got these gold watches and silver rings and free Gibson guitars. He goes on tour, makes a fortune, comes back and … he must be making a reasonable living out of it. But, I mean… [laughs]. You'll forgive me for saying this; he's a showman now. He used to give away three dozen picks from his pocket. He used to go around handing them out like Holy Communion. Gold chains. Agh! I mean, Muddy Waters wouldn't do this. B.B. is definitely Las Vegas. Muddy, I tell ya, no competition there.

"Clapton's getting back into his groove here. He's got the Armani suits. How can you play the blues with a £5,000 suit on you, you know? 'It's a state of mind,' he said. But it affected him. And the next thing he showed up in a T-shirt and jeans at Royal Albert Hall. And he's put all his big equipment away and he's just using a Fender amp [laughs]. Auto-suggestion. All you have to do is say it to him. He's a very reactionary guy in that sense, you know. I prefer him this way. I mean, he was getting to be like some guy from

Fallucci. And he was the guy … when I was a teenager he wrote in a magazine, he said, 'Jeff Beck is modeling clothes in the magazine. I wouldn't do that because I'm a blues artist.' And now Jeff's going on in a white T-shirt and jeans and Eric, who's just been through ten years of Armani suits and different haircuts and white, perfect shoes. He can't make up his mind. With beard, without beard, with glasses, without. There's a sanity problem there, definitely."

•   •   •

The band was red hot as it returned to Europe to promote the live album. With his home base still in Belfast, Gerry McAvoy decided it was time to make the move to London.

Donal Gallagher: "Gerry had been trying to find accommodations to relocate to London on a permanent basis now that he had a permanent gig. He had answered an ad. He went to this place in Stratham with a suit and tie on to see if he could get this accommodation. And he couldn't believe that this guy, Rod de'Ath, turned out to be a rock drummer! He was in a band called Killing Floor. Lou Martin was the keyboard player."

Lou Martin: "Rod had a spare room upstairs and said, 'I think I'll let that top room.' So he put an advert in *The Evening Standard* on a Friday. And on Saturday there was a knock on the door. This guy was standing there with a sports jacket, a tie, neat hair and an Irish accent. He said, 'I've come to look at the room.' So we said, 'Come in.' And in the hallway we had all the bands' gear. And he said, 'A band, eh?' And we said, 'Yeah, we're in a band.' We had really long hair and beards.

"I was born in Belfast, Northern Ireland, on August 12, 1949. My mother would play piano and my Dad would sing. One day when I was six I just picked out what she was playing. So they sent me to piano lessons. I just took to it. I went to Music College and I was going to be a teacher. But then I heard certain bands and that turned me right around when I was about fifteen years old. 'I don't wanna be a teacher. I wanna play this!' But the one thing about classical training, it does give you the technique. Whatever music you wanna play, you can play it. I was hearing Chicago blues.

"I went out and seen certain bands who were playing around the time I was a teenager. The music scene was great. The Spencer Davis Group with Steve Winwood. The Yardbirds. But the one that really did the job was John Mayall with Eric Clapton. The original Bluesbreakers. As soon as I heard that, that's what made me wanna go out and do it. I used to get *Melody Maker* all the time and they used to have classified ads for musicians in the back. I saw 'Blues band requires pianist' and I thought I'd give them a ring. The band was called Killing Floor. The first time I ever went onstage, we supported Captain Beefheart at a place called Middle Earth. It was a big hippie place in London. We ended up supporting Ten Years After, Jethro Tull, The Aynsley Dunbar Retaliation. We got an agent and went on the road.

"We carried on despite a few lineup changes. We dropped our harp player and became a four-piece. And with the wind blowing more towards rock, we changed the musical approach. We were starting to do more heavy rock numbers. And then we picked up a drummer that had just come up from Wales and that was Rod de'Ath."

Rod de'Ath: "I was born the eighteenth of June, 1950. I grew up in West Wales. My Welsh name is Morris. I was brought up in a smallholding. My father, Frank, was a concert pianist. He was a Londoner but because of health problems he moved back to my mother's place, which is in West Wales. But moving there meant the end of his musical career as far as being a concert pianist. But he did gigs. He was into big jazz band-type stuff. He started teaching me piano, so my parents told me, when I was about two years old. I was very successful on piano. I got my Royal School of Music Grade twelve by the time I was ten years old. I did my first concert at ten years old. I played 'Jesus, Joy of Man's Desire' by Johann Sebastian Bach. And 'Ave Maria' by Bach as well. And that was the first and only time I had terrible stage fright.

"The first time I got interested in percussion was when my father's drummer died all of a sudden. He couldn't get another drummer. I'd never banged anything besides a keyboard. But he had an old kit of drums. He taught me the basics for a big band dance band. And that was my first outing, that night, with his band. I was fifteen and the average age was about forty.

"I could have gone to university, etc. But much to my mother's angst, at seventeen I passed my driver's test and bought myself a car. I wanted to make my living playing music. I literally put my drums and belongings in my car and drove to London. In those days, that was the only place to be if you wanted to pursue music seriously. There were ups and downs but I managed. I was a country boy trying to survive in the city. I had never had a cup of coffee, put it that way."

Lou Martin: "So Rod showed him the room and they came downstairs and we had a chat. He asked about our band and we told him about Killing Floor. And he said, 'I play in a band.' 'Which band do you play with?' And he said, 'I play with Rory Gallagher. And I'm sorry I've created the wrong impression with what I'm wearing but I wanted to impress the landlord.' I said, 'Do you really play with Rory?' And he said, 'Yeah. My name's Gerry McAvoy.' We'd read that he had a new band but we didn't know who was in it. So that's what he said and we took his word for it. So he moved into the house. They were starting to do a tour in England.

"One night when they had a night off, Gerry brought Wilgar Campbell to a Killing Floor gig at a local pub. And the next thing, Rory was playing at Queen's Hall and Gerry said, 'Would you like to come along?' So we all went. Gerry got us in and we saw the show. I really liked it because Rory was taking everything right back to the roots. We briefly met him afterwards but there wasn't enough time to hang around. But then we had a gig at The Marquee Club. This time Rory and the band came along and he really liked us."

After a brief tour of England the Gallagher brothers were forced to deal with a situation that no one saw coming.

Donal Gallagher: "Wilgar got ill. He couldn't cope with flying. He was the only one in the band who was married. He'd brought his wife and kids over from Belfast. They'd settled in London. They were quite strange to the surroundings. Things were happening so rapidly that he was away all the time. He had a different set of circumstances and physically it was taking its toll on him. He said he couldn't fly in a plane. I suppose it was fatigue or a mental breakdown. That was the day of the Irish Tour opening. And that was the night that Irish television were using color for the first time. They were going to shoot a documentary with Rory as the subject. It was at a very critical point."

Gerry McAvoy: "Wilgar had a lot of problems but he could not stand flying. Unless that was an excuse. I really don't know. He was a very complex character, to put it mildly. Wilgar would have half a beer per night and that would be it. Wilgar was a fitness freak. He loved playing football. He didn't entertain alcohol. But I think he had problems with his marriage as well and he hit the bottle pretty bad."

Donal Gallagher: "Things were down to the wire. We were at Heathrow Airport. Wilgar hadn't shown up. We called and were told that he'd lost his nerve and couldn't cope. So Rod was called and he arrived a few hours later for the gig. He didn't even get a chance for rehearsal."

Rod de'Ath: "The first time I got a phone call from Rory was at my house in Southampton. The call was can I make myself available to get to Heathrow airport in two hours time. So I said, 'What's all this about?' I was told very briefly. I said, 'Yes, OK. How long is it going to be?' 'We don't know. A week at the most.' 'What about equipment?' 'No, no, it will all be provided.' So a car picked me up to take me to Heathrow. I was picked up in Cork by Rory's Mum and a driver who drove me, at breakneck speed, from Cork to Limerick, which was right across to the West Coast. We got to the concert hall. I was rushed straight to the dressing room. There was Rory and Gerry, all ready to go on. The concert was late. I'd never played with Rory before. I had no idea what his numbers were. He said, 'We start with this and I do a version of Messin' With The Kid and whatever.' And that's what it was like. It was being televised. We went out and did a couple of hours' concert. That was my first professional meeting with Rory. But I was a professional musician. You pay me, I'll play it. I'll do my best."

Donal Gallagher: "And because Killing Floor was a very traditional English blues band, Rory just revamped the set that night to a more bluesy set. He did a lot more acoustic. And the footage held up. I think by Dublin, which was the best part of a week later, Wilgar was well enough and had traveled over for the Dublin gig. I remember standing there with Rod at the back of the venue at the mixing board. His face dropped when Wilgar arrived. And Wilgar got his job back."

Rod de'Ath: "I got paid and Rory said thanks. Fine. I'd done my job. So that's the end of that."

At a later date as the band was readying to depart to continue the tour, Wilgar cancelled, simply stating, "I've lost my nerve again."

Gerry McAvoy: "We were going to Switzerland on an early morning flight. I got a phone call from the driver who was picking us up. He went to pick up Wilgar who lived about fifteen minutes away from me. Wilgar had a nervous breakdown because he couldn't stand flying. So we didn't have a drummer. So I said to Rod, 'Pack a case and let's go.' And Rod did well."

Rod de'Ath: "It was quite a thing for me because Killing Floor had gone through changes. Personnel. We'd just set up a showcase gig in London, Piccadilly, at a club called Bumpers. All the record companies were coming to see us. And then I get this call again from Donal. It meant that I would be away from this showcase gig. So I had to call them back. I told them, 'I can't. I've got other things on my plate.' And I was told that there would be a car outside my door. If I decided to come, get in it. My lady said to me, 'Don't be such a fucking dickhead! Go for it.' Which is what I did. Later we were on a train, I was in the bar as usual, and Rory came up to me and started chatting and said, 'Would you like to work for me?' I said, 'Sure. What's the deal?' And that was it. We shook hands and that was the beginning of seven and a half years that we worked together. No contract or anything like that."

Lou Martin: "So that left Killing Floor without a drummer. So they (Gallagher) came back and did one gig in London at The Greyhound, which was a big concert hall. It was Rod's birthday. So I went along. Afterwards we all went back to Rod's house to celebrate his birthday. Loads of drink and whatever. I was sitting next to Rory on the couch. We were listening to The Band and Neil Young records and we talked for about two hours. Actually, we talked until I more or less passed out. He must have gotten a good impression of me that night!"

Rod de'Ath: "Lou and I had worked together not only in Killing Floor but in all sorts of situations. Rory asked me about Lou and 'How is he?' And wanted him to do a gig or two. He was thinking about embellishing. Adding a keyboard."

Lou Martin: "He phoned up two days later and said, 'I'm having a rehearsal for an Italian tour we're doing. Would you like to bring your piano along and see what it sounds like?' Of course. I might get an album session or something out of it. And we just jammed every blues number he could think of. Then he phoned up again, a day later. 'We're having another blow in a couple of days time. Would you like to come down again?' I said, 'Yes.' Something was going on and I was wondering what it was. This time we did all his numbers. Which I kinda knew anyway. And then he said, 'Would you like to come to Italy?' I didn't even have a passport at the time. I'd never been out of the country in my life. I'd managed to get a passport together within a day, by sheer insistence at the passport office, and I went to Italy with them. I tried it out and I had a great time! And after ten days in Italy, he said, 'We're going to the States. Would you like to come along? And I'd like it to be permanent.' So that was me in the band for the next seven years."

Rod de'Ath: "I think it was the best he put together. I'm not one to blow my own trumpet or anything. I think it was a pretty good combination. I'm a bit biased [laughs]. We worked our asses off. During that period we were known as the hardest working band in the world. We were forever at it. That first American tour, we didn't have any roadies. We did that whole tour in two station wagons, Donal driving one and me driving the other. When we hooked up for big concerts with other bands we might get a flight. That tour was to last for six weeks but it lasted eighteen weeks. And I did all the driving. As well as playing [laughs]. And the groupies and stuff. Well, I was a lot younger then [laughs]! It was fucking great! Four and a half months. And constantly playing. It was a hard, hard tour. Oh, it was 'hard' work! But we were all young enough. What was good about it was, even though we got to play places like Madison Square Garden and the big places at the bottom of the bill, a lot of the places in that eighteen weeks were in the backstreets. The ends of beyond. It was great. We used to play anywhere. And starving to death [laughs]!"

Gerry McAvoy: "Rod actually freaked out. It was meant to be a three-week tour and we ended up staying for four months. The agents kept getting these calls from all over the States. I'd no connections at home. Family, girlfriend. But Rod had a girlfriend at home. He sort of smashed up a room one night and Don and I had to calm him down."

Rod de'Ath: "It was my choice and my family's choice. But it is hard if you have family. It puts an extra strain on you."

Gerry McAvoy: "That's the effect it has on different people. But I was having a great time. In the States for four months … fantastic!"

Lou Martin: "We were supporting Savoy Brown. They had an argument amongst themselves and decided to fly home after three weeks. Donal explained to the agency that we would play anywhere. So they just shoveled gig after gig after gig. And it was very much trailblazing. Some places we would play there would only be about ten people there. Some places there were hundreds of people. And we always did the same set. Rory's logic at the time was, 'I know there's not much of a crowd going on here but do a good show and the next time we play here there'll be five times the people.' And it worked. We toured the States thirteen times. But that first one laid the foundation."

It was a difficult situation for Lou and Rod. It was almost impossible not to be distracted by the scenery around them as they ventured from one North American city to another. Yet at the same time they were also trying to develop a consistent, live performance backing someone who rarely rehearsed with the band.

Lou Martin: "I used to ask Rory to give me a pointer. He would just want me to do it and see what it sounded like. I was more or less given a free rein to play what I wanted. He'd do two solos. Then he'd look at me to do a solo and we'd work around the tunes. I used to enjoy filling in the sound. There's two styles of keyboard playing. I like to solo but I also like playing a hard rhythm behind somebody like that, who's playing out front. It's just backing blues piano. And then have an opportunity to really let rip on a solo."

The energy was difficult to keep up with. The pace Rory was setting was quite extreme. Blind faith and self-confidence were certainly attributes. But though the pace was a normal and even comfortable one to Rory, to the new members of the band it was a challenge. Mentally, all was in synch. But physical endurance was constantly being challenged.

Rod de'Ath: "How do great adventurers manage to reach the North Pole? How do warriors manage, against all odds, to come out on top? I've no idea. There was this one time I'd been back from tour. I'd been away for about three months. I used to always try and time my flights so that I'd get back home in London sort of late afternoon, evening. I could get home, say hi and whatever, and then go out and party until I dropped. This time I got home at about six o'clock in the evening on a Monday. Say hello to everybody, blah, blah, blah. 'Right. Let's go out.' At that time a good club to go to was The Speakeasy. So I went there with my lady. We got back at about four o'clock on the Tuesday morning. Went to bed. I woke up and it was dark. It was seven-thirty or eight. I asked my lady, 'Is it night or morning?' She said it was morning and shouldn't I eat something. And I said, 'What do you mean?' And she said, 'It's Friday.' I was out completely. Don't ask me how a body or a mind manages. You push yourself I suppose. I could have gone on. If you want to do it you can do it."

The "buzz" about Gallagher was strong after the U.S. tour. The band could have easily turned around and replayed every market. But being true to his self-imposed schedule it was time to go into the studio. This release was an important one. To follow "Live In Europe" with a studio album put Rory in a very unique situation. He needed the album to reflect the band's current condition. They had just toured incessantly and the group was tight. The press and fans verbally applauded all the shows for weeks on end and anticipation for the follow-up LP was strong. "Blueprint" already had half its promotion done.

Rod de'Ath: " 'Blueprint' was my first studio session with Rory. I think Rory found it difficult to try and capture what he wanted on record. He was so live [laughs]! How do you capture that? It's tough."

Lou Martin: "It was rushed. Polydor wanted an album out by the New Year and this was early November. But there's nothing like the tour we just finished to get a band tight. And we certainly were. So an album had to be done over a period of two weeks. I mean recorded, voiced, mixed, pressed, the whole bit. And we had an English tour before Christmas. We had a day and a half off. We went into Polydor at night and went through all the numbers. There was very little rehearsal time.

"'Walk On Hot Coals,' believe it or not, started off as Rory's version of Howlin' Wolf's, 'Shake For Me.' The riff. We used to jam it at sound checks and sometimes he'd do it for an encore with the original Howlin' Wolf lyrics. So he said, 'I'm gonna use that 'Shake For Me' thing on the album but I'm gonna write some new lyrics for it.' He came up with the lyrics overnight. And he said, 'This is now going to be called 'Walk On Hot Coals.' So that was that. As far as the rest of the numbers went, he'd just play and he'd say to everybody, 'Put in what you can. Make your own part up.' And that's basically what we did. Then he went in on his own and he mixed the entire thing and managed to do it in time. The album came out in January when we went over to Germany."

Donal Gallagher: "'Live In Europe' had charted very well in *Billboard* and was bulleting every week. Also festivals were becoming quite commonplace and we were doing those a lot. In a sense, there was a lot of anticipation for Rory's next album. 'Live In Europe' had broken the ice in terms of airplay in radio. 'Blueprint' had the sound of a produced album by the inclusion of the keyboard.

"I don't feel 'Blueprint' got a fair shake. What occurred is that Polydor had gone back and taken the first two albums, 'Deuce' and 'Rory Gallagher,' and compiled them into one album called 'The Sinner And The Saint.' And they released that without any clearances. We didn't know that was coming out. And that had all the appearances of a new album. It possibly helped to broaden radio but it was confusing the audience."

•   •   •

Gerry McAvoy: "There was never time to get bored onstage because there was so much improvisation going on. And playing with Rory you wouldn't have time to get bored.

"For the want of a better word, there was some sort of 'telepathy' happening onstage. I knew what Rory was going to play before he'd played it. And I can't explain or describe why that happened. It's just something that developed over the years. He would play certain riffs at different times during the songs and I'd know that riff. It would be implanted in my brain. And the same with him."

Rod de'Ath: "It didn't take long to develop that 'telepathy.' But that has always been one of my fortes as a player. I put it down to the different instruments I learned. Horn players have often mentioned to me about my empathy with other players. So it took no longer with Rory then anyone else. But we did have a special thing, of course we did. Because we worked so constantly so long together."

Gerry McAvoy: "There were nights when not everything went so smooth. There were nights when he came into the dressing room and the atmosphere would be so cold. Rory was a perfectionist in a lot of ways and you had to be in form every night. Even if Rory coughed up himself there would be nothing said. It would be like a deadly silence until the next day. Then we'd try and iron out the situation. Luckily enough we didn't have too many bad gigs."

The tours were strong. The audiences more than supportive. But Polydor seemed to be dragging their feet. "Tattoo" was recorded and released in 1973, an album that featured a refined, confident group of musicians who were also prepared to promote the release with tireless touring.

Donal Gallagher: "I don't think 'Tattoo' was properly promoted by Polydor. I don't think Rory felt he was getting 'too' big. I think it was more disparaging between album sales and concert tickets. He always kept a governor on himself in the sense that he didn't like the big venues. I think sort of 4,000 was the max. It was slightly different if you did an open-air festival. It was a different ambience entirely. He liked the eye contact. And he certainly didn't like sharing a stage with other bands. At the end of a day, if the other bands overran, you had to cut your set short because of the union guys that had to come in. But at a club you could call it yourself. You could overrun. It was more comfortable."

Rod de'Ath: "We never had enough time. We were always very busy."

The band was faced with the reality that it had to expand its road crew to keep up with the pace of their success. Though long-time friend Tom O'Driscoll had been with the band as a full-time employee for a while, they turned to a fellow Corksman to help as the Gallagher band's popularity soared.

Joe O'Herlihy: "From about '67 to '69, I developed a *graw* for music. *Graw* is the Irish word for love. I developed a love for the technical side of it. I befriended a chap called Johnny Wright, the bass player in a couple of different groups. And through that friendship grew a kind of relationship where I hung around with the guys in the band Sleepy Hollow. It was during that period of time that we were very fortunate enough to be the kind of 'hip' band in Cork. We usually ended up playing support on Rory's Irish dates every time he came back, which was usually around Christmas time. That's where I initially met Donal and Rory and Tom O'Driscoll and got to know them personally. That would have been kind of from 1970 to '71 through to '73 to '74 until I eventually got a job doing backline with Rory which saw me

heading off, after an Irish tour, in January '74 to America. With Rory, I did pretty much everything. Doing backline, graduating to monitors and eventually to front of house."

• • •

Montreal was unique; a city that embraced many acts long before other North American cities. Genesis, Emerson, Lake & Palmer, Gentle Giant, The Police, Supertramp are but a few from a relatively long list. And Rory Gallagher was no exception. In the fall of 1974, Rory headlined the Montreal Forum Concert Bowl with Nazareth as support and Rush as the opening act. A fair evening's entertainment for $5.50.

Donal Gallagher: "I remember being very cold in there. That gig was originally in a different venue. Donald K. Donald was the promoter, I recall. With Rory's success at selling the tickets and Nazareth, who we were quite pally with as they shared the same agency as us in the U.K., they had that unexpected hit with 'This Flight Tonight.' I remember there being quite a bit of antagonism over the fact that they felt they should be headlining and closing the show. I do remember the night well. Because going from a theater-size venue into that, where the capacity was 9,000 I believe, it threw up extra problems from the logistic point of view. We were given short notice. And we were on tour with a P.A. system that was essentially used for playing theaters. And then throwing that P.A. system into a 9,000 seater, which was probably tripling the range of it.

"The actual promoter of the tour as opposed to the gig was a guy called Ray Daniels. It was Ray's first tour with a band from outside of Canada. On the back of that, we took Rush to support us on dates in the States. They did quite a lengthy tour with us. They cut their teeth then. It was their very first tour. In a way it was like giving an Irish band a break when they came over to England. And in the States, Ray felt a resistance to book Canadian bands into clubs. So they came with us."

Gerry McAvoy: "I liked it, I must admit. It's the adulation. It's the amount of people there. It's the response you're getting from 10,000 people instead of 800 people. It's a different animal. And I wouldn't say Rory hated it. He did prefer the closeness of a club where you could see the whites of their eyes. I think he enjoyed both. But when it got too large it got silly. We played a gig somewhere in Indiana, I believe. And there was something like 100,000 people there. And the stage wasn't equipped for 100,000 people. You had to get there by helicopter. It was madness. When it gets to that stage, it's not pleasant. It's not music."

• • •

The strife between the British soldiers and the patriots of Northern Ireland had reached a violent climax in the 1970's. It was essentially a bad idea to visit, never mind publicize the fact that you were there. This was evident in the lack of entertainment. No one played Belfast. The risks were too extreme. Yet every December, when Rory and the band returned home for Christmas, they would perform a tour that included Belfast.

Donal Gallagher: "It happened unconsciously. Rory liked to work. So being at home at Christmas we would do our gigs then. Also you had to think of the economics and the situation for your audience at that time. They didn't have a lot of money. People had to save up for their concert tickets. And you had to allow for the fact that a lot of your audience were students. Being allowed to go to a concert was one thing. But if it was during school periods they weren't allowed to go out on nights of study. In effect, playing at Christmas, people were on holiday. They had a few bob that they could afford. Or they were given presents of a couple of tickets. So there were a lot of social factors taken into account."

Joe O'Herlihy: "The possibility of trouble breaking out was the one thing that was always at the back of people's minds but it never happened. The music thing seemed to cross the actual divide. Rory was accepted as an Irish guy making it on the international stage. We are very conscious of Irish people doing well and he was welcomed with open arms. There was never a sense of people going in there with fears or thoughts of trouble or anything like that. What crossed my mind was, 'Yeah, we're going to Belfast. And the crowd is great in Belfast. Wait until you see these guys, the way they'll react.' And it was always like that. Great audience. Great response. Incredible emotion and complete participation. Great connection."

It seemed that there was somewhat of an imposed moratorium on violence when Rory Gallagher and his band set up shop to perform for the people who had supported him from his earliest days on the circuit. Dino McGartland is the publisher of *Stagestruck*, a fanzine devoted to Rory and his music.

Dino McGartland: "Other groups thought Rory was mad for playing in the North. It was OK to play Dublin or Cork but to play Belfast was unheard of. But whenever he played there, they sold out maybe four or five nights. It was complete mayhem whenever he arrived because people took him to their hearts. He was a fantastic performer."

Gerry McAvoy: "The first night we played Belfast in '71, there was ten bombs that went off around the city as we were playing. And you're always worried. But you had to take a step and do it. No one would play Belfast. But Rory would do it religiously every year and he was admired and respected for doing it. The thing was, it was an amalgamation for both communities, Protestant and Catholic. There was no divide on the night of the concert. And right to the end there was no divide. To music fans, it didn't matter. You might have had guys from the IRA in the audience. You might have had guys from the UDN in the audience. But for three hours everything was forgotten about and you could see that in their faces."

Donal Gallagher: "Rory was accepted by all sides. I wouldn't say he was untouchable but there was an element of that. Particularly at Ulster Hall where the Belfast concerts were. That street was bombed so many times it was known as 'Bomb Alley.' He never felt immune to anything happening but he felt he was shielded somehow. In retrospect, had Rory been blatantly supporting one side or the other, he might have fell foul to some sort of sabotage. But because they would know that everyone in that hall was a mixture they wouldn't risk hurting their own."

• • •

Donal Gallagher: "We had really started to tour in the U.S. and promote 'Irish Tour '74' despite the early Polydor situation there, as a record company, being very weak.

When 'Irish Tour' struck, it got such critical acclaim and airplay on American radio. I remember the effects of it more from Stateside than most of Europe. But parallel to that was the 'Irish Tour' movie. That took on a whole new direction because it was rare in those days for a band to film a documentary. That one was made by Tony Palmer. That, in a way, was a partner for the album.

"It was never on home video. It was only on a cinema release. Which, because being a music documentary, tended to be very limited. And it was never sold to television. But it's just been released on video and DVD as well."

Viewing the documentary, many things are obvious. The editing is confusing to anyone who understands audio synchronization. Many frames are pieces taken from entirely different songs. But it captures a typical Gallagher performance during the '74 tour except for the crowd hysteria that was exaggerated due to the presence of the film crew.

Donal Gallagher: "Rory liked audience participation but that was a bit much. But you have to remember, in the early 70s, if you put a camera on anybody at a gig … if the lights were on them they would react to cameras because they felt they had to.

"What Rory realized was that there was a lot of interest in him and that he felt that he had to do it. I know that Tony Palmer despaired making that. Rory wouldn't do things that he wanted him to do. He was trying to get Rory to go and visit these people's houses. And even the party at the end, I mean, Rory said, 'What do you mean by end of tour party?' And Palmer's view was, 'Oh, every band has an end of tour party.' And Rory says, 'No.' I was prevailed upon then by Tony Palmer to organize a party that Rory might turn up at. Which is basically what you'll see. And he participated."

In December 1974, The Rolling Stones decided that it was time to replace recently departed guitarist Mick Taylor. Many were considered and depending on whom you talk to, the list was comprised of different names: Steve Marriott, Peter Frampton, Wayne Perkins, Roy Buchanan, Eric Clapton, obviously Ron Wood. But Rory was approached as soon as the decision to find a replacement was made. And the job was offered.

Donal Gallagher: "It got serious consideration, yeah. Absolutely. The way it came about, we were home for the Christmas tour, 1974. It was into the New Year. The phone rang one night; it was certainly after midnight. It was Ian Stewart, God rest him, inquiring if he had the right number for Rory. And not an accent I recognized. Because there was a certain paranoia of kidnappings of prominent Irish people during that time, one was cautious about saying yes. I said, 'I have a way of contacting him. Who's inquiring?' 'Ian Stewart.' Rory had already retired at this point. So I ran up and he refused to come to the phone because practical jokes were always being played [laughs]. But he did come down. And he spoke to Ian Stewart who was inviting Rory on behalf of the band to go to Holland and do some recording and have a play. So that was set up for the 10th, 11th and 12th of January. We were taking a few weeks off after a long year and we were starting back in Tokyo on the 28th of January. So Rory said, 'Well, I was going to have a break but I'd be delighted to do it.'

"But the dates got moved to the 16th, 17th, 18th. And those dates got postponed again. Next thing it backed up right into the Japanese tour. So Rory ended up going on the 23rd of January to Rotterdam. And he refused to let me go with him. He said, 'Oh, these guys just want to have a blow.' And I said, 'Rory. It's dead obvious what the scenario is here.' Anyway, he took his amp and guitar on the flight and flew into Rotterdam. Mick Jagger met him and as a matter of fact negotiated the fare with the taxi driver. Anyway, he spent three days with them.

"Now as soon as he got there the press broke the story that Rory was joining The Stones and all the European papers ran with that. The press was saying it was a done deal. Marshall Chess, who was president of the Stones record company at the time, and his people were all there. And they said to Rory, 'Oh, we knew it would be you. It's a perfect choice' and blah, blah, blah. 'Where's your representative?' And he said 'I came here by myself. I just thought they wanted a blow first.' There were a lot of Stones management types who were there to consummate the thing.

"The Stones were in a state of flux themselves. When the classic rifts between Jagger and Richards were going down. I think Ian Stewart was the catalyst in that band. Charlie and Bill basically, in a sense, weren't that involved. And with all the postponements Rory wanted to get down to work. He obviously had his tour to consider in Japan. At that time Keith Richards wasn't, would you say, an early riser! Rory would spend the day with Charlie and Bill chatting about Brian Jones times. They would start at eight o'clock at night and wait for Keith to come down and plug in. I think it was very much a case that Jagger wanted Rory in the band because he liked Rory's professionalism. And Ian Stewart, who was really the heart and soul of the Stones, from a blues point of view, as their piano player and had formed that band with Brian Jones, he wanted Rory in. In the course of that Rory did say to them, 'Look. What's happening here? I've got this tour right on top of me now. We've just got another day. Would you go up and speak to Keith?' So Rory went up to Keith's bedroom and Keith was comatose. Stayed up a few more hours. Keith was still comatose. And back a third time. And Rory said, 'Well, I've got to leave for the airport. There's no cohesion in the whole thing.' He got on a flight from Rotterdam. I met him back at Heathrow Airport with a fresh suitcase. We switched planes and the next stop was Anchorage on the way to Tokyo.

"I think things could have been hammered out. What we should have done was postponed the dates in Japan. There are also factors one forgets about. The Stones couldn't get visas to Japan at the time because of their previous drug convictions. They were banned, if you like. There were a lot of countries they couldn't tour in. Rory's European sales were far greater than the Stones at that time. I think he kind of symbolized with Charlie and Bill sitting around all day waiting for the Glimmer Twins to call the shots. Rory wouldn't have been the type to cope with that. He wasn't just a backup guitarist. He'd want to participate in the songs, etc. But it was obviously clear that that wouldn't have been the case. And Keith was genuinely comatose. He was going through his bad drug period.

"One of the things that came out of that was 'Miss You.' I asked him, 'What did you play? What did you jam?' He said, 'Mick just asked me to start a riff one night. And this song had been a riff I'd been working on.' He seemed fairly convinced that was his riff and they then took that further. Because 'Miss You' was the one he was rehearsing. So Rory definitely gave them a feel for it. A bluesier track. I think it would have been a lovely combination to have seen. And Rory always said that Ron Wood was the natural 'pop' choice. But he didn't bring anything new to the Stones. He didn't get the band experimenting.

"My feeling would have been, and this is without an egotistical vein in my body about it, is that it's just a shame that Rory wouldn't allow me to have come over. And I think the reason is he knew if I'd have come over, yes, it would have been a done deal [laughs]! At the time I remember saying, 'You can do both, Rory. You could do the Stones and you could do your own tours.' And we probably could have sold ten times as many concert tickets. But there were pressures from all sides. We had agents who were freaking out. Keith Richards had gone on record saying Rory was one of his favorite guitar players in an interview with NME when they had just formed the Rolling Stones label. They asked Keith who they were considering to sign and he cited Rory as the first one. And Peter Tosh, who they did sign. And if Rory became available they would love to have him.

"But whatever feelings he had, he packed his guitar, left his hotel room and headed for the airport. And there was an element that he deserved better treatment, if you like."

• • •

Gerry McAvoy: "Years ago we were playing Birmingham Town Hall. Rory had been up earlier with Donal in a car because he was doing some TV and some radio stuff. Rod, Lou and I had driven up later in the afternoon in a horrendous fog, the worst fog they had had in fifteen years."

Donal Gallagher: "I remember the gig very well. The highway got closed; the fog was 'pea soup' thick. The roads just became completely gridlocked. They were stuck on the motorway and they couldn't get off to get a train to Birmingham."

The Hague, Netherlands, 1978.
Courtesy Theo Lagarde

Gerry McAvoy: "I had to ring Donal up at seven o'clock and we were still fifty miles away. And as we were going five miles an hour, there was no way we were going to make the gig. So Rory decided to go up and do it on his own. Acoustically."

Donal Gallagher: "The town hall was completely sold out. We were going to abandon the show. Rory might have said, 'Well, why don't I do acoustic?' We'd rescheduled the concert for the following week back in the town hall. Meantime, for all those who traveled by bus, which Rory was always conscious that people did travel to see him, that they got something from the night. So I went on and explained what had happened and that Rory was gonna come on and do his acoustic set anyway. Which we thought was going to be twenty minutes, half an hour, and everybody was going to get their refund or ticket for next week. So after an hour Rory was still going strong with material and had almost gotten the audience playing percussion. And it was such a brilliant show."

Gerry McAvoy: "But then he decided to do some electric as well. An old keyboard friend of mine that I used to play with was at the gig. Chris Morrison from when we were with Deep Joy. So Rory got him up on stage to play piano."

Donal Gallagher: "Chris got up and they did a couple of jams. I was, at this point, under 'huge' pressure from the manager of the auditorium, saying, 'Rory's running over time. Can you get him to wind up?' This was something because we'd delayed the show from starting by half an hour to give the band a chance to arrive. But Rory was literally still going strong. I slipped on to the side of the stage and gave this kind of expression to Rory, 'Look, wind it up.' Which is like a red flag to a bull! So he collared me and said, 'Right, in behind the drums!' "

Gerry McAvoy: "Donal always fancied himself as a bit of a drummer. So he got up and played drums. And this was in front of 3,000 people. I heard that it was going OK. Donal could just about manage a beat. And Rory turned around when Donal was playing and said, 'Keep it simple [laughs].' Donal couldn't do anything else but keep it simple!"

Donal Gallagher: "I'd sit in at rehearsals and play a couple of numbers with Rory and things like that. So I sat in on drums 'cuz Rory thought he could bring it to a crescendo with a drummer. With a bad drummer! He could bring the whole thing to a head and kind of rock it out, as it were. That was his intention. I sat in on the drums. And it wasn't that I was getting complicated. The road crew had a field day with me. They had me in a sitting duck position and they were putting the drums back through the monitors through echo. So I couldn't hear the beat or the rhythm [laughs]. I can't remember what I was playing or what I was playing to but I was trying to put all these fills and it probably sounded to Rory, because what he was hearing was coming through the monitors, that I was doing Ginger Baker! Just one rim shot with echo on it sounds like thirty times over. Sounds like someone's going bananas. And Rory wasn't quite sure [laughs].

"But it was some gig. I couldn't believe that a half an hour after we got off stage we were fined for over-running.

And nearly banned from doing the free show for the kids the following week."

• • •

One of the necessary evils of being a frontman is dealing with journalists. But Rory had an aversion to the media.

Gerry McAvoy: "Rory was always embarrassed by press. I'd been to radio stations with him and he always felt embarrassed about the questions that he was asked. That was just the sort of person he was. He didn't like the glamour; he didn't like the pizzazz of show business."

Having met Rory, I was immediately put at ease by his direct eye contact. Yet as soon as a paid inquisitor approached him, his personality changed.

Donal Gallagher: "He probably switched into a professional mode. He was very genuine with people; he was very warm. I suspect that he was just being guarded. Particularly with interviews being so public. Rory was also reluctant to speak publicly about his personal feelings or his private life or his family or discuss political matters. Anything that deviated away from the music."

1975

With the release of "Irish Tour '74," Rory had fulfilled his commitment to Polydor. He and Donal took the knowledge they had amassed about the record business and weighed their options.

Donal Gallagher: "We took the view at the time that Polydor wasn't in a position to put weight behind an artist. We also felt that they should have come forward saying, 'What do you want to renew the deal?' And they also felt that Rory was coming with too many albums too quickly. They wanted to dictate a release every two years or whatever. So it indicated to us that they didn't understand the nature of the beast, if you like. A lot of the big albums at the time were Warner's and we'd made friends with a lot of the Warner people who would see Rory steal everybody's thunder on the package bills. It was from the top level, from Mo Austin on down: Warner's wanted the act. We'd also spoken to Capitol. We went and saw every one of the top American labels.

"In the meantime Europe was becoming far more independent-label based. The top albums were on Chrysalis, Island, Virgin, all these independent labels. They had become far stronger than the traditional companies. Decca, EMI. So we were trying to find that compromise."

Former *Melody Maker* journalist Roy Eldridge had acquired the position of A&R director for Chrysalis UK.

Roy Eldridge: "In '74 he had released 'Irish Tour.' It was a big album. We had heard a rumor that it was going to be the last album for Polydor and they were looking to possibly move. And because I was the one who knew him from the *Melody Maker* days I was kind of deputized to see if he'd be interested in coming to Chrysalis. I'd seen a tour advertised in Germany. I jumped on a plane and went over, saw the show, found out which room Rory was in, and scribbled a note on the hotel stationary and shoved it under his door. Saying the normal things you would say. 'Fantastic show. Do you remember me? If you're ever thinking about changing record companies we're a hot, new label and we'd love to talk to you.' "

Donal Gallagher: "We had several meetings with Warner's. That seemed the route that we were going in. I was in Los Angeles conducting negotiations with Mo Austin and a whole team of Warner's people that had flown me out to do this while Rory was playing in Montreaux. We broke for lunch and I went back to the hotel. I got a phone call from Chris Wright who was one half of Chrysalis, Terry Ellis being the other half. At that time Chrysalis were our favorite for Europe anyway but they wanted to pick up the whole world. They had Warner's distribution in the U.S. but we felt we should be with the bigger company. So Chris called me and he said, 'Oh, you were at a meeting with Warner's today.' And I said, 'How did you know [laughs]?' I was quite intrigued that he knew where I was. And he said, 'Since you're in a meeting, I can tell you four of the Warner's people are going to come work for Chrysalis.' And then he explained to me the whole Chrysalis expansion. What they wanted to do, etc. But they were going to keep the Warner's distribution. That didn't sell it there and then."

Author: "Were you aware of that situation?"

Roy Eldridge: "Not specifically of that phone call but I can imagine Chris making it because that was the period in time when the company's distribution was going to be handled by Warner Brothers. We were setting up the American office and we wanted to have as many acts on a worldwide basis as we possibly could."

Donal Gallagher: "I went back to the meeting to continue the negotiations knowing that four of the people were leaving. I stayed out there for two weeks until I got to the bottom of it. And I got confirmation that they were leaving. It seemed, from a business point of view, Chrysalis were matching Warner's offers. Warner's knew that if we signed with Chrysalis they would still have the distribution. I remember after we signed with Chrysalis, they held a signing party and Mo Austin came over from Warner Brothers. All the Warner's people came. They were so positive about Rory."

Lou Martin: "As the band, we were the last people to hear about it. We were doing an English tour and were on a plane and Rory said, 'By the way, the new record company is Chrysalis and we're going to be recording a new album when we get back.' Which was good because they had some really nice people on that label. Chrysalis gave us this big party when we got to the States. They took us out in a yacht. Polydor never did anything like that!"

With a new label, a fresh start, and eagerly awaiting fans, Rory released his sixth solo album, "Against The Grain."

Donal Gallagher: "He already had that album. There was quite a gap between 'Irish Tour '74,' which was partly recorded at the end of '73 if you like, until the autumn of '75. That was the longest gap Rory had between albums. So he had stored up all this material. He was ready.

"The people at Chrysalis were very positive about Rory. They had a very professional approach and they were quite ambitious. They'd also just bought out George Martin's company, AIR. So we were tied into a lot of studio factors as well. For the first album, they wanted to wait until '76.

Rory was ready to go into the studio. He had it done inside six weeks at a studio called Wessex. It's owned by George Martin. It's an old church. They stalled the refurbishing of that studio so Rory could go in and cut his album. And because he had the material and the band was as tight as you could be, he recorded it very quickly."

Once the album was released the band took to the road, holding up their end of the bargain by promoting the album. But everyone in the Gallagher camp was very interested in how Chrysalis was going to better Polydor and do "Against The Grain" justice via promotion.

Gerry McAvoy: "I don't think they did enough for 'Against The Grain' in the States yet again. An album that did very well in Europe. But whether it was the right album at the time I don't know. But I think it could have been pushed a lot better than it was."

After touring to promote "Against The Grain," Rory wanted to return to the studio as soon as possible and try and give Chrysalis more ammunition to promote their newly signed act. But he came up against a familiar yet unwelcome idea. Polydor executives had suggested, on several occasions, that an outside producer be brought in. That may have been on the list as one reason Rory didn't stay at Polydor. And now Chrysalis had the same idea for the next album. But this time the Gallagher camp seriously considered the option and began bandying names around.

Donal Gallagher: "Contact was made with Jimmy Miller and Gus Dudgeon. A lot of those guys that had come through the early British music scene and had learned their craft at the BBC and whatever. I remember Jimmy Miller being talked about."

Author: "Would Miller's known drug problems have been a reason he wasn't chosen?"

Donal Gallagher: "I don't know that it would have been. I think it was more a lack of communication in that he had moved to the States in the 70s from the U.K. Communications weren't what they are now. E-mail, faxing. It was quite a distance. Getting phone numbers was difficult."

Rory agreed to turn the reigns over to someone of his choosing. He decided on Deep Purple bassist Roger Glover as his designate to produce "Calling Card."

Donal Gallagher: "The principle reason was we had spent a lot of time touring with Deep Purple in America. We had done gigs with them as far back as when they were known as 'Episode Six.' We had then done a few lengthy tours with Rory, Purple and Fleetwood Mac. We had spent six months on the road together in sporadic runs. So you build up friendships and alliances. And Roger, who was producing Purple anyway, had been interested in producing Rory. Roger had worked in Munich before, in that studio. We were quite familiar with Munich and the area and Musicland. Rory was into his second album for Chrysalis. And that had always been a suggestion. 'Bring in a producer and get a different sound.' "

Lou Martin: " 'Calling Card,' to my mind, was the best studio album out of the whole set. Roger Glover did a really good job on that. Roger concentrated on the instruments as well as the guitar."

Roy Eldridge: "I'd need to look at the sales history and see if the statistics prove me wrong but I thought that was a pretty good album."

Gerry McAvoy: "It was a total disaster. And that's not being disrespectful to Roger, whom I got to know quite well. But it was a mismatch in personalities, I'm afraid. Roger had a very straight, down the road idea of how something should be produced, i.e., Deep Purple. Very clean, very straight and very heavy. Where Rory had a different approach. Rory wanted things on the record. Distortion, warts and everything. He wanted to let the record breathe. But Roger had a different idea how it should go."

The one thing that was always an objective with Rory was to obtain as much of the aforementioned "breathing" on the songs as possible. His live sound had the "dirt" that everyone was trying to capture on tape. To go the other way seemed hypocritical.

Donal Gallagher: "That would be the 'produced' factor. Which I know gave Rory great cause for concern because he was never satisfied with the mixes. In fact in the end the relationship soured a bit because Roger had a 'take it or leave it' attitude. 'This is as much as I'm doing.' So Rory took the album. And in the end I think it was Chris Kimsey, who was then a budding engineer, who did the final mixes. He's worked with a lot of top-line names getting that dirty sound. Rory wanted to throw it in the dustbin for a while and dirty it up. Roger was taking a band approach to the album as opposed to an artist, Rory Gallagher."

Author: "Was Roger Glover hired to capture a band approach? Being a guitar player, Rory would mix favoring his own instrument."

Donal Gallagher: "That's true. And it was a predominant factor. But you'd have to go back to 'Against The Grain,' its predecessor. There wasn't, production-wise, too much with that. When record company people were calling for an outside producer, they were looking for the hit single. The more diluted Rory. 'Let's drive it towards the single. Let's cut the time of the songs to three minutes.'

"Rory felt himself that if he could find the right producer and engineer, he'd be happy to collaborate. But he always felt that the people that he worked with didn't have the commitment to the project that he had. And I've got to say, as Rory's brother, it was always an endurance test with Rory. You had to dispense with family links and any ideas of having a social life and strictly get down until the job was done. I know that in Roger's case, his wife was expecting a baby or something was going down. His pressures were family-oriented. So he had to say, 'Well, that's the mix and that's as far as we go with it.' And the next time that experiment was tried was the forerunner to the 'Photofinish' album. The suggestion was would he do an American album and get a 'more' American sound. And he did an album in San Francisco with Elliot Mazer. Elliot worked with Neil Young, Gordon Lightfoot, Big Brother and The Holding Company, Mike Bloomfield, Emmylou Harris and Linda Rondstadt to name but a few. And that is the album Rory put in the bin."

Cologne, Germany, 1977.
Courtesy Stefan Klimm

1977

Gerry McAvoy: "We went on to record what would eventually be 'Photofinish' in San Francisco. The original name was 'Torch.' But it was never released."

Rory had met Elliot Mazer during the final Taste tour in 1970 when Area Code 615 and Stone The Crows opened for them. Gallagher admired Mazer for the work he had done with artists he held in high regard. They teamed up at His Master's Wheels Studio.

Gerry McAvoy: "It was a confusing time. What we'd done is a Far East tour of Japan, Australia, New Zealand and flew straight to San Francisco. We were there for two months. Which was fine at the time but it became a little bit too comfortable. We had been there since October. The album dragged on and dragged on. It seemed like an eternity.

Everybody had their own apartment in a beautiful apartment block in San Francisco overlooking the bay. You couldn't ask for more. But because it was so comfortable you felt ill at ease. I would have preferred, and Rory as well, to go down there and spend three weeks, get the job done and just leave. I actually left on the 19th of December to go back to England because I finished what I had to do and Rory stayed to keep on mixing. And there was a lot of pressure from Elliot Mazer. Rory was a fan of the acts he produced and he thought it would be a successful collaboration between the two of them. But it didn't work out that way.

"The type of engineer/producer that Elliot was, he was very forceful with his ideas. I'm not saying his ideas were wrong. I mean, he had worked with Neil Young. He had worked with The Band. And because of this we had a certain amount of respect for him. But working with a European artist like Rory, it was a different situation. Working with Neil Young I imagine the situation was very laid back but with us it wasn't."

Rod de'Ath: "I thought it was going very well. Towards the end it was like, 'What's going on?' I'd like to hear the tapes, in retrospect. At the time I thought it was the best thing we'd done."

Author: "Could anyone sense any problems?"

Rod de'Ath: "No, not at all. No. None of us could."

Donal Gallagher: "I was to deliver the album to Chrysalis. They had a huge listening thing planned. They were bringing in all the national sales directors, etc. And I was just going to the elevator and Rory said, 'I'll tell you what we can do with the album.' And he literally put it in the bin [laughs]. I was shocked! I said, 'Can I play it anyway and tell them you want to go back and remix it?' And he said, 'No. That album doesn't go out. It's not what I want. I don't like it.' We almost came to blows! I said something to the effect of, 'I feel like breaking your leg.' I remember going to the record company and making all the apologies, humble pie and all that."

Roy Eldridge: "I can remember the consternation that it caused at the time. But our experience with a lot of artists is if they're making the record it's always, 'This is the best thing I've ever made. It must be out next week. This is so great.' And then quite often you get to this period where they're about to deliver it to you and they don't want to let it go. 'No, no, no. There's just a little bit more I want to do to it.' Or they have second thoughts. 'I'm not sure about this.'"

Donal Gallagher: "And coming back to a message at the Sunset Marquis from our travel agent saying, 'I've taken Rory to Mt. Sinai hospital. Everything's fine. Don't worry.' Of course it's a message that tells you nothing but scares the shit out of you!"

Ted McKenna: "What happened was Rory told me that he arrived at Sunset Marquis and he was paying his cab. I think he'd probably had a few drinks. He shut his thumb in the door and broke his picking thumb."

Donal Gallagher: "Any ideas at that point of salvaging the album were scrapped because he had to have medical treatment. It was going to take six weeks to heal. I remember flying back to London feeling like we had our tails between our legs. So the whole thing was very negative for Rory. It was his first major depression.

"You want to blow your brains out! I couldn't comprehend it. To me the material was great. I had spent time in the studio and was familiar with it. I felt there was a lot of exciting stuff and experimentation on the album. But I think that at that time he had a mental turning point. All I could do was salvage the operation like any damage.

"Because of the way the deal was structured Rory was empowered with all the rights to do what he wanted. It was his final call. He wrote the material. All he had to do was not allow his publishing to be used on the track. But you couldn't get into that. You had to respect his decision. He was a producer himself and he knew his own songs better than anybody. The mixes were poor but they could have been remixed. They were recorded well enough. I just think he

took a personal dislike to the whole situation and the scenario surrounding him.

"I'd went up and announced the thing to Chrysalis. I told them, 'We're going to take a little more time with this album. I'm sorry. Please just be patient. He really doesn't want to play anything just yet. He is not happy with it.' They asked if they could hear a track or two but I explained that he didn't want to play anything. They'd been up to the studio and had an idea what was being done and they were excited by what they had heard. And they had to respect his wishes. My intention was to go back to the hotel and sit down with Rory and look at the ways to convince him to remix or do whatever. I figured a week or two and we could sort it out. But when I'd heard he fractured his thumb and he was in hospital, we were completely snookered at that point. There was no way to go with it."

Gerry McAvoy: "It was an experiment with that album as well. It went so many different ways. It was so diverse. Mazer actually had a Mariachi band on 'Brute, Force & Ignorance.' He'd brought a fiddle player over from Ireland to play on it. It was starting to get a bit crazy. At nighttime Rod, myself and Lou would go out and go to clubs and get drunk. It became a bit of a nightmare in the end."

Donal Gallagher: "I think Rory took a turn against the whole time period perhaps. Just took an attitude towards it. And then he took about half the material from that album and used it when he recorded 'Photofinish.' I thought to bring out an album that is half another album, albeit with different musicians, would undermine one or the other.

"I know, emotionally, what it did to him. He was just very bitter. And he was bitter towards Elliot Mazer afterwards."

Lou Martin: "And the tracks on that are just starting to filter out as bonus tracks on the reissues."

Donal Gallagher: "I've used one or two of them because I felt it a shame to be wasted because they were of that era."

Lou Martin: "So by the time we got back, various things were going on. Rod and myself had been playing with these other guys when we were home from tours. Mick Clarke was one of them. He had a band called Salt. Rod suggested that we form a band with those guys and try and do something. And by that time Rory had the same band for seven years and I got the feeling that he wanted a change. A change of lineup, direction, whatever."

Donal Gallagher: "I think after the whole San Francisco thing, he just felt 'Stop. Break the band up. I'm stopping for a while.' "

Lou Martin: "So he said, 'I've decided to change the band.' And we thought, 'Well, if you want to do that, it makes a bit of sense to us.' And we parted under very amicable circumstances."

Rod de'Ath: "It was a long partnership. It was seven years. Nothing in particular had built up, not as far as we were concerned. Just time to move on."

Gerry McAvoy: "I don't think they decided to move on. I think Rory decided that for them. Rory didn't actually know which direction he was going in. When Lou and Rod went, Rory and I had lunch and we sat and talked about it. After I had the conversation with Rory I didn't know where I stood as far as staying with the band or not. And at that time it didn't really matter to me one way or the other, you know. With Rod and Lou from '72 to '78, we'd been with him seven years. Had a lot of work in America, Canada. A lot of work in the Far East. And I didn't know if I wanted to continue the path with Rory anyway. So I just sort of laid back for a couple of weeks and waited to hear what he wanted to do. He gave me a phone call to go into the studio and try out some drummers. So I just went along with the flow. And that's the way Rory worked. Obviously, you could read between the lines. You could read his mind sometimes. You knew the minute you spoke to him."

Donal Gallagher: "Gerry was always a guy that was good at keeping his head down [laughs]! While Rory severed with Rod and Lou, I don't think there was a severance with Gerry or there was a new arrangement made. And to be honest it was an area that I didn't want to get involved; with the musicians. Rory, as bandleader, that was a domain that I knew was for musicians."

Gerry McAvoy: "There was a lot of ill feeling at the time as well. About a year leading up to that, Rory and I shared a dressing room and Rod and Lou would share a dressing room. The camp was starting to divide. It was personal things. Rod wasn't happy with his lot and he wanted a bigger say in the band. I was happy to go along as it was. You didn't dare bring a song to Rory because he wouldn't use it."

Rod de'Ath: "I'm a professional musician. And during that time I was working for another professional musician. He employed me and it was his music. It was his show. It was a job. Just because you're a musician, it's still a job. And of course, as with any art form, you have your input, etc., etc. But if you're working for an artist as part of his band, how can you be owed a bigger say?"

Donal Gallagher: "I think also, too, with the keyboards at that time … we were having to get grand pianos, Hammond organs; amplification for keyboards was quite sophisticated. And I think the tail was starting to wag the dog. The entire sound check was being taken up by a piano tuner tuning up the grand piano. Then electrify everything. An hour for the drummer to do his sound check. And the star of the show is just managing to squeeze a number in before he started the concert! I think he felt the whole thing was too top-heavy. And Rory felt, 'I was one of the first guys on the block with a three-piece doing that kind of sound. Maybe that's what I'll get back to doing.' "

Gerry McAvoy: "There was a relationship between me and Rory anyway. That wasn't going to be the band in the next year. Rory knew that. It was 1978."

Donal Gallagher: "Gone and beyond. Forgotten. And Rory didn't even want to revisit the issue. I felt very

Agora Ballroom, Cleveland, Ohio, 1978.
Courtesy Brian Chalmers

caught in the situation. I remember taking the shuttle up from Los Angeles to see Elliot Mazer. And to me, this was terrible that it hadn't worked out. But you accept it and get on with life."

Ted McKenna: "If there's one song that sums Rory up to me, not necessarily clearly in a musical sense but in the sense that it sums up what he was, is 'Last of the Independents.' He was very loath to be pressured by anybody to trim or change his fundamental view of how blues should be played. My opinion was that he had the finished product and he felt that it didn't represent what he was about and that's why he scrapped it. And he had the balls to do that."

•   •   •

Being a professional athlete or a successful touring musician means an enormous amount of travel, which can cause some people to develop phobias. Fear of flying would eventually cause Rory to curb his work patterns.

Rory Gallagher: "You know the trouble I've had with flying. I've turned a lot of money down for big American and big Japanese tours. Eventually I walked into the plane and went to Tokyo and got around the world. Hard. I tell ya. It was difficult. It could ruin your career, flying, I tell ya. And I was the tough guy in the band. I used to get them on. Any time anyone got scared … one of the guys left the band because he couldn't fly. Donal couldn't fly. And I was good. But I went through some real Buddy Holly flights!"

Donal Gallagher: "It was on a Deep Purple tour that we had that one flight that got us all on edge. I'd had a horrendous fear of flying prior to Rory getting it but I managed to get over it somehow. I remember being terrified. In the law of averages, 10 percent of flights are going to be terrible. So this was an accumulation of a lot of bad flights and the lifestyle. We were going at a frenetic pace."

Ted McKenna: "For me the time to worry is when the plane goes down. Why worry about what's making it go up? When we toured we did a lot of flying. Sometimes we flew three times a day. And sometimes you get a hairy one. Especially when you have a bad hangover … you get the ones where the plane just drops like a fuckin' stone. And everybody's shit practically leaves their pants. That kind of thing does happen. What scared me is waking up … let's say we've had a heavy night with the Gallagher band. The next day, you get on the plane and you're asleep before it even takes off. I'll never forget once I woke up about probably the region of thirty thousand feet above Tokyo Bay. I had the window seat and the plane was banking 'cuz it was in a holding pattern so the plane was at a forty-five degree angle. I looked down and all I could see was the trails of ships and Tokyo Bay and I just went 'Ooh boy! We really shouldn't be up here, should we? This ain't human.' That's when it freaks you, you know, when you suddenly wake up and are totally aware of the fact that you're thirty thousand feet up in the sky above the clouds and you think to yourself 'God, how the hell do we manage to stay up here?' "

• • •

Rory still owed Chrysalis an album. His thumb had healed. He had some restructured songs from San Francisco, along with new ones. He decided to return to a power trio and started looking for a drummer.

Gerry McAvoy: "We brought Wilgar back in to see if it would work but it didn't. We brought Brendan O'Neill in and that didn't work out either."

Brendan O'Neill: "I was playing in a rock/jazz situation at the time. The band was doing fairly well. And because I felt very happy in the situation I didn't really make a big effort to join Rory at that time. In hindsight that was really strange. I don't know why I did that!"

Donal Gallagher: "Rory was working up at Air Studios at the time. The engineer was a guy called Colin Fairly. Colin could see Rory's frustration with trying these drummers every night. So he said to Rory, 'God, I know what you want on the drums. Can I play?' And he just went in and did it for Rory on a track. And Rory said, 'Quit the studio and I'll give you a job as a drummer.' And he said, 'I can't. I've got this terrific arthritic problem. I take injections once a week. I would have continued as a drummer if this condition hadn't occurred. But the guy who would be great is Ted McKenna.'"

Ted McKenna: "I was born the tenth of March, 1950, an only child. I grew up in Coat Bridge, where I live now. It wasn't until I actually wondered why Fred Astaire and Ginger Rogers made such an impression on me that I realized that it was the rhythmic aspect. I used to watch the show 'Flying Down To Rio.' I basically threw myself out of the Cub Scouts because it conflicted with the movies. The rhythm of the dance used to move me so much. I must have been ten or eleven. After that I heard my first record, 'G.I. Blues.' Then The Beatles. Listening to Radio Luxembourg and trying to eat up as much music as I could from every avenue. Jazz, blues, Charlie Mingus, Sarah Vaughan, Frank Sinatra as well as Tommy Tucker and the blues people. John Lee Hooker. All that stuff.

"I was in the process of getting into a high school band, a garage band, when I got my first kit in 1966. The bass player's Mum and Dad had a garage so we used to practice there. I was asked to join another band by a guy named Hamish Stuart, who was later the lead singer of The Average White Band. Hamish used to be in a band called The Dream Police. It was a short-lived affair. He said he wanted to go heavy metal for some reason. So he joined up with a drummer who was in a band called Tear Gas. And when I heard that Tear Gas needed a drummer I immediately joined. And that band eventually became The Sensational Alex Harvey Band.

"I went out to see Alex and we went out to a club to see one of his old pals from when he and Alex used to play in Hamburg. And I bumped into an engineer who knew another guy, a mutual friend, who was a drummer and an engineer. I asked what he was doing and he said, 'Oh, he's working with Rory Gallagher.' And he'd said that they'd been trying to find a drummer. The next day I got a call from this guy, Colin Fairly. He said, 'Would you like to come down and have a play with Rory?' And I said 'I'd love to.' "

Donal Gallagher: "I remember Ted came down and he was such good humor. He arrived and brought in his drums himself. There was no, 'We want humpers and roadies and click tracks.' He just set it up. And the tone off his drums, even before they were miked properly, was just there. It was right. It clicked there and then."

Ted McKenna: "I tell you what I was impressed with. At the end of the tryout, I packed up and started to take my gear out and Rory and Don and Gerry all helped me downstairs with my drum kit. I mean, I remember being in the Sensational Alex Harvey Band playing in Germany and I saw these huge posters all over Germany for Rory Gallagher. Rory was a big name at that point. I said 'Guys, you don't have to do this, you know.' They all helped me downstairs with my drums and it was Don, he said 'Fuck all that. We're real people. No bullshit here.'

"I got back to see my parents up here in Scotland. Don called me and said 'Listen, we're doing the Macrim Festival next week. Can you come down and start rehearsals?' And I said 'Great.' But it was real last minute stuff. And then we did the Macrim Festival, which is the very first gig I did with them."

Author: "You were being asked to create more energy with fewer personnel."

Ted McKenna: "Yeah. That's right. Fundamentally that's always been one of my, if you like, strong points as a drummer. If you have a bass player and a drummer and a guitar player that know how to set in the right part of the groove, the space, sometimes having keyboards can actually undermine the music. You have to play more but you also have to be set in your part of the pocket. And it gives more freedom to the drummer and the bass player to kind of underpin the guitar work. It's a skill. It's an art. I've seen countless bass, drum and guitar bands that are mono-dimensional. They don't have the concept but they can be a very kind of rich. So for me it wasn't a new situation. I just loved it right from the start."

After producing himself and Roger Glover's production of "Calling Card," Rory decided a co-producer would be an interesting option to consider. Gallagher was drawn to experienced engineer Alan O'Duffy.

Donal Gallagher: "Alan was one of those names that was always around. He had worked at Olympic, training with Glyn Johns. He'd worked on 'Jesus Christ Superstar' and Humble Pie and Slade and The 5th Dimension and just finished 'Venus and Mars' with McCartney. The Point Studios is where I met Alan. Alan has a very nice manner. He's a lovely man and has a special way with him."

Ted McKenna: "Alan O'Duffy. I always found him a very pleasant and gentle Irishman. He's a very nice man. Very intelligent. Very sweet man. And he was always good fun. He would tease a lot. Once I'd done my drum check in the studio, he'd very often say things like, 'OK, that's great Ted. If you just wanna take it easy the drummer will be here shortly' [laughs]. He would always have that kind of real gentle Irish way of giving you a hard time."

Alan O'Duffy: "Myself and Donal had a thought, a long time ago, of opening a studio in Ireland. That was one idea. The other idea was opening a mobile studio. We went down a few roads in that regard about twenty-two years ago. The studio I later started was called The Point."

Donal Gallagher: "We were being offered that studio at the time for a very good rate. I went down to look at it and Rory tried it. But it was a little too basic. It wasn't sophisticated enough, which is an odd thing to say about Rory. But out of that he met Alan. He liked the idea of the dark studio that had been introduced in Germany. And he thought, 'I'll get Alan and guarantee that I get a good engineer in a very good studio in Germany rather than use a house engineer.' That's the route that that took."

Alan O'Duffy: "I came in at 'Photofinish.' They still had to deliver an album. The whole album was in their heads. Certainly in Rory's head. But it was a question of recording it. So I got the job of recording an album with Rory from scratch. A lot of the time working in Germany was a one-on-one experience. The band may have been watching television or whatever and it was just Rory and myself for hours on end. He was a gifted fellow.

New York City, 1977.
Courtesy Strange Music Inc.

"My background is different. I'm a music-mixer. I had worked in recording studios since the age of seventeen with bands like the Kinks, The Spencer Davis Group and The Rolling Stones. I like melodies. I love great pop structure and I brought that interest in to working with Rory. Rory had his own path to follow. And it was my job as a mixer-producer with Rory, to be a facilitator for Rory to get his heart, his soul, on tape. I tried to do that and have as good fun as we could and make it a facility for Rory. But at the same time, having a bias in my own head, towards the idea of making it accessible."

Donal Gallagher: "I'd heard about the studio just outside Cologne. Cologne is such a nice town and we had friends there through our connections with the WDR TV people.

"On one of my trips I'd driven to a small town way outside Cologne called Pulheim. It seemed to have a nice setup and a vibe. It had a good reputation from a recording point of view. The Germans were always meticulous in their recording techniques. And we were quite used to Germany. A lot of equipment, in particular our P.A. system, we had built up in Hamburg. Language wasn't a problem. Rory had a good, basic grasp of German. So Rory came over and I drove him out to the studios. He liked it and he liked Dieter. The setup was quite homey. I think that was the attraction."

Alan O'Duffy: "Dieter Dierk is a bit of a laugh of a man who used to manage The Scorpions. Very bright and clever chap. He had basically built a studio in the back garden of his mother's house. He had cemented over the plot of land and stuck a studio on it. Then he built a concrete roof on the studio and stuck an office and a summerhouse on top of that. Then he bought the building behind the studio and converted that into a hotel. He used his mother's kitchen to provide food for us."

Ted McKenna: "She was great. She used to always make us bacon and eggs. You'd finish maybe one o'clock in the morning. We're sitting in the cafeteria area of the studio and she'd go to bed and wish us all '*Schlaff gut. Weidersehn. Schlaff gut.*' It was just like your granny putting you to bed as it were because we all lived there. I really enjoyed it. We had a great crew. Rory's main roadie, Tom O'Driscoll, Joe

O'Herlihy, Gerry and Rory and Don. It was just the warmest atmosphere you can imagine."

Joe O'Herlihy: "I was pretty much taking care of everything. Tom O'Driscoll would do quite a substantial amount of that. Tom was the main man, the boss, as far as I was concerned. The sessions went smoothly. Rory was pretty much in command of his own destiny, in the sense of where he wanted the music to go and what he wanted people to do. He was totally creative and absolutely immersed in it. Most of us had girlfriends or wives at that stage but Rory loved his music and his girlfriend was his guitar. And that love affair was 1,000 percent, forty-eight hours a day, eight days a week. That's why he was so good at what he did."

Donal Gallagher: "'Photofinish' was done very quickly. The material had been developed and honed down so it was going to be relatively easy to lay it down. It was called 'Photofinish' for a reason. The San Francisco album would have come out in March had it been ready. And then with the fracture, Chrysalis had said, 'Well, look, you've got six weeks to get the album in.' The window of opportunity was tight. So he knocked the album out in three weeks. Mixed and delivered. Rory was always the eleventh hour of the eleventh minute of the eleventh day. I mean he was just frustrating beyond belief [laughs]! He was always stringing. And it was detrimental to him in the long run. So we just delivered it in. It's just associated with horse racing. This one got to the post by a hair.

"He was a perfectionist. It's as simple as that. And it wasn't so much that it had to be perfection/preciseness. It had to be perfection that wouldn't seem to be something that had been diluted. Or sweetened. The mixes took on an incredibly introverted kind of a thing as opposed to extroverted. He was inclined to mix the things in so subtly that he was almost withdrawing so that you could barely hear him. And because he was producing himself, he was writing the material, he was bandleading, he was dictating the pace of things … you can't take up that much work in your day. He'd start an album off with great gusto. For the first two or three nights he would not stop himself. He would not discipline himself and say, 'Well, when it hits two in the morning that's my cut-off point. Time to drop everything and go home. Get a night's sleep.' He'd go through 'til five, six in the morning, get a couple of hours sleep and then start listening to the playbacks. And he'd say, 'God, did we record it that fast?' What he didn't realize was that physically he'd taken so much out of himself that his ears were possibly hearing things in a hyper state. And that's where a producer was a good idea.

"What Rory needed was not so much a producer but someone that would dictate to him what you couldn't do. I mean, there was no way in the world … I would often try it and we'd end up in brotherly rows! We had a thing where we should never be seen having a row in front of anybody else. Particularly because there was a relationship and it would make everybody feel uncomfortable. No one gets involved in between two family members. So if I said to Rory, 'Why don't you knock it off for tonight and leave well alone?' I was cast from the studio and told never to come back [laughs]! So it ended up that I didn't spend as much time in the studio as I would have liked."

Alan O'Duffy: "We did spend as long as it took to get the sounds sorted out. And get the kit sounds and set it up in the most conducive way. With a band you can take a week to set things up. With Rory it really wasn't that long a process. I would say less than a day and then we were into putting stuff on tape that we could listen back to and say, 'This is great.' There wasn't any nonsense or ego flying around to stop us from getting on with it."

Donal Gallagher: "There was an attitude, almost like 'Brute, Force and Ignorance.' Rory wanted this three-piece band to create rock 'n' roll havoc. It was exciting and he was happy. And Ted's personality brought an uplifting air to things. Rory had always preferred a drummer who was ahead of the beat as opposed to being on it or dragging the beat. And Ted was kicking the drums in a way that was making Rory kind of dance, almost."

Alan O'Duffy: "Ted can play you the drum track to any song on the planet. And he does it with such fun as well. A very musical man."

Ted McKenna: "The energy of the band, for three guys, was quite frightening. I didn't think about it at all. I just played what I felt. Rory would do a lot of takes and would pick the ones that he liked. He would take them all to his room and just sit and listen to the basic tracks. Sometimes we'd spend a whole day on one track. We'd play it dozens and dozens of times. Some things, we'd go in and then we'd head out maybe two or three times and have a coffee and a beer or whatever. And we'd head out another two or three times and eventually when Rory felt he had one in the bag … it took him a long time to make his mind up about things at times."

Author: "But wouldn't he end up with the correct decision?"

Ted McKenna: "Oh yeah. He would painstakingly decide what he thought was the right one and that's the one he went with. The key to it is always to divorce your own performance. Sometimes I thought I played a great drum track. Anybody else may want to put bass and a guitar on top of it. But he wanted to capture the three-piece together. He didn't want to do any cosmetic work. If the whole thing wasn't right then we'd do it again. That's the way Rory wanted it, which is the way to do it."

Alan O'Duffy: "It was really Rory-driven. And we used the tracks in themselves as an entity. We didn't try and create a continuity in particular. The track relates to the track. The song relates to the song. And then the next song would be treated differently. We probably would use relatively the same kit sound or the same bass sound or whatever. If a track required a certain guitar sound then we'd go for it. We wouldn't say, 'Well, we didn't use it on the previous track so we can't use it now.' And if it needed a bit more kick or drum or cymbal, maraca or something, it got it. If we felt it would move it better.

"Rory was a driven man, if you follow me. More than most people on the planet. And I respect that he had his own agenda."

Ted McKenna: "The first gig of the first tour we did was in Geneva and that was it. We were on the road for at least six weeks. And that was the first gig I met my big buddy, one of my dear friends, Phil McDonnell. Peter Collins was tour manager and Phil did sound. We had just such a knockout team of guys. We all got on so well together."

Donal Gallagher: "Pete Collins had been a junior travel agent at a company called Hep Travel. We were doing so much traveling and freighting, most of my work seemed to be logistics. Peter seemed to be very efficient. Any time I wanted help he was there and nothing was too much of a problem. And we became great friends. We were looking for somebody at that point in time that would be good on the road with the band. Be a kind of personal tour manager to Rory and the lads. I was still traveling separate to the band because of the equipment at the time. And I wanted somebody looking after the band in a good manner. So he came to do that task.

"We knew Phil McDonnell from the early days, Peter Green and Fleetwood Mac. He was the road manager for Peter Green. He stuck with Fleetwood Mac through their different forms. And the ugly one where Fleetwood Mac had none of the original members. It was a tour that got cancelled halfway. It started out where they were headliners but there was nobody from the original lineup and the fans used to get upset. Eventually they were demoted to being the opening act on this package tour."

Phil McDonnell: "I became friendly with Rory in '71 on his first ever Rory Gallagher band tour. They were working with us with Fleetwood Mac. I was twenty. Rory was twenty-one. McAvoy was nineteen. It's crazy when you think about it now. And Wilgar Campbell, who died of liver failure in 1990, though no one can confirm the date, God rest his soul, was there too. He must have been the same age as Gerry. I was tour managing Fleetwood Mac. We'd just done a gig in Detroit and come down to the Holiday Inn lobby to get some cigarettes at half-twelve, one in the morning, and Rory came across the lobby. And he just said, 'Oh, hi. How you doin'? Aren't you with Fleetwood Mac?' And I said, 'Yeah.' And he said, 'Hi, my name's Rory.' And I said, 'Oh, hi ya, Rory.' So he said, 'Are you hungry? There's a little

place around the corner. Do you fancy eating breakfast?' Rory and I went around the corner to this little breakfast place and we sat there 'til about half-three in the morning and had some great old chats. And we sort of became friends that day. As the story went, Rory used to like the sound I got with Fleetwood Mac. So in the end of '77 I got a call. Rory was going on tour for about four months or something. I just said, 'Look, lads. I've been away for six months. I just want to go away on vacation.' And they said, 'Well, just do this four months. Rory would like you to do it and then you can go on holiday.' So as it was I thought the world of him as a musician and he's one of the nicest people anybody could wish to have met, I couldn't really say no [laughs]. And I went on to do the four months and I stayed with him for nearly nine years!"

Donal Gallagher: "So we took him over to work for us. He became tour manager. I was doing sound out front. He then took over that role from me. Phil had quite good experience. The demands on me were huge because Rory, in a sense, was self-managing. He knew what he wanted to do. You were just acting like an officer and carrying out duties. And with the success the demands became greater on your time. So it was very hard to do the road and be up at nine o'clock in the morning for meetings and then advancing things. It wasn't a question of regulating my time. It just was trying to do as much as possible. I was wearing so many hats on Rory's behalf. I used to travel separate from Rory in a lot of the cases. I would always get there with the crew to make sure that everything was set up and organized properly."

Phil McDonnell: "The great thing about working for Rory was he did a two-and-a-half, three-hour show a night. And it was amazing. Even listening to the set every night of the week, it never, ever got boring because the thing with Rory was you never knew what was coming next. Rory would never have a fixed set. You see bands and they have their set list stuck to the floor. Rory Gallagher was not like that. Rory Gallagher had his set list in his head. And McAvoy and McKenna, and then Brendan O'Neill after that, Rory would just hit one string on his guitar and those guys, and I did too, just knew what was coming next. Whatever tone he was putting on his guitar, how he was tuning, whatever guitar he was changing to, you knew what song was coming. So there was never any need for a set list. We were all totally educated in sounds and guitars and tunings and stuff. So it all worked like that. And of course if Rory was one minute playing a Stratocaster, then you'd have to re-EQ the channel. You were always busy on the EQ. And also with Rory he used to have a lot of little graphic equalizers on top of his amps. As his ears used to close naturally, during a show, he would tend to add a lot of high end to his guitar. You had to compensate 'cuz what used to happen was he'd be welting it on stage. The monitors used to be flying! Monitor guys used to be talking in bars and stuff on nights off when I used to discuss the show with the crew about how it was all going and maybe talking about the show the night before. One monitor guy used to say, 'When Rory's on stage, if his mike stand fell over, if you needed to get to it, you'd have to throw a grappling hook over the front of the stage and pull yourself towards the monitors on a rope because of the volume and wind coming out of the speakers' [laughs]."

Joe O'Herlihy: "Well and truly [laughs]! Rory definitely, from a monitoring perspective, was always charged up by the feel on stage. I dealt with monitors for a long, long time there. And the one thing that I always tried to do was make him comfortable. You'd look over and you'd know by the look whether this guy was sitting comfortable or not. He was always one for making the whole thing sit comfortably. But he just lived in that space. That whole space had to be 1,000 percent for him because he was giving 1,000 percent."

Gerry McAvoy: "Oh yeah [laughs]! They were fairly loud! I had guitar through mine anyway. Rory had the whole stage filled with guitar. He had monitors, he had sidefills, he had his own backline and had some on my side as well. Which I used to turn down sneakily. He'd catch me and turn it back up again."

Joe O'Herlihy: "Depending on the environment, the condition on the night, what the stage and the venue was like,

if you were getting slapback or spill or something like that, he'd go off on a rant. But it was always to better the actual stage sound. For me, that was always an essential commodity to ensure the end result. He wasn't a high-end or a high-mid orientated recipient. It was always down to feel. And feel is kind of created in the frequencies of bottom end and low to high mid at the most. 1.5 to 1.6. It's the foundation of the whole thing. There was a good rhythm section that was solid with good drums and good bass. The guitar would sit on top of that. And you'd put a vocal on top of it so that it fits directly.

"He would have zones that he would run to as part of the dynamic of the show. And you would almost have to track him because he would like a really good, solid foundation. Kick and snare and solid bass in his wedges. He would run off to the side so you would spread that across. The image of that whole thing would move across the stage according to wherever he ended up. And that's where the actual placement of stuff like that is an integral ingredient of the show."

Phil McDonnell: "Rory could whip me up into a frenzy same as he could whip the audience. He just had that way about him where when he started to rock, you started to rock. And you used to say to yourself, 'OK, if you wanna go there, let's go there!' And you'd just ride along with him and you'd get that kick drum pumping and thumping people in the chest and you'd get the bass guitar comin' in underneath the guitar. And as long as you could hear what he was singing about and everything was clean and nobody was holding their ears, then it was happenin'."

Joe O'Herlihy: "At the time everybody was a sound guy! They bought a ticket and that entitled them to be a sound guy, a lighting guy and tell Rory what songs to play [laughs]!"

Phil McDonnell: "Wherever we went in the world Rory was adored. All the kids used to sing the same stuff at the end of the show. When the set finished they'd all go, 'Row-reee, Row-reee!' One minute you'd be in Czechoslovakia or Hungary or whatever and the next night you'd be in New Zealand. And the next night in Tokyo or Australia or

Cincinnati. Amsterdam. All the kids were universal. You could be at any gig in the world with Rory 'cuz all his fans had the same banter, you know. It was really strange."

Ted McKenna: "Rory would wear audiences out because they'd get tired of jumping about. Then he would change pace. But when he felt that the audience was getting a bit complacent he pushed the tempo. When it was cookin' he was totally in his element. He would just smile! When he would do his 'choo-choo' move, when it was up there, when it was happening and the crowd was going crazy, then he would smile. He'd gotten it where he'd wanted it. And that was good. You'd play some clubs, the one in Toronto, the El Mocambo, places like that. You'd go in there and the minute you walked on stage the place was electric! The crowds just go crazy.

"But sometimes you'd go in there and maybe you'd had a bad night before, traveling and … you know, it doesn't go. The guitar might be getting out of tune a lot or the feedback … there's always things that go wrong. Not every gig's perfect. And sometimes you get that kind of situation where you could tell that Rory's not quite happy with the way it's going. And everybody feels a bit on edge. Sometimes after a lot of gigs you get quite tired. Playing at that energy level every night … if you were doing a six-week tour of the States or you've done a back to back. You've just come from Europe and you end up in New Orleans. The change in temperature. And playing at that energy level. But we always put on a great show. If you had a tape of every single gig that we played and you put them on, I defy anybody to say when we were having a bad gig. The standard you're used to, sometimes it's hard to work. Because of the temperature, you had a night off and everybody got so drunk [laughs]. It was definitely a drinking man's band! We used to end up sometimes just back in our rooms with some beers and a game of cards and that was good fun. But sometimes, when we pushed the ball out too far, you were tired the next gig. And it took a while … well, once you're up at that energy level you could usually go out there and do it and nobody would notice.

"And then there's the other contradiction. That you would get so good at it that you didn't have the edge when you played. And that's what Rory was always looking for. That 'edge.' I used to feel that I was really on top of my time-keeping. I was feeling more comfortable. But sometimes that's not what gets the edge. Sometimes you've got to bleed a bit before it starts to flow. When it comes easy it doesn't always make good rock 'n' roll. Being nervous before a gig will usually get a good performance out of you."

1979

Being at Dieter Dierk's studio was an all-round excellent experience. It seemed a natural decision to return there for the next album, "Top Priority."

Donal Gallagher: "It started life in a different studio but it ended up back over at Dieter's. Alan also liked the environment. It was in the country. There was not a lot to do except stick with the album. They were isolating themselves in a way. They got on with the job of things. 'Let's get in, get this album cracked and done and then go home.' "

Ted McKenna: "I enjoyed the studio again. One of the things that we did was that I recorded the drums in a booth as opposed to in the main studio because we wanted to get a more ambient sound from the drums than we had on the first album. I'll tell you a funny thing that happened. The structure of the music for rock, R&B, blues, the kind of stuff we did, a lot of it works best if you play four on the floor with the bass drum. Straight force. To introduce the dynamic into it, I used to like to push the beat occasionally so you do the pushes along with the bass or the guitar. And you can either do it on the snare drum, which means not playing the offbeat, you play the push. And it's hard to do that with a bass drum if you're playing four in the floor. So I thought if I used two bass drums then I could still keep the force, to keep the pulse going. If I have to do a push and accent I could do it with the other bass drum. So I set up both bass drums and Rory nearly had a heart attack! He broke out in a cold sweat [laughs]. Because the double bass drums then meant heavy metal, right? So I was about set up with them and he took me aside and said, 'Oh, Ted. Oh, I don't know about this.' I said 'No problem.' It was just an idea that I wanted to try but because he was a purist, he couldn't associate using two bass drums."

Gerry McAvoy: "Rory wasn't too happy about that. We actually tried it live but it got trimmed after three shows [laughs]."

Ted McKenna: "We were working at Dieter Dierk's studio. I used to go out for a walk every day, which went right out of the studio, under a bridge, over the back, to the other side of the railway line all the way along to the road to Pulheim, which was the next town. Back down the main road and back to the studio. And then I'd have my breakfast. I always kinda did that to keep myself fresh, you know.

"One afternoon Rory and I decided to go out for a drink. Rory was pretty big stuff in Germany. We went out to the local town for a little stroll around. 'Why don't we just pop in here for a little Cognac, a little drink?' And, of course, it didn't take very long before people were sending over drinks. The minute they recognized Rory, it was like, 'Oh, you must have a drink with us!' By the time it got 'round to about six o'clock and time for tea, we were totally wrecked! We got back to the studio. I was really out of my face. And for some reason I ended up throwing sandwiches at Rory. Now that's not the kind of thing I would ever normally do. I was so drunk. They were trying to get me to go to bed. A couple of them grabbed me and they told me I threw them across the room. So I went out the door. And I do remember saying, 'Fuck it, I'm gonna go walk my walk.' It was raining and I only had a shirt on and jeans. I was going along the path and I slipped.

"What happened was I woke up with the sound of a diesel going past on the railway! I'd slipped down the bank and fallen asleep. And the bank went down and dropped onto the railway line. So the sound of this fucking huge diesel going past at about six o'clock in the morning … I looked around with one eye and I could see the two German train drivers laughing at me, thinking 'What kind of fuckin' state was that guy in last night?' The funny thing was I could have slipped right off onto the railway line. But then again it probably would have woken me up [laughs]. I walked back. The guys were a bit worried. Joe O'Herlihy

met me at the door. When I came to the door, they all looked at me to say, 'Are you alright, Ted? Where the fuck have you been last night?' But that's what happened when you went out for a drink with Rory in a German town."

Limitless energy allowed Rory to obtain the best possible results. Fortunately for the other members, they weren't expected to be as fanatical about their time in the studio as he was.

Donal Gallagher: "They were only called in when their parts were needed. If they were gone off to bed or not in town Rory would just save their part to be redone. But he'd be very much concentrating on the guitars he'd been laying down. Getting the lyrics right. Or the phonetics right. Or the vocal. Getting the actual sound or the tone of the instrument. Or the arrangements. And because the material is new, it's percolating as he's writing it."

Joe O'Herlihy: "Everybody was there for the one cause. I don't think there was ever a moment that I doubted that atmosphere or anything associated with it. I was there and I loved being there. And the people around me … it was exactly the same feeling."

•   •   •

Rory always had a fascination with the intellect behind international espionage. His interest was finally depicted in song when he recorded "Philby."

Donal Gallagher: "The human intelligence. The human psyche. The deviousness of the mind. As opposed to being shot by an arrow or a bullet. The criminal element. Particularly Patricia Highsmith. He was very fond of her.

"He loved the intelligence of the criminal. I remember as a kid we went to a movie in Cork called 'Purple Noon.' It starred Alain Delon. He was tickled pink with that movie. It was based on a Patricia Highsmith character, The Talented Mr. Ripley. He was fourteen years old. He was possibly reading other books at that time but I remember it had a significant impact on him.

"He was tenacious in his own way. And stubborn. I think he would have probably liked to have been the bad guy now and then and to tell people where to get off! Instead of being mild mannered and polite about it. Turning the other cheek. He never had that nature. He was a more patient type of person. I remember when he'd grown his hair long. He was about fourteen, fifteen. He had the longest hair in Ireland. He was well known for that. And certainly in Cork City, walking the street, people did everything but spit at him. I could never keep my fists to myself when walking with him. I remember we'd end up arguing. I said 'Rory, you can't let people do this to you.' I knew bloody well that if he lashed out at somebody he'd crucify them because he was a very strong, physical guy. He certainly had the back of a boxer. He'd have a made a good boxer. He did tend to identify with John McEnroe. He was all for McEnroe, who was getting terrible stick all the time. Anybody who stood their ground, who stood up for what they believed in, he identified with. The rebel."

Gerry McAvoy: "He spoke about his admiration for crime writers from the 40s. He was into Raymond Chandler and Dashiell Hammett. He was fascinated by spies. And this all took a different shade in his life as well. He also got very paranoid towards the later years. And he was fascinated with Kim Philby and that's who the song 'Philby' is about. I'm not saying that fascination became reality to him but he did start to get very paranoid about silly things."

Donal Gallagher: "Rory was incredibly well read in espionage. The whole intrigue where crime verges on legitimate crime. He was particularly fascinated and knowledgeable, before it became popular, with The Third Man, the guys who defected and were playing double agents or triple agents. He was quite an admirer of Philby. Philby's attitude. It wasn't a communist line. It was more anti-British Empire establishment. These guys would come out of Oxford and Cambridge and high-faluting universities and yet they had a very basic, socialist streak. He was intrigued by the fact that they'd give up everything that they had. And even though they were traitors to their own country he felt they were standing up for what they believed in.

"'Philby' is about Rory's own lifestyle paralleling that to a Philby-type character. Trying to make the connection in a secret place. You've only got so much information. You get to

a town. And it was also part of Rory's mind at play. Exhaustion playing tricks on the mind. The paranoia that develops out of that. The opening line, 'Ain't it strange that I feel like Philby. That I'm in a foreign shore and a knock upon the door.' "

His aforementioned admiration of Delon stayed with Rory throughout his life. He would register as "Alain Delon" whenever he stayed in hotels.

• • •

Donal Gallagher: "At long last we'd gotten material that they felt would cross Rory over to a bigger record market in the States. But it was at a point in time where Chrysalis made the worst move of their life. They left Warner's and went independent distribution. They'd lost that whole Warner's machinery, which had a knockdown effect on artists like Rory. Warner's were very keen to sign on Rory separate to Chrysalis. I regret as seeing it then as a mistake to have signed with a company who had independent distribution in America. Their ambition was to be bigger than A&M Records, independent-wise. There was more cosmetic surgery on the profile of the company than there was on the artists.

"They (Chrysalis) wanted another 'Photofinish.' Rory had gone back to spend more time in the studio for the 'Philby's' and tracks like that. Alan O'Duffy was very patient with Rory. He used to refer to Alan as Father O'Duffy [laughs]! He would indulge Rory. He would stay in the studio and the man would never utter a swear word. He was just so patient. And Rory was just hearing something else. He never felt he got it down. A lot of times you're better off going back and re-recording the song rather than trying to mix it and mix it. If you have to keep mixing, there's a problem with the recording of the song."

Alan O'Duffy: "Rory was a great humorist and a lovely fellow. He would say things like, if we were all inside the room and you had just walked into the control room, for example, he'd turn around to Ted McKenna and he'd say to Ted, 'Right Ted! Say to Dan what you just said to me about him! Go on, say it! Dan, do you want to listen to this or not? Ted, just say it! Say it again, now, honestly! Alan, you heard what he said. What did you say about Dan before he came into the room?'

Playing his prized Dobro.
Courtesy Hans Ivarsson

That was one of his standard jokes. It made everybody sort of nervous and laughing at the same time. Nice man. And particularly a gentleman. More of a gentleman than I am! But when he had his guitar on he was a different person. A guitar player that could stand beside anybody."

Phil McDonnell: "One of the funniest stories … I'd never seen Rory laugh so much in his life! He had a great sense of humor about him and he used to literally cry with a good, funny story. We were down in … it was somewhere like Hartford, Connecticut."

Ted McKenna: "I think it's clear to understand that we all might be guessing at where it happened. I think we were all pretty polluted. I've told that story a few times. It goes down kind of well."

Gerry McAvoy: "Duluth, Minnesota. I remember it well."

Ted McKenna: "The night before Pete Collins said 'Guys, to save you getting up too early I'm going to take the cases to the airport and check you in. So pack your bags tonight and I'll pick them up at eight tomorrow and then you can have another couple hours sleep.' 'OK, thanks.' We got blitzed. I went back to my room, forgot to pack. Peter arrived at the door — bang, bang, bang — 'Ted, give us your case.' So I leapt up, went, 'Oh fuck, I forgot to pack my case.' So I just threw stuff into the case, kind of in the darkness, opened the door a pinch, give him the case."

Phil McDonnell: "He stood there in a T-shirt and his underpants 'cuz we'd just woken him up, got him out of bed. So we grab his suitcase and me and Collins jump in the car and we go out to the airport."

Ted McKenna: " 'OK, see you at the airport. Bye.' Went back to sleep. Next thing I'm getting a call from Rory. Rory's downstairs. I've slept in. He's going, 'We've got to get to the airport. The taxi's here to take us to the airport.' So I opened the curtains, I looked around the room and realized I'd packed my pants. Son of a fuckin' bitch!"

Phil McDonnell: "We'd gone off with his suitcase with all his clothes in it. And he'd forgot to leave a pair of pants out."

Ted McKenna: "I opened the door and I just caught Gerry McAvoy going to the lift. I said 'Gerry, I've got a wee problem here [laughs]. I haven't got any fuckin' pants to wear.' So he went downstairs, went around the corner into an Army-Navy store and bought me a pair of black cord denims. Which would have been seven sizes too big. You could have fit another one of me in. But he was in such a rush he just grabbed a pair."

Phil McDonnell: "And they were all rolled up as well at the bottom 'cuz they were too long for him. Oh, it was fucking hilarious! And I always remember Rory cried over that! He thought that was incredibly funny!"

•   •   •

In the early months of 1980, Rory released his third live solo album, "Stagestruck."

Donal Gallagher: "The track record of Rory's live albums had shown that they were very successful. There was always a demand for Rory performing the tracks live. Not that he was better live. And Chrysalis were very keen to have a live album in their six albums. Rory was always happy to do a live album and a lot of the shows had been recorded. And with Ted in the lineup it had given it a different sound or a different feel. The heavier sound suited a live album. And Rory had done 'Irish Tour' with Rod and Lou anyway.

"You can hear Pete Collins doing the announcement on 'Stagestruck.' 'Cuz you hear, 'Wo-wee Gallaguh' [laughs]! He had difficulty with his r's! Had a bit of The Life Of Brian in it! Just a kind of humor in the band. So we left it on the record [laughs]!"

Phil McDonnell: "When Pete was relieved of his gig, as I'd always been a tour manager, Donal asked me, rather than get a complete stranger in for Rory, if I just sort of take over doing all the tour managing. Which I did for the next five years."

Ted McKenna: "We used to have a guy called Roland. Roland used to support the band quite a lot. Rory always liked to bring him along. He was a good guy. We played in the Usher Hall in Belfast and it was Rory's birthday. At the end when we came on for the second encore I think it was, Rory brought Roland on. Roland sang 'I've Got My Mojo Working.' And when we played it I became incredibly aware of the whole room and how everybody was just crazily jumping up and down. But the magical thing was every time I heard the snare drum I felt as if I was above myself looking at me playing the drums. It was the first time I saw it so objectively. It was magical. It was like primitive, you know, like being right in the center of the thing."

Joe O'Herlihy: "Music is the biggest narcotic there is. It's worse than any drug. Once it gets a hold of you it's pretty much it. It takes you to a place as well where very few people ever get there in their entire lives."

Gerry McAvoy: "Roland Van Campenhout. Roland had opened for us a few times and Rory just took to him. He was into the blues and a pretty good guitar player. We ended up becoming very friendly with him. Rory stayed out of the country for ten months in Roland's house. We used to go there and rehearse. That was during 'Blueprint.' He was just a sort of kindred spirit. A blues guitar player who was pretty good."

Ted McKenna: "Roland had a girlfriend who was a model and in fact she was on the cover of *Vogue*. She was a stunning-looking woman. And she got a crush on Rory. I remember one day I was in the bar and Gerry came by and said, 'You won't believe this.' I can't remember what her name was but he just said she'd been knocking on Rory's door asking to come in to see him."

Gerry McAvoy: "Catherine."

Ted McKenna: "And she had the French accent 'Oh, Roree, pleeze let me een. Roree!' She was banging on the door! And Rory was basically saying, 'Will you go to your bed? It's time for bed. Go to your bed.' And that's the side of Rory I never fully understood."

Gerry McAvoy: "We shouldn't have been snooping. We were at the end of the corridor, sitting on the steps listening to it. And the thing about Catherine was that she was absolutely beautiful. Why he refused her, I don't know!"

Ted McKenna: "Rory had a girlfriend at some point before I was involved in the band and she broke his heart and I think he just … that was it. He just would never let it happen again. And it's like some of the lyrics in the songs that we did. I'm sure it tends to be a reflection on that period."

Rory Gallagher: "A certain lady, who I had a great thing for, right, went off and married this guy. Then she went off and had his child. And she introduced me to the husband who showed me pictures of the child right in front of my face. And I couldn't take it. I really couldn't take it. The only reason I didn't move was she was a musician friend of mine. She must have no feelings. I mean, how do you do that? He's a nice guy; I'm not sayin'. But I spent two years in a terrible state over that."

•   •   •

In the latter part of 1981, Gerry McAvoy finally released some solo work that had been brewing up inside for years.

Gerry McAvoy: "There was actually two solo albums. One was released and the second one never saw the light of day. Terry Murphy, the guy that ran The Bridgehouse, put together a record company and approached me. It started off as a live project and it went a little bit further than that. I had written a few songs and we went into a studio and recorded five or six songs. One side was live and one side was recorded. It was something to do because there was a lull at that time. Rory wasn't doing much. I was sort of biding my time and needed something to do. It was called 'Bassics' "

Donal Gallagher: "Ted had been offered a couple of situations. After 'Top Priority' Rory was more inclined to take more time out. I'm not saying he was uncertain what his plans were but he was trying to ease off the live touring scene. So, in effect, his gaps were becoming longer and longer. I think Ted felt he wanted to be doing more and felt he could be doing two bands. He'd received a proposition from Rudi Schenker and E.L.P. turned up later on. And he optioned that. He put it to Rory that he had this offer. But it didn't force Rory into saying, 'Well, I'm going to go out and tour and I need you.' Rory just said, 'Fine. See how you go' [laughs]. That's the way Rory dealt with those situations. There was no split. He'd had another offer and Rory wasn't prepared to undertake any commitments until he felt good and ready."

Ted McKenna: "I left around about 1982. I was with Rory for nearly three years. I think the job was secure and ongoing but personally I was just getting to the stage where I felt I wanted to do something else and a different style. I liked the situation. I liked everybody in the band but I felt as if I had to move on, otherwise I would get the gold watch, you know what I mean? Gerry played with Rory for how long?

Christ! Twenty-two years. And although people knew who we were it was still Rory Gallagher and his band. I wasn't really bothered about it. But I just felt for my own career as a drummer … and subsequently I worked with some outstanding musicians and different styles.

"I went over to see Rory. His Mum was there and they made me very welcome and we went out to get take-away, carry out. And on the way back I just said, 'I want to leave the band.' I liked and had incredible respect for Rory and enjoyed playing with the guys in the band and everybody who was involved. There was no problem with that at all. But there was just this little part of me that felt I needed to go and do something else because I felt that I wasn't using my potential as a drummer by playing that style of music. And that was it. My very last gig was The Big Tent in Paris Common."

Rory had some song ideas he wanted to put on tape. He summoned Brendan O'Neill to a session and he arrived with a heavier style as opposed to the jazzier feel he carried when he auditioned at the time Ted McKenna earned the job.

Brendan O'Neill: "I said to Gerry, 'When Ted goes, mention my name.' And Rory called, luckily enough. We played a lot over a couple of weeks. And Rory being Rory, he didn't actually say, 'You're in the band, you've got the job.' After we'd had a lengthy jam session one night, he said, 'Would you fancy something to eat?' Gerry and I went with him to a little Greek restaurant. And on the way from the rehearsal room to the restaurant, he turned to Gerry and said, 'Meet Mr. Sticks.' And that was it.

"I was born August 12, 1951, in Belfast, Northern Ireland. A very working-class background. My parents both sang really well. They were listening to the radio all the time. For any child growing up in the 50s, anywhere in the world, the big thing was the radio. And there was a big pop and rock 'n' roll show … the Brian Matthews show. It was called 'The 10 O'clock Club' or something. It was on Saturday mornings. My mother would always tune into it, do her chores around the house. You heard Elvis Presley and music from that time. American music. But it was very much white. We didn't get rhythm and blues very much at that time.

"In the North of Ireland, the political situation the way it is, on the twelfth of July it was marching season for The Orangemen. And even though we were not of that persuasion, my father used to go and love to watch them march because of all the bands. They'd go marching in the streets and he'd just bring me along. And when I heard the bagpipe drummers it absolutely freaked me out! Just so rhythmic and powerful. I just wanted to follow after them for miles. I hated the bagpipes but I loved the drummers.

"I served an apprenticeship as an aeronautical engineer. As soon as I finished my apprenticeship, five months later I was in a professional showband. I knew I really wanted to get into a band and give it a crack. In Ireland at that time the first chance to play music was in a showband. And the rules for any musician in that situation was to play the Top 20 and try and mimic it as well as you could. It was a really great training ground.

"The first time I heard of Rory was 1968, when he came up to Belfast with the first rendition of Taste, with Norman and Eric, and I went to see him play. He opened for Cream on their last time around."

O'Neill was thrown into a situation that he was technically up to, but that he had to quickly learn to fit into.

Brendan O'Neill: "Gerry had already formed his opinion and his ideas, having worked with Rory for ten years already, so it was my problem to fit in with the two of them. The basic thing was to just try and complement the music to the best of our ability and to Rory's requirements. It was pretty much left to the individual to figure out his own way of getting there. Which was really great because he didn't dominate you that much. But it was a strange thing. After being with him for 'X' amount of time, you grew to know what he wanted without it being vocalized to you at all. Personally, I didn't always get it right! Rory's influences came from early rock 'n' roll music to Delta blues to Chicago blues to skiffle music to Irish Celtic music. It was very diverse. And what I learned after being with him for a long time was his musical ideas and what formed them. You were almost aware where the ideas came from. Then you could complement what he was trying to do."

Gerry McAvoy: "Rory spoke about getting another guitar player. We tried one guy called Tommy Willis. He's a fine guitar player and Rory was impressed with him. Rory had this fascination for good rhythm guitar players. And Rory was a fine rhythm guitar player as well as his solos. And the rhythm guitar player in Ted Nugent's band … Derek St. Holmes. He's probably one of the best rhythm guitar players ever. Rory always wanted that sort of rhythm thing behind him, ya know. Rory used to love to go in there and do everything live. So if you had a really good rhythm player there we could actually do it live."

Derek St. Holmes: "I remember when he was talking about getting another guitar player. I'm flattered that they would have said that. But at the same time Golden Earring wanted me to play with them as well. That's interesting because I always thought I was swept under the carpet, you know what I mean? But I got along well with Rory. We used to tour together where Rory used to open up for us or Nugent would open up for Rory and we did quite a few shows together. He had a great band. We would always jam in the dressing room. And once we'd start getting that Busch-Mills out … [laughs] he used to love that stuff!

"I'll always remember that Strat of his, man. I remember him letting me play it. We would just doodle back and forth in the dressing rooms and we found out that we liked all the same kind of early blues stuff. He was a great guy. He was always a nice, jovial guy. Never a bad word to say. They were a lot of fun. We had a lot of good times."

Brendan O'Neill: " 'Jinx' was the first thing we did. I was never on the road with them. We did nine days rehearsal and went straight to Dieter Dierk's studio in Germany. I didn't really question it at the time because it was a very daunting and nerve-racking thing anyway, to be in Rory Gallagher's band. So I suppose whatever way you set out on that road it wouldn't have mattered. For me it was still going to be a nerve-racking situation, whether it was live or studio work."

Rory invited Ray Beavis and Dick Parry to play saxophone on "Jinx," something that he hadn't done in several years.

Donal Gallagher: "He'd used sax not only on the Taste albums but on the first solo album he doubled up the altos and used tenors. They had always been subtly hidden. I noticed that, going through the albums. There was a lot more use of sax than I'd even heard. And we emphasize that in the re-mixes. And it's sporadically used in 'Deuce.'

"The sax came into play when he got into Ernie Coleman and Eric Dolphy and the jazz greats like that. And particularly the fact of improvisation, which he could obviously do on the guitar. He just liked the idea of the alto. I remember coming back to the flat one day. He'd bought a Summer's alto sax and a 'Play In A Day'-type book. We were in a very confined flat at the time so he'd play the sax into the wardrobe to absorb the sound. He didn't take any lessons. He was self-taught. It was almost instant, once he'd built his lip up. And the use of the reed. I dare say that perhaps during the showband days he'd been shown a bit so he would know the keys. Because the guitar player and the sax player had to get in tune and had learned a certain amount from the sax players in the band and knew the root chords. So I'd say he had a certain amount of knowledge. But he was very quick on that. It just seemed to be a matter of a week or two and he was playing it. And of course he had the musical head. So improvisation wasn't a problem. It was just knowing where the notes were. And once he got the feel of the keyboard element it just came very natural to him.

"I recall a review of the 'On The Boards' album that Lester Bangs wrote. I remember Rory being really proud of his comments about his sax playing. He was very positive. He felt he was equally at home with his guitar as the sax and complimented the fact that he wasn't playing, as he describes it in the review, as 'free blown shit.'"

•   •   •

Always the type of man that preferred his own company, Rory became increasingly withdrawn over the years.

Brendan O'Neill: "He was a very private man. This might sound bigheaded or whatever but I found that he was more comfortable around musicians than anyone. When he was with musicians he had this really dry sense of humor. Almost like a school-boy sense of humor and could really have a good giggle. With other people he would always be very polite. He would be unassuming. He would be a great host. He was all those things. But for some reason he could relax a bit more around musicians. He could point the finger at me and laugh at himself and laugh in situations. Often times I would probably be more quiet than him by watching and listening to what was going on."

Phil McDonnell: "I'd be traveling with him all day long. We'd do four, five hours, six, seven hour drives sometimes. Just me and Rory in a station wagon. The other lads would go in another car or whatever. I was on call for him twenty-four hours a day. That was my job. I was his tour manager and I was his sound engineer. We used to talk. We had private talks. He was Jekyll and Hyde. But I loved that about him because I'm from a show biz background. I mean, that's what it's about. It's a bit severe to say. It's like the sad clown syndrome. I don't mean to compare it with that. I know a lot of show people and it's a misconception. But I don't wanna get it out of context."

Brendan O'Neill: "Halfway through recording 'Jinx,' I remember I was looking for something for my drum kit and I couldn't find it. Once the situation was set up things like cases all got moved out. I was looking for Tom O'Driscoll, who always looked after the backline. And I said, 'Tom, have you seen…' And I heard Rory. 'Aw, he's getting into it now!' Meaning that I was starting to relax and getting others to do things for me!"

Phil McDonnell: "One thing I loved about Rory he used to stick by you thick and thin. I remember once we were doing a gig down in San Antonio, Texas. There's a certain person that wangs his way backstage. And when they get back there they come in the dressing room. All they're there for is to drink the band's beer and to eat the band's food. They've got nothing to say, really. So what these people do is they think of something to say just to justify their presence. And nine times out of ten it'll be something they say that will get you in the shit. I'll always remember this night. I used to always stand with Rory, and Rory said, 'Aw, this geezer over here. I think I remember him from last year. Hang in here with me.' So I stood there and this guy had no idea that I was the sound engineer. So Rory said, 'Oh, how are ya?' He says, 'Rory, fantastic show, man. But, uh, if anything, it was a bit loud' [laughs]. I know a lot of musicians that would have had your ass hanging from a line. 'What do you mean it was fuckin' … was it loud? Were you mixing me too loud tonight?' Rory just smiled and he looked at me with that sort of cheeky look [laughs]. The eyes used to look with that sort of a twist! And he turned 'round to the guy and he says, 'Ah well, you know what? They say when rock 'n' roll's getting too loud for ya, you're too old to listen to it' [laughs]! And the guy just said, 'Oh, yeah, OK Rory.' If he trusted you doing what you did for him then he never really questioned you. He always expected that you would give it 100 percent."

In the spring of 1982, armed with a crew of veterans and a new drummer, The Rory Gallagher Band boarded an aircraft and took their brand of high-energy entertainment to the United States.

Brendan O'Neill: "Frightening! Exhausting! Exhilarating! And rewarding. All of those things mixed up in one. It was a fantastic experience. The first gig was in Chicago. We did a show in Park West. It was the first show I ever did in America. We got there a day early. We left the Ambassador East Hotel and walked up Rush Street. I remember we went into a place called 'Arnie's' and had a proper American hamburger. And I was completely blown away! By a hamburger, yeah! It sounds pretty daft, doesn't it? The only excuse for hamburgers we had here then was McDonald's and things like that. Pathetic things really. But at 'Arnie's,' you got this burger that was two inches thick and four inches in diameter. And you went 'round and put your own innards for it yourself. From salads to anything. And fries. It was a brilliant experience [laughs]! But probably the more important experience was we went to a few blues clubs that night. And that was it. I just fell in love with the place. To be there and to be playing somewhere like the Park West. It was really fantastic.

"It's still the most difficult gig I've ever done. I've gigged with Alvin Lee and Steve Marriott in America and here. But Rory was an engine on stage. He really was. He drove everything along. And what he demanded from himself he demanded from those in the band. A real stiff pace. After a certain amount of time you knew you had to pull your socks up. There was no slacking."

As "Jinx" was released, Chrysalis was aware of the fact that if they didn't get the most for Rory and show that they were still very much behind the project, they risked losing him.

Donal Gallagher: "It was at a time where we were coming to the end of the Chrysalis contract. Chrysalis were going down the tubes very fast in America. We had expressed a lot of unhappiness at being on a label that was plying a lot of money into pop bands. We were touring three, four tours a year in America and we weren't getting any support to do that. And, invariably, we'd find that the records weren't in the stores properly. Or no radio spots. They weren't promoting or investing into Rory. They just took it for granted, 'Well, he's doing his own stuff. We don't need to spend any money on him.' So, in America, they were really losing the plot completely. And the company was up for sale.

"Meantime, in Europe, a chap called Dan Young, who was running Chrysalis in Germany, had become the head of Mercury International in New York. Between us we'd gotten a free release in America with the 'Jinx' album, which was finished and about to be released by Chrysalis in Europe. So there hadn't been time to set up a proper tour for Rory as such. But the Rush tour was going out and it had been pre-booked months in advance. It was a situation where it would be full houses. It would be a good package. But Rory really didn't want to do it. I felt that it would expose the album, which actually was on Mercury in the U.S. In hindsight, that proved to be a wrong move because Dan Young got removed from his post so we were left in a kind of limbo. And even though they had put the album out, contractually, the deal never got signed. We went from the frying pan into the fire, as it were. It was a tour of convenience. Rory wasn't that happy about it. But mixed in that tour, we branched out and did our own dates.

"Rory never enjoyed being in a position where you've got a thirty- or forty-minute slot. So in this case, we compromised by saying, 'Well, instead of having another opening act before Rory, he would do both slots giving him an hour to play.' And, in a lot of cases, what we'd do is look out and see if the venue was full, which it normally was for an eight o'clock start. And we'd start the show fifteen minutes early. So Rory would do extra time. He'd finagle another ten-fifteen minutes [laughs]. I remember a promoter saying to me once, 'Your brother is the only artist I know that doesn't threaten you with not going on stage. He threatens you with not coming off!' "

Phil McDonnell: "When he used to hit that stage … I've seen Rory absolutely flat tired. I've actually said to him before I left the dressing room to go to the desk, 'Are you OK?' Because he just looked finished and tired. And he'd go, 'Yeah Phil. I'm OK. Just a bit of a headache or something.' I'd go out to the desk. And ten minutes later he'd come out to the stage like a bull out of the traps, you know. And he'd just go fucking ballistic for three hours. And at the end of a three-hour set he would have as much energy as he did when he would first hit that stage. How the fuck he did it, I don't know. He had some incredible stamina, that man. And if a lot of people think it was drink then they're full of shit. He never used drink to get him through a show. And also Rory was totally anti-drugs. He used to read me the riot act if ever he saw anybody come near him with drugs; powder or weed or whatever. He hated it with a vengeance."

Brendan O'Neill: "I can remember you would get to a certain club or a certain venue and the manager of the venue would come in with a bag of coke or something. And Phil McDonnell would jump up sixteen feet in the air to try and get this guy out of the room before Rory caught it! For fear that he might think that one of us had ordered it [laughs]! And the guy probably felt he was being hospitable and very polite. I remember a great gig. We did a big Hell's Angels show in England called 'The Kent Custom Bike Show.' And you can imagine, full of Hell's Angels and bikers everywhere. We had a big caravan at the back. And two

of these Angels just came in with a mirror the size of a bathroom basin. With lines like tramlines. Donal literally turned the guy on his heels and back out the door again!"

Phil McDonnell: "The Agora in Cleveland. We'd been in New York for a few days doing a couple of nights there and we had a crazy day getting to Cleveland. We go down for a sound check, go back to the hotel, come back to the gig. Do the show. So by the end of the show everybody was absolutely bollixed. I walk back from the board. And every night I used to go straight to the dressing room and talk to Rory. He used to like to know how the show was and 'did this sound OK, was this guitar OK.' We'd sit and have a chat for twenty minutes. Rory's sitting there with a towel, he's wiping himself down, the sweat off his face, his hair. And suddenly this guy opens the door. Long hair. And he goes, 'DA DAA!' And I look 'round and he's carrying a mirror with fucking four lines of cocaine and nine-inches-long each. Laid out across this mirror.

"Of course he thought he was doing us a favor! I mean, you know how that one goes. But Rory was just fucking mortified! And the guy goes, 'Excuse me guys! Here ya go!' He thought we were all gonna jump up and kiss him! Give him head or something for turning us on to these lines of toot. And Rory fucking looked at me and his eyes were like two laser beams across the table at me. I just stood up and I said, 'What's the fuckin' story here? What are you doing, man? Are you fucking out of your mind?' And the guy's going, 'Oh, what's the matter, man?' I said, 'Take that shit there and get the fuck out of the room … now! Just take it and go. And I think you owe this man a massive apology because this band ain't into that shit.' And the fucking guy … you know that feeling when you want the floor to just open up and swallow you? I said, 'Look. Forget it. Just apologize to these people, take your shit and go.' And the guy just started saying sorry to everybody. 'Hey, man, I had no idea you guys weren't into this.' And I said, 'Well, maybe just fucking check it out next time.' So the guy just took the stuff … it was flying all over the place as he was running off!"

"God love him, I felt so sorry for that kid that night 'cuz it didn't matter a fuck to me. I've grown up with musicians all my life. It was just Rory. Rory wasn't into it. So I had to protect what he liked and what he didn't like. That's what you do when you're a tour manager. The easiest way to handle your artist is within the first week of being with him you keep what he likes in his reach and you keep what he doesn't like as far away as possible from him. And when you've got that sorted out, you're doing fine. But nobody could've read that kid was coming around the corner. I will never forget Rory's face that night 'til the day I die. He was fucking mortified, he was!"

Though Rory wanted a break from recording after "Jinx" was completed, the band still kept busy.

Brendan O'Neill: "Touring mostly. We were in America a lot. Europe a lot. And I'm not sure if he wasn't ready to record another record or if he just wanted to take his time. He didn't like being pressured."

Gerry McAvoy: "I'd see him quite a lot socially. We'd go out for a meal or a drink. He'd come over to where I lived and we'd go to a pub or a club where they'd have live music and we'd get up and jam. But that sort of petered out as well. Early 80s onwards he started to become very reclusive."

Donal Gallagher: "He'd gone in opposition to the 'glam rock' thing in the early 70s. T. Rex, Sweet, Slade, all of those 'licorice all-sorts' bands. So he was quite used to flying his own flag in the sense that what he was doing was considered unfashionable at that time. He had retained his cult, loyal following. He never wanted to compete or change to have to compete. And then the punk movement occurred in '77… he quite welcomed that. He was saying, 'It vindicates what I'm doing. It returns to trios and rock 'n' roll and Eddie Cochran-type riffs. It's anti-establishment and making a joke of the business.'

"But it wasn't so much that music changed. It was that radio changed things. Particularly in America. When you had all the formatting of music and AOR and all this. So if your record didn't fit through the sausage machine … Rory never really got a lot of airplay either with Taste or on his own. OK. No one likes anyone taking up all the oxygen but

he didn't resent it. He knew the shifts in music but he'd made a conscious decision that he was never going to change his core. He obviously had the input and pressures from particularly Chrysalis to make the music more radio-orientated. They kept on to refine it, make it more radio friendly and crop a few minutes here and there. When I came out to Los Angeles to cut the 'Calling Card' album, I remember playing it for Chris Wright who was keen to hear it. And he immediately went, 'Edged In Blue. We're now into an autumn release. Can we now put it back into the early part of next year? Edit the guitar intro to Edged In Blue, edit Rory's guitar solo and cut it back to three minutes and we'll have a Top 10 single in America. We'll retitle the album Edged In Blue, do a different cover and drop Calling Card altogether.' I proposed that to Rory and he hit the roof! He was adamant that the value be placed on all of his work and not just one piece of it."

There was a lot of business going on while everyone was trying to decide how the records were going to be distributed. As one who didn't care for these talks, Rory decided that now would be a good time to venture into untested waters.

Donal Gallagher: "Rory felt there was a lot of catching up to do on the European front. So we were doing a lot more shows. Europe started to open up so the territories became bigger. Greece opened up in the 80s. We went into Yugoslavia, Hungary, Poland. These were all territories that we were starting to forge inroads. Rory was quite keen to play the Eastern Block countries because he had a huge fascination with the spies and the environment. And he felt that nobody else was going in to play for these people so he was happy to do that and enjoyed the travel. He spent a lot more time touring over those couple of years.

"Going back to that period, Hungary would have been the most western, for the want of a better word, of the countries. We started off in Zagreb, Yugoslavia. We did eight shows. Sarajevo, Pécs. We went from Zagreb by train into Hungary and it was very strange. It seemed very bleak at the time. The weather was atrocious in parts. It was like being an extra in 'Dr. Zhivago' [laughs]! But it was great fun."

Gerry McAvoy: "Hungary was amazing. Not many bands had gone by the time we had went there. There was no record company promotion. We just went out and played. The reaction was a little more staid. But by the end of the show everyone was rather ecstatic. The last night in Hungary, I don't remember where it was, near the Russian border, as it was then. And I'd say that 70 percent of the audience were soldiers in uniform. We were being watched all the time. Along with the promoter there was always a Communist representative who was traveling with us. I don't know what they were concerned about [laughs]. I guess the obvious things. Making sure we didn't get up to any mischief. Make sure we didn't sneak any beautiful Hungarian women out in our suitcases."

Donal Gallagher: "To Rory, playing to the people that came out to see him was a happy experience. When you play to an audience that's starved for music or they've never seen a western/rock player or star or whatever you wanna term the person, there's a fever, a sense of excitement. People in New York or London … we're so blasé about it. You go along, you clap politely. There was that teenage-renegade excitement you get with that kind of an audience. And one thing Rory loved to do was whipping his audience. He'd whip the audience into a complete frenzy, if he could. That's what fortunately or unfortunately happened in Athens."

Gerry McAvoy: "We played in Greece once with Rory in the football stadium."

Donal Gallagher: "Jesus! They'd never seen anything since the Stones in the 60s! When the four generals ran the country … it was a military coup. We went there on the eve of the first democratic election and played the football stadium. They'd sold 15,000 tickets. It was a sell-out. But 40,000 had gotten into the stadium. There were more people on the lighting gantry than anywhere else! No security. It was the most peculiar gig. And Rory played his audience. There was a riot in the streets! We had to disappear out of Athens because we were told that there was the possibility of being arrested for causing a riot."

·   ·   ·

Youngstown, Ohio, 1984.
Courtesy Scott Pickard

Taste's former manager Eddie Kennedy died in 1985. The cause has been a matter of debate.

Charlie McCracken: "I hadn't seen him for years. I'd heard that he'd had a liver transplant."

John Wilson: "I got a phone call one night that he was dead. And that was it. I can't say I was sorry. There may have been a small twinge inside me that remembered the good times. But by and large I was more inclined to be thinking of the bad times. The fact that there were all the record sales and that we never got any money, ever. When I eventually found the truth, the bottom line, I did tell him. And likewise too, he told me how he felt. That we should have owed everything to him. That he made us and we were nothing."

·   ·   ·   ·

Phil McDonnell: "In '85, Van Morrison asked Rory if he could borrow me for a tour. I don't think Rory was too happy about it because Rory used to like his guys to be allegiant. Rory was very loyal to those people that he wanted to keep around him. Even when Rory wasn't working it was a gig where a salary went into your bank every Friday. He paid me full touring wage four weeks of the month, every month, every year. I bought a studio in London and that started doing really well. And I said, 'Look Donal, I actually feel quite bad taking a salary off of Rory. Anybody would be quite mad to say I don't need the money but I actually don't and I'm starting to feel guilty.' There's a certain code of ethics and morals about it. I made a deal with Donal that I would come off full salary and then when Rory 'did' tour, I would send Don an invoice. I got more when Rory 'did' tour for a week's work but I didn't get anything when he wasn't working.

"So I went and did this tour. Van and I got along and the tour went really well. And when he was doing stuff after that he used to call me up. When I first started working with Rory we'd be working ten months of the year. But by the time '85, '86 came Rory wasn't touring like that anymore. He'd slowed up a lot. Not as a person. I don't suppose he needed to anymore. I think Rory would have played seven days a week. I don't really know what the reason was. I finished with Van at the end of '87 and I started looking after another Irish band called Clannad. My kid brother manages them, actually. I started tour managing them and doing their production. That's how I kind of phased out of the whole Rory thing."

• • •

When Rory felt ready to return to the studio, the Gallaghers felt it time to reassess their position and make a decision that would benefit the music short and long term. Many thought that their record company choices were limited.

Donal Gallagher: "No, it wasn't restricted to choices. It was a calculated move. After 'Jinx' it did take a long time. He took a sabbatical then. 'What's the point in rushing? Who's the new company?' That was when the Chrysalises, the Islands, the A&M's, who were all Rory-type companies if you like, started being bought up by the big majors who

Rory had started to steer clear of. I think with hindsight the mistake we made was we should have gone with Warner Brothers at the time we signed with Chrysalis. We thought, 'Great. We'll have the double package here. A small company within the large distribution.' But we weren't privy to know that it was only going to last for a very short period.

"So we looked around at all the companies. Demon Records had been recommended to me by an agent named Paul Charles. Elvis Costello was part owner of the company. Rory and Elvis had met up at AIR Studios and had got along very well together and had obviously, with Declan McManus, the Irish connection and they had shared similar attitudes to music and the business. That was really the first independent deal that I did. For the 'Defender' album. And then when I looked at Europe, going to the various music markets and looking at who the independents were, I selected Intercord because they were the biggest independent. Didn't have any huge international acts on their books in the rock area. Distributed lots of labels. They were very excited about being associated with somebody like Rory in Germany. So I knew that they would push all their buttons. In France we went with a company called Musidisque. Holland was somebody else. Spain was somebody else [laughs]. In Australia we went with Festival Records. It worked quite well. But we had a bit of a lapse in America getting back the rights to the records. Then, eventually, we put it all with IRS Records, Miles Copeland's company, in America. That ultimately bit the dust and EMI swallowed it up. So thereby hangs the tale."

Author: "When you went in to record 'Defender,' did you notice a change in Rory's character or outlook?"

Alan O'Duffy: "I don't think I could give you a specific answer on that because Rory was just Rory to me. But on the more contentious stuff, if you like, Rory is a wonderfully gentle character; a great thinker and a good man. But he was a bit of a nervous fellow or hesitant or not as confident as you'd imagine somebody in his position. This is not a criticism by a million miles. But there would be things like, 'I'll just have a cup of coffee.' And he may be thinking, 'I might have a parasitamol because I might get a headache later.' There was a little bit of that. The idea of worrying in advance that something was going to happen.

"He was a bit of a hypochondriac, this is true. But I hope I was a positive influence in what he was doing. Where we'd just gone on with having fun with guitars and him playing."

Brendan O'Neill: "A lot of that album, believe it or not, was very impromptu. He would come along with a riff and we would work on that. And then he would go off on a tangent or an offshoot from it. And another tune would come from it. And he didn't block-book time then. We would just get a call and say, 'I've got an idea. Are you free tonight?' And we'd go and record. Maybe that's why it took so long. He wouldn't pressure himself by block-booking a studio for a month and go into a think-tank. We were still in London. Obviously we gigged a lot between it. That's very much the way he did it."

As a way of adding some color, Mark Feltham had been sitting in with the band playing his harmonica on occasion during live performances. This proved to be a welcomed addition.

Mark Feltham: "I was born October 10, 1955, Westminster, central London. I used to listen to a lot of country stuff at home. That's my great love. Blues came across much later. I listened to The Beatles as everyone did but my real interest came from Nashville."

Gerry McAvoy: "I met Mark when he was with Stan's Blues Band. I think it was named after Stan Webb of Chicken Shack. Then it became Nine Below Zero. I used to see them at a couple of clubs and I thought they were very good. And especially the front man, Dennis Greaves, who's still with the band. There was something there that attracted me. I used to have these jam sessions and Mark would come along and play. Rory came down to check him out. Mark is an amazing player."

Donal Gallagher: "Rory had gone to do an anniversary gig at The Marquee and Mark had turned up. Rory then invited him up for a jam at the end of the set and loved his playing. Then

Mark and Nine Below Zero had split up and Mark was looking for sessions. So Rory said, 'Well, I'm recording. I'll bring you in.' Mark is a lovely person with a wonderful manner and a very true spirited musician. Rory felt a huge empathy with him and cultivated a role for him in the band. The harmonica was a nice feature and it broadened the sound out."

•   •   •

Rory Gallagher: "I'm very fond of the French crime-cinema. And I like German films of course. It's very stylized. It's like spaghetti Westerns. I love it over and over. You could write it. Of course there's almost no dialogue. They just look at each other, the two faces [laughs]! I used to go to the movies about two or three times a week. Now I don't go to the cinema. I suffer. Videos. But I'm not interested in the Brat Pack. A couple of the new people are quite good. There are some beauties. Demi Moore. Darryl Hannah. Sean Penn I like. Who else? But I'm sort of stuck in the sixties cinema. I liked Hopper. Even now I like Hopper. But a lot of those self-conscious actors I don't like. They're all either imitations of James Dean or imitations of every rebel actor you've ever met. Like this guy who died. What's his name? River Phoenix. Interesting but I mean…I know a girl who's absolutely mad about him. I said, 'If you think that's good you wanna see John Garfield and people like that.' It's like the blues. Rock 'n' roll. A friend said, 'That's the best I ever heard.' I said, 'Well, did you ever hear of Jerry Lee Lewis? Did you ever hear of Chuck Berry?' I mean the blues goes back decade after decade. So that's what you have to deal with. Just like writing, painting, photography, everything. But of course, naturally, every generation brings up some great people and some great talent around, you know. In the eighties, not so much, I think. But now, in the nineties, it's getting better again. Are you familiar with this black painter…I hate the word black because I don't treat people like that. He died at the age of 33. [actually 28] Jean-Michel Basquiat. He worked with Andy Warhol. But the Irish actor Liam Neeson is very good. He's a very, very good actor. The film (*Schindler's List*) got a lot of awards and the Oscars wouldn't give him the award. Strange. Very strange. It's a very controversial film, of course. I miss the big screen. 'Cuz you can go out and have a nice meal."

Around this time Rory also started to become fascinated with the life and work of Nicholas Ray through the book "Nicholas Ray: An American Journey," written by Bernard Eisenschitz.

Donal Gallagher: "I know the names but I can't clue in to why. He never gave any idea why he was interested. He had gotten into a lot of writers and art and artists and books written about the artists. This is partly with the sabbaticals he had taken where his indulgence of getting into authors and broadening out his reading habits."

He was also fascinated by a German film done by director Wim Wenders about Nicholas Ray called *Lightning Over Water*. The film documents the end of Ray's life, literally following him during the last days leading to his death.

Donal Gallagher: "I think the connection would be Wim Wenders as a filmmaker because Rory loved the movie 'American Friend.' That was one of his Top 5 favorites. I was aware of the range of books he was reading. My interests were quite different. But it probably shined more from the movie aspect and Wenders' side of things. The craziness and the very dark side of that."

Rory had close friend Rudi Gerlach send him another copy of *Lightning Over Water* as he felt his copy had been confiscated.

Rory Gallagher: "I just went through all that footage. It's dangerous. I tell ya. *Lightning Over Water*. I just watched it. I normally don't watch movies during the day because it's bad for my head. And I don't listen to music much. But that's a pitiful film. It's very interesting. I was so fond of *The American Friend* and it goes over the line into that film. So the old stuff of myself...now I can face it. For a while I couldn't look...some of the stuff I don't like the way I look. I wasn't well. But the film itself is fantastic. But some of the footage of that last Bonn gig is very interesting. It's almost not unlike what Wenders was doing. Do you know what I mean?"

Donal Gallagher: "I think *Lightning Over Water* was an understanding of his own destiny or fate. Somebody was being closed in upon or didn't have long to live. I think Rory would have felt that way. It's like Fender guitars. Certainly, in the mid-seventies, they were chomping at the bit to promote his name alongside Fender's when the Claptons and all the other guys were playing their Gibsons. Or switched allegiance. Beck had switched to Gibson. Rory stuck with Fender and was a torch carrier for them. And they were slow to recognize that and he felt insulted by that. Equally he carried a torch for rock and blues at a time when it was unfashionable. When 'glam rock' was the rage and blues bands became heavy metal bands. He stuck with it. 'Who are the people that are dictating this? Who are these guys that are formatting radio? Who are these guys in A&R departments who are ignoring true musicians like myself?' He'd worked hard at cultivating tour circuits. Be it France where no one had toured. Germany, Belgium, countries like this. They really didn't have facilities for rock gigs. He'd paved the whole path. A guy that stood up for the independence of the artist within the recording industry. And that doesn't go down too well with the powers that be."

•   •   •

From the author's personal observation there were times when there seemed to have been a sadness in Rory's eyes while he was performing. A prime example is a show from 1987, available on video as *Messing With The Kid: Live At The Cork Opera House*.

Donal Gallagher: "You have to go back to the core. Rory was emotional. He was playing blues. That was his drive. He had a blues heart. Melancholy, emotion. And he hadn't been back to Cork in a long time. He was extremely nervous about that gig. It was emotional. I remember the hours before going in to the gig. We sat with a photographer friend of ours, John Minhan, from *The London Evening Standard*, who had photographed Rory a lot and was a good pal of Rory's. And he was finding it hard to understand why Rory was so glum. There he was with a sold out Opera House. A seven-camera shoot. All the ordeal, the trucks, everything that goes with it. Yet Rory was despondent and keeping low key. But I feel a lot of that was a side effect of the medication he was taking. Actually making him very remorseful inside."

Rory was beginning to feel ill on occasions and started to increase his involvement with prescription drugs. This was making him far more sensitive to his surroundings. During Feltham's solos he would often look out into the audience, seemingly looking for help and understanding.

Gerry McAvoy: "I know what you're saying. I think you're possibly right, yeah. He was back in his hometown playing for his home crowd. And I think there was a certain sadness because there were things he could deliver ten years previous that he couldn't deliver that particular night. And he felt that. Plus the added factor that the house lights were on because of the TV cameras, which didn't help. It didn't help the performance; it didn't help the ambience of the night. Rory always wanted to think that he could still do what he was doing when he was twenty-one. Which nobody can [laughs]."

Donal Gallagher: "He started to feel the pressure. Do an album. Go and promote it, which would take a year to go around the world and cover every territory. And then you were expected to deliver yet another album. It was an abnormal pressure road. I used to say to him, 'Let's go on holidays.' But Rory wasn't a sun person. Even on tour when we would be in California, we'd be upstairs at the top of the Hyatt, jumping in and out of the pool. He might come up the odd day but most of the time he'd prefer to stay in his room and write and read. Or stay out late and catch some bands that he wanted to see. He was a real nighthawk. He was never interested in going on holiday. He loved to travel but I suppose he felt he was doing that anyway as part of his job."

• • •

Rory had an incredible knowledge of primitive yet effective studio techniques. One that he learned was a Buddy Holly trick. While laying down an electric guitar track, he would mike the strumming. The noise the pick made against the strings was mixed into the song giving the guitar a little more "click" to it.

Donal Gallagher: "And in a way quite before his time because they're basic recording techniques that everybody is trying to get on their album. He was talking about it in the 70s and the 80s when it was totally unfashionable."

Rory Gallagher: "I won't work on this certain recording system that is state of the art. I will only work on … not vintage equipment but, you know, old-fashioned British Olympic stuff. And I don't mind … for mixing I will go into clever stuff. But I've been recording in the hotel. I've got equipment myself. In other words, I think some of the modern desks, the parametric as opposed to graphic, they neuter the sound. And they've ruined a lot of great rock 'n' roll and blues records. I would be quite happy to be a guitar player, a songwriter, a producer. Unfortunately it's a mixed bag with me. I haven't always got it right. But when I do get it right, it's not bad."

• • •

Rory had a long-time fascination, dare I say a crush, on Catherine Deneuve.

Donal Gallagher: "And he admired Deneuve as a person as well. I know we were in a club or restaurant in Paris with Pascal Bernard, who did all Rory's tours. And Pascal, being a Parisian and his father being in the entertainment business, knew everybody and the opportunity was there for Rory to speak to her if he wanted."

Rory Gallagher: "I learned French to meet Catherine Deneuve, right? Listen. I'll tell ya a secret. I told a French promoter … the only time I did it in my life, other then playing for charity, for prisoners and things. We're playing Paris. I said, 'You can take my share if I can meet Catherine. Just shake her hand, that's all.' He said, 'OK, I'll arrange it.' Catherine doesn't show up because the man she's mad about, Johnny Halliday, showed up. And Halliday's fine with a drink and everything. No problem. No Catherine Deneuve. What could I do [laughs]? Look, it's just a schoolboy thing. For fun I said once in my life I'm gonna have a silly … fantasy. Just be a fool, ya know? This is true. Life is very short. You can do one or two silly things. Or even more. Yves Montand said that. He said that when you go to the grave the things that you remember are the foolish things. And the good and the bad. But that's not foolish. It's expressing yourself. It's silly. But the point is that it's not business 'all' the time. I just wanted to meet her, that's all. A lot of other people like her. And it's not like I have a dirty opinion about her. I respect her. And I like her. Is that wrong?"

Donal Gallagher: "I remember on one occasion where we played at a festival in Belgium. '69 period with Taste. At that time he was playing sax. Horner Coleman was one of his absolute heroes and Horner was on the bill and staying in the same hotel. And for some peculiar reason Rory wouldn't take the opportunity to actually chat with him or hook up with him. I remember we found it quite strange at the time but he preferred to keep the distance or the respect at a distance.

"He still held that kind of 'hero-worship' factor to a lot of people. And possibly a few of the heroes that he had met earlier on didn't work out to be … that it was an anti-climax. Perhaps he just felt that he should just keep these people afar and like it for what it is."

Rory's health started to affect him even more. But as much as he tried to hide it from his bandmates it soon became very noticeable.

Brendan O'Neill: "His health got to the stage when it was becoming detrimental to his capabilities as a performer. Probably 1989/90. You needed to have been a blind man not to have noticed it. We had obviously discussed it amongst ourselves and spoke to Donal about it but only through pure concern. Donal was very much on the case. Monitoring him at all times and trying to rectify the situation. But Rory was a very headstrong man. He always believed that he would work it out himself."

By the time the band went in to record "Fresh Evidence," there were new circumstances that were preventing everyone from getting work done as in earlier times.

Gerry McAvoy: "Rory just kept a drink in him. Have another drink and have another drink. He was not very approachable. Donal would approach him many times and they would end up in arguments. He'd just rather be left alone."

But this unprecedented behavior was becoming compounded with the aforementioned prescription medication, taken for a developing liver condition, making the situation intolerable and caused his long-time bassist to consider whether he wanted to stay or not.

Gerry McAvoy: "It did, yeah. That wasn't 100 percent of the reason but it was a part of the reason. It was demoralizing to see somebody who was so close to take that road. Brendan and I spoke to him a couple of times as musicians and friends, which he could take a lot easier than from his brother, Donal. That would cause upsets right away. And Rory would say that he would get help. That was part of the reason for leaving. I was writing and I needed to express that. And yes, I wanted to become part of a band again. I wanted to have a bit more say than I had with Rory. I wanted to talk to the record company. I wanted to talk to the agents."

During the sessions for "Fresh Evidence," O'Neill stated that he felt Rory was becoming despondent.

Brendan O'Neill: "It's very difficult to put your finger on it. There aren't a string of sentences that can explain it that easily. I'm sure the wane in his career … our particular brand of music wasn't that popular through the 80s. The 80s weren't a particularly encouraging time for music with a blues influence and that point of view had a lot to do with it."

Because of record companies wanting to capitalize on the "flavor of the month," Rory was beginning to feel neglected. Yet, true to form, he kept his concerns to himself.

Brendan O'Neill: "I'm sure there was a lot of that. But, again, that's where the private side kicked in. And that's where he would sort his own problems out regarding record companies and his stature in the recording world. And when he did it and why. Because it was his band. He was the artist. So you did wait in the wings for decisions like that to know what he was doing. A lot of it was guesswork. But you can make an educated guess and look at the situation. Record companies didn't want him to tour unless he had new product out. And Rory, being the sort of man that he was, once you start to put pressure on him and badger him, well, he would react the exact opposite to the way they expected. Against the grain. He would do it his way."

Dino McGartland: "Towards the end, his name wasn't on everyone's tongue. You have to say that he wasn't as familiar as he had been but there had been gaps in-between the albums. Might have been a four- or five-year gap. So the fans were beginning to wonder what was happening. It was slowing down a lot. But at the same time, whenever he did play, it was always a bonus to see him."

Brendan O'Neill: "We handed our notice in and went on that last tour. We did Japan, Australia, Canada and the States. We'd actually discussed it with him. It was very amicable. We explained what we wanted to do musically. We wanted to form Nine Below Zero again and we wanted to get involved with writing more. Basically just have a bit more control ourselves. Just exactly what he had done himself. We wanted to pursue our own line of thought. That would have been October/November of 1990. And we did a lot of touring before we actually left. The last gig was in New York on the thirtieth of April, 1991. Rory knew we were leaving the band six months prior to that date."

While promoting "Fresh Evidence," the toll the alcohol and prescription medication was taking on him was beginning to become visually obvious and caused concern.

Donal Gallagher: "Like all of us he drank from the 60s and the 70s and not as heavily perhaps. But there was always too much alcohol all over his songs; there was always a reference. It was no mystery. The cause for concern there would have been more to his health regarding medication. Particularly in the way it was affecting his looks. The steroids that were in the medication made him look more affected. It kind of looked like the effect of alcohol. The danger and my concern was the liver damage had more cause from medication. Which is a synthetic formula. I know that one time I got him some medical attention. And the concern was more the medication causing the liver damage as opposed to alcohol. The alcohol, in a sense, while it was a deadly dose, it has some organic, natural way that the body can cope with it. But the effects with medication were far more devastating."

Rory's deteriorating health caused concern and the news was quickly transmitted to those closest to him. But by 1992 the extent of the problem was made apparent as never before.

Ted McKenna: "Phil McDonnell would tell me that he'd spoken to Tom O'Driscoll and Tom would tell him what had been happening. And gradually I got the impression that Rory wasn't in great shape. He came up here to play at an open-air festival in Glasgow. Rory was headlining. I went along to see him and I couldn't believe it. Gerry and Brendan were playing. They'd actually left the band but Rory had asked them to come back in order to do this gig. So when I arrived, lo and behold, there's Tom O'Driscoll. Great! He said, 'OK, the dressing room's over there. Go and see the boys.' So I went back and big hugs, seeing the guys again. And then Rory came into the room and he was totally out of his face. And I'd never, ever seen him in all the time I worked with him go onstage as drunk as that. He may have had an occasional Jamieson's and Coke or a whatever.

"Anyway, I'm standing in the dressing room and suddenly Rory walks in and the first thing he said to me is 'Edward!' And he never actually called me Edward. But that was just to say the point. I couldn't believe he was staggering around the dressing room. And he went onstage and he went through the motions. He sang but every time it came to a solo he kept nodding to the keyboard player to do the solo. He wasn't remotely like the Rory Gallagher that I worked with. I couldn't believe it. And so much so that when I went back to the … they had a big tent with the drinks, as they usually do at festivals. I saw Don Gallagher at the end of the bar and I didn't know what to say to him. I just felt so kind of shocked that I couldn't even go up to Don and say hi and tell him what I thought of the gig because I just didn't know what to say."

Gerry McAvoy: "It wasn't pleasant. By that stage Brendan and I had left. Rory still hadn't a band together and this was a year later. I had gotten a call from Donal to see if Brendan and I could possibly do the show. Which we obviously did. We then rehearsed for three or four days. Rory had definitely lost the plot at that stage, I think, personally. Having this young Italian violinist, which I could not understand. It didn't make sense. And the gig didn't make sense either. It was a fiasco. It wasn't good. It was the first time it had affected a performance that I'd seen."

Joe O'Herlihy: "I did stay in touch with Donal down through the years and Tom in particular. They are life friend-ships. And with people like Phil McDonnell. Though I travel a lot, I keep in touch because it's an integral part of what we do. The bigger, outer family staying in touch all the time. Certainly I was aware of what was going on."

Mark Feltham: "Yes, it was evident and, yes, it was spo-ken about amongst the band. We all knew there was a prob-lem. To be honest I saw it coming a long time."

Ironically, for someone so against drugs of any kind, Rory became quite dependent on the narcotic cocktails that he was ingesting.

Ted McKenna: "Again, this was a revelation to me. Being aware of the effects of alcohol, as most musicians are, especially rock musicians that spend a lot of time on the road, you get straight to the heart of the booze. And you tend to be able to drink the average guy under the table. But with the long-term effects, which affected me sometimes, especially in the whiskey years, you can't sleep. You get kind of wired. It's almost like a stone or something. The alcohol in your system makes you feel kind of brittle. It affects your head. You get paranoid, etc. And I suppose some guys, I never did it, but some guys might have taken some kind of downer. Just to take the rough edges off. I didn't know anything about Rory's prescriptions. In all the time I was with him we all pretty much had a drink. Had a good time. And that was it. As a band we were always capa-ble of being professional. So we never got to that stage."

Author: "I was told that for two and a half hours a night he was Rory and spent the rest of the day waiting to be Rory again."

Ted McKenna: "I think that's a reasonable description of the way he was. But most musicians are like that to a certain extent. You come alive when you do what you were put on this planet to do. Most of the time you're waiting around. You're waiting in airports. They only see you when you're onstage and think, 'Oh, that was good.' They have no idea what kind of pressure you're under when you travel every day, thousands of miles. Every fuckin' day! Six weeks at a time. Two months at a time. But that's one of the things you get used to.

"Pete Townsend said that you go on the road and you've got adulation, going on in front of thousands of peo-ple a night. You're playing to millions of people over a peri-od of so many months. And when you come back you're expected to walk in and sit down and watch the telly. It's very difficult. It's just so hard to get it out of your system. For years I've always felt I'm gonna be somewhere else because I've always been on the road. The rolling stone thing. If he (Rory) wasn't playing then he'd probably go out and drink. I was like that as well. I think one of Rory's prob-lems was he never had a relationship that was ongoing that could anchor him. This is all just my opinion. He didn't have a relationship in his life that could marry this other person that he was. That could balance it. And I can see it in myself. I'm a Pisces, too. I think they tend to be quite self-destructive when they're not channeling their energy. They either go one way or the other. That's just the way Rory was. When he was doing what he was doing, that was it. 100 percent. 200 percent. Frightening energy and positivity. But when you're not doing that, what do you do? You're not equipped to be anybody else. In the real world it's so hard to be anybody else. The social skills are the skills that make you be able to thrive on other things. Especially when you've built up the habit.

"The other thing is when you're used to drinking on the road, you drink hard and you play hard. You come off the road, you drink hard but you don't play hard. And then it suddenly becomes a problem. If you drink on the road you can sweat it out. You're always on the go. You can go out for a drink and feel lousy the next day. But sometimes you can go out for a drink and you're with people and have stimulating conversation and you do things and you feel good the next day. But I think that's the folly of it all. I think that was one of the things that killed him. I know because I have the same problem. To use drink in order to sublimate, to keep or retain. To keep down, to repress the explosive musical thing you do. It's a substitute for doing that. Drink is like putting water on the fire. To try and keep it down. I'd rather be blasting away on a drum kit."

No one could approach Rory about drinking, even to the point where Donal was being, for the lack of a better word, reprimanded every time he brought it up. This was causing a lot of worry amongst those who knew him.

Mark Feltham: "Yes, of course it did. We loved him very much. But unless you really knew Rory, although he was very humble, very soft, a gentleman, an angel, there were certain things you couldn't cross the line with. And one of them was his private life. He did what he did and that was it. You didn't dare tell him what to do with his drinking. You didn't do it. It was just an unwritten law. You didn't mention it, ever, to the artist that he was drinking too much."

Author: "At one point he checked himself into a hospital. Was this under advice or an admission that there was something wrong?"

Donal Gallagher: "Everyone was giving him advice. The peculiar thing was that right through the 80s in particular he was a regular visitor to a doctor. He wasn't somebody who had problems and wouldn't seek medical advice or medical attention. He was a person trying to keep himself very well and very fit. And keep himself from stress and physical exhaustion, which are part of being on the road. And fear of flying, etc. And this is where the prescriptions were starting. He wanted to be healthy so he wasn't overtly sort of overdoing it. He wasn't a person who did drugs as such. OK. Prescription tablets are a drug. To me it's a crime that doctors were handing out stuff that they didn't know what effect it would have on the body in the long term. And a lot of these drugs are now banned. They've now been discovered to have so many bad side effects on people.

"The problem is when you're prescribed maybe eight to ten different tablets, all of varying strengths, the cocktail, the mixture of those … no doctor is a pharmacist. At least a pharmacist could tell you what the effect of the combination of one drug over another will have or interact with another. It's a chemistry set. And if you throw alcohol in on top of it … I took it to a German chemist one time and he said, basically, 'The devil's brew.' With that kind of medication there's a drug problem, not an alcohol problem.

"Most of the prescriptions were from one doctor. There were certainly some other doctors that may have unwittingly contributed. But it was part of an insecurity that he had. I know in the case of one of the doctors he had issued him a few prescriptions because he was on tour, that he might lose them or whatever."

Rudi Gerlach: "That's the main reason why I was so heavy in contact with him. Because he knows about me and he knows about my drinking. 1990 … I was into three bottles of Vodka per day. This was heavy drinking. Then I decided to stop. Which I did. And Rory knew about it. You can see clearly on one private video when we were waiting downstairs at a hotel. The first question that he asked me, 'Do you still drink?' I said, 'No.' And then he made the sign of the cross on his body and said, 'Good God, how did you do this?' I said, 'It's easy. It has to happen in your mind.' I knew he was in trouble with drinking and stuff. But the main thing, to me, was to have contact. As a person going through all that shit, if your mother or brother came up to you and said, 'Please, would you stop it,' it won't work. I couldn't say to Rory, 'Stop drinking or stop taking your pills.' This won't work. So the thing to me was to show myself as a person who could stop. I think there was a switch in my head. You have to put it to 'off' instead of 'on.' So this is how it worked for me. And just being a little bit present, just to show him that it could work, going off of the whole shit. That was the main reason. But I knew it was getting worse and worse. And he's living all the time on his own. He was never accompanied by anybody. So he could do what he wants and no one takes care about it."

Author: "Did he ever consider stopping before it started to cause trouble?"

Rudi Gerlach: "Yes, yes. He knew about it. Often he had said in his phone calls, 'My situation, my health, are very precarious. And I have to look after myself.' And after … he would call them 'projects,' the last two albums he was about to do. 'I'd like to finish it and then I will stay off from that and look after myself because I know that I'm in bad shape.'

"I don't know what kind of pills they were. But what I saw was when I was with him in London … next to his bed was a shoebox and it was full of different pills. Maybe it was stuff like anti-depressant stuff and so. And I knew that his doctor sometimes came around and gave him injections. For whatever reason, I don't know. I never asked him about it because I thought that if he wants to start it, it would be all right with me. I didn't force it. In this case it doesn't matter because it wouldn't help. So what could you do? I have no idea about medicines. Maybe if I asked him, 'What are you taking? What are the green ones for, the red ones, the yellow ones?' And it was stuff, you know, Valium? Stuff like that I think."

Author: "Was he drinking at the same time?"

Rudi Gerlach: "In front of me he was only having a glass of wine at times. Very, very low drinking.

"I saw one thing in Belgium; that was the point where I left him. He was totally mad. I never saw him this way. I opened the door to his booth where he stayed before the concert and he was alone. He had a chair over his head and was just about to smash it through the window. And he looked at me and dropped the chair and said, 'Oh, sorry, Rudi. I think you've never seen me this way.' I said, 'No. What's going on?' And he didn't say anything. Then I went up to Donal and said, 'Come on, there's some troubles going on with Rory.' Donal went in and came out about five minutes later and Donal said to me, 'Rudi, I have to declare something. This time we don't give him anything.' Whatever that means, before the concert. I think it was related to some pills or stuff like that. So they tried to keep him away from this. The funny thing, and I have this on video, this night he did the opening song and then he took his Fender, goes to the microphone and uses it like a machine gun as he says, 'Donal, this is for you!'

"The basic thing to me, I knew he was in trouble. I don't care if it's drugs or if it's alcohol or something like that. He always asked me about it. How I stopped. And this was the point that I realized that he trusted in me. Looking back, I would have liked it if he could have asked me more. I didn't force him to talk about it. If it came to this point,

like it was in London, where we would talk about it, he would just switch it around and say, 'Oh, Rudi, I ordered room service for something to eat or we have to go to the studio …' and he'd switch off. He was always so friendly. So what can you do? Scream at him? That's the main reason I'd go to London. Because all these phone calls won't get me any further.

"There was a point where he was about to kill himself. I got a phone call on the other line and I said, 'Rory, I'll call you back in twenty minutes.' I finished the other phone call and I called him back and he was in a very terrible state from his voice. He picked up the phone and he said, 'Who is this?' And I said, 'Rudi. I am calling you back.' And he said, 'Ah, yeah, Rudi. You just saved my life.' I said, 'What?' He said, 'Yeah. The phone was ringing and it was you. I was about to jump out of the window.' This was in July, '94. So what can you do then? 'I am sitting here in Cologne, you are in London. If you were around the corner, no problem, I'll take the next cab.' This was really heavy to me because I can't do anything about it. I don't know the main problem. But such people are making their own trouble. His fear of flight. In the early days he flew around the globe. And then it became, 'I won't go to Heathrow. I won't fly. I'd like to stay here.' Terrible. But the more you are alone and the more you are talking to yourself, you put yourself into such trouble. 'I can't do this, I can't handle this.' He was a totally weak guy in this sense.

"I was not too interested in where it came from. Basically you have to see the situation as it is right now. And it should be changed immediately because it gets worse and worse. I don't care about the past but I know that something must be changed right now, immediately. That was my main point.

"When on the road, for the pills, Tom or Donal got some and kept it in their hands to keep it under control. All I could do was give him my personal support without pushing him."

• • •

Rudi Gerlach: "So what are you going to do tonight?"

Rory Gallagher: "I tell you, I have to calm down. I've got to go to the doctor in the morning. We gotta keep in touch. Listen. Look, we won't talk. We won't. You know the word 'angst?' This is what I have at the moment, OK? You know about that."

While Rory was hospitalized, former Taste drummer John Wilson wrote Rory letters looking to regain contact.

Author: "Did Rory ever respond?"

John Wilson: "Unfortunately not. But I have been told by Donal that he at one time did say that he would agree to play here in Belfast. Belfast wanted to do a concert for a peace thing or whatever. They were planning all sorts of guys. Guys from U2. And it had been suggested that Rory, Charlie and myself get together and play at this concert. And apparently Rory tentatively said, 'Yeah.' And then there was a television series called 'Rock In The North,' sort of a history of rock and pop music in Northern Ireland. They interviewed me and they interviewed Rory as part of this series. I didn't know Rory was being interviewed in England and he didn't know that I was being interviewed here. And we said exactly the same things; that it was the best band we'd ever had. And the happiest days, musically, we'd ever had. It was a pity the whole thing had to end the way it did. For me, they were great times. I'd met Rory a couple of times after the band had split and it was OK. We were able to say our piece. I said my piece. I apologized for anything that he may have thought that I had said. Or what someone told him I had said. We cleared the air from that point of view. And we got it off our chest about Eddie Kennedy."

Rory Gallagher: "Now the Taste drummer is writing me letters apologizing! The things I went through with that band, you will never know! My brother, thank the Lord, sorted all the business out. The manager's now dead. Look, I'll tell you what I feel over a cup of coffee. I've had twenty years of bad rapping. I tell ya. I don't swear. I wish I could swear. And now the drummer wants to work with me again. The very guy that stuck a knife in my back, ya know! What can you do, huh?"

John Wilson: "I would dearly have loved to have had a reply to those letters from Rory. Or even better I would loved to have seen him."

Phil McDonnell: "I only heard him say the 'f' word twice. Now that's in an industry where everybody says it every fourth word. When me and Gerry and McKenna were on a roll, which we used to be on a night off or whatever, once we started effin' and blindin' he used to go, 'Oh, c'mon fellahs.' He never liked bad language when there were women about. And he didn't really like it when there weren't women about. Out of respect for him we used to curb it a lot because of the fact. But when we'd all had a good ole skinful it used to make him laugh. We used to go, 'Oh, for fuck's sake!' And he'd go, 'Oh, ho ho ho!' It was almost like a mischievous little boy side of him. It used to make him laugh because he knew it was wrong to do it.

"The only two times I heard him say it … and he was pissed, man! Angry, not drunk. We were doing a show in Pittsburgh with Jefferson Starship. We were on-stage doing a sound check. The monitor engineer was a guy called Owsley from The Grateful Dead, the guy that had the acid factory. Owsley was out with Starship. The Mair monitor system was still in its infancy in them days. And if you're used to Martin's, which Rory would have been, the Mair system is something the ear would have to get used to. And Rory wasn't getting what he wanted from these wedges. He wasn't getting the kick from the monitors that he was used to. I used to always say that Mair was no good for acts like Rory. Rory needed kick-ass stuff with a bit more whackin' in the chest, you know. He wanted to hear the snare. Like I said it was still in its infancy. And Owsley was an experienced guy but never known for his diplomacy. Owsley went to a Fleetwood Mac party, with a few of the other crew guys from Starship, and told Stevie Nicks that he thought her mids were shot. After the gig. You know what I'm saying? 'Yeah, listen man. I was listening to you singing and I think your mids are all shot!' So that's how much fuckin' decorum he had!

"But at the gig Owsley comes up and he says, 'What's the matter, man?' And Rory demanded respect from people because he was a respected musician. He never thought he was anything special but if people would get sort of a little cheeky with him, he used to demand a little bit of respect. Which all musicians do. And Rory said, 'It's my monitors.' And he said to Rory, 'Ah, your problem is you're not using them properly. You don't know how to use monitors.' And fuckin' Rory just 'lost it!' He fuckin' lost it, man! He said the 'f' word then and everybody just went 'OH!' We all knew he was about to go apeshit just because he said that word. I can't remember the other place he said it."

•   •   •

While touring Holland in January 1995, during a performance in Rotterdam, Rory collapsed onstage.

Mark Feltham: "I was actually on the last tour with a different rhythm section. Richard Newman and David Levy. He was very, very sick by then. And I've said this before as well. I don't think he ever wanted to get well, to be honest. I don't think that it ever occurred to him that he would ever recover. I don't think he wanted to reach fifty. I don't think he wanted to grow into an old rock musician. He didn't want help from anybody. That was his thing and that was it."

Donal Gallagher: "It was inevitable. It was a matter of time. It's a sore area. In effect he had gotten quite ill the previous year. He'd had huge lay-offs off the road. We didn't tour. So he was given all the time in the world to get himself sorted. And it was very difficult getting commitments out of him. We'd say, 'Look, we're looking at doing a French tour in two months time and we need to plan it.' And that's a short window of time for a manager to get it together. And it was always down to the wire with him. So the side effects were that he became very indecisive. Or he didn't want to think that far in advance. So we left Rory alone for long periods. And when I say alone he wasn't left companionally alone. He was to be without the stress or the thought of having to be on tour or preparing for a tour. Just time to live life. But he couldn't cope with that. I would say that in '94 it was a desperate time to say, 'Let's get back on the road. Let's get out there. At least we can monitor that he eats properly. We can monitor him when he's in a hotel.' And the camaraderie of the musicians to talk the same subject. When he was in London the problem for him was that the band was scattered all over, which is a huge city and he didn't see them on a regular basis as chums or pals or whatever. So he felt slightly isolated that way. And you also had the scenario where he'd go to other people's concerts and feel, 'God, everyone else is working and I'm not.' He just became despondent. So in effect I had to force the issue. OK, his health wasn't perfect but we'd book a few clubs and do a few surprise gigs and whatever. And I felt that the therapy of doing the gigs, where he'd sweat out the toxins from his body, he'd acquire an appetite and he'd eat again. The problem with the medication was that it killed his appetite. And my argument with the doctors was, 'You're saying on one hand that this guy has a bad drink problem. If you're saying the guy's addicted to alcohol how can you prescribe medication that says to avoid alcohol?' There's no rationale there for that."

Author: "Was he the type to think, 'Well, they're doctors. They know what they're doing.' "

Donal Gallagher: "Oh, absolutely. He was very naïve in that respect. Add in the fact that he always had a tendency to being a bit of a hypochondriac … even as a kid I remember. On tour he was referred to as 'The Doctor' because anytime anybody got a cut or had a sore hand or whatever Rory would have his bag out straightaway and looking for the remedy. So he tended to be very innocent in that respect. And sometimes it's too late to tell somebody once they've got a liking for a particular thing. Or else it solves, in their mind, a particular illness or problem."

The feeling of inevitability was shared by others.

Rod de'Ath: "I felt this very early on. Probably when we were based in Hollywood. This was about '76. I was drinking so much until I had a chance to go to a doctor. And I did. I was strong enough and young enough to handle the alcohol intake. But Rory didn't."

Donal Gallagher: "I had to think positive because he was refusing treatment prior to that. I think he felt his days were numbered. It had been in the air six months prior to that, even onstage. He'd throw in numbers that you felt he was deliberately telling us a message. He'd suddenly break into, 'I Shall Be Released,' which would send shivers up your spine. And 'Don't Think Twice, It's Allright.' It was like he was giving you a message about something. He was a bit fatalistic in that respect.

"He was not a person that could cope with hospitals or anything like that. If he had dealt with it a little bit earlier than he did … the tour in January finished and he wasn't into hospital until March. He had gotten a bad pneumonia. His chest was quite bad. In that January/February I had gotten a horrendous flu. I was laid low for about three weeks. I couldn't get out of bed so I couldn't help him either. Everybody was all wired up about the whole Dutch thing sort of falling apart, as it were.

"But it was very much a drive to do that tour early in the year. We'd picked it up the previous year in '94, as I was explaining, and got him on the road. And we felt we had him trimmed down and he was thinking straight at least. What I didn't want to have happen is that, normally, we'd break for Christmas and take a break and think about touring the following year. And it would usually be May or June before we got on the road again. But this particular year I thought if we're out on the road quickly afterwards and don't give Rory time to vegetate … and the Dutch tour was relatively easy. There was only six shows. And five of the nights were spent at the one hotel so there wasn't a lot of traveling to do. But obviously it was one too far. He became very depressed over that Christmas."

Author: "How did you finally talk him into going to hospital?"

Donal Gallagher: "Coercion, I suppose. I'd given up the badgering because I knew he was just terrified of going in and I can appreciate that. But it got to the point where he had to go in. I remember looking at the man and saying so. And he said, 'Well, come back tomorrow and I'll think about it overnight.' And I said, 'You won't be here tomorrow. I'm promising you twenty-four hours to live. If you want to be around tomorrow you've got to go in tonight. And if you don't I'll ring the emergency police and ambulance.' They would pick up Rory like a road traffic victim. 'This is the choice. We've got a private hospital with a private bed booked and waiting for you. And your doctor doesn't seem to be able to cope with the whole thing anymore.' I said, 'I've got my car. I'll take you down in the elevator. No one will see you.'

"It was a few weeks before they diagnosed that he would need a liver transplant. There was a certain amount of hope that he wouldn't require it. That the organ regenerated itself enough that it might be damaged but not … and that's when the discussions came to play with the surgeon. The surgeon couldn't believe it. 'What am I doing with this young man? I've been told it's alcohol.' And I said, 'It isn't.' And he said, 'If it was alcohol I'd expect to see him in his mid-fifties. But not at forty-six.' Which is what it was at that point in time. And he said, 'This is incredible. There must be more to it.' Well I had known well before that about the medication. But you've got a doctor who was treating him. Rory was complaining of liver pains and the guy was just prescribing him coprimoxyl (sic), which is the next step down from morphine. It was pure parasitamol. But what a lot of people don't appreciate is the biggest cause of liver failure, certainly in Britain anyway, is overdosing on parasitamol.

"I'd figured it out six years beforehand. I'd gotten Rory to switch doctors and done every trick in the book. But when somebody gets hooked into one particular set of tablets it's very hard to break that cycle. I was always of the opinion that Rory could drink pints of drink, alcohol if you have to, and I never felt it was a problem. I'm not promoting alcohol. But what I'm saying is you could always figure if any band member, and they were all drinkers, had a bit too much, some soup, black coffee, you could always get the person into some shape. And particularly the next day. But when they swallow a couple of tablets you don't know what effect that's going to have on their systems. It's very hard to sober somebody up from a cocktail of those tablets. Alcohol, you've some chance."

Rory Gallagher, Gerry McAvoy, Stockholm, Sweden, 1976.
Courtesy Hans Ivarsson

Gerry McAvoy: "I thought he would pull through it. But I'm a little ticked about the whole thing because I wasn't kept informed. Which I wasn't happy with. I would get a splattering of information from Tom. I thought I had a right to know. I know that towards the end, when he was in a coma, that they brought Mark Feltham in to play harmonica. Who had known Rory for a couple of years. But I'd known Rory for over twenty years and I thought I should have been informed."

Phil McDonnell: "I knew all the time that he wasn't well. Although I wasn't working with Rory I used to stay in touch with Don and I used to call Rory and talk to him and I was very close to Gerry. We were all like brothers, basically. We'd known each other so long. It's like your own brother being sick. You just sense it more than anything. I've always been very close to Tom O'Driscoll. Still am to this day. Tom and I are like brothers, you know. And even Tom wouldn't tell me things that Rory had told him because it's just inbred in you. You just don't. If the man tells you, he tells you. If

he wants everyone else to know he'll tell them as well. It's just like a locked-in security thing you have. But I knew Rory was going down. It's one of those things you keep in touch about but you don't wanna even think that it's going on. And as I was keeping in touch it was getting worse. I didn't wanna go and see him because I can't handle things like that too well. It would have done me up too much."

Mark Feltham: "I was being fed from Donal. Initially Donal went into King's College (hospital) with Rory by himself. I would speak to Donal everyday and Donal would say, 'I've had a chat with the liver man. He tells me that he's gonna pull through. He's gonna be well again.' And I was really encouraged about this. Then Donal phoned me up and said, 'Would you like to go and see him?' So I then went up to see him. He'd had the transplant. When I saw him I was quite encouraged although he was full of tubes and things. But when I next saw him he wasn't well at all. He'd gotten this infection. Apparently after such a big operation your immune system gets lowered so any random infection can be potentially life threatening. That's what they were really concerned about and that's eventually what happened. And when I went to see him the next time he was in a coma."

Donal Gallagher: "Quite peculiarly he'd been moved from Cromwell Hospital to the key transplant hospital, which is King's College, where they have the best surgeons. That was at the surgeon's request because it was part of the thing of getting him into a hospital in the first place. Rory would go to Cromwell but didn't want to go anywhere else because it was a hospital he was familiar with. I had been in there with a back injury for a couple of weeks at one point and he was visiting me on a regular basis. It was a bit of a 'Holiday Inn' type of hospital so he didn't feel that it was an institution as it were. But the surgeons felt that his case was so critical that they had to have him at the best of facilities.

"He had recovered quite well from the transplant. The bizarre thing is that most people feel that it was rejection. It wasn't. In fact, the statement was that the best part of his body was the new organ he had. That aside, I was making arrangements for him to be transferred back to the Cromwell to recuperate. This is after about two months post-operation. So he had done quite well. And the day I had gone in with the arrangements made they said, 'No, we need to keep him another day.' He'd picked up a bug in the hospital. They had him pumped full of antibiotics but they weren't strong enough because he had been prescribed so many antibiotics over the previous years.

"So in effect the bug was out to mutate whatever the new antibiotic was. I remember the whole scenario. Watching that was quite bizarre where they were changing culture every hour. And they would go straight to a laboratory to find another antibiotic and it just didn't work."

Gerry McAvoy: "The only information Brendan and I got was from Tom O'Driscoll. He would pop down to the studio with Nine Below Zero and fill me in on certain details. But not 100 percent. He would let me know enough to let me know."

Though McAvoy felt that O'Driscoll might have been following directives on what information was to be leaked, Rory's long-time band mate felt bad about being excluded.

Gerry McAvoy: "I think it's a shame. But it could have come from both ways. I could have approached the situation myself, which I didn't do. That's guilt speaking. But because I wasn't approached I didn't feel confident enough to approach the situation. If he'd have rung up and said, 'Would you like to come up and visit Rory because he's not in such good shape? Maybe you might help.' It was a family situation. It was difficult at the time. But I hold no resentment."

Brendan O'Neill: "I'd always been in contact with Tom O'Driscoll because we're very close personal friends. And we would seek advice from Tom. 'Should we go see him?' And Tom would always try to be polite and say, 'Well, maybe it's not such a good idea right now.' But with hindsight, I realize I don't think Tom wanted people to see Rory the way he really was. Just from learning how ill he was by the end. And the people around him probably tried to protect him."

Mark Feltham: "I think it was very similar to Elvis. Elvis was a very humble man as well. Called everybody 'Sir' and quite a gentleman. Rory was exactly the same. I never saw Rory use any drugs apart from his drink. You couldn't smoke a joint around him; that was completely out of the question. He wouldn't tolerate it. And there he was, in the end, on all these different sorts of prescription drugs that different doctors were prescribing him. Which I'm sure he thought that they maybe were the answer and that he would get a little relief. But to be honest they were confusing him even more."

During the last few years on the road, Rory was carrying a shoebox full of pills not only for what ailed him but to combat potential illnesses as well.

Mark Feltham: "He was a famous hypochondriac. He used to worry about all sorts of ills. He used to carry balms and things for his skin. And then he'd have oils. He'd be a great one for old wives' remedies! 'Rub this on that, that's great for that.' And he normally had some tiger balm with him. He was a great one for ointments and old-fashioned grandmother's … he used to make me laugh!"

Gerry McAvoy: "As soon as you had something wrong with you he'd say, 'Hang on' [laughs]. He'd run up to his room and bring something back down. He wasn't like that at the beginning. This came gradually. It started around the end of the 70s."

Mark Feltham: "And a very superstitious man as well. On many occasions he would walk into the dressing room and where I'd taken my boots off to change into my stage trousers. And they would be the wrong way around of each other. The right one would be on the left and the left would be on the right. And he would go absolutely ape shit! 'C'mon, man! Bad luck! Bad luck!' So I would have to change that around. One famous time, when we were traveling through France, we were going down to do a show in Bordeaux. We were in the tour bus. And he'd only seen three magpies or four … three for sorrow I think it was. One for sorrow, two for joy. And he needed to see this extra magpie because it was really playing on his mind. Deeply superstitious man."

Gerry McAvoy: "He was a very superstitious person. You couldn't put a pair of boots on a table in the dressing room. He'd freak out! 'No, don't do it. Take them off the table fast!' A crooked photograph on the wall, he'd fix it. His mother is very superstitious. His mother actually reads cards."

Donal Gallagher: "It goes with being Irish! Particularly with a country that has the Shamrock for wishing [laughs]! Every sort of element is a good luck charm. But I think, obviously, with the blues as well. Blues music is riddled with mojos and potions and superstitions and rock 'n' roll, 'a black cat has walked across my trail.' Yeah, he was. It's part of the heritage of Ireland. And to be quite honest, this came to be exaggerated with the medication. There were a lot of phobias in Rory's mind."

After Rory had lapsed into a coma, Donal brought Mark Feltham into the room to play harmonica and try to reach him.

Donal Gallagher: "It's blind faith, isn't it? I was grasping at straws. But then every day you were grasping at straws. Every day was a critical day. Rory had been in intensive care for the better part of three months. I didn't do that as a 'Last Post' by any manner or mean."

Mark Feltham: "Donal asked me to go down to King's when he slipped into a coma. He'd spoken to the doctors and he said, 'Is there any likelihood that he can pull out of this coma if Mark goes down and plays?' They gave it their OK. So I went down to King's, took the harmonicas, got the doctors out of the room and started playing at his bedside. I played some blues and country stuff for him, you know. To try to … spark him up. I was there for about an hour doing that."

Donal Gallagher: "I believe it certainly did reach him. You could see the reaction in the well being of the man. I mean, he did improve. It's really hard to say on what kind of a scale did he improve. Certainly, from what I could see of his body heat, color, complexion, it had a dramatic effect.

"I'd been advised by the staff at the hospital that despite being in a coma the one thing they have is their hearing. They constantly encouraged me to talk to Rory as if he was awake. So I did that. And it didn't take much for me to communicate with Rory anyway. Even when we didn't speak I always felt a telepathy with him. The pleasure of hearing rather than silence would be welcomed. I'd be certain it was a comfort for him. He thoroughly enjoyed listening and playing with Mark. I think they were sort of kindred spirits, musically."

Mark Feltham: "But he never came through. And when he passed away we were all standing there with him."

Rory died on June 14, 1995.

Phil McDonnell: "I was in a hotel in the north of England. I was just sitting there watching the TV, looking over the golf course, and I got a call from my wife. She said, 'Phil. I've just had a call from Germany. From my brother. He's just heard on the radio that Rory's dead.' It was incredible. And I'm stuck up in this country hotel up in the middle of nowhere in the north of England. My heart sort of sunk. I said, 'Don't be stupid, woman. Fuckin' don't be stupid.' And she said, 'Phil, he's gone.' And it was just something you didn't want to admit to. I kinda went into a state of shock. I said, 'OK. Let me go and I'll speak to you later.' And I just picked the phone up and I made a phone call to Gerry. I told Gerry. I told Ted."

Gerry McAvoy: "I was at home. I got a phone call from Phil McDonnell, who was in tears. Eventually I got through to Donal and he told me what happened. I couldn't believe it to start with. It was a complete loss. A sad loss. I got together with the whole family to express my feelings on the whole thing. It was very sad. And I became a part of the unit for those couple of hours."

Brendan O'Neill: "Gerry called me. He had just heard. And he said, 'I've got some terribly bad news.' And as soon as he said that I just knew. But Rory being Rory, you just never believed he would die. You always thought he would fight through it. And win. Because he would often win."

Dino McGartland: "Strangely enough, I was sitting at home. He died at quarter to ten in the morning but I never heard about it until … believe it or not, a friend of mine, who's actually got a son called Rory, he called me at 11 o'clock at night. He assumed that I'd heard. So he just phoned me and he was talking to me. 'That was terrible about Rory.' And I said, 'What do you mean?' He said, 'I'm really sorry to have to tell you this but Rory's dead.' So, from Wednesday right through his funeral on the Monday, it was really sad. There were a lot of tears shed. And where I live in Omagh, which has about 20,000 people, I am the high-profile Rory Gallagher fan. All my music buddies knew I was into Rory. And the really strange thing was my friends, who I'd meet on the street, came up and shook my hand and said, 'Listen, we're sorry to hear about Rory, you know.' I felt pretty weird. They knew what a loss he would be to me. And offering their condolences."

Rod de'Ath: "I wasn't surprised. Simply because of his alcohol intake. No one called me. They thought I was dead. I had an accident and I lost my memory completely. My family actually held wakes for me."

Roy Eldridge: "Someone called me to say, 'Have you heard that Rory's really ill?' And then with the final sad news. There was a lot of rumor and gossip and speculation about drink and drugs and whatever. I'd probably known him for twenty-odd years, pretty well. Yes, he liked to drink. But no more than any rock band you can imagine and less than some."

Alan O'Duffy: "I was home in Ireland working on a series called Ballykissangel. And during that time I heard that Rory was ill. I was on a schedule of work where I didn't have a spare five minutes. And, sadly, I heard of Rory's death during that time. I recall that my son was on the set during the weekend that Rory was buried. I wanted to go to the funeral. The production manager, Howard Givens, couldn't find anybody, at all, to replace me. I told him I needed to go to a funeral. He just couldn't find anybody. And I remember crying on the set for Rory with my son. He'd been a good friend to me."

John Wilson: "I was asleep in bed. I got a phone call. It was not nice. It took me quite a few days to come to terms with it. I expected him to survive everything. He was going to have the transplant and I assumed that everything would be fine. But unfortunately not."

Lou Martin: "I was here where I am now, up in Edinburgh. I knew that Rory had been ill. I'd heard from Donal that he'd been into hospital for quite a few things and Donal had mentioned that he was going in for a liver transplant. But Donal said, 'I think he'll pull through it. He's pretty strong.'

"I didn't hear anything for a month. Then a guy phoned me up from a Scottish paper, *The Edinburgh Telegraph*, and said, 'Somebody gave me your name and number. Rory Gallagher has just died.' 'What? No. It can't be. I would have heard something.' He said, 'I'm putting together an obituary. Would you like to say a few words?' And I said, 'I'm absolutely charred. I'm speechless, really.' So I just gave him a few pointers about how great the music was and how great a guitar player he was. And then I was watching MTV that evening and I saw this thing. 'Blues Star Dies.' They had an old live piece. I looked and I saw myself onstage with Rory and Gerry and Rod. And I knew it was true. I phoned Donal up and his son answered the phone. And he said, 'I'm sorry. My Dad can't come to the phone.' So I said, 'Tell him I'm sorry and I'll call him up in a few days time.' "

Derek St. Holmes: "When I heard through the grapevine that he had passed away it was a sad day. He was one of those unsung heroes. Like these kids today, they just don't know how good he was. Everybody goes crazy about Stevie Ray Vaughan. But old Rory was something else! He was an incredible guitar player. And these kids today…if they went back and listened to some of his older stuff, they'd really figure it out."

Marcus Connaughton: "I was here in Cork, working with RTE. I was staggered. I have to say I got very drunk that night. In April of that year I met Donal in Dublin airport. He had told me that Rory had been in, had had the operation and that he was recuperating well. Rory's mum was on the flight down to Cork that I was taking. I thought it was totally inappropriate to even approach her because I'm sure she was terribly upset. So we didn't get to talk. And the next thing I knew, hearing the news on the fourteenth of June, I found it very difficult to comprehend. As one guy said to me that day, 'You expected to see him sitting on a stool at the age of seventy, swapping stories about playing with Muddy Waters and stuff like that.' And I mean, the Muddy thing was a very special period in his career. The whole thing that he actually got to sit in and play with somebody like Muddy Waters. He held that very, very close to his heart as a very special memory.

"He inspired a lot of people. It's important that his memory is cherished and that his passing is marked."

Dino McGartland: "I was playing in a band at the time. We finished the gig around midnight on Sunday and we traveled down the whole length of Ireland from the north right down to Cork. It was a seven-and-a-half, eight-hour journey. I didn't really know if I was going to go to the funeral. But when I got there, I think it was the best thing that ever happened to me.

"The funeral wasn't until two o'clock and I was there from eleven o'clock in the morning, just inside the church. There were a lot of people walking about but they didn't speak. They didn't have to speak. We knew what was going on inside their heads. It was just an awful sense of 'Rory's gone.' And seeing his coffin in the church was really hard to take in. I've been married now since 1985. It was the first time 'ever' that my wife saw me cry. And that's saying a lot."

Lou Martin: "Donal later called me and said that he had made arrangements for me to fly to Cork. He wanted me to play in the church. Mark Feltham came over as well. We played 'A Million Miles Away.' And me and Mark worked out an arrangement of another one of his favorites, 'Amazing Grace.' It was tough. It was shattering. I don't know how we kept it together. And the entire town showed up. There couldn't have been more people on the street to watch the procession go by. And the church was packed. After we did 'A Million Miles Away,' I said, 'Let's do a little blues.' We improvised like a medium blues in C. I was told later that that got to a lot of people."

Donal Gallagher: "The way that the pallbearers were handled was you mix your relatives and friends, fans, whatever. You have the first stage where the coffin's carried to the hearse. And then the hearse leaves for the cemetery to the gates. And then you can either have it driven or it can be carried up. In other words, rather than making one walk of it, I staggered it. Phil McDonnell, for instance, that was one of his wishes. To be one of the carriers. Equally, the various musicians who had turned up for the funeral who were there, I wanted to give them the chance. Devout fans that I knew. You had to spread the comfort as much as you could. There was no particular selection process but a lot of people were given the honor, if there's such a thing. But the principle pallbearer leaving the church was Ronnie Drew, with myself. Ronnie Drew had been a musician with The Dubliners. And the reason I selected him was I knew that Rory had a lot of empathy with Ronnie. Ronnie had been very good to write to Rory. He sent him literature of cultural things Rory was interested in. Or folk people that Rory was interested in. They had met up years earlier when Ronnie had decided to leave The Dubliners and go solo. Ronnie was up in Hamburg, on his own, marooned, and by coincidence we were at the same hotel. And he was completely taken aback by Rory going over to him. He hadn't known much about Rory other than by name. But he was so aghast that Rory was so straight forward, friendly, honest. They spent the entire night just chatting. And of all the Irish artists, he was the only one to ever cover one of Rory's songs, which was 'Barley And Grape Rag.' I wanted to give him that place."

Phil McDonnell: "We all sort of got under Rory's coffin and carried him on our shoulders down to the grave. And when we were all doing that, me and Tom and Donal and Ted and Gerry and that, as we were all walking along together carrying the boss on the shoulders … it still makes me choke now thinking about it. I'm a very emotional person anyway, and my eyes are welling up now just talking to you about it. I still miss him very much. I still really can't believe he's not here, you know."

Gerry McAvoy: "Being Irish you get used to it. I found the day very moving. The church was like a gig. There were so many people there. And the roads were lined for three miles. It was a very moving day and a very sad loss."

Lou Martin: "And that's another thing. Carrying that bloody coffin. Me, Gerry, Mark, Brendan, one of the guys from The Dubliners and another guy. I was the tallest so I was standing at the back. I had the pointy end sticking into my shoulder. And it must have been three-quarters of a mile. That's a long way when you're carrying a casket. And at that pace. And I kept thinking, 'He's up there looking down. I hope he doesn't catch what I'm thinking! Why do you have to be so bloody heavy?' We lowered the thing in the ground and that was it."

Mark Feltham: "Donal also asked me to play at the gravesite as the coffin went down. It was a pretty awful time just hearing this lonesome harmonica at this graveyard.

Raining as it was. It was pretty grim. That's how it all ended. Very, very sad."

Lou Martin: "Donal organized a nice wake afterwards. It was at a big hotel. Hot food, free bar. They had set up a wee stereo system that was playing his stuff. And there was a piano in there. All these people turned up. U2, Gary Moore, people from Clannad. Quite a few people from the newer bands turned up to pay their respects. After the dinner, Donal said, 'Well, the piano's there if you feel like doing something.' So I went. Gerry picked up an acoustic guitar and he started playing a few things. And before you knew it, it was a jam session. We were waiting for Rory to walk through that door with a guitar wanting to sit in. It was the best possible way to see the day off."

●　　●　　●

Lou Martin: "Nobody had heard from Rod de'Ath in a few years. Everybody lost contact with him. We heard that he'd gone to the States and we heard he'd gone to Canada. Tom O'Driscoll called me up and said, 'I've heard a story that Rod's no longer with us.' This girl that Rod was living with at the time, a girl called Ann Smith, who I thought was a bit weird anyway, she spread the story around that Rod had expired. So I called around and no one had heard anything like that. I went and checked with the Registry of Births and Deaths. There was no death certificate. So at least he wasn't registered as dead. I wondered where he was. And Donal inquired as Rod and I were best friends but I really hadn't heard anything."

Rod de'Ath: "When I died, you mean [laughs]? 1986, 1987. I just fell over running for a train and I forgot to use my legs. A serious head injury, my memory, etc., etc. I can't perform anymore. I lost 60 percent of my hearing so that was the end of my producing career. So I'm getting along in life with writing. At least I can still write. And bringing up my grandson."

Lou Martin: "After Rory had died, there was a memorial service for him in London. In Brompton, near Donal's area. All the London musicians turned up. And Tom said,

'I want you to meet somebody.' I saw this oldish character with a shaven head, a Mohawk thing. Very frail. Hardly any teeth. Worn-looking. His hands were shaking. I said hello. I thought he was an old fan. I shook hands with him. And then went outside where everyone met for a cigarette. Then somebody asked me if I'd seen Rod. And I said, 'No, I haven't.' And he said, 'You've just been talking to him.' 'Where?' 'There.' And it was the same old guy! He had a hat on. So I went over to him again. And he looked right at me. Then he looked up at the sky and I saw the profile. And I thought, 'Shit. It is him.' Looking about sixty years old. And I said, 'Oh, I'm so sorry. I just didn't recognize you.' And he just laughed and said, 'You've heard exaggerated reports of my death!' But there are some very dubious aspects as to what happened. Some people I know say he got into a very heavy drug-dealing situation. I got this from very reliable sources. It was a hit job by a rather heavy crowd from North London. They were after him for ripping them off of some money or something. But Rod's version is that he fell down the stairs at a railway station. Fell down some metal stairs and woke up in intensive care with a plate in his head. He lost the sight of one eye and generally ruined his health. He walks with a walking stick. But he met up with this nice woman called Dee, who works for Social Services, and she took him under her wing and got him all the benefits he was entitled to. I saw him recently in London. I went down and spent the night. He's OK. He can't play his drums anymore but he's come to grips with that. He's very happy with where he is and his memory is perfect."

Rod de'Ath: "That was when I resurrected myself. I decided it's time for me to put an end to all this crap and turn up. It was a very emotional time. Dee said to me, 'Why don't we fly over to Ireland for the funeral?' And I said to Dee, 'Listen. Everybody thinks I'm dead.' So when there was the memorial service, I thought, 'Right. This is the time.' It worked out fantastic. You should have seen all their faces. It was very emotional."

· · ·

Author: "Rory never married. Was his vocation his wife?"

Donal Gallagher: "Oh absolutely. You've hit the nail on the head. I think when you go through your teenage years and you blot everything else out of your life … it's your profession and your career and you just want to get out there and do it. Nothing's going to send you away. And having a girlfriend would have been a difficult thing. He wanted to travel. He wanted to tour. And didn't want to have any ties. He was the true 'rolling stone.'

"And then of course what happens is when you get into your 40s, late 30s, when life has settled down a bit, and you're more lonely and you want more company … you've become isolated and too set in your ways."

Gerry McAvoy: "He had a couple of girlfriends. He had this one girlfriend, a really nice girl. I can't remember her name. And Catherine. Catherine got fed up in trying to get Rory 'cuz Rory was old fashioned in certain ways and would shy away from the situation."

Donal Gallagher: "He definitely wanted a change in lifestyle and direction and wanted to be more hospitable and entertain people. We only lived less than a mile apart and he was obviously visiting my house on a regular basis. We always had various friends over. He enjoyed company and meeting different people in a casual basis. Living on his own he felt a little bit too isolated. It's very difficult to go into a restaurant and eating on your own. So a pub became a place where he could feel comfortable to go and meet people. Then the opportunity of the Conrad Hotel, where he spent a few years living, which I felt was a positive move at the time."

Rory Gallagher: "I expect nothing. I have problems like everybody else, you know? I have difficulties. We all have difficulties. I'm not a baby. I accept that. So I want to do two good albums. I'm prepared to work and so on. So I don't know, I'm just …"

Rudi Gerlach: "But that's the past. And now you're staying in an expensive hotel for at least a month."

Rory Gallagher: "Yes, because my roof is leaking and I'm not domesticated. I have a particular kind of attitude to life."

Rudi Gerlach: "Rory, you can't tell me the roof in your flat in London can't be fixed in a month's time. Why isn't it?"

Rory Gallagher: "Yes. Because I have other problems. I've got medical and …"

Rudi Gerlach: "But you shouldn't do it by yourself. You've got some people around you. You can hire …"

Rory Gallagher: "I don't trust people. I don't want people around me. And I've been good to people. But because I've been surrounded with people all my life … I don't like being on my own. But I have to. I appreciate the limelight but I've never wallowed in it. I just got the job done. I'm happy I have some friends. You and a few. I'm not scratching your back now! But you know me. Anyway … I can't get my flat together. I'm staying in an expensive hotel. OK. Etc. Anyway, back to the work."

Donal Gallagher: "It was an excuse, I suppose. He had an elaborate opening roof. But Rory was so private he wouldn't allow anybody in. You couldn't get a repair man in. And I was set the task of trying to fix it. It was the undercarriage of an old aircraft. A BA-111. I had submarine engineers and various people giving me advice. But it was a minor thing. The thing is that he just didn't want anybody in his place. Unless it was me or Tom, that was OK."

Rory Gallagher: "I work for the fans. I like the applause. But it's not life-blood for me. It's, uh, and I wouldn't let them down. But, Rudi, I've given more than people think. You know? OK, I'm in a luxury hotel. I've got a lot of guitars and I have a few pounds in the bank. But that's not the big issue. I'll do these albums, then I'm gonna stop. I want health for my family. I want health for myself. I want to play music. And I probably want a family myself. I don't know. I want room to move. And I want to start working again. Painting. If the Lord will allow me the talent, my nerves and health and things. I'm very precarious."

Donal Gallagher: "Recently we found that Rory had done a painting of the cover of 'The Buddy Holly Story.' He was a good artist."

Rory Gallagher: "So I'm quite happy. I'll play for the people the rest of my life. But there's more to life than that, you know? And I've written songs. I've written three in the last three days. So I just want to get this project done. I'm suffering a bit of damage, as you know. But it's all coming together. But this time 'round I'm not going to work for the company. This is why I'm so involved with all aspects. But the trouble is if you work too hard on everything … not for ego. I won't even take the credit. It's so hard to explain. I'm trying to work workshop. It's not going to be silly-billy. It's going to be saleable and all that. But I've had enough lawyers and 'make your will out' and 'who's gonna get this.' I'm a corpse now already. It's too much. But I'm also very grateful for what I have. The friends I know. But I'm a bit guilty. Being an Irish Catholic I feel obliged to get the job done.

"Anyway it's coming together OK. That's the positive. I'm not a quitter but I'm on the verge, I tell you. I owe it to the people to keep going. And I'm not a crybaby. But at the moment I'm a little bit of a crybaby, I must admit. I'm getting tired of a lot of things. (pause) Look. Let's look forward to the future. We're gonna have some good times. (pause) The frustrating thing? I'm thinking of myself all the time. I'm thinking of my family. And lots of heavy things. I wanna stay there, don't worry. But I'm gonna broaden out. This is why I'm so into this project. And this is why I love the help you're giving me and the connections and the cinematography. It's an area of my life … I used to paint as a young fellah. And you know I'm very interested. It's been a tough couple of years, Rudi, and I won't cry on your shoulder. So I'm getting through it. Don't worry. And what's sad for me is I've got … I'll tell you when I see you. But I've got some good stuff there. And I'm not a quitter. But sometimes it gets … and I'm in this hotel. My apartment, flat, it's my space. And I never had space as a young person. Hamburg, Spain and Ireland, I never had a room to myself. So I won't let anybody in there. It's a bit psychotic, I know, but I'll get it fixed. And I'll move."

Mark Feltham: "He was ultimately a very generous man. I'd seen him in many occasions where he'd stop a conversation in mid-sentence, walk across the road to give money to a busker. Always a man for the underdog. Always. A beautiful human being.

"I never, ever saw him speak rudely to a woman. Not like a rock star at all [laughs]. Absolute gentleman in women's company. In fact, if you were checking in with an airline and you were eyeing one of the good-looking girls, he would often chastise me. 'Please, this is a woman.' You had to be very careful what you were doing! He was such the absolute gentleman. And in all the years I worked with him I never heard him swear either."

Dino McGartland: "He was just like you or I. He didn't walk around saying, 'I'm Rory Gallagher.' He was the guy next door; the guy down the street. At the time, he could walk into a bar, buy a beer. He was just a normal guy. Had he been above that, the fans would never have gotten as close to him as they did. Even before a show, he'd go around the corner for a pint. And he would have met people there, talked to them, invited them back to the gig. He was just an everyday guy. Which I think was the main thing. He had time after the show to bring in the fans. Say hello. 'Did you enjoy the show? Did it sound OK?' "

Joe O'Herlihy: "Anybody that picks up a guitar in Ireland, the first thing that they reel off … Rory Gallagher would definitely be at the top of the list. In the context of why I want to be a guitar player and why this and why that."

Ted McKenna: "Most of the people I know who are into Rory have been into Rory for years."

Author: "The vast majority of Rory's fans are those that remember him as opposed to those that have recently discovered him."

Joe O'Herlihy: "That would be a very true statement. The one great thing about what's happened, and it's a sad thing to say, but the material is surfacing now in a business and an industry where accessibility is what it's all about. And I think the back catalogue and the whole thing being readily available, I think there's a huge element of good will, especially to Donal, for negotiating all that with the record companies. Getting it out there and making it happen. An awful lot of people didn't get the chance first time around because it was always very difficult in getting back catalogue on anything like that. To have renegotiated the whole thing and get it back out there is a very important thing. There's a lot of people out there who have heard from family members, 'Rory Gallagher, this, that and the other thing.' But you could never get the material. Now it's readily available. So I think there'll be a big resurgence and it's great to see that."

Charlie McCracken: "He was a very dedicated, unique musician. Some people know exactly what they want to do and how they want to do it. He was very self-centered. He led his own life. Everybody else led theirs, really. He was just a musician who wanted to continue being a musician. For as long as he possibly could."

Mark Feltham: "He was an angel sent from heaven to me. When we were doing those solos together quite often he would come over to me and I would look down at his fingers and they would be covered in blood. Especially on the last tour. He was actually hitting the bloody thing so hard in the end. And it wasn't from any drunken state. It was just passion. Right through the calluses. And there'd be blood on the scratchplate as well. Unbelievable. That guitar, when you saw it after a show … he used to reek of sweat and blood [laughs]. He was an animal on stage but a gentleman off of it."

Many fans of Rory Gallagher make a pilgrimage to Cork to pay respects to Rory and to reminisce with other fans and friends.

Marcus Connaughton: "It's very difficult to find words for it. There's a generosity of spirit with them that he would have been greatly flattered by. He probably wouldn't have known how to deal with it. But it's quite moving to see. I've been fortunate to have been living in his hometown and I've shared lots of wonderful evenings with people who suddenly picked up the phone when they got to Cork and rung me out of the blue. I wouldn't have known these people from Adam. And all of a sudden friendships had been established. I've found that at tribute shows in Holland earlier this year and in Manchester when I was over there with Barry Barnes some months ago. Dino McGartland and I have become very close. Rory's brought an awful lot of people who've never known each other together. I think that's one of the wonderful legacies that he's left."

Jack Bruce: "Rory was always highly respected. Possibly underrated, slightly. I think he was a fine player. And a hell of a nice guy, too."

Gerry McAvoy: "For me, the early 70s with Rory was a wonderful time. Everybody was young. Everything was fresh. Doing the concerts in Belfast. There was an air of excitement. There was an air of suspense. Going to the States for the first time and playing to ten people at a club in Washington, D.C. And building that up from there. Building up to mini-stadium size. That was fun. So many things stick out. So many occasions. I couldn't start to remember them all now. In the early days there was more of a camaraderie. As Rory became more popular, that started to fade away."

Rod de'Ath: "A very enjoyable time. Hard-working. A band. A band in the true sense of the word. We all worked together, supported each other, cried on each other's shoulders, had fights. We were on the road together. We were a band. And it worked."

Joe O'Herlihy: "My light from a diplomatic point of view, from a technical point of view, is Rory Gallagher. At the end of the day, he taught me everything I know or should know

or need to know in being a human. And you couldn't meet a nicer, more genuine character. And I hope what he instilled in me of my human character comes across a quarter of what he was. He was definitely a gent.

"He was extremely influential. Edge, to this day, will stand up and say the person that made him a guitar player was Rory Gallagher. He kinda looks at it in the context of a song called 'Moonchild.' Edge would break into that in sound check and everybody would join in and it would just flag me off. And they'd do their Rory imitation for the crew. Which is a testament to the guy. I mean, in Edge's mind he would have been the guitar player, the huge influence. Rory would definitely have been the person he would say, 'Yeah, that's my influence there.' "

Author: "Do you feel the renewed interest in Rory does him justice?"

Brendan O'Neill: "I think it's a bit underdeveloped at the moment. It's a very difficult thing to propel, isn't it? To keep the momentum going without an artist. And the artist that shunned, shied away from the limelight. Because he wanted to be the journeyman that he was. He was always learning. So because he didn't reach those dizzying heights of Eric Clapton and Jimmy Page and all those guys, to keep his music alive is a much more difficult thing. But I think it should be, really. When he could have been a huge artist in America, he actually took a sidestep almost. He thought that if he kept it this level, this pace, he could do it forever. So he didn't get to as big an audience as he could have. If he had played the game a bit more he would have been as big. But that was his choice."

Marcus Connaughton: "What I've done is give illustrated talks on the legacy that Rory's left. And also on the actual difficulty that someone of his age had accessing the material. Like the Leadbelly stuff, the Broonzy material, Reverend Robert Wilkins, Blind Willie Johnson. There was nowhere you could actually get access to that kind of stuff back in the 60s in Ireland. So you had to go to considerable lengths. There was a magazine called *Banjo, Mandolin and*

Guitar, an American publication. Rory used to consume that magazine because it had many of the blues artists in it. Pictures of them with certain fingerings. And he'd check out the fingerings, get a record, stick it on and practice. He was always practicing and listening out for sounds. He had a particular fondness for Son House. And his knowledge was encyclopedic about some of the Delta players. You could mention a name, and all of a sudden he'd get connections. If there was a session recorded in Austin, Texas, he would have known who was on the session. If it was Earl Hooker or if it was Texas Swing music. He knew his Texas Swing music. He was aware where this stuff was coming from, the history behind it and it meant a great deal to him. And I felt that he was carrying a torch.

"He could move from mandolin, inspired from somebody like Yank Rachell, and then move on to the Stella (1930's guitar) and getting a particular sound out of it. His bottleneck playing was amazing. And his acoustic playing, 6-string or 12-string, was just wonderful to listen to.

"I think his time hasn't arrived yet. When somebody does pass on, it takes a number of years before people rediscover. The legendary status. But he's certainly in that ballpark. It's just a matter of time before people start assessing him properly. It's only a matter of another few years before people become really conscious of the importance he had. I think also that he had a major effect on a lot of people in terms of the way they listen to music. And by the way he dressed. Many people, at the time, were looking for an icon. We were coming out of a period in our history where everything was kind of gray. And here was this guy wearing these American plaid shirts and the sneakers and the jeans and the denim jacket. And keeping the hair long. It was very unusual for somebody in that time, in Cork, to be going around wearing long hair. He kind of stood out. That was kind of a brave move on his part."

A street in Paris was posthumously named in his honor.

Donal Gallagher: "As I was referring to earlier in '94, I felt it was good to get him out and do the type of places that he hadn't been to for a while that he enjoyed. Such as France. I got Pascal Bernard to put some dates so we could go over and Rory could get a few days in Paris, indulge himself in the movies and whatever. He loved the Olympia. It was one of his favorite venues in Paris. So he played a series of gigs there. And after one of the shows this guy was looking to get a headline name to play a club called 'Le Plan,' which was in a suburb of Paris. It was its tenth birthday and he wanted to make a bit of a splash. And the request came through to Rory. Would he consider coming back to play there? Rory had no hesitation and a date was put in. Which actually wasn't convenient because I remember we had to fly from Munich to Paris during a day or two off from the German tour and honor the commitment. And did it for the guy's club. It was a great thing for him to do. And what occurred was that venue was part of some social program. It's described as the 'Marquee' of Paris if you like. Where a lot of people that have problems can go and work there through the local council or government. But they were so shocked when the news came they immediately went to the mayor and requested that the street be named after Rory for what he had done for them. And it became 'rue Rory Gallagher.' Also it housed the headquarters for the French independent promoters, all the club owners. They also wanted to have Rory's name on their stationary. So every time they sent out information, '#1, rue Rory Gallagher.' It was extraordinary.

"I received a letter in French which was stamped and authorized and notarized, as if it were a circular that had gone to a lot of people. And it wasn't a case of asking. The guy just did it. It was the most extraordinary thing for a guy to do. And it had a recall effect. In Cork the square in City Center is called after Rory. They got one in Dublin called after Rory. And there's a new area, Temple Bar, which is a nice spot in the center of Dublin. Rory had gone in and played the first Temple Bar Blues Festival, which was to help promote the area. It was an urban regeneration or whatever and he played an open-air concert to help that. So it's the entrance into that area. It's the size of an alley. 'Rory Gallagher Corner.' In Cork they were calling it 'Rory Gallagher Square.' And I pointed out that the one thing he wasn't was square! So they changed it to 'Rory Gallagher Place' [laughs]!"

Ballincollig, Southern Ireland. A reproduction of Rory's Stratocaster fret board is engraved on the right "finger" of the monument. Courtesy Dino McGartland

Phil McDonnell: "It's funny, you know. I work quite late in my job. I drive home at half-eleven, twelve o'clock. And most of the time my head is full of shit that I've got going on in my own company here. Different bands coming and going around the world, thinking about what you gotta get stuck into first thing tomorrow morning. Sometimes my mind, lying in a bath or on a plane looking out the window, staring into space … sometimes it'll just go back to those days. It was twenty-seven years for me; I was a professional on the road. There are a lot of memories in those twenty-seven years. And some of the fondest ones are from the years I was with Rory. We had some great times."

Gerry McAvoy: "It was an honor and a privilege to be a friend and workmate to such a great musician the likes of whom we will never see again. A terrible loss to us all."

STEVE MARRIOTT

"Steve Marriott was one of those rare artists who can, when you first hear him, instantly make you feel like a drought in your life has ended. It was quite a bit after my raucous youth that I first heard 'Thunderbox' all the way through, uninterrupted, and I couldn't find anybody to compare to him; to that sound, that power! Steve was his own meter, out there trying to go over the top with every number. Simply an amazing talent, tethered by nothing."

– John Keogh, September 2000

March 14, 1945. Family and friends were celebrating Kay Devo's birthday at a restaurant. Bill Marriott, in The Royal Navy at the time, was also celebrating his birthday in the same location. As glances were being exchanged across the room, Kay's father noticed and went over to invite the sailors to a party.

Kay Marriott: "My father walked over and he said, 'We're having a ding-dong.' That was the word you used in London in those days. 'Would you boys like to come along?' I think it was a Thursday but during the war, any night was party night. And they all said, 'Oh, yes, please!' And Bill said, 'It's my birthday too.' And we all hummed. But when we got married, I noticed that it really was his birthday. It's on his birth certificate."

On January 30, 1947, the Marriotts were blessed with a son whom they named Stephen. He was a hyperactive child but always seemed to find different ways to keep himself entertained. And he seemed to have a need to perform.

Kay Marriott: "Oh, yes, from a very early age. On holiday he used to go off on his own and enter the seaside competitions. And we never knew anything about it until he came back with the first prize. I think he was eight the first time he did it. My husband showed him how to play the ukulele and he entertained everybody with that. He loved it."

A daughter, Kay, was born on April 22, 1952.

Kay Mateus Dos Anjos: "He was always singing and playing his guitar. I was three as far as I can remember. I cannot remember a time when my brother was not entertaining.

"We fought like hell [laughs]. We were a normal brother and sister. Hated each other at home. Loved each other to bits. If anyone said something about him, I'd gone mad. If anyone said something about me, he'd go mad."

Kay Marriott: "At the age of ten, he progressed to the guitar. A friend of ours played in a Hawaiian band on the BBC and he showed him chords. Once he understood the concept of it, you couldn't teach him any more because he didn't want to know. He wanted to do it his way and he just went on from there. Never had a lesson after that.

"He loved it. Played it the whole time. Whatever instrument you gave him he would play. Later he even played the sitar. And he played so well. I mean, the piano. It was all chords; it wasn't just the melody. And it was good."

Stephen developed a characteristic early on that he would demonstrate throughout his life: his loving obsession with animals.

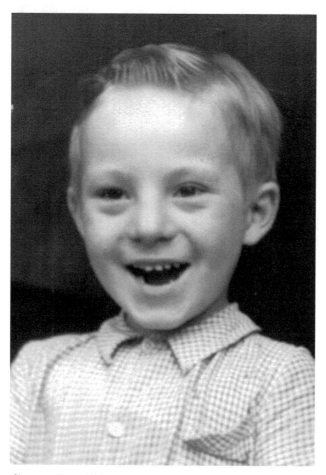

Six years of age, 1953.
Courtesy Kay Marriott

Kay Marriott: "He hatched a little duck. He saw these boys had smashed a nest and the mother had gone. And there was one egg left. So he brought this egg home. He was ten. He sat down in front of the open fireplace. And there was a little crack in it. And when we got home there was this little duck. It followed him everywhere. We put him in a big cardboard box. At night time he would jump up until he got out of this box and landed on Steve and went to sleep with Steve. He was only five or six days old. A little girl came to see it, the daughter of a friend of mine, and she picked it up and squeezed it. It died during the night and he was brokenhearted.

"Then another time he brought a baby owl home that had been abandoned. I took it to the pet shop first and they said, 'Just give it raw meat.' Which I did. But when I took it to the vet, they said it needed 'more' meat. But it was too late then. It hadn't had the right food and it died. There was a big burial in the garden for that owl. And tears. One of the

boys started laughing and Steve nearly kicked him over the hedge, he was so angry that he should laugh at something so serious."

Throughout research for this book I've discovered the importance of maternal influence on the artists of whom I write. And the recollections from these mothers don't suggest any reason to doubt the accuracy of their answers. They all possess an amazing ability to recall specific events in detail. With that in mind, I asked Mrs. Marriott to put to rest the myth that Stephen was discovered busking at a bus stop by Lionel Hart, who produced *Oliver* on the London stage.

Kay Marriott: "I've never heard that one. The only thing close to that was he used to take his guitar and go around to different flats and places, singing carols with his sister. That was the nearest I know.

"My husband worked for a newspaper at the time, *The Daily Sketch*. It was advertised in there that the theater needed boys and they wanted them with natural talents that could sing and dance and move well. We had just come back from holiday and had a picture of Steve with the guitar we had bought him. It was nearly as big as him. My husband was convinced that he would be using it as a cricket bat soon enough. But it was the love of his life, it was. Bill said, 'Send in that picture of him with the guitar just for a laugh and see what happens.' So I decided all right, not dreaming that anything would. The next we heard he had to go to an audition in the West End, at the Aubrey Theater in St. Martin's Lane. And he was accepted on the spot. He'd just gone into long trousers. He was quite small. And I told him, 'You're going to have to put your caulky shorts on. And your thumpers' [laughs]. Socks. And he said, 'No, I'm not!' So I had to tell him then what was going on. And he immediately went to the loo because of nerves. He always suffered with nerves. As soon as he got on stage, he was fine. And this was the case here. He was the only one accepted on the spot. I was so proud. I don't think Lionel Bart met Steve until he was in *Oliver*. And they became quite good friends through the years, as he got older.

"*Oliver*. He was very good. A natural. He loved it. That was a fluke. Walking in to a hit show on the West End. And he said, 'I want to do this.' I told him, 'Well, you're not going to go into hit shows one after the other. It's going to be hard. You've had no training.' My younger sister, Sheila, she gave me the Italia Conti address. And Italia Conti couldn't act as an agent without seeing what he could do. I said, 'He's been in *Oliver*.' And they said, 'That's nothing.' And I said, 'Well, he's the only one that was accepted out of all your stage boys.' So they asked would I let him go for three months, just on Saturdays, as a student, to see what he could do. I said all right. I figured that after three months of doing Shakespeare he would throw his hat in. But he loved it. They said he was a natural and they wanted him. We didn't have that sort of money. We were just a working family. And she said, 'Let us have him for a year and we'll keep him here for nothing. And for sure he'll be able to pay for himself from what he earns.' And I was so stupid, you know. Because, obviously, they were going to send him out for everything, weren't they? Getting their money back. I was so worried about him. I then had to go to work. I was a bit loath to do that. My daughter was then only nine. But he had to have £2 a day on him. He had to go to Brixton everyday, which cost money for his fare. And then there was his whole kit. All his stage stuff that he needed. All his books. His uniform. So I went to work full-time. And I think that's why we got the house [laughs]. And have been here ever since 1971."

Jerry Shirley: "Steve bought it originally and there was a mortgage attached to it. And then when he had to get out of England in a hurry one time, because the taxman was coming for something, the one thing he made sure was that his Mum's house was paid off. Lock, stock and barrel."

Steve took this as his biggest accomplishment, being able to repay those who encouraged his talent.

Kay Marriott: "Well, you help. Sometimes it's taken that the mother is pushy but I wasn't. We always worried, were always scared about the people he would meet and the different environment. But he was able to take care of himself. He'd been through it all and done it and seen it and still came out fine. I think the way you are from the beginning does help. You've got that home tie and I think it keeps an even balance. Not always but it does help.

"Whatever he went after, he got. And he more than paid for his schooling. He was thirteen when he went and he stayed until he was seventeen. And he turned down the Lawrence Olivier/Shakespeare thing. He went to the audition and he told us he'd failed. And I thought, 'Oh well, the pop is taking over.' He was getting more and more into the music. Then a fortnight later we got a phone call to ask why Stephen hadn't turned up at the theater. He'd been taken on and he'd told us that he hadn't. So we knew then that the pop had won. I think the acting, and all the training … he had done so much in films, in television, in radio, advertising. I think it put him in good state on the stage. He had presence. And I think he got that from his acting time."

One story Steve loved to tell, over and over again, was about how he had accidentally burned down his school and the newspaper article carried his head shot from *Oliver*. Not to mention the many related side-bits that would accompany the gist of the story.

Kay Marriott: "He put a match in between the cracks and there was a bit of smoke and that was it [laughs]. He's rather like his father. It's how he told a story. And each time they told it, they added a little bit on to it. They just glorified it a bit."

Author: "He said it made the newspaper and you have clippings of this."

Kay Marriott: "[laughs] No! You see, when you're young, when you're about eleven or twelve and you do something like that, when you look back on it, it does seem a big thing, doesn't it? Have you gone back to a street that when you were young was so long? And when you're older, it's not long at all!

"Steve was able, most times but not always, to say and do what he liked and be able to get away with it. If you or I were to say half the things he'd said, we'd be in trouble. But he had such a way of doing it. And he'd say, 'All right, mate, all right,' and nobody would take offense. Unless, of course, he didn't like somebody, he could be awful. I used to say to him, 'You've got to be nice to these people. They're the people that are there to help you and to push you on.' He'd say, 'I'm not going to be two-faced.' And that was it."

In November of 1962, Stephen extended his acting career with a role in an eight-part children's serial called *Night Cargoes*. In April of 1963 *Heaven's Above* was released in which Steve played a role. It starred Peter Sellers and William Hartnell, the original Dr. Who. Marriott and German teen sensation Heinze appeared in the 1963 release *Live It Up*, known in America as *Sing and Swing*. He later acted with David Hemmings in a film entitled *Be My Guest*. He had also done television on the BBC, including *Citizen James* and *Mr. Pastry*. But through it all he preferred music.

Kay Marriott: "He'd have a song on his mind and he'd get up straightaway and start playing it on the piano. And he could write it from there. He knew those notes in his mind."

Stephen incessantly practiced his guitar. He would always be performing somewhere, whether in a kitchen or an alley. He got together with a few friends and formed a band called The Moments.

Kay Marriott: "They were very good. Steve did a lot of practicing at home on his own. I got a few looks from the neighbors when I came home from work! I used to have to lock the piano up. They practiced in various boys' homes. There were pubs they could go to once they were older. I saw him play with The Moments and that was very good but I didn't take it seriously."

The band lacked decent equipment but because they played such high-energy music they had no problem getting work. They were regular entertainers at the Attic Club in Hounslow and had quite a name for themselves in Essex and East End London. In October of 1964, with the success of "You Really Got Me" by The Kinks permeating throughout Britain, The Moments recorded their own version. Through an attempt by World Artist Records management they tried to have the single released in the United States before the Kinks could get a record deal across the ocean. But terrible production squashed the attempt and the Kinks eventually attained the success that was rightfully theirs. However, the flip side, "Money, Money," achieved some success in England. The single "You Really Got Me" by The Moments is a highly valued item with collectors, and, oddly enough, *Record Collector* magazine has the flip side listed as "unknown," a sign of the records' value.

Eighteen years of age, 1965.
Courtesy Kay Marriott

In January of 1965 Steve got a weekend job at a music shop, the J60 Music Bar on High Street North, Manor Park. As far as during the week …

Kay Marriott: "Nothing very much. He was supposed to be doing acting but he was more with the groups and the boys that were playing music. He'd had a couple of days work in Lyon's Corner House, 'restaurant' as they then were. He didn't stay there very long. He smashed up more plates than he washed [laughs]."

On January 23, 1965, Ronnie Lane and Kenny Jones met Steve at the Music Bar where he had begun work just three weeks earlier to the day. After hitting it off Ronnie explained that he wanted to buy a new bass. Steve sold him one at a very low price and was fired because of it.

Ronnie invited Steve to sing and play piano with his band that night at a pub where they had a regular gig. Once he hit the stage Steve became "Jerry Lee" Marriott and trashed the piano, which turned out to belong to the pub. The band was immediately dismissed but Lane and Jones decided to stick with Marriott as it seemed that Steve was headed for a life that was sure to be exciting, if nothing else.

Steve immediately formed a group with Ronnie Lane on bass and Kenny Jones on drums. On January 25, 1965, they invited Jimmy Langwith (a.k.a. Winston) to join on keyboards, he having played with Steve in The Moments. When Jimmy introduced his girlfriend to the rest of the band, she was struck by their diminutive sizes, all under 5'6", and commented on their small faces. Being "the face," in Mod terminology, was akin to being known as "the man" in today's vernacular. Those references, along with the lyrics from "Eight Miles High" by The Byrds, "in places, small faces abound," gave the group their name: The Small Faces.

Kay Marriott: "They used to meet in my home in Allstart. They decided to do Kenny's hair in the middle to be like theirs. And he said, 'My Mum will kill me' [laughs]! They used to stand in the kitchen and I could hear them talking. What they would do if they made money. And they would always say, 'I would get my Mum a house. I would buy my Mum this.' You never heard them mention poor old Dad!"

In March of 1965, as The Small Faces were trying to find their place, Steve auditioned as lead vocalist for a band called "The Lower Third." He lost the audition to David Jones, who later changed his last name to Bowie. I witnessed an interview with Bowie where he stated he was offered the job of playing keyboards with The Small Faces and turned it down, but no one could confirm or deny this.

On May 31, 1965, after hearing about The Small Faces through other local musicians, Don Arden contacted Steve's mother and asked to set up a meeting to discuss managing the band. Since he had a certain amount of credibility because of his managerial position with "The Move," a meeting was agreed upon.

Author: "Did Steve ever talk about Don Arden?"

Jerry Shirley: "Oh, a lot, yeah. All the typical stuff, the typical stories. Hanging people out of windows and they never got paid. Just a rip-off merchant."

Exactly ten days later, on June 10, The Small Faces signed a three-year management contract with Arden. They were to be paid £20 a week and have access to an account at Lord John, a trendy London fashion store on Carnaby Street. Being a self-proclaimed "Mod" had more to do than with simple attitude. Fashion was also important.

After a few small tours Arden got them the chance to release material on Decca Records. On August 6, 1965, the Small Faces released "Whatcha Gonna Do About It," which hit the charts at number 27. They worked as much as they could and were developing quite a reputation. But there were increasing problems with Jimmy. Michael Taylor is a well-known fan and "expert" on The Small Faces.

Michael Taylor: "He started getting too big for his boots. When Steve started doing a lead guitar solo on 'Whatcha Gonna Do About It,' when they were on the television, Jimmy Langwith was waving his arms about and acting daft and trying to get all the attention onto him. From what I heard as well, they sort of used Jimmy Langwith because he was the only person who had a van to drive them to gigs and stuff."

Jimmy was by far the least accomplished musician in the band but was the most dominant in craving accolades. Once the van died, they fired him. The hunt for a new keyboard player was on.

Steve had read a concert review about a band called Boz and the Boz People, led by Boz Burrell, later with King Crimson and Bad Company. The article in *Melody Maker* raved about the bands organ player, one Ian McLagan. McLagan, because of a personality conflict, had coincidentally just quit the band. The following morning, Marriott had heard of Ian's availability and got Don Arden to telephone him and request his presence at an audition. Not only did his playing talent fit the band like a glove, their senses of humor also matched. On November 1st McLagan got the job. Though "Mac" was offered £60 a week, he refused, opting for £20 a week like the others. They started rehearsals at the Rushin Arms in Manor Park. To facilitate access for the members, they all lived at 22 Westmoreland Terrace in Pimlico, from Christmas 1965 to Christmas 1966, and the cliché lifestyle of the up-and-coming rock 'n' roll star became a reality. After a week, Kenny Jones left to live with his parents a few miles away … the only way he could get any sleep.

Kay Marriott: "That was Don Arden's idea to get them together. They can be more manageable, can't they? I mean, Mum and Dad don't know what's going on then."

Jerry Shirley: "I think Steve, in the beginning, loved Don Arden. But Don Arden was the start of the deep bitterness that Steve ended up having in him about business people in general."

On November 5, 1965, Decca released another single, "I've Got Mine." This one failed to chart and Arden started to worry. Finances wouldn't allow for another flop. He "ordered" a hit single to be written for the band. It was called "Sha La La La Lee" and was released in January of 1966. It charted at number 20 and peaked at number 3. The band was starting to be taken very seriously.

The band never made it to America. Management was quoted as saying it was due to the fact that Ian McLagan had been arrested on a minor marijuana charge that prevented the band gaining access to the U.S. McLagan contends the arrest in question didn't occur until 1967, which wouldn't have been a factor in 1966. The reason Marriott gave is that management wouldn't want the group to tour America for fear of losing control. Bands had to be booked through American agencies and the temptation of remaining in America was constantly a threat. So they never went. As a matter of fact, the band never traveled further than Belgium.

●   ●   ●

Jenny Dearden (née Rylance): "I'm from the North. I spent the first three to four years of my life in Cumberland, which is now called Cumbry, then grew up outside Manchester. Came to London to go to University College to do philosophy with psychology. Met someone who was a great friend for a long time but we've lost touch sadly because I lost my address book. A girl called Julie Driscoll. She was a secretary then for Georgio Gromolsky."

Jerry Shirley: "He was the manager of a club and also of The Yardbirds."

Jenny Dearden: "Julie started a band called Steampacket with Long John Baldry and Rod Stewart. And that's how I met Rod. Rod was my very first boyfriend. We went out together for four and a half years, during which time I packed in university. He used to walk around with this acoustic guitar in those days and play it at a pub called The Ponticraft Castle, near Lester Square. During the time with

Rod I met Steve, just as a friend, and liked him. He used to make me laugh a lot. And during Rod and my many 'bust-ups,' Steve then sort of 'declared' himself and apparently had been quite keen for a long time. We didn't have an affair; we just sort of saw more of each other. And then Rod came back and we made up again but I hadn't realized how attached Steve had become. He apparently was rather devastated. This was 1965."

Tours and television appearances occupied most of their time. The Small Faces were featured in a film called *Dateline Diamond*. By this time Steve Marriott and Ronnie Lane wanted to write their own records. They'd already had one flop with "I've Got Mine," but were determined and wrote a record called "Hey Girl." Decca released it on May 6th, 1966 and it entered the charts at number 16, peaking at number 10, the first of many successful collaborations. During this time they had been working on an album that Decca released a week later entitled "Small Faces." Their popularity soared. It got to the point where boys were adopting Steve's hairstyle. Everybody wanted to be Steve Marriott.

Kay Mateus Dos Anjos: "My close friends, who are still my close friends now, couldn't think of Steve as anything but a big brother. I loved his music but he was still my brother. I couldn't have his posters up in my bedroom, could I? And my close friends felt the same. But there were also school friends. It was a bit awkward I must admit. I loved it because I was getting all this attention but he stepped in. He'd say, 'They only want you because of me.' And I'd say, 'Oh, yeah, you're so bigheaded! That's what you think.' Obviously, he was right. At his height, I was thirteen years old. They'd ask me to meet him. To get his phone number, when he left home. And that was the difference between my friends at school. They didn't think my brother was human. 'Ohhh! Can you get me an autograph? Can you get me a pair of his socks? Can you get me a pair of his pants?' 'What? My brother?' It was very, very strange I must admit."

Kay Marriott: "The first time I saw The Small Faces I was completely overwhelmed how the girls behaved. Having a daughter of my own I used to get upset by that. It was amazing that they wanted to grab hold of them. And all I could see of my son was him standing there with his veins in his neck stuck out where he was singing so loud. And you couldn't hear anything!"

Kay Mateus Dos Anjos: "It was very mixed emotions because I was his sister watching him and critical. 'My God, that's my brother up there.' I was looking with so much pride and love and also with horror and fright. I got very frightened from the concerts and my parents did too. My father used to get up in the aisles and try to barricade the girls off. It sounds funny now but it could get very frightening because they would just surge. And you couldn't hear them play. You couldn't hear them sing for the screaming and the yelling. And you've got girls passing out in aisles and seats next to you. I couldn't believe it! I'd look at this small figure on the stage, and I'd think, 'Well, we're gonna share my Mum's toast when we get home [laughs]! With a cup of coffee.' It just seemed unreal. He was a different being, actually. Although he was my brother, you know, that I shared my bath with when we were first born. In that little poor house. That teeny bath that my Mum dragged into her teeny little kitchen. And to suddenly have all these girls screaming! So it educated me that way. And I learned to appreciate music. And people's feelings. I never went the way a lot of girls went. You know … stupid."

Author: "Are there any songs that you consider favorites?"

Kay Mateus Dos Anjos: " 'All or Nothing' has always meant so much to me."

On August 5, 1966, Decca released "All Or Nothing," their first number 1, necessitating more tours and TV appearances. By this time, The Small Faces were getting irritated with Arden, who had released "My Minds Eye" without the band's consent. They also felt Arden was ripping them off financially.

Kay Marriott: "They did work so much. They had as many as three gigs a day. If you could have seen their itinerary. It was horrendous. And the only money they had was £20 a week. This is why we said we wanted to see the manage-

ment and to find out what was going on and why they were working so hard.

"We went down and had the meeting. And Steve had told me previously that they were smoking pot. I nearly died! And he said, 'Don't worry about it. People are more addicted to nicotine than what they are to pot. And it's just something you do socially. I'll give you brochures and things and you read about it and try to understand it.' I never told his father or anybody. And when we went to see Don Arden, we parents were coming down hard and demanding to know where the money was. 'Cuz they were all under twenty-one; that was the age in those days. And he said, 'Well, you know they're all on drugs.' That's when the parents all fell about. And this is what Steve knew would happen. So I thought, 'Thank you Steve for telling me.' 'Cuz I then turned 'round and said, 'Whose fault is it then? Who wanted to take them from their parents' home? Who wanted them in a home on their own?' "

Author: "Did Arden say that to explain where all the money was going?"

Kay Marriott: "Yes. That was his answer to them being tired and overworked. It wasn't the work thing. It was the drugs and the late nights. He showed my husband and the other fathers different papers with sums of money and it was ludicrous. £2 or £3 here. £50 there. They were earning hundreds then. They had been going for a good year. Every two or three months they had a hit. And everywhere they went they were successful. They were going to Germany one minute, back in England, back up north, all in one day!"

In the meantime, the band met up with Andrew Loog Oldham, a former press officer with Brian Epstein and manager of The Rolling Stones, who, along with The Stones, had started his own label, Immediate Records. He was interested in managing the band and distributing their material. Decca released "I Can't Make It," which was supposed to be released on Immediate. But due to contractual obligations, Decca was still owed a single. The band wasn't willing to support it. Decca released another single when The Small Faces went to Immediate but the boys didn't care. They just wanted out. Oldham was giv-

With The Small Faces, Hamburg, Germany, 1967.
Courtesy Kay Marriott

ing the band free studio time, allowing them to experiment and record at their own pace. On June 2, 1967, the band released "Here Come The Nice" on Immediate Records. Mick the Nice was a dealer who sold "nice," their secret term for marijuana or speed, depending on who you ask.

Alan O'Duffy: "I met Steve Marriott and Andrew Oldham when I was seventeen at Pye Studios. The first session I ever did where I was paid as an engineer was with Steve Marriott. Steve played keyboards and guitar on the track. A very small fellow. He was great and just mad."

Jenny Dearden: "Steve was very witty. In an East End way. He wasn't just an East Ender but he very much played on that role, as a mask a lot of the time. When he had a lot of money he became much more sophisticated and had a lot more access to everything, culturally, than he had in the East End. But he still, quite often, got on that East End mask. But he wasn't that person anymore."

The new relationship with Immediate Records turned out some terrific music. "Itchycoo Park" and "Tin Soldier" gave the new partnership two Top Ten hits over the last five months of 1967. After a break for the holidays and touring, Immediate released "Lazy Sunday" in April of 1968. Steve displayed reluctance, as he was afraid it might be interpreted as a novelty song. He preferred to release "Afterglow Of Your Love."

Kay Marriott: "He always rang when he recorded and played it and asked, 'What do you think?' With 'All Or Nothing,' we said straight away, 'That's a hit.' And then with 'Lazy Sunday,' he was going to go with the other side. And his father said, 'No, I think you should do 'Lazy Sunday.'' So he said, 'Don't be silly, Dad. That was just done for a fun song.' And he said, 'Fun song or not, there's so much humor. It's a very clever song. And it's musical too. It will take off. The other one won't get airplay to get people to know it.' 'Oh, you don't know what you're talking about.' And the next thing we'd heard, they'd released it as a single.

"He never realized how much his father loved him. I don't think boys do, do they? They don't get hold of them like Mums do. Give them a hug and kiss. Steve and I always hugged and kissed. He always kissed his father but there was always a reserve with it."

Jerry Shirley: "I never quite understood where he and his Dad were at. From the point in his life when I knew him and his Dad, he worshipped Steve and everything he did. However, Steve apparently had a bit of a rough go of it as a young man with his father. His father was quite tough on him. But then again Steve was such a little bugger he probably needed it. Knowing what I know about Steve, bless his heart, it wouldn't surprise me if his parents had been somewhat heavy-handed with him as a youngster 'cuz he was a handful."

During this time ex-Yardbirds guitarist Jimmy Page took the task of getting a band together to fulfill contractual obligations and wanted to continue with these musicians in a new direction. His first order of business was to hire a singer to front the band.

Jerry Shirley: "Jimmy asked Steve if he would be interested in singing in a band with him. At that time there was talk about Keith Moon being involved and possibly John Entwhistle as well. But in any case, whatever the lineup that was offered to Steve, whilst he was flattered to be asked, he gracefully passed. At the time he was pretty involved in The Small Faces. And he was probably a bit, 'Ooh, I'm not sure about this. Keith Moon on drums? Could be a bit iffy' [laughs]! I mean from a madness point of view, not from a good player point of view. He probably didn't think there was a lot of credence in Keith leaving The Who. And I could never have imagined him doing so. Sure, The Who had their legendary fights but the four of them were as thick as thieves. They were like brothers. Absolutely one of the genuinely closely-knit bands that I ever knew. They may have fought amongst each other but you wouldn't want to say something against any of them to another member.

"With the way it was put to Steve, it was not, 'Here's my band, John Bonham, John Paul Jones and me. Do you want to sing in front of it?' It was prior to that. Whilst he was very flattered, it wasn't his cup of tea."

Author: "According to research, it's said that you used to go to Small Faces gigs in short pants."

Jerry Shirley: "That was more of a euphemism for how young I was [laughs]. I probably was still young enough that I was wearing short pants to school at that time, when I first went to see them but not to the gigs, no. I was going to see the gigs as a fan first and soon thereafter the band we were playing in, my brother and I, were opening up for them locally.

"I was born outside of North London on February 4, 1952. I started playing the drums when I was nine years old. I had gone into hospital for appendicitis. Actually, I pretended I had appendicitis and I did a particularly good job. A week later I didn't have any more appendix [laughs]! And for a coming out present, my father gave me a kit of drums.

"My influences were mostly all the black American blues/R&B, all the Stax stuff. Hal Jackson, being the drummer for Booker T & The MG's. Mitch Mitchell I loved. Kenny Jones, Keith Moon. Tony Newman was a huge favorite. Bobby Elliott of The Hollies. I was looked upon as a child prodigy but everyone looked up to me as I did up to them. It was flattering, really.

"I dropped out of school nearly two years before you were supposed to. My mother was a teacher so, legally, I could leave with the understanding that I would get tutored at home. I was fourteen years old. I started making money very young. I had my first professional paying job with the local college band who were all grand old men of eighteen, nineteen years of age. They had heard of me through the grapevine. The Key Tones! No shit! I even inherited the original drummer's uniform, a blue satin shirt which was way too big for me. They had to tuck the sleeves in the shoulders to make it fit. And a silver tie and black pants. God, it was awful! A couple of years later I spent a lot of time in Cambridge, playing around, which was a lot of fun. That's how I came to know the Cambridge lot. David Gilmour, Syd Barrett, Rick Wills, Tim Rennick and all those guys. A great place to be.

"When we first came on the scene, the band we had at the time was The Valkayrie. Very soon thereafter we changed our name to, of all things, The Little People. We became a Small Faces knock-off band; a copy band. Once we got to know Steve Marriott and the lads from The Small Faces as friends, from being fans and from opening up for them on gigs, one thing led to another and he offered to produce and write a single for us. It was a song called 'Have You Ever Seen Me' that he and Ronnie Lane wrote and it was presented to Immediate Records for release. And Andrew Oldham said, 'Yes!' We became a part of the stable by then but he didn't like the name. So he changed it to Apostolic Intervention. Why, who knows! We could have been called The Cheese Boxes, for all we cared. As long as we had a record out."

Jenny Dearden: "Steve was always paternalistic, kind and helpful in those days. He was a lovely man. Rod and I split up … finally. I ultimately had the strength not to go back again and I started working and getting my own life together. The last thing I wanted to do was get involved with another musician. But Steve literally pursued me for about a year and a half [chuckles]! I finally relented because I liked him so much. And finally I grew to love him because he was a very lovable person."

On May 31, 1968, Immediate Records released "Ogden's Nut Gone Flake," which went straight to number 1. The band had caused fanatical response akin to The Beatles yet in a much more confined area of the world. The shows were as frantic. And Steve was developing his talent at a rapid pace.

Kay Marriott: "They were just a joy to watch on stage. We went to the Rainbow. Saw him there many times. We went to the various Odeons where he performed. My mother was so thrilled. She went to most of the shows. My stepfather used to go with cotton balls in his ears [laughs]. He couldn't stand the noise! But he had to see him perform. Everybody was proud and very supportive. There always used to be about ten of the family there. He used to like to ring us when we got back home, to ask us what we thought. He knew we'd tell the truth. If it was good. If he was a bit over the top. Or a bit drunk [laughs]! But he was always a good performer so we didn't have to lie."

Author: "How did he interpret his own talent?"

Jenny Dearden: "I don't think he did interpret it. I think it was purely spontaneous with Steve. He became more aware of it as time went on. It was pointed out to him that other people thought he was talented. He wasn't the sort of boy or man who spent time analyzing or interpreting. It might have been much better if he had. He did live for the moment. He didn't really pause to think very much. He'd be working on a riff for quite a long time. He'd have it in his head and it would just come out. He wouldn't spend days sort of agonizing about it. It would just happen. And quite often, when he was writing songs about us for instance, he would leave the last verse until there was some sort of resolution. And then he would finish it off."

On June 28, 1968, Immediate released another single, "The Universal." Steve started to feel that the Small Faces had reached their peak and that they couldn't follow up "Ogden's Nut Gone Flake."

In the summer of 1968 Steve and Jenny got married, putting a legal stamp on a truly authentic romance. They purchased a home called Beehive Cottage and began an ideal existence.

As The Small Faces gained more critical success, the screaming subsided enough so that the band could actually hear themselves. Steve's biggest fear came to light. He was already convinced that the band couldn't reproduce their studio efforts on stage but he had never thought that the live performance was so void of sound. Coincidentally, Steve met someone who was building up a solid reputation for himself.

Peter Frampton: (b. April 22, 1950) "I actually met Steve at his and Ronnie Lane's house. They were living down the M-4 in Marlowe, on the way to Oxford, basically."

After developing guitar skills taught to him by a student of his father's, later to be known as David Bowie, Peter began playing with several bands in his native area. He played with The Little Ravens, The Truebeats and The Preachers, who were managed by Bill Wyman.

Peter Frampton: "Bill Wyman was the manager of the first band that I made a record with, which was The Preachers. He had been introduced to The Rolling Stones by Tony Chapman who was in The Stones at the time. And for whatever reason Tony was asked to leave and Bill stayed. Tony was replaced by Charlie Watts. Bill's a dear friend. He's like my older brother. The most loyal, honest person you'll ever meet. And he just felt that he owed Tony Chapman big time. Bill said, 'If you put a band together, I'll produce it and manage it.' And he did. We had a record out and we were with The Rolling Stones on their 'Ready, Steady, Go' special. It was the only 'Ready, Steady, Go' that was ever taped because of their availability. We went up into Michael Lindsey-Hogg's, the director's, office and I was rubbing shoulders with Mick Jagger and Keith Richards. All of The Stones and our band were up there watching ourselves. So that's how I got to know The Stones at a very early age."

At the age of sixteen, Peter quit school and joined The Herd. They gained a fair amount of success in a short period of time, earning three Top 10 singles worldwide, excluding North America. Frampton was named "the Face of 1968." Frustrated with being cared about for his looks as opposed to his music, he quit, searching for far more credible musicians to work with. Meeting Marriott suited them both.

Peter Frampton: "They had heard that The Herd … [laughs] were having trouble with management and business and all that sort of stuff."

Author: "Was that 'R&R Productions?' "

Peter Frampton: "Yeah. Ronnie Oppenheimer. Phillips/Fontana were the record company. We were being screwed but we didn't know who was doing it so we got rid of everybody. At that particular time The Small Faces were going through a lot of the same. Probably as much, if not more. And I think they'd called Andy Bown up and said, 'Do you want to get together? Maybe we can give you a hand.' Which was very nice. So Andy and I went down to Marlowe, met Ronnie Lane and Steve and their wives. I was a huge Steve Marriott fan, had always been ever since I first saw The Small Faces. And that would have been the ideal band for me to join, you know. Which almost came true, which is so weird."

Steve spoke with the other three members of the band. Frampton was who they needed. He would fill the void in the live sound and lend a high harmony to Steve and Ronnie. He would also take over major guitar responsibilities as Steve could concentrate more on his singing. But the band turned him down flat. Not willing to further divide the already meager salaries, there was to be no expansion and they didn't want it discussed again.

Peter Frampton: "Steve wanted me in, the other three didn't. That's the way I took it anyway."

Steve had confidence in his belief in Frampton's talent and wanted to help give it a chance to progress.

Jerry Shirley: "I used to go visit Steve at his cottage in Essex. I was living in Cambridge at the time and playing with Tim Rennick and Rick Wills, amongst others. He called me one Sunday afternoon and said, 'Come on down. There's a friend of mine here I want you to meet, Peter Frampton, from The Herd. He wants to put a band together.' So off I went and met Peter, who proceeded to come up to Cambridge to see me play in the band I was in with Tim and

Rick. And then he offered me to join his band. Or help him form a band of his own."

Peter Frampton: "Steve told me that I should do something else because I was wasting my time with The Herd. He said, 'I've got this drummer that every now and again, if Kenny's ill or something, we've used Jerry to sit in …' I met up with Jerry and we enjoyed working together and were soon looking for a bass player and a guitarist."

Jerry Shirley: "At this point Steve was still in the Small Faces, helping us find people to play in the band. It dragged on for a long time and we weren't finding anybody else. I said, 'Well, why don't you consider using the rest of the band too?' Which was Tim Rennick and Rick Wills. But he didn't like that idea. I was trying to get my mates involved because they were great players and they were friends. After that, nothing really happened."

On Nov. 14, 1968, Immediate released a Small Faces album, "The Autumn Stone." It failed to chart. The screaming stopped. And once they could hear themselves, Steve felt justified in feeling that the band just wasn't good enough to play live. He brought up the Frampton option again but the others wouldn't have it. On December 31, The Small Faces were playing a New Years Eve gig at Alexander Palace. During the show, while Alexis Korner had joined the band, Steve became infuriated at the inability to reproduce a stage sound equivalent to their studio work. He dropped his guitar and walked off the stage, yelling, "I quit!"

Jerry Shirley: "I wasn't there but that was it. Steve walked off stage and he was done. He quit the group right there and then. I did see Ronnie and the guys within the months that followed and there was a lot of bitterness about Steve leaving. Understandably."

Jenny Dearden: "I was with him the night he walked off the stage at Alexander Palace and said, 'That's it!' It caused a lot of bitterness between him and Ronnie, which they never really resolved. It was very sad that he and Ronnie had a terrible rift because they had been so close. But I don't think he was aware of it. Underneath, as with most people, his self-esteem was not that high at all."

After walking off, Marriott was backstage commiserating with Greg Ridley, bassist for Spooky Tooth. The two shared a mutual frustration with their current lot in life.

Greg Ridley: "We were both pissed off. We'd realized we'd both reached a peak. Bitchiness had come in to the various bands with personalities involved. They'd tried getting so far with it and gotten tired of it. Or tired of the members of it and wanted to go further on. Steve had said, 'Do you want to join a band?' And I said, 'Yeah, I'm ready for a change.' With his energy … he was a real live wire and that's what got me interested. It seemed Spooky Tooth had taken it as far as we could without any reward. Everybody had said, 'Aww, they're a good band,' but we were still living on the bread line. We got respect through our playing, which was very nice, but it didn't get us anywhere. It was time for a change."

Steve told him of Frampton and asked Greg would he at least be interested in getting together and jamming. Ridley was all for it. Aside from Frampton's talent to work with, Steve wanted to find himself in a band where he could stay in the background. He was fed up with girls screaming at him for wiggling his ass. Frampton could be the focal point.

Jerry Shirley: "The night before we went to do our New Year's Eve gig, I had told the rest of the members of the band that I decided that I wasn't gonna pursue the thing with Peter. It didn't seem like it was going anywhere. And we went and did our gig, all happy because old school pals sticking together and that kind of thing. We got back to my parent's house after the gig and the phone rang and it was Steve. He literally said, 'How's everything going with you and Peter and the band?' And I said, 'It's kinda going a bit slow. We can't find anybody else to join us.' And he said, 'How about if I join?' And my first reaction was 'OH, NO! You can't do that! You can't leave The Small Faces!' And then I got over the shock of it and went, 'OK.' Then Steve said, 'By the way, I have a bass player who wants to come along with me, Greg Ridley from Spooky Tooth.' And that sealed it for me. Not as if Steve being in the band wasn't enough already but at that time Greg was the most respected bassist in all of England through Spooky Tooth. So I had to go back to the band, and say, 'By the way it looks like I might be leaving after all.' I told them why and they were all great. 'Oh, well, you can't turn that down!' "

Peter Frampton: "I was at Glyn Johns'. He'd said, 'You've gotta come back. I want to play you this record that I just finished recording and mixing. It's a new band that we started and finished recording in ten days.' He put it on and I said, 'Who is this?' And he said, 'Led Zeppelin.' This was a momentous occasion all 'round. The phone rings after side 1. My jaw is still on the floor. Not so much from the guitar, though obviously I was thrilled with that, Jimmy's guitar. But Bonham's drumming. I'd never heard anything like it. So anyway, the phone rings and Steve says, 'We just did our last gig at Alexandra Palace, my last gig with The Small Faces. I walked off and I'm leaving the band. Can I join your band?' And I said, 'Well, of course!' So I wasn't going to play with The Small Faces but at least I was going to be in a band with Steve, which was great.

"The following day, I get a phone call from Ronnie Lane. The three come 'round and ask me to join The Small Faces. So I said, 'Why couldn't you ask me this when Steve was still in the band?' So I guess the pocketbook can lead to short sightedness because that would have been some band."

Jerry Shirley: "We were rehearsing in my parents' living room within a matter of weeks, if not days."

Peter Frampton: "It all happened so quickly. One day I was looking for some band members with Jerry and then the next moment Steve was making a phone call and we were forming Humble Pie."

Greg Ridley: (b. Oct. 23, 1947) "Elvis Presley, Little Richard, Bill Haley. When I started we used to play on washboards with thimbles and a tea chest with a string and a broom handle for the bass. It was called 'skiffle' early on and slowly progressed to the rock 'n' roll. Elvis really shook it up for me. I've got to put it down to him.

"I lived in the outback in England, in the countryside. You didn't have TVs or much music. Yer Dad might have played the violin or the piano at Christmas but that was as much musical influence as there was. My brother and my sisters used to play the old 'croony' records that they used to get. But the old rock 'n' roll really shook me up and I knew what I wanted to do the minute I heard that music. 'Rock Around The Clock' and 'Jailhouse Rock.' Yeah. 'Heartbreak Hotel.' That really stirred me! And from then all I wanted was a guitar and sing and play, out in the sticks where I lived.

"I knew that Steve was in a very successful pop band. Spooky Tooth was kind of a heavy, underground type of band, a 'bands' band' rather than a pop group. Which was a hell of a difference over here. We never would have gotten on the charts. But I did realize Steve was a powerful force with the Mod movement. I did see him play live one night before I joined forces with him. I thought he was dynamite! For a little guy to have so much balls! And voice and energy! It surprised me; it was terrific!"

Jerry Shirley: "We thought, 'All right, let's pick a song, any song. Let's see how well and how quickly we can do it.' We chose a song from The Band's 'Big Pink' record, a song called 'We Can Talk About It Now.' We had it down real quick and real well. And that's what made us realize that we had something to go on. So the thing to do next was to find a label and someone to take care of you."

The original idea for the band never wavered. It was a vehicle to promote Peter and Steve was more than happy to play some guitar and throw in backup vocals.

Jerry Shirley: "Steve went out of his way to say, 'Look, this is perfect for me 'cuz I don't wanna be the front man in a band anymore. I just want to be in the background, kick back and support you.' And it was that that made Peter say to himself, 'OK, that's great.' He couldn't ask for more than Steve Marriott as a backup singer and backup guitar player."

Peter Frampton: "I wanted to play with Steve anyway, in The Small Faces. So if it meant doing it without the rest of the guys and forming a new band, then so be it. I had no worries about being in a band with Steve. I was looking forward to playing guitar with him."

Greg Ridley: "Steve was always the main man. For such a little guy he was like Goliath on stage. His voice was so powerful and he had that little strut and stuff. Peter was kind of the pretty face of the band. Steve was the energizer. Jerry and myself, we were the heavyweight guys providing the thump behind it."

Jerry Shirley: "As soon as we started playing from the day we first met, we could have played blindfolded. It was uncanny the way Greg and I played together. We didn't plan it. We didn't sit down and say, 'OK, in this bar, you and I are going to hit this thingy.' It just happened. We stuck like glue together."

Greg Ridley: "He wanted to bang the drums and I played the bass in the way I did, with a bit of heavyweight there. And it came together nice. We got along, personality-wise, and it was great."

Peter Frampton: "Oh yeah. Jerry and Greg … we all enjoyed playing with one another. It was like being released from all our other bands. And it was like raw energy. We were just going for it. It wasn't necessarily going to be pretty [laughs]. It was just going to be what we all wanted to do. So, having been a huge fan of Spooky Tooth, I was thrilled that Greg was going to be part of it. His great voice as well. But the two of them together … it really clicked."

Jerry Shirley: "We were very backbeat, a very hip-swinging, sex, drugs and rock 'n' roll type of rhythm section. One of the primary wants the band had to have. A rhythm section that just jumped out and grabbed you by the crotch. That's exactly what Steve wanted it to be like and I think pretty much Peter too. And certainly Greg and I did [laughs]."

Greg Ridley: "We just came in with a smile and said, 'Fuck it. Let's just do it. Let's put some weight and some tight, good moves in here and get on with it.'"

Jerry Shirley: "Greg and I were all from the hip. Au naturel. And that was the primary function of that first rehearsal. To see if the rhythm section was all we thought it was going to be. And not only was it, it was better than that."

Greg Ridley: "It was very strange because no one knew what to expect of each other or what sort of direction to go in. We were all kind of tenderfoots, all tippy-toeing around at the time, before we really knew what kind of music we were gonna make. We'd never played together before."

Jerry Shirley: "You have to remember I was sixteen years old, almost seventeen, so I was on top of the world. This was the absolute cream of the crop, musician-wise, in England that I was playing with. And they happened to be my favorites. I was a huge fan of the Small Faces and Spooky Tooth and had become a good friend and fan of Peter Frampton as a musician. Once I got to know Peter and found out how good a player he was … I remember thinking all the time at rehearsals, in the studio, that I was the luckiest guy in the world. I was playing with the greatest rock 'n' roll band in the world. And there were times, musically speaking, when we hit peaks that confirmed that belief."

Author: "Who came up with the name 'Humble Pie?' "

Peter Frampton: "Steve."

Jerry Shirley: "Steve decided that the way to get a name was that we would all come up with different ideas. Write them all down on bits of paper and put them in a hat. And then write them all down on one big bit of paper and look at them all at one time and choose from those. When I saw the short list, I saw 'Humble Pie,' which was one of Steve's suggestions, although I didn't know that. And I said, 'That's the name.' And we all agreed. We were almost certainly going to be touted as a 'supergroup' because everybody in the band was well known, except me. Blind Faith had just come out and everybody was calling them a supergroup. We were trying to avoid that kind of hype and Humble Pie seemed appropriate.

"We had just put the band together. Brian Jones had only just been kicked out of The Stones. Brian called Steve Marriott to say, 'What's going on? What's happening?' They started talking and I guess Brian showed some interest in checking out the new band with a view to maybe getting involved. Steve was all excited because Brian was one of his heroes and invited Brian down to our next rehearsal. The next thing we know Brian was found dead in his swimming pool. 'July 3, 1969.' As far as I can remember he was supposed to literally come down the next day or at least within a couple of days after that. It was a real shock. Apparently he was very keen to hear the band and possibly join. From what I know now about the condition Brian was in, I'm pretty confident to say it wouldn't have worked. We would have probably figured it out. It would have been very awkward for someone that you looked up to like that to have to realize that they were so far off scratch and would have had to say, 'No, you can't join.' "

Peter Frampton: "And Ian McLagan, Mac, was so close to being in the band. He had written a song that we did on the first record, 'Growing Closer,' and I don't know what happened. I guess at the point where we were gonna say, 'OK, come on in,' that's when he and Ronnie Wood and Rod Stewart hooked up and became The Faces."

Jerry Shirley: "It took a little bit of sodding around to find the right label but it was always going to be Immediate. They had everything that we wanted in our label. They had the management skills, they had the money and they had the artistic freedom. They allowed their bands to write and produce their own records, which is what we wanted to do. We did do some shopping around. There were other people that wanted us. Island Records made a stab at it. And so did Track Records, with the Who's manager, the late Kit Lambert. A wonderful old pouf from the 60s that I had met before Humble Pie. He tried to get his evil way with me one night and I said, 'Thanks, but no thanks' [laughs]. This mad fairy would go to The Speakeasy and chat up the up-and-coming musicians and offer them an opportunity to go back to his apartment. To discuss their future and see if they would be interested in signing with Track Records. And if you were stupid like me, you'd go, 'Oh, great.' Until you realized, once you were there, what he really wanted. And if you were like me, you were on your bike and out the door real quick and in a cab. 'See ya' [laughs]!

"But he was a dear old thing, though, Kit Lambert. A very far-seeing man, actually. I remember exactly what he said to me, that night he was trying to get the better of me and didn't succeed. He was out of his mind on coke or something and out of nowhere he looked at me and said, 'The future of rock 'n' roll is in video!' And this was in 1967. For a man to sit there out of nowhere and say 'The future of rock 'n' roll is in video,' and video was barely invented at that time, was quite something.

"Andrew Oldham had the advantage of having Steve signed. So if he wanted to be a bitch about it, he could have put his foot down and said, 'Well, you're signing with me anyway.' But he didn't approach it like that. He wasn't the enemy. We knew him well. The Small Faces had just been given some tremendous artistic freedom that allowed them to make 'Ogden's Nut Gone Flake,' the best album that they ever made. It was number 1 in all of Europe. He'd already had me signed, not that it made all that much of a difference, with Apostolic Intervention. So it was a no-brainer. Andrew was the most excited to sign us even though he had the upper hand. Still, he was offering us anything we wanted. The fact that you got artistic freedom was the most important thing. And they were a young, hip company. And their receptionist was really good-looking with great legs! And they had enough money behind them to support us.

"We were making £60 a week when we signed with Immediate Records. Of which £20 a week got put into a savings account for each one of us and the other £40 we got. And that was big money back then. We got all the equipment we wanted. We got the road crew we wanted. We got the truck we wanted. We got all the recording time … you name it we had it. That's what we asked for, that's what we got. It was the equivalent to an advance. If you add it all up, it amounted to quite a bit of money."

Author: "Were you expected to pay those expenses back?"

Jerry Shirley: "Well, I don't know, to be honest with you. It never came up. Probably we would have, had any serious accounting been done. Our royalties would have been, 'Here you are lads. Here's your royalty statement and here's what we've spent.' So it would have ended up like getting an advance. It never got to that."

Greg Ridley: "As far as business is concerned, I'm the thickest bastard on the planet. I never paid any attention to contracts and agreements. I always felt that somebody else would spot the discrepancies. Usually I'd sign them and read them later and find out, 'Oh, oh. Bad news.' You try to be trusting because everybody's making money and you don't think you're gonna get ripped off. You think there's enough of it about that no one wants to take advantage. But that's how it went. I'm absolutely useless at paperwork, as my accountant will tell you [laughs]. You usually get to sign them at the wrong time. When you've just done a good gig, you come off the stage when you're a mile high and you don't know if you're signing for a washing machine or signing your life away."

Author: "After not making any money with The Small Faces, it was strange that Steve stayed with Oldham and Immediate Records."

Jerry Shirley: "Well, really it was more Don Arden than it was Andrew Oldham. All the big hits that came before Immediate, 'All Or Nothing,' they never saw a penny of that money. And they did get ripped off by Immediate too, to some extent. But that's why Steve hated himself so much about the business. He was such a trusting soul back then and then it came back and turned him sour on everybody. Obviously, some of the choices he, and subsequently we, made in business came back to haunt us something wicked. And certainly made him a very miserable bastard; bitter person. And what it did do was turn him violently against any person who was remotely business-oriented. He just didn't trust a one of them. He developed a wicked anti-Semitic humor as a result of it. Although curiously, seldom, if ever did Jewish people mess with him. I wouldn't want to repeat the black humor that he chose to develop about our 'chosen few' brothers, if you like. It was very funny; you had to laugh. But I thought he went a bit too far sometimes."

Greg Ridley: "The record company, Immediate, had faith. They handed us a lump of cash. It was the first time I'd ever seen any money in my life through playing rock 'n' roll or whatever you want to call it."

Peter Frampton: "We knew we were going to be called some sort of supergroup because of Blind Faith. I guess there were a lot of bands, at that time, that had been in one form and become successful. And then they were fed up with each other and they were leaving bands. And then their members were all forming together. So there were a lot of different bands regrouping as other bands at that time. But seeing that Steve and I were from pretty big bands, and Greg as well on slightly a lesser scale with Spooky Tooth but still pretty big, it was pretty obvious and we knew that. So we tried to steer away from any commerciality at that point and never really wished to release a single."

Greg Ridley: "I said, 'Let's do a simple 12-bar shuffle thing,' and we wrote the lyrics right there and then in the studio, and did 'Natural Born Boogie.' I don't think it was ever released in the States but it got in the Top 20 over here anyhow. That was the first thing we did. We didn't know whether to go sit on the stools and smile or go and give them a bit of the hammer. We just didn't know what each other was capable of at the time."

Peter Frampton: "But, of course, the first single that we released went to number 2, or whatever it was. And we did 'Top of the Pops.' And the thing we abhorred the most was being screamed at and of course it all started all over again. That's what we formed the band to get away from."

Greg Ridley: "We didn't know what direction we were going in. We didn't know what we were gonna sound like. Early on we started sitting, doing unplugged stuff.

Acoustics, sitting on a stool, which you never saw. Then we developed into one of the heaviest rock bands in the whole world. We wanted to get louder and heavier and more cocky. But, at first, we just put directions in a hat and would see where we went. And, fortunately, Immediate Records could afford us the time to go and try it out."

Everybody, except Jerry, was married, avoiding the classic situation of communal living amongst band members. Steve and Jenny had the cottage, which housed another building where Greg and his wife lived. Jerry shared a place with Peter. And Peter's wife.

Peter Frampton: "Well, it wasn't supposed to be with my wife as well [laughs]. I'd left my wife. Or we were split up at that point. So to start with we had the house together. In Chiswick. Then Mary and I got back together and she moved in. So I'm sure it was more irritating to Jerry than it was to me."

Author: "Cramping his style."

Peter Frampton: "Exactly [laughs]!"

Jerry Shirley: "Oh, she's the world's worst, Mary Lovett. They were a pair of prats together. I preferred Peter away from her, to be honest with ya. He was much more a nice guy, down to earth, one of the lads when he was away from her. When he was with her, he was socially conscious. Worried about keeping up with the Jones' and who was who and all that. I did share an apartment with Peter and his wife for a while. I had half the apartment, they had the other half. But that didn't last very long."

Author: "When Steve first moved to Essex was he around as much?"

Kay Marriott: "Oh, yes. He moved about ten miles away from us. He was always here or on the phone. And that's when he wrote 'Just A Phone Call Away.' He used to say to me, 'Mum, I'm only a phone call away,' if I said, 'I've not seen you. What's going on?'"

Jenny Dearden: "The music was always the goal for Steve. Not ever the money. When we bought our cottage in Essex we had to borrow £500 from somebody because he didn't have the money. It was always the music. He never thought about what was happening. Hardly any of us did then, did we?

"I honestly think that the time we spent at the cottage, when we literally had nothing, we had our animals and us, and we were struggling financially, we were the happiest. The Small Faces had nothing at the end. After all those records that they sold and all the gigs they had done, they had no money. I think Steve had about £1,000 and I had a little bit and that was it. I think that was the happiest time that he had. Without that pressure of being that person that had to be the frontman, and the one with all the energy and the one that had to be, you know, wise guy, East End, tough little Mod sort of thing. And it was the calm before the storm."

•   •   •

Jerry Shirley: "The main problem we had, business-wise, was not finding a label. It was getting Peter out of his contract with those people that had The Herd. These two guys that were songwriters/managers/producers, had Peter tied up. Andrew and Immediate Records had to buy Peter out of his contract. Till such time as that was fixed, it delayed things a little bit but it never actually stopped anything."

Peter Frampton: "I remember being bought and sold. I wrote that in one of the songs. I believe that Andrew had to buy me from Ronnie Oppenheimer. I don't know how much I was worth in those days [laughs]! It was in 'Take Me Back,' in the bridge I sang that. Basically, he was manager and record company with Tony Caulder. We never really liked Tony Caulder. He was noncreative. Whereas Andrew Oldham obviously started his career as a publicist, he always had great ideas and he was sort of a cool character. I still like Andrew. I'm sure he screwed me for money along the way [laughs]! But I find him still an interesting character."

Jerry Shirley: "We recorded the first one really quickly and it was in the can. The only thing that was holding it up was getting the right cover. And while we were waiting we just kept recording. And we kept recording to such an extent that we had another album done. Back then everybody recorded quickly even though we were taking our time, compared to previously. But it was still done quickly, if that makes any sense. And studio time back then was very cheap. It was just an expense that was absorbed by Immediate Records. We had limitless recording time. Olympic Sound Studios is where it was mainly recorded. If not there, we would be in Morgan, which had just opened. And Island Studios. We were just forever recording."

Peter Frampton: "Steve was a prolific writer to say the least. I was not as prolific as he was at the time. Greg was writing and Jerry was writing. And then there was all the numbers we liked of other people that we could do whenever we wanted. It just kept on coming. Buddy Holly numbers, old blues numbers. Muddy Waters numbers, everything. We did the whole gamut [laughs]. It was great. It was 'anything goes,' when we first formed. We were almost too diversified to get a handle on what we did."

Immediate Records not only encouraged songwriting but self-production as well. And when Pie felt they needed help in the studio, Oldham allowed the band to decide on who should guide their work.

Jerry Shirley: "Andrew, Andy Johns at the time, had already accrued a large amount of experience and was coming up off the tails of his older brother Glyn. We got involved with Glyn Johns and Andrew Johns because they were the house engineers at Olympic Sound Studios, that Steve Marriott and Small Faces had used."

When Humble Pie began to perform live they opened their sets with a twist. Though the band possessed a strong rock base, they started their performances acoustically.

Jerry Shirley: "To intentionally take away the attention from the little girls screaming at Peter because of The Herd. We tried to come off 'laid back, man' [laughs]! You know, start slow and easy and drift into this. To take away from the non-musical, screaming at them because of the good-looking side of that business and try and focus on us being musicians playing acoustically. It kind of did and didn't work."

Peter Frampton: "Also, we never did our hit single, which I never quite understood [laughs]. The point was we were basically saying, 'Look, we've got a hit single but we're not gonna do it because that's not what we want. We don't wanna be a pop band, we wanna be a rock band.' And the danger of being screamed at was becoming a 'girlie' group again. And we didn't want that."

Greg Ridley: "Steve and Peter had a lot of that. I didn't have the screamers. I came from more of an underground band. Remember, Peter was the 'Face of '68.' He was a real pretty boy. And Steve had a lot of success in the pop charts. Mostly they came to scream and to see if you had a bulge in your pants. So we tried to make it a bit more credible and let them know that we could all play our instruments and make good music without all the screaming. They would all scream at Steve and Peter. Jerry and myself, it was only our mothers screaming at us [laughs]! We didn't want them to all go away. But if they'd shut up maybe they could enjoy the music as well."

Jerry Shirley: "We did that little acoustic thing just to try to throw them a curve. To calm them down. To force them to listen. But because Greg was in the band and because Steve also was a highly respected musician, there was an equal element of the audience that did come to listen anyway."

Author: "How important was it to get to America?"

Greg Ridley: "England's so small and you've already made your mark from the stuff you'd done before. With all the screams and things it was necessary for the band to have a breath of fresh air and a bigger market. And to be able to prove to ourselves that we could actually play and sing for real. Without the hype."

Jerry Shirley: "That was the thing. Everything else was secondary. Steve and Peter and Greg had already had success in England. Humble Pie's primary concern, once we got the initial release of the records out in England, was just get to America. That was our total focus."

Author: "What were you hoping to find?"

Greg Ridley: "Fame and fortune. And a fresh challenge. To break the States, for an English band, you're doing very well, as very few do. We just wanted a fresh place to play without all the screams."

Jerry Shirley: "Lots of gorgeous women, lots of drugs. And you got to go visit places like Chicago and New Orleans, where all the great music came from."

Peter Frampton: "We virtually shut up shop in England around the time of 'Natural Born Boogie.' And we did go to America with Andrew but that was sort of a failure [laughs]."

Jerry Shirley: "Oldham was there. Not all the time. And if he wasn't there himself he made sure that someone was. He helped put together the idea of recording some stuff live at the Whiskey A Go Go. He took us to some great parties in Los Angeles when we first got there. Made sure we stayed in decent hotels. We were fairly well looked after considering the limited amount of income or money that was available at the time."

Peter Frampton: "By the time we got to the west coast we couldn't afford to pay the hotel bill. There was a Ramada Inn on Sunset. I remember getting back to the hotel, finding my suitcase outside the room, packed by somebody else and the door locked. My key no longer worked. Some of us had tickets to go back; I'm not sure if we all had our tickets. But it was touch-and-go whether we got out of the country. Finances were so low at that point."

Jerry Shirley: "The majority of the 'first U.S.' tour was opening up for The Moody Blues or the odd show here and there opening up for Santana at the Fillmore East. Then we'd do club dates on our own. That lasted for about six or eight weeks."

Peter Frampton: "I think it was a success as far as 'here we are' in America. But we didn't solidify who we were at that time. It was only one tour. It wasn't until we got hooked up with Frank Barsalona and Dee Anthony that things really started to happen."

Jenny Dearden: "I think it's always instilled in bands that they haven't made it until they've gone to the States. I didn't want to go at all. I hated being on the road in any way, shape or form. But Steve got to New York and called me up and said he hated it. There were girls sleeping in the corridors. He couldn't handle it. And could I go out there? So I finally agreed to go out and I met him in Los Angeles. And loathed it. There's no place for a girlfriend/wife on tour. You're just an appendage and slightly in the way all the time. At least they have the fulfillment of going onstage."

Author: "Did people know who you were or did you just play for whomever was there?"

Jerry Shirley: "A bit of both. Word of mouth had gotten around a lot and there was quite a bit of street knowledge, if you like, about the band already. In fact, although they hadn't been huge, Steve had been known by the way of The Small Faces having had a hit in America 'Itchycoo Park.' And Greg had been over there with Spooky Tooth. So we weren't total unknowns. But we weren't hugely well-known either."

Author: "Were you quickly adopted by the people you met?"

Jerry Shirley: "Very much so. Both musically and sexually [laughs]! The groupies couldn't wait for us to get there and the musicians were there to hear what this band, Humble Pie, were going to be like. There was a lot of very healthy and pleasant folks amongst the ranks.

"It was a rude awakening, coming to America. 'Cuz until you came here, you didn't realize how much work was involved in breaking America. Unless you were very lucky and had some kind of instant hit record, which didn't happen that often, coming here was a real eye opener. It's a huge country. You could tell by observing other bands and how long it took them that you were in for a good two or three-year stretch of nothing but touring before you started to crack the ice."

Greg Ridley: "They'd seen it all there. They'd had all the best and still have all the best. It was a good apprenticeship, going to the States and realizing what they like and what they don't like and what they'll put up with and what they won't put up with. That's what got us on the road to being one of the heavier adverts in the game."

Jerry Shirley: "The first tour was chaotic because the U.S. representation that we did have was this real mish-mash of people who were working for, and on behalf of, Immediate Records. There was no organization at all, really. And what we did not realize, until afterwards, was as we were doing our first tour of America, Immediate Records were quietly falling apart at the seams, businesswise. By the end of the tour we were informed, 'Well, it was nice to see ya but we're going bankrupt. The receivers are being called in. Have a nice life.' "

Author: "Were you given any warning from Andrew Oldham that that was going to happen?"

Jerry Shirley: "A little bit. He did keep us as informed as he could. And he was very good about helping us at the end of that tour, when it was quite obvious that Immediate Records was going under. He helped us get away from them and immediately to A&M Records for a fat amount of money. It was Andrew who said, 'Look. I want you to get in touch with Jerry Moss.' It was Andrew that got in touch with Jerry Moss and said 'Here, take this band.' So Andrew did us a tremendous favor there. We almost literally walked straight into a half-million-dollar record deal because of Andrew's recommendation and our abilities as well."

Peter Frampton: "It was a very nice gesture. We would have been unable to make a record and he knew that. He was basically giving us our career. Which I thank him for. On the other hand he kept the publishing [laughs]. So we don't thank him for that but I guess that was an asset that he had to keep. He had to give 'something' over to the Official Receiver, as it were."

•　　•　　•

In 1970, upon returning from America, Peter and Jerry performed on George Harrison's "All Things Must Pass" album.

Peter Frampton: "George and I had become friends through a mutual friend, Terry Doran. George's first production, outside The Beatles, was Doris Troy's album, 'Ain't That Cute.' So I met him by playing on that. Then he would call me up and ask me to come down to Abbey Road. I lived around the corner in St. John's Woods. I've always said that it was just that I could get down to the studio quicker than others [chuckle]. I came in and joined the chorus of acoustic guitars, which was George, Badfinger and myself, amongst others. And either Ringo or Barry Morgan on drums, Klaus Voorman on bass, Gary Wright on keyboards … I mean it was just great."

Jerry Shirley: "I was at Greg Ridley's house and the phone rang and it was Peter. He was at Abbey Road. He said, 'I'm down here recording on George's record. We need a percussionist.' I said, 'I don't really know one.' And he said, 'NO! YOU, ya fool' [laughs]! So I said, 'Oh, OK!' He said, 'Come on down. We need someone to bash a tambourine.' So I went down. There were two middle sections, a middle-eight and a bridge, on two songs. Real straightforward simple stuff. The two songs I was on were 'If Not For You,' the Dylan song, and 'The Ballad of Sir Frankie Crisp.' And that was the sum total of my involvement. Peter played on more of the record than that. He was down on those sessions several times. Eric Clapton was on the whole record, I think. If I remember rightly, that particular night, both Leon Russell and Billy Preston were playing. And then some brass players, that section from Mad Dogs & Englishmen. I think Jim Keltner might have also been playing drums. Big session. Might have been twenty musicians."

Peter Frampton: "The best memory I have of those sessions was looking over and seeing Jerry standing in between Ringo and Jim Keltner playing tambourine [laughs]. It was great! And of course, his tambourine at the other end of the microphone from Phil Spector sounded like cannons going off!"

Jerry Shirley: "The only thing I had to keep checking was to see how far my jaw was dropping the entire time I was there [laughs]. Everywhere you looked it was another hero. And they were all so nice. Very down to earth. I remember being in absolute awe of the whole thing and I remember everybody being very dear and sweet. Everybody getting along with the business of making a record. A lot of tea being drank. It was very organized and laid back at the same time.

"I remember George Harrison telling Phil Spector off … very slightly. We'd done a number of takes of one of those two songs. They all pretty much sounded the same. And Phil Spector wanted to keep doing takes. Ringo started to look at his watch because he was running late. I remember Ringo saying something to the effect, 'Well, can we hurry this up? I'd like to get home for me tea.' And George making a point of telling Phil Spector that he needed to get a grip with all these takes we were taking as Ringo needed to get home for his tea. It was very remarkable to be in the company of all those heroes."

Author: "Were you paid for it?"

Jerry Shirley: "If I was, it wasn't why I was there. Typically, when anybody plays on a session like that they get paid so that they can't come back and make claims on future royalties. But I don't remember if I got paid or not. Some of the other sessions I did for heroes of mine, I would eventually get a check. And I remember thinking, 'Why did I get paid for this? This was a privilege.' But you would normally get a session fee. I remember that happening with B.B. King. I got paid but I never cashed the check. I didn't keep it, either [laughs]!"

•   •   •

Jerry Shirley: "Once we got home from the first tour, we found out how bad it was. Immediate had in fact gone broke. We had no representation, no management, no money. Larry Yaskiel, the English head of A&M, came to see us several times and offered us a deal. It was for about $200,000. Right around that time, because we were also looking for management, Chas Chandler got involved. Jimi Hendrix's manager, The Animals. And he, very cleverly, got Atlantic

Records involved and it became a bidding war between Atlantic Records and A&M. A&M said $200,000, Atlantic came to see us. Went away. Came back and said $250,000. A&M came back and said $300,000. It kept going until it got to $400,000. A&M offered that and we said, 'Yes.' "

Peter Frampton: "The A&M signing was without Dee Anthony altogether. He was not a part of that; did not get a percentage of the record deal. When I was involved with Humble Pie we set up four separate offshore corporations. Limited companies. And all of the money that came from A&M, the advance, was split into four and went into four separate accounts. So there was never any problem there."

Jerry Shirley: "It was yearly advances adding up to $400,000. $133,333 per year for three years that we divided between the four of us. And we saw two of the three. We saw the first year and the second year. And that was the last royalties I personally ever saw. We represented ourselves. Along with an English lawyer whose name I can't remember.

"Danny Farnham got brought on board to help us as a road manager and suggested that we speak to Dee Anthony. Danny had road managed Spooky Tooth and had met Dee in 1968 or '67. They had worked with Dee Anthony on that tour, that's how come we were introduced to Dee."

John Doumanian: "I was at Columbia as a regional manager. I was the head of Phillips promotion for the U.S. Then I went to work for Rod McKuen for a couple of years in Los Angeles, taking care of his music publishing. And then I came to New York to work for a kid named Stevie Tyrell. He was the national promo guy with Scepter. He had a label and we managed B.J. Thomas and Barry Mann. Then I went to work with Bill and Dee Anthony in rock 'n' roll. Humble Pie was the first group I worked with. Never a problem. At the end, when all that other stuff started to come in, that's when it was a problem. That's when it was a joke."

Peter Frampton: "As far as signing a management deal with Dee Anthony, 20 percent of nothing is nothing so I had no reason at that point to really question. We were just so

thrilled that this big-time manager had introduced us to this huge-time agent and we were definitely going to get some visibility from this situation. As far as I was concerned, 'What could be bad about this?'"

Jerry Shirley: "Dee was the hottest manager in the business at the time for our type of rock and roll band. Spooky Tooth, Traffic, Ten Years After, Emerson Lake & Palmer, Spencer Davis Group. He had all, or part of, the management of all of those groups. He had his finger into everybody's pie. And he was great. He was really good at what he was. The one guy that you pretty much knew if you went with him, you were guaranteed to have at least a fairly decent amount of success. But most people either got away from him once they started to do well or they chose to ignore the warning signs. I loved him, Dee. I thought he was great. And it's only now I realize, 'Oh man, if only he'd let me have me royalties, I'd be doing fine.' "

• • •

Author: "When you went back to Olympic Studios to record the first album for A&M, you went in with songs that had a chance to cut its teeth on a live audience, which you hadn't done with the first two albums because you wrote them on the road. Was the energy easier to draw from because of that?"

Jerry Shirley: "Yeah. By the time we got in to do the first album, we were fast leaning towards being the already-nurtured-on-stage type of band, as opposed to before, when we were still finding our way. We were now a hardened road band. We also still had that softer, Peter-side of us in the studio, figuring out arrangements. If you listen to that first album, as there is with the first couple of albums for A&M, there's very much a bit of both. You can obviously see that we've been out on the road rockin' and rollin,' but there are still quieter, softer, more arranged type of songs. Songwriter songs. And that's where the divide started to become apparent, though we didn't see it at the time."

Greg Ridley: "I can't remember those times either [laughs]! It gets you that way; rock 'n' roll. You get a bit of amnesia. It could only have done us good. We realize that we had to go on a different course to achieve the objective that we had set for ourselves."

Author: "You went from Andy to his older brother, Glyn. Was that due to a budget increase?"

Jerry Shirley: "Maybe that was partly it but more so it was time for a change. And we wanted to work with Glyn because Glyn was so good. Andy Johns had become very busy, a bit burned at the time. And it was just a natural progression. Glyn was just someone we all had such great admiration for."

Peter Frampton: "The person that was responsible for changing the approach of Humble Pie to making records, which worked its way into live, was Glyn Johns. I remember him just getting us all together and saying, 'Look. You're too diversified. It's all very well that whatever somebody writes, you record.' He said, 'I think what you have to do is look at your best points and make a meal of those.' The list of things that we had was Steve was one of the world's all-time greatest singers so he should be the singer. Which I thought was a terrific choice. We all wrote, I was the lead guitarist that did a bit of singing, Greg was the bass player, did a little bit of singing, Jerry was the drummer. That was it. Those were our jobs. Now let's make a record."

Author: "What kind of feedback were you getting from A&M in terms of how they perceived your potential success?"

Jerry Shirley: "They were always very supportive. I don't ever remember, in those early days, being pressured by them to go one way or another. It was all very much 'go your own way' with record companies, especially A&M, back then. They were very much into developing a band. They weren't in a hurry to have the first record be a million-seller. They expected you to take four or five records to cut the cake and that's exactly what happened."

The first order of business, once Dee Anthony was involved, was to properly prepare the band for a triumphant return to America. Dee was adamant about dropping the acoustic opening. He knew the U.S. market and his resumé more than gave him the credibility to insist that his wish be carried out.

Jerry Shirley: "Yes. Very true."

Greg Ridley: "I probably said, 'That's a bloody good idea! Why send them to sleep when you first go out?' Drop the bloody acoustic and just get out there and hit them in the head."

Jerry Shirley: "I think Peter might have not been thrilled with the idea but by that time Steve was being … forced is not the right word. And manipulated is not the right word either. He was being 'nurtured' back into being more of a frontman again, not the front man, a frontman with Peter, as opposed to the frontman in front of Peter.

"In the beginning Peter was all right with it. But Steve was such a powerful … once you gave him the go sign [chuckles] he was so powerful on stage that no matter how good you were you would seem to be secondary to him. So immediately when he took over, the acoustic stuff was out the window. In America anyway. And the rock and roll, hard, kick-em-in-the-ass from no one direction was the way Dee wanted us to go. And that's the way we wanted to go. Except for Peter. And Dee was right. He was brilliant at nurturing a band live on stage. That was his forté."

John Doumanian: "Dee was fabulous. Motivated. Drive. The whole thing. Got what he wanted for the bands. I mean he fought for those guys. He was always screaming at the suits. He was great. I always give him credit for that. He was a great motivator. He'd get in that dressing room and pump you up and all that."

Jerry Shirley: "Dee had a gold whistle that he would blow on the side of the stage when you were flaggin' it [laughs]. And right before you'd go onstage he would give you the great American football coach pep talk. 'I wanna see you leave a pint of blood on that stage!' It absolutely worked. He would take us to a coffee shop afterwards. Or in between shows 'cuz at the Fillmore you'd do two shows a night. He and Frank Barsalona would take us off to Ratner's or something like that, right next to the Fillmore. They'd dissect the show, song by song. 'Now, move this one up here. Open with this one. Put this one back here. Get rid of this one.' And they literally, between the two of them, with our input, completely and entirely built the set that became the Fillmore East show."

Author: "When you went back to America, after the first A&M album, what was different?"

Jerry Shirley: "Well, first of all, we were different. We had a record company that had their shit together on the road. Promo guys showing up. They still left a little bit to be desired 'cuz we still were proving ourselves but it was a night-and-day thing. Around number two we had started to become a really good band onstage by this time and they were becoming very much excited for us and along for the ride. They cared, record companies back then, on helping develop the band live. They would have input, they would have A&R people who would maybe suggest things on stage. They were involved and that was a plus for us; that was enjoyable. And they always had great drugs. None of us knew what we were getting into with the drugs. All we knew was that we liked to smoke a lot of hash 'cuz it was fun and it made music sound good. But as far as the hard drugs go, it was new to all of us."

Author: "Would they approach you with drugs or would they wait until they were asked?"

Jerry Shirley: "Both. Depending on the rep. Some you knew. Some you'd be expecting to be showing up. There was a guy in Boston with the reds or a guy in L.A. with the coke. You got to know them. You've got to remember that back then was the height of the drug culture and everybody did everything. You were only weird if you didn't."

Greg Ridley: "We were all indulging more and more in things you shouldn't do. But there are certain things you need when you're caged up in a hotel room like a bloody animal all day long, waiting for that hour to go out and kill. So you take all sorts of substances to enable you to get through the day. We all delved into things and quite heavily."

Author: "Was Steve capable of keeping things in check on the road?"

Jenny Dearden: "Not really. I think it would cause anyone to lose their perspective. It's madness that kind of lifestyle, isn't it? You can't ever grow into yourself. You can't have any contact with any sort of routine. There's no base that you can go back to just to have some space. You're never on your own. I think it's an impossible and very destructive lifestyle. I think it's all right to do it twice a year, perhaps. I mean, they were on the road a lot more than they were at home for those two or three years."

John Doumanian: "We had a good time. They were all terrific guys to be with. The little pot was always stirring with Steve. You never knew what was going to happen. Most of the time we stayed in Holiday Inns and I'd go to the desk to pay the bill. Which usually was $300 for everybody's room. And they'd say, 'That's $900.' 'WHAT?! Oh, the telephone, $600!' It was Steve. Nobody else! Greg would never have anything. Just the room charge. Jerry was OK. But Steve, forget it. That was the shocker all the time."

Author: "Going out on a stage and staying away from the acoustic openings, you were obviously getting more energy from the crowd out of the box. How much more exciting did that make it going out to play?"

Jerry Shirley: "One fed the other. The better we got, the better the audiences got. The better the audiences got, the more the word spread. The more the word spread, the better we got. There was no MTV. There was very little airplay. It was all word of mouth, live. I can remember very clearly, around spring to early summer of 1971, when all of a sudden it went from where we would normally go on stage to a polite introductory response to as soon as we walked on stage and Humble Pie's name was announced, the place would start going nuts. The vibe was out. The reputation was starting to precede us."

Author: "Was Peter showing any discontent?"

Greg Ridley: "I never noticed. He was a lovely guy and everything else. I'm amazed at what he achieved afterwards. It was fantastic. But he was never a heavyweight guy. He didn't go for that. He was kind of different. He was brought up different, I guess. I don't want to be derogatory at all; he's a very nice guy. His roots were kind of different from the rest of the boys."

Author: " 'Rock On,' was recorded and mixed very quickly. Excess of material or was it pressure from the record company to get another album out?"

Jerry Shirley: "The speed with which it was done was because there was plenty of it. We just kept coming and coming. We did have an agenda; we did have a schedule. 'Let's get a record out by this time.' But I don't remember feeling pressured. It all found its own level. We had the material. Sound check writing or motel room writing. We had almost played all of it on the road. We had a time frame to go and record it. We had tours organized to back it up. It was all just falling into place."

Author: "By listening to 'Rock On' it seems fairly obvious that the indulgences were starting to show up in the studio."

Jerry Shirley: "At that point, yeah. Up till then, we were just a bunch of young punks. I was nineteen; everybody else was between nineteen and twenty-four years old. And we were still primarily hash smoking. Drinking. Let's have fun. Really, the main drug of choice was the music. We were just overwhelmed with the obsession of the band being as great as it could be."

Upon the release of "Rock On," Humble Pie was starting to receive something new to them: regular airplay on American FM radio. With the advent of this format the radio stations were given free reign to play whatever they wished and Pie was definitely on everyone's lips. Upon their return the band noticed the difference.

Jerry Shirley: "It was a powerful difference. You could taste the difference. Going home for Christmas before 'Rock On,' making 'Rock On,' and having it already being played on FM radio. Now we were walking into halls where we were getting a response just for walking on stage. They knew some of the material, either from the FM or because we had already been playing it on the road anyway. From 'Rock On,' onwards, at that point in America, we had become the band to see. All the bands were talking about Humble Pie. All the record companies were talking about Humble Pie."

Peter Frampton: "It was just a steady build, to be honest. When we first came over with Frank Barsalona being the agent and Dee being the manager, that's when we realized the old tried and tested routine of playing in front of as many people as you can in the shortest period of time really started to work for us. I would actually say that, from my perspective, the live show sold the records. Yes, by the time 'Rock On' came out we got more airplay. But I still maintain we were our own promotional team. We built up the following live far more than radio. We set radio off, if anything. We were very much a performing band. We were playing so much. We were based in the New York area when we came over because of Dee and Frank. You'd get a call on a Thursday. 'Tomorrow night, so-and-so's dropped out at The Fillmore. You're in the middle spot.' 'Oh, OK.' That happened all the time. We had a residency at The Fillmore East. It's definitely why we recorded there."

Greg Ridley: "We weren't immediately aware of it. Nobody told us except for the audience's reaction. As I say, Steve was like Captain Marvel out there. And we realized that they wanted to go higher and higher and have a lift and have a good time. We got to realize this just in time and started rocking! We were all capable, what with me and Jerry in the engine back there, because we had the power. Especially Steve. He always had it. And that sort of pushed Peter over the edge then, with him deciding that he wanted the gentler stuff. We certainly realized that we gotta lay it down here, give it some energy."

The tour wasn't without incidents.

Jerry Shirley: "The spring of '71, the 'Rock On' tour. We were playing the typical Whiskey A Go Go four-night, two-shows-a-night, type of deal. And we were fried. We had been on the road for a while. We weren't looking forward to it because it was a lot of hard work. It was the first night. After the show, we went up to the notorious Whiskey A Go Go dressing room. We're hanging out doing our late 60s/early 70s typical rock band thing and in walks a typical 69/70s Los Angeles groupie, looking rather tasty but very wasted. As I recall she was wearing black hose, red shoes and a short mini-skirt type of look. She proceeds to kind of fall, in an elegantly wasted fashion, onto the big old-fashioned couch that was in the dressing room. Seductively stoned, if you like. But no one felt inclined to go there. We went, 'Oh, nice. A bit too stoned.' What no one noticed was she was smoking a cigarette. As she was sitting there, it proceeded to crawl back into the couch. I found this out years later.

"We all leave the dressing room. I don't know what happened to the girl. She was probably helped out by someone. We went back to our hotel, being the Hyatt House. I got a phone call at four in the morning from our road manager, Dave Clarke, saying, 'The Whiskey A Go Go is burning down. They seem to have saved the equipment.' The next thing we know, there's a picture on the front of The *L.A. Times*, 'Whiskey A Go Go Burns Down,' and there's our name on the billboard surrounded by flames. And the record company jumped all over that. 'Humble Pie Hot … blah, blah, blah.' I had mixed emotions about it. First of all I was relieved that my drum kit and the rest of it got saved. Second of all, I was crushed at dear old Elmer and Tony and all the guys at The Whiskey who had been very kind to us. Their club had burned, which was a bummer. And I have to admit, as would everybody else if they were honest, I was kind of relieved that we didn't have to play for the next three nights [laughs]! Because it was brutal. Two long sets per!"

Greg Ridley: "I remember the Fillmore with Bill Graham in San Francisco. You didn't dare pick up your drink if you put it down because they'd spike it and you'd smash your bloody brain out! There was shagging going on and drugs going on! There were these great guys around like Taj Mahal and Ry Cooder and Grateful Dead and stuff. It was just outrageous! Loved it [laughs]!"

John Doumanian: "Bill Graham was always getting them all these great things in the dressing room. And they'd say, 'Oh, Bill's great. What a great guy!' Hey! You paid for it! Bill Graham had this stage in Oakland that he'd sell to everybody for $100,000. 'It's yours, take it.' Well, what the fuck were we gonna do with it? But he charged you a hundred for it. And then he sold it to the next guy!"

Jerry Shirley: "Everything was decadent back then. The more it became that way, the more we got into it. There were people that were starting to drop like flies. Jimi was dead. So was Janis. But it was all so new. You got to remember the mind-set back then. If you weren't drinking and drugging, if you were straight, you were weird. Now today it's the other way around. If you're drinking and drugging you're a fuck up and you're weird. And everybody is Mr. and Mrs. Corporate Rock Band America now. But back then, no. Everybody was high. It was fun. Everybody was involved in each others' music. Everybody was attentive to each other. Very friendly, healthy, competitive rivalries amongst the bands. Everybody stood on the side of the stage and watched the other bands and all that good stuff."

Bryan Adams: "Humble Pie's 'Rockin' The Fillmore' was 'the' album. It was probably the pivotal album for me as a live musician. The intro to 'I'm Ready' is a stand out."

Author: "Was it Dee's idea to do a live album?"

Jerry Shirley: "Yeah. Oh, absolutely. He had a very clear plan and the live album was absolutely the whole root and branch of it. All designed towards making that record. Where it was made, by whom it was recorded. Everything was absolutely planned. And it turned out exactly as Dee had anticipated it to be.

"It was intentional to get Eddie Kramer, to get the 'Electric Ladyland' mixing facilities, to do it at The Fillmore … everything about it was planned to a 'T.' And all based upon his prior experiences with Joe Cocker and his Mad Dogs & Englishmen and such. And though we weren't the first to do it, we were in the vanguard of those who used the live album as a platform to become huge. 'Course, our ex-guitar player proved it was the way to make the biggest record, being Peter a few years later.

"We knew the time was right. So then Dee went to go book us at The Fillmore one more time. Which gives us the summer to mix it. Which means releasing it in the fall. That was the 'crème de la crème' of our time. That summer, as we were heading into the recording of the live album, we were getting better and better, doing bigger and bigger shows. We were building like we'd never seen us being built before or since. It was very magical. Everything was going right. All the plans that we were making and everything that Dee had said he was going to have us achieve was being achieved. We were A&M's golden boys at the time. We were absolutely on a roll. Far and away the most sparkly time of the band's existence.

"Then we realized once we'd recorded it and taken it back to England and mixed it that we'd fucked it up. We'd mixed the audience right out of it. Dee came over and listened to it and we thought we were done. 'OK, next step. We press it and release it.' And to his undying credit he said, 'Where's the audience?' We all sat there and said, 'What do you mean?' What we'd done is we'd mixed it like you would a studio album."

Author: "Wasn't Eddie Kramer involved in the mixing?"

Jerry Shirley: "No, not in the first run of mixes. We did it in England with Andy Johns, if I remember rightly. In Olympic. Completely away from the New York/Electric Ladyland/Eddie Kramer environment. And we didn't put the audience microphone up, which had a hell of a lot to do with the ambience sound of the record."

Peter Frampton: "You know, I don't remember that. I remember … yeah! I sort of remember something like that. I don't remember who mixed it first. I guess it was us. When we did the mix … yeah, I'd forgotten all about that!"

Jerry Shirley: "We decided that we would have to re-mix. And we were about to go out so we would have to re-mix it in New York while we were on tour. And there was some 'to-ing and fro-ing' going on between Peter and the rest of the band about mixing. He wanted to mix some of it on his own, 'cuz I think he felt his guitar pieces would be better if he had closer control."

Peter Frampton: "I remember the editing session of 'I Don't Need No Doctor.' It was Dee, Eddie, me and Steve in the big studio at Electric Lady. It was seven minutes long, eight minutes long and we had to get it down to three and a half [laughs]! Dee said, 'If you want it played on the radio, you've got to edit it down.' I remember Eddie would be like the messenger. 'Well, should we lose the guitar solo?' 'No, no,' I'd say. Then he'd say, 'Well, we can lose a bit of the harp solo.' Steve would go, 'No, no, no' [laughs]! Dee would say, 'You want a hit' [laughs]? Eddie's going with a piece of tape around his neck, 'Should I put this back in or should I leave it around my neck? Do I throw it away?' In the end I sort of sided with Dee and said, 'Steve, we'd better do this, you know.' He never wanted to do it and I understand why. I guess I was trying to see, 'OK. If this enables us to get 'Rockin' The Fillmore' on the charts, this will enable us to be the headlining band that we want to be.' And of course it did. It opened everything up for us."

Jerry Shirley: "We did a song at the time called 'Walk On Gilded Splinters' that was about thirty minutes long. And there was a long guitar solo in the middle of it. At least a fifteen-minute guitar solo. The overall performance from the first night was fantastic but the guitar solo performance from the second night was better. What we did was we cut the entire solo from the second night and edited it into the overall performance of the first night. The tempo was exact, the tuning was exact. It was a real stunning piece of editing. It was amazing how well it fit. You could never tell. We were astonished because even though you play a song night after night and there are similarities, the fact that the tempo would be exactly the same and the fact that the tuning was the same…! That was before the wonderful world of electronic tuners. We tuned by ear and by tuning fork. The possibility of a slight variance was a lot greater back then but it was perfect."

Peter Frampton: "That's right [laughs]! Unbelievable! If you hadn't have told me … now I remember, yeah. Unbelievable!"

•   •   •

Jerry Shirley: "In the first year and a half of Dee being our manager, apart from doing everything that he did, I have to say quite brilliantly, to build us in America, his primary concern behind the scene was to work us to the position where he could renegotiate our existing deal because he didn't have a piece of it. Once he'd renegotiated our existing deal, he got all of it. And I, nor any of us, ever saw another penny [laughs]. We saw the money being spent on things but it got channeled differently. It used to come from A&M, through our lawyers and directly to us. But from the point in which it was renegotiated, it went to Dee Anthony through his lawyers and that was 'goodbye royalties.'

"Very cunningly on his part, he said, 'We're going to set up a corporation, of which you are going to be employees, for tax reasons.' And he was going to be the sole proprietor, the sole officer. As soon as we signed those pieces of paper, we effectively signed, in perpetuity, our entire rights away. That was it. End of story. Everything we did, as Humble Pie, was no longer a four-shared business partner in the group. We were just the employees of a corporation and it was our job to supply our musical services to that corporation. And it was the corporation's job, contractually, to supply the services of Humble Pie to A&M Records."

Author: "Why was this contract not shown to someone?"

Jerry Shirley: "Because we were too busy watching the cocaine and brandy going in one direction while the contracts were going in the other. And we foolishly trusted our manager at the time. We did not understand the complexities of independent representation. We didn't even understand that it was illegal, in fact, to be represented by the same lawyer as which your manager was.

"As soon as it was all signed, we had our doubts. But we just chose to ignore them because everything by this time was doing so well. We had two huge hit records. We were flying around the world in Lear jets. We were, as far as we were concerned, part of the best band in the world and we were on our way. And why should we not trust these people because they had done all of these wonderful things for us. We worked for everything but any time we wanted something it was gotten for us. We didn't understand the long-term manifestations of signing away your life. The theory of it sounded great. But by the time the practice came into place we were on such a roll and so friggin' high that we could have been told the moon was green and we would have said, 'Fine. Where's the blow?' By the time the actual deal was inked, as they say, all we cared about was playing rock 'n' roll and partying.

"My personal doubts were in the structure of that deal. I thought we were spending way too much and that the deal would never hold up. Because as fast as we were earning it, it couldn't have possibly have been invested the way it was supposed to according to that deal because we were spending it too quick."

Author: "When everyone realized that this was a very bad deal, did you guys ever have one of those gatherings where everybody was blaming everybody else?"

Jerry Shirley: "Oh, several of them. I have to say something about that. I say to this day the deal was not, in theory, a bad deal. It was just that the practice of it never worked. Dee and everything that had to do with the group was spending so ridiculously much more than our bracket of earnings really could sustain. Everything was heading for disaster. On reflection, I'm not so sure that when Dee put that deal together he sat down and put it together that it would screw us. I think he himself had the best intentions. And I think it was almost by default that when we fell apart the deal fell in such a fashion that Dee was the beneficiary. I'm sure some of it was designed so that he was protected but I'm sure a lot of it happened by accident."

Author: "Were you aware of the situation you were falling into?"

Greg Ridley: "No, not at all. Dee was just a very amusing guy that seemed to know what he was talking about. He had confidence and he could get you into the right spot at the right time. We had to start at the bottom over there, open shows and stuff, but at least he could get you on the right shows. If half of the audience that had come in to see the main act were there by the time you were on, then that was great. That was a guaranteed audience. You had a chance to go over there and kill 'em. He was very amusing and very capable of 'doing the thing.' He was a good manager."

Author: "While the band were evolving into their excesses, was Steve not cognizant of how little was being paid to the business? Did this not bother him at all?"

Jenny Dearden: "Well, the time I knew that we were going to not be so much in tune, because he used to talk to me about everything, was when, suddenly, they were taken on by new management."

Author: "Dee Anthony."

Jenny Dearden: "Yeah. I felt right from the start … and this is nobody's fault but Steve's and the rest of the band. They allowed themselves to be taken over by someone with a very forceful personality. And I understand that. They were all hugely impressed by his track record and his connections with various other aspects of life in New York. And this is where any influences I had over Steve and his business affairs were waned to the point of nothingness, really. I mean, to me, it just smacked of total irresponsibility. To have management with the same accountant, the same lawyer … it just seemed sordid to me. But there was nothing I could do about it.

"Steve didn't want to know. All he wanted to do was play the music. And he wanted to have this 'father-figure,' I suppose. It's about growing up, isn't it? It's about being responsible. And none of them did that. And I think it may not have been just them. It was the era as well. I don't think it was the thing to do. I mean, there are exceptions. The Stones. They got ripped off for a time as well. But Mick was at the L.S.C. (London School of Commerce) and they did have more of a disciplined grounding. But this lot didn't. They were just having a wild time, did far too much coke, day to day. I'm sure other people have said the same. And it doesn't put you in the frame of mind where you're able to deal with anything. The more tours that they did, the more they had to fuel themselves with anything that was available to keep going. They were absolutely exhausted! I think they did something like nineteen tours in three years. Nobody could sustain that, I don't think, without some help from one source or another."

Jerry Shirley: "I don't really want to say bad things about the man in as much, and I've said to you before, Dee was a great manager. He was a great motivator. He was just a horrible accountant."

Author: "I understand he could be very entertaining."

Jerry Shirley: "Dee could sit and tell you wonderfully funny, riotous stories all night long. He had Tony Bennett stories. He had Frank Sinatra stories. This was fascinating stuff to a twenty-one-year-old kid in the early 70s. Sinatra was still such a big star. And *The Godfather* had just come out and all of that. He had stories about all that side of his life. He had stories of when he was in the Navy. When he was a kid on the streets and this Sicilian thing and this Mafia thing. Very funny stuff. His brother too. Bill. They were a great double-act. In fact Bill, in his own way, is more entertaining than Dee. Bill's a very classic, New York, almost Woody Allen-ish humor. Very funny guy. Bill was Frank Sinatra's roadie for a while and they were both on the road with Tony Bennett all the time. So there was pretty funny stuff. About crawling the streets of San Francisco at four in the morning in limousines looking for chicks. Tony Bennett and Dee grew up together. Dee was Tony's first road manager and actual manager for a while. They parted company and Dee went into rock 'n' roll. And he threw a good party. He knew how to keep you happy. He was great. I loved the man. I absolutely adored him. And then it all kind of went wrong. We were as much to blame as him, honestly speaking.

"But right around that time it was coming to a boil as far as the personality differences in the group. It was getting a little too heavy-handed for Peter's liking, onstage and generally speaking. I remember he went to New York to mix one of the tracks but he also wanted to go to socialize because that Bangladesh concert was happening at the time. He wanted to go to New York and we were in God knows where, Iowa, or something like that. I remember there being a rift about that."

Peter Frampton: "We'd do weekend gigs and the guys would stay out, wherever we were. You'd usually do Thursday, Friday, Saturday, Sunday. And then I would fly in to New York and it would just be me and Eddie Kramer. I remember doing 'Hallelujah' and all that, just the two of us. And George Harrison had me come up to either The Pierre or The Plaza. 'Hey, how ya doing? Good to see you' and all that. He just gave me a guitar; there was a bunch of guitars in the corner of the suite. And he had every Beatles album known to man on the record player. Then I realized he was going through the numbers that he was going to do at the Bangladesh concert. So we sort of played through them. Which was mind-boggling to me. Here I am with a Beatle playing Beatle numbers. He said, 'Give me a number where I can get a hold of you.' 'Cuz I said to him, 'Do you need another guitarist 'cuz I'd love to play.' He said, 'No, Leon's brought in Eddie.' Jesse Ed Davis or whatever. So I said, 'Well, OK.' I was really bummed, you know. Like I had any cause to be bummed!

"So I go do my gigs, in the South, I come back and I don't hear from George. So I go to the Bangladesh concert and I go backstage afterwards. And George comes running up to me … (imitates Harrison) 'Where were you?' And I said, 'What do you mean?' And he said, 'It's been touch and go with Eric 'cuz he's so ill.' So if I'd have called in I would have played the Bangladesh concert."

Jerry Shirley: "I remember us coming back from that tour. We were supposed to rehearse in London before we were getting ready to go back out on another summer tour, again before the live album was released. The Who were performing that weekend at Albert Hall. Peter wanted to go see The Who play and Steve wanted to rehearse. I remember them being in an argument about that. And the gist of it was, 'If you don't come to rehearse, and you choose to go out and see The Who play, that'll tell us where you're at.' This was the argument between Steve and Peter. Sure enough, we went to rehearsal and Peter didn't show up. And that was the last we saw of him."

Peter Frampton: "I said to Dee, 'I'm leaving the band.' 'You're crazy. Tell me that again.' I said, 'I'm leaving the band.' So he said, 'Are you gonna call the guys?' And I said, 'Yeah, I'll call the guys. Obviously I wanted to tell you first. I wanna do my own album and I would like Frank Barselona and you and Jerry Moss to be involved.' And he said, 'Absolutely. I can't speak for them but I'm sure …'

"So then I called Steve and he went berserk. He thought I was crazy; he couldn't understand and all that. Basically, I'd grown up. I got to the point where it was time for me to move on. I wasn't the odd one out but sometimes I felt like I was."

Author: "Did you feel that the direction the band was going in wasn't the initial intention?"

Peter Frampton: "I did feel it, yeah. But I didn't mind the direction it was going. Everyone seems to have jumped on the fact that when I say there were numbers that I was writing that I couldn't do in Humble Pie anymore because of our direction … that really wasn't the reason. That was just an aside. That was a fact. There were numbers I was writing, acoustic numbers, as we'd done when we started. And even as recently as 'Humble Pie,' the first A&M record, there were great acoustic numbers on that. I'm sure we'd have done more in the future. But it was more the fact that I just didn't feel that I was part of the band anymore. It just wasn't fun anymore for me. Whereas the reason I so looked forward to working with Steve was because Steve is still a mentor of mine, even though I can't talk to him anymore. I'll never be able to be in any band or play in any other band situation and have someone affect me the way his talent did. He spoiled me for good. 'Cuz there's only one of him. Then there's Ray Charles, there's Steve Winwood, need I go on? You know, there's only a few, Paul Rodgers, that have that. And he sort of towered above them in his small stature. He'd been my teacher and in a way I guess I was rebelling against the person that had taught me so much. And credit where credit's due. I learn stuff when I listen to him still."

Author: "And isn't it a natural progression for one to leave the nest?"

Peter Frampton: "I think so. For me it was. I didn't realize at the time why I was doing it, I don't think. I just knew that I had to get out. And even if it meant starting at the bottom again, I didn't care."

Jerry Shirley: "We kept trying to find someone to replace Peter. People would show up at our little rehearsal hall out in the country with a guitar in hand. They'd hear us rehearsing as a three-piece and wouldn't get the guitar out of the case. They were so intimidated by the way we sounded. One in particular being Mick Abrahms from Jethro Tull. He said, 'I can't add to that. It's too good.' "

Rick Derringer: "When I was playing with White Trash, Humble Pie had crossed paths with us on the road. Steve Marriott and I had talked to each other about the possibility of doing a band together. Now, in my mind, I envisioned starting a new band together. That was when Pete Frampton was in Humble Pie. Then it wasn't long after that that I got another call. Steve Marriott had said that he was thinking about firing Pete Frampton and wanted to know if I would be the guitar player with Humble Pie. And I said, 'You know, I don't really envision the possibility of Humble Pie, in my mind, being that more exciting for me than continuing to play with White Trash,' who I loved. I did not leave White Trash to do that."

Jerry Shirley: "I do remember Rick's name being bounded around as a possible to get in contact with. Joe Walsh was the main contender. He was all for joining the band. He backed out at the last minute. We were told then it was because his management wouldn't cut him loose. I found

out years later that he thought about it a great deal. Again, he was intimidated by Steve's presence on stage. He thought to himself, apparently, 'There's no way I could play guitar at the same level, night after night, that Steve could sing and play.' And, of course, soon after that he got a job with The Eagles. So he didn't do too badly [laughs]."

Author: "How different would '*that*' have been?"

Jerry Shirley: "I know! We often wondered. As far as we knew, he was in. We were loving the idea. We would have probably all been dead, mind you [laughs]! If the drug and drinking intake wasn't bad enough at that point, Joe'd have come in … Oh, God, we'd have had a hell of a good time! It would have been a good band, too.

"The live album was done and on its way out. We had the tour booked as headliners and ready to go. So it was getting desperate. And, almost out of desperation, we made a last-ditch effort to look for somebody, just before we ditched it in and did it as a three-piece."

Greg Ridley: "We needed a guitar player even though Steve could play great lead guitar. When you're doing all the stuff he was doing, all the singing and prancing and performing, to play lead guitar as well would have been asking a lot. There's a big gap when there's only three of you and somebody's got to fill in. And if you're doing so much at the same time, he would have needed to be a bloody miracle man."

Jerry Shirley: "Steve was turned on to 'Colosseum Live,' with Clem Clempson playing some wonderful guitar on it. I remember him calling me and saying, 'C'mon over. I've found our new guitar player.' I came over to his house, he put the record on, and he said, 'This is the guy.' He got in touch with him and Clem was invited down to our first rehearsal for that winter tour of England before we came on our first tour of America. He wasn't even auditioned. The first thing Clem knew about auditioning for this band was his first rehearsal to go on the road. It was like, 'Well, we'd better not give him the option. He's in! In case he chickens out!' Then that was it, Clem was in the band."

Dave "Clem" Clempson: "Well, they may have decided that [laughs]! I was actually supposed to be doing an American tour with Colosseum and I didn't want to walk out on them and let them down. I explained this to the guys in the Pie. They were about to do a European tour, which took up the same period of time as the proposed Colosseum/American tour. So I said, 'I don't think I can join you until after your European tour.' They said basically, 'Well, if that's the way it has to be, OK. We'll wait for you. You do the American tour with Colosseum and join up with us when we get back from Europe.' But when I went and spoke to Jon Hiseman and said that I was prepared to go through with the American tour, he just said, 'Forget it. I couldn't face going through all that knowing the band was going to split up anyway.' I guess he'd decided he didn't want to go through the process of finding another guitarist. So I went back to Pie and said I would go to Europe with them. And I think we left in a week or so.

"I was born on the fifth of September, 1949, in a place in the Midlands called Tamworth. My involvement with music started when I was four. I was given a toy piano for Christmas that year. It seemed as natural a thing to me as building with blocks or drawing with crayons or whatever things that four-year-olds did. But it caused a lot of excitement amongst the teachers [laughs] who called my parents into the school and told them that I had a special talent and that I should be encouraged to take music lessons. And for the next ten years I went to weekly piano lessons.

"I did the Royal School of Music grades. It consists of eight exams and you take one a year. I'm not sure what's supposed to happen after that because when I was fourteen I'd decided that I'd had enough of all the taunts of my school friends as I walked past carrying my music case as they were all playing soccer. I always wished I could be playing soccer with them rather than going to another dreary music lesson. But I realized that I had a special feeling for music. I would often sit at the piano and doodle around and I'd get quite emotional while I was doing it. But when it came time for the weekly music lesson or practicing, I didn't really want to know. I started to get rebellious and decided to put my foot down. I just said I didn't want to do it anymore. That caused a lot of heartbreak and stuff in the family. They always

thought that I'd go on to become a music teacher. That I would make some kind of respectable career out of my 'gift.' In those days the teaching profession was the ultimate in respectability. And security as well. Little did they know.

"I had also a keen interest in the guitar as well. I was quite excited by the guitarists I saw on television which were people like Tommy Steele and Hank Marvin of The Shadows. It was at a time when The Beatles had started. The glamour appeal! So I sold my train set and bought my first guitar. And because of my background in piano, within a few days I could play a few songs. I had all the notes in my head so it was just a matter of finding out where they were on the fretboard. It seemed pretty easy.

"As soon as I'd figured out a few chords and a few tunes for myself I realized that I wanted to have other people to play with. So I got these guys together and showed them what I'd learned. We started to get invited to all the girls' parties. Which was quite … pleasant. We thought, 'This is good. We're on to something here.' And then we progressed to the Workingmen's clubs. A network of clubs which were set up for blue-collar workers.

"I was absolutely devoted to playing the guitar. Especially when I discovered the John Mayall/Eric Clapton album. All of a sudden I found something that moved me and gave me a reason to live [laughs]! I started out by emulating it because I wanted to find out how Clapton was making the sounds and the string bending. In those days, we couldn't nip down to your local store and pick up the 'Eric Clapton Plays the Blues' video. You really had to figure out all that kind of stuff yourself.

"I immediately told the rest of the guys that we were going to start playing blues. We began to drop the Herman's Hermits and Beatles tunes and played John Mayall tunes. Jimi Hendrix. Started doing that sort of stuff. Then I soon came to a conclusion that the rest of the guys weren't really up to it. It's one thing learning simple pop tunes. But when it came to improvising, that sorted out the men from the boys. It was a natural process, after getting into this music, to seek out other people who were 'like-minded.' I met up with a couple of other people in the area who already had a band going and were quite successful. They were called The Pinch. This would be about 1966.

"At some point we decided to change our name to Bakerloo. We were playing quite regularly at a club called Mothers, which was the top venue for the top bands in Birmingham. Fleetwood Mac, John Mayall, Colosseum, King Crimson. We played support to Colosseum on a couple of occasions at Mothers and a university gig in Cambridge. Shortly afterward I got a call from Jon Hiseman, asking if I'd be interested in joining the band. At that point Bakerloo was cracking up. That was a really exciting opportunity for me to move to London and play with a band that was doing all the top venues and had roadies and transits and stuff. So I jumped at that. I had a couple of great years with them."

Author: "How did you hear about the job with Pie?"

Clem Clempson: "Through the grapevine word had got to me that Humble Pie needed a new guitarist. I had been having some disillusionment with Colosseum in the weeks leading up to that so I decided that when I got back home from that tour I would call Steve. I called him one morning and he knew my name but didn't know much about me or about my playing. He fought me off, pretending to be his non-existent brother [laughs] and said he'd get Steve to call me back later. In the meantime, he went out and bought the 'Colosseum Live' album, which was very successful, and he liked what he heard. He called me back and said, 'Can you come over now?' So I drove out to Steve's house in Essex and we sat around and had a little jam, the two of us, and got on good. I just played my bluesy stuff that I'd been playing throughout Bakerloo and Colosseum. Steve said, 'Can you come to a full rehearsal with the band tomorrow?' So I turned up for a rehearsal with the rest of the guys, in London, and their press secretary was there. Their PR guy was there. And Chris Welch turned up from *Melody Maker* [laughs]. And it turned into a *fait accompli*. I hadn't even had a chance to speak to the guys in Colosseum at that stage."

Greg Ridley: "Oh, it was fabulous; it was great. A lot of ability. Very quiet on personality but very bluesy with his

playing. We had a couple of guys drop by to see if we liked their jokes and their playing but Clem got the job. I don't know who decided that but he was very proficient."

John Doumanian: "I personally liked everybody. The only guy I never really got along with was Clempson. And Bill and Dee didn't like him either. He was just one of those guys. He had that English attitude. For no reason at all. But Clem was good at what he did; there was no problem about that."

Jerry Shirley: "Clem just had a kind of a negativism that they didn't care for and the fact that he walked into the gig with all the hard work having already been done. I think they felt, and I'm not saying I believe this, Clem didn't appreciate what it was he'd got. That he never showed gratitude for it. And maybe not too good an attitude towards them. So it was a combination of those things really. Clem used to make pot shots at John but everyone else got along with him. We'd known John a really long time."

Author: "Joe Walsh allegedly turned down the job because he felt he couldn't keep up with Steve on a nightly basis. Did this intimidate you?"

Clem Clempson: "Does that mean 'after the gig' nightly [laughs]? No, not at all. I didn't consider this a competition. I kind of got the impression that that was Peter's problem as well. That he felt that he was in competition with Steve. That was never an issue for me. The most exciting thing about the chance to join Humble Pie was that I always desperately wanted to work with a great singer. To be the lead guitarist of a band who had a singer that could really go out front and do his business. I was extremely happy to be in a position with somebody that was not only capable but one of the best in the world."

Jerry Shirley: "He was in, he was done. He was on board. Equal share, equal everything. Full-time member. No, 'Let's see how it goes.' No, 'We'll put you on a salary.' None of that. He joined the band one week and three weeks later he had a house in the country and he was driving a Bentley.

Humble Pie (l-r, Steve Marriott, Clem Clempson, Greg Ridley) Dortmund, Germany, 1974. Courtesy Stefan Klimm

And three weeks after that he was complaining about the pressure. Steve chewed him a new ass about that! 'What pressure' [laughs]? We were kids, you know. Fun time."

Author: "Did Dee or A&M hint at preparing yourselves for a potential backlash from Frampton supporters?"

Jerry Shirley: "I don't remember a lot of that going on, to be honest with you. We were on such a roll and we were so into becoming tougher and heavier and having Steve take the reins that we didn't care. And we were also, deep down inside … I know I was, and think the rest were, deeply hurt by Peter. 'How dare you? How could you leave this after all this hard work?' So, whilst we put on this big, heavy, tough guy exterior, of 'Well, we're better off without him, and he was playing pretty guitar, anyway' and being real little dicks about it, we were all devastated by him leaving. But I don't remember anybody saying, 'Oh, it's gonna be terrible without him.' Everybody was very supportive. Dee, A&M. And

Clem came in, played beautiful blues guitar and we were off and running. In fact, it happened so fast that no sooner had he got in the group and we'd done our first, albeit short, headlining tour on the back of the live album, we'd already written and rehearsed almost all of the material for 'Smokin'.' And by the end of January of '72, 'Smokin'' was in the bag. It was ready to be released and we were back on the road with that. So it all happened very quickly."

Author: "Did you have to put up with hearing a lot of Frampton references?"

Clem Clempson: "No. Not at all actually. People spoke to me about it or asked how it felt but I was just having a good time. And I was getting so much support from the rest of the guys, especially from Steve, that I never felt insecure or that I had to prove anything at all.

"I think it was pretty much a continuation. They'd just had the 'Fillmore' album released, which was starting to really take off in America. It was a great time for me to join the band. Things were really happening for them. How things would have turned out differently if I hadn't joined is hypothetical, really. But I'm sure they would have gone on and been successful with whomever they ended up with.

"I was quite keen in establishing myself as 'the guitarist.' So it was great to get into the studio and start making a new album. Which was 'Smokin'.' That was one of the best times I'd had in the studio. Most of the recording I'd done up to that point was with Colosseum and they had a completely different approach. It was a very studious kind of band. But with Pie, we'd just get in there and have a great time. Smoke a spliff. And various people would drop in. Steve Stills came in. Alexis Korner came in. It was wonderful. It was like having a party.

"I remember the first U.S. gig I did with them was at The Spectrum in Philadelphia. That was pretty impressive. In a way part of me wished that I had been with them a little earlier so I could have done a bit of the groundwork. I think I would have felt more of a sense of achievement when I played at The Spectrum. But it was fantastic anyway. The whole experience was a big relief from the frustration of the previous year with Colosseum. I was playing with a bunch of guys that were easy going. And they loved my contribution. It was a great time."

Author: "Did they vocalize their appreciation of your talent?"

Clem Clempson: "Oh, yeah. All the time. That was one thing about Steve. And not to only myself. He was constantly praising the guys in the band. He would speak to Jerry and Greg in the same way. He was a great leader."

Author: "With 'Smokin' coming out so soon you were basically promoting two albums at the same time."

Jerry Shirley: "I guess we were. Did not occur to us at that time but, yes, we were. Absolutely."

Clem Clempson: "I felt like 'Rockin' The Fillmore' was a kind of summary of what they had done up to that point. Most of the songs on 'Fillmore' had been out on various albums. So maybe I didn't consider that an issue because of that fact. Obviously we were playing material from the live album but I never interpreted it as touring to promote 'Rockin' The Fillmore.' Just really a continuation of parts of their live set that they wanted to keep."

Jerry Shirley: "The Fillmore East. The very best memories. Our home away from home. I dunno if we'd played there more than anybody else but we're certainly up there. Whenever anybody backed out, they'd call us. We were guaranteed to blow the roof off, apart from everything else, and we had a good following, at that time, in New York. They either loved you or hated you, though. You could not go into that building and do a bad show and get away with it, believe me."

Author: "Due to 'Smokin' receiving airplay, how was the success noticed by the band?"

Jerry Shirley: "The vast majority of the apparent success was material. There was that quantum leap between doing really well through word of mouth and then doing really well 'cuz they've heard it on the radio. That is quite a difference right there. But I'll tell you where we noticed it. All of a sudden you were playing places like Johnstown, PA. You'd walk in and they'd know you as well as they did in New York. They might not respond as well, as they were a bit behind the times, but they knew the songs. And that was the difference of radio."

Author: "It took the pocket success and made it blanket."

Jerry Shirley: "Right. Whereas we'd be going on tour prior to that record and doing New York, L.A., Chicago, Boston. All of a sudden we went from that to doing secondary and tertiary markets. Your Johnstowns and your Des Moines. And I remember we were in for trouble if we weren't playing a major market because Steve hated playing anything but major markets. He just was a city kind of guy. I think the quality of the blow wasn't as good in Johnstown as it was in

Chicago [laughs]! And Debbie and Debbie and Debbie weren't in Johnstown like they were in Chicago! But I've always felt an audience is an audience. It was up to us to go out there and crank them up no matter where we were."

Kay Marriott: "When Steve was with Humble Pie; to see him at Madison Square Garden. That was wonderful."

Kay Mateus Dos Anjos: "I'll never forget Madison Square Garden. Thousands of people. We were all flown over. All the families. We were escorted in there by policemen with their guns out. And we all had little English flags in our hands [laughs]."

Kay Marriott: "They go on and on about The Small Faces here but Humble Pie was far bigger. I think there were 26,000 there that night. That was wonderful. And it was the first time I saw the light treatment."

Kay Mateus Dos Anjos: "The whole audience lit a lighter or a match! That sticks in my mind. I couldn't believe that. And we didn't understand what the lighters were for! My mother was saying, 'Sit down or duck' [laughs]! She thought something was going to happen because we had gone in with English flags! We'd never seen that before, you see."

Kay Marriott: "The Irish sentiment was very strong in America at that time. And I thought, 'God, the place is going to be blown up!' I don't know what I thought it was but I didn't think it was something good."

Jerry Shirley: "My father and my stepmother came over. My real mum had been dead for a while then. It was great fun. While we were on stage we could see them all in this section of seats, off to the side, and they were all waving their British flags."

Author: "Did your parents have any idea of the band's popularity?"

Jerry Shirley: "Yeah, by then they had a pretty good idea of what was going on. They'd seen us play a couple of pretty big gigs in England and they'd read the newspaper reports coming back from America. But I think it was quite something for them to actually see it. Madison Square Garden, sold out, was pretty big stuff back then."

•　　•　　•

John Doumanian: "We were on our way to Detroit, a gig at Cobo Hall. Steve lit a cigarette in the non-smoking section. All of a sudden the stewardess asked him to put it out. 'Fuck off!' The police were waiting for them when they got off. They had a sold-out show! They had to apologize. And the cops were busting balls in those days. Pie were harmless with other people. They were always charming and nice. But Steve was waking up and she caught him at the wrong time. And she said, 'Put the cigarette out.' 'Aww, fuck off!' "

Jerry Shirley: "We got, literally, chased offstage and on to a Lear jet and out of Florida one night. We got wind of the fact that the police were going to arrest Steve and possibly all of us because he was 'motherfucking' on stage."

Author: "Who tipped you off that this was going to happen?"

Jerry Shirley: "One of our road crew, Alex King. He was there and got billy-clubbed that night as a result of it. And John Doumanian. Between the two of them they organized our escape."

John Doumanian: "I was the one that decoyed everybody. Someone told me the cops were waiting, so I didn't bring the house lights up when the show was over."

Jerry Shirley: "As we came off stage they did this big diversionary tactic thing. They ran Steve off in one direction and took him straight to the airport while we went in the other direction in a car and to the airport. As we got out they backed the semi-truck across the exit so the cop cars couldn't get out to give us a bit of time. The cops were quite angry!"

John Doumanian: "I went to the hotel, checked them all out, got their bags and gone."

Jerry Shirley: "We got to this private airport, jumped on the plane and literally, as we were taxiing up the runway, we saw the red flashing lights coming after us. The cop cars were chasing us down the runway. It was like something out of a movie! Steve thought it was hysterical. He got his most fun out of creating a situation like that. He thought it was riotously funny."

Author: "How different was Steve at home as opposed to people he worked with?"

Jenny Dearden: "He was very different. Certainly with me. He was very gentle and sensitive. Had masses of animals. Loved the animals."

Kay Marriott: "He had different kinds of ducks everywhere. And cats and dogs."

Jerry Shirley: "But they didn't get fixed and they were literally swamped, especially with ducks, at one point. They didn't know how to get rid of them or what to do with them and they were way too kind-hearted to have them sent off to the slaughterhouse. So my Dad came by and found them a home."

Kay Marriott: "A horse, Bim. He used to ride down to the pub on the horse. He'd say, 'They all think I'm eccentric.' And I'd say, 'Well, don't you think you are a bit' [laughs]? He used to tie the horse up. Go in the village pub. A pint for the horse and a pint for him. Get on the horse and go back."

Jenny Dearden: "Almost the antithesis of the image people expected him to project on the stage. And, subsequently, when things were very bad between us and he didn't want to go on yet another tour, much later, with Humble Pie, he said to me, 'I don't want to go. Please say that you'll leave me if I go on this tour. I can't be that person again that they want me to be. I'm going to go mad.' But it was too late. It was the night before he had to go."

As the band readied to return to the studio to begin sessions for their next release, Steve approached the band with an idea. They had used background singers on recordings before but he now wanted to expand the band to include a trio of female vocalists. And he was in a position to be adamant about it. Steve wanted Vanetta Fields, Billie Barnum and Clydie King to join immediately. The Blackberries became a part of Humble Pie.

Jerry Shirley: "That didn't go over well at all, at the beginning. To his undying credit Steve was way ahead of his time on that one. Because everybody and their mother now has, or has had, specifically, a three-piece, black girl chorus. It was resisted by the record company and management until he was in a position where they could no longer say no to him. Whatever he said went at that point. Stephen wanted to get the backup singers in the band as early as 'Smokin'.' Finally, it all got put together for 'Eat It.' And when we really noticed it was when we went out on the road with the black girl singers. In 1972, in Beaumont, Texas, with a bunch of long-haired white boys. It did not go down well at all. It was very powerful. The audience would stand there, staring at us. 'Well, what are these niggers doing on your stage?' It was really weird 'cuz I thought all of that stuff was long gone. But it still exists today, let alone thirty years ago.

"The record company and management thought it was the wrong thing to do from the very beginning. The girls were a distraction, financially. They were a subversive force. The girls had our ear early on. They could see where we were getting screwed. The management and the record company knew they'd been around. I mean, one of them had been a Ray-lette with Ray Charles. Another had been an Ike-ette with Ike and Tina Turner. They knew their onions. And they would have us ask questions of ourselves. 'Well, how come this and this? Where's the money' [laughs]? Questions started to be asked that never did get answered properly. We never cared up till that point."

Greg Ridley: "I was a bit dubious at the time. I liked the music with a hard edge to it. And I was thinking, 'What are the girls gonna do? Are they gonna add or subtract to the band?' But when they did come in, they were great. Good singers and a great laugh. That was the way Steve wanted to progress and we went along with it. It didn't turn out so bad."

Jerry Shirley: "We all loved the girls. Steve especially. We loved them being part of the band. We loved them being friends and everything."

Clem Clempson: "I was very happy. We'd always used background singers anyway. There were background singers on a lot of tracks on 'Smokin'.' So when we recorded 'Eat It,' it was a natural move to bring in background singers for that. And when Steve suggested they come on the road with us it seemed like a good idea."

Alan O'Duffy: "Having the girls was heaven for Steve. He could phrase with them. He musically matched with their Baptist upbringing. And to hear them all together ..."

Jerry Shirley: "We were all rehearsed up. All they had to do was learn their vocal parts and we were off and running. But they were very much involved in everything. Wherever we went, they went. And that pissed the record company off. Little things like photo shoots and stuff like that. We would automatically expect the girls to be included in any and all photo shoots. They would say, 'Oh, no, this one without the backup girls.' We didn't see them as backup singers. We saw them as members of the group."

•   •   •

Author: "Except for when Steve was touring and recording, was he existing as opposed to living?"

Jenny Dearden: "Yes, he was. And that became increasingly so. It gathered momentum. The bigger they got, and the more pressure there was, when he came home ... I knew that things were really bad when I got to the point where I dreaded him coming home. Because I used to so miss him. But he'd bring this shit with him and dump it at home. We had a very idyllic life there. It was a lovely cottage with a lovely garden, a stream. And the beginning of the end was when he built the studio in the stables. Which,

when we were breaking up, he said he knew that that was what delivered the fatal blow. Because then he didn't have any sanctuary at all. People just came 'round at any time of night or day. And as soundproofed as it was, you could hear the bass. It was the end, really."

Author: "The studio became quite the hangout."

Jerry Shirley: "Oh yeah. It certainly did. We even had a club name for it. 'The Racket Club.' I mean racket as in coke, our nickname for blow back then."

"Eat It" offered a new approach to an album release. One side was rock, one acoustic, one was soul and the other was live.

Jerry Shirley: "It just evolved. We were still very hot live. We'd just done 'Smokin'.' By then we'd gotten the girls in the band. We'd done some shows with them and we'd recorded some of it. Just to see how it was. And we were psyched on recording the album. I think what happened was we said, 'Hang on. We've got this live stuff and we've got a bunch of acoustic stuff. Why don't we make it a double album?' "

Clem Clempson: "To be honest, the record company wasn't crazy about a lot of what was going on back then. I would think that they'd want us to consolidate the success we'd had with 'Rockin' The Fillmore' and 'Smokin'.' Which was a good, hard-rocking English band. I guess if I'd have been involved with the record company at the time I would have been worried about not so much the direction the band was going in, but the rapidity in which we were traveling in that direction."

Jerry Shirley: "That was when complete control was lost. At the point which 'Eat It' was put together, the new contract had just been signed so we'd lost control of our money. We'd been given complete artistic control, not that we didn't have it before. But A&M allowed us to make a record that, well, if it was a great record, underneath, there were technical problems with it. In today's world they would have never have allowed it to be released. They would have had us go in and at least re-cut it or re-mix it."

Beehive Cottage. The studio was situated above the garage.
Courtesy Kay Marriott

Author: "Was that due to where it was recorded?"

Jerry Shirley: "Yeah. At Steve's studio. All hell was breaking loose. We were spending the money that was coming in like it was going out of style. And, at the same time, weren't getting it distributed to us properly. I think our thought was, 'Well, if we're not getting our money, at least we can pick up the phone and order a studio or order a Bentley' [laughs]. And we did. So the group's money, through the record deal, financed the groups' studio in Steve's house. No sooner had it been built then all of a sudden it became Steve's studio. His rationale was, 'Well, after all, I'm doing all the writing. So by the time all the publishing money comes in, I'll have that much more owed to me anyway. So I'll just have the studio.' And we all said, 'Oh,

uh, OK.' Which, I guess, there's a certain amount of sense to that argument, although it was never mathematically worked out. He just ended up with the studio in his house. What we didn't do was we did not have it acoustically scoped, we never had it tested acoustically. So what sounded great while you were in the studio, once you got it out and tried to cut it, sounded like shit."

Author: "So why was it released?"

Jerry Shirley: " 'Cuz no one could say no to anybody. We're all high as kites on the enormous amounts of cocaine."

Author: " 'Eat It' didn't sound up to par but no one noticed until you were told. Who told you?"

Jerry Shirley: "I know who told me. Hearing it on the radio in America is what told me. I heard 'Get Down To It' in the back of a limousine going to a gig in Detroit. It scared the hell out of me. I realized how off the actual sound quality was. The thing was, you see, we didn't listen to it anywhere outside Steve's studio until it was released."

Author: "It never occurred to anyone to get fresh ears?"

Jerry Shirley: "No. We were so self-wrapped. It never occurred to us because it sounded great in that room! But that room was so deceiving, sound-wise. It was very bass-light so you could put lots of bass on it and it would still sound good. But once you take a record out of a room like that and try and play it through a normal system, all of a sudden it sounds like it's made out of woolen socks.

"There was some great material on that record. And with the technology available today … see, you couldn't do a lot to a record after the fact. Not anything like you can today. The correctability was limited. Short of going in and remixing the whole thing. It was too late for that. This is the extent to which we had ourselves and A&M and everybody so self-wrapped. Now, in today's world that never would have happened. They would have said, 'Stop. You're not releasing this. And this is why.' But back then they didn't do that."

Author: "Did it sound good while you were recording?"

Clem Clempson: "Some of it did, yeah. But I did have reservations on some of the tracks. I think overall we were quite happy but there were problems with the motives as well. It was really the fact that we weren't going to the studio as a band and working as a band and leaving as a band. Basically, when the rest of us left, Steve was still there. When the rest of us had enough and needed to get home to rest, Steve wouldn't feel the same and would often want to carry on. Some of the stuff that Steve had done in those circumstances was OK. And sometimes we didn't like some of the things he'd done. But it became difficult because we had gotten to that position where we had to take a stand about certain things. And up to that point, we had always been united."

Author: "The quality of the recording was 'different.' "

Clem Clempson: "It was something I was concerned about. When I listen to 'Eat It' now, I still feel exactly the same. The studio wasn't really up to the standard that was required."

Due to the strain of his marriage falling apart, Steve ensconced himself in his studio and would literally stay up for days at a time. But the energy he needed to accomplish this task was being chemically fueled like never before. He was going through vast amounts of cocaine.

Jerry Shirley: "We allowed Steve to compensate for the mess his personal life was in. We decided that the right way to go was to give him all the reins, entirely, on that record. Let him do whatever he wanted. 'Here, Steve. Put all your energies into this record. An acoustic side, a live side, whatever you want to do.' And that's how that record came about. He engineered it. I guess we were still 'group producing' it but it was more totally Steve than any other record we'd ever done. Although let me say, to add to that, Steve had also changed by then. He'd become very out of control for a while there on the coke and everything. The lunatic was definitely running the asylum at that point. Bless his heart 'cuz I love him dearly. And if I say anything ever that sounds like I'm putting him down, I'm not. I'm being honest about what was going on."

Clem Clempson: "He was playing other people's parts, sometimes. Parts that other people were expected to do. Steve was up and ready to go. Wanting to be creative, he would sometimes do it himself. I mean, there's no reason why he couldn't have done that occasionally but because it was done after everyone had left it kind of created some bad feelings."

Jerry Shirley: "But he didn't do a lot of other people's parts. We all very much played on it. There was never any resentment. It was just that we allowed him to mix everything and allowed him to have the production say and the way a song was done."

Clem Clempson: "His intentions were never malevolent in any way but he was just full of energy and wanted to keep on working. And that's the way Steve was. I mean, he was very sort of spontaneous and if he had an idea for something on a particular track, he would want to do it. He wouldn't want to wait until the next day when the rest of us got back to the studio. But that did cause a bit of resentment. This was supposed to be a four-piece band. The strength of the band was, despite the fact that Steve was always the face of the band and the frontman and the leader, it was very much a band."

Jerry Shirley: "We were all coming from that awful place where ego and too much fun could put you in. And that's when we thought we were invincible. Everything we thought we did was golden. Us make a bad record? It didn't happen."

Author: "Why were the excesses being tolerated?"

Greg Ridley: "I think because we liked it! And you did need something to keep you on a high, which you had to be, we all thought, to achieve what we were trying to achieve. We were trying to be the greatest band on the planet and play to all those massive crowds that would turn up. Obviously, you couldn't have just finished your typing job and gotten up onstage and done that. So you need a little bit of help, whether it had been from a bottle or 'talcum powder' or if you wanted to get nastier. But it didn't get nastier than that so that was fine."

Jerry Shirley: "And it wasn't entirely our fault because underneath it all, it was a good record. There were some good songs on there. There were some good performances. The Blackberries sounded great. But the actual sound quality of the record … by this time, radio had become huge and it mattered. For a fun record, where it's just you, me and the lads listening to it, no problem. When you're talking about commercial entity, and it's following a big record … it had something to live up to. And all of those things backfired on us. It bit us in the ass.

"As soon as the record was released and it went to the charts with a bullet at number 10, everybody was happy. The following week it stayed at number 10 but lost its bullet. And the week after that, when it dropped to number 140 or something, then all the noises started. 'Oh, dear, things are going drastically wrong.' We went to Japan and did a tour that was way out of our league, financially. You know, spending $100,000 and only earning $20,000, that kind of stuff. So the voices of discontent did not start until after the toss had bolted. Everybody was happy for us and having a party until they could see that things were going wrong. Then they all ran for cover."

Author: "Management and the record company didn't agree with the addition of The Blackberries. They weren't happy with the sound, the direction. But nobody could say no to Steve. In retrospect, did this instigate the beginning of the end?"

Clem Clempson: "Yeah. I think that had a lot to do with it. People did find it very difficult to say no to Steve. He had a lot of 'courage of his convictions' and sometimes things he said would appear completely crazy to the rest of us. But he was the way he was. And in a way that's what made him what he was and that's what made him the performer that he was."

Jerry Shirley: "The tours were still great. We were still playing great. We were still drawing good audiences and we had the added bonus of having The Blackberries which, from our point of view, we enjoyed that. And so did the audiences in the big cities. In the secondary markets is where they were looking at us a bit screwy."

Clem Clempson: "Touring was different but it was still fun despite the reservations that there may have been about the girls being on the road. I mean, they were great people and we had a wonderful time. We used to love being with them. Before the girls joined the band, we'd started to use a Lear jet. And that was a lot of fun because we used to get these ex-Viet Nam pilots that would do all kinds of tricks for us. Aerobatics. And we used to have a wonderful time."

Jerry Shirley: "It was Mick Brigdon who introduced us to the wonderful world of Lear jets. I hold him responsible for that little nest of vipers. It was great fun and they weren't that expensive. It was right before the oil crisis so they were only a little more expensive than first class tickets all 'round.'"

Clem Clempson: "So when the girls joined the band, we had to get a bigger plane. And that was really boring because you couldn't do all these stunts. We decided that the best thing to do was to get two Lear jets! Then we started to travel with two Lear jets and we'd have to split up. And we didn't like being split up 'cuz we used to have such great times singing together and stuff like that. So we discovered that if we put all the bags and equipment into one of the jets, we could squeeze into the other one. So we carried on like that for a while."

Author: "Why did Steve call Clem 'the bitch?' "

Jerry Shirley: "At that time he was very into all vocal mannerisms pertaining to black American slang. He walked and talked and mimicked that which the girls would say backstage between themselves. Excuse me for saying this, but 'nigger' talk. Nigger this, nigger that. 'Hey, what's up nigger?' And all points in between. And he included himself. You know how black people regularly and openly refer to each other as nigger this and nigger that? Well, he got so close to them, apart from the fact that he was their boss, that they allowed him into that small, elite circle of white people who are allowed to be included. Black people will talk to each other like that. But if you presume and jump in and say it yourself, they'll look at you and say, 'Who you calling nigger?' In fact, the girls got on him on a number of occasions about keeping it behind closed doors. They told him off a number of times for talking like that onstage. He had gotten very into almost being a caricature of himself as a James Brown, 'hey, what it is,' onstage. Frankly, a lot of people got down on him in reviews and stuff because of that."

When "Eat It" was released, it didn't come near to previous Humble Pie sales.

Clem Clempson: "We weren't totally unaware of the reasons. We weren't shy about discussing it. We were trying to figure out what to do to put things back on course. But then we came upon more stumbling blocks. I know that Jerry and myself were convinced that recording at Steve's house was a mistake, for all kinds of reasons."

Author: "So he found a new way to bring his work home."

Jenny Dearden: "Exactly. It negated the whole object of what the cottage was originally intended for."

Clem Clempson: "It seemed to us that the obvious thing to do was to go back to the commercial studio where we'd done 'Smokin'.' But Steve was dead against it. He couldn't understand why we would want to do that. He was very happy with his situation but he reluctantly agreed."

Author: "How did Steve react when it was suggested that the band go back to Olympic?"

Jerry Shirley: "Not well. He was not amused. In fact, he did everything he could do to avoid going back to Olympic including when he did go back there he intentionally misbehaved. He didn't like stepping out of Beehive Cottage at all."

Clem Clempson: "But it didn't work. He obviously didn't want to do it. I can't remember what happened. He didn't show up on the first day or he showed up on the first but not on the second. So then he would start to get other musicians up to his studio so he could carry on having his fun in his own studio. His attitude was that if we weren't prepared to go and indulge him at his place, he'd bring people along that would do it. And there was no shortage of them. And no shortage of stimulants to keep them going, to stay up with Steve, which was something else he enjoyed."

Jenny Dearden: "I feel eternally guilty about Steve basically because I know how I felt at the time but I just had to get out. I think it the hardest thing I've ever done was wrench myself away from Steve. He was everything that I ever cared about.

He was a very powerful character, Steve. And as much as anything, it wasn't him. It was the amount of substance abuse, which I had no control over whatsoever. I mean, we used to smoke dope in the 60s. But I knew nothing about the chemical stuff. It was not part of what happened, living in the country. So it took me a long time to understand, really, why it was that he went on this radical personality change. And it was radical. He would disappear for three or four days and come back looking so rattled and terrible. Because of the studio. When things were bad, I was sort of 'persona non grata.' "

Author: "Was there any way to get him out of there?"

Jenny Dearden: "No! There were always people there. And there was constant awareness, in the middle of this idyllic setting, that this horror story was happening for days at a time within eyesight of where I was trying to carry on this normal existence. Taking the dogs for a walk, feeding the animals …"

•   •   •

Author: "When were you first made aware of the band's management concerns? This was a situation that you had inherited."

Clem Clempson: "That I inherited, absolutely, yeah. Which has always been [laughs] my source of consolation. Because there was nothing I could have done about that. After 'Eat It,' when we started to feel a bit burned out, it became obvious that there was a lot of pressure from management to maximize our position, our earning potential as a top live act in the States. Basically, they wanted us to stay on the road. I think I had something like twenty-six American visas in my passport in the three or four years we were together, which shows you how many times we toured back then.

"I suppose that was really the time when certain divisions started to appear within the band. They didn't seem to be serious divisions at the time but the cracks were definitely starting to appear. Steve was becoming concerned about the management situation and management were becoming concerned about Steve's behavior. And the rest of the guys, we were kind of a bit confused! Steve did take us to one side and voice his concerns and sent us away thinking, 'You've got a point there.' And Jerry Shirley would often voice the management side of things that could be equally convincing."

Author: "Did that cause resentment from Steve with you?"

Jerry Shirley: "Absolutely. I was trying to put a practical, well-managed point of view across and Steve was putting his anti-management point of view across. And he and I fell out about such things many times. It happened a lot. It was sad because a good portion of Steve's fears, you could argue, eventually came true. But not to the degree that Steve believed in. He believed it to the point that there were literally millions of dollars stashed, not only with Dee but with A&M, that were owed to us. And that just was not the case. You could do the numbers a million times over and you couldn't generate these millions of dollars that were supposedly sitting there that we weren't getting. Steve had convinced himself, or others had convinced him, where he truly believed that there was this enormous hoard of millions of dollars somewhere. Not to say that a lot of money didn't go amiss or was ill-spent or ill-invested or whatever."

Clem Clempson: "We started to see a way of easing the situation at first. We tried to kind of make ourselves a bit more independent of management by trying to establish some kind of set up in England and in Europe. But, of course, that caused all kinds of problems and conflicts as well because management didn't want that. They didn't want us to be involved in any situation from which they weren't profiting."

Jerry Shirley: "Greg and Clem were getting fed up because the whole money issue was becoming a big issue by then. Bad feelings starting to creep in. Steve was getting more and more out of control. Coke. His marriage had fallen apart. And instead of diving into more work and more coke and more recording, what we should have done, easy to say now, is we should have given the guy time out to let him try and save his marriage. Because his marriage did not survive and he was never, ever the same again. He made a brave effort of getting over that marriage but he never actually did. Not 'til his dying day. He was just never the same guy. She was the love of his life."

Author: "Had he been given the option to take time off to save his marriage, would he have taken it?"

Jerry Shirley: "Yes, I think he would have. In fact, he was desperate for it. And we all failed him by being so caught up in making hay while the sun shone; basic insecurity, really. Common wisdom today is once you have a successful record the last thing in the world you wanna do is rush the next one out. You take your time and make sure it's right. A combination of things pulled us all in the direction of work, work, work, work, work."

Author: "Was everybody thinking this way?"

Jerry Shirley: "Yes and no. Everybody in the perfect world was quite happy to keep working. I certainly had no problem being on the road. I loved it. Clem could have taken it or left it. He would have probably leaned a little more towards taking time out then I personally would have been. Greg … as long as he could have his missus with him, he was happy to keep rolling on the road. And then you had Steve, whose entire life was completely crumbling around him as a direct result of cocaine abuse. And he didn't know how, where or why it could be achieved. All he wanted was out of the 'rock star on the road' bit and into his marriage. But it was a hopeless situation. He was damned if he did and damned if he didn't. He didn't know how to repair his marriage but he knew in order to do so he would have to take this huge time-out. But he had himself set up so that even if he had taken the time out, the slightest sign of problems, he had his rock 'n' roll world to jump into literally in his backyard."

Author: "And with more than enough people to encourage him."

Jerry Shirley: "Oh, absolutely. He had all the encouragement he needed to keep rockin' and rollin', sure. And Steve's only way of dealing with a problem with someone was completely confrontational or just blow it off. You know. 'Fuck you, fuck you.' That was it. All or nothing. Sitting down and having a quiet, intelligent, lengthy, compromising, seeing-both-sides-of-the-fence type of solving a problem talk was just not in Steve's scheme of things."

Kay Marriott: "Jenny was smashing. She was the love of his life. That was very sad. She was only twenty-four and he was nineteen when they met. But a man has to be a little bit older, sometimes. If a woman is younger when she's married, she's a lot older in her ways. I think she can cope better. But he'd been around from an early age, doing all sorts of things, meeting all sorts of people. So he was quite experienced for his age. Steve really fell for Jenny and adored her."

Kay Mateus Dos Anjos: "He was only twenty-one when he married Jenny. She was five years older than him, therefore ten years older than me. I always felt very in awe of Jenny. I liked her very much. She was very nice. Very kind. We got on well. With the age difference, we'd get along better now. I haven't seen Jenny since they split. But in the years they were together, she seemed to idolize him. They were very in tune. They had the same ways. They had the same ideas about how to make a home. About their animals. They were very laid back. It was so sad when it went wrong. Very sad."

Jerry Shirley: "He was away too much and there was too much drugs, too much infidelity and it all caught up with him. She started to get angry because she could see that success was ruining his personal life and he was lashing out at success and lashing out at his personal life too. He turned into a person he would not normally have been. He became violent with her, which was the last thing in the world that would have been on Steve's agenda years previously."

Greg Ridley: "Well, we were all having problems. Whether it be women or drugs or your mortgage ain't paid or you're getting stale or you want something to excite you."

Jerry Shirley: "Jesus, everybody and their mother was getting high back then and no one was prepared to concede that it might be a problem. Plus which, the perception of having enough money to do anything you wanted to do at any time meant that, at that time, and this is a very dangerous place to be, is when you either do have, or seem to have, enough money to be able to afford a habit like that. Then the money side of it is not an issue. Your life doesn't become ruined the same way an everyday Joe's life does. The rent doesn't get spent because there's more rent money to spend. So it just becomes a simple question of abuse."

Kay Marriott: "Drink wasn't the curse with Steve. But he could kick it for months on end and be fine. But then he'd go a binge. Not alcoholic. And he wasn't very nice in drink, unfortunately. Most people aren't, are they?"

Pam Cross: "He was a happy drunk, too. But he also had this split personality. If he got too drunk and had too many pills, he would get really mean."

Jerry Shirley: "Steve's 'happy drunk' … there were degrees of it. In the early days he was just a typical, seeing the funny side of everything, using the best of his sense of humor, so on and so forth. And then later in life, the happy drunk was becoming the cynical, anti-Semitic humor, behind closed doors type of funny. And then the angry thing was very destructive. Smashing up rooms, causing trouble. Melvin would take over. The famous alter ego, 'Melvin the bald wrestler,' who would magically appear at his door, out of nowhere, to explain why the room had been completely destroyed. It wasn't Steve that did it. This, literally, was true. It started by him claiming that his room had been destroyed by a bald wrestler called Melvin who appeared at his door mistaking his room for a party room and he smashed the room up. So from that day on Steve's alter ego became Melvin. You'd call up the studio to find out whether or not it was worth going there. You'd ask the question, 'Is Melvin out tonight?' Or, 'Careful, Melvin's out.' "

Author: "So that would tell you whether or not it was worth going over?"

Jerry Shirley: "Right. Or, if you had no choice but to go over, what you had to expect. 'Cuz Melvin was not a pretty sight. Believe me. And being part of the inner circle did not prevent him lashing out by any means. It meant that maybe his threshold of lashing out would be extended but by no means, because you were close to him, did that mean that you didn't get Melvined. He respected no one when it came to that."

1974

Author: "The 'Thunderbox' record sounds like it was an extremely fun time."

Jerry Shirley: "A lot of fun. Literally. You got that dead right. It was a lot of fun making the back tracks for that record and the various levels of recording. By the time it was all said and done, finished, we had managed to get around the sound problem in Steve's studio. But the record didn't sell and the record company and management and everybody involved took one more step from it. They stopped getting behind us at that point. They'd given up, pretty much. It was all over but the crying. There were no, as the record company would say, 'hits' on that record."

Author: "Was there a conscious effort to make 'Thunderbox' funkier than the previous releases or did the writing just evolve in that direction?"

Jerry Shirley: "Yeah, it just was. I didn't sit there and say, 'I am going to personally play tighter or funkier.' That's just the way we were going. It was the way I was personally going. I was particularly proud of the drum tracks because they'd gone up a notch. They were a little slicker, a little funkier. We did a few things on that record, as a rhythm section, that we had yet to do that worked in that kind of funk area."

Author: "Some of the grooves you and Greg laid down, in 'No Way,' in 'Groovin' With Jesus,' 'I Can't Stand The Rain,' all of them. They 'stink of the groove.' "

Jerry Shirley: "Yep. They were absolutely as tight as a duck's bum, some of the grooves on that record. And so much so that when we were making the tracks, Greg and I would just smile. Things would be happening. It was as if we had no control over these bits of rhythm section, these bits of bass and drums that were just being played together as if we didn't have anything to do with it. They were coming through us, if you like."

Clem Clempson: "That was us trying to push the band back in the 'Smokin' direction. And I thought it was a noble attempt. But it was really a case of the band being past its creative peak. I think we were happy with the direction. Greg was beginning to sing more, which was something that he personally wanted. I was writing a bit more, which is something that I personally wanted."

Jerry Shirley: "We were desperately trying to get something back, whatever that thing was. First of all, soundwise, we made a conscious effort to eradicate the sound problems that we discussed on 'Eat It.' Simplistic things like the compensation for the bass-light room. Making sure the EQ was corrected. In terms of material we definitely did try very hard, although obviously not hard enough, to pull back the reins and get more into the groove of back then. The general scheme of things. The writing. The sound. The arrangements and everything. I think what it was we were trying to get as far away from 'Eat It' as we could. There were some tremendous moments on 'Thunderbox.' I mean, 'I Can't Stand The Rain.' Even 'co-writer' Ann Peebles, bless her heart … one of my proudest moments was right after 'Thunderbox' was released. She was in London and doing an interview for *Melody Maker* or someone. And what they did was ask her to be a reviewer and gave her, like, ten songs to review. One of the ones they gave her was Humble Pie's version of 'I Can't Stand The Rain.' And she said, 'Oh, wow, I love that record! The groove is so cool! The rhythm

section is so down!' Greg and myself, we were just in seventh heaven over that."

Alan O'Duffy: "I recorded 'Thunderbox' but Steve mixed it. Steve was, 'Get out of my way, I'm mixing this. It's my studio.' And he couldn't be told no."

Jerry Shirley: "Of all the engineers that got the best out of me, sound wise, the two who were the best at getting my drum sounds were Eddie Kramer with the live album and Alan O'Duffy on 'Smokin' ' and 'Thunderbox.' He's recorded some pretty serious drum sounds in his time has Alan. He was one of the handful of people who was responsible for the technique it took to record a Charlie Watts or a John Bonham or a Ringo or a Mitch Mitchell. There was that little circle of them. And only they know how to get that wonderful, natural drum sound."

Alan O'Duffy: "Once upon a time, my singular drug experience was in Steve's studio."

Jerry Shirley: "It was hysterical. But they were warned!"

Alan O'Duffy: "Someone came into the studio with a hash cake. I like cake. I like a Guinness cake that my wife makes. And I thought, 'Well, I don't smoke but I do like cake. So, hey, have a bit of cake.' So I had a bit of cake. Great. We carried on."

Jerry Shirley: "They were chocolate brownies that had hashish in them. Jenny made them. And she was world-famous for her hash cookies. They were very, very strong. Hallucinogenic strong. And neither one of those guys had ever gotten high in their life, John Doumanian nor Alan. I don't know if they'd ever taken a drink let alone get high. Both as straight as it comes. And just as they'd started to eat these things we warned them, 'No, no, no. You don't know what you're doing there. It could get ugly.' "

Alan O'Duffy: "I had the last of the cake. And I was saying to people, 'Well, I feel the same.' 'Cuz they all knew I didn't take anything. Eventually the girls got there; I don't know, around six o'clock in the evening. And when they came in I played the track. At this point I was feeling pins and needles and I said to Steve's assistant, John, 'Oh, you run the track, mate. I feel a bit funny.' I then went downstairs to the band who were in the anteroom of the studio and I said, 'I don't feel so well. I feel a bit funny.' They knew I'd had the cake and they knew I didn't take drugs and stuff."

Jerry Shirley: "They had this long leather couch in the studio. Before you knew it they were both lying along it going, 'Ohhh! I want my Mommy! Help! The world is coming to an end! Armageddon is with us' [laughs]! They were trippin'!"

Alan O'Duffy: "And I said, 'If I'm not feeling a bit better within the next half an hour I want to be brought to hospital' [laughs]! And they all laughed at me like mad. And it went on and on. I started to drink water to try and flush it through my system, loads and loads of water."

Jerry Shirley: " 'Oh, call an ambulance.' 'Oh, no, we don't wanna do that' [laughs]. I mean, they ate a whole plate full. And these were so strong you only needed to eat one-half of a hash brownie to get high for a day. But they were both piggies, especially John Doumanian. He was the guy with the famous quote … he'd be sitting in a restaurant and he'd have the menu and he'd look at the entire menu, hand it back to the waitress and say, 'Yes, that will be fine. And I will need an Alka-Seltzer' [laughs]! 'And coffee.' "

Alan O'Duffy: "Anyway, the session finished. I had nothing to do with the session because I had missed it. Steve had me stay upstairs in his house, in one of the bedrooms. And I wanted to go to the toilet in the middle of the night. So I went to try and open the door and it wouldn't open. And it transpired that the door needed to be pulled rather than pushed. An appalling state of mankind to tell you that I had to piss out the window! And when I went home the following day the only person who really understood where my head was was my dog. I felt funny for several days afterwards. I just wanted to be back to my normal self."

Author: "When the band returned to the road, this time to promote 'Thunderbox,' were the tours as strong or were the lack of sales evident?"

Jerry Shirley: "That was when the real writing was on the wall. They did not promote it. It didn't get airplay. It didn't sell. At the same time, for the first time, we started to notice that we weren't selling tickets with the same strength as we were before."

Clem Clempson: "We saw that things weren't going well but we knew that anyway."

Jerry Shirley: "We went out and toured all of '73 with 'Eat It,' and we made it look like it was doing well. They had managed to hype it into seeming like it was doing better than it in fact was. The ticket sales were still doing pretty decent and we were playing big halls. And when we went back out in '74 with 'Thunderbox,' that's when they talked us into getting rid of the girls and going back to the basics."

Greg Ridley: "The hit single that would have made us like Zeppelin never happened. We thought we were worthy but it never happened. Everybody loved us playing live. Everybody thought, 'Great band.' But business-wise and money-wise, the hit single to sell the mega-album never bloody happened. We had albums that went to number 40 with a bullet but it didn't really cream off all the profits that management would have liked and obviously would have kept us going longer. We all had to start selling off things and moving out and whatever. We never had a grand lifestyle out of Humble Pie, that's for sure."

Artistic integrity caused many bands of the time to become "anti-single." By being an "album band," the statement being made was the refusal to sell out for the almighty dollar. Many bands lost their way as a result of someone picking a song for them and convincing the group to release it as a single. In many cases that decision ruined careers.

Jerry Shirley: "Exactly. They get on a catchy three-minute number and 'BOOM,' the rest of their career's over. Look what happened when 'Frampton Comes Alive' first came out.

It was correctly viewed as a solid piece of musicality. And then they started to pick singles from it and edited them down. They took 'Do You Feel Like We Do' and released a shorter version. And they picked 'Baby I Love Your Way' as opposed to 'I'll Give You Money.' That was a great track. Rocks on, ballsy track. But they went with [sings] 'Baby I Love Your Way.' So there's a great example. Whilst it didn't seem apparent right there and then when it was happening, it's easy to say with 20/20 and all of that, it was downhill all the way from Peter's point of view. Before you know it they were rushing out another album. And sure enough the first thing, the title track, really schmaltzy [sings] 'I'm In You.' "

Author: "You've attained an incredible amount of individual success. When did it become a bit much?"

Peter Frampton: "When 'Frampton Comes Alive' went through the ceiling. As Cameron Crowe so wonderfully put it on *Behind The Music*, 'I was snapped to the nose-cone of a rocket and I went through the ceiling.' And there was nobody else up there but me. From the beginning of '75 to the end of '76, those two years were an incredible ride. At one point I said to Bob Mayo, 'What did we do, eight or nine in a row?' He said, 'No. Twenty-seven.' And some of those were doubles [laughs]. I remember we did one on the east coast, an afternoon one, rented a plane and flew and did one in like Denver or something in the evening. We were just a touring force. And who was complaining? It was just so exciting. But when 'Comes Alive' took off it seemed I had no time. I was touring and I was interviewing and I was TV'ing and I was all this and magazining, whatever. There was not time allotted to regroup. You've got the biggest-selling record of all time and everybody's rushing me back into the studio. That, right there, is the whole problem with what happened afterwards. I would have liked to have taken a couple of years off at that point. And I should have. But Jerry Moss's feeling at the time, rightly for him, wrongly for me, was that he felt the longer you wait the harder it'll be to follow it up. Maybe there's some truth to that. Who knows; we'll never find out. But if I had the wisdom that I now have about being able to look back at everything I went through and everybody around me, I would have done nothing. I would have gone and lived in the Bahamas for four or five months. Written when I felt like it. No pressure. Because it's very hard to turn the faucet on and off."

• • •

Clem Clempson: "I don't remember being aware of the record company saying that 'Thunderbox' wasn't what they wanted. I don't remember us being that close to the record company. We had Dee Anthony. He was kind of the buffer between us and the record company. I don't remember Dee ever saying, 'The record company isn't happy. You've got to rethink this.' "

Jerry Shirley: "The feels on that record in general were very strong and I also think the record could have done much better than it did. It's always easy to excuse a record; there's always a reason why it didn't do what it didn't do. 'This was wrong, that was wrong,' instead of being honest and saying it was a lousy record. But it was by no means a lousy record. It was a great record. But what had happened was that the politics had started to come into play. We were falling apart at the seams, internally, and it was no longer hideable. There was a lot of dissension going on behind the scenes regarding the management. Everybody knew about it. It wasn't for our ears only. Everybody from Jerry Moss on down knew what kind of trouble we were in because Steve's troubles with his marriage were not kept behind closed doors. Everybody knew about it because we were very much a family. Everybody was involved in our lives. I'm so out of touch with the big leagues but it seems to me a much more clinical business, a cold environment, compared to back then. I mean, Jerry Moss and Gil Friesen and Abe Summer and all of them knew, first hand, what was going on. They had tried to help, talking to or counseling if you like, Steve and Jenny both. And I don't think presidents of record companies call husbands and wives and try and reconcile them in today's world.

"The politics of it had gotten so that the record was probably, from inside the record company's point of view, written off before it got a chance to get going because by then Steve had … well, not just Steve. We had all managed to summarily piss off every area of the record business and probably radio stations too. And Steve, very clearly, had stated that he would only tour America, if at all, once that year. On top of all of that, the band had actually broken up right before the album was released. Just as we were trying to put right what had gone horribly wrong with the whole financial situation, which I've already explained. The Japan trip and the $100,000 in debt."

Greg Ridley: "Money is very embarrassing. And, of course, you don't realize what you spend on the road. Or you think you're being ripped for this and ripped off for that. I mean, you will get ripped off. But, of course, what you squander you're not even aware of at the time. And there was a lot of squandering."

Jerry Shirley: "We'd gotten this meeting with Dee and Bert Padell, the accountant. And Steve was not being loud or aggressive or any of that but he was being awkward, shall we say. I was obviously hot and bothered about the whole situation. Steve turned to me at one point and said, in a very kind of catty way, 'Well, I'm sorry, Jer. I didn't realize I had been hanging you up so much.' That was old hip speak for pissing you off. I just completely freaked and said, 'You're not just pissing me off now. You've been pissing me off for years, you cunt!' And the look on poor Steve's face … 'cuz he really didn't realize the extent to which he had been impossible to deal with in our lives and for how long. The way I said it, it was like at that moment he realized that someone very close to him had been pissed off at him for so long. And he just said, 'Well, if that's the way you feel, then I'll just quit. I don't want to piss anybody off.' So I lunged at him and he lunged back and Bert and Dee grabbed me and prevented me from slapping the shit out of him, thank God. And I stress, we did not actually exchange blows. In fact, we never did. There's a lot of people that have interest in our inside story that say Steve and I did physically fight. That actually never happened. We came very close and I definitely had to be dragged off him a couple of times. I did swing at him a couple of times. But never, ever did I hit the man. And that

was it. His reaction was quite understandable, which was, 'I'm out of here.' And my reaction was, 'Fine, so am I.'

"Dee had already booked a tour of America. Our initial reaction was, 'We just won't do it. Cancel it.' The group was done. In fact we were looking for a new lead singer. We had started to approach Bobby Tench. And it was very embarrassing because I went to see Derek Green with A&M in London to discuss the situation. We had come forward with the idea of perpetuating the group with a new lead singer. And he was all keen. 'Oh, good. Who have you got?' We told him we got someone really exciting. And I'll never forget the look on his face when I said, 'Bobby Tench.' He looked at me. 'What do you mean?' I said, 'Why? What's the problem?' Well, he had just signed Bobby Tench to A&M with a group called Hummingbird. We had forgotten to mention the fact that we were trying to get Bobby Tench to Bobby Tench. We were shooting in the dark. It was like our wish list. We didn't even know Bobby back then and we certainly had no idea that he had signed a record deal with A&M. So that idea didn't go very far."

Author: "When Steve quit following an argument with Jerry, they had considered approaching you to replace him but you had just signed with A&M with Hummingbird. Were you aware of that?"

Bobby Tench: "No, I wasn't. We'd signed a three-album deal at that point. That was after Jeff Beck. But it was a regular thing between those two. They were always arguing but they couldn't do without one another. They needed to do that sort of stuff to be on the edge."

Jerry Shirley: "To Dee, quite rightfully I suppose, he scrambled around for ideas for us to at least get back together for one tour; call it a farewell tour is how we did it. And it was left up to me to eat crow, if you like, to call Steve and say, 'Look, why don't we let bygones be bygones? We've got a tour booked for us anyway, so let's go out and tour and see how we do. We at least need to talk long enough to get this tour done. Let's call it a farewell tour.' And he said, 'Yeah, man, I suppose. But I have to talk to my band about it.' And I said, 'Your band?' And he said, 'Yeah, I've just joined a new band.' Being very coy, not saying, 'I've just joined the Stones.' And of course he didn't have a job at all.

"Steve was hanging out with Keith Richards from time to time, jamming and going over to his house and up all night. The only person that could out-Steve Steve was Keith. Steve could stay up for five days straight, without so much as thinking about going to bed. Keith could go ten. And that's literally true. Apparently Keith's record was he did not see a bed, well not to sleep in anyway, for ten days straight. And you would never have known. Didn't affect his performing onstage, I mean. I'm sure if you were close to the man you could certainly tell.

"Anyway, Steve and Keith were hanging out. Keith loved Steve. Mick Taylor had just left. And a long list of candidates, including Peter Frampton I might add, were being considered. Of course, Ronnie Wood was always there and eventually got the job. But Steve went and did an actual proper audition. And apparently he had been forewarned by everybody, but in particular by Keith, not to overdo it on stage because of Mick. 'Cuz Mick will not be upstaged by anybody. So Steve said, 'Yeah, no problem, man. I'll just kick back, play some rhythm, do a little backing vocal if you want me to.'

"So. They get to the rehearsal place; sure enough they start playing. Steve's doing as he said he would and it's going really well. So the more encouraged he gets and the more of a smile there is on Keith's face, they start to get into it a bit. Keith himself is quite a performer. So as they get into it Steve lets the chains off and starts to be Steve on stage. All of a sudden he's leaping all over the stage and he's thinking that it's going down well and everybody is loving it. And the more he thought they loved it the more he played to the gallery. He's singing full on and he's literally Mick Jaggering all over the stage and guess what … he didn't get the job! But he thought he had got it for a while. I don't know if that's because Keith told him that he got the job and he didn't have the heart not to tell him or it was just Steve assuming that which he shouldn't have assumed. But I have an eyewitness

of it. Alan Rogan, the guitar tech for The Who. He's done Pete Townshend and Keith and Joe Walsh … all kinds of people. He described the scene to me. That's why when I tell the story it sounds like I was there but it was Alan. He said it was hysterical to watch. 'Cuz Steve Marriott is, or was God rest his soul, the only person who would be capable of upstaging Jagger. Not only as a performer but as a singer. I mean, God, Mick can't shine Steve's shoes."

Author: "But it's half of Mick's band and he's not going to let a sideman show him up."

Jerry Shirley: "Absolutely. And he would show him up. I mean, Mick's a great singer, don't get me wrong. And if nothing else Mick Jagger is a complete original. However, strictly technical ability as a singer, putting him next to Steve when Steve can match him note for note in terms of individuality and all, just a pure, 'Who's the better singer?' There's no contest. Steve's got everyone. So Mick Jagger is not a big mountain to climb [laughs]."

Peter Frampton: "I was driving into Manhattan from Westchester and had NEW glued … that was the station you listened to. And they had 'Rock News,' or whatever and I had to pull over. 'Excuse me [laughs]? I gotta call somebody!' I'd heard I was on the short list of five people, which was quite amazing to me. Then I thought, (pause) 'Bill' [laughs]! It was a great feeling.

"When I was doing 'I'm In You' and Mick was next door mixing a Stones live record at the time, I said, 'Mick, are you gonna sing on my album?' He said, 'All right.' So I said, 'I gotta ask you. Was it true, was I on the list?' And he said, 'Yeah, of course you were.' And I said, 'Well, why didn't I get the job' [laughs]? I never auditioned. I think they played with Ronnie and it was like within the first few seconds they all went, 'This is right.' They had other suggestions of which I was one of but I think that Ronnie was so perfect that straightaway they realized that."

•　　•　　•

The Small Faces of Steve Marriott — #1, 2, 3 & 5, San Diego, CA, 1973. #4, Los Angeles, CA, 1973. #6, San Francisco, CA, 1975. Courtesy Karen Dyson.

Jerry Shirley: "We did that one tour of the U.S. in the spring of '74 and that was the only tour that year that we did in America."

Clem Clempson: "There were several occasions of flare-ups between different members of the band. I remember having a row with Steve about something to do with money. He had said he couldn't work with 'breadheads' anymore. I think we were basically trying to pay the rent at the time [laughs]! Which was starting to become a problem. Up until the 'Thunderbox' time, we had been kept very happy with wads of cash, even though we didn't have a clue how much money we were making or what was happening to it, and the assurance that everything was taken care of. But then that suddenly started to dry up and we actually started to find ourselves in a debts match in England. That again

caused a lot of internal problems. We all had different ideas on what we had to do to deal with it. Though I don't remember Dee Anthony ever standing up to Steve. He would always sort of blame Steve when he was speaking to the rest of us for any kind of problems we were having. 'You know how long this guy spends on the telephone?' And as soon as anyone breathed a word of that to Steve, all hell would break loose. At that stage we didn't have any idea what the truth was at all."

Kay Marriott: "I despise those people, really. 'Cuz they just live off of the young ones, don't they? Like leeches. But sadly, they need people like that. With so much money around, how can you get honest people interested? We had honest people with them in The Small Faces and they went crooked because of the money. It's such a sensation. And in America, it just attracted all the wrong people. The big people. They control them. So what can you do? Without the talent, they wouldn't stay there. But they put them there. His father used to say to him, 'You've got to watch your money. You've got to watch what's going on. And stop signing things. Study it first.' And he'd say, 'Dad, my job is to play and entertain. I pay people to look after things for me. Other than that, I don't understand a thing about it. I just hope that the people I'm paying can and do.' How can you argue with that?"

Author: "Was there any one particular thing that caused Steve to lash out at success?"

Jerry Shirley: "First, the obvious, but we didn't see it at the time, you have to backtrack twenty-five years and remember what everybody's mind set towards cocaine was. That it wasn't harmful. That it was just another close cousin to marijuana. Accepted and encouraged at every level. It was the great panacea of everybody. It was the great communicator. Business decisions were not made unless that was involved. How could you possibly make a sound business decision without having the appropriate amount of blow to make the decision for you?

"So to get to what you were saying about what 'one' thing, that was an enormous difference. Prior to 1972 cocaine was either not done at all or only once every six months, if that. It was not part of our drug vocabulary. At all. So along with that came the money to afford it. So not only did we have this new habit that we didn't understand at all but, to make matters worse, we could afford limitless amounts. Because we had the money and back then it was really cheap."

Author: "And plenty of people around to make it available."

Jerry Shirley: "Everybody from presidents of record companies to roadies and all points in between. I remember walking into a sold out show in the southern part of America and the promoter coming up and greeting us at sound check and saying, 'Congratulations, tonight's sold out.' And instead of putting a hand out to shake with, the hand that he put out held an ounce of the purest cocaine in the world. It was, 'Thank you very much guys. We appreciate it.' "

Author: "Was coke also at the root of Steve's getting violent with Jenny?"

Jerry Shirley: "Oh, absolutely. Steve very much did have a pre-existing anger problem. His only way to go was attack. All the way down to the basic simple 'little guy against the rest of the world. Attack is the best form of defense. Blah, blah, blah.' But the quiet, somewhat matured hash-smoking hippie that I previously described to you at that time when he was at his happiest, his private life from 1968 through to 1971, had suddenly been supplanted with this very aggressive bloke."

Jenny Dearden: "I went back a couple of times just to see the animals, when he wasn't there. And I was just beside myself. I sobbed all the way back to London. Leaving the animals … they were my children. And leaving him was the hardest thing I'd ever done. But I was drowning. I still loved him. But I couldn't live in that unhealthy bubble anymore. He would not deal with life outside. Most of the time he was away I was living a perfectly normal life and seeing normal people and normal friends. And appreciating my surroundings. The countryside. He could have been living in the middle of a slum. He never noticed in the end.

"He was very difficult to help. He was incredibly stubborn. And he always had to be right. What really finished us off was every tour he did, he'd had lots of affairs. I was incredibly lonely. And towards the end I'd hardly went out at all and I got very depressed, introverted. A friend of mine whisked me up to London and I met somebody at a party who then pursued me. This was sort of what it was like to be admired, really. Anyway, I couldn't hide it. Steve had come back a week later and he went ape shit."

Jerry Shirley: "He wasn't prepared to face the fact that he might be the problem. I think what actually happened was he pressed her one night. 'Well, you can tell me.' And she did! And he slapped the shit out of her.

"To give you an example, when they were going through the breakup, this is how bad it was. There was a meeting set up between Jenny and Steve where Steve was on the road and she was being flown to New York to supposedly have a reconciliation. It was all over by then and everybody knew it except Steve. In terms of being able to accept it. A last chance grasp at reconciliation. And it was set up to take place at Dee Anthony's apartment in New York."

Jenny Dearden: "I was followed everywhere I went by a six-foot gorilla. I was ferried off on a plane to Nassau to keep me out of the way. I was then taken to New York to see Steve, who had written two book-fulls of 'If I said I loved him, I'd be back on a pedestal again. If I didn't say I loved him …' There were reams and reams of horrendous stuff."

Jerry Shirley: "Steve had been sat down by Dee, by us guys in the band, by the road manager and everybody. And he'd been made to promise that he would, no matter what happened, would not lay a finger on her. At that point it got so bad that the only terms that Jenny would agree to be in the same room with him alone, so they could talk it through, was if she got a guarantee that he would not touch her. And so, on that understanding that Steve be more behaving like his quiet, hippie self, she agreed. 'Of course. I wouldn't dream of such a thing. My whole marriage depends on this meeting' type of attitude. They walked into the room and within thirty seconds he was beating the crap out of her."

Jenny Dearden: "It ended up quite unpleasantly and I got out. He was so coked out. So if he'd had handled that differently, if I had handled it differently … but it's very hard to reach somebody when they're doing that much coke every day."

Jerry Shirley: "That's how psychotic that drug can make people. Like all people who do a lot of coke, of course they do lots of alcohol to level themselves out. And so yes, his alcohol consumption soared as a direct result of the same old coke story."

Jenny Dearden: "The fact that he brought over all these really heavy guys … that's not a thing that one can respect. It was big bullies being brought in to crush me. I was already quite crushed. So it wasn't really necessary, you know [laughs]. But that was the sort of atmosphere that he was surviving in. It's the only way he knew how to do it.

"After everything, the saddest aspect is the fact that before all the bullshit and tours of the States and the too many drugs, he was an extraordinary person with an extraordinary talent. And that's the horrible irony, isn't it? That in promoting the talent, everything else that goes with it is destroyed."

Author: "And it borders on the cliché as well. It happens to so many people."

Jenny Dearden: "Exactly. And that is the part that has always interested me. What is the common denominator? Obviously, it's the frailty of human nature. Even the strongest people succumb in the end."

Jerry Shirley: "They were a great couple. During that period from 1968 to 1971, those three years, it was just magic. If you listen to his love songs from that period, it just oozes. He was a great love-song writer. Everything from 'Tin Soldier' through to 'A Song For Jenny,' and all points in between. Tough love songs, gooey love songs. He was great at it because he meant it. I think the first song he wrote for her was 'Tin Soldier.' That was a song he wrote to 'pull her.' It was his way of getting the point home. Any young tart listening to that song being written for her and seeing it performed on television … if she doesn't fall for that, then she's gay! And 'Afterglow,' from The Small Faces. It should have been a huge hit. And though it was in the sense that it was on that album, 'Ogden's Nut Gone Flake,' and they did release it later as a single, it didn't get any push behind it. It was a beautiful song."

• • •

Jerry Shirley: "Dee suggested that we go check into Billy Joel, of all people. Obviously, that went nowhere. And immediately thereafter Steve was back in the fold anyway."

After Humble Pie toured to promote "Thunderbox," everyone had pretty much made up their minds that they would all take another stab at it. Steve returned to his studio and started working on three albums simultaneously. A rock-oriented Pie album, a solo release and a Marriott/Ridley record. I was curious why no one saw this as being counter-productive.

Jerry Shirley: " 'Cuz we were completely off our trees at that time. Everything was so self-destructive at that point. Everybody was doing everything in a dozen different directions and nothing was getting done. And no one was facing the issue at hand, which was the fact that the group was falling apart at the seams. I remember I was making, what I thought, was a manly attempt to try to get the group to have a look at what was going on, financially, and get other management involved. But whenever we did try, we failed miserably. And Dee had us truly locked up, contractually, anyway. It was a nightmare of a time and no matter what got done, it seemed counter-productive. Steve's way of dealing with things was buying an ounce of coke every other day and burying himself in his studio. Therefore, when you've got nothing but carte blanche studio time and all the coke in the world, all you do is record. So, suddenly, he had a solo album, he had his album with Greg and he had the band and all kinds of stuff going on. And none of it got done very well. There were great bits here and there but there was no one focus on one record."

Greg Ridley: "He and I were two lonely souls. We used to sit there with a sack full of whatever would make you feel better and just play to the two of us. I would play drums one night or he would. Then I would play the guitar or whatever. And we had the recording desk, of course. We'd just sit there for almost a week at a time without sleeping. He and I would just go through different things. He'd say, 'Let's try this chord,' and then we'd go off from that. We did spend a lot of time together up in the recording studio. Which was great."

Jerry Shirley: "We went in and started recording what ended up to be 'Street Rats.' By now, A&M had put their foot down and Jerry Moss said, 'I insist that you hire a producer for the next record.' And we grudgingly said, 'All right. ANDREW OLDHAM!' That's like saying, 'OK, we'll hire a producer' and then chuckling behind their backs and hiring your cousin Vinnie! Andrew was one of the lads. He let us get on with it anyway we wanted to. Although, with undying credit to Andrew, he did make a tremendous effort to try and have us make a well-produced, well-structured, well-written record. But the rot had long since set in and it was just no good at all. He tried, he failed, let's put it like that. There was all kinds of nonsense going on. We were cutting tracks in London and my drumming would be on it. The tapes would end up in New York, having some session drummer overdub on top of mine, and then … that's just me. God knows what happened to other people's parts."

Clem Clempson: "What the 'Street Rats' album was was pretty much a compilation of tracks that Greg and Jerry and myself had done. And a lot of stuff that Steve had at his house with his various musician friends. And there's a lot more of that stuff on 'The Scrubbers Sessions.' There were tracks there that Steve had recorded with other people at his house that he kind of replaced other people's performances with those from guys in the band. It was all crazy then, you know. I don't think anybody's heart was in it. That was the problem."

Jerry Shirley: "It was so bad that when they came to do the photograph for the album cover, which is the four of us squatting down and we've been cropped into the background of a street? Well that, in fact, is not the four of us squatting down together at all. What they did was send a photographer out to each one of our houses and took an individual shot of each one of us and cropped it into making it look like we were in the same room at the same time. No one cared. No one was talking. We'd already broken up. We'd agreed to allow the album to be released and to do a farewell tour. Other than that we were pretty much done."

Most of the excess material that was recorded in Steve's studio was later issued as "The Scrubbers Sessions." But one glaring omission was the presence of Jerry Shirley.

Jerry Shirley: "It was getting way out of control and I just couldn't handle it. Way too much partying. And the music that was being made was just not on. Some of it turned out all right but Steve was doing mountains of blow and he was staying up for seven days straight. And there's nothing more ugly in this world than what we used to call a 'Five-Day Marriott.' It was just uncomfortable. A lot of not very nice people hanging around. Dealers and this and that. I had to pass."

Jerry had set up a meeting with the thought of seeking new management to stop the bleeding. Clem and Jerry arrived ready to do business. Greg didn't show up at all. And Steve arrived completely trashed.

Jerry Shirley: "That was in 1975 so I was all of twenty-three years old. Steve was a grand old man of twenty-eight. And what seemed like insurmountable problems at that time, combined with the drugs, combined with out-of-control egos all-round, probably could have been easily solved with a quiet chat over a cup of tea in today's world. But back then, all joking aside, the rot was so deep … it had gotten to kinda like driving a car down a hill when the brakes had definitely failed.

"This was the most important meeting we had ever gotten together over. The whole thing was either gonna make it or break it and Bill Curbishley had stuck his neck out a long way to jump in and act on our behalf. This was not just a quick meeting to decide on the catering. This was big stuff. And Steve had such a 'What's the big deal, flippin' attitude towards this meeting. 'Oh, we're having a meeting? Business?' That was becoming Steve's total attitude. The word 'business.' Anything about asking for a sensible meeting of the minds about what was, after all, a multi-million dollar thing that was fast slipping through our fingers … Bill Curbishley looked at me, I looked at him, we looked at each other and said, 'Oh, man. There's no talking to this guy right now.'

"Bill Curbishley was fast becoming the main man with The Who. He had unofficially been their manager for some time. This was not some schmuck who was involved here. This was Bill. And he had gone to great lengths and great risk because we were still signed to Dee. So Dee could have sued Bill for poaching his act. And then there was the fear

side of Dee, which Bill didn't care about. You couldn't scare Bill like that.

"We'd met earlier that day at Steve's studio. For two reasons. One was to play the backing track we'd done for Roger Daltrey on his upcoming solo album. It was a song called 'Do It.' I don't know if it made the record. Our version didn't because it was too much like The Who. We went out of our way to 'Who it up,' if you'd like. It was a great backing track and Roger loved it but he said, 'I'm sorry, Steve, you've gone too far, out of respect for The Who.' When Roger left was when we were to have our all-important meeting for Bill Curbishley to report on what happened in his meeting with Dee."

Clem Clempson: "They were the only people we knew of that we thought would be big enough to take on Dee Anthony. And they agreed to see if they could help us out. Steve was wrecked and Greg didn't turn up at all. And it was at that point that they said, 'Well, you know, there's nothing we can do at the moment.' "

Jerry Shirley: "I said to Clem, 'That's it, I'm out of here.' "

Clem Clempson: "Jerry and myself just went down to the pub and had a drink. And that's where we first said, 'That's it. It's over.' "

Jerry Shirley: "And Clem said, 'Well, if you're out, I'm out.' Which was very nice of him. 'If you're not here, what's the point.' I don't think he meant that from a musical point of view. He meant that from a business sense. If it got to where I thought I couldn't figure out a remedy, no one could because no one had been as close to a) the business side and b) Steve.

"But we neglected to realize they had booked us for one more tour. So we agreed to do that, as a farewell tour, again, and that was the end of it. The tour was great. It was a farewell tour and because of that we did sell tickets again. And we did play great again."

Author: "Was the farewell tour a relief or sad?"

Greg Ridley: "Definitely sad. Thinking that you're on the decline, going down the ladder. It was bloody sad; it was terrible."

Jenny Dearden: "Steve could not be on his own. I had a call from Dee saying, 'Please, Jenny, come on this tour with us because he's not going to be able to cope on his own.' And I said, 'Dee, I've left. I'm trying to get myself together.' By this time I was back in London. I was fairly distraught but trying to keep myself going. So I suggested that he take this girl called Sally. She brought somebody around to see me, she was going out with him at this time. And he called me up when Sally went off to the States and I ended up seeing him."

Jerry Shirley: "I'd forgotten about that. Do you remember the cover of 'Thunderbox?' There was a brunette who was not facing the camera; her ass was facing the camera. That was Sally. She was also a very good artist. And she had one of the greatest pair of legs I've seen in my life. Wonderful friend. She worked for Steve and Jenny as a dog sitter. And then when Steve and Jenny broke up, that's when she sent Sally along to … what was the name of that girl in John Lennon's life? May Pang. Yoko Ono sent May Pang in. Well, it was nothing like that [laughs]!"

Author: "What were you doing during your down time then?"

Jerry Shirley: "Playing soccer, going to the pub, and trying to figure out what the fuck I was going to do with the rest of me life. I had started to meet a few people, musician-wise, which ended up being the next group I was in, a group called Natural Gas. But I just remember being pretty much in a daze about everything, just being very devastated by the fact that this great group, that we were so close and dedicated to just a few years before, had fallen apart into this badly managed, drug-hazed mess. Though we still played great on stage. We never, ever 'didn't' play well. We might have still been playing the same songs but we still went on and performed our asses off, no matter what was going on."

Author: "Was it promoted as a farewell tour?"

Jerry Shirley: "Oh, yeah. And there were lots of teary nights. 'Sorry, man, I never meant to …' you know. Everybody was so disenchanted with the money thing and the management thing. And it was time to move on anyway."

Author: "It must have been a relief as well."

Jerry Shirley: "In a way, yeah. It was a bit of both. But until it happened, I didn't stop to realize. When we broke up, in '75, my life was over at twenty-three. I'm going, 'What the fuck is this all about?' It was particularly devastating for me, once it all sank in. Steve and Greg had been around the block a bit more. Let's face it. As lead singer/lead guitar player, bass player/singer, they had much more potential to move on and do something else than a drummer did. Just common sense tells you that."

Author: "When it was all over, what did you have to show for it? Besides the obvious good memories, good experiences."

Jerry Shirley: "Not a whole lot. Because everything I did have to show for it got quickly sold or liquidated because I had no money. There were no royalties coming in, no tours. At the beginning of 1975, I had the spoils of the war. The house in the country, a Mercedes, a Rolls Royce, a Range Rover, a BMW, a marriage, a kid, money in the bank and all points in between. At the beginning of 1976 I was sitting in the living room of a rented home in upstate New York, surrounded by a few boxes. The wife had left me [laughs]. Seems like a bad country song! There was no money in the bank. The house in England had been sold. 1976 wasn't too bad, playing with Natural Gas. But I went from having the world by the tail in January of '75 to having, literally, nothing in January, '77. Pretty astonishing. In two short years, between the ages of twenty-three and twenty-five, a pretty rude awakening was at hand [laughs]! Fortunately I got brought up on a pretty down-to-earth background, down-to-earth folk, and I could see it for what it was fairly quickly. Otherwise, I dunno what I would have done.

Humble Pie (l-r, Steve Marriott, Jerry Shirley, Greg Ridley, Clem Clempson) San Antonio, Texas, 1975.
Courtesy Karen Dyson

"When the band first broke up we were in debt to A&M Records, so it didn't matter who was getting the royalties 'cuz no one was getting the royalties. Once the debt to A&M was paid back ten, fifteen years later, in the late 80s/early 90s, we were in a position where we should be getting the residuals everybody else tends to get nowadays. We were told that the record company would pay it off. And then, when we went to try and get our royalties, we found out that all of these contracts were not only bad for us back then, but more importantly, they were really bad for us now."

John Doumanian: "It's their own fault. They never took care of business and they spent money like it was from a bottomless well. Those guys did spend dough. At the end, everyone's charging. Bills are coming in and there was no money coming in. It wasn't totally Dee's fault. They gotta

assume some of the responsibility. When they got the money to go home, the cash in their pocket, it was wonderful. All is forgiven."

Clem Clempson: "It's very easy to cite all this as the reason for the band's demise but I think there was more to it. I don't think it was just a case of the band being destroyed by Steve's excesses or anything like that. I think it's true of most rock acts that they only have a short period of real creativity and the height of their popularity coincides with that. And very few acts, really, have been capable of maintaining the high standards year after year and constantly exceeding people's expectations. There are hundreds of Humble Pies and they may all have their personal reasons that they attribute to their downfall. But usually it's just because they have a creative period and they get popular.

They get some hit songs and everybody wants to hear them. And they just fail to live up to it for whatever reasons. The combination of the pressures of touring. The internal conflicts of egos. Believing their own hype. All these things are contributing factors."

Kay Mateus Dos Anjos: "I think Humble Pie were ahead of their time. I loved watching Humble Pie. I thought they were fantastic. They were much cleverer than The Small Faces. Much more musical, everything. When I was seventeen, eighteen, I thought, 'Oh, my God, I'd rather listen to 'All Or Nothing' or 'Sha La La La Lay' than '30 Days In The Hole.' But now I prefer Humble Pie to The Small Faces. I found them very exciting. Also, the audiences were quiet."

Author: "What can you tell me about the solo album Steve put out in '75?"

Jerry Shirley: "It was extremely expensive. There were some good songs on it but it got horribly over-produced, at least on one side, by a pair of American guys. And it came back to bite the group in the ass because of the way the record deal was structured. Our huge Humble Pie recording contract that Dee renegotiated for us had cross-collateralized itself, a nasty word never to be included in the vocabulary of a rock 'n' roll musician. In other words they can take the loss from one record and deduct it from the profit of another one. And in this little nest of vipers they could take the loss from a solo record and take it from the profit from a group record. Well, at the point when the group broke up and we released our last group effort, being 'Street Rats,' which barely broke even if not went into debt a little bit, we were only maybe a year or so away from paying back Humble Pie's debt to A&M. However, Steve went off and recorded 'Marriott' and something like half a million dollars later it didn't sell squat. It took the band's profit fifteen years to pay off Steve's solo debt. So instead of it taking until 1990 for the group account to become in the black, it would have been, conservatively speaking, in the black a full ten years before that. Not the smartest contract signing I ever did."

• • •

Michael Taylor: " 'Itchycoo Park' got re-issued and Steve was asked if The Small Faces would mind getting together for a video. Steve got in touch with all the old members and nobody was committed to anything. So they reformed under the guise of doing two videos, 'Itchycoo Park' and 'Lazy Sunday.' And during the shoots, they talked about reforming and maybe doing an album or two. Ronnie Lane didn't want to do it as a full-time thing. MS was beginning to set in with Ronnie, which no one else was aware of. One day in the studio Steve thought Ronnie was drunk and there was an argument. Some say there was a punchup. Ronnie left. The other three got Rick Wills in and continued on. They released two albums, 'Playmates' and ''78 In The Shade.' But the former glory never returned."

Author: "Apparently Steve had a really hard time with Ronnie that they never had a chance to resolve. I've heard from several people that Ronnie was quite rotten about Steve when he died, saying something to the effect of 'Good riddance.' "

Jerry Shirley: "That's how deep the resentments were between them. Which is a great shame because Steve loved him. Steve was so generous to Ronnie about sharing the talent and the spotlight with the writing. When push came to shove, Steve was doing the majority of it. And that's not to say Ronnie wasn't talented. He was. But they're both at rest now."

Ronnie Lane died at his home in Colorado on June 4, 1997 after a twenty-year battle with Multiple Sclerosis.

In 1977, A&M Records and Dee Anthony decided to capitalize on Peter Frampton's success with "Frampton Comes Alive" by collaborating with Robert Stigwood and his triumph, The Bee Gees, and steer their clients into making a movie based on arguably the most important album in recorded music history, *Sgt. Pepper*. The movie has been repeatedly called the "worst film of all time." Many claim that the blame can be worn by the participants, both in front and behind the scenes.

Jerry Shirley: "When Peter fucked up the 'Frampton Comes Alive' period, royally, he had built himself up quite a nice reputation, some of it not deserved, some of it

San Antonio, Texas, 1975.
Courtesy Karen Dyson

deserved. Peter fell foul of, in his way, the exact same thing that we fell foul of. Certainly excesses were going on all around him. Whilst Peter himself was never in as deep as we all were, from a point of view of personal drug intake, he certainly was allowing himself to do enough to where it was clouding his decision-making. And he made dumb choices like choosing to do *Sgt. Pepper* as a movie as opposed to doing Woody Allen's *Annie Hall*. Woody Allen, at that time, couldn't get more hip if you tried. And instead of doing that, which would have been a tremendous career move, he took the money. Three-quarters of a million dollars or something like that and star billing with The Bee Gees. Please!"

Author: "Did you turn down a role in Woody Allen's *Annie Hall*?"

Peter Frampton: "No, I didn't. It's a bit of a mystery. What happened was Woody was doing *Annie Hall*. Our mutual friend was John Doumanian. John was my assistant. And while I was doing *Sgt. Pepper*, he brought Woody to the set to meet me. He was very, very quiet. It was such a thrill to

meet him. John said, 'I'll be back.' He drove Woody off back to his hotel or whatever. And John said, 'Well, what do you think?' Woody said, 'He just exudes money' [laughs]. That's the way he saw me. I was just this money machine! Then John was the one that told me that Woody wanted me to play this rock star that Diane Keaton … if you remember she goes off to interview the rock star at Madison Square Garden. You never actually see that interview because they tried it with an actor and it didn't work. This is what I was told by John. He wanted to do it with me. And I said, 'Oh, my God, I'd love to do that.' Then what I've heard is that it was shot down. I don't know whether this is true or not, it's just what I heard, that Dee wanted a million dollars or whatever, and then didn't even bring it to me. Whereas you could have thrown *Sgt. Pepper* out the window! I should have quit that film and done the small part in Woody's film, if the truth were known. Even if Woody had asked me I'd have done it for nothing. Obviously. And he would have probably paid me nothing. Because to be in a Woody Allen movie would have been incredible visibility."

Author: "And from my point of view would have reinforced the credibility that, unfortunately, you were starting to lose."

Peter Frampton: "Well, yeah. And the obvious thing was that it would have been a self-deprecating role. You're in a Woody Allen comedy. He's gonna make fun of me. And even then, I've never taken myself that seriously. I would have loved to have done that."

Author: "There's nothing like being mocked by the best."

Peter Frampton: "Exactly! Hell, Woody Allen wanted me! Anyway, I would be thrilled if you could find out if that's true. If not, then I don't know where I got that. And I think it was John that told me about Dee turning it down. But I could have dreamt all this, who knows!"

John Doumanian: "No, that never happened like that. Woody would have talked to me about it and I would have talked to Dee. I don't remember talking to Dee about money or anything. I don't think it ever got that far. Maybe it was a conflict in who was where and where they were doing it, probably. If Peter were available and it was right he would have used Peter. But I don't remember the exact details."

Jerry Shirley: "At the time that movie *Sgt. Pepper* was released and premiered the week before is when Peter had his car accident. He had gone down to the Bahamas, where he owned a house, to supposedly surprise his then-girlfriend. 'Hi, honey, I'm home.' And when he got there he found some shocking things, upsetting from a relationship point of view. Evidence of infidelity, shall we say. It devastated him and I don't blame him. I would have been devastated in his position. And poor Peter proceeded to go get drunk, pop a couple of Valiums and then try to drive home and crashed the car. And, God bless him, the only reason he's here to talk about it is that Dee's housekeeper, I think it was, who had finished for the day and was driving or walking home, saw the car that Peter had driven off in a ditch. Apparently had he not been spotted by the housekeeper, he would have been dead.

"To cut a long story short, he had to be private plane-rushed to New York to do some vital surgery on his arm because they didn't trust the facilities in Freeport. And after all it was his arm. It was a career-ending situation; had they not done it right he would have not played guitar again. He was checked into The Lennox Hill Hospital and they got the surgery done. He's still in hospital up to his eyeballs in morphine, as you can imagine, having had this very intricate surgery, and the movie is premiered. Of course, he couldn't go but his entire family was invited from England. Peter asked me if I would go to spy on it for him; give him an idea how it went down, so to speak. And I'd like to think that he knew that I knew him well enough to be honest with him. We got into the movie house, sat down a few rows back from the Bee Gees. And within no more than five minutes of the movie starting, the place was breaking out in what started as sporadic laughter. Now, they weren't laughing because of comedic excess [laughs]! And the sporadic laughter started to develop into flat-out belly laughs of how bad it was. And no more than ten minutes into the movie The Bee Gees got up and walked out. They were at least brave enough to then go over to the aftermath party at Roseland. Peter's parents

got up and left. I have to say that some of them did have to leave ahead of time in order to get to the party but that was like an excuse that was used by everybody. We stayed till the end and watched the whole thing.

"Later on I tried to visit and/or call Peter to let him know, as tactfully as possible, what happened. Well, I couldn't get through to his room. They certainly wouldn't allow me to visit him that night, though I did try. And they wouldn't put a phone call through either, for whatever reason. As soon as they would take calls, eight or nine o'clock in the morning, I'm on the phone. I spoke to him briefly and he said, 'Come on over.' He wanted to hear it from the horse's mouth. So I went in to the hospital and as I walked into his room he was laying in bed looking very dejected and before he asked about the movie, I said, 'What's up? Why you look so down?' He said, 'Do you know, no one called me? No one came.' Not his mother, his father, Jerry Moss, Robert Stigwood, Dee, nobody took the time to visit him, call him or anything. Now I don't know if that was because they were too embarrassed or they didn't know what to say or whatever. But then he finally asked me, 'Well, how bad was it?' And I said, 'Well, Peter. Considering the material you had to work with, I mean the dialogue, which there was none, you did a good job' [laughs]."

Peter Frampton: "A lot was kept from me. The best thing I heard was at the point when my character Billy Shears was on the roof, wrapped up in his grief losing Strawberry Fields, and I go to jump, somebody in the audience yelled, 'Jump!' That was the response I got! [laughs] 'Please jump' [laughs]!"

Jerry Shirley: "The bit they all laughed the most at, and I don't know how familiar you are with that miserable movie, there's a bit towards the end that goes along with 'Golden Slumbers.' She's laying in a glass casket and he's over the casket looking and he's singing, [sings] 'Oh, the golden slumbers fill your eyes.' Oh my God! At that point the whole fucking place urinated themselves!"

Author: "When did you realize 'this is not a good idea?' "

Peter Frampton: "Before we started shooting. I just knew. I tried to get out of it. The Bee Gees, unbeknownst to me at the time, I found out later, they tried to get out of it. But there was no way. Our managers were Robert Stigwood and Dee Anthony, who were the producer and the executive producer of the movie."

Jerry Shirley: "Don't forget that at the time not only was it the worst movie ever made, and it's still to this day considered the worst movie ever made, it was also the most expensive. Which is a double whammy. And when you consider the material they got to work with was the greatest record ever made, how they could go from that so far off to where it became that bad … its anybody's guess. A perfect example of how bad in the error column Hollywood can sometimes be."

Author: "Also a case of the blind leading the blind."

Jerry Shirley: "Oh, absolutely. Peter had never acted before. Neither had The Bee Gees. Dee had taken on the role of executive producer. Which means absolutely nothing; it's just pure ego. Stigwood had made movies before. But you think he would know better, right? I think it was John Doumanian who told me the reason why Stigwood got away with as much as he did was because of the phenomenal success of *Saturday Night Fever*, which he also produced. He was given carte blanche by all these Hollywood moguls. You know how that works. *Saturday Night Fever* had been the biggest grossing blah, blah, blah. So that was literally the blind leading the blind there."

Author: "A complete conflict of interest."

Peter Frampton: "Absolutely. And there was no way those guys were gonna let any of us leave."

• • •

Steve Marriott's personal life returned to being involved in a relationship.

Pam Cross: "He met Pam Stephens on a plane. She was an airline stewardess. He liked Southern girls. And they both had the same temperament. They would just sit there and scream and cuss each other out and then they'd be back together again."

Jenny Dearden: "Ultimately, we (James Dearden) were together for eighteen years and I had two children with him. But Steve called almost every night for the first two or three years, usually in the middle of the night. And when James would pick the phone up Steve would say, 'Hello, mate. Can I talk to my old lady, please?' He called me up the day before he was going to marry Pam and said, 'I'm meant to be marrying Pam tomorrow because my visa's running out. I'm just calling to see how things are and are you going to stay with James?' "

Pam Cross: "With Pam there was not a major love there. She was probably pregnant with Toby by then anyway. They were oil and water. It was just ridiculous. I could never see how they had time to have sex. They were too busy fighting. And that's probably the only reason they had Toby. It was a fluke. It wasn't, 'We're happily married. Let's have a kid.' Uh uh. That would have been Jenny."

Author: "Do you feel that Steve married Pam more out of necessity to remain in the United States?"

Kay Marriott: "No. Pam and he were together when Toby was born. They were together about three years when they got married. So, no, she was living here (England). But they went back to America because she was so miserable. She was used to Atlanta and the warmth. She couldn't take our climate, which can be very damp. It must have been very hard for her."

Jerry Shirley: "His Mum's correct about that. First of all, when he was first with her, it was that he needed to live in England, not him to live in America. Now what they may have done was that they may have not bothered to get married until such time that they decided to get out of England

and move to America and therefore to make his green card accessibility easier. But they were long and deep into that relationship. It wasn't, 'Oh, let's get together and get married so I can have a green card.' "

Soon after Steve became a father for the first time.

Kay Marriott: "Toby was born February 20, 1976. Toby just had a little girl, Zoe."

Pam Cross: "Steve has a kid in Detroit but he kept saying it wasn't his. That kid is about three or four years younger than Toby."

Jerry Shirley: "A Lebanese girl I think she was. He does have a child. I don't know if it's a boy or a girl but, yes, he has a child in that area."

Jenny Dearden: "I hadn't been able to get pregnant, ever, and I had gone and had tubal surgery. I had literally come out of the hospital that day with Rory, my son, and Steve called. 'Hi. How are you? I'm buying this house in the States. It's just like the cottage! I'd like you to see it some day.' And I said, 'Steve, I'm exhausted. I've just got out of hospital. I've got a baby.' And he said, 'Oh. All right then, love.' And he put the phone down. And I knew that was it then. Once he knew I had a baby, he finally accepted that my relationship was a solid one. And I never heard from him again."

Jerry Shirley: "Steve was embarrassed. That was the depth of Steve's desperation in terms of the way he felt about Jenny. It's very clear to those who knew him, and combined with 20/20 hindsight, what Jenny's leaving did to Steve. And he was classic, right off a Hollywood script … the guy was never the same. From the day it was over-over, that was it. I mean, he could still sing great but he never, from that time onward in his life, had quite the same creative spark in him. He was a very changed man in terms of his bitterness towards things. He was the most devastated I have ever seen anybody over the break-up of a relationship. 'Cuz everybody gets over it for crying out loud!"

1979

Author: "What prompted Steve to reform Humble Pie?"

Jerry Shirley: "He was broke. He was living in California, outside Santa Cruz, collecting the deposits from 7-Up bottles to get his cigarettes. Pretty awful. The poor bugger. I mean, a guy that talented, literally living in a little shack, a very nice little shack, in the hills of the Redwood Forest outside of Santa Cruz and going nowhere, doing nothing. He'd gone to San Francisco to put a band together with Leslie West. It never got much further than the rehearsal stage before it fell apart. So Steve ended up stuck in Santa Cruz. I was living in New York at the time. The phone rang one day and it was Steve. The band I had, Magnet, was falling apart at the seams. And the management we had, which was somewhat connected to Leber-Krebs, Aerosmith's management, got wind that Steve had called me and said, 'Well, great! Fuck this Magnet deal. It's not going anywhere. Get Steve together. We'll manage it and get you a record deal.' So they got Steve a ticket to fly to New York. Myself and Steve met with David Krebs on a Friday afternoon in his office and he put us to the test. He said, 'I want you to go away for the weekend and write a hit record. I want you to come back on Monday morning at nine o'clock, bright and early. I'll book some studio time for you, go in and record it and we'll take it to a record company or two.' So, having been challenged like that, we went to my house in upstate New York for the weekend. I had a couple of ideas tossing around and so did Steve. And this one idea I had in particular Steve grabbed and turned it into 'Fool For A Pretty Face.' We went in on a Monday morning, much to Steve's chagrin … he was not happy about being up at nine in the morning to record [laughs]. But I managed to toss him into it. We went in and cut a great track. And that one song got us a record deal."

Clem Clempson: "Steve and Jerry had linked up together and they called me. I was actually making plans with Bobby Tench to put a project together. So when they called me I said that I was working with Bobby and I was reluctant to just blow him out and do the Humble Pie thing instead. And they decided it would be great to have Bobby in the band as well. So Bobby and I flew out to meet with the rest of the guys in San Francisco. The whole thing was a nightmare. First of all, I got a phone call the day I arrived from some tax inspector there, saying that I owed the IRS a fortune as not a cent of tax had been paid throughout the whole Humble Pie period. Which was a massive shock. And then we got into the studio and it was still kind of where we left off years before. There was still too much indulgence and not enough music. I couldn't get excited about it. I stayed for two or three days and decided I didn't want to be involved and I just came home and Bobby stayed."

Jerry Shirley: "As soon as Clem got back into Steve's company, he couldn't handle it. Couldn't handle being around Steve. They all went home for Christmas and Clem decided he didn't want to go on with it. I called Bobby Tench and said 'If Clem doesn't want to continue doing it, where does that leave you?' And he said, 'Aw, fuck Clem. I'll have a go at it.' So we had our line up, which was Bobby, Anthony Jones, me and Steve."

Bobby Tench: "I was aware that they were interested in having me in the band but I didn't see how it was gonna work with all those guitars. But it sounded quite nice, actually. Then Clem decided he didn't fancy doing that rocky stuff anymore. He was more into Larry Carlton-type stuff."

Author: "Did Steve call you?"

Greg Ridley: "He never got 'round to that but I did hear the rumble in the jungle. I wish it would have happened because it would have been even better. Money was never the object. We just expected to have some money but that was never the driving thing behind the band. It was just being successful and being liked and play some good music."

Jerry Shirley: "Anthony Jones joined the band in 1980 having been a friend of mine through my days in New York. He was in a great late punk/early new wave band called The Planets. CBGB's type of band. They were really good.

Very influenced by The Move and The Who and all of that. When I was in Magnet we needed a bass player and Anthony got that job briefly before the band broke up. Steve and I needed a bass player to do the sessions for 'Fool For A Pretty Face' and 'My Lover's Prayer.' We recruited Anthony and as a result of that session he got the job in the band. Steve had told me at the time that he had contacted Greg and he wasn't interested. I found out later that Steve never even contacted him, which I find interesting. I couldn't quite figure that out."

Author: "It would be interesting to know why he didn't."

Jerry Shirley: "I know. As bad as Greg's memory is, I can't imagine that he would have forgotten a call from Steve Marriott in 1979/80 to ask him if he wanted to get the band back together. He would have remembered a phone call like that. What would have been Steve's motive for not wanting Greg in it or saying that he'd contacted him when he hadn't, I don't know. I do know that he'd gotten along very well with Anthony but that was in almost a sick … he treated Anthony like his nigger. 'Jump? How high?' "

Author: "Did he comply with that for the opportunity to play with Steve?"

Jerry Shirley: "Oh, absolutely. You name it, he'd do it. And it was actually unnerving to witness. Bobby Tench personally took great offense to it. The guy's nickname was Sooty, for crying out loud! Bobby would tell him off many times. 'Don't let him treat you like that. You're no one's nigger.' Anthony didn't seem to care. He was too dumb to realize, half the time. So Anthony got the job with Humble Pie. He was no Greg Ridley but he was a good bass player. He fit the bill. He looked good on stage, that kind of thing. Couldn't sing for shit but I guess that didn't matter with both Steve and Bobby Tench in the band. And he survived through that reincarnation of the band until 1981. And then when I got the band back together in '88 with Charlie Huhn on vocals, that was with Anthony on bass again. And very, very sadly, God rest his soul, Anthony passed away in a freak accident whereby he contracted meningitis through, believe it or not, giving

'Avin' a 'Appy Christmas! 1983
Courtesy Kay Marriott

someone mouth to mouth resuscitation. He saved their life, caught meningitis and died as a result of it. In November 1999. It was devastating. He was working at some kind of nightclub and this guy just went down, collapsed, and he needed CPR. Anthony knew how to do it, gave him mouth to mouth, lip to lip, and ever so dead three days later. And he'd been through a really rough time. He'd gotten really bad into crack and stuff and gone to prison and he'd gotten himself clean. He was just about to celebrate his first full year of sobriety and this happened."

Clempson soon found himself working with a hero of his.

Jack Bruce: "The first time I met Clem he came to my house to audition. I was putting a band together and I wanted a guitar player. In fact, he didn't become the guitar player of that band. But later on I was looking for a guitar player and he joined my band with Billy Cobham and David Sancious. That was in 1980, '81. We toured a lot together with that band. We toured in Europe. We toured in the States. And he's been with me in other bands I've had too. The last time I actually played with him is a few years back now. He played in my

50th birthday concert. And we made a record of that, called 'Cities Of The Heart.' Clem played some of the finest blues guitar I've ever heard. I think he's a vastly underrated player."

Steve Marriott offered Tench the job of lead guitarist.

Bobby Tench: "I got along well with Steve. We always had a laugh. And I loved working with him. The two voices together worked. I thought we played quite well. I enjoyed it very much. I don't really know what the intention of the project was because I came in when it had all been discussed. I think it was just to do some playing. Everyone was sort of a bit … bored."

Author: "And Steve wasn't in a good situation."

Bobby Tench: "No. But when was he ever? He was never that good with money, we all knew that."

The production credits are given to Humble Pie and John Elijah Wright.

Jerry Shirley: "He was an engineer from England that Steve had used originally at Joe Brown's studio in Essex and he had done the engineering work on the reformed Small Faces records. He had moved to California with Steve and got a job as a resident engineer at the studio in Modesto that we used (Villa Recorders) and subsequently became our engineer and co-producer."

Author: " 'Fool For A Pretty Face' must have made everybody feel good."

Bobby Tench: "Yeah. Steve had an idea with Jerry and that was it. Just went into the studio and it came out. Simple as that. Sometimes the best things are the simplest things and that's a fine example."

Jerry Shirley: "It was promising. 'Fool For A Pretty Face' was kind of a hit single. It got into the Top 40 and the album started to do quite well. But there was no follow-up single to speak of. And we started to misbehave again [laughs]."

Bobby Tench: "This goes without saying. You've got to rest sometime. Have an early night. But Steve thought he had endless amounts of energy. He didn't understand what it was doing to him. It never bothered him to have to sing the next day. It would bother me. If we were up too late and had a show the next day, my voice would be shot."

Jerry Shirley: "By the time we got to the early 80s Steve was like a chameleon who changed to suit his surroundings. First of all, onstage, when it had to do with Bobby Tench, he wouldn't dare go too far into the 'bitch, nigger this' because Bobby'd rip his head off. In fact, that actually happened one night. They got into a fistfight because of something that Steve said on stage. 'Aw, I couldn't understand why Bobby got uptight about it.' Whereas everybody else, including the 18,000 people who were witnessing it, could well understand why Bobby wasn't too pleased.

"We did well on the road, as a special guest with a headliner. And we did some of our own shows in big clubs or small theaters. We got through to the following year and we recorded another record called 'Go For The Throat.' Which was a pretty decent record. But the record company chose to drop it at birth because Steve had been particularly rude to the Senior Vice President of Atco Records the Friday before its release. And he sent a memo around his office on Monday morning, after the record release party, which is where Steve was rude to him, and the memo basically said, 'Dump this record. Don't work it.' So whether it would have hit had they worked it, one will never know. Pretty soon after it came out, we toured behind that record."

"Go For The Throat" gives production and engineering credits to Gary Lyons.

Jerry Shirley: "We got hooked up with Gary through Leber-Krebs. We had already made the record once, producing it ourselves, and it had been rejected. And we were told we needed to employ a producer to do it again with. Gary Lyons had done a lot of work with Leber-Krebs, not least of all Aerosmith."

Author: "Why was it rejected?"

Jerry Shirley: "Because they didn't consider the production up to scratch for the time. We'd produced it real raw, rough and ready. I guess it wasn't slick enough."

Author: "On that particular album there's a song called 'Lottie and the Charcoal Queen.' Is that a reference to your wife?"

Jerry Shirley: "Yeah, that is my wife and Steve's wife. Steve's wife being the Charcoal Queen, Pam. Simply because she burned everything she cooked [laughs]."

Author: "How were the tours during that time?"

Bobby Tench: "They had us doing everything. We were doing an enormous amount of dates. We traveled on buses. And what we couldn't get to on a bus we flew and the bus would meet us there. We were out with Ted Nugent, Aerosmith. We were out with everybody. But after a while we felt overworked 'cuz we had to start writing on buses and that wasn't conducive to getting good material together."

Jerry Shirley: "By this time Leber-Krebs were pretty much supporting us, financially, and they could only put up with doing that for so long. And then we had all our equipment stolen, including the Ryder truck, in New York City one night and that pretty much ended it. We couldn't survive. It was all done by the summer of '81."

After Humble Pie had broken up, again, Jerry returned to England and formed Fastway with Eddie Clarke from Motorhead and later played in a group called

Wasted with Pete Way from UFO. Steve stayed behind and formed Packet of 3, a take off on an English slang term for a package of condoms. During the initial version of Packet of 3, Jim Leverton was hired on as bassist and vocalist and Fallon Williams was drumming.

Pam Cross: "When I first met Steve in the eighties, he was still married to Pam and they lived out in a farm in a place called Griffin, which is about forty-five minutes south of Atlanta. It was Pam and Steve and a friend of his named Mike and his wife. Toby was out there and Mike and his wife had a baby. A little commune kind of thing going on out there. It was very strange. Toby was a blond little munchkin by then, three or four. Pam wouldn't put up with Steve's crap. She was in and out of that house I don't know how many times. And then finally she got totally pissed off and went 'Fuck you' and left. But that took years. She was married to him for the majority of the time that I knew him. Toby was just this sweet little kid running around. He looks nothing like that now which is why I was surprised when I saw him. Tall, skinny. The head part, just like Steve. But he didn't look anything like that when he was little. It was so weird seeing him all grown up, brown hair and tall. I mean, Steve was 5' 4". And Pam's not that much taller. Where he got that tall part I don't know."

Author: "What kind of a dad was Steve?"

Pam Cross: "He liked playing with him. It wasn't dad, it was more playmate. Toby was four, Steve acted four. He used to chase him around the house and that kind of stuff. Toby could never get near Steve's guitars. God forbid! That was the worst thing in the world. But apparently when Toby got older they started connecting a little bit more. Toby was going over to England and seeing him. That's how that finally came into fruition. You can't be a playmate with your kid forever. But that definitely finally worked itself out. Pam always gave Steve access to him but he really didn't take it that much. He didn't really have a lot of money then either. That had a lot to do with it."

Jerry Shirley: "As soon as he'd wear a father's hat he was hopeless at it. He was way too heavy-handed or he couldn't

deal with it at all. Typical Steve. Extreme in everything he did. I don't know anybody who actually knew him who would say he was a great father 'cuz he wasn't. By his own admission he was hopeless at it."

• • •

Kay Marriott: "Steve broke his ankle in several places. He jumped over a two-foot fence and landed funny."

Jerry Shirley: "This is not when I was with him. This is was when he was living in Atlanta and he was going out as Steve Marriott some weeks and Humble Pie the next. He had a full leg cast."

Kay Marriott: "He had to perform in plaster up to his thigh and he stood that for six months."

Bryan Adams: "I saw Steve only once in Houston, Texas, with a mock Humble Pie lineup. He had a broken leg and hobbled onto the stage, sat down on a stool and propped his manky leg up on another stool and then proceeded to sing one of the most amazing concerts I'd ever seen. I jumped on stage at the end of the night with him. I can't remember which song I jammed with him on but it didn't matter. I'd sung with one of my heroes."

In 1983, Steve returned to England after his marriage to Pam dissolved. On May 1, 1985, Steve and Manon Pearcy became parents to a daughter, Molly. After playing the pubs in England he called upon an old friend to take the act back to the U.S. The call of the road returned.

Jerry Shirley: "And again I got a phone call out of nowhere from Steve. I'd heard he'd gotten this little blues three-piece together, A Packet of 3, and he called. So I went down, rehearsed with him and it ran almost two years."

Pam Cross: "I was twenty-seven years old and was road managing, for the first time, with Humble Pie. One of the cool things about Steve was he always treated me like an equal and like one of the guys. I didn't realize how special that was at that time. Back in '87 when you're out on the road being a female road manager all the people were say-

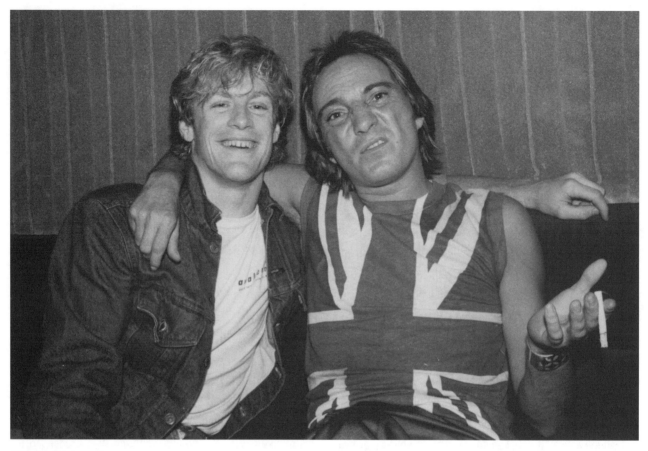

Houston, Texas. 1983
Courtesy Bryan Adams

ing, 'Oh, you must be doing somebody in the band. Oh, are you the secretary?' And Steve would laugh and say, 'You do what she tells you to.' He was always backing me up. He never belittled me, ever. That part was just so cool that I had that kind of respect from him. And I didn't really understand that part until later. About what he was doing for me.

"He wouldn't drive. Everywhere he went he took a cab or got somebody to go take him there. And he'd get drunk and I'd have to go pick him up. One time I took him back to my apartment and he started playing bagpipes with my cats! He turned my cats upside down, had their tails in his mouth and was blowing on them. That was too funny. I was mad at the time. 'Put my cats down! You're gonna bite their tails!' He said, 'No, I won't.' But he was really drunk so you never knew what was gonna happen, if Melvin was gonna come out or not. One time he tried to head butt me and he missed and hit the wall and we all started laughing. 'I hurt my head!' 'Well, you were gonna hit mine!' He loved to head butt people."

Steve would spend a lot of time in the Atlanta bars, usually visiting his friends, The Georgia Satellites, who would frequently ask him up onstage to jam. The Satellites wanted to use Steve on their first album but they didn't have any money and Steve demanded to be paid for his talent and name. The relationship started to sour and Steve was soon no longer being asked to join the band onstage.

Pam Cross: "The record was incredible. They'd been playing the set for five years. It didn't surprise me at all because we used to go and see The Satellites every Monday night at this place called Hedgins. By then Steve was living in Atlanta, right off Peachtree Street, and the club was probably ten minutes from his house. An easy cab ride. And if he wasn't out on tour he knew they were playing there and he'd go down and hang out. I would always have to go and pick him up."

Jerry Shirley: "I wanted Steve to be doing what Eric Clapton was doing in terms of putting his life back together and Steve just wasn't having any of it. He really wasn't interested in the mainstream at all. He positively kicked against it. Steve was as happy as a clam when playing with a little three- or four-piece blues band in pubs in and around England and Europe. And I have to say not only was it a lot of fun but he was making a nice living too. He had no need for the big stuff."

Pam Cross: "Steve was happy in clubs. He didn't like the big auditoriums and the stadium stuff. He liked where he could see the people and get to see their reaction. He got more of a buzz saying, 'You see that guy out there? He's singing every word!' That kind of thing. He told me before when he did the big places that it wasn't as personal.

"Steve was basically an old black man. He didn't like being a little English guy. He wanted to be an old, black bluesman. That's what he always aspired to be. That's why he played the way he played and sang the way he sang."

Author: "Do you think his energy wore him out?"

Jerry Shirley: "Yeah. It was exhausting being around Steve but what it must have been like to be Steve, God only knows. Because you can't get away from you, can you [laughs]? He had to put up with Steve twenty-four hours a day, seven days a week. At least everybody else had the choice, if they wanted to, to leave. But he couldn't leave. I think he was pretty much bored. He liked the quiet life, the truth be known. He'd go down to the pub with his dog and that kind of thing."

Author: "I've been told that if he didn't like you he'd tell you."

Pam Cross: "Oh, he would terribly tell you. If you were Jewish he would start talking about Hitler. He had one of those Hitler tour shirts. It was like, "Hitler's Invasion – 1944." And it had all the places that he bombed. He would wear this stuff on stage. And he would tease then road manager Bill Hibbler all the time because Bill was Jewish. He was always saying that Bill was stealing his money because Bill was a Jew. Everybody caught the joke but it rubbed Bill the wrong way. None of the rest of us took it seriously.

There was no money to steal. He was making about $1,000 a night at this point and playing really crappy clubs. He did good business but the club owners wouldn't pay him any money. The only thing Steve knew how to do was play.

"Steve always buddied up with somebody in the band so he could pick on everybody else. He wouldn't do anything by himself. When he had Jim Leverton he always had an ally. And they would pick on everybody. Everybody was fair game."

Jerry Shirley: "It was almost schoolyard mentality. He always had to have one guy on his side against the rest. And it was often a very awkward place to be in. Once he thought you were on his side, your opinions didn't matter anymore. You'd committed yourself to Steve's cause and that was it. So if you started to question where he was going with whatever it was that he was up to, all hell broke loose. Steve was an absolute master. The two things that Steve was the best in the world at were singing the blues and pissing people off. And close to those two things was guitar playing and keyboard playing and songwriting. Having said all of that, he was also a deeply compassionate man about animal welfare and stuff. He wasn't good with kids but he was great with animals."

Pam Cross: "They didn't pick on me. I'm the only one and I'm not really sure why. Plus I gave him Valium [laughs]! He would drive me crazy. 'OK, I'm gonna give you Valium to shut you up.' The opening acts would try to pay homage by bringing him blow and all that kind of stuff but they never got anything while I was with them. Steve said, 'This is a weird tour. No one is offering me drugs.' And I said, 'Isn't it, though? I don't know what it is. Here. You can have your vitamin and go to sleep now.' And that placated him. He couldn't figure it out."

Angry tour bus drivers, because of Steve's habit of falling asleep with a lit cigarette in his hand and burning seat cushions, were constantly berating him. It became routine to repeatedly check Steve for burning cigarettes.

Pam Cross: "And he smoked non-filtered Camels! Nasty. They smell terrible. Or him and Jim would be rolling their own like English guys do. I was always on the hunt for tobacco papers. But he smoked more pot than anything else. Sitting in the back of the bus. Joint or cigarette. And there had to be a bottle of brandy at all times.

"He liked playing court for a little while after he got done. It took him about thirty minutes to cool down and change clothes. But he didn't like talking, doing chitchat, for too long. He would go into 'Steve mode' and do the little entertainer for a little while then get bored. If he hadn't pulled a girl by then he was done and ready to go."

Author: "How was he handling his indulgences back then?"

Pam Cross: "His drug problem was always more drinking than anything else. He loved Courvoisier. He didn't have a cocaine problem when I knew him. Like I said, I kept it away. He didn't need it anyway. I was more likely to sit there and hoover it down so he couldn't do it [laughs]. People were giving it to me to give to him. I always had it but they never knew. I told the soundman and I split it with him. Mark Ballew was doing sound. He worked for him almost as long as I did. John Skinner was the other roadie. John worked for him for twenty-one years. He did everything. He did the guitars and all of that stuff.

"At one time I was working with Steve, Gregg Allman and Stevie Ray Vaughan. Let's talk about three of the most dysfunctional people I can think of! Heroin with Stevie. Gregg was always toasty. And Steve popping anything anybody would give him. One night Gregg and Stevie were playing together at The Agora in Atlanta. Stevie had just finished the 'Let's Dance' thing with Bowie. Bowie wanted him to go on tour for $150 a week. Stevie told him, 'Fuck off.' I hadn't seen Stevie yet. He was making $150 a night and we had just picked him up. Steve was in town and said, 'I wanna go and see Gregg and Stevie play.' And I said, 'I don't know about that, Steve! I really don't think this is that great of an idea.' And Alex, my boss, said, 'Steve is not allowed to go backstage because all three of them are gonna get fucked up and I'm sure Steve has a pocket full of pills.' Of course, he'd have a pocket full of pills. When would that be new?

"The whole night he was saying, 'Oh, they're so cool. I really wanna meet Stevie.' And he started getting drunker and he'd popped all these pills. And I said, 'You can't go backstage.' 'Why not? Why not?' Just arguing with me. 'Alex said you can't go backstage because you're a bad influence on Gregg and Stevie' [laughs]! I had to keep our clients apart because they were a bad influence on each other. So by that time he was about to fall on the floor. Steve had said, 'Somebody just gave me a bunch of pills.' And I said, 'What were they?' 'I don't know. I ate them all!' 'Oh, great. You have no idea what you ate and now I have to watch you so you don't die!' And then he starts drinking beer. I picked him up and took him home and the next day he'd forgotten all about it."

Author: "During this time he was notorious for going on swearing tangents. Would what prompt him to do this?"

Pam Cross: "He did that just to do it. It was pure shock value. 'Fuck' became a normal word in my vocabulary. It took me years to stop saying it from being around him. Everything was 'Fuck this' and 'Fuck that.' You didn't say 'bloody' because that was a bad cuss word for English guys. That's all he did was cuss. I'd tell him, 'Be nice tonight. If you don't have to cuss, please don't.' And as soon as he got on the P.A. he'd start. The promoters would complain and he'd start laughing."

Author: "What were the ravings about?"

Pam Cross: "Anything. If somebody had a bad shirt on he'd make fun of him. It didn't matter. And he'd do that whether he was drunk or sober. It was one more thing with shock value for little Steve to do. If the manager would get pissed off, they'd still book him again because they made money off of him."

Author: "What about if he was picking on somebody from the crowd?"

Pam Cross: "They liked the attention. 'Cuz Steve Marriott actually saw them! The rock god! And those were the people that would come backstage and try to talk to him. 'What? That fuckin' bloke is actually out there and he actually thinks I'm gonna talk to him?' And he'd start laughing. That's what he did. He had that malicious little streak, trying to rub everybody the wrong way."

Author: "Would he ever back off from the teasing when it upset people?"

Pam Cross: "Oh, he'd keep on! He would keep on and keep on and keep on. People's problems gave him something to work from. If he knew of any kind of insecurity you had or anything bad that you really didn't want to deal with, he'd pull that out and pick at it and pick at it and make the sore even bigger. And if you tried to tell him to stop it he wouldn't. That just egged him on more. The fact that I didn't have a boyfriend was the only thing he could pick on me about.

"When the tour ended in Toronto in November of '87 I don't think he'd met Toni yet. I figured I'd see him the next year. And then he married Toni and I didn't really get to talk to him that much anymore. He said, 'I really loved Jenny but she couldn't put up with my stuff.' Jenny was always the love of his life. Pam was just a fluke. Toni was just a twisted, perverted need. I don't know what he was thinking. He was lonely again. He had to have somebody around him that would kiss his butt and I'm sure she did it quite well. He always had to have somebody like that. He didn't like being alone. That has to be the reason he married Toni.

"The next thing I heard was that Steve and Frampton were in the studio. And I thought, 'This is a good thing. He didn't want to do a record before. Maybe something has changed.' The first thing that came to my mind was that he was broke again. Peter put a couple of the songs they finished on one of his records. I had to go buy that just because it had Steve on it. And Steve sounded great."

With Packet of 3, Toronto, Ontario, 1987.
Courtesy Pam Cross

Author: "What was the goal?"

Peter Frampton: "The goal was to see if we could write together. And we obviously proved that we could still write together. And I maintain that we wrote closer this time than the first time around with Humble Pie."

Jerry Shirley: "It all fell apart at the seams because they started offering Steve and Peter lots of money. Steve was once quoted as saying, 'They offered me another million dollars,' or whatever the figure was. He said, 'They did that before and look what happened.' But they were also watching him like a hawk. The deal was no drinking, no drugging."

Author: "Was the collaboration contingent on Steve behaving himself?"

Peter Frampton: "Yeah. The thing was that he agreed. 'Look,' I said. 'It's during the day. I don't care what you do when you go home. Why don't we just try …' If one person has a drink and the other one hasn't during the day, it's difficult to work. And we were working so well before until he started doing that again. Unfortunately."

Jerry Shirley: "Steve resented a) the fact that he was being watched so closely, and b) he was scared to death of the idea of going out there into the big time, again, with lots of money. By that time, he was happy. He was going into bars, playing with his little three-piece band. And whilst the idea seemed like a good idea at the time, once the reality set in … 'Oh, dear, I'm going to have to go and do it all again.' So he self-destructed. I think he was behaving when he first went out there but soon after he started misbehaving and that was the end of that."

Author: "Was Peter getting on his case as well?"

Jerry Shirley: "I wasn't there so I don't know. But from what I understand, everybody was on his case. And typical Steve, 'Well, if you're going to accuse me for it, I'm gonna go do it!' And off he went! Steve was not the type of guy to throw the gauntlet down, for whatever reason. But if you suggested that he shouldn't do something, he'd go ahead and do it just to spite ya.

"Peter enticed Steve out there to go and make a million bucks again. And that wasn't Steve's want; he just wanted to make a nice record. Put all these pressures on Steve. Did not handle Steve at all well. Didn't pay attention to the human side of it. Steve was being thrown into the deep end again, in Los Angeles, being offered all kinds of money to go out there and give it another shot. The big time, man! And he was getting twitchy about it. It was not where Steve wanted to be. And all Peter cared about, from what I can understand, was being real hard-nosed about, 'We're gonna do it right, and no drinking, no drugging.' I'm not saying it's right or wrong. It was wrong in terms of getting a result out of Steve. Steve gets there, he sees Peter, he sees the business people offering him all kinds of money and he sees Peter siding with them. And that was a major mistake on Peter's part. And then

when it came down to a screaming match, Peter just wimped out. He didn't have the guts to deal with whatever it was Steve was not happy with. 'What's the problem? Let's find out.' He just let Steve go on his merry way and the next thing he knows, after having had this row, Steve went on a bender for two or three weeks in L.A."

Peter Frampton: "We did get three finished tracks out of it. The only drag was that one of them, a sort of a Buddy Holly type number, he never sang that. That was supposed to be his lead vocal. I've tried it and of course it doesn't work. But the idea was that we were talking. We had people lining up for record deals and publishing and everything. So it was just a case of when and where, really. And then we had a little set to, as we always did. We didn't necessarily come from the same tree. We were very different people. And that's why we worked so well creatively together. And this time was no different. I'd completely stopped drinking and doing anything and Steve hadn't. So, unfortunately …"

Pam Cross: "Frampton was sober and Steve was still popping Valium, doing blow and drowning himself with Courvoisier while he was in L.A. They got into a great big fight and Steve said, 'Fuck this, I'm going home.' And he stayed drunk on the Concorde."

Jerry Shirley: "He arrived after a long, very drunken flight home and he was exhausted. He got into a bit of a 'barney' with the missus. They'd been drinking and popped the odd Valium and they had the odd line and that kind of thing. When he finally got back to his house … I'm not saying he was blind drunk but he'd been on a night out, so he was pretty whooped. Jet lag and everything else. So exhausted that he fell asleep with a cigarette on."

In the early morning hours of April 20, 1991, Steve Marriott died.

Jerry Shirley: "It was accidental. Had he been not out all night, maybe it wouldn't have happened. Who knows? I found out the gory details from the fire department when I was over there for the funeral. They found him in his bedroom. There was a walk-in closet and it had the water

San Diego, CA, 1973.
Courtesy Karen Dyson

heating tank in it. It's called an 'airing closet' in England, where you put your clothes to air them out. They found him in there, curled up in the fetal position, on the floor. So, what probably happened was, in the confusion he crawled in to what he thought was the door 'out' of the bedroom or he crawled in there thinking he would be protected. They had to identify him by his teeth. The only consolation, the authorities told me, is when you go like that, the smoke inhalation literally knocks you out long before being burned up."

Jenny Dearden: "Bobbi Korner, Alexis Korner's widow, called me, weeping. And a newspaper called. I don't know how they got the number because I had it changed twice. A friend of mine, who is also a journalist, called. I thought he was being very sympathetic but he was calling for the wrong reasons. And then Jerry called, just beside himself. So distressed. He finally came over and we went to the funeral together."

Jerry Shirley: "I was in Cleveland, at a friend's apartment on a lazy Saturday afternoon, when feeling no pain was not a problem, kicking back and minding our own business, and the phone rings. Minutes later, my friend walks in the room, ashen white, staring into space, and he said, 'It's Peter Frampton. Steve's dead.' He handed me the phone and it was Peter telling me about it. Devastating."

Peter Frampton: "I was on the phone to my brother in England. I was in an apartment in Hollywood at that point and I got someone beep in on call waiting. And I said, 'Wait a second, Clive, let me see who this is.' And it was someone, I don't remember what paper he was from; it was an English daily. This voice comes on. 'Hello, Peter. I just wanted to ask you what are your feelings on Steve Marriott's death?' I said, 'Excuse me? Hold on.' I got rid of my brother. I said, 'Steve's dead. I gotta find out more. I'll call you back.' So then I said, 'Well, this is the first I'm hearing of it. I have no comment to make whatsoever. And I have to find out more about this. Thank you very much. Goodbye.' And the guy was still pushing, 'But, but …' 'Goodbye.' And he said, 'I wanna let you know before anybody else does.' 'Thanks a lot, buddy.' So that's when I found out. And that day I spoke to Ronnie Lane, Mac and Kenny. It was a horrible day. I was unbelievably sad. I thought that I'd got my partner back again. We were meant to play together. And every time we did, it happened. I mean, I'm not saying success, necessarily. I'm talking about creatively it happened."

Greg Ridley: "I was at home here and I heard it on the radio. I just couldn't believe it. After all the practice he'd had, and what he'd done, and the number of times I had to carry him off to bed and throwing him into the sack … I couldn't believe that could happen to him. It was shattering. He was a fantastic little guy."

Bobby Tench: "It was on the radio. Steve didn't like flying, so he had to take whatever, Valium, to fly. He hated to fly. So I heard on the news and spoke to Jerry after that."

Clem Clempson: "I was in my local snooker club in London. I'd had a few drinks and the news came on the television. I was absolutely stunned. It was a shock. But there was a kind of vague predictability about it. I mean, there'd been a few hairy times with Steve on the road. I wouldn't say he had been close to death or anything. Things got a bit dangerous from time to time."

Pam Cross: "As soon as it happened I started getting calls. Everybody called me. And I didn't have enough money to fly over for the funeral, which really pissed me off because I really wanted to be there. But at least he got a decent obituary in Rolling Stone. I was quite proud to see that."

Kay Marriott: "He said to me once, I think at the time he was twenty-eight, and he said, 'Mum, if I die tomorrow, I've done everything I've wanted to do and I've had a wonderful life.' 'Don't talk like that.' I always had the fear that he would. Because it's such a fast life, isn't it. But he made it to forty-four. And then that was an accident. Such a loss. Such a waste. When you're not here, people start realizing what they had. Because years ago, it was always, 'Aren't they like The Who? Aren't they like Status Quo? Aren't they like this?' Never like themselves. They're always like somebody else. And that really used to annoy me. 'Cuz I don't think that there was anybody that sounded like Steve."

Jerry Shirley: "His funeral was sold out. Standing room only! And the amazing thing was, out of nowhere, between fifty and a hundred Mods showed up on their scooters, literally right out of *Quadrophenia*. They lined up on either side of the church and in back of the church, very respectful, with their heads hung. And then the funeral proceedings themselves. His wife had put together a choice of music. In the middle of it there was a kind of musical repose, where you could hear what the vicar was saying. And then it broke into The Small Faces original version of 'All or Nothing.' The whole place just collapsed. I mean, there wasn't a dry eye in the house. I sat right next to Kenny Jones and I looked at him, he looked at me and we were sobbing like children."

Greg Ridley: "The funeral was depressing but I tried to bring a smile to it because that's the way Steve would have wanted it. It was real sad. We were all sickened to death thinking, 'How the hell could he fall asleep one night with a fag after he'd done it a million times?' I could hear him up there in the sky saying, 'Ah, bullocks' [laugh]!"

Jerry Shirley: "Peter must have felt really bad about the fact that, at the very least, he didn't resolve issues. The last thing he knew was he had a row with the guy. And to walk away from a friend, having had a big row, and the next thing you know, that friend's dead and you don't get a chance to resolve any issues that he may have wanted to, it's a rotten place to be."

Peter Frampton: "But the bottom line is I absolutely, 100 percent believe that we would have gotten back together again. 'Cuz before he left to go to England, he did call me. And he said, 'Did you just call me?' And, of course, I didn't. 'Oh, I was just seeing how you were.' And that was the last time I spoke to him. I think he was fishing. It was too 'good.' If he'd had a clear moment there, or when his next clear moment would have been, I think that we would have finished it. I would have pushed for it, anyway."

Author: "Did you approach anyone to finish the tracks that Steve couldn't finish?"

Peter Frampton: "No, I couldn't do that. It would be wrong. It's like there's been no Led Zeppelin since Bonzo died. And rightly so. There could be no replacement. I have a whole DAT of songs that Steve wrote over the last few years of his life, which are unbelievable. And I have some plans for various people to get them. I have nothing to gain from it. The Marriott estate is handling all that. But if I can bring some of these songs to some really good bands or singers that really respect … like Chris Robinson. I know him. And he's such a huge Humble Pie fan. I told him about it the other day. There's a song that I know would be terrific for him. So I'm gonna try and get it to him."

Author: "As a member, did you have a sense of how good a live band you were?"

Clem Clempson: "No. I've always been amazed at the amount of people that have come up and said that they thought it was the greatest live rock band they'd ever heard. I mean I thought we were good. I always thought Steve was one of the best rock singers I'd ever heard. But I've always been self-critical. I'd always heard other bands that I thought were at least as good. I went to a Jeff Beck gig the other night and a guy came up to me and said, 'I just want to thank you for all the pleasure you've given me with the Humble Pie years. And the 'Eat It' album more than anything else.' And I thought that this was fantastic. He was telling me how much trouble he was having getting a newer copy of it."

Kay Mateus Dos Anjos: "Steve loved his career. He was handling it himself, which he wanted. He loved the closeness to his audience. He didn't want great, huge audiences anymore. He loved the pubs and the small clubs. I went to most of his gigs before I moved to Portugal. He loved it. Managing his own money affairs. He was so happy. He was living well and doing what he loved. Because at the end of the day, it was the music. Money didn't come into it really. It was his music. That was the love."

Pam Cross: "I didn't realize what a phenomenal talent he was until he died."

Derek St. Holmes: "He was a hoot, man, he was something else. He was an incredible, incredible singer. He was just a live fast/live hard kind of guy, ya know. All the good ones are dying, man!"

Author: "Steve *must* have considered himself talented."

Jenny Dearden: "Well, he did but it was something he was quite humble about, really. I mean, his music was the most important thing to him. I think he sort of took it for granted. Somebody would teach him how to play some-thing, another instrument, and within a day…I mean, one is not an expert, musically. But he would seem to be playing it beautifully and fluently. He learned to play the sitar, obviously not like someone who studied it for years, but he played it beautifully in a relatively short time. He would take lessons from somebody for two or three days and then he'd be sitting in the garden playing it. He just sort of had a natural aptitude to sort of pick up on anything."

Bobby Tench: "I loved him as a guy. He was fun. After the band disbanded I used to go see him play around London. He's one of the best British artists I've seen. Singer/guitarist."

Alan O'Duffy: "I thought the world of Steve Marriott and he was such a gifted fellow. He was a white black man. He could sing in several styles. One of them was cheeky Cockney. [sings] 'Wouldn't it be nice to be friendly with my neighbors.' He could do all that. But then he could turn around and sing like Otis Redding. In a flick of a switch. He could play piano great. He played bass and guitar. And he had such energy and such charm. He was a great guy."

Kay Marriott: "He had such a big sound. I don't know where he got that from. It was absolutely Negroid, you know. I know you mustn't say that these days. It really came from inside him. And for somebody so small. A terrific voice and he really let it go. He could do all sorts of things with his voice."

Bryan Adams: "Steve's voice had an unmistakable quality — it was a perfect combination of soul and blues that is rare in white singers and can only found in the real R&B singers."

Kay Marriott: "He did it all. He knew what he was getting when he was playing. Whether it be in a hall or a pub, he loved it. And it was always packed. He said, 'As long as I've got these hands, I'll never want for anything. I can always walk into a pub, sit down at the piano and earn a few bob.' I don't think he would have gone busking but he would have gone into a pub as an old man and gotten his supper probably."

Cleveland, Ohio, 1983.
Courtesy Brian Chalmers

Jerry Shirley: "For a little sod, he was definitely a handful! He was a handful to love, let's put it this way. He wasn't physically tough. I mean, he would scream at ya, yell at ya, he'd have a go if he could. I've known a lot of physically small guys who were as hard as nails and he wasn't like that. He would have liked to have been. But he could intimidate you just by screaming at you [laughs]."

Clem Clempson: "It was lots of fun. It's an experience that I wouldn't have missed for the world. And it's a shame that we couldn't have achieved more than we did."

Author: "Any regrets?"

Greg Ridley: "Yeah, that we never got back together again and really did it with enjoyment and even got some money out of it next time. We would all have loved it. Because we were all at loose ends after Humble Pie…we were all nowhere. Didn't know what to do, get a proper job or what. After you've been to the top of the mountain and you fall off the other side, it's very strange. I'd have loved it if we'd put it back together and really rocked them all again. With a big smile and a big purse at the end of it."

There have recently been some tapes discovered from the early Humble Pie days that possibly contains the ultimate example of Steve Marriott's talent.

Jerry Shirley: "Ray Charles' 'Drown In My Own Tears,' no doubt about it. The one thing Steve wanted to do with Humble Pie was to pay homage to that song by reproducing it as closely as we possibly could to the original. And we pulled it off. But it got lost in the shuffle. We were in between records; we went on the road. While we were on the road, Immediate went bust. We came back, ran for cover, got the fuck out and got on A&M. It got swallowed up in litigation. And it survived. As far as I knew it was a piece of 8-track tape that could have gone anywhere. I didn't even know if there was a mono mix of it that survived. And not only did it survive, but it did so in its multi-track form."

Peter Frampton: "I know that people will have a lot of things to say about Steve and not so complimentary, maybe. But the bottom line is we all have our quirks. With his talent, which was supreme, came a lot of baggage. But I think of many true artists, whether they be musicians, painters, writers, whatever, I think out of pain comes some of the best art. And Steve had his share of pain. And for whatever reason, he was the way he was and he couldn't change that. And God alone knows, people tried [laughs]! But Steve was Steve and that's it, you know. I just thank God that I had the opportunity to work with him. Be his friend and experience working with that sort of talent."

Jerry Shirley: "Singularly, the greatest white blues singer ever! There was everybody else and then there's Steve. He was, by far and away, the best at what he did. He was the Ray Charles of white blues singers and no one else is even close. Everyone is in one league and he's in a league of his own. And it's not just me who believes that. You ask any of the rest of them what they think. Ask Rod Stewart, ask Paul Rodgers, ask Bryan Adams, ask Chris Robinson. And they'll all tell you the same thing. He was 'the man.' He was the Jimi Hendrix of white lead vocals. Jimi stood out on his own. So did Steve."

RICK DERRINGER

"Johnny and I had played 'Hang On Sloopy' as kids. But I had no idea how talented Rick was until hearing him play. I'll never forget that evening. 'This guy is a really great guitar player.' And from that point on we became friends. I really have a great deal of respect for Rick. I think he's one of the most versatile, complete guitar players that I've had the pleasure of working with. He knows enough advanced chord theory. He can play jazz. He knows all the authentic blues licks. He's a great country player. He plays a folk-picking style of guitar. He plays really great pedal-steel. He's a very complete player."

−Edgar Winter, July 1999

Rick Derringer: "It was an easy-going life. My dad, John Zehringer, always worked on The Nickel Plate Railroad. When he was seventeen he was the youngest section foreman they had at that time. He worked on the railroad 'til he went away into the service."

Janice Zehringer: "He was drafted. He was being shipped to Taipan or somewhere and the war ended while they were en route. So they went to Hawaii instead."

Rick Derringer: "He ended up painting jeeps mostly. And when he wasn't working for the Army, on his time off, he picked pineapple! When he returned, he continued to work on the railroad until he retired, in 1991. My mom, Janice (née Thornburg) also worked while I was growing up. Most of the time at Westinghouse. They were married when Dad was twenty-one and Mom was eighteen. I was born a year and a half later, August 5,1947, in Celina, twenty-two miles away. Fort Recovery didn't have a hospital. Randy was born November 21, 1949 and Robin on December 15, 1960."

Janice Zehringer: "That was where the railroad was. And that was where my husband was born and raised. His whole family lives in Fort Recovery, Ohio. At the beginning there

was only one Zehringer family but they were Catholic so they had huge amounts of children. There's a building there that has the name Zehringer on top of it. There's a road that has Zehringer on it. It's just a small town."

Rick Derringer: "We lived on 3rd Street until the end of the eighth grade, 1961."

By means of a company transfer to Muncie, Indiana, the family moved to nearby Union City where Janice was born and raised and settled in a house on Willow Drive.

Rick Derringer: "My mom came from a little bit of a musical background. Her brother played guitar, my Uncle Jim. She sang with him when she was growing up."

Parental encouragement is crucial once a child has been given the opportunity to develop an artistic interest. In the previous chapters the mother seems to have sighted that creative spark and liberally nurtured it. In this case both parents involved themselves in aiding their sons to showcase their talents.

Janice Zehringer: "He always wanted a guitar. When my brother would come to the house and play, he just was all eyes and ears. So we went to the music store on his ninth birthday and bought him an electric guitar and an amplifier."

Rick Derringer: "It was a one pick-up, no-name electric [laughs] and a Gibson amplifier. I think it was actually a Harmony but it literally had no name. Just gold paint on the headstock."

Janice Zehringer: "And he went to sleep with that guitar! We had a closed-in porch with a couch on it and he sat out there with that guitar. When it was time to go to bed I looked out there and he was asleep and the guitar was still in his arms. And I don't think he's put it down too many times since."

Rick Derringer: "We immediately called someone up in our hometown, a mechanic at the Ford garage. We had heard that Gene Feely played guitar. My dad took me and my guitar and we went up to this guy's house, knocked on the door and said, 'Are you Gene Feely?' 'Yeah.' 'OK. We heard you play guitar. Would you mind showing my son something?' And he said, 'Sure.' I remember sitting on his front porch and he showed me probably three chords and how to put them in a song formation. Then he said, 'Go home and practice these chords.' I remember going home and practicing those chords and having them down immediately. It came really easy to me."

"The next day we traveled fifty miles to where my Uncle Jim lived in Dayton, Ohio,and asked him if he would show me something. He showed me the song 'Caravan' and the other one was a song called 'Bye Bye Blues,' both as instrumental songs, chord-style lead guitar playing. He showed them to me and within a half hour I remembered them. And then went home and played them that night 'til I knew them. So by the third day I was playing real instrumental lead-guitar songs. And by that weekend I could have gone to wherever my uncle was playing and gotten up on stage and jammed with him and passed the hat. So within weeks I was playing professionally. But it's not like I didn't practice. That's all I did. It just came that fast. It stuck like glue and it was easy for me in as much as I can say I did not struggle. It was fun."

"My Uncle Jim died in 1999. His time came up. A lot of little health things. He died peacefully and everything was OK."

The guitar was far more than a dalliance. It quickly became an obsession.

Rick Derringer: "I played all the time. As soon as I got home from school I played the guitar. I would still go out and play sports and play with my friends. But as soon as I got back to the house, I'd pick up the guitar and play. If there were TV shows on, I'd play with the music of the TV show. I played with 'Ozzie & Harriet' because Ricky Nelson was on there. I played with 'The Lawrence Welk Show,' which I always thought was cool 'cuz they had a guy who played a Fender guitar."

As a result of first-hand exposure, younger brother Randy developed a need to become involved in music yet failed in his first attempt.

Rick Derringer: "When Randy first started, he started playing accordion for some strange reason. I don't think he knew why either. My folks got him a small accordion that he could handle. He started playing it a little, he took some lessons, but very quickly he realized, 'Why did I pick up the accordion?' "

Randy Zehringer: "They used to have accordion music on television a lot back then. I saw a picture of one and it just seemed like something I wanted to try. I started taking lessons but I wasn't really advancing on it. I was really young then. Maybe eight."

Janice Zehringer: "That's what I wanted when I was a child. Somehow I never got it. I thought I could convince him to try the accordion. Well, he played it when the music teacher was there and that was about it. So we decided that maybe that wasn't what he really wanted."

Rick Derringer: "And then he started pounding on cardboard boxes with spoons and realized he wanted to play the drums."

Randy Zehringer: "I got a set of drums for Christmas. I played on them that night for later than I could normally stay up for and Rick just started playing songs. We played as a duo for quite a while."

Union City, Indiana, 1958.
Courtesy Janice Zehringer

Rick Derringer: "My mom taught us about singing and harmony. In fact, she was the first person that really helped get us started singing, my brother and I. I can remember when we were real young she would sing along with songs in the car and eventually she started showing us how to sing harmony parts. And that's really where we started singing more than just melodies. Musical theory training was in the car with my Mom telling us how to sing harmony.

"My Dad supported me just being there to help, kinda like a road manager. He was always there to take us around to different places to try to get up on stage and play, and then later on helped driving us to shows and stuff. We played at Kiwanis Club meetings or somebody might want a couple of kids to open up the new Ford garage coming into town or something like that. We played a lot, right away, from when I was nine. We didn't have a name when we first started playing. It was just Rickey and Randy Zehringer."

Rick received some formal lessons in Celina but the instructor quickly ran out of things to show him. As soon as Randy showed a spark of talent in drumming, the brothers were enrolled under the guidance of a woman in Union City who taught them both. They quickly absorbed all she had to offer.

Janice Zehringer: "So then we took Rick to Richmond, Indiana. That's the last place he took guitar lessons. The teacher told us that he just could not teach Rick any more. He said, 'He comes in, honestly, and shows me. Someday I expect to see him on television.' "

Randy Zehringer: "We hadn't lived in Union City a really long time and Rick got with one of the neighbors we used to see a lot of and wanted him to get a bass guitar."

Dennis Kelly: "They were across my backyard from me. One summer day I heard somebody playing a guitar and looked over. Rick was sitting on his front porch playing. I walked over and introduced myself and that was the beginning. As time passed by we talked and he said, 'You know, if you get a bass guitar and learn how to play we could start a band.'"

Rick Derringer: "If he could talk his parents into buying him one, I would consent to showing him how to play it a little bit."

Dennis Kelly: "Rick said that was what they could use as far as filling out the band. I found a place in Union City where I ordered a real cheap bass. Rick basically taught me the basics of playing it."

Rick Derringer: "At that time The Ventures were popular and I decided that it would be easy to try and play an instrumental together. We wouldn't have to worry about any vocals, just playing. So I got out my Ventures album and went to what I figured was the easiest sounding one to learn. It turned out to be a song called 'The McCoy.' I showed Dennis how to play the bass part. The very first time we played that song together we were so awestruck and inspired by how much it sounded like a real, full band. And we decided right there that if we called ourselves The McCoys, we would have ourselves a theme song, 'The McCoy.' It didn't matter that it was the only song we knew. We just decided that it was enough to call ourselves a band. So we started learning more songs, putting together a set of enough music that we could go out and play as a three-piece band, The McCoys."

Dennis Kelly: "I remember the first job we played was a dance in Union City. We played strictly instrumental and Rick and I played through the same amplifier."

Randy Zehringer: "So when Dennis caught onto those songs we started doing more popular places. Back then if you had an electric bass you could get pretty good jobs just about anywhere. We had a job just about every weekend. It just kept getting bigger and bigger."

Dennis Kelly: "My parents said, 'You learn how to play this and we'll buy you the best one we can get.' So I played with my bass for a while. One time when we were in Dayton, I found a red Fender Jazz bass and a Bassman amp that they bought for me. I was a sophomore in high school at that time."

Rick Derringer: "He didn't just get something. He got the best. And I was corralled into showing him what to play."

Dennis Kelly: "Rick taught me the basics of it and I seemed to catch onto playing bass. I had a little bit of experience but he was very patient. When I was in junior high I had played trumpet and when I was a little bit younger my parents bought an organ and were giving me organ lessons.

"I used to fantasize about being in a band which I think is a fantasy that any number of high school-age boys have. But to realize that was really awesome. I know a lot of bands that are starting up now. The major difference is that they don't have a really talented guitar player and they make up for it by being loud. We were never really loud at the expense of the quality of sound."

Janice Zehringer: "They would practice either in our basement or our garage. I had a babysitter at that time for Rob when I worked. And she told me, 'All the neighbors come out to hear the boys practice!' I never had a neighbor complain, ever. There were times when I would hear them and think, 'Gee, that sounds pretty good!' "

Dennis Kelly: "Most of the kids at school, and again we're talking about a very small town, they really seemed to downplay it a lot. They would not allow themselves to be impressed by where we were going and by what we were doing. As a result, ironically, we played very little in our hometown."

Rick Derringer: "We did play at local 'sock hops' and things like that but there were no real venues there to play. We played very near there a couple of times."

Dennis Kelly: "In a very short period of time we became the top band in the area. When I say 'the area,' I mean Dayton, Ohio. And I think the entire phenomenon was due to Rick's talent on the guitar. Randy was an OK drummer. I was an OK bass player. But Rick was as phenomenal then as he is now. If you can imagine a kid of fourteen or fifteen at the time, that good at the guitar, it was incredible."

Visual presentation became something that was becoming important. Image. Some cared, some didn't.

Rick Derringer: "We just went and bought the clothes [laughs]. There was a store in Dayton that carried things that a lot of bands went to, as a matter of fact. I believe it was called 'Ridge Clothing.' We could go there, periodically, and shop at that store and pickup a coordinated look. We wanted to look good!"

To promote a flashier moniker, on the advice of an agent, the band became The Rick Z Combo in 1963. And, simultaneously, an opportunity of steady work presented itself, giving the band a chance to get tight in front of an audience.

Rick Derringer: "We played every Saturday night at the local armory in Greenville, Ohio. We didn't have monitors, that's for sure. We had some kind of P.A. system with some speakers that were made for us. They were nice enough speakers with closed backs. And they worked pretty good. I think we had a kind of a Bose or something like that as an amplifier. The sound came from the amps and we did the vocals through the little P.A."

Janice Zehringer: "After they had played there once, they asked them if they'd play there every week. They played dances every week for I don't know how long. But they really did help them raise the money to build that pool at the YMCA."

Rick Derringer: "And the concerts were so successful that they went ahead and built a Greenville community swimming pool with money that was generated from that series of concerts we played. We didn't even realize what that money was used for. It was only later on that my parents told me they had used the money generated from those concerts to build the Greenville Ohio Community swimming pool.

"At one of those concerts, a kid came up and just started banging on an off-stage piano. His name was Ronnie Brandon. And because we wanted a fourth member in the band and he presented himself we said, 'OK, you can come and join us.' He went out and bought a little portable organ of some kind and we became a four-piece band."

Ron Brandon: "I had a broken wrist but I started playing with them at that time and it basically took off from there. They lived in Union City, Indiana, and I lived in Greenville, Ohio, which was only eight miles away.

"I was playing with them right away but it took a while before I got paid for it [laughs]. They were getting $60 a night for a three-piece and they had booked for several months in advance. So I worked for a couple of months without any pay because they couldn't get more than the $60 and that's the way it went."

Dennis Kelly: "When Ronnie Brandon joined us my parents had an organ. So a lot of times we would practice in the living room of my house. I can remember on summer days we'd be in there practicing and cars would come up and stop out front and listen."

Ron Brandon: "We were basically considered the backup band for the radio station in Dayton. For WNE and WING. If anybody came into the area that didn't have a musical group behind them they always called us 'cuz we learned the songs real fast."

Janice Zehringer: "After they had gone to Greenville I went to a radio station in Dayton, Ohio. There was a disc jockey there named Bob Holliday. He promoted dances and concerts and he would have name groups come to Dayton and play. I finally thought, 'They sound as good as the others on the radio!' So I boldly walked into the radio station and asked to talk to Bob Holliday. I told him that I wondered if they couldn't play at one of his shows. I said, 'I know they look little and I know they're young but they can play really well.' And he said, 'I'll think about it.' He called and was going to let them play one night. And they opened for … not a well-known group. He stood there and he watched them. And he came over to Rick's father and I and he said, 'I'm going to have The Beach Boys here next week. I wonder if they could come back and open for The Beach Boys?' 'Well! Of course they can!' So that's how they really got started."

Randy Zehringer: "The first one that was really exciting was when we were with The Beach Boys at Swordsville Lake. We had never really seen a big name act or anything up till then."

Dennis Kelly: "Down between Cincinnati and Hamilton, Ohio. It was a theme park. I remember we'd go out between sets and ride the roller coaster. We also did an opener in Dayton for The Four Seasons. We did an awful lot of backup work. Ray Stevens was an example. Terry Stafford. What we would do is we would learn their songs during the week and be their backup band when they would come into town."

Rick Derringer: "In the summer following that we were playing a series of shows in Dayton, Ohio, at a place called Forest Park Arena. A lot of bands came through the area who were big recording acts that didn't necessarily travel with their own bands. The promoter would supply a local group who would open with a set and then back up the headliner. That's the kind of thing we were doing. People like Chuck Berry, The Strangeloves, The Drifters, Roy Orbison, Lou Christie, The Beach Boys, The Byrds, among others. It was very cool."

Randy Zehringer: "We did some television shows in Dayton and Cincinnati. We might have won one or two. We were just starting out. I was so young at that time."

Janice Zehringer: "WLW, at the time, was probably the biggest station in Cincinnati. They had called them to come down to perform on a show that was called 'Bob Rowan.' Bob Rowan was pretty well-known for about three states and well-acquainted with Dick Clark. And while they were waiting to go on the air, Rick must have visited the restroom a dozen times! He was so nervous. And Randy got nervous but Randy would just crack his knuckles and bite his nails.

"They were so little when they started and so young when they joined the union. Randy was the youngest member they'd ever had. I think he was only about twelve or thirteen. And everybody insisted they had to join the union because they were making far more than union scale. They had bookings on up for a good while. Rick and his Dad and I did that on the phone from home. Just people who said, 'We want them for this, we want them for that.' Our phone rang all week from people that would want them to play at some kind of a show or a function."

Author: "Though you were young, had you yet seriously considered music as your vocation?"

Rick Derringer: "Well, we did it so much that certainly it was something I envisioned. But my parents, being very pragmatic Midwesterners, encouraged me to think music would probably only be a hobby and I should have some other vocation in mind. I had been accepted into the Dayton Art Institute, a five-year art school, which is what I was going to do when I graduated from high school. You had to do a pretty ornate, inclusive portfolio of different styles of your work. I had to have a little painting, a little drawing,

just a lot of pictures of different things that I had done. I think there were probably some scholastic scores you had to meet. But the main thing for them was the portfolio. And my portfolio was accepted and I was ready to go to school. I liked all of it. I had planned to do something in commercial art, which would have been all kinds of things. Ads for magazines. Could have been greeting cards, really. One of the things I was interested in was architecture. In the most complicated form, I might have been some kind of architect. And in the simplest way, I might have been just a big general commercial artist."

Their exposure to statewide television audiences called for the group to make and release a single to a growing fan base.

Janice Zehringer: "They had wanted to record for so long and they tried to make a recording on their own. Which didn't do badly in the area we lived in."

Rick Derringer: "We had recorded it ourselves in Ohio. It was called 'I Know That I Love You.' (The B-side was 'What Can I Do'). We pressed them up ourselves. We called our record company Sonic Records. Those were the first songs I ever wrote. When it came time to actually start working on songs, my Mom sat down with me and helped me write some lyrics. And 'I Know That I Love You' is one of those songs that she gave me some advice about."

Dennis Kelly: "We rented time at a recording studio in Columbus, Ohio. I still have a copy of that."

Rick Derringer: "I think my Dad has several left but I don't have one."

Janice Zehringer: "When they made the record, we went up and had a guardianship drawn up at a lawyers' office. So when they would give us checks from performances we would put them into accounts for them. If it was an uneven number, like $73 short of a hundred, my husband would add that to make it an even amount. They never had to be concerned where their money went. And to this day I think people believe that we lived off them! But it's what you'd do

The Rick Z Combo, 1964.
(clockwise from bottom, Randy Zehringer, Rick Zehringer,
Dennis Kelly, Ronnie Brandon)
Courtesy Dennis Kelly

for any child that worked. I read about people that take their children's money when they're young and spend it. How could you do that?"

In the early summer of 1964, the band came across a group touring the United States.

Rick Derringer: "The Corronados had a couple of hit records in the mid-60s (Love Me With All Your Heart). They had the job of doing some live performing at The Texas Pavilion at the World's Fair in 1964. And they said that if we were ever in New York City, they'd love to have us come by The Texas Pavilion and play a set. So we did that. On that particular trip, The Corronados asked if we would want to record a song, a single, and they would try to place it with a record company. We did 'Yesterday, Today and Tomorrow.' I don't think they ever got it out on a real label."

Dennis Kelly: "I'd love to get my hands on a recording of the stuff we did in New York. We ended up with one press

from that, one promotional copy. We had some decent songs on there. We sounded good."

Janice Zehringer: "They would call and say what they were going to do and this and that but then they never heard anything more from them."

Rick Derringer: "But it did give us the opportunity to get to New York City a year before we did 'Hang On Sloopy.' So it didn't seem like such a big, foreign place to us."

• • •

Rick Derringer: "As time went on, we learned that other people in town played music too. Dennis had the ability, when I showed him how to play a song, to learn it. But the other guy that we knew and heard about very quickly was Randy Hobbs (b. March 22,1948). His Mom lived in a little trailer in the poorer part of town and she couldn't afford to buy him much of anything. But he found somebody that had an old six-string Danlectroguitar. He managed to take some strings off that and tune the others down low enough that it sounded like a bass. And he was learning really complicated songs. All the Motown hits and things like that on his own. The first time we heard him play or got the chance to jam with him, he already knew how to play really cool stuff. As it turned out, we were getting quite popular around the area and with my Dad's help we had an ability to get gigs and were working a lot. Dennis Kelly, who was a couple of years older than us, had started to think about going away to school. All of a sudden we had to think about canceling gigs."

Dennis Kelly: "When I went to college I was coming home every weekend to play and it really got to be kind of a hardship. I told them, 'Why don't you get Randy Hobbs to fill in on Friday night gigs and I'll play on Saturday nights?' We did that for a while. Then I don't know if the quality was suffering a little bit or what, but the Zehringers were wanting me to come home from school during the week to practice. It reached the point where I decided I had to make a decision as to what I was gonna do with this band. That was really when I decided to step down. And to be honest, a major part of making that decision was that the Viet Nam War was going on at the time. That gave me a deferment and kept me from coming home in a box."

Rick Derringer: "Hobbs was a little bit like the town hood! He was like a kid in the movie *Grease* [laughs]! He wore the leather jacket. Greased his hair back. Smoked cigarettes on his way to school. He was kind of the town bad guy. He didn't really do anything to get himself in trouble or anything like that. It was just an image he liked [laughs]. We always found him to be a really nice guy when we finally met him. Maybe it had to do with the music. Maybe it had something to do with being some kind of a rocker. I don't know. He eventually did get into motorcycles and things like that. Maybe that's where the leather jacket thing came from. But that's the image he certainly had."

Randy Zehringer: "In Union City everybody was pretty much regular people. They didn't have people that, I don't know how you could say it, somebody that you wouldn't want to be with all the time. I guess he was kinda like that. But he was really dependable as far as practicing. He never missed a job or anything like that. Just being a bass player and a good singer meant nothing if you weren't there."

Then came another name change.

Rick Derringer: "One of our promoters encouraged us to change it. We chose the name Rick and the Raiders. Paul Revere and the Raiders hadn't happened yet. And that was the name we were going under when I was graduating from high school in the summer of 1965."

Rick and The Raiders met another touring group. This meeting would change their lives.

Rick Derringer: "One of the groups touring in the summer of 1965 was a group called The Strangeloves. The Strangeloves had recorded and produced 'I Want Candy' and 'The Nighttime' and a couple of other big hits. They were not Australian sheepherders, which is what they billed themselves as. They were actually three record producers from Brooklyn, New York, who were called FGG Productions. (Bob Feldman, Richard Gottherer and Jerry Goldstein.) And FGG Productions had established a

relationship with Bang Records, Bert Berns' label. The first hit on Bang Records was a song called, I believe, 'My Boyfriend's Back' by The Angels. FGG Productions produced that record for very few dollars. It was some nurses and stuff that they knew and used as the vocalists and it became a huge number one hit all over the world. So Bang Records had a lot of confidence in FGG Productions to produce records. Bert Berns had written a song the year before that had become a number one R&B hit by The Vibrations, a black group. That hit was called 'My Girl Sloopy.' But because of Beatlemania, he knew that if he could get a bunch of young white guys that looked like The Beatles to do 'My Girl Sloopy,' that record could be a huge hit all across the board, not just an R&B hit. The Strangeloves were his pet producers for the label. So he sent them out on a little tour. And he had said, 'Look, if you can find a bunch of white kids that look a little like The Beatles to do 'My Girl Sloopy,' I'd like you to produce that record for me.' "

Ron Brandon: "They just couldn't believe that we were that young and that good [laughs]. It seemed that anything they wanted to do that night, we could do it. I was nineteen, Rick was eighteen, Randy Hobbs was seventeen and Little Randy was sixteen."

Rick Derringer: "They were impressed with us as musicians. But they were trying to impress us with what they were able to do also. I think somewhere in their head they probably had the idea of being able to take advantage of a bunch of kids. But at the same time, they had the ability to take us back and make this hit record. We were certainly impressed and really excited about it. They asked us if we wanted to come to New York with them and record 'My Girl Sloopy.' It sounded like a great idea. I immediately turned to my dad and said, 'What do you think? Is that going to be possible?' This was in late July of 1965."

Janice Zehringer: "And it just so happened that John had a vacation the next week. So we took them to New York, the whole band."

Rick Derringer: "And our little trailer pulling our equipment! We stayed at a hotel on 73rd Street, a place that they recommended we go. It was pretty convenient to everything. It was pretty much up to us to take care of ourselves. They might have actually paid for those hotel rooms but I'm not even sure of that.

"Then we had meetings with The Strangeloves. The first thing we decided was that the title, 'My Girl Sloopy,' wasn't appropriate. Because it sings 'Hang On Sloopy' all the time. So the first constructive decision was to change the name to 'Hang On Sloopy.' Then they decided that Rick and the Raiders certainly wasn't a usable name because Paul Revere and the Raiders had arrived and become a big hit. So looking through old photos they found one with our original drum head on it, which said The McCoys. 'This is you guys?' 'Yep. That's us.' So they said, 'Well, this is the ideal name. We can envision even having a girl group going out as an alternative called The Hatfields and we could have a whole feud between The McCoys and Hatfields in the press!' We all laughed amongst ourselves and also thought, 'Well, that would be cool.' In actuality they never tried that. But we would have gone along with that kind of stuff [laughs].

"Within a couple of days we recorded the basic track for 'Hang On Sloopy,' and within a couple of more days recorded the vocals. Immediately after we recorded it, everyone in the control room all jumped up and down and yelled, 'NUMBER ONE!' And we thought, 'This looks like it's gonna be an easy business for us.' We didn't know that didn't happen every time! But within a matter of weeks after it was being played on the radio, it really was number one. So then we changed our opinions and figured, 'Wow, this must be how easy it is. You go in and you record a song and everybody yells 'Number One' and the next thing you know, it's number one. This is some easy business here!'

"It was August, 1965. I know 'cuz my birthday had just occurred. Had the version of it finished within a week or two and probably out in early September 1965. Very quick because they were fighting a battle with people doing it simultaneously. As it turns out, a lot of other groups thought this would be a good song too. The Yardbirds recorded it on one of their albums. They luckily didn't release it as a single. A Canadian group called Little Caesar and The Consuls released it in Canada as a single at exactly the same time we did. (The group featured Gene McLellan and Robbie Robertson.) They called theirs 'My Girl Sloopy.' So we had a little bit of an edge right away because our name was more appropriate. But the battle was on. Who's going to get the hit single out of this? Was it going to be Little Caesar and The Consuls, who looked like the Beatles? Or was it going to be The McCoys, who looked like The Beatles?

"Well, one of the things that helped us win that battle was Bang Records was a strong little label. It had a lot of power behind it. Bang stood for **B**ert Berns, **A**hmet Ertegun, **N**esuhi Ertegun and **G**erald Wexler. Originally it was a little offshoot from Atlantic Records and a brain child of all these really high-powered executives. So when it came down to doing battle in the marketplace for who's going to be a big strong hit, we not only had the title going for us of 'Hang On Sloopy,' but the writer of the song, Bert Berns, owned his own label. And these powerful guys, Atlantic, were behind the label. So within a matter of weeks ours was almost number one in every country in the world that sells records.

"Until we had a real manager from the FGG Production guys there was no real manager. My dad and I would both acquire the gigs and keep the books. It eventually went to a guy that FGG found, his name was Roy Rifkin. He managed Little Eva as well. And he was specifically working for FGG Productions, we found out later on."

Ron Brandon: "I hated New York City at first but I got into it. We worked out of there because that's where our producers were. They hired a frontman to be our manager. They wound up taking it all."

Rick Derringer: "When we first hit New York we signed with the William Morris Agency. My first agents were David Geffen and Wally Amos, who became Famous Amos, the cookie guy. My first PR man was Robin Leach. He had asked for old photos of us. My folks gave him everything they had. He had promised that they would be returned to them but they never were. And my mom, to this day, we're talking thirty-five years later, she will still, every time she sees me, 'By the way, did you talk to Robin Leach at all in the last few months? See if you can get those photos back.' "

Janice Zehringer: "On our way home, they played this song at a dance in Washington, D.C. with The Strangeloves, who were appearing there."

Ron Brandon: "It wound up in the Huntley/Brinkley news report that night. We were probably the only rock 'n' roll group to ever hit the Huntley/Brinkley newscast!"

Janice Zehringer: "And The Strangeloves told them, 'This will be on the air, so you'll want to keep listening.' So we didn't think … that quick! By the time we got home, they were playing it on the radio. It was just a week. You can imagine all these teenagers in a car and hearing a song they just had recorded on the radio for the first time."

Randy Zehringer: "It was kinda like the Loretta Lynn movie, 'Coal Miner's Daughter' [laughs]! You hear it on the radio and you start jumping up and down and everything."

Janice Zehringer: "But the problem was that we had lived in a small town. When you talked to people and you said you were going to do something, you could believe it. So when they made the record, I would say the biggest mistake we made was when they signed their contract. We had no way of knowing at the time that the recording company and the manager and the producer were all hooked up together along with the lawyer. We had no lawyer. It was 'their' lawyer. So believe me it wasn't the best contract in the world. All of the recording that's been done since 'Hang On Sloopy' and that over the years, except for the initial money, they never ever received a penny for.

"I blame myself and their dad because we were adults and should have understood. I never had a lawyer in my life for anything but a couple of occasions when I needed one for some minor thing. But if you had a business and you let the managers have a certain way, then it just stood to reason that you were telling the truth. I guess it's naïve to think that way

but we had no reason to distrust these people. As it turned out, we did.

"But that's what they wanted so bad. If it had been for ourselves we might have delayed and said, 'Well, we have to think this over. We gotta go get an attorney.' But We didn't. And it was a mistake. But at the same time, these people know who they are. That's something. And it got him established. Rick has worked all these years because of it. It wasn't all a mistake. But at the same time it's sad what people will do to young people. I think if you're dishonest with an adult, it's one thing. But when you're dishonest with a young person whose whole future is at stake it's another. I couldn't do that. But then I couldn't be in that business."

Ron Brandon: "It had hit so fast that we really didn't believe it had hit. And it was a pretty phenomenal record. They said it had sold six million. We got a gold record out of it. A lot of bootlegging went on back then. Bang was pretty notorious for that. They had Neil Diamond for a little while. I think Neil got hip to what was going on so he bought himself out."

Rick Derringer: "And then we were called up to come out on the road and tour with The Strangeloves as their opening act and backup band on our first official outing as 'Hang On Sloopy' was taking off."

Author: "Who found you a place to live?"

Rick Derringer: "They did. It was The Hotel Forest. It was a little residence hotel right in midtown Manhattan. I remember the songwriter Doc Thomas lived in a hotel room right above us. We traveled so much that it was convenient. And ultimately we got to the point where we found ourselves apartments. I think they were keeping us close by to keep an eye on us. We were pretty young."

The guys were suddenly thrust into a foreign situation. Relocating to New York City showed a definite commitment both from the band and the parents.

Rick Derringer: "They had nurtured this whole music thing and been behind it to such an extent that the success with 'Hang On Sloopy' was looked at as the greatest blessing a kid could have. They had a little misgiving because my brother Randy hadn't graduated from high school yet. What they said was, 'He's gonna kind of be in your care. You watch out for him.' Our producers offered to have our first road manager in The McCoys, who was a tutor, to spend time with both my brother and Randy Hobbs. They were also enrolled in the Professional Children's School in New York City, which is the best school of its kind for children that happen to be in Broadway plays or touring with the circus [laughs]! And they both fit into that category. So they took their lessons at P.C.S. when they were in Manhattan and were tutored by our road manager, Eddie Rabkin, when we traveled."

Eddie Rabkin was a member of the doo-wop group The Linc-Tones, who later became The Tokens and had a hit with "The Lion Sleeps Tonight." Rabkin and fellow member Neil Sedaka left prior to the name change.

Rick Derringer: "The story I got from Eddie Rabkin was that Neil Sedaka's homosexuality was a real turn-off for him. And that's why he left the band."

Ron Brandon: "He was supposedly a tutor but he didn't do anything."

Janice Zehringer: "I went with Randy to New York when he enrolled in that school. The man (Rabkin) traveled with them but the tutoring part I don't know too much about. They were only supposed to travel 'so' much but they were going all the time. And that's when I found out what those people were like. I had quite a few conversations on the phone with them about Randy not being in school, not getting the tutoring he was supposed to have. But by this time they had convinced me that it was working out. That Randy and Randy Hobbs were going to school. Which is true. They did. While they were there. But if someone is working 'til late at night and riding all day in a car, there's not much opportunity to study. So it didn't work out very well."

Randy Zehringer: "He was educated to tutor us but we weren't very good students. I could get by in school and get pretty good grades but it wasn't something I was all that interested in. I guess like everybody else you have some things that you're more interested in than other things. I never looked forward to studying. I think I went more than Hobbs. I finished one year of that. They had kids from *As The World Turns* studying their scripts for the next day. I felt like a lot of the people there would lean towards their career before they would go for school. But they also had students that went there and took music courses, theater and things like that. We did a commercial for some kind of acne medication. To this day they still mention us as having gone there."

Rick Derringer: "We continued as the opening group for The Strangeloves and we would do 'Hang On Sloopy' in our set. But that was only for a few months. And those were clubs, usually. A hundred to three hundred people. Quickly, after 'Hang On Sloopy' came out, we started doing our own shows. Mostly still clubs but bigger clubs. We did a *Murray the K Brooklyn Fox Show*, a theater show that they did three times a day with many other acts. And we did a *Murray the K Fox Motown Revue*. The headliner on that *Motown Revue*, with all those other Motown acts, was Peter and Gordon. It was a weird show. We played 'Hang On Sloopy,' which a lot of black people thought was a black song. Us being little kids and talented, they extended us a great cordial welcome every time we hit the stage. When we first went out, we played for quite a few black audiences that had assumed that we were a black act. We got a great reception each time. We also did a Dick Clark tour of some kind. A bus tour. We also did another bus tour that consisted of us, The Outsiders, Shadows of Night, and the Mysterians. We did another one that was us, The Beaubrummels, The Seeds, and Freddie & the Dreamers."

Liz Derringer: "I always liked music and rock 'n' roll especially. I saw Rick one day on *Shindig*, fell in love and said I was gonna marry him. I was only fourteen. Everybody thought I was insane.

"I went to *The Murray The K Show* where all the bands used to play in Brooklyn. I don't remember the exact second meeting Rick, but I remember following him around a lot once I did meet him. I think it was in this place they used to always hang out a lot, The Satellite Diner or something. Downtown, Flatbush Avenue. I remember I kept coming to see Rick wherever he was. He was seeing a girl at the time. I wasn't too happy about that but I did everything in my power to get him to care about me. It took a long time but it worked. By the time I was seventeen, I was married. February 2, 1969."

Rick Derringer: "We did *Hullabaloo, Shindig, Where The Action Is* several times. *American Bandstand.* And all the local rock shows when we traveled. Mostly all lip-synch. But not totally. We did *The Mike Douglas Show.* Mike Douglas called us over to chat. Jack E. Leonard, who was kind of like Don Rickles in some ways, said that my brother's hair looked like an eagle created a nest there and landed on his head [laughs]. We all thought that was kind of cute. I remember I had a terrible sore throat. One of the things our producers and managers didn't really take into consideration was we were young. We hadn't been used to singing every night. We hadn't been taught how to sing properly and not blow our voices out. A lot of times I'd be put in situations where there would be important shows and I would have no voice at all. It would just be so blown out, so destroyed. *The Mike Douglas Show* I remember because I was very embarrassed by the fact that I was on national TV, not lip-synching and I had no voice at all.

"Never did *Ed Sullivan.* Probably just one of those things that if we had the opportunity, while we were big enough to do it, we were out making money somewhere else. It's not a bad thing, necessarily. What FGG were really into, when I look back on it, was keeping us working on the road as much as possible. And sometimes that would mean that we wouldn't have the opportunity to do some things. Like the *Sullivan Show.*"

Randy Zehringer: "When in New York we had to have enough work to pay our bills. That was something we had

our minds on a lot. We were living there for three or four weeks at a time and not working. It was costing us more to live there than we were making. But we wanted to get apartments there. Rick was staying at his girlfriend's apartment and she was staying with her mother."

Liz Derringer: "His band would stay in a hotel and he'd stay with us 'cuz my mother would cook him all the dishes he liked."

Rick Derringer: "I wasn't really living there. We had two apartments in Greenwich Village. But it was about that time that I started getting closer with Liz. I probably stayed overnight there occasionally. Naw, I didn't even do that. That would have been strange. We spent a lot of time together, that's for sure. She was only a few blocks from our house, literally. So I could certainly go over there and spend days and eat meals and stuff like that. But we were in no way living together. Her mom never would have allowed that and that wouldn't have been right."

Randy Zehringer: "Randy Hobbs had an apartment up on somewhere around 50th or 56th. And Ronnie Brandon had an apartment uptown."

Rick Derringer: "And shortly after that was The Stones tour."

In the summer of 1966, The Rolling Stones began their fifth North American Tour. The McCoys shared the opening bill with The Tradewinds and The Standells.

Rick Derringer: "The Stones had just started their new label called Immediate Records. Their manager, Andrew Loog Oldham, heard 'Hang On Sloopy' and decided that it would be a great record to release as their first single. So Immediate Records was the label it came out on in England. The Rolling Stones decided to help promote the record and they used us on their entire 1966 U.S. tour to open for them. So The McCoys had a lot going for them."

Aside from the prestige of being associated with a tour of this magnitude by sharing in the media blitz, The McCoys took advantage of the occasion to learn from the headliners.

Rick Derringer: "We learned how to present ourselves in an even more high-powered way. The Stones are great and certainly time has proven that. And we might have been copied after the good boys, The Beatles. But we certainly learned all the stuff The Stones had to present as kinda the bad boys of music in those days. We learned how to work that crowd. Mick Jagger has certainly proven over the years that he can do that like nobody else. And that's certainly one of the reasons why I'm still here today. I have always been a very kinda pragmatic student from the Midwest. And every little bit of opportunity that's presented to me along the years I've used as a way to learn a few more lessons. Even though I might not have had the huge success that I have always looked for in my career, I've used all of those opportunities to learn lessons and learn from my mistakes. And I'm still working toward that huge success today."

Randy Zehringer: "We had played to audiences that big before. For instance, we played at Maple Leaf Gardens in Toronto with other shows and had pretty much filled them up. But it's one thing to have people come in to see Gene Pitney. With The Rolling Stones there's a lot more excitement."

Ron Brandon: "That was kind of an experience [laughs]. We traveled two months with them. We stayed in New York for a month and flew out to gigs from there in a private plane they had leased out of Florida and did the shows every night. Back in the plane and back to New York. And then we worked another month out of California back this way."

Randy Zehringer: "I think it was a DC-3. We were all in that little plane all the time but nobody really talked to us [laughs]. Three of them stayed together all the time and their drummer and bass player were separate from them. They weren't exactly walking down the aisle shaking hands with everybody."

Rick Derringer: "I didn't interact that much but I certainly got to know the guys. Including Brian, who was on that tour. And to varying degrees, people interacted as much or as little, I guess, as The Stones would allow. There were no rules or anything that said you couldn't talk to anybody or stuff like that. We were all in awe of them. And, in some ways, we didn't interact as much as we could have because we were little kids."

Though the band were hardly rookies, the circumstances that go along with being on a tour of that size were prevalent for the first time.

Rick Derringer: "We saw it going on but we really didn't do anything like that. I didn't drink anything 'til I was almost twenty-one as a matter of fact. That's where that song came from that I wrote on The Stones tour. 'Don't worry, mother, you're son's heart is pure' [laughs]. It's Stones-influenced, lyrically. But we certainly saw those things going on. Heard about the Stones hiding stuff in the lining of their clothes. And we were certainly presented with a lot of groupies and stuff like that for the first time."

Ron Brandon: "You'd go back to the hotel and there'd be three girls in your room. They would bribe the bellhop or something. But it didn't worry us. It would worry me now. Back then you didn't have anything like AIDS so you didn't have to worry about it."

Rick Derringer: "We were all impressed with Brian Jones because he was certainly an individual up there. Each guy had a distinctive personality and he had his own. The Stones actually talked a lot about how Brian was a little perverted, sexually [laughs]. They would like to brag about that to other people. They would say, 'You think you've got stories? You think you've had experiences? You should talk to Brian over here!' That was one of the things The Stones were most proud of … how sexually active and adventuresome Brian was!"

Randy Zehringer: "I remember when we were in London, England, to finish that tour Rick ended up in the hospital for more than a week. He had gotten his vaccination for his passport and it made him sick. We were supposed to play all over. Six weeks or something. And after two shows he got real bad. The rest of them went back and me and Eddie stayed there and waited for Rick. We lost that part of the tour."

The band quickly returned to the road upon returning to the U.S. to capitalize on the favorable reviews they had garnered from The Stones tour. Apart from their music, they were becoming known for their onstage exuberance, which was somewhat rare for a group of such a young demographic.

Rick Derringer: "We happened to be innocent young kids who liked what they were doing enough for it to be contagious. And we were talented. There's no way to get around that. It's still the same today. A producer can understand the viability and the commercial aspects of a young group in the marketplace. That producer can go out and create a record and find a young group to kind of fill in the shoes of whatever that artist is called. That doesn't mean that they have to be talented. Sometimes the record is great and the group isn't very talented. And sometimes both the song and the group are talented. And that is exhibited today with a group like Hanson, who are characterized for being not that talented. But, in reality, they are talented. Or The Backstreet Boys, who are really very talented people. So we were Hanson [laughs].

"They were always intending to promote us as that kinda perfect young bunch of kids. The problem in the music business was 'Yummy, Yummy, Yummy' and a lot of records like that had started to come into the marketplace. There was a band actually called The 1910 Fruitgum Company that had become real popular. And a lot of bands like us. If your managers and promoters weren't smart enough to promote you as a 'hip band,' you were being characterized as a bubble gum band. And I think that's what happened with us. People were so interested in the short buck that they weren't interested in looking ahead and promoting us in the proper way. And we got characterized as one of those bubble gum groups. Even though we had hits, 'Fever,' 'Come On, Let's Go,' 'Up and Down,' we had kind of a built-in downward curve. And we ended up rebelling against all those people and ended up taking The McCoys to make esoteric records for Mercury Records. We made two albums over there as The McCoys. One was called 'Infinite McCoys' and one was called 'Human Ball.' And those were just total, flat-out vehicles for us to get out of that bubble gum group kind of mold."

Ron Brandon: "I think we just wanted to succeed. It wasn't too bad being a bubble gum group back then. We were too young to know the difference. FGG Productions pretty much handled everything. We'd just split up the account every so often. FGG took 25 percent of the gross. William Morris took another 10 percent of the gross. And what it all boils down to was that there wasn't a whole lot left. You got your traveling expenses and everything out of it. That was just the price everybody paid for fame back then, I guess. I was just a kid. I was seeing the country and going over to England and stuff like that."

1967

Rick Derringer: "The keyboard player, Ronnie Brandon, wasn't a very good musician. Soon after we had made it, we were playing onstage and we realized he wasn't very good. So we fired him immediately."

Ron Brandon: "They just called me up and said that my services were no longer needed. It didn't sit too good with me but what are you gonna do? What I really think happened is we were trying to get out of our contract with FGG Productions and Bang. The rest of the boys were all underage. I was the only one that was twenty-one at that time. The parents had signed the contracts. But the contract they signed was only to state that they were legal guardians of the boys and they did not sign the main contract. So their lawyer said, 'Get rid of Ron and you have no contract.' I think that's what actually happened. They didn't tell me that. They just said that my services were no longer needed. Our road manager called. Then Rick got on the phone after. I called him a few fruitful names [laughs]! I kinda pouted around for a few days about it. They actually did me a favor. Things were starting to slow down. And they were into things I wasn't into. And it eventually caught up with them. Drugs. Little Randy and Big Randy, they partied too much."

Liz Derringer: "Randy (Zehringer) started doing drugs early on but Rick didn't."

Greenwich Village, 1967.
Courtesy Liz Derringer

Randy Zehringer: "We had an idea that we were gonna try and go as a three-piece. Just drums, guitar and bass. So that was kinda awkward to tell Ronnie that. The road manager we had at that time, Mike Conwell, he looked forward to doing things like that [laughs]."

Rick Derringer: "The parents didn't feel like some of the tutors, who were previous road managers, were doing a very good job. And they also weren't confident with the way the money was being handled. So we decided we wanted our own road manager. Mike Conwell told my parents that he would be willing to do that road manager job for us and we hired him. He did have experience as a concert promoter but not really as a road manager. It became a little too stressful for him. I understand that later on he had become kind of a Woodstock follower, a summer of love devotee, and had become well immersed in that whole psychedelic culture. LSD and stuff like that. He committed suicide, is how I've heard it, with some kind of note referring to a popular book that was out then

called *The Other Side*. It was about what happens after you die."

Randy Zehringer: "So we tried that for a while with just three people. It was all right but different people told us that we needed an organ or a piano. So we got Bobby through somebody in New York. He was from Atlanta and had been working there."

Rick Derringer: "We found Bobby Peterson and hired him because he was really a great player. He joined us about the time we did the albums for Mercury Records. He plays on both of those records. We didn't try to make a hit. We made kind of psychedelic, somewhat jazzy music on those two albums."

In most situations of the day musicians would usually stay with their label so as not to risk being left out in the cold. But The McCoys somewhat arrogantly felt that they stood a better chance by seeing what their value was worth.

Rick Derringer: "Our contract was up with Bang Records, with FGG Productions. We went to Bang and said,

'We would love to sign with you but we'd like to give other record companies the opportunity too.' We didn't know what we were doing. Bert Berns offered us the opportunity of staying with Bang Records. He said that we'd been cheated severely by FGG Productions and he would show us the books if we would simply sign back with him. Being very naïve, we said, 'Well, that doesn't sound like we're really letting everybody else have a shot at us [laughs]!' So we ended up signing with Mercury Records and never going back and looking at those books. Which was really a dumb move on our part. Very, very stupid. And probably not a good career move 'cuz Bert probably would have tried his best to make us very successful."

With the release of "Infinite McCoys" and "Human Ball" on Mercury Records, the band was trying to leave their current audience and develop a new one. The audience they were leaving behind had faces. The audience they wanted to attract didn't exist yet.

Rick Derringer: "We had no clue [laughs]! We only knew that letting people characterize us as a bubblegum group meant that we weren't going very far. Our records were going to sell less and less. All we wanted to do was break out of that mold. We really didn't have an idea of how to make a hit single. Obviously, we hoped that our music would be successful and liked. So it was an attempt to be more musical and get out the music that we felt we wanted to do as opposed to doing the music we were being told to do.

"We didn't have hits. But it did give us the opportunity to get out of that mold and to get into a place like The Scene, where we did play a lot. And it was through The Scene in New York City that we met the guy who was going to become our manager, Steve Paul, who introduced us to Johnny Winter and Edgar Winter. And that was where we had the opportunity to get out of the problems of being a bubblegum group. We just discovered The Scene walking down the street while we were looking for something to do. We heard music coming out of it. Went in and realized we'd struck gold! We found our hangout!"

Randy Zehringer: "We had been there when a lot of groups played there. Jimi Hendrix would play there. Randy Hobbs had known some of that group. So I guess that must have helped getting a job there."

Rick Derringer: "A very hip crowd of people. All the hip musicians went there. And a lot of late night people. Steve Paul was one of those kinds of people that would only allow his accepted crowd into the club. And that included press. Critics at the time. People from within the record business. Obviously, all the people that played in groups. And up and comers, all the successful people.

"Steve Paul came from a PR background. He was very clever and he certainly had an aptitude for promotion. And became a whiz kid at it when he was seventeen. He was making huge amounts of money. When the psychedelic age came in, he believed that he was somehow doing it for the money and the wrong motives. So he wanted to involve himself in a business that was more appropriately humanitarian, we'll call it [laughs]! And that to him was music. He wanted to get involved in music because that was hip. He decided to have a club and he created exactly the situation he wanted."

Edgar Winter: "He was very creative in that area. He was a very unorthodox kind of manager. Which I liked [laughs]. He referred to himself as 'organic director!' He was great to work with."

Rick Derringer: "Immediately we saw The Doors, Jimi Hendrix, Traffic, Jerry Lee Lewis. Everybody was hanging out there. Led Zeppelin was there, hanging out. Janis Joplin, Sly Stone. Of course Johnny Winter. Edgar Winter, when he arrived in town."

Liz Derringer: "Oh, God, it was incredible. Everybody who was anybody in rock 'n' roll came to The Scene. And the jam sessions were unbelievable. At night, when Jimi would get up, when the bands were over and start the jam sessions. Rick would always play with him and Randy Hobbs. It was really crazy. It was too many drugs. Too many women, too much insanity back then."

The McCoys, 1968.
(l-r, Randy Hobbs, Rick Peterson, Randy Zehringer, Rick Zehringer)
Courtesy Liz Derringer

Edgar Winter: "It was the place to go! The Beatles. The Rolling Stones. And in a lot of cases the British people who weren't known in the States would come in and jam. There were a lot of magical nights at The Scene. And it was definitely a unique experience. I remember Johnny jamming with Jimi."

Rick Derringer: "After talking them into letting us play one night, we were asked to play any night we wanted to. That's why we got the name as the house band. We were there a lot. We jammed with everybody. People were surprised to see a bunch of young kids play the kind of music we were playing. And that's how Jimi Hendrix got to hear me play. That's how the mentions in all the Jimi Hendrix books and stuff came about was because we became pretty good

friends. Jimi would come and try out new song ideas and stuff in that jamming atmosphere down there. He certainly got the opportunity to hear me play a bunch of times and profess to people that I was one of his favorites. It became a great meeting place for everybody. Janis Joplin asked my brother Randy to join her band. Jimi Hendrix asked Randy Jo Hobbs to join his band for 'Band of Gypsies.' But we were all very loyal to The McCoys.

"I know Jimi Hendrix recorded the whole scene between him and Jim Morrison that people have talked about in several books. Jimi was playing and he was recording himself that night in a jamming situation. He had one of his hats on that he used to wear, that little cowboy hat kind of thing. Jim Morrison came in and decided he was going to come up and start singing with Jimi. And Jimi had a pretty good attitude about it. For awhile. Everybody knows that Jim Morrison was a heavy drinker and he was pretty wasted that night. Could hardly stand, let alone sing. But Jimi was letting him do it. Then at one point Jim Morrison just decided he was gonna go over and kinda knock Jimi's hat off [laughs]. So he walked over and knocked Jimi's hat off his head. And now Jimi had that Afro with the shape of a hat on his head! Most people wouldn't have appreciated it and Jimi didn't either. And the bouncers didn't dig it. So they came up to try and get Jim Morrison off the stage. He was still holding on to the microphone stand and trying to stay there singing. They carried him off physically. They had a guy on each arm and a guy on each leg. And he was lying down while being carried out, still holding the mike and singing [laughs]! Till the cable ran out! And I know Jimi recorded that whole scene."

Steve Paul started to want to scope his work and become involved in the newly developing world of music management.

Rick Derringer: "He wasn't managing anyone but Tiny Tim. He wasn't kind of like a real manager. Basically he had The Scene and Tiny Tim played there every night. Later on Tiny Tim was kind of stolen under Steve. That's why Steve decided he wanted to become a manager. He felt, 'I found Tiny Tim and now someone's stolen him.' He had heard about Johnny Winter in Rolling Stone. That's when he decided to go find Johnny Winter."

Liz Derringer: "Steve came up with something very special. Nobody had seen it before.It's not that hard to promote it when it's that special; what he had. And he knew it. His biggest talent was realizing it and going and get Johnny and convincing him to come up here."

Rick Derringer: "Brought him to New York City, did something good with him. Then The McCoys sought Steve out through that success. We said, 'We need somebody like you.' Steve was starting to work with Edgar and The McCoys joined in at about the same time."

Edgar Winter: "I was born December 28, 1946, in Beaumont, Texas, and Johnny as well. As far as I know. He likes to claim that he was born in Leland, Mississippi, because that's where he was conceived and where he would have been born. Our parents were very liberal and very supportive. Very loving, very musical. My mom played clavicle piano. My dad sang in the choir. He played guitar, banjo. He played alto sax in a swing band in his youth and that's basically my first memories of music. Sitting in my mother's lap and just being big enough to peer up over the keyboard and associate what her hands were doing with the music that I was hearing. Our dad showed us our first chords on ukulele, both Johnny's and mine first instrument. I was about eight, Johnny three years older. We played ukuleles and sang Everly Brothers songs as kids. Johnny graduated to guitar. I became interested more in piano. Then became interested in saxophone and in jazz in particular. I thought nothing of picking up two or three instruments at a time. It seemed a completely natural thing to me.

"There was a DJ on the black station, KJET, pretty well-known, Clarence Garlow. He had that song 'Bon Ton Roulet.' He used to play three or four records and then pick up his guitar and play live on the air. The station was right down the block from my grandmother's house. Johnny was very aggressive back then. The first time, he went upon his own and played a few of Clarence's songs for him. And the next time he brought me with him. We'd go by once every other week. We used to play live on the radio. It was really a fun thing, live radio! I think there should be more of it."

Like Rick, Edgar's vocation seemed to have been clearly presented to him at a young age.

Edgar Winter: "It was just a natural, everyday part of life. There was no dawning moment that I realized that I was gonna be a professional musician and pursue it as a career. We started playing professionally when I was eleven at club socials and after football games and sock hops and so forth. It was in high school that I decided that rather than go on to college to pursue a career in that fashion, I chose music. Most of the guys that I was playing with were Johnny's age. The first band I organized, White Trash, was basically a revival of the high school big band that I played with. Johnny, on the other hand, was really interested in the primitive Delta-style blues. He listened to all the guys like Lighting Hopkins, Howlin' Wolf and Muddy Waters. I gravitated more towards jazz oriented/R&B people like B.B. King and Bobby 'Blue' Bland and Ray Charles. Ray was probably my foremost influence. But I loved playing with Johnny. He was really my primary influence and one of my musical heroes. And remains so."

It was difficult for musicians to have record company executives come around their turf for a listen. But an article in *Rolling Stone* magazine drew a lot of attention to Johnny.

Edgar Winter: "We had been playing the southern club circuit. I was living in Houston, Texas. Johnny went to Austin. That's when he decided to put together a blues trio. And I think most of that arose from the article that was in Rolling Stone. That was the point where he was discovered and became known. Several different management people approached him. He made the trip to New York and signed with Steve Paul. Johnny then invited me out to New York to play on his new record. Johnny was always very gregarious, outgoing, aggressive. He always wanted to be famous. He used to read all the magazines. I, on the other hand, was very shy. Introverted. A serious musician. I thought that I would probably be a starving jazz musician. I was content to remain in the background. Johnny was always the front man, the bandleader. He did the majority of the singing. I was maybe singing two or three songs a night. I would rehearse the band. And because of that there really was no sibling rivalry."

During the summer of 1969, Edgar joined brother Johnny onstage at Woodstock. But the performance was excluded from the Woodstock movie and album.

Edgar Winter: "Steve Paul thought that Woodstock was going to be looked back on in an unfavorable light and he advised Johnny not to sign any releases or any promotion, any publicity, any records, any movie rights, anything. And Johnny, of course, since Steve was the business manager, accepted the advice and didn't. There's probably footage somewhere unless they just got rid of it because they knew that they would never have any rights to use it. I would love to see that stuff. And I'll bet somebody could find it. I've never gone to the trouble to try to track it down. It was an interesting experience and certainly one I'll never forget. Because the whole thing was so disorganized, I didn't really have this sense of any great historical event until I got up there on stage. And When I looked out there, it was just a literal sea of humanity as far as the eye could see. And I said, 'Wow. This is really something.' "

Rick Derringer: "Johnny and Edgar had both been brought down to hear The McCoys play at a club called The Club Tarot in lower Manhattan. That's probably the first time we met them. And then they asked if we wanted to move into a place called The Quadrangle, which was where Johnny had a house across the swimming pool from another house. The McCoys took over one house and Johnny had the other. And that's where we started playing together.

"Johnny was known as a blues musician. Steve Paul probably said, 'You know, that really has a built-in kind of limited audience. And this music business is just exploding. You being the very commercial, promotable character you are, Johnny, if your music was a little more rock 'n' roll-oriented you'd go a lot farther.' And that specifically meant record sales. So they were looking for some way for him to venture into that, to be more commercial. But at the same time to still retain his respectability and the quality of music he had presented. We were looking for exactly the opposite [laughs]. We wanted to be more respectable and hipper than the bubblegum image that we had but at the same time we wanted some way to retain all the musical quality that we thought we had. It was a marriage made in heaven. Johnny became that perfect vehicle for us and we became that perfect vehicle for him. He gets to venture more into commercial music, rock music, and we get to venture more into respectability and 'hipness' just by becoming a band."

Author: "Why was Bobby Peterson left out of the amalgamation?"

Rick Derringer: "Bobby Peterson, who had come from Roy Orbison and the Candymen, was a little bit nutty and he just basically had a nervous breakdown in the middle of rehearsals for the record. So the band was Johnny Winter and Randy Z., my brother, Randy Jo Hobbs, the bass player, and myself. Bobby Peterson was dropped as he went into a hospital."

Author: "Did he display erratic behavior during The McCoys?"

Rick Derringer: "Nothing in particular. We just heard a lot of those stories about his past. He didn't do any nutty things during the time he played with us. Our music was so crazy at that time it was kind of an outlet for his nuttiness and his particular brand of 'wild thinking.' So he was happy. And maybe the thought of going into this band with Johnny Winter, where all of a sudden we were going to be more contrived in some ways and controlled in our approach to music … 'I don't know if I'll be able to take this.'

"I've heard stories that when he was a little kid, he would be driving down the road with his parents and he would open the door and jump out of the moving car. Another story I heard about, there was a stack of air conditioners in a department store display. And he, as a little kid, decided to pull this stack of air conditioners down upon himself. So he was always a little crazy anyway. He was so intelligent, he was crazy. Sometimes they're both the same. Bobby was that kind of guy. He had a super intelligence. Mensa society. But it also made him very eccentric and nuts. He went into the Armed Forces at some point, got drafted or something like that. They couldn't deal with him either. He got kicked out. So in general he was just that kind of a guy. And I think, for some reason, it all came to a head about that time we were starting the Johnny Winter band. I don't know if he ever came out of it either. He was kind of a street person down here in Florida, where he last lived. He'd go around town and show up at all the restaurants and bars and play music for his upkeep. Not hired, necessarily, but kind of like a freeloader. But he always had a good heart. And because he was a sweet, loveable kind of guy, everybody forgave him for how nutty he was."

Hooking up with Johnny Winter gave The McCoys the credibility they needed to shake the bubblegum image they had been saddled with.

Liz Derringer: "People considered them a kid's band, like a one-hit wonder. But people started finding out that Rick was a pretty serious musician and they started respecting him for that. He wanted to make records."

The advantage of having Rick in Johnny's corner was quickly evident as Rick could act as the intermediary between Winter and the people that worked in the studio.

Rick Derringer: "I think Johnny just said, 'These New Yorkers are trying to take advantage of me.' When he went into the studio, he said, 'They're not really listening to me. They're not paying attention to me. They're trying to tell me what to do.' Things like that, I think, were going through his head. So he looked at me like, 'Well, here's a guy who's working on my side.' I think he just figured I was a guy who would listen. I think just being a guitar player/musician in his band helped. Being from the Midwest didn't hurt, that's for sure. He looked at producers and engineers as kind of executives from the record business. He looked at me as a rock 'n' roll guitar player. He saw me as a lot more on his wavelength. That I would listen to what he said and convey those ideas to the producers or engineers.

"I was inspired by Johnny. He had an idea of what direction we needed to go in. He knew that it didn't have to be a narrow kind of version of rock 'n' roll. It really could be something that we created. We were creating something new in some ways. It wasn't a kind of rock 'n' roll that necessarily existed before we did it."

Upon entering the studio Rick found himself performing more than music as he co-produced the album.

Rick Derringer: "What had happened was we had gotten to watch the whole recording business grow from 4-track recording, which is what we did in The McCoys, originally, all the way through eight and even into twelve. The two records we did for Mercury we produced ourselves. So when we started working for Johnny, his problem was he didn't feel like anybody in the music business could speak his language.

Rick Derringer and Johnny Winter.
Savoy Theater, New York City, 1982
Courtesy David McGough

He spoke Texan [laughs]! And he felt like his points weren't getting across. So when he decided that he could talk to me on his level, and when he found out that I helped produce the McCoys records for Mercury, he asked me if I'd help him as co-producer. He gave me the opportunity to get out there to show that I could do things on that level.

"I specifically was there to bring more of a rock sound to Johnny. And Johnny would only allow it to go so far. I was at least good enough to know what that meant. I could play enough blues to make it viable and honest. But at the same time I was there to bring enough of a rock 'n' roll element to it to make it more commercial. The first song I wrote for Johnny was 'Rock 'n' Roll Hoochie Koo.' That, lyrically, was just a title satisfying those ends. 'Rock 'n' roll' to satisfy the rock 'n' roll that I was supposed to be bringing into the picture, and 'Hoochie Koo' to satisfy the kind of blues sensibility that Johnny was supposed to maintain. Then I had to figure out what the song would be because the title was to answer that need. And it worked out great."

At this point in time Rick adopted the name "Derringer."

Rick Derringer: "After I started working with Johnny Winter, I was going out on the road with him a little bit. And people would recognize me. But because the name was hard to pronounce, they wouldn't say, 'Hey, Mr. Zehringer,' because they didn't know who that guy was or how to say the name. So they didn't say anything! And it's always been my thought that if I was put in a situation where it meant something I would have a more professional name because of those reasons. And that's when I had the vision of a Z dropping away and a D moving over, and Zehringer became Derringer that quickly. I think it had to do with that little derringer on the Bang Records logo having some influence. I just put two and two together and thought it would be a cool name to have. I didn't do it legally or anything. But on the first recording with Johnny, I used the name Derringer. And immediately people did start coming up and saying, 'Hey, Derringer!' And it proved to me that it was effective."

Right out of the box the performances garnered rave reviews by critics and fans alike. The cohesion between the musicians stood a cut above the rest.

Liz Derringer: "I remember it was really unbelievable, charismatic. They used to get in such a frenzy and so crazy that Rick used to run between Johnny's legs and Johnny would jump over him. And they'd do a lot of battling dual guitar stuff. It was pretty incredible and it was growing."

Rick Derringer: "We were essentially out playing all the time. I didn't have very much free time."

As Johnny was gaining notoriety, brother Edgar was also building up a credible reputation as a musician to be reckoned with. This eventually gave Rick another avenue to pursue production interests. Edgar had the musicians to record his debut, "Entrance."

Edgar Winter: "That was the band I was playing with in Houston when Johnny migrated to New York, The Goldenaires! 'Entrance' was probably the most innocent album that I've recorded. I wanted to put together an R&B band. That whole area in Texas is a hotbed of music. Authentic country. Authentic blues. Close enough to the Mexican border for that hot, Latin rhythm thing. Jon Smith, the tenor saxophone player, is from Louisiana. He and I have known each other since we were kids in high school. Jon and I played in rival bands. Jon's grandmother at one point was having a heart-to-heart talk with Jon and said, 'Jon, what are you doing with your life? Are you still playing with that white trash?' She's actually credited with coming up with the name. I broke up! 'Yeah! White Trash! That's what we are and that's what we should be!'

"I played with a lot of black musicians in Texas and there were a lot of clubs which discouraged interracial bands. A lot of times I'd want to sit in with the group and the club owner would say, 'Well, we don't think that's a good idea.' And they would refer to those bands in disparaging terms. 'You playing with them? You're no better than white trash!' So we loved the name. It was like our badge of honor."

Edgar didn't have to look far to find the right person to help interpret his music as a producer. He gladly handed the reigns over to Rick.

Rick Derringer: "They would tell me, 'We wanna go for a kind of New Orleans sound, or a Stax/Volt kind of approach here.' And they would let me try and interpret that. He pretty much let me do exactly what I wanted to do. He didn't hamper me at all or try to say this is right or wrong."

Edgar Winter: "At that time it was advised that artists should not produce themselves. I felt entirely capable and ready to produce my own stuff. My thinking was that if I'm going to have a producer, I want to have a musical producer. I really respected Rick and I knew that he understood the music and that he would do a great job, which he did. Rick had a very minimalist approach to production. He would, for the most part, just sit back and listen. Let the engineer get the sound. He listened to my ideas. I tried to stay out of it [laughs]. Try is the operative word! I am pretty opinionated about things. I have a pretty definite idea about a lot of things. But that was the reason that I had Rick doing it. Just out of love and respect. He was the best guy to do it."

•   •   •

As "Johnny Winter And …" started a tour in 1971, Randy Zehringer got ill.

Janice Zehringer: "Randy had encephalitis. After he got out of the hospital, he came home from Connecticut and stayed for maybe six months. Then he went back to New York. He was going to try to work. And he called me one day and said, 'Can I come home?' I said, 'Of course, you can come home.' And we realized that he wasn't going to be able to play. It was too much for his nervous system. The noise from the drums was one thing. And then the huge amplifiers and everything. He takes medication to this day. Not anything powerful or anything like that, just pills that keep him a little less nervous. He was hospitalized with a nervous breakdown probably five or six times after that."

Bobby Caldwell: "I think there was also a little more to it than encephalitis. Like too much of everything in life. Disconnected him a little bit from reality."

Randy was finding that his body was beginning to deteriorate due to the excesses he had put himself through the previous few years. Physically, he was starting to fall apart. Whether these excesses were relevant to his contracting encephalitis is a matter of opinion.

Liz Derringer: "Very relevant. He just broke down. He was going too crazy."

Randy Zehringer: "We were supposed to play as The McCoys somewhere in Connecticut. We were sitting in the dressing room and all of a sudden I didn't feel welland told them that they couldn't go on with me that night. So I was in the hospital there in Connecticut for three or four days or a week maybe. Then I went to Dayton. I was in the hospital there for a couple of weeks."

Liz Derringer: "He didn't remember a lot back then. He was too screwed up. But we were too young to know it was a serious problem. We did see it coming. There was a lot of signs. I remember we were in L.A. and Rick and I drove back to New York. Randy didn't come with us. He said he was going to get on a plane the next day. We didn't hear from him for a long time. And we were all pretty worried about him. I heard he was hanging out with Danny Hutton, Jim Morrison, all those people and going wild. And he came home and we asked him where he was and he said Arizona. He said the TV told him to go there. He was so out of it. Couldn't make any sense out of something like that."

When Randy was originally admitted into the hospital the nature of his problem escaped medical detection.

Liz Derringer: "They didn't know. He was in some sort of catatonic state. They kept a curtain around his bed. They opened it during the day and he would get up and close it. He was not eating or anything. They were feeding him intravenously. Very bizarre, you have no idea."

Janice Zehringer: "He's lived with us ever since. He does everything he wants to do. Goes everywhere he wants to go. Drives a car and everything. He volunteers at the Mental Health Center not too far from where we live. He's there about three or four days a week and he gets along fine. But it's too bad. He still loves music. He still enjoys going to see Rick. But as far as being a part of it, no, he can't. But he's fortunate because he could be dead. We're just glad he's here."

Liz Derringer: "She (Janice) blamed a lot of it on me. She just didn't know what was going on in New York City. It wasn't just me. It was everything. I certainly didn't do as many drugs as Randy did. And I didn't hang out and go crazy with the people he did. He did it on his own. In those days it was 'sex, drugs and rock 'n' roll' of the 60s. And Randy was a victim of the 60s. We were all doing the same crazy stuff. Eventually he (Rick) got pretty screwed up. But Rick's screw up was drugs and drinking. I didn't do drugs and drink, no matter what was going on. It was a very confusing time for everybody. Everybody was doing everything. I regret a lot of that now but what could I do? That's what was accepted then. And I think it hurt a lot of people."

The next order of business was finding a replacement for Randy.

Rick Derringer: "The Allman Brothers turned us on to this drummer who they had heard about and they said he was just great. He was in the Florida area. His name was Bobby Caldwell. And that's how we found him. He turned

out to be a super, super drummer. He played with us into the 'Johnny Winter And … Live' album."

Bobby Caldwell: "I grew up in Winter Park, Florida. Started playing drums and an interest in music at about the age of six. I had known the Allman Brothers for a long time because they're from Daytona. Duane was always telling everybody, 'You gotta get Bobby.' Finally, they were playing with Johnny and he told Johnny about me. Most of the places they asked about me in the South said most of the same things as Duane did. Fortunately for me they called and I went down there and that's how it happened. I joined Johnny Winter And … probably when they were the biggest drawing group in the world, when I was about eighteen.

"I was prepared for it. I'd been on the road to New York several times with different groups I'd recorded with. There's a little bit of a change. Not so much lifestyle but people not knowing people. All of a sudden you're with a different group of souls, learning their ways and them learning your ways. Trying to work as a unit. But it wasn't that big a thing. My only responsibility was to play the best I could and make the band the best I could make it. That was really all I was interested in doing. And if I picked up a few chicks along the way it wouldn't hurt either."

Columbia quickly released "Johnny Winter And … Live."

Rick Derringer: "We had recorded some shows that we thought would be great audience shows because that's part of a live album. The interaction between the band and the audience. So we picked some shows that we thought were great shows where the audience reacted well and where we had a fun time playing for that audience. So dates at the Fillmore was obviously one of those shows. It wasn't like we had recorded a trillion shows and used the best ones. We used bits from the several shows that we recorded."

Edgar Winter: "It really displayed that combination of Johnny and Rick at their best doing a thing together."

During this time rumors were rampant about the drug problems Johnny had developed and was struggling with.

Rick Derringer: "We thought Johnny pretty much had it under control. Obviously, he was dabbling with heroin. But that's all we thought it was. Just dabbling. We didn't see it excessively, hardly at all. It wasn't until he announced to us that he had a problem and he was going to stop the band and check himself into a hospital that we knew that the problem was to that extent."

Bobby Caldwell: "There's no way you can run an organization when everybody's partying. You don't know that at the time it's happening. We always played well. But Johnny got to the point where he had to take time off. If we had been drinking fruit juice everyday and jogging three or four miles, we probably would have been better off. But …

"I think it caught everybody off guard. I don't think that any of us knew to what degree the problem was. Everybody was partying. And whatever they were doing, everybody was doing it. I don't think anyone knew that Johnny was contemplating taking some time off, saying to Steve Paul, 'I need to take a break from this,' you know what I mean? The shop was just closed up."

Rick Derringer: "I still don't think the problem was as drastic as he let on. I believe that what happened, because he had told us a little bit about it, was that we were in England, touring. And he got a chance to see how they dealt with their drug addicts in England. They put them on a maintenance program. They allowed them to come and pick up their drugs, at cheap prices, from a pharmacy. Johnny returned from that trip to England and he said, many times, 'Man, that looks great. You never have to worry about dealing on the street with people. You can just go and the government's gonna give you the drugs for the rest of your life.' He said 'Boy, that's what I would like.' So, in effect, I don't think he had as much of a problem as he let on at that time. I think it specifically was just something that he envisioned as a great lifestyle, strangely enough. And he used that opportunity to check himself into a hospital to put himself in some kind of situation where he could get stuff from legitimate sources rather than having to deal from the street. And that is basically what he still does today.

"It's sad to say. It's not legal. In the U.S., it's supposed to be a weaning-off process, when you do methadone. But I think he's been able to find doctors that are unscrupulous enough. And when they get nervous about being found out, Johnny is able to find new doctors that will start him all over again. He goes into the hospital and gets slightly detoxed so that he can come out and act like he's starting over and go to a new doctor. And he's been able to maintain that lifestyle of getting methadone from the state for twenty-five years."

Author: "But Johnny wasn't the only bad soldier in the lot?"

Bobby Caldwell: "Oh, no! We were all doing the same thing. Whatever was out there, we were taking part in it. And that's without any judgment. I've been a major health freak for twenty-five years and I don't regret any of the stuff I went through. It was just an experience. It was just something we all did."

Rick Derringer: "I dabbled. Like anybody that came from the 'Summer of Peace and Love,' I got the opportunity to try a little of everything over the years. But most of the things have taught me why I don't want to do them. That's why I don't have any trouble with drugs or alcohol anymore because I certainly learned why. I've seen enough people die. I've seen enough people destroy their own lives. I've seen enough people who can't even tie their own shoes, let alone continue with a career. So I know all the reasons why you don't do those things. Sensibly and intellectually."

Edgar Winter: "I knew in general what Johnny was going through. I had a lot of conversations with him. He was very aloof at that time. The thing that was strangest to me was he had such a drive to become famous. And having achieved that, it just didn't seem to be something that made him happy. He didn't know who to trust. He didn't know who his friends were. He really felt isolated. I was always there to help and support him. He knew that if he ever needed me, I would always be there. And I continue to tell him that every time I talk to him. I love Johnny. Without him, I wouldn't be where I am. He really encouraged and supported me."

"I couldn't believe that it happened. And it's still so bizarre to me because Johnny had such a strength of character. He has that artistic sensitivity and everybody deals with success and fame in a different way. I personally don't subscribe to that tortured artist, the people that think that you have to go through all of this pain and hardship in order to be an artist. I just think that that's a very self-indulgent, self-defeating attitude."

When Johnny walked into a rehab center, the band was done.

Edgar Winter: "I thought that was a great band and I think that had it continued it could have been one of the absolute top rock 'n' roll bands in the world. I mean, the synergy with Johnny and Rick ... they had great songwriting potential, great energy. I really liked it when Rick's brother, Randy, was playing drums. And it was great after, with Bobby Caldwell. He was more of a power kind of drummer. But Randy had more of an earthy, funky kind of feel that I happen to like. It's one of my favorite albums, that first album. Really great songs. Funky music. I love that album."

Author: "When things started to wane on Johnny's part, were you consciously beginning to work on a solo album or just recording songs to see what you could come up with?"

Rick Derringer: "It was both. I really had been writing more and more after the success of 'Rock 'n' Roll Hoochie Koo.' And after having the opportunity to write songs with Johnny for 'Johnny Winter And ...' records, I just really started writing. I've always been the kind of guy that's hard to pin down exactly what style I'm in so I was writing different kinds of music. And it became obvious that that was all going to be useful for a possible solo album. Then Edgar called me up and asked if I was interested in playing with White Trash."

Edgar Winter: "Floyd Radford wanted to work on his own music. Rick really loved that band and Floyd knew that he was ready to step in so he wasn't going to be leaving me in a lurch. And it was a good thing for all concerned.

"Rick was about my favorite guitar player other than Johnny. And he was familiar with the band. He had produced it, he played a lot of the solos and things. Real signature things like 'Keep Playing That Rock and Roll.' That was Rick Derringer's solo. 'Good Morning Music.' There was no other guitar player that I knew of that could have been better. At a time when we were going through all our drug phase and craziness, Rick was like the voice of sanity. He was just very positive and very together."

Rick Derringer: "So I went straight from Johnny out on the road with White Trash. Well, I woke up one day and I realized I'd been on the road for seven years! And that's without any major breaks. We'd go home for a week here and there but most of the time we were out there touring. It really did get to be a heavy schedule. And I called up my road manager, in the middle of the White Trash experience, and said, 'THAT'S IT! I would like to get off the road. I love playing with this band but I can't take this anymore!' They convinced me to stay with the band until we finished the 'Roadwork' album. Which is what I did."

Edgar Winter: "I knew Rick wanted to do his solo stuff. But I've never been able to see why bands don't stay together and have the individuals do their solo projects. But I respected everybody's desires to do that. I felt that the best thing was to move on."

Rick Derringer: "So I took about a year off. And during that year off, I planned and finished the writing for the solo album which became 'All American Boy.' "

Author: "Were you exhausted physically or mentally?"

Rick Derringer: "I was young enough and strong enough. It certainly wasn't the kind of thing where 'This guy's ready to drop over!' I'm a healthy kind of guy and I always have been. It was just a mental thing. I'd been under the 'travel, travel, travel, travel, travel' so much, seven years straight, I just said, 'I gotta stop this. I would love the opportunity to be home for a while.' And that's what I did. I certainly didn't need a break from anything work-wise. I kept right on working and writing that album. As a matter of fact, when I started recording the 'All American Boy' album, I was working almost simultaneously on 'They Only Come Out At Night' with Edgar Winter, producing that record too. So the work schedule didn't stop too much."

Author: "Who was the road manager you called while with White Trash to say you needed a break?"

Rick Derringer: "Teddy Slatus [laughs]! Teddy Slatus was originally the bus boy at The Scene. He would bus glasses back to the kitchen. But he was conscious enough at it that Steve Paul eventually said, 'You know, I think you should be the manager of The Scene!' Steve was always the boss and Teddy was pretty much the maitre'd. Teddy would dress in a suit and do what Steve said. Seat people and stuff. When Steve Paul started managing people like Johnny and Edgar Winter and sending them out on the road, he needed to feel like he had the same confidence in somebody that he could send out to watch his bands. So he asked Teddy to be the road manager. Then when Johnny Winter decided that Steve ultimately was more controlling than he wanted, he said, 'Who better to be my manager than Teddy?' I think the only requirement that Johnny said was that he wouldn't manage anybody else. That he would be 'his' manager. 'I'll have my own manager and it'll be Teddy.' And that's how Teddy became a manager."

Rick had mostly been in control of production duties the previous several years but, for some diversity, decided to bring in an impartial ear to help put his solo album together.

Rick Derringer: "This is funny! It originally started out with a concept. Like I said, my music goes a lot of different directions. So the concept was that we were gonna be produced by many producers. To travel around to all the famous producers who were my favorites at that time and play for them the songs that I had written. Let them pick out the ones that they thought would be hippest for their style, that they would be most interested in doing. And through this idea I had gone to Paul Samwell-Smith, who was with Cat Stevens at that time. He picked out a song. I let Felix

Pappalardi pick out a song that he wanted to do. I had gone to Jimmy Guercio, who was producing Chicago, and asked him if he wanted to do a song and he picked out one. Coincidentally, Bill Scymcyzk was working on a Joe Walsh album at Jimmy Guercio's studio at that time. So I was easily able to go over to Bill and ask him if he wanted to do one. They'd all picked out songs. So then we started trying to schedule who would do what and when. And it just seemed like every time we had a schedule set up with one of them, and remember, these were all very successful producers at that time, their act would conflict and we would have to cancel the date. Or, I was a pretty busy kinda guy, my schedule would conflict. We kept postponing and we didn't get one song recorded with this concept thing.

"It was about that time that I happened to be back in the Caribou Ranch area, which is where Bill was recording. And Bill said, 'Look. I'm right here recording all the time. Forget about that concept; let's make this album. I'll start tomorrow, if you want to.' And that's really just what we did."

"Rock 'n' Roll Hoochie Koo" became the first release from "All American Boy." Having success with a song twice was not only rare but also quite gratifying.

Rick Derringer: "Completely gratifying. I have a suspicion that it was much bigger than we ever knew. That was a time in the record business when record companies were heavy into bootlegging. The president of CBS, I forget who it was at that time, told me, 'You know, 'All American Boy' is the most popular album at the college my daughter attends. Every kid in school has one.' And it almost seemed, as we went on, that it was popular everywhere. And the single, 'Rock 'n' Roll Hoochie Koo,' to this day, still seems to be popular. (Author's note: The song recently received an award for having been played one million times on the radio.) But it was never reflected in sales or on the charts. I've always had the assumption, and lived under the assumption, that it was one of those records. We've never been able to pin it down or prove it. Sam Goody got into tons of trouble around that time period for bootlegging. There were also operations going on within record companies that were proven later on. I always assumed it was even bigger than we knew. I think it was reported that it sold half a million albums. I think it probably sold several million albums, conservatively."

As a sixteen-year-old musician and fan, others and myself were obsessed with trying to figure out exactly what was said through an effect during the guitar solo on "Teenage Love Affair."

Rick Derringer: "'I wanna eat you right now [laughs]! Don't you fuck with me, buddy!' It's actually what it says! I'm not necessarily proud of it as I get older. But nonetheless, that's an impetuous youth speaking boldly through a hard-to-understand voice box!

"I then decided I'd like to go out and play some music and capitalize on the success of 'Rock 'n' Roll Hoochie Koo' and that album. But I didn't have a band of my own."

Author: "Tell me the process you went through to form 'The Edgar Winter Group.'"

Edgar Winter: "Dan Hartman was the first. That was through a demo tape that he sent Steve Paul. Which when I heard it, I thought, 'This guy's great. A real talent.' And there were hundreds of tapes from Dan! I flew all over the country looking for people. Ronnie Montrose I knew from when he played with Van Morrison and Boz Scaggs. And he had previously played in a band with Chuck Ruff. And he recommended Chuck."

Chuck Ruff: "I was born May 25, 1951, in Reno, Nevada. My father was a Dixieland drummer and a disk jockey and M.C. He had his own advertising agency, 'Bill Ruff Productions.' One day I was looking for a wrench in the garage and there were these drums. I talked him into giving me those drums 'cuz he wasn't playing anymore. My dad was working at a radio station in Pittsburg, California, KKIS. He would bring home promo albums of stuff that his program director wouldn't let him play. And one of the albums happened to be 'The Johnny Winter Progressive Blues Experiment.' I went nuts! And I knew that something was going to come from me knowing about this guy."

"Went to San Francisco in 1967, became a hippie and started working for Bill Graham at The Fillmore as a janitor. While working at the Fillmore I became good friends with David Rubinson, a producer with CBS. David's secretary, Annie Rudder, had access to his Rolodex. With a couple of other people we were looking to put a band together and needed a guitar player. And listed under 'Carpenters and Electricians' was Ronnie Montrose. He'd only been playing guitar for about eight months but he was really hot. He had hair down to his butt, living in the Haight-Ashbury area, and he was one of the strangest guys! He was a borderline genius kind of guy. He knew a lot about carpentry and electronics. The band became Sawbuck and we recorded one LP for Fillmore Records, a CBS subsidiary through David Rubinson and Fred Katero. Ronnie got into some bad feelings with Mojo Collins, the leader of the band, and split with our bass player, Bill Church. They went off and joined up with Van Morrison.

"When the band broke up, I was literally starving to death so I returned to Reno to be close to my family. I got a gig with a band in these really sleazy places for about $30 a night around Reno. While we were playing a bar called The Burly Bull, I got a phone call. It was Ronnie Montrose. And he said, 'Edgar's putting together a rock band and he wants me to play guitar and he wants to try you out on drums.' So they flew me out to New York and I auditioned."

Edgar Winter: "And for a while Dan Hartman was playing guitar. Dan and Ronnie on guitar and Randy Jo Hobbs was playing bass."

Rick Derringer: "Dan Hartman (b. Dec. 8, 1950) was one of the more talented people, musically, that I have ever worked with. He really is right up there with the best of them. He came from a really positive, healthy family in Harrisburg, Pennsylvania. They taught him the power of positive thinking. Great writer. Great producer. He used to send a demo and a letter every week and timed it so that it would arrive at Steve Paul's desk on Monday morning. Every week [laughs]! I mean, he thought about it that consciously. It had a little heart logo on it. He was just a kid. He was working at a bank

Dan Hartman, Backstage, Mobile, Alabama, 1974.
Courtesy Chuck Ruff

in Harrisburg and playing high school gigs and stuff. Steve finally listened to one of them one day and liked what he heard. He brought it over and said, 'What do you think?' And the demo that he played for me included 'Free Ride' almost note for note like the way we recorded it. The song 'Autumn' was on there. A lot of the stuff that ended up on 'They Only Come Out At Night' existed on that demo, almost note for note like we ended up recording them. He was an amazingly talented guy."

Edgar Winter: "It was a five-piece group. And before we did the first album, Johnny Badanjek from Mitch Ryder and the Detroit Wheels was playing drums. He played on 'Free Ride.' The first two songs we did before we actually went in to do the album were 'Free Ride' and 'We All Had A Real Good Time.' Then we decided to switch Dan to bass."

Chuck Ruff: "So they flew me out to New York and I auditioned. I never really got a firm contractual offer but I was there and learned Dan and Edgar's tunes and learned the show."

Edgar Winter: "I really liked Chuck. He had real good energy and he seemed to be the right drummer. And that's when we finalized the group. I felt that a four-piece was more focused. And I thought, stylistically, Randy Hobbs was a different kind of player. I was looking for people with more of a universal feel as opposed to people who had a niche or a particular kind of groove. And Randy is a great groove player. But I thought it would be a more focused group with guitar, bass, keyboards and drums. That's just what I thought it should be."

Author: "Was Rick your immediate choice to produce 'They Only Come Out At Night?'"

Edgar Winter: "Oh, yeah. I wasn't looking for any other producer. I didn't see any reason to change. We had a great relationship and I knew he understood everything I was doing.

"'They Only Come Out At Night' was definitely calculated to be a successful album. It was the one that I said, 'OK, you guys. I'm gonna give you the album that you've been asking for. This should be the one.' And I just did all of the obvious stuff on it and it worked. I love the album. I think it's got a lot of great songs on it. We put everything that we had into it as a group to try to make it something that would have that kind of appeal. And it ended up being very successful. For which I'm very happy."

After several attempts the group got to enjoy the benefits of Top 40 success when "Frankenstein" became a certified hit.

Edgar Winter: "It was one of Rick's favorites. We didn't even record it with the intention of putting it on the album. It was just a song that I had written years before. I played it with Johnny in the blues trio. I played it at Woodstock if I'm not mistaken. We used to call it the 'Double-Drum Song.' Johnny would do the first part of the set. And then he'd say, 'And now I'm gonna bring out my little brother, Edgar.' I'd come on and do a couple of Ray Charles songs. And I was looking for an instrumental. I wrote the song with Johnny in mind. I was looking for something that would fit in the blues context. Something simple and bluesy. A power-guitar riff (hums the tune). I played Hammond B3 and alto sax and did a dual drum solo with his drummer, Red Turner. So we played that instrumental. Years later I was walking around a music store looking at all the new keyboards. I saw the Arc 2600 which had a remote keyboard that was really light. 'Now if I could just pick this thing up and put a strap on it and play it like a guitar.' I was really tired of sitting down and being stuck behind a bank of keyboards. And why do guitar players get to have all the fun? I was looking for an instrumental to showcase the synthesizer so I revived the old 'Double-Drum Song.' It was just a song that we used to play when we'd come into the studio. We'd plug in and spend hours getting sounds and stuff. And it was a song we enjoyed jamming on and playing. So we had two or three versions of it. And they were all fifteen minutes or so long.

"So after we got through with everything, we were saying, 'Well, we need another song but that song's like fifteen minutes long.' And Rick's saying, 'Yeah, but it's so cool. It's got really cool parts.' Now back in those days the only way to edit anything was to literally cut the tape. So we started hacking away at it until we had about forty pieces of tape lying all over the control room, draped over the backs of chairs. 'Now, here's the main body. And this has the bubbly section. The acid bath.' We were just joking about it. [Sings] 'The leg bone's connected to the ankle bone.' Trying to figure out how to put the thing back together. And Chuck Ruff said, 'Wow, man, it's like Frankenstein!' Drawing from the analogy of an arm here and a leg there. Assembling a thing out of parts. And as soon as I heard it, 'Hey! Frankenstein! That's it!' It has that lumbering kind of [hums tune] monster vibe! So, the monster was born! And we got it down to four or five minutes. I just said that we'd put it on as the last song. 'Cuz I thought 'Free Ride' would be the hit. Maybe 'Hangin' Around.' 'Undercover Man' was a good live track.

"So we released 'Free Ride' first and it didn't do anything. And we released another couple of songs. The album had been out for six months and Steve said, 'It's pretty much run its course. You oughta start thinking towards the next album.' And then the underground FM college stations started playing 'Frankenstein.' And the AM stations picked up on it but they wanted a shorter version. A two-and-a-half or three-minute version. So we had to try and re-edit it even further! I got it down to a certain point and finally I threw my hands up in dismay and said, 'I'm not gonna cut it anymore. This is as short as it can get and retain the musical integrity of the song.' So we sent it to all the radio stations. And the DJ's started cutting it. There are hundreds of different versions. The edits were very bizarre. They would cut in the middle of synthesizer glitches. They made no sense, musically, to me. But it ended up being a huge hit and I think that part of the appeal was the fact that the edits were so bizarre they were ear catching because they didn't make sense. They were unexpected. And that was the story of 'Frankenstein' and how it came about. And if it goes to prove anything it's simply that a lot of times when you try to envision and try to calculate and second guess an audience and determine what you think is gonna be successful and what's gonna be commercial, sometimes it's just the stuff that you don't put any attention on and that you just enjoy doing that ends up being the stuff that works the best."

Rick Derringer: "Edgar had done some dates for 'They Only Come Out At Night,' but for some reason there was a little dissension in the ranks. There were some problems between Edgar and Ronnie, personally. In fact, Ronnie had stopped playing with the band."

Edgar Winter: "I didn't know why Ronnie wanted to move on. After talking to him years later, he felt that he was unappreciated. It had nothing to do, as far as I was aware of, with me. I think that Steve Paul's vision of the band was that the strength in the band lay in the co-writing between Dan Hartman and myself and he was not encouraging Ronnie to participate in the overall direction of the band. I never felt that way but evidently Ronnie had gotten that idea. He never voiced it to me. I got along great with Ronnie and I always liked him. The thing I liked most about Ronnie was he had this sort of rebellious outlaw vibe that I liked. And that was the main thing in comparison to Rick, who is a very disciplined and organized player. Ronnie was the total opposite. Very unpredictable."

Chuck Ruff: "Ronnie left because he and Steve Paul did not get along at all. Ronnie wanted more of a cut. He had been working on a bunch of songs with Edgar and only one of them got on the record. So he was kind of pissed off about that. And he felt like he was being slighted and not being treated the way he wanted to be.

"We were on the road in Houston, Texas, opening for West, Bruce and Laing. Ronnie and I were roommates. And I happened to have overheard a conversation between Edgar and Steve Paul. Steve was running Ronnie down left and right. I didn't like it at all because Steve was saying all this shit behind his back. 'We're gonna fire that guy.' It was Steve Paul backstabbing and saying, 'This guy said this about you,' and 'That guy said this about you.' Just a real shit-disturber. One of those guys that shakes your hand with one hand and stabs you in the back with the other one. I immediately told Ronnie that they were gonna fire him. So before they could do that, he quit.

"They were gonna call a big meeting and lay down the law to Ronnie, that he was gonna get fired. So one day, as we're walking through an airport, he just quit. And as soon as he did that they all started looking at me. 'Hey, asshole, why did you tell him all that shit?' But they should have known better to talk about that kind of shit in front of me. He was my best friend. What was I supposed to do?

"I ended up getting the new guitar player into the band. A friend of mine from high school, Jerry Weems. He was a really good guitar player and a really good singer. He recently passed away from liver failure. Rick was producing us and kinda playing guitar with us once in a while. It was a weird situation. We did a taping of *The Midnight Special*. We played 'Frankenstein' with Jerry, whose hair was really short. And Rick came out and joined us on 'Rock 'n' Roll Hoochie Koo.' Anyway, we were in Winnipeg and Jerry and I took a few days off to go back to Reno. And while we were in the airport Jerry disappeared off the face of the earth. Nobody knew where he was. Turns out that for two weeks he had been held in solitary confinement in a military stronghold. The whole time he was on the road with us he was AWOL from the Army National Guard. So they cut all his hair off. Then he hooked up with us in L.A. and we did that program."

Rick Derringer: "I then decided I'd like to go out and play some music and capitalize on the success of 'Rock 'n' Roll Hoochie Koo' and that album. I was able to call up Edgar and say, 'Look, since I played on some of the stuff and produced it, doesn't it make sense that we do it together?' And rather than create a band of my own that I didn't have, I simply went out and worked with Edgar. I had worked with Dan Hartman and Chuck Ruff and Edgar making that record. And even helping him put together the band. So it really felt like my band as much as Edgar's band. We called it 'The Edgar Winter Group featuring Rick Derringer.' And I was able to go out on the road and support 'All American Boy' and 'Rock 'n' Roll Hoochie Koo' at the same time as helping Edgar with his music."

Edgar Winter: "I always enjoyed working with Rick in whatever band it was. I thought he was great in White Trash. I knew he would be great in the new band. A great strength of his is his versatility. I tried to balance that. We'd do an album. Dan would write three or four. I would write three or four. Rick would write three or four. And we tried to keep that balance going so that everybody would feel that they were being given the opportunity to contribute."

Author: "Was your joining the group contingent on being able to support your album as well as supporting theirs?"

Rick Derringer: "We didn't have to make any contingencies like that. 'Teenage Love Affair,' 'Rock 'n' Roll Hoochie Koo' and some of the songs from that album were successful enough that Edgar wanted to do that."

Edgar Winter: "I told him that I knew of his interest in his solo career and there was no reason why he couldn't continue to work on that and be in the band."

Rick Derringer: "We really did enjoy being out there and being successful. That's part of it. It's not only the music. When you're a young man and you're involved in the spillover from Beatlemania and just the phenomenal success of the music business at that time, it really is that much fun. It doesn't just look like it's that much fun. And then the other

1973

The Edgar Winter Group, 1974.
(top-bottom: Chuck Ruff, Dan Hartman, Edgar Winter, Rick Derringer)
This postcard was sent to fans who had written in requesting autographs.
Courtesy Chuck Ruff

part of success is, all of a sudden, you have lots of money to spend. We were buying outrageous clothes to perform in, spending money creating musical instruments. Basically living your dream! I couldn't wish a better thing for any young male than to be living that kind of experience."

Edgar Winter: "At that time we had a concept and we had the means to really produce a show. I loved the theatrical aspect of putting together a show. I'm not doing that today. Mainly because I can't afford that kind of production! But it is fun to do."

Author: "You returned to help Johnny on 'Still Alive and Well' and 'Saints and Sinners.' Was it a request or an offer?"

Rick Derringer: "He wanted me to continue working with him. We did 'Still Alive and Well' as he returned from the hospital. We thought that would be an apt title. And then 'Saints and Sinners.' I loved Johnny. Like I said, there was never a problem between me and Johnny in those days at all. And I looked forward to the opportunity of helping him make those records."

During the sessions for "Saints and Sinners," Rick and Dan Hartman wrote what would become the follow up to "They Only Come Out At Night." As soon as Johnny's album was finished, The Edgar Winter Group returned to the studio to record "Shock Treatment," again produced by Rick.

Rick Derringer: "As a producer I have a very basic philosophy. And that is you want to be able to close your eyes and you want to be able to see the band. A bass drum is physically bigger than a snare drum. So I would like to be able to close my eyes and see that. Acoustic guitar is not bigger than the drum set, so that wouldn't be right to hear that. In other words, I feel like size relationships should be maintained. And there's an easy way to do that as a producer. And that is not to get involved in too much outboard EQ and things like that. To use good mikes that you can use without EQ's. Carry that philosophy through. Then all the size relationships haven't been tampered by using EQ and are maintained. That includes the voice and everything else.

"All of us had come through different levels. The McCoys had come in through the whole bubble gum thing, into Johnny, into White Trash, into my work with Edgar in 'They Only Come Out At Night.' Dan had come from the same album but he wanted to evolve. Edgar started out as more of a jazz, avant-garde kind of musician with 'Entrance' and then got involved with those commercial endeavors. I think everybody was looking to create some kind of music. I wanted to be respectable. I know that Edgar wanted to satisfy his leanings towards jazz and classy kind of music. At the same time, we all still wanted to think about maybe we can still be commercial. We were trying to be all things to all men. It's a little hard to do."

Edgar Winter: "It was a continuation and we wanted to progress some. We certainly didn't set out to do just a part two or a sequel. We tried to keep the basic spirit of the group. That's all we were really concerned with.

"I think that the production was different. Shelley Yakus engineered that. It was the Record Plant instead of The Hit Factory, which had a completely different sound. And we took a lot longer to make that album. Much longer. I personally have always felt that songs should reflect individual production. I actually enjoy an album that has a variety of different production techniques as opposed to an album which sounds like it's pretty much all done at the same time. There are people who don't agree with that concept and say, 'Well, it just sounds scattered. It's not focused. It's not cohesive. It should all sound like it was done in one session.' But I don't necessarily agree or disagree with that. I think it just depends. There are certain songs that you want to have different. If you've got a song with a country vibe, I don't think you should try to produce that the same way as you would something with a jazz or contemporary or fusion kind of feel.

"It seemed to me that we probably worked on that for five or six months. 'They Only Come Out at Night' we did in six weeks. It took long to do because everybody was doing other projects as well. I was doing things for 'Jasmine Night Dreams.' I'm sure Rick was doing stuff for his next solo album, 'Spring Fever.' Everybody had other interests and considerations, other things in mind. We were having fun. I don't understand people that complain. If you're not having fun doing it, go home! I love playing. If I didn't, I wouldn't be out there. All these people are pampered. They've got a hundred people taking care of their every need. They're just babies. You don't like it, don't do it. Music is fun! It's supposed to be fun. That's what it's all about. I never thought of it as a career or as work."

Rick Derringer: "Everybody started having very definite ideas on what they thought the record should sound like. Technically. From a production point of view. And they started voicing those ideas more, individually. So on the 'Shock Treatment' album, for instance, you hear Edgar saying, 'I want my songs to sound like this.' And his songs he would really control. Dan would be saying, 'I think my songs should sound like this.' And he would have control over that. We didn't have a unified sound like we did on the white trash records or the kind of oneness that we had on 'They Only Come Out At Night.' 'Shock Treatment' became more a 'hodgepodge' in some respects. Everybody wanted to do what he wanted to do. I don't think that worked in favor of those records. I think it worked against them."

Author: "Was promoting that particular album easier than previous touring because of the money?"

Edgar Winter: "I wouldn't say it was easier. It was definitely more intense. There was a lot more involved in it. We had a lot more stuff to do. And we were definitely looking at it in a more serious way. Back with White Trash all we cared about was the authenticity and the sincerity of the music. With The Edgar Winter Group there were many more elements. Of course the music was the first and most important. But the theatrical value… it was a lot of fun, figuring out different things to do to improve the show. We were always working on it. We were very serious about it. We recorded every set. I used to have an enforced policy of making everybody sit down and listen to the show to refine what we were doing. The tape doesn't lie."

The group started to garner quite a reputation for being able to provide the latest in production gimmicks, a complete entertainment package for those who attended its concerts.

Rick Derringer: "The band wanted to be as flashy as anybody else. One of the things Steve Paul liked to dwell on, as a manager, was, 'A good musician belongs in the pit.' And what that meant is you can go to any Broadway show and hear great musicians but you never see one. 'Cuz those great musicians end up in the pit. So what makes the guy on the stage? He's more than a great musician. He is a great

Backstage, Mobile, Alabama, 1974.
Courtesy Chuck Ruff

As a young developing guitar player who had seen The Edgar Winter Group several times, I was taken with the sound Rick delivered from the stage.

Rick Derringer: "I played real loud [laughs]! I worked those amplifiers real hard. I used flangers and choruses and things like that. One of the ones I particularly liked was 'The Jet Phaser!' That had a 'speed up/slow down' button that was kind of like a Leslie. Which had a quick 'vibratoish' kind of fuzzy sound. You'd push that button and it would gradually slow down. And I did use echo too. I still use some kind of overdrive for solos. I find it helps give me a little extra sustain. And just a touch of delay occasionally. But that's about it as far as the effects. I really don't like the guitar through choruses and ring-modulators and that kind of stuff too much at all."

Some of the benefits of being in a successful rock band were money, dressing room catering and "peripheral benefits."

Rick Derringer: "I was very unconscious of those things. I have no idea how much I ever charged for a gig. I don't remember how much salary I ever made with any of those people. All I cared about was that I got there and there was a place to tune up and change, if we changed. The perks for me were specifically being able to play in front of that big audience and to feel like they looked up to you like a star. And that you were respected as a musician. Beyond that, the basics, the real things that a male gets, there are tons of groupies. And there certainly was enough sexual gratification. You hear about males who never feel like they had the opportunities to try things. And as they get older they end up doing stupid sexual things. They end up messing up their marriages by fooling around because they never felt they had the opportunity. Well, we were never in that situation. So, as an adult, I feel that it's real easy for me to be faithful to whoever my companion is. Because I have had the opportunity to try about every kind of girl there ever was [laughs]! And I was able to sow my wild oats like every teenager's dream! All that stuff were certainly the perks that were there. There was drugs. There was alcohol, if that's what you wanted. Anything a person wanted was available."

entertainer. So we were always schooled first and foremost in being entertainers. When it came to flashy clothes or the state-of-the-art flashy instruments or anything that had to do with entertaining as well as sounding good, we were right there. On the forefront. We were thinking of all those kind of things. We traveled with the world's largest mirror ball [laughs]!

"I was just out there trying to do the best I could each night. I probably would have taken more control of my career and my music rather than being directed by other people. If I had thought about it more on those terms, frankly. But being from the Midwest I was always the kind of person that figured, 'Well, we don't know everything there is to know and there's probably somebody else that knows more about things than we do.' And I was always looking to those people who I thought knew more than I did. It took me a long time before I realized, 'You know, in reality, we are pretty much on the same level. And we all pretty much know about the same stuff.' If you want to feel confident about being a grown-up, a man, then you better start taking responsibility and start making some of your own decisions."

Author: "You stated that during your drug phase Rick was the voice of sanity."

Edgar Winter: "It was a phase that I went through. It was such a commonplace thing. Everybody in Johnny's group, we all did drugs recreationally. When I first started I was a very conservative, brainy kind of a kid and very anti-drug. It took me a long time to agree to try any drug. Marijuana was the first thing that I did. And there was a whole different attitude towards drugs at that time. There was a certain innocence about it. I was interested in it as a mind-altering and mind-expanding type of experience. I never knew it as something that would be harmful. Until I saw a lot of people doing hard drugs. Doing heroin. And as I saw that kind of influence start to develop, I realized that it was a serious survival issue. In the mid-70s I stopped all drugs except marijuana, which I put in a different category from all the other drugs. I pretty much experimented with everything. I did psychedelics and I thought they were really interesting. And I don't regret having done any of that. But at a certain point I just came to realize that it became really difficult for me to write. I had to really discipline myself. I had to sit down and set a certain amount of time aside. And it wasn't always an easy process. After having stopped drugs, I became an unrestrained and prolific writer as things began to flow very easily. Now there are also some songs that I know that I never would have written had it not been for drugs."

Chuck Ruff: "Back then it was mostly cocaine. We were in Washington, D.C., and there was this guy whose nickname was Squirrel. He would follow us all over the east coast. He introduced Dan and Edgar to PCP. Ronnie and I weren't into it, but Edgar, Dan, Randy Jo Hobbs, Squirrel and a couple of roadies were on it."

Edgar Winter: "It was definitely one of those things that had a certain creative state that you can reach. Unfortunately, it's hard to maintain that. It can be inspirational in the short term but it can really become, in the long term, very counterproductive. I think it's different for every person but that's the way it fell out for me. And eventually I stopped doing marijuana as well. I've been completely drug-free since '83."

Chuck Ruff: "As a band, we never had anybody procuring anything for us outside of maybe one driver who used to get us some pot every once in a while. But other than that, all the other stuff we ever got we got on our own. We just seemed to have connections everywhere and it basically fell into our laps. When you're in the spotlight like that and you've got money to spend, for some reason people come out of the woodwork and start giving you things. We used to get mostly cocaine and pot. It usually happened around hometown areas. If we went in an area like around Ohio where Rick was from, all of his friends would show up. If we went around an area like San Francisco where I knew a lot of people, all of my friends would show up.

"The balance right until the very end was Dan. Because if someone had some coke, me, Edgar and Rick would do it. And if somebody had some pot, we'd smoke it. It was one of those situations that you've got all this money. You know all these people. And you don't have to pay for anything. It's the weirdest thing. As long as you let them hang out, you can drink and do drugs and have chicks and it don't cost a dime. And then when you're starving to death, nobody will talk to you. It should be the other way around. People should be trying to help you when you're all fucked up."

Edgar Winter: "I just thought of Rick as being a very positive, energetic person and he seemed to handle it well. In later life he got much more heavily into drugs. He just went through that phase later in life than everybody else did. Now, thankfully, he's just playing as great as ever, singing great. The last time that we played together, I made a point of mentioning to him that I was so happy to see the real Rick Derringer back to 100 percent of who he is."

When "Shock Treatment" was complete, Rick ensconced himself in the studio doing pre-production for his next solo album, "Spring Fever." Despite all his success there was something standing in his way.

Rick Derringer: "I never had quite enough confidence to think for myself. I was hungry to be a big star on my own. The mistake I made in those days was thinking that there was always some manager out there or some record executive or some A&R man that knew more than I did. So a lot of times

I would listen to them as opposed to using my own brain and following my own instincts. What that led me to do was become more involved with a kind of a glam-rock thing than my nature would have taken me. I think in doing that it looked like I was pandering to get a hit. I was pandering to get a hit! That's right! But I think I would never have done that if I wasn't so weak and so kind of insecure about my own ideas at that time. I thought, 'You just listen to these guys. They know what they're doing and you'll get there.' I found out later on that I didn't like where they had led me. And that's when I stopped, pretty much, that style of recording."

As someone who bought the album within a few days of its release, the album's front cover came as bit of a shock.

Rick Derringer: "It was very surprising in some ways. Francesco Scavullo. He was on the fashion end of the society scene in Manhattan. My wife Liz was certainly a part of that whole scene. So I knew of Francesco and had met him on many occasions. When I went in to do that album cover I specifically said that I wanted a casual-looking thing, regular guy, just kind of sitting around with his shirt unbuttoned a little bit and relaxed. Nothing too presumptuous or weird. I went into the photo shoot saying those words. The next thing you know, Way Bandy was there doing hair and make-up. And Francesco's stylist, who was probably his boyfriend at the time, was picking out a shirt from his own closet. And Francesco's cuff links. And the next thing you know, the photo looked like that! The whole direction it took was very surprising to me. When I look back at that particular album cover, which I see many times, I go, 'How did I let this come out?' But that's what we all thought was the right thing at that time."

Liz Derringer: "I thought it was a beautiful picture. Scavullo had done it with Edgar but he went so far out with the 'They Only Come Out At Night' cover that it was accepted because it was so freaky. But Rick just looked like a very pretty girl. It wasn't his image. And that was the problem. Nobody knew it at the time. Francesco Scavullo! But they made him look too much like a girl. Way Bandy and Laurie Hobson, their make-up. Way really put too much make-up on him. And they pouffed his hair too much."

Rick Derringer: "The back cover was certainly more of what I'd have liked to have seen [laughs]. In retrospect, once again, I wish I'd have had more of a handle on things and had taken more control. So many times we've said, 'This is what we like.' And we were always overridden. Steve Paul would like to go out and get so many opinions from people and he would like to feel like everybody liked what he did. And in reality, I found out later on, what he was doing was bringing us to a middle ground rather than have anything that stood for anything at all. When you are well-defined you will have strong reactions, both positive and negative. But Steve would dilute it and water it down so it came so close to the middle that nobody really liked it and nobody really didn't like it. And I allowed myself to be put into that position before I realized that. I don't know if 'Spring Fever' made Steve go that one direction or it was a case where he, as a homosexual himself, really thought that was the way we should be going."

•   •   •

Author: "On the albums 'Jasmine Nightdreams' and 'The Edgar Winter Group Featuring Rick Derringer,' the individuality of the songs was extremely evident in terms of production. How did this sit with you?"

Rick Derringer: "I was happy about it. I thought it was fun. That was when Dan Hartman had actually started building a studio in the Edgar Winter bandhouse. And we started working together on the record up there. Whoever wrote the song got the most input about how it was recorded."

During this time Rick finally began to consider putting together his own band as opposed to being part of an ensemble.

Rick Derringer: "Promoting 'Jasmine Nightdreams' was actually the time period When I started to think that going in other directions was a good idea. When I put my band together, we were pointed in that real heavy rock thing. And I went there probably against my better judgment. I liked what we did but I would have done something more well-rounded, if it were up to me. And probably a little more grown-up at that point."

Before everyone went their separate ways, The Edgar Winter Group combined with Johnny Winter's band to record some live material of classic rock 'n' roll songs which was entitled "Together."

Rick Derringer: "At that time we were all kinda going our separate ways and Steve Paul just thought it would be a good idea to do a record that brought us all together. I don't know if we were ever thinking 'for the last time.' But The Edgar Winter Group had gone its way and I was starting out on my kinda solo endeavors and Johnny certainly was always doing his own thing. The idea then came to somebody, 'Why don't we all actually do a live album and pool our resources and see what we can come up with?' "

Edgar Winter: "I always wanted to do it. I guess it was my idea. I always try every opportunity to work with Johnny. I just thought all of our fans would really enjoy hearing that. And we've all worked together. It just seemed like the logical, fun thing to do."

Author: "What officially caused the Edgar Winter Group to break up?"

Rick Derringer: "Just everybody going their separate ways. Dan really did. Edgar started to get more disenchanted with the pop thing and really wanted to start, as evidenced in 'Jasmine Night Dreams,' going in that jazzier direction a little bit. And everybody felt a little constricted by the management and the business end, I believe. Dan really became more involved in his own studio. By then he had moved it out of the Edgar Winter bandhouse to his own house, which he called 'The Schoolhouse,' in Connecticut. He started working on his own writing and developing his own projects. He became more and more involved in doing it all himself. 'Instant Replay,' 'Relight My Fire,' and just great, great, great records. There's no way to get around it. I loved Dan. He was a very talented guy."

Author: "One of my favorites of his works was the "Gravity" album with James Brown."

Rick Derringer: "Yeah! [sings] 'Living in America!' He wrote that one, sure. He wrote one for Tina Turner, 'Simply The Best.' Great record. And he did The Teenage Mutant Ninja Turtles! The first Ninja Turtles record was Dan Hartman.

"I just think it was a time period where we all started to go our separate ways. It wasn't anything like you hear with some bands, 'They had a big huge fight and will never play together again!' I think it was just everybody's growing independence and it was kind of a natural progression. Everybody got stronger individually and started working on their own things."

Edgar Winter: "As simple as that. And I never saw any reason for it because it was my contention that I don't see why a band can't stay together and everybody can still record their own solo album. I had just done 'Jasmine Nightdreams.' We did the 'Together' album and had just done 'The Edgar Winter Group With Rick Derringer.' And I physically tried to make sure that the songs were balanced. If you talk to Don Henley, who wrote most of the hits, he would say, 'You need to do the best material rather than trying to ensure that everybody has an opportunity to write just because they write.' But in our case they were all great writers. In many cases I preferred their songs to my own. I think everybody was into making a personal mark and statement and felt that being apart of a group was not the best platform to do that from. They all wanted to move on and be their own man. Which they did!"

In 1975 Rick finally took the initiative to put together a band with which he could use to strictly represent his own music. He called it "Derringer."

Rick Derringer: "I had done some work on 'Shock Treatment' and 'Spring Fever' at the Record Plant. And through that project I had gotten to know Jimmy Iovine, one of our tape ops at that time. He went on to become an executive at A&M and produced trillions of hits over the years. But Jimmy Iovine, at that time, was practicing to be an engineer. So he asked me one night to come down, as a producer, and give him a hand and kind of oversee him. He was doing practice sessions at night with some guys. And it turned out those guys he was using included Vinny Appice, Carmine's little brother. So I got a chance to hear that band and hear how good he really was."

Vinny Appice: "I was born in Brooklyn, New York, on September 13, 1957, Friday the thirteenth. That explains why I've played with all these weird bands! Grew up in New York. I'm eleven years younger than Carmine. I used to go see Carmine play and I got really inspired and said, 'I wanna play drums too.'"

Carmine Appice: "Vinny was really young when I was with Vanilla Fudge. I was on TV, magazines and on the radio, playing live gigs in New York. He used to come. He used to tell my mom that was what he wanted to do."

Vinny Appice: "It was great. 'Wow. You get paid to do this? You make a living doing this? This is what I wanna do.

"I hooked up with a nine-piece band, had four horn players in it. And this is how I got to meet Rick. The name of the band was Bomf. A weird name. My friend Angelo was the bass player. And he knew a guitar player called Joey Dambra. And Joey knew Jimmy Iovine. Joey called Jimmy and said, 'I've got this great band. I'd like to do some demos.' Jimmy was nice enough to give us some time up in The Record Plant studios, for free, to record our demos and engineered it for us. So we laid down some tracks. And two things happened.

"On one of the playbacks Rick Derringer was in the studio next door. He walked in and he heard it and he liked the drums. 'Who's the drummer?' And somebody said, 'It's Vinny Appice.' 'Aw, cool. That's Carmine's younger brother.' I wasn't there that night so I didn't meet him.

"At the same time the owner of The Record Plant, Roy Cicala, liked the band and signed us to a management deal which he gave us a room upstairs, for free, to rehearse in. And while we were upstairs we got a phone call one night that said, 'Hey, you guys wanna come down? We need handclaps for a song that John Lennon and Elton John are doing.' The song was 'Whatever Gets You Through The Night.' So we came down and went right into the studio and started doing handclaps. John was there and he said, 'Where'd these guys come from?' He was told, 'That's the band rehearsing upstairs. Roy's managing them.' So we did that and went back upstairs. We were rehearsing a couple of nights later and John and Yoko come walking in while we're playing. We were freakin' out! I was sixteen at the time. So we played some stuff for him. And he used to come up all the time. Hang out, listen to us play. An opportunity came up where he needed some people to be in a video with him; to be the band. So he asked us to do it. And we shot it at The Record Plant.

"John was also producing Roy Cicala's wife. She sang. Her name was Lori Burton. She didn't have a deal or anything but Roy wanted to lay down tracks. So we were the band. We went into the studio with John and worked out about seven songs. It was pretty amazing for me. I was freaking out, sixteen and working with him.

"Too bad I didn't bring a camera [laughs]. But I really didn't want to bother him. I was around it a lot because of my brother being in the business. He used to bring Jeff Beck to the house to eat and things like that and all these famous musicians at the time. So I was trying to be cool and never brought a camera, which I regret now. But I do have a video of us playing together so that's good."

Rick Derringer: "I had also met Kenny Aaronson, from the bands Stories and Dust, and had talked to him. And he said he would like to be in that band."

Kenny Aaronson: "I was born April 14, 1952, in Brooklyn, New York. Every morning before I went to school we always had Murray the K on. He was the New York-based disc jockey. He was the fifth Beatle. I remember even as far back as going to kindergarten. I heard rock 'n' roll music, doo-wop, Elvis, The Ronettes, Phil Spector records. I loved rock 'n' roll on AM radio at that time. I appreciate how those recordings were done and the musicians and the work, the arrangements that went into this music. The technology was so limited, although it was state of the art at the time. I'm still fascinated with those old records. I still cherish my collection of 45s. I'm such a Phil

Spector fanatic because of what he created. And every one of these records has upright bass on them. There were no rock 'n' roll upright bass players. These were jazz cats doing sessions on the side. I think that's really cool stuff to think about at this point in time. And that's what I grew up on."

Rick Derringer: "So, basically, the first guy that said yes was Kenny."

Kenny Aaronson: "I had been playing with Leslie West for a while. One weekend I was home and I got a call from Rick out of the clear blue sky. It was, 'Hey, Kenny, it's Rick Derringer. I'm putting a band together and I'm wondering if you'd be interested in being in it?' And I said, 'Sure.' I didn't hear from him for a little while. He was off checking out some other people for the band."

Rick Derringer: "And then I went to track down Vinny."

Vinny Appice: "I had come out to California. Somebody told me about this band Axis in Louisiana, a three-piece band with Danny Johnson and Jay Davis. I had gone back to New York and Danny called me and sent me a tape. I liked the stuff that I heard and I said, 'Send me a round trip ticket and I'll come to Louisiana and play with you guys and see how it gels.' So I hooked up with Danny and Jay. It worked out really well. We played together and I liked the music. Really liked Danny. I played with them for about six weeks down there. And then, one day, Rick called my mother's house, in Brooklyn, to get a hold of me."

Carmine Appice: "He said, 'Hi, this is Rick Derringer.' And my mother was hip on the rock 'n' roll back then. She used to follow my career. And my mother says, 'Oh, you must want to speak to Carmine.' Rick said, 'No, no, I know Carmine. I wanna talk to Vinny.' And she kept saying, 'You sure you wanna talk to Vinny?' "

Vinny Appice: "So finally Rick convinced her that it was me he was after. She gave him the number in Louisiana. I was outside on the porch and somebody said, 'Vinny, Rick

Derringer's on the phone!' 'Rick Derringer? Holy shit!' I ran to the phone and Rick told me he's putting a band together and he'd like me to play drums. And he's looking for a guitar player and bass player. I said I was playing with Axis. Really cool guitar player. Good bass player. He suggested that he come down and check us out. So he flew down and the whole town was freaked out. Rick Derringer comin' to Shreveport [laughs] to check Axis out!"

Rick Derringer: "So I flew down to Shreveport to hear Vinny. But I also found Danny Johnson, and I said, 'Man, this kid is great!' "

Danny Johnson: "I was born on June 14, 1955, in Shreveport, Louisiana. My earliest influences were people like Elvis Presley, Chuck Berry. I liked the harder-edged singers like Wilson Pickett, James Brown. Stuff that was biting and exciting, the records my older brother was listening to. And then I got into the psychedelic bands like Cream. That was a big one for me. And Jimi Hendrix.

"I was in Louisiana and the sun was going down. I heard these chords. A minor, C, D, F. 'The House Of The Rising Sun.' I was moved by this lonely guitar calling out at night. I stopped what I was doing and walked up to this sound. And there was my cousin, ironically named Robert Johnson, playing this guitar. And I thought, 'If he can do it, I can do it.' So he started me off, giving me lessons and kinda got me going.

"My brother had a friend who was a really good guitar player and I would bribe them. They would have some whiskey and I would say, 'Hey, I'm gonna tell on you guys if you don't give me a guitar lesson!' And my dad got me a guitar lesson from a cousin of mine, Walter, who was really good. I always hung out with guys older than me. It's like Rick once said to me, 'When you're young, hang out with the older guys and learn from them. And when you're old, hang out with the younger guys and feed off that young energy.'

"Rick came down, saw us play and said we were really good. I thought he was just gonna take Vinny off. The next day I was holding my daughter Celeste on my knee, trying to keep her from crying, and Steve Paul calls me. Who, at the time, was the most major guy you would ever want to have call you, being a broke, down-in-Louisiana guitar player. The owner of Blue Sky Records. He had the whole stable. 'Hey, this is Steve Paul. I manage Rick. He said he went down and saw you play. Do you want to come along?' I was pretty much stunned. I didn't realize I was gonna get that offer. I had my band Axis that I believed in."

Rick Derringer: "I said, 'I'm sorry to say it but I've already asked a bass player to join the band. I'd love to have you in the band but you're going to have to do it with Kenny Aaronson.' "

Danny Johnson: "The bass player, Jay Davis, who's my brother-in-law, said, 'You go ahead and go.' "

Author: "When he invited Danny and Vinny he made it clear to them that he had a bass player for the band and didn't want to use Jay Davis, their bass player. What do you think you showed him that made him adamant about keeping you?"

Kenny Aaronson: "It's interesting that you brought that up. I never really thought about that but you're right. I always thought of Jay Davis as being a very good bass player. And to be honest with you, I'm not really sure what it was about me that Rick was positive about having me involved and really just wanted Vinny and Danny. At this point in time, after all these years, I would have to ask Rick."

Rick Derringer: "There was a big record out called 'Brother Louie.' It was a great single but it was a great musical record. The track included some nice playing between the drums and the bass and I found out Kenny was playing bass. One of the things I was most interested was having great players in my band. Jay Davis was a good enough bass player in some ways but had absolutely no personality on stage. Kenny Aaronson was one of the first guys I called to see if he would want to be in a band because one of his key selling points that gets him all these gigs is that he's an unbelievable entertainer! Kenny is one of the most fun people to watch on stage that you'll ever

see. He moves. He's got a great personality that's all his. Plus he's a great bass player. I had to make a decision and the decision was to go with Kenny."

Danny Johnson: "It was tough leaving Jay behind. Being down in Louisiana, you might as well have been in Africa. So to get to New York City and work with Rick Derringer under Steve Paul's stable was a great opportunity. Axis was good and everything but we had no decent agency. No management. We'd traveled around and owned a van and a P.A. and we had each other. But we also had wives and kids."

Vinny Appice: "We were young. It was a really good opportunity for me and Danny. We figured, Let's do this and see what happens. Right after that Jay Davis wound up playing with Foreigner. Jay was making $50 a week before the first record came out, so he quit [laughs]! Oops! Wrong move."

Danny Johnson: "I went on ahead to New York and auditioned for Rick and got the gig."

Author: "What direction did Rick tell you the band was going towards?"

Danny Johnson: "He made it clear to me that all his flamboyant clothes were down in his basement rotting. I said, 'Is it possible that I could have some them?' And he said, 'I prefer that they just stay there and rot.' He had that stuff from the Edgar Winter Group. He felt that they got too glammed-out with some of their outfits. He wanted to put together an uncontrived band who wore blue jeans and T-shirts. A rock 'n' roll band with a New York attitude.

"Rick is probably one of the best musicians I've ever known as far as being able to just tear the guitar up. I'm friends with Van Halen. And Eddie Van Halen is the best Eddie Van Halen there is. But Rick is versatile. He can play like Van Halen or Johnny Winter or Rick Derringer. He can do anything. He also plays bass, piano. But what always amazed me about him, as a musician and a producer, is he can see a band. He took me to CBGB's and introduced me to punk rock. There's no virtuosos in the band. The singer's mediocre. The drummer is barely chunking along. And he can say, 'That's cool.' He can feel something when it's primal and tell that there's something there. He was into a lot of bands that I thought were not as good as Led Zeppelin but it turned out to be Blondie or Tom Petty or The Talking Heads. These were bands that he was turning me on to. The Ramones. Yeah, they played the same song for an hour but they had a certain energy. And to this day I'm glad that he took me around that kind of stuff. It was all about attitude as opposed to how well someone can play the guitar or how perfectly they can sing."

Rick Derringer: "Danny was a real adventurous kind of guitar player. He had his own style. One of the things I liked about him was he had his own kind of presence. He was a good-looking guy. He held himself well."

Danny Johnson: "I've always been kind of an insecure guy. I knew I was good for being a nineteen-year-old guy from Shreveport. But on his level, I pretty much thought I was a punk kid. Which I was. But he saw something. I've always felt kind of indebted to him because he helped me along and got me going. Got me some good equipment and took me from the club scene into national arenas and magazines."

Rick Derringer: "I wanted somebody that was good at writing. He was the lead singer in his band so I also got somebody who could sing. But as far as his guitar playing went… I hadn't heard Eddie Van Halen yet. In fact there wasn't a Van Halen band as a recording entity yet. And Danny was doing the hammer-ons technique. I hadn't really seen it that much before."

Danny Johnson: "Guitar players are emulators. I had seen some guy in a music store, Arnold and Morgan Music in Garland, Texas, put his finger on the neck. I don't remember what he did but I thought it was cool. So I started fooling around with it. A couple of years later I saw ZZ Top and I noticed that Billy Gibbons was doing it. He didn't do anything flashy. He would just hit a note and bend it to the fifth.

And then go to the seventh to where it would go up to the whole tone. It sounds good on record but I think it's more exciting live. It's more of a showpiece or something."

Rick Derringer: "I later learned that Eddie Van Halen was coming to see the Johnny Winter band and the Edgar Winter band whenever we played in the California area, he being from San Bernadino. In the middle of my guitar solo I had been whipping into 'You Really Got Me' by the Kinks. Every time I'd whip into that song the audience would go nuts. I didn't know Eddie Van Halen had been out there and seen us play a few times. Unbeknownst to me, when they recorded their first album, they did a version of 'You Really Got Me.' Now somewhere in me I want to feel like, well, I was the guy that influenced him to be struck by that song because I had been playing it in my solo. When I went out on the road with Danny, it wasn't too long after that Eddie started touring with us in Van Halen. The first tour we did together we shared the headlining bill. Their record had just come out and one night we would open and the next night they would open. I wasn't that conscious of their first record immediately. It took me a little while to hear it. But in the middle of my guitar solo on the nights that I would open I would, without even thinking, go into 'You Really Got Me.' After a few nights Eddie came back and started saying, 'What are you trying to do, steal my song from me?' Because they were getting ready to release the single of 'You Really Got Me,' which they eventually did. But I always thought it was certainly egotistical on my part to think that Eddie was influenced by me to choose 'You Really Got Me' because in reality both of us had taken it from the Kinks. It wasn't my song. We were both stealing it. But at the time I had been doing it before I had even heard of Eddie, that's for sure."

• • •

Vinny Appice: "We moved to New York and started rehearsing up at S.I.R. Rick just wanted to have a good rock band. It was fun. We rehearsed at night and I couldn't wait to go down there and play. We did some writing over at Rick's house 'cuz he had a nice studio set up. Rick wrote most of the stuff but we put it together at rehearsal. Danny wrote a couple of tunes on the first record and that's how we got that far. It was kinda like working with John Lennon at the time. Here you are working with Rick Derringer and all the stuff he's written."

Danny Johnson: "We were ordering all of our food out. I remember our orange juice bill being $500! We were young and didn't think. 'Whatever you guys want, we'll just pay for it later when we tour.' $3,000 worth of cheese blintzes, $500 worth of the cookie bill. We were all kids, still eating cookies and drinking cokes. And paying for Ryder trucks and all this stuff. It was really expensive."

Kenny Aaronson: "Wow, that's pretty funny [laughs]! The blintzes were probably me because I liked ordering from the Carnegie Deli. Steve Paul and Teddy Slatus always made sure we had whatever we wanted in rehearsal. Back then none of us were drinkers or anything like that. I hadn't reached my party mode yet! Whatever we did we smoked pot. Rick and I were pot smokers."

Vinny Appice: "We didn't know what was going on. 'You guys need new road cases?' 'Shit, yeah! Give me five of them!' 'Hey, you guys hungry? Let's order from the deli.' So every night … I mean, somebody was paying for it. 'Hey, you guys wanna eat?' 'Sure.' "

Author: "Did Steve ever mention that, one day, you would have to pay this back?"

Vinny Appice: "Naw! Who fuckin' cares? We're having fun! I think the cab fare bill for the album was $30,000! Everybody was taking cabs. It was a huge bill [laughs]. But you know what? It was fun. And what are you gonna do?"

Danny Johnson: "We did our first album. It was supposed to be done with Bill Scymczyk and they cancelled us at the last minute. 'He's busy with the Eagles,' and kind of blew us out. Rick and Steve are pacing around like 'What are we going to do, call Pete Townsend?' And I'm going, 'I know a great producer.' 'Who?' 'Rick Derringer.' It's like they

were wanting to do something else but it worked out for him to produce the first album. Harry Maslin came along to help engineer but Rick produced it and we did it at the Hit Factory."

Vinny Appice: "Rick would bring in the songs pretty much as you heard on the record.There were some things changed here and there. He let me play what I wanted to. Rick didn't really control that so much. He let me play. And if he had an idea he'd tell me and we'd try it. And if it sounded good we'd do it."

Danny Johnson: "The first album went so fast I didn't even know I was on it."

Vinny Appice: "Yeah, the album was done real quick. I think it was done in five weeks or something. I didn't know anything about drum sounds. It was my first record. And the drums are real dry on it. It was before the big wet sounds come out. It was just a bunch of mikes. They told me what I needed to do and I did it. And that's the way it sounds, ya know."

Author: "You brought a real chunkiness to the songs as a rhythm player."

Danny Johnson: "I have a lot of confidence as a rhythm guitarist. That's another thing that Rick helped me with. Once upon a time, I wasn't as good and within ten seconds he made me a better rhythm player. We were in S.I.R., playing, and I took a solo. Everything was fine. Then he took a solo. And he stopped the song and said, 'I have a problem. When you solo, what happens?' I go, 'Well, everything's cool.' And he goes, 'Yeah. 'Cuz I'm playing rhythm and I'm giving you the groove and I'm backing you up. And then when I take a solo it's like you're playing with no authority and you're just meandering.' I just thought in my mind, 'I should play this rhythm with authority while he plays the solo.' And I'm looking at the door and I'm thinking about the ride back to Shreveport and I became a solid rhythm player in that instant.

"You gotta keep in mind that here I am, nineteen years old up there. And here's Rick Derringer next to you! In his prime! I mean, [chuckles] he was hot! I remember him going to the mailbox and throwing royalty checks on the table. It would be no big deal. There would be $10,000 from this gig or album royalties. He was really going. So when he would play, I had to give it all I had."

Vinny Appice: "I think we finished the album some time in April and we were out on the road in June. We started off doing a month of clubs. I remember we were in some hotel room and Steve Paul came in and said, 'We got the Aerosmith tour!' And then he told me all the cities and I was jumping on the couch. 'Ah, shit, man, we're going to Chicago!' I'd never been anywhere, ya know. It was really exciting! Then we started opening up for Aerosmith. It was the first time I was on the road and it was incredible."

Kenny Aaronson: "For the over three years that I played with Rick we toured constantly. We were always on the biggest tour of that year with the biggest act of that year. I'm talking Foreigner, Peter Frampton when the live record was made. I'm talking Aerosmith's 'Rocks' tour. We opened up for Zeppelin for two days in a row at Bill Graham's 'Day On The Green.' Boston. Whoever was huge at that time, between '76 and '79, we were on those shows. And in between we played every club that meant anything to rock 'n' roll in every state in the United States. We played our asses off! From the biggest places to the smallest dumps. If there was good rock 'n' roll happening, we would be there."

Rick Derringer: "We felt like the longer you do something right, the more it adds up, the more success will come your way. We were trying to be the best we could on the best possible tours we could get. We became the most widely used opening band in that time period."

Danny Johnson: "Rick used to say, 'If you're the opening band, look at it this way. Let the other people pay for the PA and the lights and all that stuff. And then we get their audience. Then, when they're onstage, we can get their women and their food and dressing room.' He wasn't a guy to ever go there but I think he would just try to make it appealing to us. Aerosmith probably hadn't eaten anything out of the dressing room in four years at that time, if you know what I mean. They did something else. Back then."

Carmine Appice: "I'd see them pretty much whenever they played L.A., if I was here. They did some great gigs. They were doing gigs like at The Whiskey A Go Go and the next night play with Aerosmith at a big stadium. It was pretty exciting for my brother. I believe he was only seventeen."

Danny Johnson: "That band probably could have been a headliner in my opinion. Maybe not the big, big places yet but Rick and Steve Paul were really in sync in those days. They wanted to make sure that we were always in a good situation."

Seeing Derringer open for Aerosmith was the first time that I, and thousands of others in the audience, had been exposed to wireless guitars.

Rick Derringer: "There were wireless units previously out for microphones and stuff but they never worked very well. They were radio-type units. It was a guy, Ken Schaffer, in New York City. He had done some work with the True Diversity system, which is the first wireless unit that worked. They used two different channels that silently switched back and forth using the most optimum reception that either of those channels was receiving at any given second. They could switch back and forth silently a hundred times a minute if they had to, always finding the optimum channel. And because of that it made the first wirelesses really useful and a practical thing. Schaffer came to us, because we were playing a lot, and asked if we would want to be one of the first bands to use the wireless. And we said 'Yeah!' We thought it would be a great thing. We bought three and we were using them on the road as one of the first groups out there using them."

• • •

Author: "How quickly did the band go from blintzes to the other extreme?"

Kenny Aaronson: "Things happen. You're out there partying and you're playing with all kinds of people and you get introduced to whatever and you experiment. It happens to everybody. I'm glad I'm alive to talk about it. But I have no regrets. I had a great time."

Vinny Appice: "I like to have fun and party with the best of them but I never got into anything heavy. Never let anything affect the performances."

Kenny Aaronson: "Rick and I were the party animals, eventually. Danny and Vinny … those guys weren't doing anything of any sort. Vinny smoked pot. Danny was into Jesus at the time. Or thought he was. And Rick and I sort of did whatever we did. But then again we were also older and we just had different attitudes about it."

Author: "Were the 'perks' of being on the road a surprise to you?"

Vinny Appice: "No. That was really interesting. It didn't affect me much. I never walked around and said, 'Hey, man, I'm fuckin' cool as shit.' I just thought, 'I love playing. These people love listening to it.' I was pretty lucky and enjoyed what I did and it didn't affect me in that way. And Danny too. He was just so happy to play and be appreciated that it wasn't a big ego thing. And then on the other hand we never made it really big. We did a club tour then the opening for Aerosmith. We were making a name for ourselves but we never went out and headlined arenas, limos and private jets and that type of lifestyle."

• • •

Rick's wife, Liz, exposed Rick to a side of New York that was extremely foreign to him upon arrival but he seemed to adapt quite easily.

Author: "There was your crowd and her crowd. Did everybody fit?"

Rick Derringer: "Yeah. Everybody wanted to be a part of the same crowd! Basically it was just kind of like New York's little social scene and we were considered in the center of it somewhere. Everybody wanted to be there."

Danny Johnson: "He used to have this cool place where it had a grand piano and some drums. One night we had a jam. We had played Madison Square Garden that night with Aerosmith. Rick had invited everybody over to his house to kind of hang out a little bit. It was John Belushi singing, Steven Tyler on drums. I was playing guitar, Brad Whitford was playing guitar, Rick was on piano, David Johansson was playing harmonica. When I lived at his house I stayed downstairs and Rick and Liz stayed upstairs. So when someone would knock on the door I'd go open the door and after a while I said, 'Do you guys know anybody that's not famous?' It would be Todd Rundgren or Johnny or Edgar or Mick Jagger. The list goes on and on."

Rick Derringer: "We were in the center of Manhattan. By '75 or so, when Danny Johnson came to town, everybody knew where we were."

Liz Derringer: "One night we had Mick Jagger, Andy Warhol, Truman Capote, John Phillips and his wife Genevieve, and Robert Maplethorpe and Patti Smith and everybody was there. Debbie Harry. It was pretty amazing."

Rick Derringer: "Steven Tyler was seeing Bebe Buell, on and off. And I guess at the same time she was married or living with Todd Rundgren [laughs]. I was on the road. And my ex-wife, Liz, offered Bebe Buell our house as a meeting place for Steven and Bebe. So our bedroom was where Liv was conceived. And because of that, I'm her godfather.

"It was at a time when Steven's career was not as successful as it came to be. Bebe told Todd that Liv was his child and she was raised as Liv Rundgren, not Liv Tyler. Todd paid the bills. Todd paid for the toys. Todd was the dad. And then after Steven got successful again, Bebe decided, 'Ya know, I've always thought she looked a lot like Steven. I think I'll have a paternity test done to verify who she is!' I guess Steven, at the time, balked at the idea and had to be dragged in to have that paternity test performed. They found out she was indeed his and she became Liv Tyler. But I saw an interview with Liv on MTV. They were asking Liv what it was like to have Steven as a dad. And she told the whole audience, 'Oh, he was the greatest dad to grow up with!' It was a disservice to Todd, who raised her as the dad and thought he was the dad, and she thought he was the dad. And Bebe, because of really opportunistic reasons, decided at the last minute to claim who the dad probably really was. And then, for show biz reasons, probably, here's Liv not even mentioning Todd or any of that part of her life. Now, I gotta tell ya, Steven's a good friend of mine. And Todd is a good friend of mine. And Liv is my goddaughter. Bebe is a friend. So I'm not trying to say anything necessarily bad about any of them. I just think it's a wild, show biz story."

Liz Derringer: "It was terrible. I was in a place where no one would want to be, that's for sure. I cared about all of them. I introduced Steven to Bebe. Went to school with Steven. It was a professional children's school here called Quintano's on West 56th Street. It's not there anymore. And you know Bebe's reputation; I don't have to tell you. She stayed with Steven for a little while. He was doing too many drugs, she couldn't take it and she left. And when she went back she was pregnant. She didn't know who the father was for sure. Todd said he'd give the child his name. Which he did. And I guess as the years went on, he loved Liv but he wasn't providing for her the way Bebe felt he should. And by that time I think Bebe needed to know who the father was. And I think Liv needed to know. Steven certainly didn't wanna do it. But what man does? But, believe me, he's happy he did it [laughs]. He loves her to death and they've had wonderful success together."

1976

The band tried to maintain its momentum by returning to the studio to record their second album, "Sweet Evil." Still looking for the magic formula, Rick handed the production reigns over to Jack Douglas.

Rick Derringer: "I just loved his work with Aerosmith. I thought he was a great producer. I approached Jack and he decided that he really wanted to help. I also talked to Bob Ezrin, who was producing Alice Cooper at that time, and he was interested. But this was one of those cases like Scymcyzk. Douglas was right there and ready to go."

Vinny Appice: "Jack was cool. Since we were close with Aerosmith, we met Jack a lot of times and he'd heard us and Rick thought it was a really good idea. And so did we. He was real easy to work with. He didn't get involved in the song arrangements or changes that much. He was more involved in the sounds of the album."

Danny Johnson: "I think he brought a mystical quality. In New Orleans they call it the 'Grih Grih voodoo powder.' English call it the 'fairy dust.' He just brought a strangeness there. Rick was more of a straight-ahead rock 'n' roller and really, at the time, had a lot of R&B. I think Rick could have done some neat up-tempo R&B stuff where he was actually playing the bass guitar. He really had a lot of that in him. But he had a rock 'n' roll image. A lot of what Rick was capable of doing didn't really fit his image. Jazz, long instrumentals and funky things. We worked some of it in there, some of the funky stuff. Jack Douglas brought about some of those layered, trippy guitar parts and unusual sounds. Like on 'One Eyed Jack.' Rick had a lot of toys and a lot of guitars. Jack was doing a lot of stuff like shooting a Marshall stack into a glass wall and miking the glass. Or shooting a Marshall stack into a grand piano and hold the sustain pedal down with a bag of sand and get the reverb off the strings. Very involved. Our first album was a little dry compared to 'Sweet Evil.' "

Kenny Aaronson: "What Jack Douglas brought to the table for us was his way of using production techniques to introduce us to, 'How would John Bonham get this drumsound? Well, this is how I'd do it. I'm Jack Douglas.' He would take Vinny Appice's drum mix and run it through a guitar amp. Put the guitar amp in a concrete stairwell with a mike at the end of the stairs and he'd mike it and he'd mix it in with the dry mix."

Vinny Appice: "Yeah, he did all sorts of stuff like that. And if you listen to that album a lot of the drums were a lot deeper and bigger. The whole album is a lot more bottom heavy. And it's a little darker."

Kenny Aaronson: "There was also the encouragement for Danny Johnson to write 'cuz he had a couple of good tunes that were on that record. But I have to say I was never happy with my bass sound. That was the one thing that really bothered me about 'Sweet Evil.' It wasn't fat. It was thin. I was using a Jazz bass and I always found it was too thin and honky-sounding. It didn't have any bottom. It didn't have any growl. I really didn't like it at all."

Vinny Appice: "That's the way he did things. He got the bottom end from the bass drum and he had the bass kind of being percussive. But it's definitely on the lower end of the spectrum as far as the sound of the album."

Kenny Aaronson: "I didn't have the balls to say what was on my mind back then. That comes with time and confidence. I tend to be a very shy and laid-back person. For a very long time in my life I never really had a lot of confidence. And because of that it kept me from expressing opinions about stuff. You don't want to be the guy that's complaining. And it's not good to complain unless you have an answer for it. If you don't know why or can't figure it out, don't say anything. So a lot of times I would let things go by and I would live with it. And to this day I have a hard time listening to anything I've ever played on because I don't like the way it sounds. And that album in particular."

Author: " 'Sweet Evil' has a lot of terrific riffs and hooks. Good songs. Again, why the lack of commercial success?"

Rick Derringer: "Part of the problem with the whole thing was a purely business one. Blue Sky Records. When I went in to sign my record deal as a solo artist, I was being managed by Steve Paul. And Steve Paul told me, 'I started this record label and it will be our record label.' And he used the word 'our' and convinced me it wasn't just his record label, it was 'our' record label. I went in to have a meeting with Steve one day, to talk with Clive Davis about their wanting to sign me. And Clive told me, in front of Steve, 'You can sign to Columbia Records, CBS, which is where I want to put you, or you guys can start this label, Blue Sky Records.

I think it would be better for you to do this thing with CBS and me rather than the independent label thing.' And I, like a stupido, said, 'No. Steve, my manager, says it's going to be 'our' label! So we're gonna do this together.' So I went with Steve rather than with Clive.

"When a parent company says, 'You will be a subsidiary of us,' they also require that subsidiary to be a company too. They will supply the distribution and they will help out in any way they can. But the subsidiary has an obligation to do something too. In this case they expected the subsidiary to do some publicity to help promote the record; to do some work on their own. In Steve Paul's case with Blue Sky, it became apparent that all that was happening was he was using every facility of CBS and not doing anything himself. He was asking CBS to give us huge amounts of money to make the records, advances to actually create the thing. He was asking to use their art department to do the artwork. He was asking them to promote it. He was asking them to press it. And really doing nothing as a company. And I think that caused some real resentment from CBS. I think they stopped working on it from their end. They weren't promoting it. They said, 'You guys have to do some of this work as a record company.' And we weren't. So from a purely business point of view, we blew it!"

Author: "Do you think that was also why the promo people weren't getting airplay?"

Rick Derringer: "That's exactly why. That requires money. If CBS had it on their label, like Clive had originally wanted, they would have. That's part of what they did. But I wasn't on their label. I was on Blue Sky. So they required Blue Sky to do that. Blue Sky never justified spending that kind of money 'cuz Steve was too interested in putting it in his bank, frankly. So that was what happened. I love Steve for all the good things and all the opportunities he gave me. But as a record company exec, he didn't do his job.

"We really were getting to the point where it was just about to mean something. We were ready to break! That's when Vinny and Danny decided to go back and reform Axis. They had left their bass player behind and they always kept thinking about it.

'Til finally they said, 'You know, we'd really like the opportunity to try Axis. Use the success we've garnered with you, Rick, and see if we can take that with our band to a new level.' And that's pretty much what broke up the band. They pretty much messed up our battle plan. I was then thrown into a situation where I had to stop for a while. And what we did was we made the 'Derringer Live' album. Which was not in our plans. But we had talked them into staying long enough to at least finish that record. It would give us time to go ahead and reform."

Kenny Aaronson: "They thought that they were just ready to move on. I know that Rick was very hurt about it. Rick found those guys, took them out of basically the boondocks and made a great band with them. Really relied on them. Gave them a lot of exposure. Rick probably felt, 'All right. You guys think that … fine. Go ahead. We'll get somebody else. Good luck.' And ultimately it didn't work for them. Danny Johnson's never really done anything where he became what he thought he had the potential of being. Danny was doing some unique things back then. If he still wanted to leave he might have been able to leave for something actually substantial. Tell me. How many people know about Danny Johnson? I think he would have profited if he'd have stuck around for another year or so. Both those guys would have. But these guys had egos and thought they were better off doing something else. And after that second record they were gone."

Vinny Appice: "It was after 'Sweet Evil' and we went on tour again. We were playing clubs again and blah, blah, blah. And we were saying, 'Hey, man, what's going on? We've played clubs already. We should be doing better places than this.' And towards the end of the tour, months later, we're still doing a lot of the same places. And we were thinking, 'I don't wanna play clubs the rest of my life. Why don't we just get our old band together and try it on our own? We've got a little name going and this and that.' So I think from being young and impatient and we weren't making any money … and then we found out we had to pay for a lot of the stuff from the Carnegie deli and the cases and road expenses. We had been asked, 'What do you want? A cut of the band or a salary?' 'Oh, a cut of the band!' Well, who knew? And who cared?"

Rick Derringer: "I was never a great businessman, like I said. I was always conscious of just having that opportunity to be out there playing the music. If I was losing money anywhere, it was being reinvested into my career. In this particular case I had invested quite a bit of money in those guys. I bought them their amplifiers, their drums, their guitars. And in each case, when they left a lot of times, they'd feel like they had earned those instruments. They would take them with them. And being kind of a chump, easygoing guy, I would usually let them do that. I can say that I lost quite a bit of money. Real dollars giving them equipment and rebuying for new guys. But that's kinda the way I always was. It wasn't really the smartest business move but in the end I always looked at it as a kind of investment in my career. And I didn't really want to make enemies. I wanted to leave on good terms, usually."

Vinny Appice: "I think Rick said, 'Hey, man, if that's what you wanna do, I'm not gonna stop you.' That kind of attitude. I think he knew we were young and on fire [chuckle]! From what I heard later he was upset because he really liked the band. We were kinda upset that we weren't making any money."

Liz Derringer: "He was very unhappy. But you know, Danny kept saying he wanted to go back and do his group again."

Danny Johnson: "I had been around the rock 'n' roll lifestyle for a while at that point. I was raised very religious and I was getting to where I wanted to tone it down a little bit. I'm not saying I was a goody-goody kid but they did call me 'Danny Chapstick.' I just wanted to get back into doing my own music and get out front again. After talking about it, I thought that maybe it was a good time to put it back together with Jay Davis and go to California or something. I didn't know it was going to be that heavy of a thing. I told Rick that I was thinking about pressing on and that I would stay long enough to help him out until he could get someone. I didn't really think that I meant a whole lot to him at the time. I was insecure and naïve. I thought it would be easier for him to get somebody else and move on."

Vinny Appice: "I think at the end of that tour, when we were talking about leaving, that was when we started recording the live stuff. They said, 'We're gonna do a live album.' All right, no problem. And then when it started happening we weren't getting along with Rick quite as well, obviously, because he was pissed off we were leaving. I guess on paper we were broken up. We did the live shows and the tour ended and that was the end of it."

Danny Johnson: "The vibes just weren't real good. And I felt like the bad guy. 'Cuz I was."

Vinny Appice: "On the 'Derringer Live' album, there's a big picture of Kenny and a small one of Danny. And nothing of me! So I guess I was the bad guy. It wasn't just my idea. Danny wanted to leave too."

Danny Johnson: "I was following my heart. I wanted to get away from the whole scene of late nights and the things that go on. I later went through all that but at the time I was kind of innocent to the whole thing. For years Rick and I didn't talk at all. Then we gradually started talking again. And now we're getting along real good. As a matter of fact I'd love to work with Rick on something. Play on one his albums or have him play on my album."

Author: "So no bitterness?"

Rick Derringer: "No."

Danny Johnson: "And after the Derringer band we re-formed Axis. With Vinny and Jay and myself."

Vinny Appice: "We went to New York and recorded 'It's A Serious World.' And we loved it. I thought that album sounded really good. But it was a small indie label. They didn't push it very much and there were a lot of business problems that we didn't know about. Then we went out on the road with a lame agent and we were playing some real die-holes everywhere. The business part of it was not happening. The record company didn't know what they were doing. So we moved back out to L.A. It went on for a couple of years and we weren't getting anywhere. Then I got a call from Black Sabbath. Now I've gotta make a decision. 'Now what do I do? Do I do this? This is going to be big, obviously.' So I made the decision to leave and do the Sabbath thing."

Author: "What did you take away from the experience of playing with Derringer?"

Danny Johnson: "I took away a lot. I learned a lot about recording. Touring. Performing. How to walk onstage and give it your all. And I think the main thing I learned from Rick was there are a lot of crybabies out there. People do interviews, 'Oh, man, we've been traveling all day.' He used to say, 'Screw it, man! Yeah, it took us a long time to get here but we wanna have a good time! And we can't wait to get up there and play and have all those pretty girls looking at us!' He has a real positive attitude about everything. I was kind of a moody guy back then. Now that I'm older I can see how my personality caused people to get tired of my moodiness. I thought it was OK to be like that. But later I realized that it affects other people.

"I think Rick is a genius onstage and in the studio. If it has anything to do with music, it's an incredible thing. His playing, his singing … he just has this thing he can turn on. We had a good thing together. It was kind of like bookends. We were quite different in our lifestyles and in our playing and in our writing. But they went together really well."

Vinny Appice: "I learned a hell of a lot. Before then I'd never been on tour. How to write songs and put them together. How to record in a studio. Rick was a great teacher. He had so much experience. He was just a great person to work with. Especially me being at a young age I was trying to observe and learn as much as I could."

Rick Derringer: "When Danny left the band, the first guy that filled in for him was Mark Cunningham."

Kenny Aaronson: "We loved Mark. Mark was great. Mark I knew just from being local. He wasn't the most technical guitar player, he just did things with a lot of feeling and a lot of energy and a lot of love for it. We had a good time with Mark. He was so into everything and just wanted to be a part of it."

Rick Derringer: "Mark was really into the whole Jimmy Page thing. He dressed like Jimmy Page, his hair was like Jimmy Page, and he played a Les Paul, the closest-looking one to Jimmy Page. He pulled out the violin bow to play it. He was very impressed by Jimmy Page. But we were impressed by Mark. I really always felt like we should be entertaining the audience. And that's what I saw in Mark more than anything else. He really was a showman. He wanted to impress the audience. He wanted to be an entertainer. He got Danny's old wireless. And one of the things he thought of was, 'Why, in the middle of our guitar solos, don't we just toss the guitars? Exchange guitars in midair.' And I said, 'Well, that's a ballsy move there. That would be a brave thing.' And I gotta tell ya, it took quite a bit of nerve to try it the first time. One of the things people don't realize is, when you throw a baseball to a catcher, one guy throws and the other guy catches. Very seldom, except in juggling acts, does anybody ever take the baseball and throw it at each other simultaneously. When you throw the ball, you watch where you're throwing it to make sure it went to that other catcher's hands. But if you both throw the ball simultaneously, you can't watch that. I can tell you it's not the easiest thing to do. It's probably why we don't see bands do it all the time. There might have been a lot of bands try it but have hit themselves in the head with guitars or broken a couple. A pretty ballsy move every time we did it [laughs]."

Author: "How many did you and Mark drop?"

Rick Derringer: "Maybe one at some time or another. But we had to be on our toes. And we certainly had almost dropped them probably every time we did it. We'd have to compensate immediately. We'd have to run to where we'd see that new instrument flying to catch it almost every time. And we'd have to then confer with each other. 'OK, Rick, tonight when you threw it to me, I had to run way over toward the right. So the next time, imagine you're throwing it toward the left.' "

Vinny Appice was replaced by Myron Grombacher.

Kenny Aaronson: "I rehearsed drummers without Rick. He said, 'You audition these guys and let me know what you think.' Myron was about the last guy that came in. We couldn't find the right person. I wanted somebody that not only could groove but that could play their ass off. It was either people could play but they didn't know how to keep time or they kept time but they were so boring they didn't do anything, they didn't have the right combination of things at the time. I thought Myron was the guy."

Rick Derringer: "Myron had been very interested in acting and that drama kind of direction. So he brought that kind of experience with him. He started out just performing specifically without even knowing any music. In other words he really was an entertainer in the truest sense. So when he came for the open tryout was where we recognized him. He would climb all over the drums. He was very dramatic. He wanted to make contact with the audience and that really was always as impressive. To me, like I say, music is as much a communication with the audience as it is an aesthetic kind of head-trip. If it doesn't work with the audience then to me it's kind of a pointless exercise. It's about communication."

Author: "When you moved on to 'If I Weren't So Romantic I'd Shoot You,' you hooked up with Mike Chapman and Nicky Chinn. Was it experimenting to find somebody that could bring that winning sound to the table?"

Rick Derringer: "Exactly. We were looking for that producer that could do that. But in some ways, once again, I wouldn't necessarily like all the directions they were taking me in. But rather than do battle with them, we really fell into that trap where, 'Well, you must know what you're doing, Mike, so we'll do whatever you say.' And in the end, it's not one of my favorite albums. Mike has something to do with that. We did everything we thought was right and so did he. But it didn't become an interactive relationship where we were involved enough to make it what we wanted it to be."

Kenny Aaronson: "We were listening to these records that Mike had done at the time and had success with. Suzi Quatro and Sweet and all this stuff. And we thought that maybe Mike would be great. And some of his magic would rub off on us. But of course it didn't [laughs]!"

Rick Derringer: " 'If I Weren't So Romantic I'd Shoot You' was a lyric written by Bernie Taupin and Alice Cooper. I'd met Bernie and I knew Alice. I was seeking outside lyrics to try and find something that was inspirational. And that was one of the lyrics that came my way. I just thought it was [laughs] a cool one! So we used it. And it's one of the more interesting songs that I've recorded. And certainly is an interesting lyric. There aren't many lyrics out there written by Alice Cooper and Bernie Taupin, who are both great lyricists."

Author: "With the totally different sounds of 'Derringer,' 'Sweet Evil' and 'If I Weren't So Romantic,' did you feel you were attracting a broader audience?"

Rick Derringer: "No. I think what I was doing was turning people off. They started to get the impression that I didn't know what I was. That I didn't really stand for one kind of thing. I think they sensed that I was trying too hard for success and not just simply playing the music that I thought they deserved. So that whole experience had been a great learning experience for me. And what I've tried the last five to six years is really to get into doing the music that I wanna do. And the music that I found out on the road that the people really like. And not so much just trying to get a hit! I think doing the best music you know how to do and being true to your heart is how you theoretically can get a hit. But this whole thing about just pandering, making it look like you're trying to get a hit so bad, is not very attractive."

Author: "But you didn't feel that it would come back to bite you on the ass?"

Rick Derringer: "Oh, no. We did the best we could. We thought we were doing what the record business required of us. A guy told me a story once. He said, 'Your problem was you were listening to these A&R men.' I said, 'I thought that was what you were supposed to do.' He said, 'No. An A&R man is really a frustrated musician. He's usually a lawyer, someone who hasn't made it as a musician, that always looks up to a musician and knowing that the musician knows more than the A&R man knows. When an A&R man says to you, 'There's a problem with this demo you're bringing me. It needs the guitar to be louder,' what the guy is really saying to you is he does perceive a problem somewhere. But if you go in there and turn the guitar up because he said that's what the problem was, that A&R man is going to go, 'Well, he doesn't know any more than I know!' And he said, 'What you have to do is you have to learn that when he perceives a problem that means that there probably is something that needs to be fixed. But it's your job to figure out what it is. Go in there and fool the guy by finding what it was that he never suspected. Then you've won the A&R man over.' And that's probably pretty correct."

Kenny Aaronson: "We were like two different entities. We were this band that would grope around trying to find a sound in the studio. And we would inject some new tunes from whatever that current record was. But we would still do this live set with this long guitar solo at the end. The live approach was completely over the top, head banging, take no prisoners kind of thing. We just went out to kick ass. That was it. We were not subtle."

Rick Derringer: "I think there was some major problems in the record company itself. We certainly were making records that everybody still tells me all the time how much they love. And that was one of them. I hear that all the time. People love 'Lawyers, Guns and Money.' And I certainly liked it by Warren Zevon. It's why I did it in the first place. So, I really do feel one of the major problems was within Blue Sky Records."

Author: "From your commencement with Johnny Winter you were always in the CBS corner. Had you ever considered approaching other labels?"

Rick Derringer: "No. Steve Paul had managed to get us a lot of advances. He could get a big chunk of that as his commission each time. And we had a nice long-term contract over there. Most of the artists I was working with were over there. So we didn't try to go anywhere else. We were ensconced in that company. I was always a guy that was so happy being a part of the music business and out there, successful and playing and stuff, that I didn't question what was going on around me very often. I've played concerts as much as anybody in the world has played concerts. I had enough money to pay my bills. My accountants did that for me. So I never bothered to find out how much I was charging. It wasn't important. All that was important was being able to do them."

Author: "In retrospect, would you have taken a different approach?"

Rick Derringer: "I would run my own business. Would I have changed things when I was younger? You can't. But if I had been a smarter guy or had a little better managerial direction, somebody would have told me these things and I would have taken more control in my own business. I would have been more cognizant of those kinds of things. I would have tried to stay true to my heart a little more. I was the kind of guy that would never really discuss those kinds of things. I was very proud. I would never admit, in those days, that I was having problems. I would only admit how great things were going and how much I loved my life. Those were always very quiet and private thoughts. I wish I had been more open about those kinds of things because people probably would have told me, 'Hey, Rick. You better take more control in your career here.' But I was very proud. Never let on to anybody about those kinds of thoughts.

"I think they (Blue Sky) advanced tours and they were always interested in making money on their tours. But I don't think they were ever interested enough in the careers they were creating for their bands. They had a short-sided interest."

1979

The next solo release was entitled "Guitars and Women." Rick and Rick Neilson from Cheap Trick co-wrote two of the songs that appear on the release, which was produced by Todd Rundgren.

Rick Derringer: "I went to write some songs with Rick. He had a couple of songs that he thought were perfect for us that they hadn't done. So I heard those two songs. They were the kind of rock that the record really didn't have at that point. I thought they would be perfect. Also, Rick and his guys had become friends and we were close. And they felt like their success and their name would also help me generate some success with the record. So they were just trying to be helpful in more than just supplying songs. Todd and Rick Neilson and I, we were all thinking in the same direction, all trying to achieve the same goals. But, once again, we had to be in tune with the record company and I don't think they were able to hold up their end, quite frankly."

Liz Derringer: "When Rick did the record with Todd Rundgren, that was a great record. I'm really surprised, and everybody else was, that it didn't do better. 'Guitars and Women.' There were great songs on there. I wish that record had done better because he deserved it."

Rick Derringer: "Kenny was on some of the 'Guitars and Women' record. But Donnie Kisselbach was there for the majority of it. I felt that 'Guitars and Women' had more vocal stuff and I wanted a band that could help me with the vocals. And that included Jimmy Wilcox and Benji King. And that became the band to specifically fill that void. I wanted guys that could all sing as well as play."

Kenny Aaronson: "I don't even like talking about that record. I was on the outs and I was not being treated nicely by Rick at that point. Rick was basically firing me from the band. He said to me, 'You can do this record if you want to

Cleveland, Ohio, 1979.
Courtesy Scott Pickard

but you're not gonna be in this band any longer.' I decided I would try recording on that record knowing I was being fired. That was the end of it with Rick for me. I would tell him to his face. I have no qualms about it. If he has any brain left he should remember the way I was dealt with. And he would know why I'm saying what I'm saying now. He was letting go of me after me being with him for a long time. But I did half that record and it was very uncomfortable for me. I don't even like being associated with that record.

"He was just moving to another place, felt he needed to do something else and I wasn't right for it. And he probably thought it was time for Kenny to move on and it would be

better for Kenny. And in that sense he was right. It was time for Kenny to move on. But I didn't know it at the time. I was so hung up on being part of a band that I was probably afraid of what the future might hold. So in a sense Rick did the best thing by doing it. But it was very hurtful to me at the time. And I don't forget that. So I still have to express that side of it although it allowed me to become a better musician sooner than later."

A really good record passed unnoticed. Frustrated that bringing in producers wasn't working, Rick produced his own work on "Face to Face."

Rick Derringer: "I never wanted to not produce. It was just that one with Todd specifically to try and bring in a team. Even if we weren't getting the success we wanted, we had set a goal for ourselves and established a direction. And I think in the 'Face to Face' record, we continued in that direction. We weren't out there pandering. We weren't doing this 'heavy metal' kind of rock thing. We were trying to be more musical and achieve the goals that we had set for ourselves. So I didn't really keep thinking that we necessarily pursue finding other people to help. I had felt that they had come in and done their job and they had helped me establish a direction that I liked."

Author: "Was the band maybe a little radio exposure from making a difference?"

Kenny Aaronson: "If we'd had the right record. But I don't think we ever really did. I never really thought much about that stuff. I cared to play live and to rock and to travel and to tour and to party every night and to get chicks. That's what we were into. We were kids, man. We're on the Aerosmith tour. We're opening up for Zeppelin. We're on the Boston tour. We're on the Peter Frampton tour. We're on all these big festivals with Jeff Beck and all these different bands. We were there when everything was happening. We loved the lifestyle. We loved going from town to town. Another show, another night in a hotel. 'Let's hit the road.' We were just so into it."

Author: "So you were playing the music for all the right reasons?"

Kenny Aaronson: "Oh, man, that's rock 'n' roll! That's what it's all about! When I played with Rick I can't even think about how many people I played in front of in three and a half years. It must have been a million. We didn't stop. We played the biggest coliseums and the smallest clubs. Whenever something was happening in any city, we were there. And we kicked ass. It was great.

"We never found ourselves as a recording band. We were a high-energy live band. We were great as headliners in clubs. And we were great as a support band for larger acts. We never found our true selves and were able to record that. And build upon that. That's the thing that never happened with us."

But with yet another disappointing result, a serious change was due.

Rick Derringer: "We had no contract. Steve had always said, and it ended up being a good thing, 'Why do we need a contract to say that we're obligated to be together? If it's not working for you, Rick, then it probably isn't working for me either. As a manager.' He had this with all his artists. 'So if we come to that point, why would I want to keep you with me? Or why would you want to stay with me?' Whether that's a great philosophy or not, from a business point of view, it really became easy for the day I wanted to go out on my own. I didn't think Blue Sky was really helping me and I wanted a little more independence and a little less of being told what to do. It was easy for me to call up Steve and just say, 'It's not working for me. And so I'm going to exercise that option and try to find some other direction. Some other manager or some other record company.'

"Even if I didn't have a contract with Steve as a manager, I still had a contract with Blue Sky that they used with CBS to supply Rick Derringer records. So that's what I used to leave Steve as an artist. When the record contract ran out, I called Steve and said, 'Now we'll part ways because we can do it ethically and legally.' The last work was the 'Face To Face' album.

"Steve likes to be mysterious. He never liked his picture taken. He wanted to concentrate on his artists. He wanted them to have the limelight, not him. And he always used Bob Dylan as an example of being mysterious. He said, 'If you don't tell a writer something, they're going to have to make up something. And sometimes what they made up is better than what you'd tell them.' In the case of Bob Dylan, when Bob first came on the scene in the 60s, he didn't give any interviews at all. And so the stuff that was written about him was totally fictitious in most cases. And it turned him into this mythological folk singer character from points unknown!"

Danny Johnson: "Steve Paul's very, very eccentric. He probably wouldn't talk to me if I called. I remember he wore very expensive suits and house shoes. He would drag his clothes bag through the airport and this really expensive suit would be all dirty and wrinkled. He just would throw it away and buy a new one. I don't get it. But I thought he was a great manager. I wasn't really managed by him; I was just in the band. But they were in sync pretty good. Later I think Steve was really more getting into movies, probably a little bored with the rock 'n' roll thing. He was getting more into David Johansson, who was Buster Poindexter. And I think he was more getting into that Broadway thing 'cuz he goes all the way back to managing Tiny Tim and stuff like that. Which we know he must have some kind of talent to make that thing happen."

Chuck Ruff: "When I got married to Moni, we had a great bash. Edgar and his then wife Barbara were there, as were Rick and Liz. Rick's brother Randy was hanging out with Steve Paul, if you know what I mean. They were there. Ronnie and his wife, Jill, and their kid Jesse was there. Bill Church, Sammy Hagar was there. That was the first time I ever met Sammy. He was one weird dude [laughs]. This was May 6, 1973. And a lot that were there aren't with us anymore. Dan was there, God rest his soul. Jerry was there, God rest his soul. Why is it that all the good guys have to die and the boneheads like Steve Paul end up with all the money? The reason he won't talk to you is that he doesn't want to have to face the truth."

1982

Rick Derringer: "Rich Little had a TV show in the late 70s, early 80s, and I met Cyndi Lauper while doing that show. She was with a group called Blue Angel. And she was pretty impressive. Blue Angel's records had kind of dwindled and they weren't doing as good as the record company had hoped. And I think they were being dropped, actually. And everybody was trying to get her to do a solo thing. She was so loyal to Blue Angel, she said, 'I'm not gonna do it.' So I said, 'I will help you try to do one more demo with Blue Angel. I understand you want to be committed to this band, and all I know is, you've got some good songs. So let's go in and make a demo.' So I ended up taking Blue Angel into a studio that I was working in at that time and we did three or four songs. I thought they came out great but I don't think it changed people's minds in the record business. She then went ahead and met David Wolff, who really wanted to help her. He was pretty well-connected over at Epic Records. And what they did was they took the demos I did for Blue Angel. David had enough 'talkability,' we'll call it. He was able to sway her opinion and talk her into doing the 'solo thing,' finally. And she was swayed also by the people at Epic. 'Cuz they really were interested and they had a lot of confidence in her ability. So those demos that I did for Blue Angel were, in effect, the ones that got her a record deal."

Author: "How did you end up touring as Cyndi Lauper's guitarist?"

Rick Derringer: "We had been in touch quite a bit. Her and David Wolff both were into the wrestling. And wrestling and rock were getting closer and closer together. David had looked at my work and said, 'Rick seems like the perfect guy to come in and produce these wrestlers [laughs]!' So David called me up and got me involved with the WWF wrestling album, which I produced most of. Cyndi produced a couple of songs and a couple of other guys did a song each. And then the second wrestling album, I pretty much produced the whole album.

"Cyndi went out on the road with the band that did the second album, the 'True Colors' album. The guitar player was a kid from Canada, Aldo Nova. He wore leopard-skin tights. I remember [laughs] long-haired, rock 'n' roll guitar-playing guy. Had a couple of hits on his own. Pretty big records. They had started on their tour in Japan. And I guess Aldo just did not get along with David Wolff at all. One day he got on the bus and in the middle of one disagreement with David Wolff called him a 'fuckin' Jew bastard.' David didn't like that very much but said nothing about it at that second. But at the first opportunity he called me up and he said, 'Do you think you could fly to Australia, which is where we're going next, to do the rest of the world tour?' And I said, 'Well, I don't have anything else that important that I'm doing right this second. And that sounds like it would be fun.' He thought that if I could see one show, that I'd be able to start the very next show. So he put me in the audience, way back in the back, in Sydney, Australia, and he had me watch the show. And after he said, 'Do you think you could start tomorrow in Melbourne?' And I said, 'Yeah, I don't think there'd be a problem doing that. I think I know the stuff enough. You know, we could fake our way through it. It would be fine.'

"So then he called up Aldo and said, 'Well, I've got Rick Derringer to come in and fill your shoes [laughs]! Aldo got together with me afterwards and said, 'You know, I would normally be mad at somebody else taking over this gig, this is my gig.' But he said, 'You're the only guy that I can ever imagine being able to fill my shoes [laughs]!' So I completed the rest of the world tour. That was the tour where we ended up doing the 'Live From Paris' video. I think it's a really good video. It shows her singing some of her best stuff. And it's a great band that she put together for that video."

Author: "How did the idea for DNA come about?"

Carmine Appice: "After I played with Rod Stewart my following in Japan at that time was really big. Rick was basically living here (Los Angeles). I used to see Rick here and there. I'd had this tour lined up for Japan in March of '82 in support of my solo album. The promoter in Japan called me up and said, 'Look, can you put a supergroup together? Call it Carmine Appice and Friends, Rock Supersession Volume 1.' I thought about who I'd like to play with. Rick was a person I'd always admired as a player. So I asked him if he'd wanna go and he said 'Yeah.' We took Tom Peterson. We took Eric Carmen, which is an off-the-wall choice. And Dwayne Hitchings, who, at the time, was my best buddy and co-writer of a lot of songs. So we went to Japan and played about six or eight shows, including The Budokan. And it went so well that I said to Rick, 'You know, I'm releasing the album in America. Why don't you come on tour in America with me too?' "

Rick Derringer: "We came back to the U.S. and started playing a little more with Tim Bogert over here. Carmine had a solo album out at the time. I found that the production wasn't quite up to snuff. So I suggested that I help him with his next record."

Carmine Appice: "Spencer Proffer said, 'Maybe you and Rick should do a record together. We actually wrote some songs, put it all together and recorded it in ten days and called it DNA."

Rick Derringer: "I still envisioned making Carmine's record and I still think that would have been the best idea. 'Derringer 'n Appice' was kind of forced together for this one record. It wasn't really a thing we had envisioned doing for the rest of our lives. Our hearts weren't in it as much as it would have been if it were just simply a Carmine Appice solo record."

Carmine Appice: "We got a deal on Boardwalk Records. We did a video. 'Doctors of the Universe' came out and started doing really great on radio, man. It was going up in the Top 40 airplay. And the fuckin' record company went out of business [laughs]! Me and Rick were like, 'I can't believe it!' 'Cuz this was a big shot for us. We were on MTV five times a day with the video. We had the airplay goin'. And we had already done shows with the support of my tour. The attendance was great when we did these shows. And then

when the label went out of business it was very hard to find another label in midstream so it sorta fell apart."

Author: "Was there a chance DNA would have continued?"

Rick Derringer: "If the success would have remained with it, yeah. You come out, you get the idea, you put out the project ... if people love it, and they only have one way to show that is by sales, then you go ahead and continue with it. And if they don't, which is shown by lack of sales, then you just kind of toss it to the side. It's that way with my song-writing. I write a lot of songs. But the ones that stick, the ones that people prove that they like by buying them over and over again, are the ones we continue playing. Now we have an opportunity for a new medium to gauge these things. And that would be write-ins on our Web site bulletin board and things like that. Those are the people we're playing for."

Carmine Appice: "A lot of us from that era, now we're like the old football players. Normally our record deals are not with majors because the majors are signing young kids now. So you do big indies, you deal with the bullshit. But as long as you can make some decent money and go out and play, that's what it's all about. I feel I've been lucky. I've been able to do this for thirty-something years now and Rick's been doing it longer than me."

•   •   •

As Rick was one of the first to expose me to noticing guitar effects, I was curious if he built his own pedal boxes.

Rick Derringer: "I did for a while. Eventually I had a whole huge guitar system that I was taking around with me. Every kind of effect that I liked. And they could all be patched together in different ways. It was very sophisticated. Cost quite a bit. Eventually it was stolen. The whole equipment truck at that time was stolen. And I was never able to replace that again.

"We were playing a concert one night at The Palladium in New York City. I lived on 13th Street in the West Village. The den of my house was right on the sidewalk level, with the windows facing right out onto the street. A beautiful wooded block we lived on. After the concert, all the road crew and band had come back to my house to have a cola before everybody went home. We were all sitting around in the den. The equipment truck was parked in front of the house. It was a beautiful summer night. We had the windows open. And we heard the truck start up. Everybody looked around the room. 'Who's starting up the truck?' And at the very second that we realized we were all there, the truck pulled away. Everyone went running out into the street to hop into available cars to try and chase this truck. But by the time they all got in their cars and started driving, the truck was out of sight. Eventually one guitar was recovered. The police told us that they spotted a known convicted burglar driving down the street. They pulled him over for a routine check and he had that one guitar in his car. But did that lead to having any of the remaining equipment to be returned? No. We lost everything."

A benefit concert was recorded and released as "Derringer & Friends" on King Biscuit Records. The benefit was held to raise funds to replace the stolen gear.

Rick Derringer: "That's exactly right. It was a pretty good benefit that was held at The Palladium."

"A lot of people came to help out. Hall & Oates were there. Ted Nugent. Carmine Appice and Tim Bogert. Ian Hunter. Carla DeVito. Lorna Luft. My manager Jake Hooker and I put this together. He was married to Lorna at the time. We had a full house that night. Of course, you can't donate the cost of the people's salaries. Ushers, security. We did have some direct costs. But after those costs were paid we ended up with enough money to buy everybody a new amplifier. Everybody got a new guitar. The drummer got a set of drums. Nothing like what was stolen. I mean, we had really classic instruments stolen. Custom-made stuff. Custom-made guitar racks, effects racks. Things that could never be replaced.

"Eventually I got to the point where I am nowadays, which is I use very few of those kinds of things. The opportunity to use everything I wanted to only showed me that the more things you put between the guitar and the amplifier, the less guitar comes out. So my approach nowadays is to put as few things between the guitar and the amplifier so you hear more of the guitar. And less of the effects."

Author: "How do you compensate for some of the effects?"

Rick Derringer: "I don't. Jeff Beck told me once that he really preferred the sound of the clear guitar as opposed to the sound through any effect. The guitar synthesizer taught me the same kind of thing. When the guitar synthesizer came along I grabbed one o those right away and started playing it in the shows. I'd stop in the middle of the shows and do a guitar solo. And I thought, 'Now I'm going to be really cool and have this big dramatic sound available to me all of a sudden. It's going to be the guitar playing the synthesizer.' And I went out and did that enough times to learn that the audience wasn't hearing guitar anymore. And rather than being very impressed they were just very confused. So I really learned the validity of the guitar. The guitar is very cool all by itself. Unadorned, without effects. And sometimes those effects weaken, just dilute that authority and attractiveness of the guitar. People love the sound of the guitar. Enhancement doesn't necessarily help it."

• • • •

Rick's session work resumé is as impressive as anyone else's. His introduction to this work was a session he recorded for The Osmonds.

Rick Derringer: "I was working with Jerry Goldstein, the ex-producer of The McCoys. I had just started working with Johnny Winter. He called me up and wanted to know if I wanted to freelance on several records that he was producing in California without FGG. He asked me if I wanted to play guitar for a group called The Osmond Brothers. They had appeared on the 'Andy Williams Show,' so people knew about them, but they hadn't really 'made' it. Jerry was producing a song called 'Flower Music.' He told us how great the Osmonds were and how genuinely nice and gentlemanly they were. The great manners they had. And he admonished all the musicians before they got there that they were very religious and they didn't say any foul words, and they didn't wanna hear any of 'em. 'So all you musicians, be cool in their presence.' Everybody had to watch their language and be nice [laughs]!"

(l-r, Lorna Luft, Edgar Winter, Rick Derringer, Dr. John, Todd Rundgren, Bebe Buell.)
Benefit concert, The Palladium, New York City, 1982.
Courtesy Rick Derringer

Author: "Do you remember what you got paid?"

Rick Derringer: "Jerry paid me pretty good. $700, probably."

Rick has done session work for numerous acts: Alice Cooper, Kiss, Steely Dan, Meatloaf, Todd Rundgren and Barbra Streisand to name but a few. I was curious as to whether it was the challenge or the variety that interested him.

Rick Derringer: "In those days it was really a combination of things. Whenever an artist would present themselves and it was interesting … like Barbra Streisand or Air Supply or Bonnie Tyler, a lot of those things came through my work with Jim Steinman, who was fun to work with. But it was also an attempt to try different things. I've worked with a lot of different artists. I was doing some jingles at that time. I did a Budweiser commercial where I played the jingle as an

instrumental but sounding like ZZ Top. That was kind of fun to do. I did a lot of stuff for some jingle houses in New York. To me the music business is good because you don't just have to do one thing. You don't have to be just a guy that plays guitar. You can write. You can produce. You can publish. You can travel around and do concerts. You can discover artists. You can play on other people's records. It's just such a big ballpark. It's a way of keeping it interesting.

"After a while I grew disenchanted with playing on other people's records. And that was just because it's hard to be bossed around, frankly. They have an idea of what they want you to do. You'll come in, and they'll say, 'I want you to play this kind of a solo.' Me, as a guitarist, I would think, 'OK, I understand what you mean' and I would do what I thought was the best in that respect. If they said, 'No, try something more like this,' I might try that thing. But I obviously thought that what I did at first was better. And just that whole style of working, trying to please somebody else, I got tired of doing that. And I stopped doing sessions a lot, for a while, just because I wanted to be my own boss and not have somebody else telling me what to do [laughs]!"

Author: "How did you get involved with Al Yankovic?"

Rick Derringer: "OK, I'll tell you the story of Weird Al. Weird Al had been interested in playing the accordion and had interest in writing the parodies. But mostly he was a real Dr. Demento fan."

"Weird" Al Yankovic: "I started listening to the Dr. Demento show in my early teens. A friend of mine told me to turn on KMET. 'There's this guy playing all these weird songs on the radio.' So I turned it on and there was Dr. Demento playing all these comedy and novelty recordings that I'd never heard before. Some really bizarre things. And I thought, 'Well, this is really different. You never hear this kinda stuff broadcast over the radio.' My mom wasn't really fond of the show because it could get a little off color. So I sometimes would have to hide my little clock radio under the covers at night and listen to the show. And it was a big part of my life. That was my Sunday night, listening to Dr. Demento.

"I played the accordion and came up with funny little songs once in a while. Before long a friend said, 'You know, you should send your stuff to the Demento show.' And he twisted my arm enough that I recorded a song in my bedroom and sent it in and he played it on the radio. Which blew my mind, you know. A fifteen-year-old kid getting a song played on the radio. And it kinda took off from there. Dr. Demento encouraged me to send him more. And the sound quality got better and better. And by the time I graduated from college I had a couple of nationally released records."

Rick Derringer: "He used the Dr. Demento show to play his first parody song on the air, 'Another One Rides The Bus.' And because the Queen song has a big bass drum that's featured, he used a fist on the accordion case to simulate the big bass drum and he played the music on the accordion. Besides the lyric being funny, 'Another One Rides The Bus,' what I really thought was funny was the whole picture. Weird Al, in his funny little voice, singing it, playing it on the accordion instead of the pompous, over-produced rock record. And pounding on the accordion case instead of the bass drum. I found that whole thing very funny. And so did the audience. It became very well-requested. I believe Dr. Demento released it on one of his records. But it gave Al the idea that he wanted to make a single. So he wrote a song called 'I Love Rocky Road,' which was a parody of the hit record 'I Love Rock 'n' Roll.' Jake Hooker, along with Al Merrill, is the writer of that song. In order to release a single of a parody, because you are taking someone else's song and incorporating your own lyric, you have to go to the original writer and work out a new publishing deal or a writer deal. You have to get permission. Can you call yourself half-writer? How much of the royalty is to be shared? Things like that."

"Weird" Al Yankovic: "And Jake also managed, at the time, Rick Derringer. So when my manager, Jay Levy, contacted Jake to get permission, Jake got excited by the whole idea. 'Well, this is a really great concept and I can see this really working. And I'll bet Rick Derringer would love to be involved in the project.' "

Rick Derringer: "Jake brought the tape to me and played it and asked what I thought. I really liked it. As a kid, my parents had a big Spike Jones collection. He took the best musicians of his day, like Gene Krupa on drums, part of the Tommy Dorsey band, just the best musicians and he made comedy records. And they were very good, musically. And they were very successful as far as sales went. People loved them. And growing up I was conscious of records like 'Purple People Eater' and 'Ahab the Arab' and on and on. Alan Sherman's records. All those kind of records. I thought they were really funny. And one of the things that struck me about them was that once they come out, they have no competition. If you bring out the latest rock 'n' roll, heavy metal kind of song, there might be twenty other heavy metal bands competing with you that day. But a parody artist usually has no competition in the marketplace. So if he brings out a song that's really funny, that's the one!

"So I said, 'This is a great idea. You've found a great novelty artist.' And I also thought it would be a great addition to my production career. But I said, 'This is stupid to make just a single. Let's do an album. Does he have enough material?' And sure enough he had plenty of great songs. We went to Cherokee Recording Studios in Hollywood. They thought it was a good idea too so they didn't charge us for the time until after we had made the record. We were able to make an entire album."

"Weird" Al Yankovic: "The sessions were very quick. In retrospect I'm certainly not embarrassed by it. It certainly doesn't have the production value of any of my later albums. The whole thing was done on spec and nobody wanted to waste any time. Cherokee was basically giving us the time for free unless we got a record deal. In which case they would get paid a premium rate. A percentage of the album [laughs]. Cherokee ended up doing quite well for their faith in the project. But at the time everybody was basically working for free and everything was done very quickly. I think we did ten basic tracks in three hours. We went through one, maybe two takes of each song. 'Well, maybe that one was a little fast but, you know, it's good enough!' I could be wrong but I think we recorded and mixed the whole album in, like, a week [laughs]. And it was fun. It was exciting. I'd never done an album before. And it was a real thrill to be working with Rick. I'd been a fan of his since I was a kid. The whole experience was really great."

Rick Derringer: "We shopped the album around and Scotti Brothers ended up being the label that picked it up. And it was exactly like we had figured. The first one was a big hit. I went on to do five albums with Weird Al. We won two Grammy's. One for the best comedy album. That was the one that included 'Eat It.' Number 1 hit single. And a Grammy for the best video for 'Who's Fat?' "

"Weird" Al Yankovic: "It's pretty amazing. It's cliché but it's the respect of your peers. People in the Academy are vot-

ing for it. It's definitely ranked up there with my most prized possessions. It's really a thrill to have won. Unfortunately, I mean this is a whole different rant, they changed the category several years ago from 'Best Comedy Recording' to 'Best Spoken Word Comedy.' Which means I have virtually no chance of ever winning a Grammy again or even being nominated. Which I'm upset about. It's like the 'Yankovic Exclusionary Rule.' All comedy except Al [laughs]!"

Rick Derringer: "I thought this was really going to help my production career. But one of the reasons I stopped working with Weird Al was I was getting artists coming to me and saying, 'Hey, man, can you produce my album? What have you been doing lately?' And as soon as they'd hear about Weird Al, they'd say, 'Oh, you've turned into a "novelty producer!" And here I am back in the whole bubble gum thing! I've got this whole image stamped on me, for right or wrong, of something that's got negative connotations. I couldn't believe it! Here we were, re-creating the biggest hits of the day … Quincy Jones records. Police records. It doesn't matter who the artists are, we're re-creating their records and making big hits at the same time. And all of a sudden, I'm looked at as something less than a real producer! It was ridiculous. It was absolutely crazy. And I lost my interest in the whole thing."

"Weird" Al Yankovic: "I decided pretty quickly that I wasn't going to have a recording career with just an accordion and a guy banging on my case. Ever since 'Another One Rides The Bus' took off … when I did that song on the Dr. Demento show I wasn't thinking I was recording a master of a song that was going to be with me forever. But that's kinda what happened [laughs]."

Rick Derringer: "Also, we got to the point where I found that what was funny in the beginning wasn't being pursued anymore. As Weird Al got more successful his record company allocated a bigger budget every time. All of a sudden we were now in the studio doing a Quincy Jones/ Michael Jackson parody but we would actually be using Quincy Jones programs for the synthesizers. We would be trying to simulate the music exactly. What I found funny about it was the accordion. The contrast of taking these slick songs and doing them in a funny way. It was not only the lyric but the whole picture was funny. But we weren't pursuing it anymore. We were spending days and days on end with Weird Al trying to get his vocal more perfect. And I'd be going, 'Al, you know, this isn't funny [laughs]!' "

Author: "Was he becoming a parody of himself?"

Rick Derringer: "I guess in some ways you can say that. It's true. His records aren't selling as well anymore. They aren't as funny anymore is why. He can still do a funny video. The ideas are still there. But he has just gotten into this whole Hollywood thing of making it so slick and so perfect that the ingredients that made it funny just aren't there anymore."

"Weird" Al Yankovic: "There's actually two schools of thought. They're both funny to me. To me it's a kind of a practical joke for somebody to be listening to the radio and hear one of my parodies come on and get sucked into thinking, 'Oh, this is Nirvana. This is the Chili Peppers.' And all of a sudden it's nothing like either one of those. And I try and add little quirks here and there. I'll replace the guitar solo with an accordion solo. Or do something a little out of the ordinary so it's not such a faithful re-creation. Like I said, there's two schools of thought. 'Another One Rides The Bus' is still a funny arrangement of that song. But since I've been doing this so long I've got a track record of quality, if you will. It would be difficult for me to go back to that kind of production."

Rick Derringer: "So I was becoming less and less infatuated because Al wouldn't listen to my input, my direction. He really wanted it to be slicker. And he wouldn't allow me to make it less slick in order to make it funny. And the whole image of the novelty producer I did not like at all."

"Weird" Al Yankovic: "It was certainly nothing personal and it was certainly no reflection on his talent as a producer. It just got to the point where I felt like I could hold the reins by myself. Rick did an amazing job. But after all that time in

the studio I was feeling more and more comfortable and I guess I kinda became a control freak over the years. The same thing happened with my directing career. My manager directed all my videos in the 80s. Even though most of the creative input was coming from me, he was the guy in control. And at a certain point I just felt like I was able to direct myself. So it was very similar to what happened with Rick. I love Rick and it would be great to work with him at some point in the future. But I almost felt like I was wasting his time 'cuz I knew what I wanted and I pretty much knew how to get it."

Rick Derringer: "I used to tell people that the only novel thing about this is how hard Al works as opposed to the other artists I've worked with. He works twice as hard or harder. From that point of view, he's so conscientious, it's incredible! But I found that he was using that against himself."

"Weird" Al Yankovic: "I work really hard. I pay a lot of attention to detail. When I come into the studio I'm very prepared. I've got my three-ring notebook with the plastic dividers. I've got the charts written out. And I know what I want. It pretty much blows my mind how expensive studio time is. I still remember what it was like to work for $5.00 an hour in the mailroom. And to work in a place where it basically costs you forty bucks to go to the bathroom [laughs]! I like to walk into those situations knowing what I'm going to be doing and how I'm going to be doing it. Who's going to be doing it. What time they're going to be showing up. I just try to be as organized as possible."

Author: "So you *did* work in the mailroom at Westwood One."

"Weird" Al Yankovic: "Yep. I also graduated with a degree in architecture and proceeded never to use it. I worked for a couple of years doing whatever I could to pay for the music."

Rick Derringer: "There was an album in there called 'Good Dirty Fun,' when I was working with my manager,

Jake Hooker. He had some ties with Japan. We specifically recorded that with Japanese backers who advanced the money for that record. It was a record that I wrote most of the songs on. And it was a pretty good record. In fact, that's one of my favorites of all the albums. That one with 'All American Boy' is right up there at the top. 'Guitars and Women.' Those are my favorites that I made as solo records. I made 'Good Dirty Fun' while I was working with Weird Al.

"And when I stopped working with Weird Al, I specifically went right out on the road and started working and touring. It was during that touring that Mike Varney contacted me to see if I wanted to do an album for his label. 'Cuz I wasn't going to go out and do a bunch of demos of songs that I think are hit records and take myself around, as if I'm starting over, to all the major labels and try to compete with a bunch of young kids that the audience is going for. I said I refused to do that. I'm going to go out there and create a career that exists kind of from the grass roots up. I'm going to go out and get the livework and find an audience that likes what we do and let the thing grow in a more organic process. And that really is what's happening now. Mike Varney did find us and ask us to do those records. Which we did. And that led to the album that's out in Europe called 'Tend The Fire,' which we hope to have out here soon.

"I was managed by Teddy Slatus at that point. We had a couple of years where we were working together. Peter Fish and I went ahead and actually started making the record without any record company involved. He's the co-producer and owner of the studio. National Recording in the middle of Manhattan. They do *MTV Unplugged* and some VH1 programming. And then Teddy helped us shop the thing around and came up with Mike Vernon, the guy who started Code Blue Records. Mike Vernon was responsible for bringing the original Fleetwood Mac with Peter Green into the light. And I believe he did John Mayall's Bluesbreakers. A lot of the original, real roots music that came out of England, Mike Vernon was responsible for. He came to the U.S. and hooked up with Atlantic Records here. So we thought it was going to be a great situation. Here's this legendary guy who had a lot of good history behind him and

was with one of my favorite labels, certainly. Atlantic. But as it turns out he didn't really promote the label very much over here. Code Blue just dropped the ball. So Atlantic dropped Code Blue. And, as it turned out, it was a day before our record was to be released in the U.S. So 'Tend The Fire' got dropped at the same time. In some ways that's bad because it didn't get released in the U.S. properly, but in another way it's good because it wasn't just tossed aside. So we still have the opportunity to do something with it and we're still working on that now."

•　　•　　•

One of the sadder results of the demise of "Johnny Winter And …" was the way it affected Randy Jo Hobbs.

Nevin Doll: "I met Randy Hobbs in '78 at a favorite hangout called Tommy's Pastime, a beer joint there in Union City. Still there today. He'd come in there and we'd sit and usually drink screwdrivers at the bar. Randy Zehringer was still in the area at that time. I probably didn't meet Rick until about '79 or '80 when he used to come back for Muscular Dystrophy shows and The Union City Merchant's Day Parade.

"In 1978, Randy was pretty much shoved out, packed and sent home. And that's when he pretty heavily got on drugs. Cocaine and heavy drinking. He was pretty much a mess in '78. And as a matter of fact so was I. But he didn't push too hard as far as his future went in music at that year or after that. He just pretty much played in local bands. He lived with his mother. He had to. He didn't really have any royalties, so to speak, from anything. If he did it was very, very little. Whether it had been from the McCoys or Johnny Winter, I don't even know.

"He did a lot for people around there. He did a lot for me. He was pretty much a special friend at that time. Very bighearted. We had a lot of good times together. There was never a serious moment. If Randy tried to get serious anybody who was around him or whoever he was talking to would end up laughing. He was a complete cut-up.

"The best memories, that I recall him talking about, were during the 'Johnny Winter And … Live' album. He loved to host and keep the party going. And that's pretty much what they did during that tour. He talked a lot about the stage. There was many a time when he'd set his guitar down and go out into the crowd while the music was playing! Shake hands and dance and do whatever he wanted to do down there. And they had to coax him back on the stage. I said, 'Gosh, Randy, where does that leave everybody else?' And he'd say, 'They'll be alright.' I imagine it didn't go over well with them. And he talked a lot about the end with Johnny. It wasn't Johnny's decision because Johnny had a heroin problem at the time and for a long time. And I don't know that Randy didn't have a heroin problem. I'm pretty sure he did. He didn't by the time he came home but he was pretty ripped up over it. And Teddy Slatus pretty much cut corners. There are five words, 'under the urging of Teddy,' which ended Randy's career. Teddy kinda controls everything. And I think that a lot of people can see that because Johnny was powerful at one time. Not just physically but mentally. And this guy comes in in the middle of a $600,000 Columbia contract and takes it over. I call him 'the puppetmaster.' And not to degrade Johnny. That's just the way I feel. Randy just went to pieces after that. He was sent home with his bags. And it was pretty much all downhill."

Author: "Would it be fair to say that he never recovered from that?"

Nevin Doll: "No, he never recovered. Exactly. He was bitter about it. There wasn't much bitterness to Randy but you could hear it in his voice. He'd say, 'Well, I still call Sue once in a while.' She was Johnny's wife at the time. He called Sue a lot. And Sue was pretty much upset for Randy having been thrown out. But that ended Randy. And he never had a good word to say about Teddy."

Edgar Winter: "It was distressing to see Randy in later years. When I did see him, he seemed to want to be playing more and wanting to do things. But his health was declining and he didn't seem to be completely himself. At that time I had grooves that were a little more progressive, and Randy wouldn't have been the right player for what I was doing. But we'd always sit around and joke and laugh about good times. I knew he had his share of problems but I never thought that he was on that kind of a negative downward spiral."

On August 5, 1993, Randy Jo Hobbs was found dead in a motel room.

Author: "Was Randy an inevitability?"

Rick Derringer: "Yeah. He was so incorrigible. He was such a nice guy on one hand, kind of a sweetheart. But on the other hand he just was never able to shake his fascination with drugs. He eventually moved back to the Midwest and couldn't afford to buy expensive drugs anymore, as he was living off the welfare state. And infatuated with prescription medication. He became really talented at being able to go to doctors and get all kinds of things. He would create, in himself, an imaginary facial tick, for instance. And then, because of that, he'd be able to go to a doctor and get some kind of medication to take care of that. Next thing you know, he'd be walking around with an inflatable splint on his leg. 'Oh, I need pain medication for this knee problem.' And it made him less and less of a vital, alive guy and more of a zombie."

Nevin Doll: "Scripts. He had parties and had a bowl of pills on the table. Different mixture of things. It was like hors d'oeuvres. And that's how he lived it every day. It was unbelievable. And drinking heavily on top of all that as well. I remember the true friends he did have would avoid him because they knew he was gonna be dead. And this was six years before he even died. They knew he was on his way out. Union City is an industrial town. Small. Depressed. And Randy, a legendary bass player, comes back to this depressed town and he's in real big trouble. And there's nobody there to really help him out. Union City had a lot of thugs that Randy hooked up with because the friends he did have avoided him. 'We're hanging around a big rock star. We'll give him anything he wants.' And that's pretty much what ended Randy. It started slowly but it ended quickly."

Rick Derringer: When we had heard that he had a heart attack at that age it became pretty obvious to everybody that, once again, the heart attack was related to another problem. In this case it was drugs and alcohol."

Author: "How did he die?"

Nevin Doll: "From what I heard, asphyxiation. He was in a bar with several of these so-called *friends* that he had. And I think he played a little bit of bass that night from what I heard. I wasn't there. He left these people there. They had a motel room they had rented there in Dayton. And when these guys came back he was face down on the motel floor. That was it. I don't know what's on his death certificate. But he just couldn't take it. His body gave up. He just didn't know when to stop and it stopped him. His forty-five-year-old heart just gave out. It was quick and easy. It was a small service. Quite a few people there. Buried in a Catholic cemetery outside of Union City. He's got a small but nice stone. Practically killed his mother. She was probably about seventy. She still can't talk about it. She lived every moment with him. They were pretty close."

Two days after interviewing Nevin Doll I received the following e-mail from him.

Nevin Doll: "I froze on our telephone conversation the other day. I felt reluctant to say what I had to say. I said I did not want to be the one to finish Randy's life with a down note. Although you said there is always the bad with the good, I felt the need to thoroughly look back upon the situation. My wife of thirteen years can remember our parties at his mother's trailer. At one time she had sneaked out her bedroom window and Randy thought she should go home as not to get into more trouble. The next night Randy asked if she got in trouble. She said, 'No, they didn't realize I was even gone.' Randy thought that was awful that her parents didn't notice. Leaving oneself to undoubtingly believe that Randy was bighearted and not just drug crazed. He had many of times talked about the little girl that he had wanted and the family of his own he craved. Who knows, he may have had one and never known it.

"One other thing Randy would demand if you were to party with him is that there always had to be a 'babysitter.' That is why Randy's parties were known as the 'Babysitter's Club Parties.' If you were to walk into Randy's house, you always expected there to be a bowl full of pills setting upon the coffee table. Black beauties, percodans, etc. So there was always one person selected, flip of a coin, whatever, to be the person to watch over the rest. At least he was responsible over the crowd. He would also get out his guitar and play, also sing, little ditties of destiny. He could also play a six string and sing very well. He wasn't just a bass player. Speaking of destiny, he would talk a lot of destiny when he was fucked up. He often asked, 'Do you believe that destiny is what you make of it? If destiny is real, than why in the hell am I back in this God forsaken town of Union City?' Just think, he started out with his mother here in Union City and it ended here as well. In 1965, 'Hang On Sloopy' fought with the Beatles' 'Yesterday,' on the number one chart. I remember one time at Tommy's Pastime, we were drinking a few, and Randy noticed the house band playing 'Hang On Sloopy,' and said, 'That's pretty good. They oughta record that.' On that particular day I didn't even think he knew what the song was. Randy was sent home a broken man, physically, mentally, and financially. Johnny Winter was a strong backbone at one time, until Teddy Slatus got a hold of him. I know that Johnny had all the help at the time for his heroin and other drug habits. Randy said that once he was hooked there was no help offered and the best thing to do was send him packing. This took the high life away but it didn't take the drug addiction away. So Randy was left to fend for himself. Randy was the most thoughtful and caring person, no matter how high he got! And one thing I can say is Randy walked upon the stage the night he died and played for a house band in Dayton, Ohio, and he walked off that stage and later fell dead. Teddy has to have a crew practically carry Johnny to the stage. I guess Randy didn't die in vain; he left an impression upon a lot of people. He was only controlled by the drugs that fueled his system and not by some puppet-master. I miss Randy very dearly and I feel that I must stop because I am getting pissed. Randy was like a war veteran that came back from Vietnam."

On March 22, 1994, Dan Hartman died of an AIDS-related illness.

Rick Derringer: "I had actually seen Dan several months before he died. He had told me that he had a cold and he couldn't shake it. I said, 'How long you been sick with this cold?' And he said, at that time, something like three months. And I said, 'Whoa, that seems a little long for a cold.' Then he

Randy Jo Hobbs 1948 – 1993.
Courtesy Liz Derringer

went through a period where you'd call him at his house and it always seemed like he'd try to pick a fight. Like he was trying to keep people away from him. I think he was trying to keep secret what was happening. And slowly it became visible that Dan was sick and there was something wrong. That he was not good. So it wasn't totally a surprise when it finally happened."

Author: "But you weren't aware of the seriousness of his illness?"

Rick Derringer: "No. Dan made it well known after the end of the Edgar Winter Group that he had come out of the closet. We had only known him as a heterosexual guy with the normal kind of girl problems that most guys have. Then at some point he announced to us that it had always been a struggle but he was really a homosexual. And he really came

blatantly out of the closet and didn't have a pretense of fooling around with girls anymore — at all. One of the things he became involved with was his friends were Freddie Mercury and people like that. We still got problems with it but that was the time when people didn't know that much about it or how to stay away from it. It was spreading like wildfire among that community. And that was at a time when Dan was really living that lifestyle. So when we found out his disease, whether it was pneumonia or whatever, was related to his having AIDS, people weren't really surprised."

Edgar Winter: "I didn't find out anything about that until after the band had long since broken up. Dan was, as far as any of us knew, straight during that entire time. He had a girlfriend. He had a bad relationship experience, which may have contributed to that whole thing. I really loved Dan and

I think he was a great talent and I miss him and his music. I think he left a great musical legacy. He was a very talented guy. Great producer. Great writer. Great player."

Chuck Ruff: "I didn't find out about it until I was in New York City playing with Hagar and opening up for Boston. Liz Derringer was working for *Interview* magazine and Edgar had just met Monique. I had Liz in one ear and Edgar in the other, in the dressing room, both telling me about Dan. My jaw was lying on the floor. I couldn't believe it. I felt this must have happened because of Steve Paul. And they both sort of gave me a nod and a wink. They never really confirmed that it had to do with Steve Paul. It was one of those things where some people think they have to do everything in the world to become a complete person. To me there are some things I don't even want to know about. Ignorance is bliss! But Dan never came out to me. When I found out that Dan had actually died, I couldn't believe it. I miss Dan. I loved the guy. He was a really cool person."

Liz Derringer: "This is when AIDS first started. We had never heard of it. And that was the biggest shock of all. I was in Westport the other day and I realized how much I missed Dan. It was horrible. He was a great guy. I had a lot of fun with Dan."

· · ·

Author: "With the constant work that Rick consumed himself with, it must have been awfully difficult to keep a relationship together."

Liz Derringer: "In the beginning I traveled a lot with him and I went to most of the sessions and was there all the time. But as time went on it gets so boring when you're not involved. And it did put a strain on the relationship. But it lasted for twenty-something years. Rick is a good kid. Until he got screwed up. He was a really great guy. He's funny. Talented. Liked to have fun. He fucked up too. He got on drugs too. At some point he started drinking and it got progressively worse over the years."

Author: "Why did he not start that until much later than everyone else?"

Liz Derringer: "Because of the business. What it does to you. It's a popularity contest and you're in one year and you're out the next. The critics would slam him for things. It's horrible. To be so high, with number one records, and then to be so low and nobody wants you. Imagine what that would do to you. And he hasn't changed. Times change.

"He had a great relationship with Steve Paul all those years. And Steve was very good to him. And the record company was very good to him. The records just started selling less. Maybe the music wasn't as good. Maybe Rick couldn't put his heart and soul into everything. It's very hard."

Rick Derringer: "I think that in some ways I was my brother Randy's keeper so I've always really tried to live by example rather than tell him what to do. So all through my early adulthood I really was pretty straight in every way. I have seen promotion things for Pat Travers, a promotional cocaine mirror. That was the society that existed at that time in the record business. So it was kind of hard to not, especially living in New York City, become involved in it to some extent. I can say that from my point of view I never did it because I was compelled to or was so depressed or in any of those negative kind of ways. I looked at it always as entertainment. Recreational they used to call it in those days."

Liz Derringer: "It was the drugs that really screwed it up more than anything. There was a lot of free sex, love and

Liz Derringer and Dan Hartman. Westport, Connecticut, 1974. Courtesy Liz Derringer

rock 'n' roll back then. And I don't think any of that was healthy for anybody. But everybody was doing it. Whaddya gonna do? That's the way it was and you couldn't change it. Especially in the world we were in. I started doing drugs at the end of my marriage because I thought to myself, 'This is one way I can save my marriage.' I was a reporter at CNN at the time. My executive producer was getting into it. He and Rick would be doing it all night and I felt like I had to keep up with them. And I got pretty hooked. Then I said, 'This is ridiculous' and I stopped. But Rick kept going and going and he met Dyan, which basically was his downfall. It really hurt him. Very much. And it's a shame. Everybody warned him. It was unbelievable that he would go with her."

Rick Derringer: "Rather than trying to make anyone look bad, I will say simply that Liz didn't want children, and Dyan, who had just come out of rehabilitation and was healthy at that time, did. I felt that a relationship based on fidelity and children was the responsible thing for me to pursue. I started going with Dyan who was in a group called Roxx, an all-girl band from the San Francisco area who had been picked by a Japanese firm, Shinko Music. They were there for a couple of years pursuing that before they came back to the U.S. They rebelled against the whole thing because they needed a personal life for themselves. Dyan and I were married."

Liz Derringer: "If probably he hadn't married this girl he would have been a lot better off. I stayed friendly with a lot of people. He didn't. And he should have. Mike Green from the Grammy's is still a close friend. I stay in touch with people like Clive Davis and Seymour Stein and see them all the time. Go out. Instead, that girl got him into a lifestyle where he never saw anybody. He dropped out of working with the Grammy's, which was a great, respectable thing for him to do. It really upset me."

Rick Derringer: "As far as moving away from New York City was concerned, I was more interested in improving my health than maintaining contacts with people in the record business who had no concern about my personal well-being. I moved away from a bad lifestyle in Manhattan to a healthy one in Myrtle Beach, South Carolina."

Liz Derringer: "And more than the insanity and the craziness and being broke and having to sell everything to pay his taxes, more than any of that, and more than being left for Dyan, the thing that hurt me the most was that he hurt his career. I was really and truly disappointed. 'Cuz I had tried to, as best I could, guide him all those years. I introduced him to a lot of people. And he did a lot of great things. But disappointment was what I felt when we broke up because he fucked up his career. That really hurt me. He was too talented to let that go. For him to throw it away on her … I mean, I know you've heard. She is a piece of work. I used to say to people that I sound like a bitter, scorned woman. I remember I said that to Edgar. And Edgar didn't know because he had never met her. And after he met her he called me up and he goes, 'Liz! I thought you were just saying that. My God! I told Rick to come and live here and we'll lock the doors and I won't answer the phone [laughs]!' And then he went and married her. Nobody was too thrilled with her."

Rick Derringer: "The first opportunity I had to get away from (drugs and alcohol) I chose to take that opportunity and did. Very easily and successfully. In my case it was right before my daughter was born. And it seemed exactly like the right thing to do. It certainly wasn't anything like I had to go to any 'AA' meetings or any rehabs or anything. Just simply stopped doing whatever I was and to the point where nowadays I don't do anything. I'm absolutely zero tolerance. Completely straight. No drinking at all. Not even beer. No drugs of any kind. No smoking of any kind. Including tobacco. I just feel healthy and feel great.

"Dyan hid her character faults from me until it was too late. By then I was a father and had a commitment to my daughter that superseded anything else. In 1997, Dyan began a relationship outside of our marriage. It turned out to be a blessing in disguise, allowing me a way out of a very bad situation. It took more than 2 years, but the marriage was dissolved, allowing me major custody of my daughter, Mallory.

"Leaving Liz for Dyan was definitely a big mistake, but no one can ever turn back. On the other hand, if my life hadn't gone in the direction it did, I would never have had the opportunity to meet my wife, Brenda.

"Divorces are always crazy and having a child torn by it makes things even worse. I was very depressed and didn't know what to do, so I began praying for help, literally getting on my knees and asking Jesus Christ what to do. The answers not only came but He immediately sent Brenda into my life. That's when everything began to change for the better. Brenda is everything that Dyan wasn't. She's intelligent, responsible, health-conscious, doesn't smoke or drink and has no vices or addictions. She's a nonstop hardworker, and best of all, she's a moral, devout Christian who cares about everyone and is great with kids. Brenda and I were married Valentine's Day 2000. We have two children; a little boy, Martin, eight, and a girl, Mallory, nine. Having Brenda and our family has helped me focus my life in more productive, positive and healthy directions. We're creating a future that gets better all the time. We're very much in love, working and praying every day to make our bonds even stronger."

Brenda Derringer-Hall: "I've never known anyone with more inner strength and beauty than Rick. He is God's gift to the world, with or without any musical talents. A true, shining star that never burns out."

Rick Derringer: "To put it succinctly, Brenda is the greatest thing that's ever happened to me."

•   •   •

Rick Derringer: "Blues Bureau Records offered to do something with me people don't get a chance to do."

Mike Varney: "I started my company in 1980. The first record I put out, 'U.S. Metal: Unsung Guitar Heroes,' I think sold 8,000 to 10,000. Back then, records wholesaled at four bucks and you paid a dollar to have them made. There wasn't a lot of money in there but enough to get something started."

Rick Derringer: "In the music business, 99.9 percent of the time, the record company wants you to sell as many records as you possibly can. Mike Varney's record company really does not do that. He wants to sell as many as it sells and that's it. All he wants to do is the kind of record that he likes. He wants to make a profit on it and if that's 15,000 or 30,000 records, he's totally happy. He's achieved his goal. That's like a dream come true for an artist. You really don't have to feel like you're trying to compete with the big boys. You're just out there making your music and everybody's happy that you're doing it."

Mike Varney: "I've always been interested in Rick. I'd been working with Pat Travers. I'd been discussing doing something with Leslie West. I'd been trying for Trower but I could never make it happen. Frank Marino was somebody that we had on the L.A. Blues Authority records. So Rick was somebody that was the 'crème de la crème.' And that's something Blues Bureau was focusing on, those kind of guitar players.

"My thing with Rick is we sort of agreed that it was gonna be in the blues style. I trust him to be one of the greatest guitar players ever. The only thing I've ever really done as far as input is picking songs. Sometimes we do it together. I wanted to make enjoyable records that he's proud of and that he can always look back on as being something good. I just figured that Rick would be really great to have focused on doing a blues/rock record rather than trying to reinvent with a pop song or a hit or whatever. We should kinda get back in and do the kind of music that made me a really big fan of his. I gotta tell you something. Rick came in with almost no songs, maybe one or two ideas. And within eight or nine days, he had written those records and was rehearsing them and playing them like a champ. I mean, that guy would come in and by the end of the day there'd be another new song. It's incredible. This guy's turning out world-class material. He's got so much to offer.

"I think Rick did have the credit he deserved at one point in time. He was one of the biggest names in rock 'n' roll. He toured with Led Zeppelin. He hung out with The Stones. Rick Derringer's a guitar icon. I think like with everything else time and record labels have a way of taking the steam out of artists. They want him to change with the times or whatever. And then all of a sudden the artist ends up in a situation where he's sort of wondering how he fits into the current music situation. A lot of these artists found themselves in a strange world. What do you do? Do you change styles to be contemporary or do you keep doing what you know? I think the records we did with Rick sort of return Rick back to what he knew."

Author: "When Rick recorded 'Blues Deluxe,' he did a lot of covers. Were these songs that he wanted to do?"

Mike Varney: "I consider Rick Derringer has a classic voice and a classic guitar style. And I wanted to hear him do some of these covers. So Rick came up with some songs and I came up with some songs, we kind of put them together in a hat and shuffled them up and there would be the record. Rick would come out for a week or ten days and the record would be done, start to finish.

"We know that there's an established fan base there for Rick. We don't have to reinvent the wheel with him. We know what we need to do to get the stuff out there. We have really good distribution. And one of the reasons why we work with Rick is because Rick does get out there and he works really hard to promote his product. He's been very visible in front of a lot of people over the years. So we have a walking billboard."

Rick Derringer: "I think things are really good. We're not going around and begging anybody for anything. We're making good music and people love the concerts. I have a great audience. We don't have a problem working. Our price goes up a little all the time. And I'm spreading out in more areas. I'm looking at other artists to produce. Writing songs for other artists. I've got some stuff in some movies happening. Things are good and the music is spreading out in different directions. And that's the way I've always liked it."

Author: "How did Edgar's 'Live in Japan' album come together?"

Rick Derringer: "He joined us and we did a show together where we included 'Rock 'n' Roll Hoochie Koo' and 'Hang On Sloopy' and 'Teenage Love Affair' and 'Jump, Jump, Jump' and a lot of my songs that people wanted to hear. And we also did 'Free Ride' and 'Frankenstein' and 'Tobacco Road' and incorporated it into one show. And while in Japan, we met the owner of Shinko Music, Shu Kisano. And Shu said that he would be interested in doing a live album for us. He brought in a huge remote truck and did, in one night, the video and the recording for what became 'Edgar Winter and Rick Derringer Live In Japan.' "

•　　•　　•

Rick Derringer: "I've become more involved with Christian music. I grew up as a Catholic, went to Catholic school for eight years as a kid. And I kind of drifted away from that for a while. And in the last few years I've become more interested in the Bible, specifically, and not the organization of the Catholic Church. And that's led me to be more interested in using my music to spread that word. I think right now we have so many problems with people's concerns of the media in general, being a bad influence on society and on children in particular, that I think music is changing. I hear music on the radio reflecting, as I travel around, more and more Christian stations all the time. And the music on those stations sounds more and more like secular radio. The line between secular and Christian becomes more blurred all the time. One of the directions I'm going in is I'm trying to create a music that doesn't necessarily say the word Jesus in every song. But the messages are a good message that stands for something that can truly help people that listen to it and like it. And makes them feel good."

Author: "Is it safe for me to assume that you're much more comfortable in your own skin?"

Rick Derringer: "Yeah. I feel very good about that. Over the years we came through the 'Summer of Peace and Love,' and all the way through the abuses of the 70s and 80s. I feel good and thankful that I survived all those years with all those people that didn't necessarily survive. And I try and do the right thing. I try and allow myself to appreciate what I have. I've had a great life. And I've been able to do all kinds of things in that life. I started traveling when I was sixteen and I've had the opportunity to use those travels to visit the most interesting cities in the world. I enjoy traveling. I like to go to museums and the theater, parks, beaches, everything that's out there to do. I like to sight see when we go to other countries on days off."

Vinny Appice: "I think Rick is so talented. He wrote all these cool songs and came up with these ideas. And plus he's a fuckin' great guitar player. Back then he was blowing everybody away. And a great producer. And he sang. I wish I could do half of that. I thought he was such a talented musician. A great teacher. I was really fortunate to work with him as my first professional band. Here's a guy that really knows his stuff and all the facets of the music business."

Carmine Appice: "I always liked Rick. I thought he was a great producer. He did all that stuff with Edgar. As a matter of fact we were considering Rick, at one point, to produce the second 'Beck, Bogert and Appice' album."

Liz Derringer: "Phenomenal. God gave him a talent that He gives very few people on this planet. And Rick was totally dedicated to music. He was never without a guitar. Twenty-four hours a day. Literally. He was extremely devoted to his art. He's a good songwriter. Some of his songs were great. Some of those 'Guitars and Women' songs were great. And obviously 'Rock 'n' Roll Hoochie Koo' is a classic. He's done some great things."

Chuck Ruff: "Rick is the most underrated guitar player. He's like the Charlie Parker of the guitar. He just knows that instrument. A virtuoso. He can play 'Lullaby of Birdland' all in chords without moving his hand out of position. He practices constantly and probably learns something new every time he practices. It's like he was born with it in his hands. It's an incredible thing to watch him play and hear what comes out of his guitar. I have nothing but respect for the man. I know many guitar players that idolize him. And he's one of the nicest guys I've met in my whole life."

Author: "What do you want people to know about you that they probably don't?"

Rick Derringer: "My writing partners. Patti Smith and I have written together. Larry Sloman. They call him 'Ratso,' who now has become famous for helping Howard Stern with his books and his movies, as a writer. Larry Sloman and I have written a lot of songs together. Also, Cynthia Weil, who is famous for writing with her husband, Barry Mann. She wrote some songs with me. Also, Alice Cooper and Bernie Taupin and I have written tunes together.

"And that I haven't made it as big as I want to make it. I'm not in the middle of some kind of comeback because I've never been there. I'm still striving to be a better conveyor of my music. And through the communication of my music, I hope to reach more people than I ever have. I'm that kind of guy. I've always avoided doing the oldies shows because I'm not an 'oldie' [laughs]! I still feel like I'm striving to break new ground and trying to get to an audience that I haven't gotten to yet. VH1 has asked me several times to do 'Where Are They Now?' and I just keep turning them down. I am not gonna do it. First off, I think they put these people in a terrible, negative light. If I make it to the level I'm talking about and am satisfied to say, 'Hey, I've really made it,' then maybe someday, in the future, I can do a 'Where Are They Now?'

"But right now, I'm still totally active. I feel like I'm on the cusp of a whole new area. I'm pursuing artists more than ever. I've got artists that I'm developing right now. To try to get their music out there as a producer. I'm becoming more involved in managing and guiding their careers. We also book ourselves mostly and would like to help those other bands as an agent. I am still designing musical instruments. I'm working on a new guitar right now that is totally different than what has ever been built. Christian music has become very important to me. I believe that this world is going toward that kind of music at an amazing speed. Some people may think I'm nuts to say that but I believe that our society has problems nowadays. We hear about them every night on the news. We don't hear about the good things. Music seems to influence people in all the wrong ways.

I believe that there is a necessity for music and media that leads people in the right directions. And the right messages. And a positive approach. It's something that parents are going to seek out so they can feel comfortable about what their kids are listening to. The world needs to feel good about what it's listening to. I believe I'm at the right place at the right time with the right message."

Author: "It seems like this is your way of keeping us from going to hell in a handbasket."

Rick Derringer: "That's right [laughs]! It is my way! And if I can be a good example to people and be a 'convincer' for them to do the right thing too, then that's more proof that I'm doing the right thing.

"Where Liz felt bored with studio work, Brenda and I have found that we work together really well. She's a great lyricist and we've written many songs. "Dawn of Love" has already been released on the Derringer, Bogert and Appice CD. That record is called 'DBA – Doing Business As.' But I'm most excited about our future. We are writing really great songs and are releasing a Contemporary Christian CD called "D I G I T" which stands for "Divinely-Inspired-Guy-In-Training." We wrote all of the music on the record together, and it's a real 'step up' in quality."

Brenda Derringer-Hall: "Rick and I have started our lives fresh and anew and really do, pardon the pun, make absolutely beautiful music together. I count it a most tremendous blessing to love, work with and assist someone so wonderful, a 'living legend' that has touched so many lives. He is a perfect gentleman as well as an excellent coworker, husband, parent and lover. Our adoration for each other overflows and increases daily. We get an incredible rush when we write and record together and have it work and come out so beautifully."

Still going strong. St. Paul, Minnesota, 2000.
Courtesy Thomas E. Wheler II

Rick Derringer: "There's a lot of good things happening in my life. We wanna try to use those to continue in the right direction. To create some kind of momentum. We pray and work towards the fruition of those goals [laughs] everyday! We are currently more alive and the record company is more aware of us than ever. The stuff with Blues Bureau certainly has helped. The re-releases of the old records certainly has helped. And it's great. I really do still want that new label deal with a company that can go out and promote to radio. So that we can become more successful than ever. I know I have a lot of fans out there. We wanna see them back into the fold!"

ROBIN TROWER

"It still amazes me that coming into his own more than thirty years ago and releasing more than twenty solo albums Robin is still changing. Still growing. Staying true to his convictions; still going his own way. Robin plays with power and emotion. A truly unique guitarist/ songwriter, he possess the gift to gently, subtly lure you, with but a single note, on a willing journey into his mind and soul. I have never heard anyone who 'feels' the notes like Robin does. Just listen to him once and you'll see what I mean."

–Steve Shail, October 2000

Robin Trower: "I was born March 9, 1945, in England. When I was two my father, Leonard, decided to immigrate to Hamilton, Ontario, Canada. We moved on to New Zealand after a couple of years. My father and mother, Olive, broke up. My father got me and my brother, Michael, and we went back to England and started afresh. I was going on seven or just seven.

"I was a big Elvis fan. He always had a guitar around his neck. Elvis is what made me want to play the guitar. I asked if I could have one and my father got one for me. It was a Rosetti, what they call a 'cello' guitar. I had a book and I seemed to pick it up pretty quick. It only took a few weeks. As a kid I never practiced [laughs]. It came naturally. I never actually sat down and tried to work out somebody else's thing from their records. I was just more interested in making my own things up. I did copy people but in a more obscure way. I'd hear guitar players and I'd absorb it as a sort of a 'whole' thing but not the detail. People like B.B. King. I never sat down and worked out what he was actually doing but I was really heavily influenced by him. You sort of absorb his thing and take it on board as part of your own thing.

"I liked Steve Cropper a lot, from Booker T. & The MG's. All the great rock guitar players. Cliff Callup with Gene Vincent and Scottie Moore with Elvis. Those are the ones that stand out. And then a little bit later Chuck Berry came along. Bo Diddley. I was very lucky. I had a friend, Tony Wilkinson, who in the early 60s was importing stuff from Memphis. I was getting to hear all this stuff that just wasn't available in England. Then a little later in the 60s it started to be imported but I got a bit of a jump-start there. And that's when I first heard B.B. King, James Brown and people like that. I remember the first time he played me 'Think' by James Brown. I couldn't make head nor tail of it. It was like something from another planet. It was so out there but it had a huge effect on me hearing stuff like that."

Author: "Would the attitude of the music affect you as much as the playing itself?"

Robin Trower: "Yeah, I think probably the attitude, the soulfulness of it, the beatness of it. Once I heard stuff like that I just was not interested in pop music. I realized that The Beatles were really good but I just wasn't really interested.

"I started having bands from about fourteen. I finally put together The Paramounts. I think I must have been sixteen. There was a band I used to think was a great band locally: The Rockerfellers. They were all four or five years older than me. They were the inspiration for putting together

The Paramounts. I met Gary Brooker when he was playing with a friend of mine, a guitar player called Tony Short, and he was the only piano player I knew. I asked Gary if he would take up singing so we could be like The Rockefellers. They had a piano player who was the singer. It's all very simple. We had Mick Brownlee on drums and 'Graham' Diz Derrick on bass. We changed the drummer for B.J. Wilson after a little while. I can't remember how we came across B.J. I think we must have advertised because we went up to London and auditioned a couple or three drummers and B.J. came in and he was the best. He was only sixteen at the time, I think. We were lucky if we played once or twice a week to begin with. Then we got a record out and we did a few more dates for a few months but it didn't really last very long."

Author: "My research tells me that your father bought a café."

Robin Trower: "At the time when The Paramounts were just getting going with a record and that, we had a place called The Shades and we used to play down in the basement. I think it used to be Friday or Sunday nights. Once or twice a week anyway. That and the odd pub gig around the South End. I was actually working in the coffee bar. I had been a window cleaner before that with my brother."

Author: "Did you ever have any other vocational aspirations besides being a musician?"

Robin Trower: "No, never."

Author: "You were determined to restrict your set list to black R&B."

Robin Trower: "That was the music that we were mad about. We thought this was the best music around and that we wanted to try and do stuff that was like that. They were our heroes: James Brown, Bobby Blue Bland, Ray Charles. We just wanted to emulate them. I really think we were doing what we loved, just the music we thought was great."

The Paramounts went into a studio and recorded their version of "Poison Ivy" by the Coasters, a song all the band members felt they could help popularize. Ron Richards from Parlophone Records picked it up and released it.

Robin Trower: "Once we got 'Poison Ivy' out we started to get out and about a bit more. We played with The Stones a lot, and as they were moving up they'd give us work and what have you."

As the 45 achieved fair success in London and environs, everyone decided it was time for an album. In July of 1966 the band entered Abbey Road studios, with Glyn Johns engineering, and finished the record in just five hours. The LP featured the first Trower original; a song co-written with Gary Brooker called "Don't Ya Like My Love." But the released single was another Coasters song, "Bad Blood," which was banned by the BBC, as it was construed to be a euphemism for VD.

Robin Trower: "It was always just a laugh really, anyway, wasn't it?"

Author: "Was there a sense of newfound excitement working with people like Glyn Johns and having the band become a little more defined?"

Robin Trower: "Not for me, I don't think, no. Possibly for Gary. He had more of a sense of ambition and moving up. I was just interested in playing the guitar; that's all I ever really concentrated on."

Though Brian Epstein was enjoying success with The Beatles, he wasn't resting his laurels and was constantly searching for new and upcoming talent. He expressed interest in The Paramounts but only as an addition to his "stable."

Robin Trower: "We were signed for a little while with his agency (NEMS) and we got the Beatles tour probably because of that."

The Paramounts were picked to tour as the opening act for The Beatles on a UK tour in 1964. Contrary to what one would assume, The Beatles didn't play to a sold out audience every night.

The Paramounts (l-r Gary Brooker, B.J. Wilson, Robin Trower, Diz Derrick).
Courtesy Frans Steensma Archives

Robin Trower: "I don't think everywhere was sold out, no. You've got to remember that most people probably wouldn't want to go because you couldn't hear them because the girls were screaming so loud in the audience.

"They were very friendly. I always remember George and Ringo, particularly, would come up to our dressing room and play records and stuff."

After that Beatles tour, the band was feeling discouraged and disillusioned. As soon as their repertoire of songs was no longer being considered sacred, they all quit. Robin was previously quoted as saying, "I was getting more and more into the blues; B.B. King, Otis Rush, Albert King. They were trying to make us into a pop group. Just wasn't for me."

Robin Trower: "We weren't getting very much work. I wanted to get into playing more blues and writing my own stuff, so I split and formed a band called The Jam."

During this time, Gary Brooker joined an impressive lineup: Roy Royer on guitar, Keith Reid as a lyricist, Matthew Fisher on organ, Dave Knights on bass and Bobby Harrison on drums. They were called The Pinewoods and released a single, an original piece of music entitled "A Whiter Shade of Pale."

Matthew Fisher: (b. March 7, 1946) "I had piano lessons because I was a kid and my mum thought I should have piano lessons. One of the earliest influences I can remember was when I went to see the film, *20,000 Leagues Under The Sea*. James Mason in this submarine playing this organ; that made a big impression on me. I was aware of pop music but I was more into classical. When I got to be sixteen I got into rock music, mainly through The Shadows. From that I went over to The Beatles and from The Beatles to a lot of the American music that influenced them. By the time I got to be about twenty-ish I'd been a rhythm guitarist, originally. I'd changed to being a bass guitarist. Then I'd decided that I wanted to be a professional musician and it seemed to me that it was easier for me to get work as a keyboard player than as a bass guitarist. Keyboard players were very much in demand. Because I'd had piano lessons as a kid I could play keyboards but I never thought about playing them in rock music. But it seemed to me that if this is what people wanted, then this is what I would do.

"There was a lot of organ-based rhythm and blues happening so I was getting into that. I met Ian McLagan and he was very encouraging. He said, 'You really should go out and buy yourself a Hammond because people are crying out for Hammond players. You'll never want for work if you get yourself a Hammond. You'll have it made.' So I took his advice. My grandmother very kindly lent me the money and I bought this Hammond. I stuck an advert in *Melody Maker* and I got loads of replies. The phone just didn't stop ringing! One of the replies was Keith and Gary from Procol. They came down, sort of gave me the spiel and said, 'Oh, yes, we're gonna be big. Blah, blah, blah.' I'd sort of heard it all before. But they also brought down a very basic demo of one of their songs. Just Gary singing to a tape recorder, playing piano. You couldn't really hear the quality of his voice or anything [laughs]. And I liked the song. I liked the words and the tune and everything. I'd taped it and listened to it again over the next couple of days and decided I rather liked it. So although I'd be looking for instant money, I didn't go through all that trouble to get a Hammond and live out on a limb, I thought I'd give it a try for three months to see if anything happened. Otherwise I'd be off. But as it happens something did happen in three months. And the rest is history as they say."

Author: "With the band essentially being controlled by Gary and Keith, do you feel your ideas were getting the attention they deserved?"

Matthew Fisher: "No, not really. At the time that I was in the band I would think that it was a very democratic band in some ways. It might not have been politically but musically it was. I think how it seemed to work out is that fairly specific

directions were being given to the bass and drums. But, really, when it came to me, I could do whatever I wanted. And I had good instincts, so what I did was usually the right thing."

In May of 1967, as "Whiter Shade Of Pale" was being released, the band officially became known as "Procol Harum," the prefix being Latin for "far from these things." On June 4 they made their performing debut opening for Jimi Hendrix at London's Saville Theater. As the recording was being delivered to the stores, Brooker felt a change was needed to solidify the lineup. Drummer Harrison and guitarist Royer were replaced with B.J. Wilson and Robin Trower, respectively.

Robin Trower: "While I was in The Jam, Gary had a hit with 'Whiter Shade Of Pale' with Procol Harum and he called me to join them."

Trower initially exhibited a little hesitation as he was worried that the dominant keyboard sound would never allow him the chance to showcase his guitar playing. Yet he was assured that he would have opportunities to do so even though there were two keyboard players in the band.

Matthew Fisher: "They probably don't think as much of him as Rob does. But no one thinks as much of Rob as Rob does [laughs]! When it was decided to change the personnel, to get rid of Bobby Harrison and Ray Royer, we had some auditions. Gary got in touch with Rob and B.J. We all unanimously wanted Robin. We just thought that he was absolutely right. I always thought that Keith thought pretty highly of Rob. He was writing songs with him and everything. I think with Gary there might be a case of sour grapes. Let's face it. Rob, at his biggest, totally eclipsed Procol and Gary probably finds that a bit hard to take. It's very difficult to know exactly what Keith and Gary think."

In November of 1968 the band released "Shine On Brightly." The guitar sound was audible in the mix yet restricted.

Robin Trower: "They were definitely a keyboard band. There's no doubt about it. Piano and organ."

Author: "Do you feel Robin was satisfied with his role?"

Procol Harum, 1967.
(l-r, Matthew Fisher, Gary Brooker, B. J. Wilson,
Dave Knights, Robin Trower.)
Courtesy Frans Steensma Archives

Matthew Fisher: "I don't really know. I think as his playing developed and he sort of got a bit more ambitious he wanted more room. And there really wasn't enough room in Procol. But he seemed pretty content all the while I was in the band."

Robin Trower: "I was just happy to be doing it. Get to go and play in America and go to big studios and make albums. When you're young, I was just happy to be playing guitar. That's all."

Matthew Fisher: "We just wanted a good guitarist. A guitarist that, when it was his turn, could really step forward and do the business. We wanted someone that was really powerful. Obviously, the material didn't feature guitar all the time but in the moments when it did we wanted someone that could really make the earth move. And Rob certainly did that."

Robin Trower: "I don't think I'm any different in my overall view of what music, and especially live music, is about. It's all very much based on kind of 'James Brown Live At The Apollo' being the ultimate standard of live music. You can't call James Brown rock 'n' roll but you know what I mean. The ethic of it. What you try and achieve in terms of a rollercoaster ride. He set the ultimate standard, which, in my opinion, has never been reached since. Then I went on

to add to what Hendrix did with 'Band of Gypsies' and it's all sort of starting to stack up. 'B.B. King Live At The Regal.' Those three albums had a huge influence on me as being sort of the very best that music can deliver."

Author: "Many of your fans would put you in that group of people. Does that compliment make you uncomfortable?"

Robin Trower: "Well, you can't see yourself in those sort of lights. It's nice if people think you're maybe a bit special. But, no. To the work of my heroes I'm not even game, really. I think all music, since a certain period like the 60s, has achieved the heights and I'm a part of that underachieving bunch."

Author: "Do you feel that you've been unfairly compared to Jimi Hendrix?"

Robin Trower: "Well, he was one of my big influences. Him and B.B. King. They're very much a part of my music and Hendrix would be the biggest influence I would say. You try and put your own thing on it. I think there are some tracks I've done where it shows a lot but there are a lot more tracks where it really isn't that apparent."

Robin then met a man that would prove to play an important part in his career.

Derek Sutton: "I was born in Scotland, January 5, 1942. My dad was in the Air Force so we moved around a lot. I went to eleven schools before I graduated from high school."

Author: "Moving around as an Air Force brat, was it disorienting or did it sort of prepare you for the life of a partial nomad?"

Derek Sutton: "Both. One of the biggest problems with moving around is you never form any real long-term friendships. You never have a home. I know nobody that I knew during the first eighteen years of my life. That's the major problem. The good thing is that this business is entirely on the road, still is and will always be. And because of the thick skin you grow as an Army or Navy brat or whatever, you are better armored to meet the rigors of the road. That is, as opposed to a person who has lived a comfortable, non-moving lifestyle.

"I went on to university in Newcastle. During my college years I met and became really close friends with Terry Ellis. I ran all the entertainment in my college for three and a half years. Terry and I had planned to set up a business together, basically becoming a college entertainment agency. I got a broken heart and went off to Calgary, Canada. So Terry hooked up with Chris Wright and they created Chrysalis. They were doing quite well when Terry called me out of the blue and told me he had an artist that stood on one leg and played the flute. I flew down from Calgary to see Jethro Tull open for The MC5 in Seattle and that reawakened my love for the music business and artists. We started corresponding and when they wanted to open an office in New York they called me and offered me the gig. In February of 1970 I opened the Chrysalis office in New York."

Roy Eldridge: "I was a journalist with *Melody Maker*. Then a number of us left to start a magazine called Sounds. Over the course of my three years at those two publications I'd done a lot on the three acts with Chrysalis at that time: Jethro Tull, Procol Harum and Ten Years After. I was about to leave Sounds to go and work for another record company. United Artists had offered me a job. I'd spoken to Chris and Terry and said, 'Look, I'm thinking of leaving to do this and I just thought I should tell you.' They said, 'Come and start a press office for us at Chrysalis.' So I did.

"Chrysalis, in those days, was a management company and an agency before it was a record company. Then there is the classic story of how it became a record label because they couldn't get a deal for Jethro Tull. They had come in contact with each other and then decided to form what was then called The Ellis-Wright Agency, which specialized in booking English 'blues-boom' bands. The 'crème de la crème' of who they managed was Ten Years After, Procol Harum and Jethro Tull. They had a deal for Ten Years After, which was with Decca in the U.K. and subsequently Columbia in America. They had a deal for Procol Harum with Decca in the U.K. and A&M in America. But they couldn't

get a deal for Jethro Tull. They talked their bank manager into giving them an overdraft and they recorded the first Jethro Tull album themselves. They then were shopping it around to various labels, one of whom was a now defunct label called MGM. They go down in history as having agreed to sign the group and printed up some white labels for what was going to be the first single. But they had spelled the group's name wrong having it listed as 'Jethro Toe.' Those singles have some rarity value now.

"In the end they persuaded Chris Blackwell, from Island, to give them a distribution deal. And the deal that they did, and having been in this situation many years later I know how you have to give in to these things 'cuz you don't think it's ever going to happen, was 'When we have a dozen hits on your label, you'll give us our own label.' Without really expecting it to happen. Jethro Tull were beginning to explode. They were about to get the key spot at The Redding Festival. So when I joined them they were very much a management company and an agency and sort of a record company by default.

"But the record company was beginning to build. Just a few years later they were putting acts on the label that they didn't manage. Leo Sayer, for instance. Steeleye Span. This was the early 70s. The label grew very quickly as this was a very hot time for Chrysalis. They opened up in America. I don't think anyone was doing A&R in the U.K. It kind of happened because they were managers and agents and they got offered acts. It wasn't structured like a formal record company."

Author: "But wasn't this a huge conflict of interest?"

Roy Eldridge: "Yes, it was [laughs]! But at the time you can imagine if you were the group or the young manager, all the group wanted to do was get the next gig. They wanted to get the Marquee residency. So, yeah, down the line it did become somewhat of a conflict of interest but, at the time, everyone had grown up together."

Derek Sutton: "I then went on to learn the business at Chrysalis, being a contract road manager for a couple of years. When they took on their own publishing, I ran the publishing operation. I started working with Robin when Chrysalis took over management of Procol Harum in 1970 and that was how I met Robin. At that point Chris Wright was wholly responsible for Ten Years After. Terry was wholly responsible for Jethro Tull. Procol Harum demanded that somebody visibly important in the organization should be solely responsible for them and they picked me. The very first tour I did with Procol was in 1970. We played American University on May 1 and Abbie Hoffman and crew tried to take over the stage, which was at an outdoor amphitheater. And when we got back they had trashed our dressing room and stolen one of Robin's guitars.

"In those days, rock 'n' roll was not the business that it is now. It was a very 'cowboy' business. It wasn't the suits and Ticketmaster and get paid by check. We're talking about counting out crumpled ones and fives with a guy with a .38 Special on the table at the end of the night. It was a totally different kind of business.

"In September 1972, when Chrysalis opened their own record company, I was second in command. When the professional they hired as president, Ron Goldstein, got tired of dealing with Terry and Chris, I, by default, got to run the record company. Ron lasted less than a year but I learned a lot from him that allowed me to run Chrysalis Records U.S. So from '70 to '75, I was working for Chrysalis and learning the business"

Author: "Who controlled the pace of the record company?"

Derek Sutton: "The pace was controlled entirely by London; London signed all the acts. One of my mandates was always to find new acts but my A&R talent has never been as good as Terry's. Terry Ellis is one of the most brilliant A&R men in the world. He took more risks and found and developed more artists than any single individual I've ever known."

Roy Eldridge: "The two principles of the record company, Terry and Chris, and people like Doug D'Arcy and myself and the artists were all about the same age and all growing up together. This was all happening for us. This was all so exciting. 'We're seeing these artists grow and grow and we're seeing hot acts in the U.K. becoming hot acts in America.' Which, of course, was the Holy Grail."

Author: "Who was managing the band at the time of your involvement?"

Matthew Fisher: "We started off with Jonathan Weston. Then we went to Tony Secunda. And then we went with Ronnie Lyons. And then Ronnie Lyons kind of went into partnership with Benny Glotzer. And then the partnership broke up and we were back with Ronnie Lyons again. Around that time I left the band and then they split with Ronnie Lyons and went over to Chrysalis."

Author: "What was Procol's main problem with maintaining management?"

Derek Sutton: "Individually, they're great. As a collective they're a bunch of fucking assholes. Print it. There was no reason for Keith Reid to go on the road with Procol Harum and he generally got in the way. He thought he knew a whole lot more than he did. The band had an ego. If you separated the band into individual components, the ego was not there. If you put the six of them in a room, suddenly it was as if Yoko Ono was in the room and everything changed. The individuals were all sensible humans. But you put the five individuals plus Keith into a room and start discussing Procol Harum business."

Author: "Due to a succession of managers and bad business decisions, Procol Harum soon ended up in severe financial and emotional trouble. Did you involve or distance yourself from these matters?"

Matthew Fisher: "That's a difficult question, really. I don't think I ever really understood what was going on as far as business was concerned. I was never really that interested in it. I just went on gut feeling as to whether I thought people were doing the right thing or whether they weren't.

But as I say, aren't we getting into politics here? Procol was not very democratic, politically. It was musically, if you see what I mean.

"I think what it came down to was that there were various things that I wanted to do, and all the while I was in Procol I was kind of committed to doing these other things. Which I found as a waste of my time. I mean, we had to go out and do all these tours. And these would be quite long, some of these tours. Well, long by my standards. Say, ten weeks. That's a long time to be away from home, away from all the things I like to have at my fingertips. And it's ten weeks of basically traveling around, never being in one place long enough to really do much. I never really liked life on the road. I didn't mind it for short tours but after a few weeks I'd really had enough. I found it frustrating 'cuz I felt a bit like a fish out of water all the time. That I couldn't be swimming whichever way I wanted to go at any particular time. I just liked to be in a situation where, if the mood takes me to get involved in something, I could go off and I could buy a book and read things and forget about anything else. It's a strange kind of commitment being on the road because you are basically committed to just a couple of hours a day. But the rest of the time you're not free. You've got to be part of the entourage. It's like Charlie Watts said in a documentary. Someone said, 'You've been doing this for twenty years.' And he said, 'Yeah, that's right. Five years playing and fifteen years hanging about.' And that was about the truest thing I've ever heard about life on the road."

Author: "Was there a gap between what Robin was trying to do and what the rest of the band was trying to do?"

Derek Sutton: "Yes. Procol Harum was controlled by Keith Reid and Gary Brooker. And anything that didn't fall into their very strict and very blinkered control-freak idea of what Procol Harum should be wasn't welcome. I was also calling lights for them as part of my road manager duties and if I tried to do anything that was in any way theatrical they would get really upset."

Author: "Did they feel that it took away from the focus?"

Derek Sutton: "From what they thought the focus was. I thought I was enlivening what was otherwise a boring performance to anybody other than the stoned, the crazy Procol fans. And Robin was doing the same thing. By the time I got in there he was struggling to keep his guitar voice muted enough that it took a place in the spectrum of the sound of Procol Harum.

"Procol Harum was in severe financial and emotional trouble. They had had several managers by the time Chrysalis took them over and they'd only ever made any money in America. There were all kinds of people here that were looking for a piece of them. I remember being served with papers at the Fillmore East the first day of a two-day run there. We met with our attorneys the next day and everybody was in a totally destroyed, emotional state when they went into the first of two performances on the second night. It had destroyed Barrie Wilson. He was in tears in the lawyer's office and just couldn't focus on the fact that there were people who had the right to take money away from them because they hadn't paid their bills in the past. And that night was one of the most phenomenal Trower performances. Robin put every ounce of that emotion in his guitar. Still thinking about it now, I'm really close to tears myself."

Author: "What was touring like then?"

Robin Trower: "It was great [laughs]! We got to go to America. You can't imagine how exciting that was because all the music made by our heroes, the aforementioned, was coming from America. It was just great.

"The first thing that hits you is the size. The scale of everything. It's so huge after England. Our first show was in New York. I was a little bit daunted by it. It had a real feeling of violence, which I hadn't come up against ever before. All through the night you'd hear cop cars, sirens, guns going off. Kinda puts you on your back foot a little bit. All the major cities are caught up in the violence but in those days it was unheard of, anybody having a gun! It was a bit scary. I'm much more comfortable traveling around the States now then I was then. You gotta remember with long hair … especially when you're going down South in the 60s, you know. It wasn't trouble but it was like you were looked at in a sort of 'aggressive manner.' And it was kind of intimidating. But that's gone. In America I prefer to travel by road but that's mostly because I find it so tiring. The constant airports. Going up in planes and all the rest of it. We now plan the tours so I can go by road. I find I have more energy for the gigs."

In March of 1969 Matthew Fisher decided that he didn't want to remain in the group; that he would prefer to pursue avenues more conducive to what he wanted to do. And he felt justified in doing so.

Matthew Fisher: "I was always sort of bitter about the whole 'Whiter Shade Of Pale' business. I don't know if I felt I should have gotten more money out of it than I did, but I think what really hurt me was the fact that I never felt I got the recognition I should have got for my contribution to 'A Whiter Shade Of Pale.' It was nagging at me all the time. That, plus the fact that I didn't really enjoy life on the road very much, it was always there. Every now and then I'd say, 'I've had enough of this. I'm getting out.' And then usually what would happen is that somebody would persuade me to come back. It was Rob on one occasion."

Robin Trower: "I don't remember what I said but I remember talking him into staying on after he quit, yeah."

Matthew Fisher: "I also had this feeling that the band wasn't really going anywhere. That was a lot of it. I mean, sometimes they would say things like, 'We're getting much better tours now. We're gonna get a new manager.' There was one point where they were saying that 'Dylan manager' Albert Grossman was going to be managing the band. That was one of the occasions when Denny Cordell talked me into not leaving. He seemed to think that there was this interest expressed by Albert Grossman. I don't know where that idea came from because we did this tour and right at the end of the tour we ended up in New York and we went to see Albert Grossman and he wasn't interested at all. And neither should he, really. He had The Band. How many two keyboard bands does any manager need?"

Derek Sutton: "They were briefly managed by one of Grossman's people, not by Grossman himself. That was just before they were managed by Chrysalis. And it was Grossman's office that actually attached the box office at The Fillmore East because they hadn't been paid."

As Matthew left, it was decided that Dave Knights be replaced and Procol Harum became a Paramounts reunion.

Robin Trower: "We went down to a four-piece. We got Chris Copping to do bass and organ and got a bit more of a rock 'n' roll edge to it, I think. That lineup was a good band. Not that the earlier one wasn't good, but there was a bit more toughness."

In June of 1970, Procol Harum released its fourth album, "Home." On it contained a powerful song with a driving guitar riff that FM radio picked up on. "Whiskey Train" was a tune penned by Trower and Keith Reid that allowed Robin to do what he had always hoped to do: allow his guitar prowess to be noticed. Trower was feeling a little more confident about his place within the band.

Author: "When 'Whiskey Train' was successful did you feel you had proven the guitar to be more than capable of fronting the music?"

Robin Trower: "I don't think I thought about it in those terms. I just liked doing it. Liked writing it. Liked playing it. That's all it was really. As long as I get to play a bit of guitar, I'm happy."

In 1971, they followed "Home" with their most successful album, "Broken Barricades." The song "Simple Sister" was an instant FM hit.

Derek Sutton: "I still think that one of the greatest tracks of Procol Harum is 'Simple Sister.' And that's entirely a Robin Trower riff. It's a great riff. If Procol had given him his due, he would have been able to stay within the band. The band would have reached new heights and Robin would have been OK. But Keith and Gary had a very constricted view of what Procol music was all about, and they had no intention of stepping outside of their own comfort zone."

There was also a particular track that was catching everyone's ear. 'Song For A Dreamer' was a tune that Robin and Keith Reid wrote as a tribute to Jimi Hendrix after his death.

Robin Trower: "We were getting ready for the next album. Keith and Gary were doing a lot of writing. This was for 'Broken Barricades.' We had done one of Hendrix's last shows and he died two weeks later. Keith was very moved and wanted to write a tribute song to him. He had a lyric, which fit perfectly with a musical idea I already had, which wasn't particularly a Hendrixy thing. So what I did, and this is where I picked up a lot of influence from him, I borrowed some albums of his. I only had the first one. So I studied them to try to make 'Song For A Dreamer' as close to him as possible as a tribute."

Author: "Considering the timing, why did the record company not release it as a single?"

Robin Trower: "I've no idea. There's no sense asking me anything about the business side of things because I've never had any interest in that."

Within a few months, Robin decided that he wanted to go on his own. He became tired of the organ and piano sound and of being restricted to playing with people who weren't willing to expand and try new things.

Derek Sutton: "They didn't want him out front. They saw the guitar as merely a support instrument to the organ/piano crossfire. They didn't see that the guitar in the hands of a master like Robin could and did drive the emotional power of some of Keith and Gary's songs to an entirely new level. To a level that was more accessible to people whose musicianship was not the level of a Matthew Fisher. Bringing classical organ overtones into things was not everybody's cup of tea. But a raging guitar, even muted to the point to be within that same spectrum, was still much more acceptable and accessible to an American audience."

Matthew Fisher: "I still play with them on occasions, but you get the feeling that there's sort of a straightjacket around people which didn't use to be there. Mick Grabham now feels that while he was in Procol he was trying too hard to do what they wanted him to do rather than just be himself. It's difficult to say who's to blame there. Like I've always said, if there's something I've got no nerves about is playing organ in Procol Harum because I've defined the role. Whatever I do is OK because I made that role. And Rob may very well feel the same. But when people like Chris Copping or Mick Grabham joined the band they all felt, 'Oh, I've got to carry on this tradition.' So you can't really say that with Keith and Gary it was totally a case of them being restrictive or control freaks or whatever they were. I think a lot of it is just the psychology of some musician coming into another band and gets the feeling that he has to carry on where someone else left off."

Author: "And they were large shoes to fill."

Matthew Fisher: "Well, that's not for me to say. It's a question of the picture. The picture already being there and you take something out and you want to put something back in. It's different when you've joined a band and it's a blank canvass and it's up to you to paint the picture."

Author: "Why did you stay with Procol Harum for as long as you did?"

Robin Trower: "I think because I felt it was good for me. I was writing a bit more each time and my playing was improving. I used to go down really well in America with Procol and I just felt it was good. There was a trigger there as to why I went on my own, and that was because B.J. Wilson decided that he was going to leave Procol Harum. And that's what started my mind thinking, 'Is it worth going on? Blah, blah, what should I do? Well, I'd like to do something on my own.' That's probably some of what made my mind up. Then B.J. actually changed his mind and decided to stay in [laughs]. But I'd already made my mind up to go then. I was writing more guitar ideas. There just wasn't room in a keyboard band. I felt I had a bit more to say than there was room for. It was no good trying to force my stuff on them.

They were known for keyboards and a bit of guitar, but not mainly being a guitar thing. I wanted to have a three-piece. I wanted to be where the guitar was the instrument. But I was quite happy with them for the time I was in Procol Harum."

Derek Sutton: "Robin is an exceptionally loyal person. He also is very single-minded. Once he gets into a paradigm, it's very hard to move him out of it. I don't know if that's fear, I don't know if that's lack of confidence. After all these years I really don't know because he's such an incredibly and intensely private person. I know a lot about Robin Trower but I don't know that. I had to work on him for five years to get him to agree to go back and play on Procol Harum's reunion album. And when they screwed him over the way they did it basically took away my credibility for quite a while. But that's the kind of person that Robin is. He doesn't want to look back. I'll say to him, 'You know, we really need another "Whiskey Train" or we need another "Simple Sister." We need an upbeat pounding track rather than the more thoughtful kind of tracks you've been writing recently.' And he just has been there, done that. He's not going back there, mate."

Author: "Though you were accomplished by the time you joined them, did you still look at Procol Harum as a learning experience?"

Robin Trower: "Oh, yeah. Definitely. All the thing about going in to proper big studios to make albums and touring America, touring all over. A very good experience."

Derek Sutton: "Procol Harum never made any real money. Their real money went to Keith and Gary who got all the publishing. One of the things that very few people realize is Matthew Fisher does not get a penny of publishing for 'Whiter Shade Of Pale,' even though his organ riff is one of the major parts of the music."

Author: "Was that a case of Matthew making a bad deal at the time?"

Derek Sutton: "No! It's just the fact that the law says that a song is the melody line and the lyrics. The arrangement is not a part of the song. And because of the greed of Keith and Gary and their disbelief that arrangements mean anything, they don't share with anybody. He could have argued for credit. But at the time, we're talking about the late 60s, there really wasn't a business awareness amongst the artists. Even Keith and Gary lost half of the publishing and they were also robbed left and right."

Matthew Fisher: "I mean, technically, they would argue that they wrote the song before I joined the band. The argument would be that 'A Whiter Shade Of Pale' with my organ solo is a completely different song than 'A Whiter Shade Of Pale' without my organ solo. But that's not an argument they would contemplate. Keith and Gary had this little 'clique' put together. It was them against the world, including the rest of the band. I felt we were partners. They still feel like that and I can't quite understand why. We've all known each other thirty-odd years. So Gary's known Keith six months longer than I have. Well, big deal [laughs]! Why those six months seem so vital that he puts Gary into this completely different category than what he puts me in, I find it all very strange. The real trouble was that I didn't stand up for myself as much as I should have. I guess I expected people to do the decent thing. It took a long time before I realized they weren't going to do the decent thing. But by the time I realized that it was all a bit too late.

"I used to feel very bitter about it but I don't feel bitter about it now. I take the view that I think I'm one of those people that even if I had gotten the money it probably would have ended up in somebody else's pocket anyway. That's the story of my life [laughs]! I was managed by Ronnie Lyons and he basically took all the money I had. So if I had all that money he would have gotten that as well. And whatever I would have been left with, when I got divorced my wife would have gotten that! I wouldn't be any better off now, anyway. So it's not really the money. I feel a bit bitter about the lack of recognition but even that, these days, isn't so important because I'm not really in the music business anymore.

"I didn't even know Derek knew about it. He never mentioned anything to me. Rob wasn't actually there at the time but I think he found out. Gary was never that keen about Derek but I never really knew why. I always thought it was a bit of a shame."

Derek Sutton: "Gary hated my guts because I told him that he should leave his wife at home so he could get on with the job at hand. I don't know if you saw the MTV interview with George Martin done by Martha Quinn. It was the best interview that Martha Quinn ever did, I think. George was just so gentlemanly and so genial and open. She said, at one point, 'What was it that broke The Beatles up?' George looked up and looked her straight in the eye and said, 'Well, it was the women, wasn't it?' And Frankie Brooker was one of those kinds of women. Or is one of those kind of women. If you put Gary and the other guys in a room and had to make a decision, we'd make a decision that would come out right. If Frankie was around, Gary was gonna have to go back and explain that decision to her. And if he wasn't trying to get half of everything for himself and let the other half go to the band, she wouldn't let him rest.

"I'm told that Gary has written some incredibly good symphonic music. I have no doubt that he's a really strong, powerful musician. But as a human being, he's a munchkin. It's Spinal Tap. Jeanine is the epitome of the wife. If you cross Dennis deYoung's wife with Gary Brooker's wife, you'd have Jeanine but she wouldn't be blonde. When a man has to defend himself to his bedmate, it's really hard to do what is right. Because her idea of him is completely outside the bounds of reality. A bad case of bringing home to work is what it is.

"We were crowded. We were traveling in a single station wagon. And when you throw an extra body in there, suddenly everything is grossly overcrowded. And when you deal with a woman with haughty ideas of her own space, it causes all kinds of problems. 'What is she doing here? Excuse me. Isn't this a band meeting?' This is Ian Faith talking in Spinal Tap. 'Exactly what is she doing here? She is not a member of the band. What is she doing here?' I have to tell you that sixteen years ago, when I worked on the picture, it was funny."

James Dewar with Stone the Crows, circa 1970.
Courtesy Frans Steensma Archives

Robin started a band called Jude with singer/guitarist Frankie Miller, who had a reputation of his own.

Robin Trower: "That was a very informative time; that was an exciting time, really, even though it didn't achieve anything very much. We were both managed by Terry Ellis and Chris Wright. I had a meeting with Terry and said that I fancied blah, blah, blah. And he said, 'Well, I've got a young singer that would be interested in doing something.' So he put us together."

Robin and Frankie hired ex-Jethro Tull drummer Clive Barker and singer/bassist James Dewar.

Robin Trower: "We talked about getting a bass player and a drummer. And the bass player we wanted was Jimmy. He was a friend of Frankie's and he knew he had a great voice. Great for harmonies and what have you. He was still with Stone the Crows at the time."

Originally from Glasgow, Scotland, Dewar (b. October 12, 1946) played and sang with many local bands. In 1963 he co-fronted a band with Marie McDonald McLaughlin Lawrie. Though only fifteen, she warranted the band to be called Lulu and the Luvvers. They signed with Decca and released an album in early 1964. In 1967 he formed a cover band with Frankie Miller and ex-John Mayall drummer Colin Allen, playing the songs of Otis Redding, Sam and Dave and Wilson Pickett, to name a few, and called themselves Sock 'Em JB. After only a few months, Miller left, and while auditioning new singers, Les Harvey and Maggie Bell sauntered in. It clicked and Power was born. In 1969 Peter Grant went to Glasgow and signed them to a management and record deal, renaming them Stone the Crows. Maggie Bell was quoted as saying about Dewar, "He's one of the finest singers I've ever heard." But eventually Dewar felt his role in the band diminishing and left in February of 1971.

Frankie Miller felt that he had to get Dewar into a band and invited James to join Jude.

Robin Trower: "The band never really worked. I thought Frankie was a great singer. I hoped that it would be good. You put together some ingredients that you hope are gonna work. But throughout I would never have found Jimmy Dewar if I hadn't have done it. It's Frankie that brought Jimmy in. And, really, Jimmy was the key for me to be able to go solo. You know, his voice. The bass playing. What really made it special, that early stuff.

"I don't think I had a real concept of what I was up to. I knew I wanted to write and perform soulful music. I don't think my style had formulated enough by then. It wasn't until I got together with Jimmy Dewar and Reg (Isidore) that it started to really come in, got a bit of a stamp to it."

Derek Sutton: "Frankie Miller was a drunk. Robin could not deal with a guy with a great voice who could not ever keep time or place. I mean, the guy lived inside a bottle. And to my understanding Robin truly respected his ability to sing but he needed more than that on a human level. The ability to keep your word and actually come into the studio and to be on time."

Matthew Fisher: "Frankie's a strange guy. I think he's one of these people that doesn't think too much about what he

does. He just does it. He's a very naturally spontaneous kind of talent. Also he did a bit of acting. He was in a TV play. I only caught the last couple of minutes of it but I thought he was pretty good. Mind you, he was only playing himself."

Author: "You say it didn't really work. Is this why Clive Barker was replaced?"

Robin Trower: "Yes. I'm not sure what I was looking for but I did want a bit more of an R&B drummer. Jimmy Dewar came across Zoot Money, a local London musician, and he asked him if he knew any drummers. He gave Jimmy Reg's number."

Reg Isidore: "I was born April 4, 1949, and grew up in England. I come from the soul era and it just grew from there. Both my brothers are musicians. We're a musical family and it ventured from there onwards.

"I just got a phone call one day to go for an audition. It was around the time that I think was a progressive era, way back in the early 70s. Musicians went out and did what they could. At the time I was playing with Joe Jammer."

Robin Trower: "He had that big, fat beat. Which was great."

Author: "Had you considered giving the group a name as opposed to using your own?"

Robin Trower: "No. I decided that after the previous band with Frankie, it split up and it didn't work, you can't always guarantee that musicians are going to stick together. If I wanted to replace musicians or if you lost a musician because he was fed up, you've gotta start from scratch again. So I decided if I could do it under my own name, I could go on and on and on. Which I have managed to do.

"The first time we played was supporting Jethro Tull. We did quite a bit of rehearsal but those gigs were what really kicked it into shape."

Author: "When playing live, were the songs structured or did you leave room to stretch during your solos?"

Robin Trower: "There are some stretched things which have no specific shape or length but most the songs are pretty structured. Certain length of solo and all the rest of it."

As with all European bands that had visions of success, crossing the Atlantic and trying to make an impression on American audiences was the ultimate test of talent. Just being able to make a dent into the available audience almost guaranteed some form of success.

Reg Isidore: "That's another thing that just happened. That was all to do with the company and the people that were in charge of the whole thing at the time. It was important because we did crack it. There are a lot of bands that went out there and it didn't happen for them. A lot of English bands. It was important to be selling records."

Author: "Were you comfortable with Jimmy as a writing partner?"

Robin Trower: "Yeah. He wrote some great songs, especially on that first album. It only took a few months to come up with most of that stuff."

Author: "Were you satisfied with what you laid down in the studio?"

Reg Isidore: "No, I was very restricted in what I was doing. It was the first time we went into the studio for stuff. I hadn't done a lot of playing in the studio. I'm more or less a busy kind of drummer, and when you're cutting an album you've got to discipline yourself. You start leaving things out and not playing so much. It was in the material we were writing at the time. It was what was required to play. And more so than a rhythm section, it all sort of geared itself around Robin's guitar. It was very much like 4/4 to the beat. It had that edge to it though. Jimmy wasn't a technical bass player as such. He just laid down that 'meat' stuff, that big thing, and we worked all right together. That was the magic of it."

With a budget from a newly signed deal with Chrysalis Records, they went into the studio. Matthew Fisher was offered the job of producing the sessions for the album that would come to be known as "Twice Removed From Yesterday."

Matthew Fisher: "I'd been away working in America for six months or so. Rob just phoned up and said he was getting ready to do some recording."

Robin Trower: "I got along well with Matthew and I thought he did a great job on 'Salty Dog.' I just wanted to work with people I knew."

Matthew Fisher: "The sort of producer I was at that time was the sort of producer Rob wanted. Which was a kind of a go-between between the musicians and the studio. Rob was very untechnical and didn't really know much about microphones and things. He wanted someone with a foot in each camp. That understood the music on one hand and understood the technology on the other. To give him the sound that he wanted. He needed somebody that understood what he was trying to do, and that could see the recording process was sympathetic to that. You could, for instance, take a band that was really great, stick them in a studio with engineers who are technically good but maybe they don't understand what they're trying to do, and give them all the wrong sounds. Good sounds but completely inappropriate for what the band is trying to do. I certainly never told Rob what to play or anything like that. I regarded it as I was providing a service."

Derek Sutton: "When Robin was first signed to Chrysalis, I was working for the company in L.A. We got the first record and it was a good record. I was also involved in booking the tours and making sure he got the necessary supporting engagements and that kind of thing. Robin hates the fact that I put him on tour with Ten Years After [laughs]! He said it was an awful bill but that's part of what we did, and it helped get Robin in front of a larger audience."

Robin Trower: "I don't remember that."

Derek Sutton: "He thinks Alvin Lee gets by on flash and good looks, and quite honestly Robin thought he should have been the headliner and Alvin should be the support act. In terms of talent. Ten Years After was riding a huge wave after the Woodstock movie came out. They were selling out 10,000 to 15,000-seat buildings and they were truly a phenomenon. And we at Chrysalis were using that as a lever to get a lot of our opening acts out there. There were all kinds of acts that went out on Ten Years After tours and Robin was just one."

· · ·

Author: "Tell me about the first time you played a Strat."

Robin Trower: "Actually, the first time I played a Strat was in The Paramounts but I had it stolen. I didn't have it for very long. But the next time Procol was on tour with Jethro Tull. Martin Barre had a Strat as a second guitar. I picked it up one day at sound check. It was on the stage and I just picked it up and I immediately fell in love with the tone of it. It seemed to have a much more vocal tone to it. I was playing a Les Paul myself at the time and it had this sort of more vocal 'cry,' which I really got off on. So I went out as soon as possible and bought myself one and have played Strats, more or less, ever since."

The piercing sound Robin had been trying to achieve with Procol Harum was finally becoming a reality. "I Can't Wait Much Longer," "Daydream" and "Hannah" are all songs that display thunderous grace from Robin's guitar. Yet European radio didn't cooperate.

Robin Trower: "I don't think it got any airplay. It only took off in America."

In 1974, Robin Trower released "Bridge Of Sighs," a collection of eight original songs that form as powerful a collection of music as any album of that time or since. Matthew Fisher hired Geoff Emerick, former recording engineer with The Beatles. Emerick and Trower were definitely on the same page when it came to experimenting with guitar sounds. Each song is a masterpiece, as is the album as a whole. The mixing of the record and the performances were superb.

Robin Trower: "He did a great job producing the first couple of albums but we were lucky. Especially with 'Bridge Of Sighs.' We had Geoff Emerick, who had a huge input with how that album turned out. He was brilliant. He actually got

the sound. I wouldn't say we particularly had an idea of how it should sound. That's why 'Bridge Of Sighs' sounds so different from the first album, because of Geoff."

Matthew Fisher: "Geoff came into it fairly late. We'd already recorded a couple of tracks at Olympic. Geoff had been working at Apple. Apple was wound up by then by the Official Receiver or something. The Beatle thing was all falling apart and Geoff came to work at AIR. At the time I was sort of planning my first solo album using this drummer, Geoff Wetner. His brother was a tape op at AIR. So his brother told Geoff about Geoff Emerick joining the staff at AIR, and Geoff told me. So I thought, 'Wow. The Beatles engineer!' Geoff didn't record any of my album but he mixed it. And although we already had a couple of tracks in the can, we switched from Olympic to AIR and Geoff did the engineering for most of it."

Author: "Was working with the band an easier task second time around?"

Matthew Fisher: "I don't think it was much different. I suppose we spent more time on things. Rob's band was never one to work things out in the studio. They were always rehearsed. They actually would go and play the stuff live before they recorded it. So really all we had to do when we got to the studio was set the mikes up and go for a good take. Everyone knew what to do. I was particularly fussy. I used to wait until one sounded particularly right to me. That had something that I thought, 'Yeah, this is the one.' And sometimes it might come on the second take or sometimes not until the fifth or sixth."

Robin Trower: "Matthew'd sort of sit there and say if that was the take. Whether the parts were working well. Basically oversee the performance and make sure it sounded good. I think it is a good idea to have an objective viewpoint. I really believe in that. It's very hard to judge your own work. You can hear it two weeks later and decide about it but the minute after you've performed it, it's impossible to actually know what its effect is.

"I was always there. With 'Bridge Of Sighs.' I remember we all sat there at the desk and moved the faders and did the mixing. Me, Geoff and Matthew. But Geoff really was the guy. He would set it up and I would say to him, 'Can I have this guitar louder?' And he'd say, 'Turn it up as loud as you like' [laughs]. He was the one that set the sounds up. Give us the effects. Stuff he had brought from The Beatles."

Author: "Did you have a sense of how good that album was at the time?"

Matthew Fisher: "You can go make an album and you can think, while you're making it, that it's your best and it sounds really good. But if you put it out and nobody likes it, it colors your own judgment. And the reverse can happen. You can think, 'Yeah, this is pretty good,' and then it goes triple platinum. It's difficult to be objective about what you do. There were a lot of things on that album. I can remember really being impressed by what Rob was doing. Specifically, the track 'In This Place.' He put down loads of tracks at the end. Just layered things on top of each other again and again. He was playing a tune on a bass guitar through a wah-wah pedal, which Geoff Emerick was kind of going crazy about. 'It won't work, it'll never work!' And it did work [laughs]. Rob was incredibly inventive on that album. And the same with the track 'Bridge Of Sighs.' On the fadeout section of that he was coming up with all sorts of weird ideas. On that very long fadeout, there are things going on in the background and him standing in front of a microphone and mumbling. But it all sort of works."

The opening riff for the song "Bridge Of Sighs" was a melody that Robin carried in his head for close to half a year before he could come up something to turn it around with. It was important that the music meshed with the opening notes and formed a perfect union.

Robin Trower: "It's what I call the bridge/chorus part. It's a straight lift. It's the only time I've ever lifted something straight from another record. And it was 'Down And Out In New York City' by James Brown."

Author: "Wouldn't you agree, though, that everything has pretty much been done before?"

Robin Trower: "Oh, yeah [laughs]. It's very hard to come up with anything completely original."

Author: "When 'Bridge Of Sighs' started to take form, did you know how good the album was?"

Robin Trower: "No. I remember being in the middle of doing it, I said to Matthew, 'How good is this album, do you think?' And he said, 'Well, it's not "Sgt. Pepper" but it's going to be very strong.' And that gave me a sort of sense that I'd done some good work."

Derek Sutton: "I have an image in my mind of the day the tapes for 'Bridge Of Sighs' arrived. We had an office on Hollywood Boulevard in a major office building. I can actually picture, in my mind, sitting behind my desk, putting this reel-to-reel tape into my player and turning it on. And the hairs on my body standing up when the first few notes came out! We had been asked by the building not to play any music really loud. I cranked this thing so I could really get it. Everybody from the floor came in with their mouths open! People from all kinds of businesses. It was just outstanding! Michael Papale, head of promotions at the time, came running into the office screaming, 'Jesus Christ, what's that?' We knew what we had got."

Author: "Chrysalis knew immediately that 'Bridge Of Sighs' was great. Were you made aware of how the record company felt?"

Robin Trower: "No. I didn't have a lot of contact with them. I didn't seem to be able to communicate with people that weren't musicians. I was somewhere else."

Reg Isidore: "I honestly would have to say that I didn't know it would have that effect. It's a good album but it took me by surprise, actually."

Author: "How quickly did you get this packaged and on the road?"

Derek Sutton: "Right away. People in the music business have about a six-week attention span. If you don't get something out and happening in six weeks, they're already moved on to the next thing. You're not new anymore so you can't be important. So we wanted it out there. We had a plan. We had a release date. What we had to do was pull back dramatically from where we were because we didn't want to let anybody else know what we'd got until we were ready to let them know. The only Warner's person it was played for was Russ Thyrett. Russ had just moved to the West Coast. At that point he was a 'wet behind the ears' promotion guy but a major Trower fan. He's always been an amazing promotions person and he was head of promotion at Warner's for many, many years under Mo Austin. Then when Mo left, he sort of moved up. He's now chairman of the board. He's one of the great, truly music-oriented heads of music companies in today's world and he's a great guy. He's just a great human who has his life in very good perspective, I believe. Russ just freaked out! He was ranting and raving on how this was gonna change the way guitar was seen. It was wonderful."

Author: "Was there a big-budget promo campaign behind this?"

Derek Sutton: "In those days the only big-budget campaigns were for AM artists. Basically, if it wasn't pop you didn't get a budget. But you didn't need budgets in those days. Most of FM radio was still driven by a closeness with the street; attached to people that valued music. It wasn't a case of you needed to advertise. You just had to put things on the air. The audience knew and the jocks knew. You just had to play good music. That's how we got it all happening. I mean, there's no way that Chrysalis could have put this together if they had needed to put big budgets. If I remember rightly, our operating budget for the year was $400,000, including all salaries, office space, etc."

Robin Trower: "Mostly we were third or second on the bill. I remember doing a tour when 'Bridge Of Sighs' was in the Top 10. We were opening up for King Crimson and Ten Years After."

Derek Sutton: "Robin played everything from the rock 'n' roll clubs to the 'enormodomes.' The Fillmores to The Forums. Those kind of places. There were places in every major city where the bands always played, just as there are today. With the difference being in those days the clubs expected to pay a living wage. And they didn't take on acts that didn't have any chance of drawing people. That was the days before tour support, the thing that has totally destroyed the touring industry."

Author: "Why do you say that?"

Derek Sutton: "Because it's obvious. I was laughing the other day. I read a *Cashbox* interview with me from way back. It was just when tour support was coming in. I said, 'Look. Here's how it works, guys. Right now the clubs choose which artists to put in their clubs because they've got to pay them. If they don't think they can make any money, they either will go with the agent or the manager or the record company because they trust those people to make sure they don't get hurt. Or they don't play the act. What happens now is that every record company throws out tour support. All clubs expect the bands to play for nothing. For the record company to pay for them. So there is no discrimination at the street level at all for live shows. There's no skin off any club owner's nose if he plays Band A, Band B or Band C. So he goes to whoever has the biggest budget. It doesn't matter how good the band is or what their audience draw is in the neighborhood. The only thing that matters to the club owner is he's gonna get his bar. Everything else is paid for. If he can steal a little bit from the record company here and there, he's making a living.' "

Author: "I understand bands will pay for the opportunity to perform."

(l-r: James Dewar, Robin Trower, Reg Isidore.)
Courtesy Frans Steensma Archives

Derek Sutton: "It's called 'pay for play' and it's happening to a lot of places. What club owners do is say, 'If you want to play here on a Thursday night you have to buy a hundred tickets at face value and we don't care what you do with them.' So the band has to come up with $1,500. If they sell them to their fan club, for instance, for ten, it costs them $500 to play."

•   •   •

For the first time, Robin and the band got to enjoy the benefits of airplay.

Derek Sutton: "Radio was all over it! It was an absolute staple for radio. There were three tracks that were played to death. 'Bridge Of Sighs,' 'Day Of The Eagle' and 'Too Rolling Stoned.' And 'Daydream,' from 'Twice Removed,' got played a lot. They went back to the first album looking for something that was in a different kind of tempo. 'Daydream' is such a brilliant song. One of Jimmy's best ever vocalizations. And you're hearing my personal preference coming through. I love that song.

"At that time, radio was in a space where they would play three, four, five tracks deep off an album and play them consistently. Not just one track, play it to death, next track … until people got sick of it. They would actually get into an album. Different from today of course."

Robin Trower: "It's quite a thrill when you think people are that into it. I also sort of felt that we were a bit unique in what we were doing."

During the "Bridge Of Sighs" tour, situations occurred where it was decided that Reg Isidore needed to be replaced.

Matthew Fisher: "This is where we have to be careful what we say. Basically, Reg just fell apart. I thought Reg was fantastic on those first two albums. I loved his drumming. I thought he had incredible feel. He just started to lose it. I've worked with him since and he's just not the same as what he used to be. I've often wondered what exactly is responsible for this. He drinks a lot, or has done. I don't know if that's got anything to do with it. I don't know if it's a chronic lack of confidence. His older brother, Conrad … he was following in his footsteps. Whether he always felt number two to him, I don't know. Whether it was Rob's ego got totally out of control … he may have found that a bit hard to handle. Whether it was the fact that wherever the band went it was like … all the people at Chrysalis, Derek's not like this, they just said hi to Rob and they just ignored the other two. And he hated flying. I've never been on a plane with him, but the stories I've heard from the crew and Jimmy. When he got on a plane he'd actually turn green. He was so frightened of flying. I've been scared of it myself but he had it really bad. And things have a habit of changing. You meet some musicians. You form a band. You rehearse and play a bit. It's all amongst the mates. And all that can suddenly change when you start making millions selling records. It's so many things that I don't know what to attribute it to. He went from being a fantastic drummer to being an embarrassment."

Robin Trower: "Reg and Jimmy sort of used to be at loggerheads at shows and that. And after shows. It was getting sort of a bit fraught so I decided that we better replace Reg."

Reg Isidore: "I wanted to get back and have my feet on the ground and it went too far for me. They put down that I had personal problems and stuff like that but it just wasn't going to where I thought it was gonna go. The pressure was just too much. It was nothing to do with me; it was just the situation. It wasn't where I wanted to be. I was getting very versatile. I wanted to be doing a jazz/rock kind of thing and this guitar thing started to get to me. There was no melody there for me. I wanted to see more colors. That was basically it. And I knew I was much better than that. I was being very restricted. It was just the right time to get out."

Robin Trower: "Otherwise there was gonna be a punch-up [laughs]! I couldn't face any of that."

Matthew Fisher: "Jimmy used to find it particularly difficult being in the rhythm section. Rob could just wail away and not worry too much about what everybody else is doing. But Jimmy and Reg had to work together. Jimmy used to come off stage sweating from the effort of trying to keep up to what Reg was doing and follow him. Jimmy was singing as well. I can understand that. I'm very sensitive to drummers. You get the right drummer, you forget about it. You don't even have to think about it. Everything just fits. You get the wrong drummer, every second you're wondering, 'What's this guy gonna do now?' So I can understand how Jimmy found that really hard to take."

Robin Trower: "I think Reg was sort of a bit too wild and Jimmy used to find it hard to know where he was. And while he was singing and playing bass, it made it quite difficult for him."

Bill Lordan: "As far as I know Reg flipped out for lack of a better term. He couldn't handle all the freedom and the success that they were having in America. When they got on tour, Robin said it became like a tug-of-war onstage, a musical kind of fight where Reg's will was kind of going against Robin's. I've met Reg a couple of times and we've talked and he seems normal enough. But sometimes the freedoms and the rigors of the road … and maybe it was partying and the women and drugs, everything that affects you … he just couldn't handle it. And Robin, at the end of a tour in Milwaukee or something, said, 'That's it!' They'd had a bad night onstage and he said, 'I can't go on anymore with this drummer' [laughs]! It started off good. They recorded a couple of albums and it was good. But I think it was the road, the touring, that kinda broke him down. Reggie just needed a break and had to get away. They sent

Reg back to England and Robin cancelled the rest of that early tour and started the audition process in L.A."

Reg Isidore: "I was really tired. I didn't lose myself but it was getting there. I had to find myself again. And it wasn't all about rock 'n' roll. It wasn't about being a pop star. It wasn't about the money. It was just to do with the fact that I'm a home kind of guy, a domestic guy. I just wanted to come down and have my feet on the ground and meet decent people and just be ordinary. It was going towards a certain planet and I'm glad that I got off that train. I might not even be alive today. It just got weird. I really wanted to play some funky music again like when I first started. I just wanted to be this guy who knew nothing about the big time. Go back, play me funky drums. I wasn't into it for the money. I was into it for the fun thing when I started playing. And I still love music today. It's not about being a pop star."

Author: "Were there restrictions when you played live?"

Reg Isidore: "Yes. When playing live you try to get it as near as the records. And sometimes on live gigs things can go wrong. So it's up to you to try and keep it together. Some nights it was magic. Some nights just didn't happen. I'm more of a studio drummer. Although going on the road in them days and being a kid, it's big time stuff. You really disciplined yourself and cut it. Being twenty-one, twenty-two at the time it was an adventure. I don't think we really knew what we had until we lost it and it just went weird [laughs]."

Author: "Did you battle with stage fright at any time?"

Reg Isidore: "I've done that lots of times [laughs]! There were a few times I had stage fright where my legs turned to jelly and stiffened up on me. It would occur because of the expectations of what we had to give. I knew what I had to do but it was being with the other players. When you go out and play with colleagues and if you flip for one second, you can throw the whole thing off. If you do the first number and that goes down all right, then you've got to do the second number. Sometimes it don't work out."

Bill Lordan, Stockholm, Sweden, 1976.
Courtesy Hans Ivarsson

Robin Trower: "But I don't actually think the band was ever as good after Reg left. I think there was a magic about that unit. As I say, he had this fat backbeat and a great sound. And I was reminded of it. I had to mix a live album from '74 that Reg was on. We put out a double live album from '98 and '74, and there was something about the combination of the three of us. There was definitely a magic there which I never achieved again, I don't think."

All differences put aside, it was time to take on the task at hand and hire on a new drummer.

Robin Trower: "We were in L.A. and held an audition. Bill called me first and spoke to me on the phone and said he was playing with Sly and all the rest of it and we were impressed."

Matthew Fisher: "I went to the auditions. I saw all the different drummers they had and I didn't rate Bill the highest of all of them."

Author: "Then why was he taken on?"

Matthew Fisher: "Because it was Rob's decision. Rob had his reasons why he wanted Bill."

Robin Trower: "I was very impressed with the fire. And he had a great facility. Chops. He reminded me of an old time, big band drummer. And, of course, his pedigree coming from Sly and the Family Stone."

Bill Lordan: "I was born on May 22, 1947, in Minneapolis, Minnesota. I was twelve years old when I started drumming. The big influence was my mom. She encouraged me in my music. She always thought that because I didn't have construction-worker hands that I'd be some kind of artist. When I started to play, the music that was happening was R&B, soul music. At twelve, thirteen, I was playing with guys eighteen to twenty-one, making money, playing wherever we could. If we played in a bar, I had to stay on the food side when I wasn't playing to get around the laws. This would have been in the late 50s and early 60s. Ended up with a band out of Milwaukee called The Esquires. They had a number one song called 'Get On Up.' We did The Apollo Theater in New York. We toured the 'chittlin' circuit' down South. I was the only white guy in the band. We were in Washington, D.C., when Martin Luther King was killed. I had to hide in the back of the van 'cuz they were wasting any white person they saw while all the looting was going on. It was pretty hairy at times. I still remember bathrooms that said 'White' and 'Black.' It was at the tail end of that era."

Every once in a while there comes an opportunity when a musician gets to lend his talent to enhance that of an idol's. This came true for Lordan at an audition for Jimi Hendrix.

Bill Lordan: "I had a friend in Minneapolis, Joey David Southern, who knew of myself and Willie Weeks, a bass player and studio musician who now works with Wynnona Judd. He's worked with Stevie Wonder and Chaka Khan and a lot of good people. Joey knew Jimi Hendrix through Buddy Miles, and we asked if he could get us an audition with Jimi. It happened to be at the time when Jimi had fallen out with

Noel Redding, and Mitch Mitchell was in England because his wife was having a baby. He was looking to start a new band called Gypsy Sun and Rainbow. He wanted to audition some guys so he flew us to New York and we jammed at the Café A Go Go in Greenwich Village in July, 1969. He really liked my drumming but there was a problem with the bass spot because he had Billy Cox, an Army buddy, there. So even though Willie Weeks was a better bass player, there was kind of a snag in the whole thing.

"At dinner that night Jimi said, 'I want you to play drums.' I'll never forget that. But he said, 'I got this bass player, Billy Cox.' He looked at Willie Weeks and said, 'Can you play special effects bass or rhythm guitar?' That kind of ticked off Willie and he said, 'If I can't play bass, I don't want to play at all' [laughs]. To Jimi Hendrix, right! So we decided to stick together as a unit and we went back. I got a call through the agency that Jimi Hendrix had called me to come and play Woodstock. He eventually ended up calling Mitch back from England to do that. There was a policy with the agency not to give out personal numbers, so I never really got that message. But it was a great inspiration for a young kid from Minneapolis to go to New York and play with one of the all-time greats."

In 1973 Lordan became a member of Sly And The Family Stone.

Bill Lordan: "I joined up with Sly in L.A., at Paramount Studios. Sly walked in with the entourage and he didn't have a drummer. I talked to one of the bodyguards and they said, 'Do you want to play?' I went in and sat down behind this drum set and cut. There was all this commotion in the control room and they called me in. Sly turned around and said, 'You're in the Family Stone. I want you.' Boom! I was in the band.

"I thought we were the best band in the world. Everybody in that band was so incredibly good. There wasn't one weak link. We could do no wrong. And working in the studio was working with a genius. I actually worked closer with Sly than anybody else because a lot of the songs were written with the drums and the rhythm first. I could really do my thing, which was part of what I did with Robin. Sly used

to call me 'The Lord.' And he used to tell me, 'Lord, go play sloppy tight and raggedy clean' [laughs]. But it makes perfect sense! He'd sit down at the drums and he'd play this incredible rhythm and he'd say, 'Now, you interpret this but put your polish on it. Your chops.' I learned a lot. When people describe my drumming they say, 'Bill, you play with forty-foot pockets.' There's a depth there. It's not one-dimensional."

Author: "What caused your involvement with Sly to come to an end?"

Bill Lordan: "There wasn't much going on. We'd just got off the Sly tour and a friend of mine called that worked at S.I.R. and said, 'They're auditioning for this guy, Robin Trower.' I let Sly's management know. And Steve Fargnoli said, 'Chrysalis Records and Robin Trower? Ah, great break, Billy. Go for it.' And when he said go for it, it was as if they knew Sly was in a slump or getting ready to go off the deep-end. I jumped ship because the opportunity was there and it was a chance to do the kind of music I wanted to do.

"I was one of thirty-five guys that heard about it and got down there. I asked where I could get a hold of him and was told to call the Continental Hyatt House. I asked for Robin Trower's room and he was listed. I called him and he thought I was a black guy 'cuz I had the slang from hanging around with Sly and everybody. So I went to the Hyatt House, brought the scrapbook and showed him the Hendrix pictures and everything I'd done in the soul days. Kinda got to know him. When I played I won them over, hands down. Coming out of Sly And The Family Stone, I was kind of like an L.A. session man and that my being heavy into partying … Robin didn't know if he could handle me [laughs]. We were all kind of wild back then. No shortage of ego and attitude! The next thing I know they flew me to England. We ended up in an old Victorian church rehearsing to do the upcoming tour."

As with any new rhythm section, the ability to synchronize is the deciding factor as to whether or not things can gel. With Lordan's experience heavily based in funk and R&B, the result of joining with Jimmy Dewar was something all involved parties were anxious to observe.

Bill Lordan: "Jimmy Dewar was very solid and almost primitive. He held down the fort and Robin and I would take off. He wasn't technically a great bass player or tremendously soulful but he played really big open notes on his old '62 Fender P bass that he had, which was a great bass. And having to sing and play made him keep it simple. He had good timing. When I first jammed with him at S.I.R. he was very deadpan. He didn't have much expression and he didn't look very excited about me or anything else [laughs]! But as I got to know him, he was one of the best relationships I'd had. We were like family. And a sweeter guy you will never meet anywhere in life. Jimmy was the salt of the earth. He wrote a lot of good lyrics and came up with a lot of great vocals. His sound was totally unique and unmatched by anybody else to this day.

"Coming to join Robin out of Sly, the hardest thing was the slow, burning songs, which he used to call the 'slow burn.' I wasn't used to slowing down like that. I was used to more up and funky. Sly used to say, 'If you can't do your stuff, stick to the arrangement.' And the more people you play with, the less you really have the freedom. But in a three-piece I was able to really fill those patterns on the high-hat and the bell and the cymbal. If Rob was on certain pedals, the tangs and the chinas would give it breath. So we really did develop a unique kind of thing, which came from the roots of everything we'd done. But then that was kind of experimental, where we developed the sound from whence we first got together and jammed. Robin said he liked my foot.

"And then the way Robin played … that part-British rock and soul and blues. Jimmy was a very simple bass player and allowed Robin to soar and take off at the top because he always held it down for us. His voice was the other key. He was a background singer and he couldn't even sing lead. Robin played notes on the guitar and said 'Here, sing these notes.' He actually taught him how to sing lead by playing the guitar notes. And when you combine my drumming with the forty-foot pockets and Robin's guitar and Jimmy's vocal, I think that's what caught on and why it sold as many as it did. People loved it. It had the power and the passion and it was very ethereal. Spacey kind of tunes that the words didn't have to mean anything, Robin said. They just sound good. So it doesn't have to have some deep meaning.

"We started in New York. We opened for a lot of people, like Wishbone Ash and Foghat, in hockey arenas. Later we toured baseball stadiums with Jethro Tull. There weren't any clubs. We went right on to theaters. He was kind of already on the way. Not quite there. We toured all of the U.S. and did a lot of touring in Europe. Australia and Japan came later. My favorites were the theaters because that was where you got the best sound. Three- to five-thousand-seat theaters where people could see you and it didn't sound like a big barn with an echo chamber."

Robin Trower: "It's almost impossible to get a really good guitar sound in those really huge places. All we could be was loud. You couldn't have any nuance with it at all. I got sick of it and in the end it's why I just checked it in. Got fed up with it."

Author: "You don't play wireless. Do you keep the wire to retain the high end?"

Robin Trower: "Yes. I try and get as few gadgets as possible between the guitar and the amp. I had one phase in the 70s where I had a huge amount of pedals to get all these different effects. I'd had a long pedal board that I'd had especially built."

Author: "What kind of rack were you carrying?"

Robin Trower: "It was custom made. I had a tech that put it together 'cuz there weren't any racks then. The trouble was if you hooked more than two or three up together you'd get the signals off. So he invented a system by which there no would be no signal loss. I was using about six or seven different effects.

"We had our own huge monitor system built so we could make it work. It's quite difficult with a three-piece. It can be, if you're not careful, a bit empty. I liked the idea of playing for that many people. The excitement. And the fact that that many people had turned up to hear you play is fantastic. But artistically it was very difficult. You felt like you were a bit on autopilot and not really being creative. You couldn't create. You had to deliver the goods. Keep the energy up high. But you have to put so much more energy into it to make it work in that situation."

Bill Lordan: "In the early days people were still getting to know us. We had buttons that said, 'Who Is Robin Trower?' We were breaking ground and taking it a day at a time and a town at a time. Building it up. There was a void from the Hendrix days. We pulled all those people in. It was a good time for that style of music. Robin hit the vein and it just seemed to take off. The reaction of the crowds and the number of people that were showing up … we'd walk out on stage to a standing ovation and lit matches. The crowd noise was almost deafening! And boy did they love 'Bridge Of Sighs!' There was a warm feeling that people really loved what we were doing. Then the venues got bigger and we started to headline. I remember once in Washington, Billy Joel was on the bill and he wanted to headline. So we said, 'OK. We'll go first.' But he declined because people were mainly there to see Robin. At the time Robin was hot and Billy Joel was known but not as big as he went on to be. I don't remember ever being blown off by anybody. We did the Day On The Green at Oakland Coliseum for Bill Graham in '76 to 63,000 people, where we made $200,000 that day. I saw the check but I didn't see much of the money. We were headlining over Fleetwood Mac, Gary Wright, Dave Mason and Peter Frampton. Robin always held his ground."

Author: "Did Chrysalis have a lot of promo reps showing up at the gigs to visually show their presence?"

Robin Trower: "Yeah. We used to get the local reps come in all the time. Especially when you're in the Top 10. They come out of the woodwork! I think you're always going to have that happening around a successful rock act. But I used to finish the gig and go back to the hotel.

"Looking back at it I wish there could have been a slower rise. I even felt at the time that we got to the top of the bill too quickly. We should have hung about second on

the bill a bit longer. But, unfortunately, no one would have us second on the bill."

Bill Lordan: "It did happen fast, I'll tell you. But I think you have to ride the crest of that wave while it's there. Chrysalis was definitely wanting to put us into the big arenas at the superstar level because of the greed factor. They wanted to make a lot of money. The manager always said that Robin paid for the Rolls Royce that the president drove from 'Bridge Of Sighs' [laughs]. It seemed like one day it just took off."

Robin Trower: "What I think I'm paying for is being incredibly badly managed and handled. In terms of Chrysalis."

Author: "Robin claims that he never cared for the business side of things. Because of trusting the wrong people was the band aware of how he was getting the short end of the stick?"

Bill Lordan: "Yes and no. What happened there was that there was a big renegotiation of the contract. We always heard from day one that Robin didn't have a very good deal to begin with. The points were low and it was just a bad deal. And when he really started to sell and they were making a lot of money the manager, (Wilf Wright) then went into this 'renegotiation.' I think we were living in California somewhere in Malibu during that time. And he thought he'd come out a lot better on his publishing and everything.

"Wilf Wright used to work for Chrysalis as an employee. They were pretty upset when he took Robin as a personal manager because that was definitely a conflict of interest to them. They kind of allowed it because Robin wanted it and they didn't want to upset Robin. But they were not happy with the split in management going to Wilf Wright, who promised Robin the stars and the moon. 'Oh, they're ripping you off. Let's do an audit.' I always felt that from that day that they didn't promote us like they did before."

Author: "And the renegotiation wasn't retroactive."

Bill Lordan: "No [laughs]. I felt like I should have been rich; made these guys a fortune and I ended up with nothing. And Robin is pretty much in the same boat. I never thought we got a good shake from those guys. After the renegotiation things seemed to get a little better for that period, but then we were on the other side of the peak. If we had been financially set then we could have rode it out and milked it. We were all living like it would last forever. I certainly thought it would. All of us were spending a lot of money. Robin rented Liza Minelli's house or Diana Ross. He was in Malibu Colony and he brought the wife and kids over. Although they never really settled because British people will always go back to England. Just the way of life; it was not as conservative as they wanted for their kids at that time, who were small. One time he also lived in Florida on Star Island. He rented a big house there. It was extravagant living for a while. We thought, 'Well, we're making the money. I guess we've got it.' But it all came crashing down. I had a big house that I lost and Jimmy the same way. He had a Citroen Maserati that he had to give back. I went from a Mercedes to a Volkswagen. We were all affected by it. I was always in the dark with the accounting and never knew where I stood with it."

Author: "How different would your life have been had your agreement with Chrysalis been properly put together?"

Robin Trower: "Well, obviously, I'd have been a lot wealthier. There's loads of money out of that album that I should have earned. But that's life, isn't it? It can't all be about that. It's got to be about the things that matter. Family, children and health. Look at Muddy Waters. Did he end up being rich? And there's a guy … he's a giant in the world of music. He probably didn't have two cents to rub together. So I feel lucky. I've made a great living from it.

"I was just with Chrysalis. But there was a real conflict of interest 'cuz they managed me and they were the record label as well. It was all a bit dodgy."

Author: "But it was at a time when you wouldn't have suspected that things would go wrong."

Robin Trower: "No, that's right. I think the turning point for me, when I look back career-wise, was when Chrysalis decided to stop being distributed by a major label. And go independent. And, unfortunately, my album, 'Long Misty Days,' was the first one that they released. My career took a nosedive from then on."

Bill Lordan: "But we did have that feeling that it could go on forever. We did Australia, Japan, all of Europe. Man, it just seemed like it was never gonna stop."

Author: "Do you feel that the success of 'Bridge Of Sighs' prevented you from getting the proper attention for the material that followed it?"

Robin Trower: "In looking back, I don't think I made an album as good as 'Bridge Of Sighs' again. I think there were good tracks that maybe compete but never an overall album that was as good. The main pressure was that you had to have hits on the radio. And that got in the way a bit of the sort of records I was trying to make. But radio changed quite a bit. They wouldn't play moody stuff and they became very much more commercial after that period."

Author: "As success came your way, how different were the people around you becoming?"

Robin Trower: "Well, you got treated more and more like a prince [laughs]. 'Be careful. Don't upset him.' You get all that crap. I don't know if it's annoying. It's not good for you, put it like that. But the people from home were treating me the same. I was just so busy. Touring. Writing. Recording. And what with trying to spend the rest of the time with your own family, you never have a lot of time or space in your head to think about a lot of stuff."

Derek Sutton: "I think when artists hit the big time, they think it'll go on forever. They don't understand that this is as temporary as the winter snow. It is definitely finite. You need to husband the resources that you have and be able to look at yourself with a very cold and calculating eye and say, 'OK, am I flavor of the month? How long is this gonna last? Do I want to take the money and run? Do I want to try and parlay this into a twenty-year career? What's the strategy here? What am I going to do with all of this power and money and glory?' They can't figure it out, and the people that should be helping them figure it out are paralyzed and petrified that they're going to lose what they worked so hard to get if they give them the wrong advice. And the wrong advice under these circumstances is generally something that'll make the artist angry. It's a very interesting balance of emotional and financial involvement. This is not a business business. It's a highly emotionally charged arena.

"I'll give you an example from Robin's career. Robin was playing at one of the sheds in the Midwest. This was on the '20th Century Blues' album. I had a PR person working for me who was out to raise some print for Robin. She got to the rock critic for a particular newspaper. This guy was Mr. Big in Louisville and controlled the most important print column on rock in the city. She called him and he said, 'Listen. You can take Robin Trower and you can tell him that as far as I'm concerned he doesn't exist. I would never print a word about him in my entire life.' So I called the dude and said, 'I've known Robin for thirty years. I have never had anybody say something like this to me before. Just purely for my own information, I'd love to know what Robin did to you to cause you to carry such a hatred for him.' And he said, 'Well, a long time ago when Robin Trower was a big star and I was just a college student, I did an interview with him and Jimmy and Bill. They just laughed and joked and didn't take me seriously.' And that was that. That is the level of emotional bullshit that artists go through every day. Most rock journalists are rock journalists because they can't get a real job. There are an awful lot of dropouts, people that don't have skills, who get by in this business who would not get by in any other business."

•   •   •

Author: "What was the attitude when you went in to record 'For Earth Below'?"

Bill Lordan: "Pretty much upbeat. But the album was actually kind of experimental. Robin was already going off in some kind of different direction, with more of an R&B approach. It was in L.A. at The Record Plant. Everybody was flown over from England and rented houses."

Author: "Did you feel you were living beyond your means at that time?"

Robin Trower: "No, not really."

Derek Sutton: "They had three houses in Malibu. They had drivers. It took three weeks in lockout time at one of the studios to get a sound. People were telling Robin how much money he was wasting all the time but he didn't care. Remember something, please, and that is to English musicians from that period, the only money you ever made from a record was the money you got from the advance. And if you could con the record company into giving you a damn good time for a long time while you make a record, you've scored. When Humble Pie did their last tour of America for Dee Anthony, having been raped for every tour they'd ever been on, they just said, 'To hell with this. We're gonna spend every penny we get and we're gonna leave Dee Anthony with a debt instead of a profit.' That's the kind of mentality that Robin came from. With Pie, there wasn't any money to pay for it. Dee almost had a heart attack! It was the same thing with Procol Harum. Procol Harum used to do things like be on tour, and we'd come into New York and they would have a competition to see who could have the biggest room service bill. They would do dumb things like that. And they'd say, 'Well, how come we have to pay for this? Why doesn't the tour pay for it?' It's more an attitude of they know they're gonna get screwed by somebody and so they're gonna have a good time while they're getting screwed. 'We'll spend the money now because we know we're not gonna get it anywhere else.' 'Bridge Of Sighs' was so huge but no one ever told Robin that he wasn't making any money from it."

Matthew Fisher: "There was a lot of pressure on them. It wasn't the same relaxed atmosphere that had been going on in previous albums."

Bill Lordan: "I don't think the band had developed into the style that I thought was better depicted on the later albums. Matthew was there to produce. It felt like the beginning of something good. We were all looking forward to the future and the tour coming up. The wave had started. The interest and the excitement of the people that were into it. The jobs were getting better and bigger and the response was really incredible."

Robin Trower: "Obviously, we were trying to make another great record. But I don't think I had enough time to prepare for it. I had just come in off the road and hadn't really had time to sit about and come up with new songs. But that was the way they were managing me. 'He's a machine. Get him back into the studio and get another album out.' You were either on the road or you were in the studio. They had no idea of the 'art' side of it, what goes into creating it."

Author: "They weren't interested in investing the time to have it develop?"

Robin Trower: "They just didn't have any idea. They didn't have a clue. They thought, 'This guy can just turn this stuff out.' And that was it. They didn't think, 'Oh, give him six months to cool off and get regenerated.' They had other acts. But how many of those got better and better, do you think? Not many. It's a money machine, isn't it?"

Author: "But after a while you would hope that they would see a pattern."

Robin Trower: "Yeah. Maybe they did eventually, but it was certainly too late [laughs]! I just don't think people thought in those terms in those days. That we, as people, needed time to create stuff. I think artists nowadays have more control over what they do. An artist today would say to their manager, 'Look, I need a year before I go back in

there.' They put their foot down. They're much more in control of their own destinies as it were. 'Cuz they've learned. They've seen what's happened to the previous generation."

Author: "Do you feel indebted in any way?"

Robin Trower: "No [laughs]. I'm sort of bitching a bit now but I've had a great career. I've gotten to play guitar as much as I've wanted to."

As the band when in to record "For Earth Below," two glaring omissions were engineer Geoff Emerick and the studio he worked out of.

Robin Trower: "Matthew and I both thought that some of the drum sounds that were coming out of America were good. I just felt that there was so much great stuff happening at the time in America that it would be a good change. And I knew I didn't want to make the same album over again."

Matthew Fisher: "I was quite keen on the idea to record in America. I was interested in American recordings as opposed to British recordings. But I was kind of presented with a *fait accompli* most of the time. 'We've booked the studio and we're going to go over to Hollywood, blah, blah, blah.' It's difficult to think thirty years ago what I would have done if I'd actually been asked. I don't know if Hollywood was really the place. It was a really nice place to hang out. They were living in these houses with swimming pools and the rest. But was it really appropriate for the music that we were doing? Maybe if we'd have been in Chicago there might have been a better vibrancy. I don't want this to sound like they went against what I was saying. I got carried along by what was happening. I suppose I could have objected if I'd wanted to. It all seemed to make sense to me at the time. But in retrospect I don't think that was the best thing to do."

Robin Trower: "I don't think there was a depth of great material on 'For Earth Below,' but I thought there was some very good stuff on it. The whole idea was an attempt to do something different from 'Bridge Of Sighs,' which was not a good commercial move if I were just into cashing in. But I wanted to do something that was away from 'Bridge Of Sighs.' You like to think you're moving forward all the time."

Author: "How was 'For Earth Below' taken by Chrysalis as a follow-up to 'Bridge Of Sighs'?"

Derek Sutton: "(long pause) Not well. There was a certain amount of Procol Harum-induced death wish in Robin. Self-sabotage. My remembrance of that time is that it had taken us a while to get this album together and Robin had refused input from everybody around. And rather than building himself a base of support, he had alienated a bunch of people. I don't remember any details. I just think that he had not done himself justice. I remember that there wasn't a track on the record that people could seize on like they could seize on 'Bridge Of Sighs.' And the result was, 'This is a sophomore effort,' even though it wasn't, 'and it's a bit of a duff album.' "

Robin Trower: "I remember Chris Wright saying to the guy that was tour managing me at the time that he thought I'd blown it with that album."

Matthew Fisher: "It's a bit difficult to compare the two albums because 'Bridge Of Sighs' is such a classic. It was a number of things that all came together. A lot of Rob's ideas crystallized and the chemistry with the band all kind of crystallized. It was a magic time where everything really just happened. And I suppose the material was written over a longer period of time as well. But all sorts of things started to change after 'Bridge Of Sighs.' I get the feeling that Rob got more into writing the lyrics as well as the music. I think he wrote a lot of the lyrics on 'For Earth Below,' where I think Jimmy wrote the greater portion of the lyrics on 'Bridge Of Sighs.' I don't actually listen to it anymore. But then I don't listen to 'Bridge Of Sighs' either. I don't listen to music much at all besides classical, so we're kind of groping in the dark here. I can't tell you what I think of the album, but what I remember of it. And what I remember of it is I think it had some good things on it. But it just didn't have the magic for me. Whether that was the change in

drumming style between Reg and Bill, that might have been part of it. It was just sort of a looser feel we had with Reg. I kinda liked that. If you compare those two albums just from the point of view of the music, that's the sort of difference I'm talking about between 'Bridge Of Sighs' and 'For Earth Below.' It's a bit harder. It's a bit more rigid. It doesn't have the same kind of swing to it. So that's one thing why I would prefer 'Bridge Of Sighs.' "

Bill Lordan: "It went gold. They say any album that follows a big album will automatically do that much business. Which might be true. Like I said, we were just starting to develop the style. A lot of the songs that were on there came out of jams and rehearsals. Where Robin later became more songwriter-oriented with structure. We'd do a song just around a guitar riff and Jimmy would write words. If it felt good we went with it. So it became more the 'guitar stylings' of Robin Trower. But we weren't disappointed on a creative level."

In early 1976 Chrysalis Records released a live recording of a performance that took place in Stockholm, Sweden, on February 3, 1975, entitled "Live." The album concentrated on the music from "Bridge Of Sighs."

Both photos taken February 3, 1975, Stockholm, Sweden. Courtesy Hans Ivarsson

Derek Sutton: "I think what happened was that the financial wizards in London realized that they weren't going to get cooperation from Robin as an artist to produce a second 'Bridge Of Sighs' to satisfy an audience and build on the sales base. What they wanted was to capitalize on the enormous success of 'Bridge Of Sighs' and pull in as much money as they possibly could before Robin self-destructed. So they found this great Swedish recorded show and they put this record out. We took it with great glee here because, as you say, it was 'Bridge Of Sighs' revisited. Gave us a chance to rework the live versions of the songs and show just what a brilliant guitarist the man was at a time when guitar was pretty much peaking. And that's what we did."

Bill Lordan: "The 'Live' album was a filler because we needed something quick. A Swedish radio station had recorded us one night on an 8-track, which we bounced to sixteen later. To this day most Robin Trower fans say they love the live album because they say it sounds like the band. It sounded live. In the studio it was always a compromise. Like there was a blanket over us or something. In the studio it's hard to get the excitement of 10,000 people standing in front of you. The adrenaline wasn't there. I thought we were more of a live band than a studio/Steely Dan kind of band or some band that could come up with the big hit songs in the studio."

Robin Trower: "That was actually our idea. One of our live shows in Sweden went out on the radio and they happened to have recorded it properly. We heard it and decided it was good enough to put it out as an album. So we got a hold of the tape and remixed it, re-did some of the vocals and stuck it out."

Matthew Fisher: "I was supposed to be mixing it. Rob said, 'If you're going to produce this live album you ought to come on the road and do the sound for us so you can get to know what the band's live sound is all about.' So I did. And then after all that he said, 'Oh, I've decided I want to mix it myself.' And, frankly, I think the mix he did is crap. 'Cuz I know what the band sounds like. I heard them every night. And what's on that record is not the sound of the band. That may be the sound that Rob heard when he was onstage but it's not the sound that you heard out front. The sound sounds too 'up front.' I spent two months touring all over America hearing the sound of Rob's band in a big hall with an audience, and I know what that sound was. You cannot tell, from onstage, what the band sounds like out front.

"My impression on hearing the record was that he wasn't interested in capturing the atmosphere of the hall. Presumably they've got a couple of mikes at the back of the auditorium picking up the audience noise and the ambience and all the rest of it. And you can hear these mikes only coming in between tracks, while they're applauding, just so you can hear the applause. And they go back down again when the music starts. And they just don't go down. They fucking vanish from sight completely! It doesn't sound anything like a live band at all. It sounds virtually like it's in mono. I can't say I like the way he mixed that.

"The thing about Rob is that there's something strange about his ears. He hears things differently than anyone on the planet and he can hear things that no one else can hear. It's not that his ears are bad. Maybe they're too good. But I can't see why it's a good idea to have someone in charge of the sound that's got ears that are radically different than anyone else's. You really want someone who hears things the same way as everyone else does. That is not Rob. But I wouldn't say they're bad. They're weird. They're different. Actually, they're very acute. He can hear things I can't hear. We were in Los Angeles and there was some rock show on a little crummy TV set with a two-inch speaker. And it was live. He started talking about what the drummer was doing with the bass drum. I couldn't hear a bass drum. He could hear it. This is what I'm talking about. Rob's got incredible ears; they're just not like anyone else's."

Author: "What happened to cause you to stop working with him?"

Matthew Fisher: "He just didn't want me to anymore. All I know is my side of it, which is … I mean, I was always a bit paranoid. I can remember once I was up at AIR Studios and someone said, 'Oh, you're in this weekend with Robin Trower.' And I said, 'Am I? First I've heard of it.' And then I thought, 'Oh, my God. Is he going to work with someone else and hasn't told me?' The next day I get a phone call from Rob saying, 'By the way, we're in AIR this weekend.'

I never quite knew when Rob was going to decide that he didn't need me anymore. So I really wasn't very surprised when I finally got a phone call from Rob saying that he wanted to mix the live album himself. And that was it, really."

Derek Sutton: "That was a decision made by Matthew Fisher. And it might have been by Robin. I think Robin at that point found out how much Matthew was getting paid compared to everybody else and got really disgusted with the whole idea. Matthew was getting one third of the total available artist royalties, and Robin and the band, who had been on the road slogging it out, only got two thirds of the share between them. It was a total fuck deal. I didn't find out about it until the middle of 1975 and it was the only time that I was ashamed to be a member of the Chrysalis family."

Author: "Sounds like it still bothers you today."

Derek Sutton: "It does. It bothers me that Robin has never profited from his labors. All of that money is gone. I assisted Wilf Wright and helped them transition out and get a decent contract, I think. It really bothers me that so many people in this industry who are in a position of trust look on the artist as the way I would look at Mike Tyson if I was managing him. Some short-term creature to be exploited to the max and discarded. That was definitely the way Robin was treated by Chrysalis, and he has suffered from the sting of that all his life. He never trusted any of the business people after that."

Author: "Was he aware of it at that time or was it something he learned?"

Derek Sutton: "It was something that I think he learned when the money started flowing and it didn't come to him. He realized that there was something wrong in the equation. Then he got a decent contract but he's never gotten any record sales after that. Chrysalis was managing him and I was not in the loop at that point. I had become a corporate citizen, in other words. I was building the company and I wasn't as involved on an artist level as I would have liked to

have been. But Robin was allowed to be incredibly self-indulgent. The bills were enormous.

"They modified the contract way after the majority of the sales were done. When Robin left Chrysalis, he had made no money. I think he was £400,000 in debt when he left. That's been worked off in the intervening time and there is now a very small royalty stream going to him. Basically, for all of the fat years, Chrysalis took all the money. What money they didn't take, Robin spent unwittingly on self-indulgence. In the studio, in his mode of living while recording. And he didn't know."

Matthew Fisher: "I never heard from Robin again as far as doing any work with him. And after the live album, he did 'Long Misty Days' with Geoff. Which is a strange album. Jimmy brought around a copy of 'Long Misty Days' and I sat through and listened to it and it sounded like no one was having any fun on it at all. It sounded very, very serious. No sort of humor in it at all. I remember thinking the opposite when I heard 'Victims Of The Fury.' I thought that was a real step in the right direction. I thought that the feel had really come to life again. I saw the band live just as they had that one released. They did a gig at the Hammersmith Odeon, which I went along to, and I thought they were playing well at that time."

Bill Lordan: "When Robin later did the 'Victims Of The Fury' album, that was a blatantly obvious attempt to go back to the 'Bridge Of Sighs'-style album. And if we'd have done that album instead of 'For Earth Below,' it might have been two platinums in a row. With me coming in the band, it changed the sound somewhat. Chrysalis might have been disappointed but I don't think we were. But it didn't do the numbers."

• • •

Derek Sutton: "At one point, I was running all three of the Chrysalis companies. I was acting as an executive tour manager, if you like, and running both the New York and the L.A. offices of Chrysalis. So my monthly schedule was ten days in New York, ten days in L.A. and ten days on the road. Before the days of fax. Before the days of e-mail. I was having a wonderful time. Those probably are the most productive years of my life and certainly the most busy."

Though being a huge part of the reason for the success of Chrysalis Records, Derek Sutton decided to quit the frantic pace and begin his own management company.

Derek Sutton: "I went out on my own and had three clients to start off with. One of those was Styx and the rest is history."

After consecutive world tours, the band returned to the studio. Robin co-produced the sessions with engineer Geoff Emerick and Chrysalis released "Long Misty Days."

Author: " 'Long Misty Days' seemed to be a bluesier album than the other ones. Was that an intentional direction?"

Robin Trower: "I think you just make the album to the songs that you write. That's basically it. You come up with material and you say, 'Yeah, that's a nice idea. I like that. It's got a nice feel or vibe' or whatever. I'm just drifting through it all, really. I'd come up with ideas at home and I'd come up with ideas on the road. It was wherever I had a guitar and a quiet room to work in, really. I can't remember if I ever did put them down. I think if I worked at home I had a reel-to-reel that I would put ideas on. But I mostly just kept them in my head at the time."

Author: "What are the differences between working with Geoff Emerick and Matthew Fisher?"

Bill Lordan: "Matthew tried to have more of a say where Geoff would let us do our thing and captured it. Then gave Robin a 'yes' or 'no' or an opinion, if he was asked. And Geoff had a way to get that magical sound and didn't have to do much as Robin was doing it. Matthew, being a keyboard player, he wanted to play a little keyboards on it and Robin didn't like to have a keyboard on it. It confines you to the chords and affects the sound. Robin knew how he wanted to sound at that point in time."

Robin Trower: "I think I fancied having a bit more of a say about the production side of it. I thought Geoff would take care of me, you know. Make sure I didn't do anything silly with all his experience."

Bill Lordan: "Matthew, being a musician from Procol Harum, did great on 'Bridge Of Sighs.' And Robin needed coaching at that point in time. But Geoff was different in that he was a great engineer and just kind of captured what you did and wasn't as hands on. Matthew would have definite ideas. Robin would have had more freedom with Geoff, who kind of let him be himself and really captured some great performances. Really understated. He had a way of getting the sounds. He was a great engineer, having worked with George Martin. He was the other side of the magic. As Robin said, 'Half of playing the guitar is your sound and the other half is your choice of notes to play.' Geoff was instrumental in getting us that great sound."

Author: "Was it frustrating to have other people, basically for the sake of argument, to have the final say?"

Robin Trower: "No, not at all. Matthew did a very, very good job. And all the producers I've worked with, you hand over to them. I just at times fancied producing myself because at the end of the day it's down to your taste as a producer how the thing finally ends up."

After a very successful association being distributed by Warner Brothers in the United States, Chrysalis decided to end the association, a decision that they never recovered from.

Author: "Can I have your take on why Chrysalis ceased being distributed by Warner's?"

Derek Sutton: "Money and politics. That simple. Terry Ellis had a business plan in his head. And that business plan involved becoming a very big record company. As long as they were at Warner Brothers, Terry could not possibly get what he wanted because the hierarchical structure at Warner Brothers had been in place for a long time and was not gonna be changed. Warner Brothers was one of the few record companies where people stayed. Even promotion staff stayed there for years. There was no way that Terry was gonna be able to manipulate his way past the lower levels of people waiting. Mo Austin was too good a company head to allow that to happen. Terry wanted to be in charge, so they needed to go to a different kind of distribution. One where there wasn't as powerful a leader."

Author: "Would it be fair to say that he was trying to make his company the biggest independent company around?"

Derek Sutton: "Absolutely. As opposed to just another imprint under the Warner banner."

In early 1977, Robin called the band together to again make some changes. He felt he wanted to get away from a sound that he felt was restricting his development. He had music that was different from what he was known for and felt it was as good, if not better, than what had been previously released. First off, he hired Rustee Allen to play bass, allowing James Dewar to concentrate more on his singing. He then booked time at Criteria Studios in Miami and hired Don Davis to produce. A change of venue and the different ambience that goes with a new city would be the perfect manner to launch Robin's new musical direction. And hanging around Miami isn't that tough a task to endure. All were in favor and the work began.

Robin Trower: "I thought it might be interesting to take on board some of the more current rhythmic patterns that were going on and I was interested in all that. Rustee was recommended by Bill, and we tried him out and it was great. That was a really big part of what made 'In City Dreams,' going down that road."

Bill Lordan: "Jimmy mainly didn't want to have to sing and play bass anymore. He wanted to bring in the extra guy to take over the bass duties, so he could just concentrate on singing. But then he didn't know what to do with himself, so we bought these congas and stuck them in front of him. Jimmy wasn't really a conga player but he would hit on them just to make it look better. We got Rustee Allen from Sly, which was kinda through me having played with Sly."

James Dewar. Stockholm, Sweden, 1976.
Courtesy Hans Ivarsson

Rustee Allen: "From what I know, it was an experimental thing. Robin wanted to try and enhance the sound. He wanted to add more … I don't want to use the words 'black influence.' He just wanted to enhance his music. With a funk player in the rhythm section it would have given him what he was looking for. Mind you, not only did he add me but he added a black producer, Don Davis. And Jimmy Dewar was listening to a lot of Johnny Taylor too. There was something that he was looking for to add to his sound.

"I was born March 3, 1951, in the south of Louisiana but I came to California when I was about six years old. When I was a small kid my parents would have a couple of friends come over and they would play cards. When it would be bedtime I would beg my mom to let me stay up, and lay in front of the stereo and listen to music. At that time they would mostly play stuff by Ray Charles and Charles Brown, B.B. King. Somehow my mom got me a bass and a Fender Piggyback Bass amp. I used to catch the bus from where I lived all the way to west Oakland and back up these wanna-be Temptations groups and wanna-be Ben E. King's.

"I went from Johnny Talbert & The Thing to the Edwin Hawkins Singers. In the meantime I was messing with new funk concepts with this drummer, Willie Sparks, who was called Willie Wild. He was a Sly And The Family Stone freak! Little Sister, Sly's sister, needed a rhythm section. Fred Stewart was kind of commandeering that project. Next thing I know I'm over at Sly's parents' house and I'm the phone with Sly Stone and he's telling me, 'Yeah, I know you can do this.' I'm telling him, 'Of course, I know.' But I'm not sure and I'm scared to death!

"To make a long story short, the way things ended up I really became a part of the family. His mother and father, their love and care about me. Sly himself. The drug thing; it was there before I got there. It was there while I was there. It was there after I left. It just came to a point where the drug thing just got a little heavy, a little bit too diverse at the time. Sly started to make some bad decisions. His sister, Rose, her and her husband decided they were gonna pull out. Hamp Banks. They called him Bubba. He approached me and said, 'We're getting ready to pull out.' And I said, 'Yeah, I think I'm gonna do the same thing.' So we just kinda all split and tried to do something else."

Author: "How did you get the job with Robin?"

Rustee Allen: "I remember we were on a plane flying somewhere to do a gig and Bill Lordan had a cassette of a Robin Trower album. I heard the guitar playing and said, 'Man, who is that?' I distinctly remember Freddie Stewart coming over and saying, 'What are ya listening to that shit for?' I said, 'Man, this is as soulful as anything else.' I loved it a lot.

"So I go home and I'm off. Kinda kickin' it with some friends of mine. I go into this shopping mall and go into the record section. And we see 'Robin Trower: Live at the Oakland Coliseum.' And I said, 'Hey, that's my friend Bill Lordan. He was with Sly And The Family Stone.' And I said, 'Man, I would love to do something like that.' A few weeks later I was getting a call to audition for the band. Me and Willie Sparks had a new group called Willie and the Wild Bunch. We were up in Vancouver, Canada, at the time I got the call for the audition. They arranged the flight. Flew down

from Vancouver early that morning to the sound stage. Did the audition and they said, 'Great. Everything's cool.' I flew back to Vancouver and played that night. After the engagement in Vancouver with Willie and the Wild Bunch, I flew down to L.A. and waited for Robin to finish the last few dates on their tour and then flew back to England."

Author: "What's your proper first name?"

Rustee Allen: "Something I don't like to talk about [laughs]!"

Author: "Did you play any gigs before going in to record 'In City Dreams'?"

Rustee Allen: "Actually, we did. We did some European stuff. We went to Brussels, Belgium. Did some stuff in Germany. We did a gig in Paris.

"For the most part everything was fine on the road. I was a little younger than the other guys. I was almost in 'Candyland.' I was playing music that I loved. It was high energy. It was major venues. From waking up and getting on the plane to hotel check-ins to the soundcheck to the gig … I mean, everything was like clockwork. It was the way it was supposed to be. It was incredible how everything was coming to fruition. I remember when I finally did the first album at Criteria in Miami. We had excellent accommodations. It was work but it was what I was put here to do. I remember I made one little mistake. I'm all the way in Oakland and they fly me all the way back to Miami to repair two or three little notes. Robin picked me up, he'd had his Jaguar shipped over from England, and telling me, 'Rustee, be very careful. You can make a lot of money. Just be careful.' And I'm reacting like, 'Cool, I'm gonna be OK.' I'm thinking in my mind that I'll be able to get my house and take care of my mom and all these sorts of things. But what actually came to pass was quite a letdown."

Author: "What did you hope Don Davis could bring to the table as a producer?"

Robin Trower: "He did an album called 'Eargasm' by Johnny Taylor and I just thought it was a wonderful album. Just so beautifully put together. All the sounds were great. Very soulful. And I felt he might be able to notch it up a gear for me, you know what I mean? Plus 'In City Dreams' was all kind of R&B-flavored. I thought it might be a unique combination of putting my sort of rock/blues things together with a proper R&B soul producer."

The "Don Davis" session resulted in a different musical direction for Robin. The music is more melodic and less grinding. The cohesion of the rhythm section is as tight as it had ever been, but the "in your face" drive that had been so prevalent in his previous works was simply not there. The music was more "trancelike," allowing you to get swept away in all the instrumentation. Dewar's singing came across in a sweeter manner and was very effective, but this was not what Robin Trower fans expected. It's terrific to hit a formula that works and allows one to attain success, but being formulaic is exactly what Trower didn't want to become. "In City Dreams" was recorded and released with that specific direction in mind.

Simply put, the fans didn't go for it, though they still turned out to enjoy the concerts that Robin and his band were putting on with regularity around the world. The shows were as energetic as ever, but it seemed that the average Trower fan was content with repetitious playings of "Bridge Of Sighs." While touring to promote "In City Dreams," King Biscuit Flower Hour aired a concert from that tour, which was released nearly twenty years later. The majority of the songs are from "Bridge Of Sighs." Though there was a decline in album sales, Trower was adamant that this was the way to go.

Rehiring Don Davis as producer, Trower decided on yet another change of venue for the next album and booked time at Wally Heider Studios in Los Angeles to record "Caravan To Midnight."

Derek Sutton: "Well again, Robin wanted to go black. He really wanted to go with that kind of production. This was a whole big deal to get a black Detroit producer to produce Robin Trower. Nobody in the company thought it was a good idea. That's really what it came to. Back then there were two businesses that were coexisting and were mutually exclusive. There was a black music business and a white music business. The color bar was equally high on each side. I think that record was probably more relevant four or five years ago than it was when it was made. Before the onslaught of computerized music, when there was a great ebb and flow between the black and white music businesses, when guitar was not an immediate torpedo. I think that that record could have been rereleased and been much more successful. And it might be able to be more successful again as guitar is coming back into focus and the entire culture has been permeated with black music.

"Robin is never comfortable artistically repeating what he's already done. He's always looked to try and do something different. He is more interested in an artistic sensibility than a commercial sensibility. One of the things that Chrysalis expected of Don Davis was to have him sort of shorten and punch up some of the songs, which he did in fact do. But what might be a single today wasn't a single then. Robin wants to be in charge and wants to stretch but only within a certain comfort zone. Or just a little bit beyond. He's never that interested in making major changes. If you've noticed, all the changes in Robin's career have been gradual ones. Because of the gradualism there have been some albums that really fall halfway between two places and therefore are pretty lame albums.

"He's not a prolific writer and the metronome of having to pound out an album every eighteen months or two years is quite often very difficult for him. The creative process, as I love to tell people, is not a sausage machine. It isn't a machine of any description. It requires that the artist experience new things. It requires that the artist extend himself emotionally. It requires that they actually find a theme, that they have something that's important to write about. And that doesn't happen every day. The big problem during the 70s was artists weren't considered true artists if they didn't write their own material. And Robin still has that kind of an attitude. It's very hard for him to conceive of doing somebody else's material. There's another reason for it but he won't even do 'Simple Sister' or 'Whiskey Train' because he would be contributing to Procol Harum pockets."

Author: "When 'Caravan To Midnight' came out there were conflicting maneuvers between management and the record company. Were you privy to what was going on?"

Rustee Allen: "No, I was kept in the dark about any of the business side of things. Even in my younger days, that was something I never had the initiative to get involved in."

Author: "In retrospect do you think it would have been a better thing for you to get involved?"

Rustee Allen: "Absolutely. Because then I would have gotten paid [laughs]! I had contracts signed. Even the way that went down … I used their attorneys, their accountants, their everything. I trusted everything that was said to me. You've got to remember I was this twenty-five-year-old kid from pretty much a poor home. And I'm thinking that because of my musical ability I would be taken care of, business-wise and whatever. I got taken better care of with Sly And The Family Stone, although I never signed any contracts. Sly made sure I got paid and treated me like I was like one of his brothers. It definitely would have been to my advantage to be more aware of the business side of music."

Author: "Did you possess this blind faith in the people supposedly taking care of things because everybody else did?"

Rustee Allen: "Yeah, pretty much. I know that Bill Lordan, shortly after I got into the group, had bought his first home in Lemon Grove, California. And that was a direct result of him getting his proper royalties after he recorded his first album with Robin. So I'm thinking, 'Well, he's gonna take care of me the same way.' And that didn't happen."

•   •   •

Author: " 'My Love.' Just a great groove and vocal structure. Was this done in combination with Jimmy and Don?"

Robin Trower: "I don't remember Don having a great influence on vocal structure. Just on performance. His main thing was putting the whole thing together — performance, vibe, groove. I think me and Jimmy wrote that song. That was Jimmy's idea, the sort of vocal phrasing and melody."

Author: "The punches in the song, the way they fit in the vocal gaps, was that intentional or did it just turn out?"

Robin Trower: "One of the reasons why I wanted to bring in a bass player was to free up Jimmy to be out of sync. 'Cuz previous to that we could never put the vocals down as we were recording. And of course you tend to get a bit of a linear thing when you're not going around the voice, you know? So the great thing about 'In City Dreams' and 'Caravan To Midnight' is that, as we were cutting the backing tracks, Jimmy would be singing. I think that was one of the things that sort of makes it different from previous albums. Without a proper backing track, you couldn't concentrate on both and get them both great. So we used to just lay the backing tracks and put the vocals in afterwards."

Author: " 'Fool' is a beautiful song. Who was it written for?"

Robin Trower: "I don't think it was written for anybody in particular. Jimmy might have been writing about himself. Yeah."

Bill Lordan: "We used a percussion player named Paulhino deCosta. Man, he was magical!"

Author: "Were you confident with what you had at the end of that album?"

Robin Trower: "I think so. I think at the time we thought it was good, you know. And Don was pleased with it. But looking back now, I don't think it's as strong as 'In City Dreams.' I think the playing's great on it. I don't think it's enough really strong songs on it. That's the weakness of it."

Though Robin refused to comply with the wishes of the record company about most suggestions, he did, whether intentionally or not, release two tracks that seemed to have radio written all over them. Yet "My Love" and "Fool" were ignored.

Robin Trower: "It didn't get on the radio at all, that album. I think you've just got to be lucky to be in step with what you're doing, with what radio's into at the time. And I don't think either of those albums were anywhere near in step really. It was already starting to be more corporate, wasn't it? And it's very corporate now. I don't think about it as being bad or not. I look at it as a challenge. Getting on the radio is a different challenge but it's still a challenge, as it was in the 70s."

Bill Lordan: "We thought we definitely had something commercially viable for radio. I thought they were closer to radio songs than other albums that we had cut. It gave radio something they could probably get their teeth into. But the music business … if there was lack of coordinating, promotion, airplay. Or maybe it didn't click with the people. But a lot of people we talk to love that album and have that album. It was one of the ones I signed last March, backstage, when I saw Robin with one of the fans that was there."

Author: "Some say 'In City Dreams' and 'Caravan To Midnight' would be far more successful had they been released today as opposed to then."

Robin Trower: "I have heard that said. Especially 'In City Dreams.' I know Don Davis himself thinks so. I know it sounds like I sort of blow my own trumpet but maybe they weren't quite right for the time, certainly."

Due to the lack of success of "In City Dreams" and "Caravan To Midnight," Robin was beginning to express a lack of conviction in his musical choices.

Bill Lordan: "I think Robin started doubting himself and me and everybody. And he asked Don Davis, 'If you had Bill on a session, how would it be?' And Don said, 'Well, I wouldn't cancel it. But it wouldn't be, ya know.' 'Cuz they were used to these black session guys that play a certain groove. I never considered myself a drummer where I could come in and play on anybody's thing and be great, be the first guy they call. I had too much of a signature style. But if I can get on something where I can do what I do best, then I shine. With Bobby Womack, they used to call me in to do some funky things and another drummer, black or white, would come in to do the straight stuff, which I found hard to do. So during that time with Don Davis, Robin started to doubt himself and the direction we were going. And maybe

starting to doubt me too. I think that was kind of misguided. I think we were fine the way we were and we could have developed that way. I don't think we needed to change. 'Cuz ya know what? If it ain't broke, don't fix it. We had something great. All we had to do was stay in that direction."

Robin Trower: "I felt that it wasn't really successful. The albums didn't sell well. I think those two albums were a statement unto themselves. It was just something that I wanted to do. I think by the end of 'Caravan To Midnight' I'd run out of steam on that, to be honest."

Author: "Was it around this time that the crowds started to get significantly smaller?"

Bill Lordan: "Yeah, I would say it started to taper off during that time. We still drew well. We were out in buses and had more production. Smoke and backdrops and lighting. I remember we did one tour where there were $1,000,000 in cost and we ended up making zero! It all went to the semi-tractor trailer drivers and the lighting guys and sound. We had Pink Floyd's P.A. on the road and we hung it from the ceiling. And the hype was that it was the largest P.A. system on the road in the history of rock 'n' roll to date. But the venues did start to get smaller. With the recession and disco, everything kinda took a dump and we were affected about as much as anybody."

Rustee Allen: "I remember in Boston we did a show. And from the first note to the last note, and most of our gigs were like that, we came on there like straight gangbusters, man! Flawless performances. It was so much fun. And the next day I looked at the write-up and it said, 'There was a definite funk/blues presence by the bass player, Rustee Allen.' They said some nice things about me and made me say, 'Wow, I really am adding something to this. They can't be just saying that to make me feel good!'

"For the most part every gig we did was high energy, kick-ass! Robin never played the same thing the same way night after night. What he did was he just took what he was feeling and took it to another spiritual level that I just loved."

Author: "The majority of the live show at that time still contained a lot of songs from 'Bridge Of Sighs.' Did you feel you had to do this to give the audience what they paid to hear?"

Robin Trower: "Oh yeah. 'Cuz that was the big album. Those were the hits and everybody's going to play their hits. Unavoidable. But it's not that I didn't want to play them because all the ones that I played live, I still play them now. There are four songs off 'Bridge Of Sighs' that I always do and it's fun to play. I still love to do 'em. To be honest I think they're vital cornerstone foundations of the set. I couldn't do without them. They work just so fantastically well live."

Robin then surprisingly called for the return of his three-piece band.

Bill Lordan: "It wasn't anything personal or that Rustee was a problem. I think Robin just decided to let Jimmy go back. Rustee lived in Oakland and Robin was over in England with Jimmy. So he wasn't as close, geographically. I think Rustee did really well for the time he was in there. He definitely added. Robin just decides to change the bass player or change the drummer. Although the one thing that keeps coming back is Robin doesn't really sound that much different with a different drummer or different bass player. That really doesn't change it. He should have changed in the writing and the production. He could have kept the same band and made a change. But to just change the rhythm section … if he thought he was doing something new and different and fresh I don't think it had that effect. If anything, it wasn't as good as what he already had. But Jimmy went back on bass and Rustee went back to Oakland."

Rustee Allen: "After 'In City Dreams' I was told that every six months I would get a royalty check. When it came time to get the first royalty check I didn't get anything near what I was supposed to get. Wilf Wright. We were at the Sunset Marquis and I went to his room and he gave me this small amount of money and told me that they couldn't afford to take me on the next tour. Of course, I was totally blown away at all of that. That was after we had done 'Caravan To Midnight.' And I

basically hadn't gotten paid for the first one. I thought that time would catch up and I would get my money.

"I ended up going to Michael Krassner, a San Francisco attorney, and told him I had a contract and blah, blah, blah. And he said, 'They approximately owe you about $90,000.' He was faxing their offices trying to get to the bottom of it and we never got any response. So after the statute of limitations ran out they came back on tour to the States. And I never got it. I was so hurt, man. I had total faith and trust in everything. Every musical ounce and fiber I had in me I put into both projects. There was some instances where I should have actually gotten co-production credits because I was coming up with chord structures and little things to enhance what he was doing. But to me it was all part of throwing what you had in the kitty to make a wonderful product. I was just a naïve guy that played bass."

Derek Sutton: "Wilf Wright was a young man who was in the wrong place at the right time. Wilf worked with me at Chrysalis for many years as a contract road manager and he worked with Robin for a long time. He did his very best to get Robin out of the Chrysalis contract and into something that was less rapacious. But because of the times, Wilf had some substance abuse problems. Something that Robin has magnified dramatically and everything that ever went wrong was always Wilf's fault. Let me give you an example.

"Robin Trower never, ever played shows in the month of August. Didn't matter what it was. 'Don't come to me with shows in the month of August.' His kids were off school so he was gonna stay home. Even when it came down to a $250,000 offer from Bill Graham at Oakland Stadium … wouldn't even think about it. And at the end of the year when they were not showing the kind of profit that they wanted, Wilf would say, 'Well, we had all these cash offers in the summer and you wouldn't take them. You wouldn't take July because you had just done this. And no August.' And Robin would say, 'That's not my problem, mate. I need the money.' One thing that I know that Robin blames Wilf for, and I really and truly do not believe, was Wilf's responsibility for the loss of Robin's guitar collection. Robin had a bunch of Fender Strats, good ones, and they were in the S.I.R. locker. Eight guitars disappeared. The only people that had keys to the locker were two roadies and Wilf. And, of course, it couldn't have possibly been the roadies! Everybody knew that Wilf had a coke problem. So Robin took from that, and will gladly tell you if you ask him, that Wilf sold his antique guitars to put up his nose."

Author: "But you don't think Wilf did that."

Derek Sutton: "I do not think Wilf did that. I am still friends with Wilf Wright. I like the man. I believe him to be completely honest. I know that he made a bunch of mistakes but Robin chose an untested, untried manager, somebody who had been a road manager all his life. I don't believe that Wilf is the best manager in the world. He was and still is a great tour manager. So whatever management decisions he made that were not good he has to bear the blame for. But I also think that a lot of this, 'The coffee is cold in the dressing room. It's Wilf's fault,' I think that that's where it came from. I also think that Wilf was unfortunate enough to have negotiated a great contract, and then being served up with non-commercial albums that didn't sell."

Roy Eldridge: "I think Wilf's still around, basically in America, as a manager or a tour manager."

Derek Sutton: "A contract road manager for $3,000 to $5,000 a week. Arista, Columbia and two or three other management companies keep him on call all the time. He has more work than he can cover. It's a way to make a living when you absolutely have no life. You're on the road all the time. As he said, he has a million miles in airline tickets but he doesn't have a girlfriend."

Author: "Do you think that all these bands having been robbed in that particular time have gotten people to understand how things worked to avoid that from happening in the future?"

Derek Sutton: "Oh, yeah. And the problem is that the pendulum has now swung fully to the opposite direction. The artists feel like they're in charge, bringing in these high-powered lawyers to negotiate contracts, not realizing that a lot of the contracts they negotiate, although the lawyers are winning brownie points with their clients, they're actually short-circuiting the career-building process. I'll give you a simple example.

"There are no managers now who get what is called 'in perpetuity clauses.' An in perpetuity clause makes the manager a partner with the band on the product produced during the manager's management term in such a way that he gets paid for as long as there is income on the product. Their involvement in the earnings of projects is cut off very soon after the artist fires them. Now that seems like a great idea until you realize that that means the manager is forced to make 'take the money and run' kind of contracts. The only way he can protect himself and make sure he's going to get paid for his work is to get the money up front. I have yet to find a 'take the money and run' kind of contract that is good for a long-term career. So a lot of these guys will negotiate monstrous front-end load contracts both in publishing and in records, which virtually assures destruction of the artist's career. And that is done entirely because the lawyers are so clever that they don't realize that humans have incentives that are financial and that nobody is going to work for nothing. You know, all artists are ingrates. There is no artist that that does not apply to. They simply will use you for as long as they can. And then when they're done with you, they dump you and move on. As a manager I have to understand that while still loving my artist, knowing that I'm going to get fucked at some point. I still have to deal with the legal side of that in protecting my own financial interests. So the lawyers come along and they do these wonderful contracts and they grin and they laugh at one another as they get 'em, not realizing that they're savagely beating up the people that they're supposed to be protecting."

Author: "Why is this so difficult to get? Seems fair to me."

Derek Sutton: "Because the lawyers have made it into a thing that is a 'boogie man' to artists. There's no group in existence who would deny the drummer his royalties forever. He may have played five days during the making of a record, didn't write any of the songs, didn't create anything other than maybe his own drum parts. If he was a member of the band at the time the record was made, he gets paid his artist's royalty share forever. But, of course, a manager only works for a few weeks therefore he's not worth it. That is the current thinking. It's my considered opinion that the lawyers that started all of this are the ones that have shortened careers dramatically. Because the net result to a manager not having an in perpetuity clause is that they have to accelerate all income into the present. So they go out for the biggest advances they can get because that's the only way they're gonna get paid. So everybody is trying to go out and do a rape and pillage situation and nobody gives a fuck about the artists' career because they don't share in it. I won't sign an artist if I don't have an in perpetuity clause. I won't work with somebody that is too stupid to understand that if I'm not a partner for their long-term career, I may make financial and other decisions based upon the short term that may hurt them in the long term."

Author: "How far back do you think that started to become prevalent?"

Derek Sutton: "Mid-80s. When the artists began to completely control the business."

Author: "Was there ever a time when there was a happy medium for a while?"

Derek Sutton: "Yeah, there was. In the early 70s and mid-70s. It may swing back. This whole business is cyclic, so it probably will. Right now I suppose you're in a position where producers are in control because artists are not particularly important. Songs and producers are probably more important, as you see. Who are the people that are lauded at all these things? It's not the artist per se. I mean, we need them to do the performances but it's Puffy and it's Mutt Lange and the producers that get the major credit. They're the ones that are making the fat living and they

don't have to do much of the work … no touring, no promotion, no schmoozing. That's the way it works. There's always something going on where the artist is sidelined."

1980

Author: "Was there a particular reason why you went back to London to record 'Victims Of The Fury'?"

Robin Trower: "I wanted to work with Geoff Emerick again. We were all living in England at the time, except for Bill, so it made sense to record in London and prevent Geoff from having to travel. I thought I was doing the right thing at the time but I wasn't doing 'me.' I didn't get back to doing me until we had our own label. Derek had the idea of having our own label where I could make the music … just exactly what I wanted to do. All through the 80s I was playing the record company's 'gotta get played on the radio' game. And I hate it. All that stuff. I wish it would just leave the face of the earth, really."

Author: "But in retrospect, when you wrote the songs, were they as good as you felt you could get them?"

Robin Trower: "At the time I thought that we had some strong material. But you can never tell what the combination of musicians and singers, producers, engineers, etc., how it's gonna affect the outcome of the album."

Author: "Was returning to the studio with Geoff Emerick for 'Victims Of The Fury' an attempt to get back to that 'Bridge Of Sighs' sound?"

Bill Lordan: "Absolutely. It was a conscious effort to try and write another 'Bridge Of Sighs' and get it back to the one album that struck a chord with all sorts of people. It wasn't to copy 'Bridge Of Sighs' but to recapture that feeling. Like I said, if that album had come out right after 'Bridge Of Sighs,' it might have been more successful for all of us. But in a career you might only have one 'Bridge Of

Sighs' in you. You might never get back to that. Or keep it going. Hendrix. If he hadn't died, I wonder if he could have kept up that standard of excellence?"

Author: "Jimmy only has one co-writing credit on 'Victims Of The Fury.' What was going on that was causing him to become less and less involved?"

Robin Trower: "Keith Reid took over the lyrics. I always wrote all of the music. It was just an experiment, really. It had nothing to do with the relationship at all. It was just a case of trying something else."

Author: "What inspired you to get together with Keith Reid?"

Robin Trower: "It was interesting. It was to spice it up a bit. Add a different ingredient and see what came out. I am constantly experimenting with the lineup and the formula and messing around with it. You can't keep making the same album over and over again. People don't want it."

Author: "Sadly some people do."

Robin Trower: "Well, that's something I wouldn't be interested in doing. You want to do something that's going to give you a bit of a lift. A bit of a kick. Something different. 'If I have a go at this maybe it'll be great.' You're always hoping that you'll do something great [laughs]! And if you don't you go on to the next one and maybe that will be something that will turn out to be great."

At this point in time Derek returned to working with Robin as a full-time manager.

Derek Sutton: "You're never given the position of manager. You either earn it or you take it. The artist is never going to give you the right to manage them. You have to prove to them that you are capable, that your decisions are more valid than theirs and that your skills and expertise are equal to or greater than theirs in the area of business. And it's a battle that managers lose all of the time. Because in the end when the artist is successful, they think they don't need the

manager. There are plenty of other people that'll come along. And so the person that is a manager at some point is faced with the same kind of situation that I had with Styx. Which was I could either shut my mouth and continue to draw a high six-figure salary and let the band self-destruct, or I could actually tell them what I believed and try to get them to do the things that I believed they needed to do for their career. Run counter to the person who controlled the band and get myself fired. Once the artist is a hit artist, they are totally in control. Nobody else is going to control them. Right now Robin Trower listens to every word I say and actually will do some of the things that I ask him to do. At the time when he was enormous, he wouldn't listen to anybody. He did what he chose to do and everybody else said, 'Yes, sir.'

"After I got involved with Robin, one of the first things I tried to do was to rationalize his financial situation. And the pressure I put on the then-business manager was part of the reason that the guy spent seven years in jail for stealing money from clients. He stole everything that Robin and the band had. And he also stole £1,000,000 from Pink Floyd. Finished off doing seven to twelve in the clink. But Robin couldn't regain anything because the crook used all the money to buy property in the south of Spain in the name of his wife. Robin lost everything he'd ever made. But, nonetheless, I would love to see him have some kind of an annuity from the business to which he has contributed so greatly."

Author: "Most of the people that I've spoken to have recurring stories in similar situations, either it be with management or the record companies, that were not in their favor. And the two schools of thought are 1) either they didn't care or 2) they were just grateful for what they had, kept their mouths shut and did their jobs."

Derek Sutton: "My feeling is that artists generally are very trusting people. What they do, or at least the artists from the 70s, they didn't believe that they needed to do any business. They were too busy creating their art. They trusted the people that they were working with and they had no reason not to — in the early stages. But then when the money started to flow … there are an awful lot of people in the business who don't really like artists and basically don't give them very much credit. And certainly try to divert as much of the cash flow as possible into their own pockets. All you've got to do is look at the way the industry is today and see the vast salaries being paid to major record moguls. They're greatly out of any proportion to what the artists get. And what has happened has been that the people that are in the business value the business more than they value the artists that create the product that supports the industry. And there's this whole lovely côterie going on. The current crop of executives loves the fact that the artists are virtually interchangeable because that way they have even more power. I think that's just endemic. I think that's the way it is. I think it's the kind of people that are in the business. It is one of the fatal weaknesses that people that are the artists have. There are very few artists that can be like a Mick Jagger who can run a business as well as creating popular art."

Author: "But why would these artists not have asked the odd question?"

Derek Sutton: "They have no reason to. They're focused entirely elsewhere. Their entire focus is on the pressure to create. They're always being asked to make more music, more music, more music. And that is a difficult task. So they leave the business with the classic stories."

Author: "Could it have been a guise at times where management would keep the artists in homes and the like so that they wouldn't ask questions?"

Derek Sutton: "I don't think so. I think you're giving too much credit for intelligence to the managers. You have to remember, I've said this before and I'll say it again, there aren't a lot of very bright people in this business. There never have been. The people that fly by the seat of their pants, they may be street smart but they are not very bright. I don't think they have the ability to plan that kind of a thing or the understanding. Especially not back in the early 70s.

Everybody was in it for different reasons but it was more fun and games and 'Boy, this is amazing. Let's do this until we get caught' kind of thing. You just did what came naturally and for a lot of people that was grab whatever you can get. If somebody isn't smart enough to stop you from taking it then you take it."

Author: "Everywhere I've lived it seemed that there was some sort of 'musicians community' where they would, on occasion, be able to sit down and talk amongst themselves. Did that exist back then?"

Derek Sutton: "Oh yeah. Especially if there was something specific to talk about. I mean, music, particularly. But they didn't talk business."

Author: "And they never noticed precedence? Because there was a time where everybody was getting ripped off. And I just can't seem to get over this self-fabricated hump of why it never dawned on anyone because the mistakes kept getting repeated."

Derek Sutton: "Because there's no communication. Apply that to a regular corporation. How many people within a corporate entity are going to sit down and discuss their salaries and benefits with other people? They don't. It's only when there became a series of real bright and really controlling attorneys that the information was widely spread.

"When Styx was first really big on the road we carried with us a tour accountant. By three or four years later this guy had a file on every building in the country and knew what all of the expenses were before he went in. Now this was totally unheard of until the late 70s, early 80s. First of all touring wasn't the multimillion dollar business it is now. The dollars were much smaller. But the overall sophistication of the business was very low. It was definitely a cash and carry business. In the Ten Years After case I would very often be carrying seventy, eighty, ninety thousand dollars in cash in the saddlebags on my shoulder. At a time when you could buy a house in L.A. for that kind of money. And the bank used to freak out. I'd come in dressed in a Georgia

State Prison shirt, faded jeans and clogs and start pulling out wads and wads of bills. There were no checks and balances. Tickets were roll tickets. The same was true of the record companies. There are stories about companies having double sets of books, manufacturing one set of records and selling and paying royalties on another set of records that were going out the back door. And nobody ever knew where the money went. That's the way the business was back then. It was run by a bunch of crooks. Everybody felt really lucky to be doing what they loved doing and getting paid for it.

"You can go all the way back to Chuck Berry. You can go back to Buddy Holly. All of them. The actual royalties that those people were getting paid were abominable. It still happens even today. It's probably worse today than it ever has been, even though it's institutionalized because the family of powerful lawyers and record companies are symbiotic. There's nobody really and truly representing the artists anymore because managers are reliant on the lawyers to get them the deals to keep them in business. And the lawyers are reliant on the record companies to keep them in deals and keep them in business. Nobody's really arguing for the artists. And what's happened over the last fifteen years is a lot of expenses that used to be a part of record companies' daily business have now been passed on to the artists. Things like promotion and the cost of making videos. It's not anything but a promotion cost. Tour support. All paid for by the artists. But when it comes down to the record company hiring any kind of promotion people, charging them back to the artists, and independent marketing people and charging that back to the artists, all they're doing is, with the connivance of the attorneys, is basically legally stealing from the artists.

"Another thing. Why is it, for instance, that a producer who is in the studio makes a record and is never a part of the business again, gets paid from the first sale of a record? The artist has to recoup all of the costs of making the record and the video and the tour support and everything else before the artist gets paid. And even when it's been repaid, the record company OWNS the master!! But nobody's fighting to change it. We're talking in the year 2001, when we're dealing with sophisticated attorneys, sophisticated management, sophisticated artists, that don't fight the system.

"The moment the artist has a big hit the power switches from the record company/manager to the artist. And very often that is to the artists' detriment because they then start doing things that are self-indulgent and screw themselves up. They are so busy trying to impress their musician friends that they forget that the audience is not employed by the musicians. But there are no record companies who can manufacture artists. This doesn't happen. This guy that's made Backstreet Boys and 'N Sync; that's one man with an organization. Everything else depends to a very large extent upon songs and it depends upon a creative process that is not controlled or understood very well by the suits."

•   •   •

Derek Sutton: "We worked together for a couple of years. It came to an end after the 'Victims Of The Fury' record. We parted company and we were separated until 1984 when I got the call that he wanted to tour and would I do the American business. Robin had drifted around, hooked up with Keith Reid. Keith offered to manage him. And as soon as Keith Reid and Robin agreed on the management, Keith called me and asked would I do the work [laughs]? I said that the only way I would do it was if I was given complete carte blanche to do it myself and present him with a profit making tour. And if I paid myself off the top. So there's that gap. And from '84 until now it's been continuous."

Trower's wanting to try something new led to another lineup change, this one involving his signature singer. Robin felt that a different vocalist was the way he wanted to go.

Matthew Fisher: "Rob is one of these people that every now and then he likes to make changes. He feels he needs a change. And somehow you get a feeling that he does it for the sake of it. Just because he feels that he's had enough of something and he wants to go off in another direction. I suppose there's a lot of other factors involved. Maybe he was getting bored with the sound; that by getting another singer he could change the sound. It's like when he got Rustee Allen to play bass. I couldn't really hear the difference. Which is not to say that there is no difference between Jimmy and Rustee. As bass players, I suppose in the right context, they're poles apart. But, really, when you start having Rob's music and you've got fairly fixed bass lines, it really doesn't make an awful lot of difference who's playing them. It could be Rustee Allen, it could be Jack Bruce, it could be Jimmy. They're all gonna sound pretty much the same."

Derek Sutton: "I don't really know what was happening with Jimmy. He was going through a very difficult part of his own life. Jimmy had always been a heavy drinker but Robin felt that he couldn't get anymore out of the unit than he had and he needed to try something different. And even though Jimmy had a great set of pipes, he wasn't a creative singer. Robin had to coach a lot of what he sang. A lot of the phrasing and a lot of the delivery was induced by Robin. And so in many ways Jimmy was an instrument that Robin played."

Bill Lordan: "I think Jimmy kind of deteriorated because of not taking care of himself. I think Robin just couldn't work with him anymore. His voice was gone and I think he was drinking too much as well. It became a problem where it affected him."

Robin Trower: "I spoke with Jimmy and told him that I wanted to do something different."

Bill Lordan: "So Robin had to make a choice to go ahead and do something else, to think of who else he could use. And one day on the radio he heard a Cream song and he thought, 'I'll get Jack Bruce [laughs].' So he got a hold of Jack and we got together and played him the songs. He thought they were great and we went to the Kinks' studio in Hornsey, England, at Konk Studios and we laid it down. That was one of the easiest, fun albums and the greatest bass player I ever worked with. So effortless."

Jack Bruce: "I really don't have a problem playing with any good drummer."

Robin Trower: "I also thought that it would be great if Jimmy could do a solo album. Chrysalis were interested in him doing his own album."

Dewar hired John Platania and David Hayes, friends who were playing with Van Morrison at the time, along with Andy McMasters from The Motors, who helped write material and drummer Dave Mattacks from Fairport Convention, to play on the record. Dewar covered The Stones, as well as Buddy Holly and The Drifters and a recently penned Dewar/Trower song. The result was entitled "Stumbledown Romancer." The album was recorded at Matthew Fisher's home studio with Matthew producing.

Matthew Fisher: "I think how that album happened was more through the instigation of Ronnie Lyons. Ronnie was managing me and he was friendly with Jimmy. And we had this studio together, me and Ronnie. I think he saw it as a project to get some money out of Chrysalis for. So that's why that happened."

The album wasn't released.

Matthew Fisher: "They didn't like it. It doesn't sound like anything Jimmy was doing in Rob's band, does it?"

Author: "Wouldn't that have been the intention?"

Matthew Fisher: "I don't know if it was much of an intention. We just thought, 'Let's do this and let's do that.' We did things. We never really planned it as an album."

In early 1981, Robin and Jack Bruce, along with Bill Lordan, entered Konk Studios and began work on "BLT." With the exception of a song that Robin had co-written a year earlier with James Dewar, the other nine songs were new and intended to show freshness in the direction Trower was now taking.

Derek Sutton: "At that point in time we were trying to get Robin to experiment. If he wasn't gonna have Jimmy, which was, other than the guitar, the most recognizable thing … a lot of people used to think that the voice was Robin. We wanted him to go out and do something different. Commercially we needed something to restore interest in Robin Trower. Jack Bruce had been in a couple of supergroups. Jack Bruce is a bass player/singer, which is what Robin is comfortable with. It seemed like a really good idea at the time."

Jack Bruce: "I met Robin many years ago when he was with Procol Harum but I didn't see him for a long time. He approached me to see if I'd be interested in making a record with him. And so we in fact made that record which was quite successful."

Robin Trower: "I thought it would be an interesting thing to play with Jack, one of my heroes. I got his number from somewhere. I called him and asked him if he'd be interested. I met with him and played him some of my music, some of my ideas and we went on from there. We didn't rehearse for that album. He just came into the studio. I don't think he spent a lot of time on it. We just banged it down live mostly and then mixed it."

Author: "Who came up with the name?"

Robin Trower: "I did [laughs]. I was being sort of jocular with it but I thought it was a fun idea."

Bill Lordan: "Robin said he did, but I say I did. He took the credit. Immediately I thought of BLT and a bacon, lettuce and tomato sandwich. But Robin would say that he came up with the name. And I guess from there they came up with that cover. But it sure was a natural and it could be a good nostalgia tour."

Though expectations were high for selling concert tickets. "BLT" never toured.

Robin Trower: "I just wasn't sure about the album at the end of it. And I was sort of going through a patch of not wanting to go on the road. I didn't really feel like it."

Jack Bruce: "Robin felt that we didn't have enough material. Which in fact is ridiculous. I've got over five hundred songs [laughs]. And he's got a few himself! But at that time he wasn't really too keen to tour. I had my own band and my own record at that time too. So it was difficult for me to actually tour. But I would probably have been prepared to tour with that band but it never came up, really."

Derek Sutton: "Interesting thing. Jack Bruce had never seen Robin play until 1998."

Jack Bruce: "I saw him not so long ago in San Francisco. He was playing there and I went along to see him. And he was playing absolutely beautifully. A fantastic show."

Derek Sutton: "And when Jack actually saw Robin play in San Francisco, he came backstage afterwards and said, 'Shit. I wish I'd seen you play before we recorded together. It would have given me an entirely different idea of what we could do.' "

Bill Lordan: "At the same time we did the album, Jack had a group with Billy Cobham, Clem Clempson and David Sancious. They had recorded an album for Epic, 'I've Always Wanted To Do This.' His other project had an offer to go out on tour right at the same time, and he really wanted to go out and play with that lineup, which didn't do that well as far as the numbers went. It was kind of a flop, actually. This would have been our comeback. This would have been a great tour. We could have done the old Cream songs and the best of Robin and "BLT." And when Jack did come and said he could go Robin said, 'Sorry, mate, it's too late. The opportunity, the window, had closed and passed us by.'"

Author: "But the lineup certainly would have enticed people to buy tickets."

Robin Trower: "Yeah. It would have meant going on and playing some of his old stuff and some of my old stuff, plus some 'BLT' stuff. I don't think that really appealed to me. The idea of 'Truce' was to put together enough material. But I actually wish I hadn't done that second album. I think 'BLT' was as far as that combination could have gone. And I was right."

Jack Bruce: "The first one was very successful. We did a second one and that one wasn't quite as commercially successful."

Author: "Why did Bill leave after the 'BLT' album?"

Robin Trower: "I just decided to try a different drummer. I went back to Reg to see if he could bring back some of that old beat. To see if that worked nicely. It was just falling with the formula all the time. When I looked back at the first album, it just wasn't quite it."

Reg Isidore: "The whole thing had to do with Robin and it was to do with Jack and it was to do with their managers. I don't think the egos went together. It just didn't happen. I was just along to play drums. Do the album. It was supposed to be a touring band but it just didn't materialize."

"Truce" was an album that displayed a new sound for Trower, far more involved than his previous releases. One would think that the co-production credit attributed to Jack Bruce may have been the difference.

Jack Bruce: "I wouldn't say I was more involved in the production. I'd say there was too much production on that one compared to the first one. And 'BLT' was good because it was simple, straight ahead. For guitar, bass and drums kind of records, it's best just to get in there and record it. But Robin had some slightly different ideas for the second one. One of them was to use a click-track for the drummer to play to and I've never liked to play to metronomic time. I don't think the record worked too well."

Robin Trower: "And that was my fault as well. That was down to me. I thought the only way we could really get big, clean beautiful sounds was to do everything sort of separate. But not a good idea. At that time most modern records were being made that way and I thought that there must have been something in it. I'd heard records that worked very well having been done that way. So, 'Let's give it a go!' It ended up not being a very good album. To my mind. I think the material wasn't very good. There were a couple of good things on there. I've realized, in recent years, that I have never put enough time into writing and preparing material for an album. It's only these last two or three albums. The one I'm working on now, 'Go My Way,' is the most time I've ever put into getting the material sorted out before recording."

Author: "After 'Truce' you took a couple of years off. What occupied your time?"

Robin Trower: "I spent most of the time with the kids. Kids just growing up. Just mostly that."

Bill Lordan: "We all had to look elsewhere for other projects and other things to do. And there could have been some contractual things about getting away from one manager and he got back with Derek. There might have been other reasons but I think he just needed to clear his head and have some time to think about what he wanted to do next. I never heard from him that I was fired or that it was over. We never really spoke. He isn't real good with confrontations.

"I joined a Christian band for a while, the Darryl Mansfield Band, and we did contemporary Christian music and toured all over the world. That was kind of a good thing to get into. It was very supportive. Everybody was clean and sober and I met some good musicians, guys that I'm still in touch with and work with. It kept me going for quite a few years. It was a difficult time with the recession and disco all through the 80s."

Author: "I admire your commitment to experiment."

Robin Trower: "It's cost me [laughs]! There are a lot of albums I wish I hadn't done actually. Lots and lots. I'm OK about the first Jack Bruce album because that was an experiment and it kind of worked. The second one didn't work. We didn't work hard enough to try and get the music to gel between the two of us. Where with the first one I felt he came in on my thing as more of a session player/singer and did a great job. The songs I'd written weren't the greatest. It kinda worked in a way, some of the tracks. The second one we tried to do as a band, more and more as equals on the thing and write together. But we didn't work hard enough on that side of it. I wish I'd never done hardly any albums of the 80s. I hate most of them. 'In The Line Of Fire,' 'Take What You Need,' all that stuff."

Derek Sutton: "There are a couple that he truly hates. 'Beyond The Mist,' which was something that Keith and I cooked up because we couldn't keep touring if we didn't have something to put out. We got some outtakes and some live stuff that we put together on a CD and had it independently released because we didn't have Chrysalis. The other one would be 'In The Line Of Fire,' which was a Davey Pattison album with Robin playing on it. Made at the behest of Atlantic who wanted Robin Trower to play with session musicians and concentrate on songs rather than concentrate on playing the guitar."

Author: "Why was there no tour with 1983's 'Back It Up'?"

Robin Trower: "Probably because I didn't want to go out there. I would say that would be the fundamental of it."

Author: "Would this be relative to what you said about those albums of that time?"

Robin Trower: "I was pretty pleased with 'Back It Up,' I must admit. At the time I thought it was a good record. I just wasn't inspired enough to go out on the road, yet if it had had some success I would have gone out with it."

With no radio support and no tour to promote the album, Chrysalis Records dropped Trower from their roster. Robin returned to England to decide where to go from there.

Author: "Why was Robin let go from Chrysalis?"

Roy Eldridge: "This is probably something that had gone on between Derek and Chris and Robin. 'Is this working?' Again this is something I didn't deal with so I can't really tell you."

Derek Sutton: "To be brutal, Chrysalis couldn't make money from him anymore. Robin had become very reclusive. He still wanted to live his lifestyle but he really didn't want to go out and work. I left his environs because I had a big argument with him and told him that if he didn't work, he wouldn't eat. He got very upset with me. I didn't speak to him for a couple of years."

Robin Trower: "Basically, they just decided to let me go. They gave me the option of doing one more album or going. And we decided it might be good to go. But they took so long, dragging their feet, about finalizing that. It was not good."

Author: "Were you surprised?"

Robin Trower: "No, not really. I guess they decided that they didn't need me in the family anymore [laughs]! I was informed through management."

• • •

Author: "How did you hook up with Dave Bronze?"

Robin Trower: "I knew him through my brother, who is also a guitar player, locally. We got together. I tried him out on some rehearsals.

"I would talk to people and they'd say, 'You know, so-and-so's a great drummer. You should try him.' It's all that kind of thing. Try them out. Put them on a couple of tracks. If you like them … Bobby Clouter was actually a very good drummer but I never toured with that album (Back It Up). They have to make a living. They go on to something else and by the time you turn around, they're not available."

Trower took singer/bassist Dave Bronze and drummer Martin Clapson into the studio and recorded two new tracks to be released along with the aforementioned live tracks that Derek Sutton and Keith Reid scanned and agreed upon. The album was entitled "Beyond The Mist" and didn't do anywhere what the Trower camp expected. It was obvious that Robin needed a vocalist to take over the void left by James Dewar. Bronze more than sufficed on bass but a singer to carry the weight was needed.

Author: "You then released 'Passion,' a new album on a new label with a new band. How did you decide to go with this lineup?"

Youngstown, Ohio, 1984.
Courtesy Scott Pickard

Robin Trower: "A friend, Johnny Rewind, had played me a tape of Davey Pattison and I liked what I heard."

Davey Pattison: "I was born November 18, 1945, in Glasgow, Scotland. I was first exposed to music through my family. My mother and my aunt had a little duo where they would go to parties and sing Andrews Sisters kind of things. I didn't realize it was influencing me until much later on. The only thing in Britain that was playing what I call rock 'n' roll was Radio Luxembourg. Every Sunday night Jack Jackson would play American rock 'n' roll music. Little Richard is the guy that got me going. I was taken to see him when I was a little boy. I remember thinking, 'God, I don't know what he's doing but I want to do that!' To me, Richard is definitely the true 'King of Rock 'n' Roll.' It was very American to me. I looked at Richard, Presley, Chuck Berry

and thought immediately about America. And the glamour that we thought America was. I think everybody here thought that America was all like Hollywood.

"About 1965 I got this regular gig playing guitar and singing in a Top 40 band at a little bar in Glasgow called The Burns Cottage, and that's where I met Jimmy Dewar. Frankie Miller. Guys from the Average White Band. Everybody was hanging out at this little bar.

"I started writing songs in the early 70s. I went down to London, through Jimmy Dewar, and recorded an album of those songs with Matthew Fisher. He produced the album with the hope of maybe getting a deal in America but it never saw the light of day. But Bill Lordan gave a copy of that tape to Bill Graham. I got a call from Bill in the middle of the night, asking me if I'd be interested in flying to San Francisco. Graham was managing a band with Ronnie Montrose, which would eventually become Gamma. I took the offer and flew out. Ronnie and I started to write songs together and that became the first Gamma record. I've been in San Francisco ever since.

"In 1982 Ronnie was getting tired of getting little or no support from Electra and I was getting a little tired of the hard rock thing. I'd known Robin for a long time through Jimmy. Jimmy and I were pretty close pals. I'd been working here (San Francisco) with a friend of mine called Johnny Rewind. Obviously, not his real name. He had a studio in Mill Valley, California, and he and I were in there pretty much every day getting ideas going, writing songs. He was friends with Robin and gave him a copy of what we'd been up to. I don't think Robin was overly impressed by the music but was impressed by the voice. I got a call from him asking me if I'd be interested in singing on 'Passion.'"

Robin Trower: "So I got in touch with Davey and invited him down. I had been doing some work with Dave Bronze and he was the one who brought Pete Thompson by."

Author: "The album certainly took on a bit more of an edge with this lineup. Was that circumstance or a conscious direction you were hoping to go into?"

Robin Trower: "I'm not sure it was a conscious decision. With Davey on vocals you have a natural edge to the sound."

Davey Pattison: "The music always appealed to me because it's very deep, very bluesy. So when Robin called me up to do it, I was thrilled. I knew I would enjoy it and I could do it. My first two sessions were wonderful. I had a great time."

Author: "Were you a part of the band as opposed to a hired player?"

Davey Pattison: "Nobody said a word. Dave Bronze was on bass and Pete Thompson was on drums. Everybody looked at each other and said, 'Yeah, this is going to be very, very cool.' So nothing had to be said."

Author: "Where did producer Neil Norman come from?"

Robin Trower: "I think he just contacted Derek about producing 'cuz I didn't have a record deal."

Derek Sutton: "Neil called me and said, 'I want to make a record with Robin Trower.' I said, 'Where's the money gonna come from?' And he said, 'My record company.' I said, 'Who's gonna produce it?' And he said, 'I am.' 'All right then, let's go into the studio and try a couple of tracks.' We did two or three tracks, it seemed to be working and they were prepared to put up the money to do the job so away we went."

Author: "How quickly did you start promoting this on the road?"

Davey Pattison: "The same year, 1986. We started in Cincinnati. We were playing mostly clubs, some theaters. In the summer we'd do some 8,000-seat sheds in a co-headline kind of thing where we'd work with The Allman Brothers or something like that. Johnny Winter. I'm a guy who likes the road, so it was a lot of fun for me."

In November of 1987, terrible news arrived in the offices of Trower's management. After almost two decades of drinking, drugging, poor diet and the other cliché trappings of a rock star, James Dewar suffered a stroke. Though disputed by some, he suffered another stroke soon thereafter, leaving him unable to care for himself. Fortunately for Dewar, since he had spent the vast majority of his wealth, these terrible events occurred in Scotland, where socialized medicine will take care of him. He was, and still is, institutionalized. The news hit Robin and those close to Dewar very hard. Many close to Jimmy could see some form of harm being inevitable, but they had never thought that he would be so incapacitated. Trower had always hoped in the back of his mind that a reunion with the original lineup might one day be possible but that option has now been closed.

Davey Pattison: "It affected his memory. He's in a wheelchair, can't walk anymore. It's awfully sad. I hadn't seen Jimmy since Gamma toured Europe in 1981. I was home last May, back in Scotland, and I was going to see him in hospital. And my friend, who knows us both, said, 'You're better off not going 'cuz he won't know who you are.' So I would rather remember him the way I remember him. Which I think is probably better for me 'cuz we were pretty tight for a long time."

Author: "Were there noticeable signs of this ever happening?"

Robin Trower: "No. Not when I knew him."

Derek Sutton: "Robin has never had problems with substances. Other members of the band have but Robin has never had problems with substances."

Bill Lordan: "Robin never had a problem. Jimmy and I were the partyers in the band. But nobody was addicted or did anything that harmed the performance. Jimmy, being a Scotsman, called Scotch the nectar of the gods. Me coming out of Sly where we had tried a little bit of everything, it never got in the way and it was never a problem. Jimmy's health problems later on, I think, were more from his drinking, smoking and a bad diet and not really taking care of himself. I was never a cigarette smoker. In school I was athletic. I played football, track and basketball. I'm tall and thin and was always in good physical shape. And drumming is like an aerobics workout so I always kind of stayed in good shape. It was only later on when it started to take a toll on Jimmy."

Robin Trower: "He liked to drink and whatever else but it never, never interfered with his work. He was a real pro, Jimmy. He might have a bottle of beer before he went on, but didn't overdo it and not perform great."

Author: "So this was all extracurricular?"

Robin Trower: "Yeah. You know, when he was at home off the road and we weren't doing much he got bored and that may be a part of the problem."

Author: "Back when you were playing with Jimmy were there any signs, because of the way he was treating himself, that his health was going to catch up with him?"

Rustee Allen: "Other than a fifth of Scotch on stage [laughs]? Yeah, I guess in subtle ways. You could almost sense that his potential wasn't being utilized. He was used to playing bass and singing. If he wasn't playing he was kind of lost. He wasn't this great stage performer where he would jump up and do the splits and all this kind of stuff so he would kind of fall back into the wings and whatever. I remember one time we were listening to a Revox two-track of a gig and he was saying, 'I can do that.' And I said, 'I'm sure you could, Jimmy.' But these subtle things like that made me feel that he was missing playing bass. He felt lost without that in his hands. Like I said, he would have a fifth of Scotch on stage and I didn't realize he was consuming that much."

Author: "Not to sound morbid but he was lucky that his strokes happened in a country that will take care of him."

Robin Trower: "Yeah. I imagine if that sort of thing happened to you in America, it's a different kettle of fish. He would have been on the street. I wish he was still about and singing with that beautiful voice."

Davey Pattison: "Jimmy Dewar, in my opinion, is the best white singer I've ever heard. Without a shadow of a doubt. A very quiet, unassuming man. Soulful, deep. Certainly moody. I miss him. I miss the Jimmy that I know."

Robin Trower: "Yeah, he's certainly up there. It was an exceptional voice, an exceptional thing."

Author: "The combination and uniqueness of your playing and his voice was very effective."

Robin Trower: "That's right, very effective. There's no doubt in my mind that the lineup that worked the best, that had the best overall sonic and feel was the first lineup. Reg, me and Jimmy. That combination of guys was without a doubt the one that worked the best. There was a magic about it. It was one of those things. A match made in heaven. He was a sweetheart, no doubt about it. A lovely man."

Bill Lordan: "It's too bad that his demise was because of his health and other things. When he left Robin to move to Scotland he got into some used auto parts business. A guy named Joe MacCourtney. I remember that little guy. He took advantage of Jimmy's good nature, which wasn't hard to do. Jimmy was the salt of the earth."

Davey Pattison: "Joe MacCourtney used to manage me too."

Author: "Prior to this business, was Jimmy well off?"

Davey Pattison: "I don't think he was rock-star wealthy. When he moved back to Scotland he got involved with Joe MacCourtney and bought this mansion of a house. And when he lost his money he couldn't afford the house anymore. So he made some bad choices. You want to buy a house you know you can stay in for the rest of your life. But Jimmy was a very trusting guy, so I guess he was trying to look towards his future with a view that his career in the music business was pretty much over. He was looking for something else to get involved in and a little panic sets in when that's what you've done all your life and suddenly it ain't there anymore. So I think he probably started to panic a little bit. Joe's still around I think but not involved in the music business anymore."

Author: "Have you been keeping abreast of Jimmy's situation over the years?"

Robin Trower: "Yeah. We hear, from time to time, from Mattie, his wife. I suppose we speak a couple of times a year on the phone. And my wife speaks to his children sometimes on the phone so we're pretty much up to date."

Author: "Do you feel he's comfortable?"

Robin Trower: "I think he's being looked after, from what we've heard."

While conducting my research I discovered that few people rarely visit Jimmy anymore, mostly because of his lack of awareness of those around him. But I was very curious as to whether he could sense music or certain activities that might trigger any kind of response. I had spoken to the hospital director who was unaware of Jimmy's particular case and he passed me off to a very kind woman who knew that Dewar was formerly "some sort of pop star." I explained to her the true situation and she was most impressed. She contacted a doctor who would be aware of his particular case and I was told that he would contact me in the very near future. I never heard from him. Prior to going to print, I contacted the hospital again and received the following reply from Marian Allan.

"Dear Mr. Muise.

You enquired of a patient in our hospital. I am sorry to say that the individual is not in a position to give consent to your request and staff have not had recent comment from the family so that your enquiry might be passed to them. In conclusion, therefore I regret we cannot help you with your enquiry."

Just prior to this book going to press, I was put in touch with Brian Denniston, a man who has been a friend of Dewar's since 1966 and is a regular visitor to the hospital. Contrary to the popular opinion that he isn't capable of communicating, Jimmy understands where he resides though he's not exactly sure why he's there and the duration

James Dewar, 1977.
Photo ad for "Gandoff The Wizard," a leather store in
Royal Oak, Michigan.
Courtesy Bill Lordan

of his current stay. I was hoping Denniston could shed some light as to why the family couldn't be contacted for permission for me to get some information on Dewar's condition.

Brian Denniston: "I don't know the real situation regarding the family. I haven't seen his wife, Mattie, for several years. I initially wanted a photograph of Jimmy to send to Bill Lordan, of whom Jimmy is very fond, but that, like your request, was rejected on the grounds that I would have to get permission from the family and the hospital board would have to be consulted for deliberation. With regard to Jimmy's actual condition I have to say it's not great. He can walk, if aided, and will converse, although sometimes it's only one word replies to questions. 'How are you today.' Short pause. 'OK.' Other times he will say more. It is true to say, though, that he never was a big conversationalist as Bill or Davey Pattison will testify.

"I have to say that as far as the hospital goes they're very security-orientated and I myself don't really get much info from them. Except one of the male nurses told me that he doesn't see visitors very often.

"I only wanted to tell any fans that Jimmy is alive, although not at his best, and should hopefully not be forgotten with reference to the major part that he played within the Robin Trower Band during his tenure."

When Denniston asked about playing with Trower, Jimmy responded, "I'd go back tomorrow, aye I would!"

1988

Author: "Was the band progressing when you went in to record 'Take What You Need'?"

Davey Pattison: "Oh, absolutely. We were used to playing with one another. I thought it was progressing. This lineup that Robin had was the best band he ever had. That's my opinion. I think Robin needed somebody like myself, if not me, just to push a little bit the show side of it. Because Robin is a shy kind of guy. I have so many reviews here saying that I was exactly what Robin needed. A pushy guy! I think he needed a cheerleader. I used to get the crowd singing all the time and he needed that. When Jimmy was there, Jimmy was the same as Robin. Really quiet, unassuming guy. I'd been around the arena situation fronting a hard rock band. With Gamma. With Robin I took a step backwards from that. I wasn't running around the stage but I was kind of mouthy."

Though Pete Thompson played on the album, Robin brought Bill Lordan back into the fold to tour.

Author: "By bringing Bill back in the band was it an attempt to return to an earlier groove you had set?"

Robin Trower: "There was a certain excitement about his playing. Yeah, I think maybe that's what I was looking for."

A drastic event occurred in 1989 that affected many artists. Chrysalis was sold to EMI.

Roy Eldridge: "A number of things happened. The principle thing was Chris and Terry weren't getting along very well. After the early days of the management company, when they were both looking after groups and putting

themselves under enormous stresses and strains, when that settled down and they became record company executives, Terry had very much run the American end and Chris had very much run the U.K. and European end. Then there came a time when Terry wanted to come back to the U.K. so we had them both working here. Their relationship just wasn't the same. The company was in acute danger of being pulled apart. In fact it was going to be pulled apart so it was obvious something had to happen.

"In the end, Terry was bought out. It could have gone either which-way. One time they were going to try and split it in half but in the end, through a lot of private conversations that the two of them had, it was agreed that Terry was going to be bought out. There'd been some pretty hairy moments in terms of cash flow. America, although I've referred to it earlier as the Holy Grail, is also a very expensive place in which to operate a record company. The sheer size of the country, the promotion, your marketing expenses are pretty high. The company had been really hot with the Benatars, the Huey Lewis's, the Billy Idols, Blondie. We couldn't have been much hotter over there or indeed over here because we were having similar success with Ultravox, Spandau Ballet and vice versa. So it was a particularly great period in the company's history. But it was expensive and we needed to get a new partner in America. Terry had by this time gone, paid off. I think Chris thought that EMI, being an English company, would be the right sort of partner. I lived through that period over this side of the water and it was pretty dire.

"America never worked for EMI, period, I don't think. And it was very painful. Every act that I had on the label wanted out of EMI America. You had the acts that were concerned about the future of the company when it was an independent. When it went with EMI, we went from one uncertainty to a different uncertainty. This was kind of corporate uncertainty, with a different style of management. Chrysalis had always been very much an independent record company and very personal and very hands-on. But then you went to an EMI culture which was much more corporate, a less 'artist-friendly' culture with tougher deadlines and not so flexible in its way of operating. That was pretty grim actually.

"EMI had bought the first 50 percent in '89 and they had the right to buy the remaining 50 percent in '91 which, of course, they duly did. I was the managing director of Chrysalis Records at that time in the U.K. and then became the managing director of Chrysalis Records under EMI management as well, from '91 'til '95. And that was a particularly painful period for me because at that time in the U.K. we had our own sales force, our own international team, this whole range of people who through absolutely no fault of their own, because of the way these things happen, had to be made redundant. EMI didn't want them. What EMI wanted was this brand and its artists. And so I had the very painful task, within the four years I was in that culture, of having to make people redundant who I had grown up with. Now I'm not blaming EMI entirely for that because that's business. There were good parts of the EMI experience. But my overall feeling about it is one of sadness because it absorbed Chrysalis and the artists from those days, whether it be Sinead O'Connor or Jethro Tull, World Party or any of the preceding acts, are no longer there. So I think it's a bit of a mockery, the Chrysalis-EMI of today. But I would think that, wouldn't I?"

1990 saw the release of "In The Line Of Fire," a collaborative effort of outside forces all chipping in for the common good. Famed producer and engineer Eddie Kramer, whose work with everyone from Hendrix to Led Zeppelin is legendary, was available. As he had always considered Trower one of his favorite guitarists, Kramer jumped at the chance to work with Robin.

Author: "How influential was Eddie Kramer in choosing the players that actually played on the record?"

Robin Trower: "He decided that he wanted to bring in different bass and drums and he was adamant about it. That was that, basically."

Davey Pattison: "We were in L.A. Bill Lordan was on drums, Dave Bronze was on bass. Eddie Kramer came to see the band."

Dave Bronze: "As I recall Kramer came to one show, The Country Club in Reseda, and subsequently made his decision."

Davey Pattison: "And I guess Eddie wanted to use his session guys as a rhythm section. Which kind of upset me at the time, but it wasn't my decision. Robin was on Atlantic Records then and they were pulling the strings. There is only so much you can say when your career is on the line like that. At that point there were no other deals around. Eddie brought in John Regan on bass, Tony Beard on drums and Bobby Mayo, who was fabulous, on keyboards."

Dave Bronze: "Robin must have had his own reasons for seemingly acquiescing so readily to this decision. I'm sure more went on than I know about, but history would seem to indicate that the decision was not a good one."

Author: "Was Kramer's track record the credibility he needed for you to go along with these changes?"

Robin Trower: "Yeah, I think so. I mean, it was something he was adamant about. He'd come to hear the band live. We tried out two different sets of bass and drums in rehearsal. And settled on who we ended up using on the album."

Author: "How difficult was it for you to stand back and let someone else do everything?"

Robin Trower: "It was something I wanted to try. To bring in a producer that was going to be in control with it. I was just going to be the artist. I was prepared to do it and did it with good grace. But it seems a bit forced to me. As I say all that stuff that I did in the 80s … put it this way. I'm far happier with the albums I've made, the last two and this one that's about to be finished. And being in complete control of it and doing the music that I want to do."

Author: "Why such limited touring to promote 'In The Line Of Fire?' "

Davey Pattison: "Because we were getting absolutely no support from Atlantic. I was calling up friends at radio stations here in San Francisco and saying, 'Hey, why aren't you playing me?' And they would say, 'We don't have it.' Atlantic Records weren't even sending it out to the radio stations. I was appalled of their attitude towards that. 'In The Line Of Fire' took two years to put together. I'd fly to London, rehearse, Robin would write some more, I'd throw my coppers in there. And when it came out, no one knew it was out. We'd go to L.A. to do these videos that cost God knows how much, but nobody saw it. They weren't out promoting it. The music business sucks, mate."

Robin Trower: "I'm never involved in that end of it. I'm usually, by that time, thinking about what I'm gonna do next. So that one's already by the by. To be in the position to make records is luck enough, it really is. There are so many musicians out there that can't even get to make albums. You just consider yourself lucky. I'm very fortunate in the way Derek looks after me and makes it possible for me to make albums regardless of how many they sell."

Author: "Why was 'In The Line Of Fire' not promoted by Atlantic?"

Derek Sutton: "Because when they got it they realized it was a piece of shit. Robin Trower records are guitar records. They're not Davey Pattison singing great songs with Robin's guitar back in the mix someplace. It wasn't a Robin Trower record, it was a Davey Pattison record. And as much as I love Davey's voice, I think the record was engineered all wrong. Eddie Kramer is brilliant when he's brilliant, but he's just completely bland when he's not."

Author: "Was he hired to get the end result you just mentioned?"

Derek Sutton: "I don't know. But what we finished off with was a vocal album. It was not a guitar album. And the biggest problem of all of that was the fact that we had made a very good album in the previous album, 'Passion.' That was a very good Robin Trower record. If we had not had the tie-up with GNP/Crescendo, that record would have gone to Atlantic and probably would have been a gold album. But we were dealing with a family-run record company that was based in the black jazz business. Once they have a master they're not gonna let it go. They would not hand the ball off to somebody that could have done a better job than they could. It would have made them more money than they could have ever made for themselves but they didn't want to hand away the master. And the interesting thing is that the attorney that GNP/Crescendo uses traditionally is a professor of law. And I found out three years later that he was the guy that David Geffen always used to hire to do a contract that he didn't ever want to complete. This guy knitpicked so much and takes so long to do every draft that everybody gives up and goes home before the contract is ever finished [laughs]!"

Author: "In the three albums you sang with Robin you had no songwriting credits."

Davey Pattison: "I was encouraging Robin to do more of that because a lot of the stuff he was coming up with was real good. I didn't want to upset the apple cart."

Author: "How did your association with Robin come to an end?"

Davey Pattison: "He stopped for a couple of years. He went back to work on Procol Harum's album and then he was co-producing Bryan Ferry. So there was a couple of years where there was nothing going on. And at that time Crescendo Records in L.A. brought out a 'Best of Gamma.' Ronnie Montrose and I got back together and we started touring with that. We knew that, at least on the West Coast, there would be a lot of action going on with it. Lots of radio and video play. The gigs were incredible because people hadn't seen it in fifteen years. So I did that for almost a year. Then I got fired from that because I didn't want to be playing music that was twenty years old and I couldn't get a record deal, as usual. The record business had moved on from that kind of music. But that year with Ronnie was a lot of fun."

Author: "You returned to Procol Harum at that point to record an album, 'Prodigal Stranger.' Was that something you had to be talked into or did you go willingly?"

Robin Trower: "I don't think I had to be talked into it. I very much liked the songs that they played. Keith brought some songs for me to hear and I thought they were excellent. And I'm not actually sure, when I think back, that those demos weren't better than the actual tracks that we ended up with on that album. Admittedly, there were drum machines and stuff, but I thought the demos were very strong. And I think, in some ways, what we ended up with on that album wasn't quite as strong. I've got no way of being it or playing one side of it against the other. That's the impression I've ended up with."

Derek Sutton: "I worked for five years to get the Procol Harum reunion thing put together with all of them in it, and they brought Robin in at the very, very last minute with no space for him to create at all. They just wanted his name on the album. That's all they wanted. Even after he had had greater commercial and artistic success than Procol Harum ever had. So that was the mindset."

Matthew Fisher: "When we reformed to do 'Prodigal Stranger' and we ended up being managed by (the late) Bill Graham … I couldn't understand why we were going with Bill Graham. As far as I was concerned, he was a promoter, not a manager."

Derek Sutton: "I think it was Mickey Briggs from BGL that did the management for Procol Harum on that tour."

Matthew Fisher: "And we needed a manager. I'd have been a lot happier, myself, if we'd been going with Derek. But from what you say [laughs] that was never in the cards! Which is a shame.

"Obviously, they wanted Rob to play on the 'Prodigal Stranger' album. But whether this was just a marketing move or was genuinely for musical reasons that they wanted him, your guess is as good as mine. To be honest, I don't personally think Rob's particularly good for Procol these days.

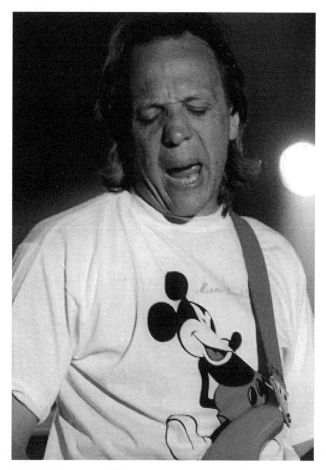

Nashville, Tennessee, 1985.
Courtesy Gary Morton

He's been on his own too long. His whole style's kind of evolved around being a guitarist in a three-piece. And to suddenly stick him back thirty years and say, 'Look, you've just gotta play in this slot here,' I don't think he's that same person. He's not the same player anymore. No reason why he should be either. And we never tried it with him on the road. We all thought it would be a total disaster. He's about a million times too loud [laughs]. He had just moved over into a completely different kind of arena to what Procol is. Procol is actually a quiet band. It might be loud out front through the sound system, but onstage it's pretty quiet."

Author: "But it's obvious why they would want his name to validate the promotion of the original lineup."

Matthew Fisher: "Yes, absolutely. But, to be honest, I wasn't convinced by what Rob did on the 'Prodigal Stranger' album. It didn't really gel for me. As far as I was concerned, I think I was really looking to sort of fit into what was going on. It was more like Rob was there for his little cameo appearance. And that's what it was. If you like Rob, well, there he is. Did it really sound like a part of what's going on? I really didn't think it did."

Robin Trower: "It was all right. It was good fun. I wasn't there very much. We cut one of my songs and I did some overdub guitar. But by the time I got in, there really wasn't much space left for me. It wasn't like a long period of time or anything. I think I might have been there a couple of weeks.

"I think they'd hoped that it would work out; that I would go out on the road and everything with them. By the time it was all done I realized there wasn't much in it for me, musically. So I decided to go on with my own thing. The two things conflicted."

Derek Sutton: "Gary Brooker and Keith Reid told me, when I went to complain to them about the way they were mixing the 'Prodigal' album, that Robin Trower was not musician enough to play for Procol Harum."

Author: "Were they serious?"

Derek Sutton: "They were absolutely dead serious. That's the kind of attitude that Gary and Keith used to make one another project. It's hard to understand … it's twenty-five years ago now, thirty years ago. But there's a death wish amongst those people. They don't want to be successful. It's the old 1970s thing. 'If you're successful you must be selling out' kind of attitude. They couldn't keep management because they wouldn't allow management to manage. They kept making demands that were absolutely unmanageable. Their idea of what their own value is, is completely out to lunch. On their most recent tour of America they toured with Jethro Tull. Ian Anderson used every opportunity to try and get Gary or Keith or somebody to go and do the promotion that is necessary if you're gonna survive in today's world, and they turned it all down. 'Procol Harum doesn't do that kind of thing.' Yet they were demanding a big fee and in terms of ticket draw they weren't worth half of it. So

that's part of the thing. The body of work that Procol Harum produced up until about 1978, I suppose, is truly wonderful. I think they deserve a place in rock 'n' roll history. But in terms of them as people, they're not people that I would want my kids to use as role models.

"That's the reason he (Matthew Fisher) left the band in the first place. And when he came back, Gary and Keith just used him. I spent five years of promptings and ringings up and beggings and handlings to try and get a Procol Harum reunion with Matthew and Robin. Because as far as I was concerned, with Barrie gone (died October 8, 1990), Matthew, Robin, Gary and Keith, plus whatever extra musicians they needed, was a damn good Procol Harum. But they did not want to give Robin any kind of space. They basically cut all the tracks and said, 'OK, you can throw a solo in here, you can throw something in there. We'll give you a bit of a writing credit on this one.' I was there when the record deal was cut because I was gonna manage them. And when they wanted me to give the royal shaft to Mr. Trower, I resigned. And because I knew what the inside numbers were of what they were getting, when they made an offer to Robin that I thought was truly outlandish in its miserliness, I hit the roof."

Author: "Does Gary Brooker resent Rob for his success?"

Derek Sutton: "I don't think Gary knows Robin's been successful."

Author: "Can he be that close-minded about it?"

Derek Sutton: "Absolutely."

Robin was credited with performing and assisting in the completion of two albums for Bryan Ferry, "Taxi" in 1993 and "Mamouna" in 1994.

Robin Trower: "Ferry actually got me in as a session player to play on some tracks that he was working on, and we kind of hit it off. I think he thought that I was the kind of musician with the kind of ears that he was looking for to help him on his project. So he asked me to come back, and I did a few days, and eventually I was there all the time [laughs]! It was great fun, a real pleasure and an honor to work with someone so gifted. I'm very proud of 'Taxi' and 'Mamouna.' "

Trower decided that he was going to record and perform for himself and those that truly appreciated him for his art. He and Derek Sutton started their own label, "V12 Records," and with Livingstone Brown on bass and vocals and Mayuyu on drums, released "20th Century Blues." This was an album that Robin had always wanted to make and never had the chance.

Robin Trower: "I did a thing in Europe called 'The Night Of The Guitars,' which featured six different guitar players and using one backup band. Livvy and Mayuyu were the rhythm section. And while we were on tour, Livvy was playing B.B. King's 'The Thrill Is Gone' on the bus. I was sitting there with him and he said, 'I think I'll do a dance version of this song.' And I said, 'Well, if you want somebody to play guitar on it, I'll be only too pleased.' So we did. We did a great version of it. And that led to us working on an album together for me."

Robin then started a worldwide club tour that received great reviews. This was the answer he had been looking for. Let the past go, don't try and live up to the 70s and enjoy the progression his art was making. The music was drawing not only the core fans but blues fans that had never heard Trower play music in that vein before.

Author: "The fans have always loved what you do. Do you take them into consideration when you write?"

Robin Trower: "No, I must admit. I have to really think it's something I want to do. I have to think it has the potential to be something that I could really be proud of. You have to feel, initially, when you're working on a piece of material that it is something that has the potential to be really good."

Author: "So, by giving your taste priority does it validate the authenticity of what you're doing?"

Robin Trower: "Well, I think the best stuff I've ever done is something I've really loved."

Author: "Can you give me an idea how much material you've released that you don't like?"

Robin Trower: "At least half of it. A lot of times, especially in the early days, there was no time to really work on material so you ended up with quite a few songs that were just rushed together. Not enough time spent writing and you end up with inferior songs on quite a few of the albums. As I say, during the 80s some of the stuff is really good. And some of the stuff I don't like at all. This is always hindsight, of course, and it's 20/20. But since working with Livvy I started to really get back to where I started off being. Just started to write songs I really got off on. And also the thing about writing my own lyrics and getting back to that as a constant."

Author: "Does that make the music more personal?"

Robin Trower: "Yeah, it does. I think the lyrics that I write marry better with the actual idea of the music itself and the feeling of the music. After trying many different combinations of working with other people, writing and all that, producers, I decided that the best stuff I've ever done was the stuff where I more or less did the whole thing. Where the songs, the words, how it was supposed to go, the whole arrangement, everything came and built."

Author: "In retrospect would you have spent more time writing lyrics as well?"

Robin Trower: "Let's put it this way. I'm glad I'm doing it now. I don't believe in crying over spilt milk and saying, 'Oh, if I'd only … and I wish I'd have done this' and all the rest of it. I'd rather just sort of say, 'Well, you know, the stuff I'm working on now is good.' And I'm very happy with these last three albums that I've done. All of the V12 stuff … I like it."

Author: "What objectives does V12 have with regards to your music?"

Robin Trower: "The only reason that label exists is to put out records that I make. We've never had any ambitions to turn it into a proper label, as it were, with other artists or anything like that."

Derek Sutton: "It got to the point that nobody wanted to release Robin Trower music. We had two records on GNP/Crescendo. The first of which was quite successful. After we played out that hand, nobody wanted to touch Robin. Nobody was interested. And the only available opportunity was that we should do it ourselves. So we did.

"The first record was '20th Century Blues.' Robin worked very hard to make a commercial record and also fit it in with his needs and creative expression. I put up some money. I actually believed we could get some radio. I got a pretty substantial advance from a distribution company and used all of that money for promotion and marketing. The record started to sell but I needed a jackhammer to get money from the distributors! I put more money into promo and marketing. But then I ran into the brick wall; I didn't have enough warm bodies on the street. I could only hire the indie promotion and marketing people. They take on too much because they need to get their overhead covered. So I had nobody actually waving the flag. And I ran into the problem that radio stations had been so highly leveraged financially that their spot load didn't cover their overhead. So they needed paid promotions from record companies and I couldn't do it. So the record stopped at about 45,000. By then the distributor went into bankruptcy and we had all our product tied up and had a lot of other problems.

"With an artist like Robin, he's never going to be mainstream because he's not interested in the music of now. He's only interested in his own creation and he doesn't make artistic compromises at all. You have to find a way to market to a niche market that appreciates what he is. And it's extremely difficult, in a radio-driven marketing arena, to find alternative ways of reaching an audience, even that niche audience, when their major exposure to music is radio. That may change with the advent of the Internet and the availability of direct marketing channels of music, but I still see the market that will allow us to stay alive being created from radio exposure.

"I think CD's are a commodity. People buy them on price alone. They go where they know the cheapest price is. They go for what they want and I don't think there are anywhere near as many impulse buyers except in the classical, traditional and 'best of' categories. The problem that we have is that the media has been preaching for twenty, twenty-five years that music should be free. And people object to paying $15 for a CD. They don't mind paying $8 for a first-run movie, which is over and done with in two hours. But a music work, which will last them a lifetime if they choose to listen to it, they think that $15 is too much money. And they're told that it's too much money by our friends in the media. Every six months to a year there's a campaign by the various magazines and the press people. 'Music's a rip-off. It shouldn't be this much.' Bullshit.

"The plan that I had was we were going out with '20th Century Blues,' and that we were going to spend every penny that we could get our hands on marketing the record and pulling in names from the shows. We collected, over the course of that tour, over 10,000 names and addresses from people who had put their name on a mailing list at the shows. I know Robin has a dedicated fan base and I wanted to reach them and find out if we could market directly to them. I sent out two mass mailings to the 10,000 people mailing list and got a dismal response. Almost the same dismal response from that targeted mailing that I would have gotten with no target whatsoever. I was shocked. We spent so much money getting this together. I really expected to get 3,000 to 5,000 people just on the idea that Robin Trower had a contact fan club and that they were going to be able to get his records direct. It didn't work then and I'm not prepared to invest the money again. The premise was that we were going to become self-supportive from their orders. There were 800 numbers. You could get the CDs by Visa or MasterCard. You could order them by mail, direct, by check or money order. We were making it as easy as we could, for the people who love Robin, to get the music direct. The weakest link is reaching the people. But it didn't work for us."

Author: "After all these years does Robin get irritated with requests for tracks from 'Bridge Of Sighs?' "

Derek Sutton: "No. He doesn't pay a lot of attention. Robin goes into his own world when he's onstage. One of the things that I've tried for many years to get him to do is to have him try and bring the audience to where he is. Turning it into a joint experience rather than a solo experience for him. It's just very difficult for him to reach out to the audience and say, 'This is about my music and this is about me. Come on in and join me. You're invited to take part.' But he's much better now. He's much more relaxed onstage than he ever was when he was huge. His major problem is one of shyness and reserve. Talking to the audience and bringing them in makes the experience more satisfying for both.

"I think the biggest influence on him in that fashion has been Livingstone Brown. Livvy has been around for a lot of years and is a consummate performer. And Livvy had backed up my pounding on Robin to talk to the audience. Let them know what's going on. Tell them about the songs. Let them be a part of this, more than a paying guest. And I think Livvy's the one that has encouraged Robin the most to be more participatory in the live performance process. Robin sort of takes the attitude of, 'The music speaks for itself. The music is everything. I am the music.' Although he's a brilliant player, he is not somebody that I would consider a brilliant performer. He doesn't perform and he never has. And that's one of the reasons he's not more recognized as a player. The people that are recognized are the people that have a knack for self-promotion."

Author: "How long did '20th Century Blues' take to write?"

Robin Trower: "Quite a while. A couple of years I think. If it's the right ten, twelve songs that you're happy with, it's gonna take a couple of years. Inspiration doesn't come every day. You've got to wait for it to come, basically. Especially when you've written a lot of songs already. Coming up with new ones is very difficult."

In May of 1997, Robin engaged the services of Reg Isidore and recorded "Someday Blues," again to be released on his own V12 Records label.

Robin Trower: "Funnily enough, I bumped into him. He came along to one of the shows I played with Bryan Ferry in London. I hadn't seen him in a long time but he had been in my mind when I was thinking about who I would get for drums for this blues album. There's a particular kind of drummer that you need for that, to make it sound authentic. And I thought that Reg was probably the nearest I'd get to it in this country. Obviously, there are guys in America a-plenty that you could pick up, but Reg definitely had that feel."

Reg Isidore: "He called me. I did see him at The Odeon with Bryan Ferry. There was something that he said that he wanted to do. Years ago, he said that he wanted to do a blues album. The way I see it, Eric Clapton and Gary Moore … there's a big blues revival thing happening with these guys and they're all doing these blues albums. Rob thought I was the right guy for it and gave me a call and asked if I'd like to play on the album. And I said, 'Yeah, boom, boom, boom.' And again, like 'Truce,' it was supposed to be a thing that was gonna go on the road. And after the album I never heard no more. The next thing I knew I had some friends of mine calling from the States and said that my name was advertised as playing at certain places with this outfit. That was like a misrepresentative kind of thing. 'What? You're joking!' I didn't hear from Robin after the album."

•   •   •

Author: "A little while back King Biscuit released a live concert of yours from 1976. Did you have any involvement in that?"

Robin Trower: "The only thing I was involved with was checking the final mixes and passing them or not as the case may be."

Author: "So you did have final say?"

Robin Trower: "Yeah."

Author: "Robin, Jimmy, Rustee and yourself was the line-up on the King Biscuit album."

Bill Lordan: "Sure was. And Rustee used to do quite a good bass solo in 'Messin' The Blues,' which I co-wrote with Robin and Jimmy. It was a jam one night in the studio where Geoff Emerick had come back from the pub; he was pretty tipsy when he came back. I came up with this beat and Robin kicked in the lick, Jimmy jumped in and Geoff quickly turned on the tape recorder and captured it. And then we had to do brain salad surgery. We had to splice it up to put the verse here and the chorus there 'cuz it wasn't in the right order, but it was this great jam we came up with. Robin gave me credit for the writing on that because it was sparked, as were a lot of the songs, by the drum groove or the beat that I came up with. From the black days. Robin really liked the soul stuff that I did. The Bobby Bland, the Sly, the stuff that had that kind of groove to it."

•   •   •

Author: "How are you feeling about the new album, 'Go My Way'?"

Robin Trower: "Very good. I'm very proud of it. Put a lot of effort into it. More effort into that album than any other album I've made. I wanted it to be great and Derek wanted it to be great."

Derek Sutton: "Robin is a pretty straitlaced guy. He has a paradigm in his head of what he and his music is and are. And he won't budge off of that. We went out with Peter Frampton just a couple of years ago. And after one show he told me, 'This is the wrong place to be because these kids won't listen to me. They only want three-minute pop songs.' So, basically, I don't think Robin Trower would be comfortable supporting anybody because his almost jazz free-form style is not echoed by any other band. At least nobody that could headline over him and draw big crowds. So it's really difficult to understand what he expects when he's playing support. People get big because they play tunes that are hummable and recognizable and what have you. And if you're going to go out there and try to make a living and get big too, you've got to either do the same thing or else lead that crowd into a different place with your artistry. And it's very difficult to see where a twelve-minute version of 'Bridge Of Sighs' fits into that.

"I've been talking to Robin over the last couple of months about the possibility of us doing a three-guitar tour next summer in the sheds. Let's put three really great guitarists together. And every name I've mentioned, 'No, I couldn't work with him, mate.' He would accept going out on the road with B.B. King, but I don't know that his crowd would buy Robin Trower records. You ask him who his favorite musicians are and he comes up with the great crooners, the great singers. Virtually everybody he likes is dead."

Author: "What's it like dealing with radio these days?"

Derek Sutton: "What is the lowest possible word you can think of? Radio has become a numbers game that has nothing to do with music."

Author: "Are there any stations with a program director, a music director, that you can approach and appeal to their sense of what's good and what's bad?"

Derek Sutton: "How would they know? They're not music people. The great P.D.'s are gone. They've all become consultants."

Robin Trower: "It's very hard to get your foot in the door. Maybe in the 60s or 70s you would get a DJ playing whatever he liked. He could put your record on if he fancied it. But now it's got to fit in with the playlists and it's difficult. A whole different set of rules there now."

Author: "Do you have a sense of how good the music is that you play?"

Robin Trower: "I think I do. I'm aware that what I've done … I've carved out a niche, explored a place where very, very few, certainly rock 'n' roll musicians, ever get to. I'm aware of that. I'm aware that there's a depth, a soulfulness to what I do."

For "Go My Way," Robin recruited Richard Watts to replace Livvy Brown.

Robin Trower: "Livvy's become a big-time producer. He's signed a young girl singer called Kate to a very big record deal and they're just finishing up her album now. He's doing fantastic. Which I always knew he would. I knew I had him on borrowed time."

Author: "You must be pleased with Richard Watts."

Robin Trower: "Very. He's worked out fantastic. I knew it was a risk but I felt it was a risk worth taking. I think you've got to take chances. Obviously, you've got to be lucky and come across people with talent but, you know."

Derek Sutton: "The only problem that I have with Richard is that Robin won't allow him to blossom. Yet. But I think Richard is going to grow into a very competent and very … I don't know if he's ever gonna be a star."

Author: "Does he want to be?"

Derek Sutton: "Yeah. This is his first real tour, so it's hard to tell. It's his very early days. Yet he's very much under the thumb. He's overawed by Robin, both on a musical level and on the fact that he's his dad's age. Robin met Richard through Robin's son. So I don't know whether he's gonna blossom and become really incandescent onstage. But I think his voice is wonderful. I think he's learned an enormous amount this year and I think he'll be able to contribute a great deal to the Robin Trower sound over the next little while. His minimalist bass playing has allowed for a complete change in the overall sound and set because Robin now has to fill up more space. And it also leaves the drummer, Alvino Bennett, room to fill up more space. It definitely has gone back towards the original concept. Jimmy was a minimalist bass player too. So it's gone towards that thing where it was guitar and drums doing most of the fills and the bass was simply giving a meter. Whereas Livvy is such a brilliant bass player. There were always a lot more bass notes and it forced the drums to pull back a little bit and in

some places even made the guitar pull back. So I think that Richard is enabling Robin to stretch better."

Author: "How's the road treating you these days?"

Robin Trower: "Good. I love to play, that's the whole thing. And if I don't play live, I know my chops are going to go down the tubes. So I'd rather play live or give it up. 'Cuz it isn't gonna be there for any other situation."

Author: "The traveling, the running around, the horrendous deli trays."

Robin Trower: "I never touch deli trays [laughs]! It's sheer desperation to eat off of those things. I take life pretty easy, don't worry. I go down and do the gig."

Patrick Rule: "He doesn't stay away from deli trays? No [laughs]! Let me put it to you like this. There have been nights we've eaten everything on the deli tray and he's come up and made a cheese sandwich because all the meat was gone. He'd say, 'Well, who ate all the meat?' 'Robin, you never eat from the deli tray.' 'Well, I want a sandwich tonight.' "

•   •   •

Author: "Do you play much anymore?"

Reg Isidore: "Yeah. I do gigs and stuff in the pubs in London. I do charity gigs. Jam here and there. When I'm not doing my carpentry. I'm still the baddest drummer on the planet! I'm telling ya [laughs]! I am! I'm a serious drummer. It depends which way you wanna go. I'm more into sort of Caribbean/jazz. I play anything basically. Depends on the material. It's like putting it in the pocket. It's like a Jekyll and Hyde with me sometimes. I hate the drums and I love the drums."

Rustee Allen: "Since '94 I've been playing bass for Bobby Womack. I've been doing hundreds of demos for people here (Oakland, California) and I've been writing some songs to get my little thing together to try and get it

Robin Trower and Bill Lordan.
Los Angeles, California, 2000.
Courtesy Kate Williams

released. Right now I'm getting ready to get involved with this bass player/producer who's got a group called Yahoo Bar-B-Q now. He just finished his CD and I did three tracks for him. And I'm working on my piano skills and trying to stay on top of the reading aspect of music and everything. 'Til I ain't here no more to do it!"

Bill Lordan: "I released a CD with two Robin Trower songs on it. One is 'King of the Dance' from 'Caravan To Midnight,' and 'Messin' The Blues.' The rest are originals. I've got a guitar player friend and a bass player friend who I've played with over the last fifteen years in both the Christian band and a band called Fortress, which was signed to Atlantic. And this guitar player, Eric Turner, and I are about the same vintage, same age and influences. We put together a seven-song CD that we're calling 'The Bill Lordan Experiment.' We funded it by ourselves and recorded it quick and it's really come out great. I'm really excited about it. It's on my Web site. It's kind of a Hendrix/blues/rock style. A three-piece and Eric sings. With the technology available, I've got the best drum sound I've ever gotten."

Author: "You and Bill were a great rhythm section. Do you ever keep in touch?"

Rustee Allen: "No. It's funny because I think me and Bill jelled better as a rhythm section with Robin than we did with Sly. He did well with Sly, don't get me wrong. With Robin there were bass lines and patterns to follow but you had more opportunities to express yourself. With Sly it was pretty much structured. I'd listen to tapes where he would play a lick or fill or something and it seemed like it was always me and him on time. Going into something and coming out of something, it was like we were one brain almost. But I never stayed in touch with Bill. There were things that were said that even at the time it would be better for me not to make waves or anything. There were like certain little racial remarks that were made that, when I think about them now, I can understand why somebody would say something like that. That's part of why I never went out of my way to stay in touch with him."

Davey Pattison: "I just brought an album out. 'Mississippi Nights.' Paid for it myself. Put a Web site together and I'm selling them on the net."

Reg Isidore: "Music is my life, man. I'm a very talented guy. I don't just do music. There's lots of things that I do. In so many ways I'm fortunate to be gifted. I don't put my eggs in one basket. I just got tired of the politics. Just got really tired with the business. I don't make a living from music anymore. I'm a carpenter and joiner. That's what I did before I started music and that's what I'm doing now."

Author: "What has Robin learned from his career?"

Derek Sutton: "Robin has a deep and abiding faith and it has become much deeper and much more consuming in the last five, ten years. But he has this wonderful ability, when I'm going out of my mind trying to make a decision, that he will say very calmly to me, 'You make the decision, then you wait.' And that's what he does."

Author: "Is this something that you've had most of your life?"

Robin Trower: "Well, I won't say that, no. It's something that's developed obviously being married to a Roman Catholic. Eventually, I got accepted into the church. Don't get me wrong. I was always a religious person. I'd always had a good, really strong faith. But not specific. I started going to mass with the family. It just seemed a natural thing. I sort of flowed into it. I would say it's made my path forward a lot more defined. It has more of a sense of place."

Author: "So you're much more comfortable in your own skin."

Robin Trower: "Yeah, exactly. See the thing is about Catholicism is it gives you a real set of boundaries as well as a sense of the boundlessness of it all."

Author: "Has he always been so calm?"

Derek Sutton: "No, not at all. In fact, earlier in his career, he was incensed at anything that took away from his sound or his playing. We used to carry half-inch-thick sheets of steel to put out on the stage to avoid radio interference through his highly tuned pick-ups. He carried a guy on tour with him for quite a few years while he was playing the huge places who they called 'the boffin.' His primary job was to tune out radio interference and make sure the guitars, with the pick-ups tuned the way Robin wanted them, giving him the sound that he wanted, didn't also produce a local FM radio station coming out of the same body. Robin used to get incensed by things like not being able to turn up to eleven. He had no grasp on the reality of the day to day. Everything had to be perfect. And the other thing was … everything was the actual playing. It wasn't the promotion. The interviews and the other things were just a pain in the ass. Now he understands that it's a major part of the game. Robin is a 70s artist where the music speaks for itself. Music is what counts. 'If people want to hear my music they'll come see me.' "

Author: "What type of a person is he to hang with?"

Derek Sutton: "Very, very laid back. Good sense of humor."

Author: "Twisted?"

Derek Sutton: "English."

Author: "That could be taken two ways."

Derek Sutton: "[laughs] The person to best ask that to is one of his tour managers. When you spend five hours a day in a car with somebody, you'll find out what he's all about."

Patrick Rule: "Oooo … it's wicked [laughs]! It's very British. As a kid I grew up with Monty Python and Fawlty Towers and all that kind of stuff so I was kind of hip to the way they are. It's very dry and he's very kind of witty about it. There are times when he will take a cheap shot at you for the sake of a joke. Which is fine. I guess the best way to describe it is if you don't know that he's joking, you might take offense at the things that he says. There's a lot of sarcasm."

Derek Sutton: "He doesn't listen to music on the car radio. He has started to in the last year or two but generally he doesn't listen to music. The kind of music he wants to listen to is not the kind of music he would normally be associated with. He'll listen to big band music. He'll listen to jazz. The great crooners. He doesn't listen to the old blues players or modern pop or modern rock stations. He's just not interested. He prefers music he has respect for. One of the things you'll find when you talk to him is Robin has very little respect for current artists."

Patrick Rule: "He's a brilliant man. For somebody that's had as little education as he has had, he's just brilliant. I mean, he's well read. He's very much into the classics. Not just literature and that kind of stuff but music and everything. He's very much into classic radio. On the long trips we pop in some of these old-time radio tapes. Jack Benny, Burns and Allen. A lot of old crooners. A lot of older, good stuff. Late 20s, early 30s."

Author: "Aside from having the greatest job in the world, what has music brought you?"

Robin Trower: "Being involved in music, and without sounding pompous about it, but being involved with an ear for music. That special gift if you can appreciate it. It's a non-stop treasure trove, isn't it? I keep hearing stuff that's just so thrilling and so enriching. I was listening to a bit of opera today that was on the radio and it was unbelievably good. There's a nonstop feast out there for anybody with ears."

Author: "Is applause as addictive for you as to others?"

Robin Trower: "I'm not sure that I've ever really been bothered by it one way or the other. My whole thing in getting up onstage is to really feel, by the end of the night, that I've played really well. Obviously, you want to go down well but that is the overriding thing. It's no good coming off thinking you haven't played well even if you've gone down a storm, as they say."

Author: "A lot of people I speak with about my book are authentic fans of yours and are very supportive in what you do."

Robin Trower: "That gives me a nice feeling. That's nice. When you feel you've left a bit of a trail somewhere, [laughs] you know what I mean?"

Author: "Do you consider it a bit of a trail? Nothing more?"

Robin Trower: "Yeah, nothing more. I think it has been just a bit of a side trail, what I've done. But it's great that it means something to people. That's about as much as you can hope for as an artist, I think."

Patrick Rule: "He's a very particular gentleman who likes to do things a certain way. On the last tour, over fifty-three dates, we developed a real serious routine. He likes Bob Evans. He likes Cracker Barrel. That could be two places where you really wouldn't think a rocker would want to go to. But he likes those places. Especially Cracker Barrel. He likes to keep things clean. He likes to keep his hands clean. We carry Wet Ones and that kind of thing.

"You also have to remember. I've been on two major tours. I've been all over the U.S. two times now. He's done it thirty, forty, fifty times. He has done this country over and over and over again. And he does it because he loves his fans and he does it because that's what he does. So when you have a gentleman who's that used to the road, he develops a certain way. We stay in a certain hotel. We have certain places where we will eat and we have certain places where we will not eat. He doesn't like the really long drives, but who would? I drove around 17,000 miles on the tour. We had a couple of nights off in Myrtle Beach and he took the car once."

Author: "You have an incredible amount of integrity. Were you getting this kind of feedback from your contemporaries?"

Robin Trower: "Very, very occasionally. But not in any big way. Around that period I wasn't socializing around musicians very much. I didn't know many people personally.

"I think I lost an awful lot of integrity in the 80s, to be honest. But I think, overall, the overview of what I've done, hopefully, doesn't stand up too badly."

Author: "What has all this taught you?"

Robin Trower: "I think, for me, it's the old saying, 'unto thine own self be true.' I think if I've learned anything, it's certainly that. It's been the right thing for me."

Author: "Do you have an easier time judging your own work today?"

Robin Trower: "I think I'm able to be more objective about what I do, yeah. I'm a better producer of my own work now. I can be very objective about it."

Derek Sutton: "He knows he's one of the greatest guitarists around. He used to say he was the greatest guitarist. I don't think he does that anymore. But I think that in terms of his musicianship, he knows that he's as good now as he's ever been. Although he did say to me after he listened to the King Biscuit Flower Hour tapes for the first time, 'You know what? I was full of piss and vinegar back then.' Which is a good old English expression. And it's really true. There's a lot of energy and excitement in those early tracks. Robin's much more relaxed now and much more controlled and in command. He's not living on the edge anymore. That's really the difference. In those days he was pushing the envelope. Now he firmly stays inside the envelope most of the time."

Author: "From observing your catalogue and from speaking with you, I admire your constant desire to reinvent yourself."

Robin Trower: "That's what I strive for. Thank you for the compliment."

DRAMATIS PERSONAE

Aaronson, Kenny: Bassist with "Derringer" and Rick Derringer solo material from 1975-1980. Played on six albums.

Allen, Rustee: Robin Trower bassist from 1977-1978. Played on two albums.

Appice, Carmine: Formed "DNA" with Rick Derringer in 1982. Released one album.

Appice, Vinny: Drummer with "Derringer" from 1975-1977. Played on three albums.

Brandon, Ron: Original keyboard player with "The McCoys." Played on their first two albums.

Bruce, Jack: Bassist and vocalist with Robin Trower in "BLT" from 1981-1982. Played on two albums.

Caldwell, Bobby: Drummer on "Johnny Winter And...Live."

Clempson, Dave "Clem": Replaced Peter Frampton in Humble Pie in 1972 and remained until the band broke up in 1975. Played on five albums.

Connaughton, Marcus: Irish music expert and announcer on Irish radio's RTE in Cork.

Cross, Pam: Road manager for 1987 "Packet of 3/Steve Marriott" tour.

Deardon, Jenny: Steve Marriott's first wife and commonly known as "the love of his life."

de' Ath, Rod: Rory Gallagher's drummer from 1972-1978. Played on five albums.

Derringer, Liz: Rick Derringer's wife of over twenty years commencing in 1969.

Doll, Nevin: Long-time friend of McCoy and Johnny Winter bassist Randy Jo Hobbs.

Doumanian, John: Worked for Dee Anthony; road managed Humble Pie.

Eldridge, Roy: Former writer with *New Music Express* from 1968-1971; grew from press officer to A&R Director with Chrysalis records from 1971-1989.

Feltham, Mark: Harmonica player with Rory Gallagher from 1984 until Rory's death in 1995.

Fisher, Matthew: Original keyboard player for Procol Harum and produced four albums for Robin Trower.

Frampton, Peter: Original Humble Pie guitarist from 1969 to 1971. Played on five albums.

Gallagher, Donal: Rory Gallagher's brother and manager.

Gerlach, Rudi: Met Rory in 1977 when a cameraman with WDR's broadcast of Rockpalazt. Became Rory's closest friend and confidante.

Isidore, Reg: Robin Trower drummer from 1973 to 1974 and again in 1995. Played on three albums.

Johnson, Danny: Guitarist, singer and songwriter with "Derringer" from 1975-1977. Played on three albums.

Kelly, Dennis: Original bassist with "The McCoys." Left before "Hang On Sloopy."

Kittringham, Eric: Original bassist with "Taste" until August 1968.

Lordan, Bill: Drummer with Robin Trower from 1974-1981. Played on eight albums.

Marriott, Kay: Steve Marriott's mother.

Martin, Lou: Piano player with Rory Gallagher from 1972-1978. Played on seven albums.

Mateus Dos Anjos, Kay: Steve Marriott's sister.

McAvoy, Gerry: Rory Gallagher's bassist from 1971-1991. Played on fourteen albums.

McCracken, Charlie: Replaced Eric Kittringham as bassist with "Taste" in August of 1968 until the band broke up in 1970.

McDonnell, Phil: Soundman and road manager with Rory Gallagher from 1977-1986.

McGartland, Dino: Founder and publisher of *Stagestruck*, a fan magazine dedicated to keeping Rory Gallagher's name alive and introduce new fans to his music.

McKenna, Ted: Rory Gallagher's drummer from 1978-1981. Played on three albums.

O'Duffy, Alan: Engineered and co-produced "Photofinish" and "Top Priority," as well as engineered "Defender" for Rory Gallagher. Engineered "Smokin', "Eat It," "Thunderbox" and "Street Rats" for Humble Pie.

O'Herlihy, Joe: Audio engineer with Rory Gallagher from 1974-1978. Soundman and road manager for U2 from 1978 to present.

O'Neill, Brendan: Rory Gallagher's drummer from 1982-1991. Played on three albums.

Pattison, Davey: Robin Trower vocalist from 1986-1990. Sang on three albums.

Ridley, Greg: Humble Pie bassist and vocalist from 1969-1975. Played on ten albums.

Ruff, Chuck: Drummer for The Edgar Winter Group.

Rule, Patrick: Robin Trower's road manager from the late 90s on.

Shirley, Jerry: Humble Pie drummer who played with Steve Marriott up until 1987. Played on eleven albums.

St. Holmes, Derek: Formerly with Ted Nugent, he was once considered as a rhythm guitarist to join Rory Gallagher's band.

Sutton, Derek: Former head of U.S. operations with Chrysalis Records; Robin trower's manager since 1978.

Taylor, Michael: UK expert on The Small Faces.

Tench, Bobby: Guitarist and vocalist with Humble Pie from 1980-1981. Played on two albums.

Varney, Mike: President and owner of Blues Bureau Records which released Rick Derringer's blues catalogue.

Wilson, John: Replaced Norman Damery as drummer with "Taste" in August of 1968 until the band broke up in 1970.

Winter, Edgar: Long-time Rick Derringer colleague.

Zehringer, Janice: Rick Derringer's mother.

Zehringer, Randy: Rick Derringer's brother. Drummer for The McCoys and first "Johnny Winter And…" album. Left band he contracted encephalitis.